Warman's
Flea Market
Price Guide
2ND EDITION

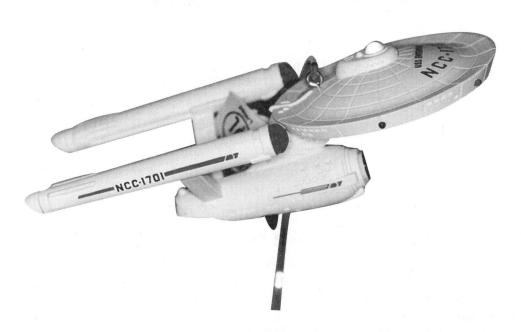

DON JOHNSON & ELLEN T. SCHROY

Published by

krause publications

700 E. State Street • Iola, WI 54990-0001
Telephone: 715/445-2214

Please, call or write for our free catalog of publications. Our toll-free number to place an order or obtain a free catalo
800-258-0929 or please use our regular business telephone, 715-445-2214.

Library of Congress Catalog Number: 99-63752
ISBN: 0-87349-246-3

Printed in the United States of America

Cover Illustrations

Front: Metal clock in a Victorian house motif, Golden Nov. Mfg. Co., Chicago, $150.
The Rifleman lunch box, $330; thermos, $140.
Pepsi-Cola thermometer, tin, $175.
A Charlie Brown Christmas, 1st edition, $25.
McDonald's Halloween plate, plastic, $5.

Back: Red Ryder Lucky Coin, $10.
Coca-Cola 6-pack, 1995 Winston Cup Champion, J Gordon, $20.
Czech Letovice teapot, 6-1/2" high, $25.

Contents

Abbreviations

The following are standard abbreviations used throughout this book.

3D: three-dimensional
adv: advertising
approx: approximately
attrib: attributed
C: century
cond: condition
cov: cover, covered
d: deep
decor: decorated
dia: diameter
dj: dust jacket
doz: dozen
ed: edition, editor
emb: embossed
ext: exterior
ftd: footed
gal: gallon
ground: background
h: high
horiz: horizontal
hp: hand painted
illus: illustrated, illustration,
   illustrator

imp: impressed
int: interior
irid: iridescent
k: karat
l: long
lb: pound
litho: lithograph
MBP: mint in bubble pack
mfg: manufactured,
   manufacturing
MIB: mint in box
MIP: mint in package
mkd: marked
MOC: mint on card
n.d.: no date
No.: number
NOS: new old stock
NRFB: never removed from
   box
op: operated
opal: opalescent
orig: original

oz: ounce
pat.: patent
pc: piece
pcs: pieces
pg: page
pgs: pages
pr: pair
pt: pint
qt: quart
rect: rectangular
Soc: Society
sgd: signed
sq: square
unp: unpaged
vol: volume
w: width
yg: yellow gold
#: number, numbered

❖ <u>Acknowledgments</u> ❖

Like black-and-white snapshots from childhood, this project has been filled with moments worth slipping into a special album and storing safely away, so we can recall them again in the days ahead.

SNAP. We owe a debt of gratitude to collectors and dealers for the enthusiastic response to the first edition of *Warman's Flea Market Price Guide.* Without your support, this second edition would not have been possible.

SNAP. We say thank you to our editor, Karen O'Brien. Though we've worked from afar, your time and vision haven't gone unnoticed.

SNAP. We are grateful to everyone who helped us obtain photographs for this book. Among them, Barry and Barbara Carter, owners of the Knightstown Antique Mall, Knightstown, Ind., were instrumental. Thanks!

SNAP. We tip our hats to Tom Johnson for moral and technical support. Broadband is a good thing.

SNAP. We are indebted to Liz Johnson for her countless hours of writing and editing. Your name belongs on the cover. Thanks for being our silent partner.

SNAP. We are humbled by a loving God who has given us life and talents. We once again acknowledge His work in our lives and in this project.

Ellen Tischbein Schroy
Don Johnson

<u>Introduction</u>

by Don Johnson

The two-dollar swizzle stick brings back a million dollars worth of memories.

The small plastic stirrer is marked "Indianapolis Motor Speedway Motel." Despite having lived in Indiana my entire life, I've never been to an Indy 500, but I've been on the track several times. My first trip to the famed oval remains the most memorable, and the one that's linked to the swizzle stick.

When my high school cross country team advanced to the state finals, we drove to Indianapolis for the championship meet, spending a night at the Indianapolis Motor Speedway Motel. After dinner, a group of us took a walk, quickly making our way to the track, where we climbed under a fence, over a wall, and found ourselves standing on one of the steeply banked turns of the legendary Speedway. For a bunch of kids fresh from the country, it was 100 percent adventure.

I hadn't thought about that nighttime excursion in years. But, fond memories can rush back when we least expect them. Pulling the Speedway Motel souvenir from a box of swizzle sticks triggered my mind, instantly sending me back to the track as a teenager.

There's a lesson here. The most valuable things we find at flea markets aren't always for sale. Often, the real treasure is the memory that an object brings to the surface of our minds.

Maybe that's why we love flea markets so much—because they're filled with so many possibilities. Sure, you can find good stuff at fancy antique shows and mega-super-colossal antique malls. But there's something refreshing about a flea market.

Take a walk with us. Don't worry, you won't have to scurry under any fences. We're heading for one of our favorite places—a flea market.

It's a family thing

One benefit of today's flea market is the emphasis placed on the family. While some dealers at higher-end markets twitch nervously at the sight of strollers and young children, most flea markets are promoted as events for everyone, young and old. Look around the next time you're at an outdoor flea market. Notice the number of parents pulling children in wagons. And, pay close attention to the smiles on those kids' faces.

Where else are kids encouraged to dig through a box of fast-food toys or spend a portion of their allowance on a 10-cent baseball card? An ice-cold drink or a soft pretzel is often all that's needed to give them a boost when they're wearing down.

No segment of the antiques and collectibles industry does a better job catering to the interests of children than do flea markets. These microcosms of the antiques trade offer youngsters appealing items at reasonable prices. For many adults, their love of collecting germinated in childhood and blossomed into adulthood. The legion of flea markets across the United States assures a bright future for the antiques and collectibles trade by creating tomorrow's collectors today.

And the fun isn't just for kids. If you haven't been to a flea market in a while, you're in for a treat. What are you waiting for?

Let the games begin

The thrill of the hunt continues to drive the antiques and collectibles market. People delight in the search for treasured items. Nowhere is that hope more alive than at a flea market. Whether you're looking for a Sesame Street record you remember from your childhood or a goblet to fill the void in your collection of American pattern glass, flea markets offer the realistic hope that the search will be successful. Better yet, chances are good the item can be purchased for a reasonable price.

Don't assume this book is another run-of-the-mill price guide. It's much more than that! *Warman's Flea Market Price Guide* contains valuable information about attending flea markets, and we've honed this edition specifically toward your needs as a flea market shopper or seller. We understand that flea markets are fun, family-oriented events. With that in mind, we've kept the tone lighthearted. A sufficient amount of information about each topic has been provided, complete with notes relating to periodicals, collectors' clubs and reference books. However, the listings are the backbone of the work, since that's what flea market enthusiasts really want.

In compiling the listings for *Warman's Flea Market Price Guide*, we put our fingers on the pulse of the marketplace, carefully checking to see what's being sold at flea markets. There's not much sense in listing prices for potholders if no one is collecting them. Instead, we've focused on what's hot, like NASCAR collectibles, which has its own heading in this edition. Other new categories include Architectural,

Flea markets remain the perfect venue for finding an affordable treasure. These common sports cards are available for pocket change.

Pokémon, Sunday School, Ethnic, Ladders, and Pull Toys.

Photographs are a key component of this work. *Warman's Flea Market Price Guide* contains more photographs, and this book illustrates more categories, than does any other flea market price guide. From the beginning of this project, photography has been a priority. While detailed listings are vital, clear photographs are invaluable for identifying an item.

In preparation for this book we asked you, flea market buyers and sellers, to tell us what you think. That input allowed us to fine-tune the end product to fit your needs. This isn't just another general-line price guide with the upper-end merchandise stripped away and the words "Flea Market" added to the title. From start to finish, we've focused on creating the best flea market book possible. Included is inside information about what's happening on the flea market scene, what's being offered for sale, and the value of that merchandise.

Our goal was to accurately reflect a typical flea market. We were literally thinking on our feet as we prepared this book. We walked hundreds of miles during a multitude of flea markets, talked to countless dealers, and listened to innumerable shoppers while observing the collectibles landscape.

You'll find an intriguing mix of merchandise represented here, from things that are readily available to scarce objects that, much to the delight of collectors, do occasionally surface at flea markets. Values in this price guide begin at 25 cents for trading cards and range upward from there, highlighting the diversity of items that can be found even within specific categories.

Methodology 101

How do you combine roughly 700 photographs, nearly 800 categories, and countless listings into one cohesive unit? We started with "A." It's a pretty basic concept, but one that works just fine. Categories are listed alphabetically, from ABC plates to Zeppelins. Within each section, you may find the following:

Category: In an effort to make this book as enjoyable to read as it was to write, we intentionally omitted dry discourses on a category's

history. If you wanted to do research, you'd be at a library, not at a flea market. Levity aside, that doesn't mean we shied away from useful information. Instead, we utilize a mix of key facts and fun tips. If you're not smiling as you read this book, we haven't done our jobs. For anyone wanting additional insight into a topic, we include information on periodicals, reference books, and collectors' clubs.

Periodicals: The advantage to periodicals is their ability to keep abreast of a changing marketplace. Newsletters are great sources of insider information. Weekly and monthly trade papers and magazines can also help you understand the market. We included those publications we consider helpful.

References: Due to the seemingly infinite number of books about the antiques and collectibles industry, we limited reference works to current titles we believe provide the most useful historical information as well as accurate prices. Most of the titles listed are readily available from booksellers, and many are offered for sale at flea markets.

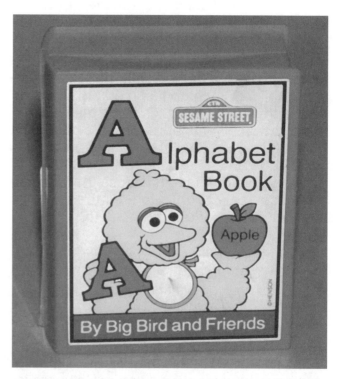

A is for Apple! Simple enough. *Warman's Flea Market* takes a straightforward approach in providing the information you need when you hit the flea market trail.

Diversity makes flea markets interesting. Don't be surprised when a dealer displays a $10 Mission Orange bank next to a $350 oversized Brush-McCoy frog.

Collectors' Clubs: It's hard to keep a good thing to yourself. Collectors love to share their enthusiasm with others, and collectors' clubs offer the perfect avenue for that. We've included many clubs, but there may be others we are not aware of, and new groups may become active. Use our suggestions as a starting point, but don't hesitate to ask fellow collectors and dealers about other clubs they may know of.

Reproduction Alert: Reproductions remain a problem throughout the antiques and collectibles trade. When we were aware of reproductions within a specific category, we used this alert to call your attention to their existence.

Listings: Looking for the heart of this book? You just found it. The individual listings are short but sweet, giving detailed descriptions that aid in identification. You'll find the listings presented alphabetically, each with a current value.

What's a flea market?

Attempting to define a flea market is like trying to describe all restaurants with a single statement. Sure, McDonald's and the White House kitchen both serve food, but there's a world of difference between the two.

Flea markets suffer from the same identity problem. They come in innumerable varieties, from multi-thousand-dealer events at Brimfield, Massachusetts, to the local volunteer fire department's annual flea market and chili supper, featuring only a handful of merchants. The first may attract full-time dealers, while the latter may appeal to neighbors who have just cleaned out their garages. Yet, good sales and exciting buys can be made at both events.

Typically, flea markets are stereotyped as having low- to middle-market merchandise displayed in a haphazard manner. Imagine a herd of nude Barbies sprawled on the bare ground under a wobbly folding table holding a scattered array of chipped glassware and musty *TV Guides.* However, that's not always the case. In today's market, a shopper is just as likely to find a selection of 19th-century mechanical banks grouped in a professional setting, complete with risers and lights.

Additionally, a number of events considered flea markets are actually seasonal antique shows, such as the Sandwich Antiques Market in Sandwich, Illinois. Ask someone in the Midwest to name his favorite flea market, and Sandwich is likely to be it. The Sandwich Antiques Market remains dedicated to providing both affordable and quality antiques and collectibles, while filtering out those dealers who carry bottom-of-the-line material. Is Sandwich a flea market? No, but it exhibits many of the qualities that attract flea market dealers and shoppers—a well-established event with indoor and outdoor spaces, good facilities, and the promise of finding a bargain.

The reputation of a particular market often dictates the quality of the merchandise presented. Better-known flea markets typically attract upper-end dealers who are just as comfortable at sophisticated antique shows, while lower-end markets tend to adopt a more laidback approach. Booths may have a cluttered look, and there may be more merchants selling items from outside the antiques and collectibles field, everything from ferrets to football jerseys.

Flea markets also run the gamut from daily markets held in strip malls to monthly shows at 4-H fairgrounds. Outdoor summer markets tend to be a favorite with shoppers. During good weather, the flea market becomes a haven for families wanting to do something together. Children who normally whine at the suggestion of going to an antique mall or auction will often put on a happy face when told the destination is a flea market.

Long live Flea Markets!

Flea markets are alive and well. That's good news in an industry that is undergoing none-too-subtle changes, due in large part to the Internet. In a day when many antique malls are losing dealers who have decided they can more easily do business selling online, flea markets still appear to be strong. What's their secret? Actually, it's the Internet!

An increasing number of people have discovered fun and profit through selling antiques and collectibles on the World Wide Web. Although they might have started by cleaning out the attic, they're soon looking for additional sources of inventory. Flea markets have proven to be the perfect place to find inexpensive items for resale.

Nor have seasoned collectors abandoned flea markets. Shoppers still root through showcases and burrow under tables for prizes waiting to be found, sometimes at a fraction of their value. The thrill of the hunt continues to lure collectors and dealers to their favorite flea markets.

Those flea markets that serve as tag-team partners with more traditional antique shows are also doing well. Consider the Springfield Antiques Show & Flea Market, held monthly in Springfield, Ohio. While shoppers find a variety of upper-end antiques there, from American art pottery to country furniture, the show also attracts a number of dealers selling more affordable wares. Looking for Beanie Babies? They're there. Need vintage hardware for a kitchen cabinet? No doubt, someone has it. Interested in Little Golden Books? Bring a large bag to carry them home.

Many promoters who combine traditional antique shows with flea markets are careful to limit the number of dealers selling new items, such as T-shirts and shrubbery. Because they are offered a range of items across a broad spectrum of prices, shoppers have the hope of finding exactly what they're looking for. Not even the Internet can dampen that enthusiasm.

Even better than a game of chance at a carnival, flea markets offer the hope of finding "A Prize Every Time."

The Flea Market Zone

If Rod Serling were still with us, he might sum things up this way: "There is a fifth dimension beyond that which is known to man. It is a dimension as vast as collectibles and as timeless as antiques. It is the middle ground between wanting and owning, between seeing and sacking, and it lies between the pit of man's coveting and the balance of his checkbook. This is the dimension of collecting. It is an area which we call The Flea Market Zone."

Is there a signpost up ahead? Collectors hope so, and they get excited when it reads "Flea Market" in large, bold letters. However, there are more efficient ways to find flea markets than by relying on chance. For starters, several guides have been published that cover American flea markets. These books are valuable for the detailed information they provide, listing flea markets, locations, dates, times, admission rates, dealer rates, and contact information. Check your favorite bookseller for titles and availability.

Trade publications are another excellent source of information. National and regional publications contain a fair number of advertisements for flea markets. In addition, don't overlook the free tabloids available at many flea markets, antique shows and antique malls. Ads for smaller flea markets and festival-related events can often be found in these publications.

Of course, nothing beats a good recommendation from other collectors and dealers. Ask around, especially when at a flea market you like. Talk to the dealers to find out which markets they prefer and which venues offer similar types of merchandise.

Don't go quite yet

You've done your homework. You've found a great-sounding flea market. You managed to finagle a Saturday off from work. The rest of the family is dressed and ready to go. Have you forgotten anything?

How about a phone call?

Sure, the flea market guide states that Billy-Bob's Flea-Spectacular is open every Saturday and Sunday. However, circumstances do arise that cause flea markets to change their hours, move to a different location, or even go out of business. There's nothing more frustrating than driving 100 miles in the wee morning light, enduring two hours of your kids drubbing each other in the back seat, and drinking three cups of lukewarm coffee, only to find a "CLOSED" sign hanging crookedly on the chain-link fence surrounding what used to be Billy-Bob's. Such experiences can generally be avoided by confirming the details of the market ahead of time.

When contacting the promoter, double-check the date, hours of operation, and admission fees. If you aren't familiar with the area, ask for directions. And remember, if the drive involves much distance, find out if you will be changing time zones. Otherwise, a road trip from Illinois to Michigan could find you arriving 45 minutes after the gate opened instead of 15 minutes early, as you had planned. Time zones have crushed more than one collector's hopes of getting into a market with the opening surge of shoppers.

While you're at it, don't forget to check the weather forecast. It might be sunny when you leave your home in San Jose, but Pasadena could be in the midst of a thunderstorm. Rain and outdoor flea markets are natural enemies. A quick check of The Weather Channel would have shown you that a low-pressure system had stalled directly above the Rose Bowl Flea Market and Swap Meet. Sure, the event might be held "rain or shine," but that doesn't mean you feel like slogging through puddles on your day off.

Getting comfortable

Boy Scouts are pretty intelligent kids. They've got that neat hand sign, and they're good at expecting the unexpected. We should all be so smart.

Veteran flea market shoppers also know to be prepared. To begin with, they dress for success. Nothing will kill a day at a flea market faster than being uncomfortable, whether you're too cold, too hot, or suffering from achy feet. Dressing appropriately for the season and accounting for changes in the weather are essential components of an enjoyable hunt for flea market treasures. Two rules are key: dress in layers, and take a change of clothes.

Before you "GO!" to your favorite flea market, it's always a good idea to "STOP!" and make sure you have the essentials you'll need for a great day of shopping.

Many flea market shoppers are early birds, wanting to jump into the action as soon as possible. When arriving at a Wisconsin flea market in the chill of the morning, a wool sweater and a cup of steaming coffee will keep you warm. But once the coffee cup is empty, Mr. Sun peeks from behind the clouds, and the temperature climbs, it's likely your wardrobe will become a hindrance. Suddenly you're concentrating on the hot, itchy sweater instead of the under-priced Art Deco candlesticks you just walked past.

At the very least, expect the temperature to fluctuate during the day. Layers of light clothing will prepare you for any variations in the weather. It's better to wear a light jacket that can be removed and carried in your cloth bag or backpack, serving as packing material if needed, than to be stuck in a heavy hooded sweatshirt all day because it's the only thing you tossed on that morning.

Never wear clothes that haven't been worn and washed several times. Everything should fit and be comfortable. A new pair of jeans might be a little tighter than you had imagined, or an unwashed T-shirt could cause an unexpected rash. And don't even think about breaking in a new pair of shoes at a flea market. You're just asking for trouble (read: blisters) if you think your new Nikes are going to travel miles of hot pavement and acres of uneven terrain at an outdoor market without revolting against your toes or heels. Comfortable, well-worn walking shoes are your best bet.

Don't forget something to cover your noggin, also. On cold days, nothing keeps you warm like a stocking cap. In hot weather, a wide-brimmed hat will protect your head, face, and neck, lessening the possibility of sunburn and headaches. At the very least, a baseball-style cap affords shade for your face, and it can easily be stuffed in a back pocket when no longer needed.

In addition to those items you're wearing, pack a second set of clothes to keep in your vehicle. Give yourself the option of warmer or cooler clothes, depending on the weather. You may start the day wearing long pants, but by noon the shorts in your car might feel more comfortable. A quick trip to change will be time well spent. Don't forget to pack an extra pair of shoes and socks as well. More than one rainy day at the flea market has been salvaged when the cloudburst stopped and the shopper changed out of soaked sneakers and into a dry pair of shoes and socks. Better yet, pack a pair of boots. You'll be glad you did when the other shoppers are slogging through a rain-soaked field with mud oozing between their toes.

The right stuff

The right clothes are important, but wise flea market shoppers know that it takes more than a comfortable pair of khakis to ensure a good day shopping. Here are some other items you'll find useful.

Cash: Money talks. Cash speaks a universal language that everyone understands. Do more than just take along enough to get you through the day, keeping in mind that you'll probably eat and put gas in the car before returning home. Make sure you have a sufficient number of small bills, as well as some change in your pocket. Ones and fives come in handy when buying low-priced items, especially if a dealer has a handful of twenties or doesn't want to break your $100 bill for a postcard tagged $1.50. The quarters jingling in your pocket will speed the transaction at the concession stand when all you want is a glass of iced tea before heading down the next aisle.

Reach for the sky! You'll be reaching for a dunce cap if, after years of searching, you finally stumble across a pair of Roy Rogers cap guns, but didn't bring enough cash to seal the deal.

Other funds: Although not all dealers accept checks, many do. Before leaving home, make sure you have a sufficient number of checks with you. Credit cards are honored by some dealers, primarily at the larger events; however, don't expect to use your VISA at many of the smaller flea markets. An ATM/debit card offers the best of both worlds. When you unexpectedly find a Pairpoint cornucopia just as you are running low on cash, the dealer will likely hold it for you while you dart off to the nearest automated teller machine. Many large flea markets now have ATMs available on the property.

Meals and snacks: Flea market food ranges from fantastic to repulsive, and to make matters worse, what some markets charge for a hot dog and a cold drink could finance a small Third World nation. Depending on the market, a better solution might be to pack your lunch and keep it in a cooler in the car. A quick trip to the parking lot will take less time than waiting in line for a greasy cheeseburger.

Pack high-energy food that's easily digested and, if desired, can be eaten while you walk. As a snack, fruit is always a good option, as are many sports-related energy bars. Don't forget to take along some drinks. A thermos of coffee, tea, or even soup is great for chilly mornings, while a cooler of iced soft drinks or juice will be worth its weight in gold by the end of the day. And don't forget the water. Not only will it quench you thirst, but it can also be used to clean and cool your face, neck, and hands on hot, sunny days.

After a long day of shopping, you may be too tired (or too poor) to stop at a restaurant. A cold drink and that box of crackers you stashed in your vehicle might be just what it takes to see you through the miles home.

The car kit: If you've spent much time at flea markets, you know how important it is to pack some things in the car "just in case." Among the items to consider are sunblock, Chap Stick, a travel-size medical kit, pain reliever, antacid, a small package of facial tissue, a container of anti-bacterial wipes or hand cleaner, bug spray, and even a hairbrush for those windy days at outdoor markets.

A box of your most frequently used reference books can serve as your traveling library. And don't forget to toss in some empty boxes, newspapers, wrapping supplies, and tape to pack your purchases safely for the trip home. A clipboard or several sturdy pieces of cardboard will protect items that are easily bent.

Some shoppers also include a black light, Bakelite and gold test kits, plastic bags for holding small items, maps, a flashlight, a tow chain, gloves, hand warmers, an umbrella, and a small bag of tools with screwdrivers of various types and sizes.

Tools of the trade: Although your goal is to travel as lightly as possible, you will still want to carry a number of items with you. Begin with a cloth bag, fanny pack, or backpack for storing needed tools of the trade as well as your flea market finds. Some shoppers prefer to use collapsible carts.

Do you find yourself in a pickle at large flea markets? With a multitude of items piled hither and yon, the approach you use to cover a flea market can mean the difference between going home with a treasure and leaving empty-handed.

A pen and a pocketsize notebook are useful for jotting down information on a dealer's location or for noting a specific item you want to quickly research using the reference books in your vehicle. A small tape measure can be used to determine whether the yellowware bowl you're considering is the size needed for your nesting set, or whether the Victorian marble-top table will fit next to your sofa. A collapsible jeweler's loupe will prove invaluable in reading small marks or enhancing details in vintage photographs. Some shoppers prefer a magnifying glass with a battery-powered light.

A magnet can be used to determine if a painted frog doorstop is cast iron or brass, and a set of batteries will come in handy for testing toys or other battery-operated collectibles.

Handing out a want list or cards printed with your name, telephone number and what you collect can help secure items after the event. Most business supply stores and copy centers can create inexpensive versions. You might also want to carry an inventory to refer to so you don't purchase duplicate items.

Durable paper towels can be tucked in your pocket, serving a multitude of functions. They can be used to wrap your newly acquired Davenport Cigars match safe so it doesn't get scratched, wipe a runny nose, clean up blood from a cut finger, or serve as a backup when the Port-A-John is out of toilet paper.

Dickering doesn't have to be ugly. If your heart's set on taking home this little critter, a well-mannered approach to bargaining might save you a few dollars.

Communication: Cellular phones and walkie-talkies have become standard equipment for many flea market shoppers. The cell phone allows you to inform your spouse when you're running a little late, to ask a friend if he's interested in the Creature From the Black Lagoon model kit you just found, or to call to have someone check a reference book you forgot to pack. Walkie-talkies and other two-way radios allow teams of shoppers to stay in contact with each other, checking to see if a Pepsi tray is a good buy or whether a team member still needs a specific Camp Snoopy drinking glass.

On your mark...

When it comes to flea markets, most veteran collectors attack the event with forethought. There's method to their madness. Here are some of the approaches used.

Run and gun: In the run and gun, the shopper hurries down the aisles, glancing in each booth for certain items, but not stopping unless he sees something he wants to buy. Sometimes he resorts to shouting, "Got any...?" as he's scurrying past. After going through the entire show, he'll begin a second loop, this time checking each booth more carefully.

Slow and steady: In this approach, the shopper figures he has a better chance of finding something if he methodically looks at all of the merchandise in each booth. This method allows him to scrutinize the items in each booth, but by the time he gets to the last aisle, several hours may have passed. He feels what he might miss in those latter booths (because it's already sold by the time he gets there) will be offset by the treasures he discovers early on.

FDS (Favored Dealer Status): Knowing certain dealers carry the type of merchandise he's looking for, the collector will immediately head to those booths. This is generally a good approach, and the dealers are easy to find since most flea markets allow them to reserve the same booth space for each show.

Walking advertisement: In this method, the customer wears a shirt or sign noting what he collects. Who could miss a neon-orange shirt with large black letters that read, "Old Cameras Wanted." Dealers with cameras for sale will eagerly flag down the shopper. No doubt, the resulting sale will be a Kodak moment.

A little diplomacy

It's well understood that most flea market dealers are willing to lower their prices. Surely you've had this experience: You're shopping a flea market when, out of curiosity, you pick up an item. Immediately, you are hit with a rapid-fire, "Icandobe'eronthat!" Translated, it means, "I can do better on that." It doesn't matter if you're holding a $125 Blue Ridge teapot, a $10 PEZ dispenser, or the gum wrapper your daughter just dropped on the ground, the phrase speaks volumes about the fact that flea markets are places where prices can be negotiated.

Some dealers will automatically volunteer to provide a discount, while others may have signs announcing, "Ask for a better price" or "No reasonable offer refused." Yet, often it's up to you to make the first move. Here are some rules for the game of dickering.

Rule No. 1: Politeness is everything. This is a good rule to follow in all your dealings at a flea market, from negotiating with a seller to ordering a hot dog at the concession stand. Put a smile on your face and enjoy the day. When seeking a better price from a dealer, a cheery countenance can work wonders. Talk to him with the same tone and manner you would use when asking a friend for a favor. You can never go wrong when treating people with kindness and respect.

Common courtesy will also put you in good stead when seeking additional information about an item that's for sale. You might want to know who previously owned a particular cedar chest or whether an oil painting has had touch-up work. Do as your mother told you, and mind your manners. A non-threatening approach will help put the dealer at ease and could put you both on the path to a sale.

Rule No. 2: Play with a poker face. Conceal your enthusiasm until after you've purchased the item. If you spot a Chef egg timer you recall from your grandmother's kitchen, don't squeal, "OH MY GOSH!" and immediately rush into the booth to gleefully snatch the piece off the table. To a dealer, that's tantamount to announcing, "I hereby waive all my rights to bargain on the price of this item." The dealer knows you want the egg timer, and he sees a sale coming at full price. Instead, wait until you get the little Chef character back to the car before jumping for joy.

Rule No. 3: Be willing to pay a fair price. Don't let your pride keep you from owning something you want, especially if it's already affordable. If you find a Hummel lamp worth $475 that's only priced $200, it's okay to ask if the dealer will negotiate the price. However, don't be offended if he tells you the price is firm. Pay the $200 and be happy with your bargain. Remember, collecting should be fun. Don't let the absence of a discount ruin your day.

Rule No. 4: Know how to bargain. There are a number of methods that work for buyers. The one we prefer is a straightforward, non-threatening approach. Politely call the item to the dealer's attention and ask, "Is this your best price?" The dealer then has the option of quoting a lower figure or telling you the price is firm. If a discount is offered, we recommend you either accept it or thank the dealer and walk away.

Some people delight in dickering back and forth until a price is agreed upon. If that's your style, and the dealer doesn't mind, the best of

Closely examine items before reaching for your wallet. The scratches and wear on this 7Up sign should be noted before you put it under your arm and head for the car, not after you get home and hang it on the wall.

luck to you both. But keep in mind that some dealers will be insulted if you respond to their offer by undercutting it with a counteroffer.

Rule No. 5: Bargain seriously. Don't ask for a discount unless you are truly interested in buying the item. Otherwise, you're wasting both your time and that of the dealer. We've all seen it happen. Someone picks up a Hubley airplane tagged $165 and asks the dealer, "Can you do any better on the price?" The dealer says he really wants to move merchandise, so he'll take $85 for it. The customer then mumbles something unintelligible, sets down the plane and walks out of the booth. Obviously, the individual never intended to buy the toy.

And that's final!

They're just three little words, but they can have a big impact on your life. We're all familiar with the phrase "All sales final." The general rule at most flea markets is that the deal is finalized when money changes hands. If you experience buyer's remorse or find an identical item for less just two booths later, don't expect the seller to refund your purchase price or give you a rebate.

Even if the item is later determined to be a reproduction, your avenues of recourse may be limited. While reputable dealers will refund the purchase price if an honest mistake has been made, others will point out that you should not have bought the piece if you weren't sure of its authenticity.

The best thing you can do is to carefully examine all merchandise before you buy.

Would you check on that?

You've found a McCoy cookie jar, the sticker price seems fair, and the dealer appears willing to negotiate. But before you strike a deal, there are some other steps you'll want to take.

Examine the item: Carefully check over prospective purchases. If the price seems low, the piece may be damaged. Examine glassware and pottery for chips and cracks. Check toys to see if all the parts are original and to determine whether the item has been repainted. Look for stains and holes in textiles and make sure you're dealing with an authentic item, not a reproduction.

Beware of reproductions such as this Uncle Sam with Carpet Bag mechanical bank. This example should be priced $20 or less, simply for its play value. An authentic example in very good condition is worth $2,800.

Ask about it: Even if you are convinced the item is perfect, ask the dealer if he's aware of any damage. You might have missed a hairline crack or a carefully concealed repair. An honest dealer will tell you what he knows and most dealers are honest.

That Latin phrase

This is the part of the book in which we get to use the Latin phrase every antiquer knows, *caveat emptor*—let the buyer beware. Although flea markets are enjoyable and hold the promise of turning up a prized collectible at a reasonable price, there are also some pitfalls that seem more troublesome than in any other segment of the market.

We want to stress that most flea market dealers are honest, reputable sellers who enjoy what they're doing and wouldn't think of jeopardizing their business by cheating a customer.

However, it's important to discuss the proverbial "one bad apple" that can spoil the rest of the fruit in the barrel.

Reproductions: Reproductions, fakes, and fantasy items are often found at flea markets. One must understand that sales of reproductions are not dependent on the items being represented as old merchandise. Quite the contrary. At some flea markets, reproductions are stacked ten-deep on the table and are offered at wholesale prices. That repro tin windup penguin may be bought as new here, passed off as authentic there. *There* may be no farther than three aisles away, so *caveat emptor.*

Knowledge is your best defense. If the price seems too good to be true, even at a flea market, then maybe it is. When examining an item, use all your senses. Look at it. Are the details crisp, or does a cast-iron bottle opener have the worn molding of many recasts? Examine the hardware. Are the screws in a mechanical bank the right type for when the piece was made? Study the lithography. Is the printing of a die-cut sporting goods sign a little fuzzy, indicating a later printing method? Feel the piece. Does the wear on the base correspond to the age of the planter? Some old merchandise even has a slightly different texture than the reproductions. Using your nose can also provide some clues about the item. Does a small curly maple candle box have the smell of a 150-year-old piece, or is the scent that of freshly cut wood or new varnish?

Tall tales: Unscrupulous dealers always have a story to tell about their merchandise. Listen carefully, and *caveat emptor.* You might be told that a crystal goblet traveled across the Atlantic Ocean with a family of Pilgrims aboard the Mayflower. But, if that goblet is pressed glass, you can rest assured it's not as old as the dealer suggests.

Some mistakes are made honestly, but they're mistakes nonetheless. How about the Lucy doll with a 1963 copyright date. The price tag read: "Lucy, 1963, all original, $45." But, Lucy's dress was fastened with Velcro tabs. Does anyone see a problem here? The Velcro shows the clothes to be of a more contemporary design.

Copyright dates are tricky things, and worth a brief mention. They indicate when a particular copyright was issued, not necessarily the date of manufacture for the object on which the copyright appear.

Look for clues that indicate an item's true age. For instance, a Royal Staffordshire platter marked "Dishwasher Safe" is definitely from the second half of the 20th century, not from the 19th century, no matter how old the transferware pattern looks. Knowledgeable collectors are always on the lookout for price tags with incorrect information. Among the common mistakes are pressed glass said to be cut glass, molded pottery marked as hand-thrown, machine-molded glassware claimed to be mouth-blown, plastic tagged as Bakelite or celluloid . . . Need we go on?

Knowledge is your friend. The best purchases you will ever make are good reference books. Some of your most productive time will be spent with dealers and collectors who allow a hands-on examination of authentic antiques and collectibles. Armed with knowledge, you can shop any market safely.

Absolutely positive

Don't let "The Bad and the Ugly" scare you away from flea markets. The nasties are far outweighed by "The Good" that can be found at these events. Topping the list of those positives is the family atmosphere at flea markets. Here's the perfect way to spend a day with loved ones. Because flea markets offer something for everyone, even children enjoy tagging along. The hunt for inexpensive collectibles will keep them interested for hours.

Although children seem to have a natural interest in the merchandise at flea markets, they don't always have the stamina to spend an entire day walking aisles and darting into booths. One popular solution is to take a wagon. Your youngsters will enjoy the ride, especially at outdoor markets. Toss in a coloring book or handheld video game, and you've made great strides toward boredom-proofing the day. Add a small cooler with juice and snacks, and you'll be a hero in their eyes.

Strollers can also be used, and they're particularly good for infants. But whether you're pushing little Susie in a stroller or pulling Johnny Jr. in a wagon, don't be surprised if you get the evil eye from at least a few shoppers.

Some adults think children should be banned from all markets. Don't let such cavalier attitudes ruin your day. Remember, you're spending time with your family, and there are few things in the world more important than that. Behaving courteously when maneuvering through the show and using common sense when parking your children to examine an item will certainly be appreciated though.

Due to the inexpensive nature of some of the merchandise, flea markets are good places for children to learn the value of money. Permitting them to spend their allowance on a collection of their own teaches them to make decisions regarding how that money is used.

The other side

What's more fun than shopping at a flea market? How about selling at one? Most flea markets are a mix of full-time dealers running a business and one-time sellers looking for a way to get rid of the stuff that has piled up in the garage. As such, these markets are perfect for anyone looking to make a little cash from the extra things around the house.

Selling your unwanted childhood toys might be a great way to put a little cash in your pocket. But before signing up for a booth at a flea market, make sure you know what you're doing.

Here are some tips to help you succeed if you're new to the role of flea market dealer.

Finding fleas: The first thing you need to do is decide which flea market you want to try. Check flea market directories and trade publications to see which events are held in your area. Before making a commitment to take a booth, attend several flea markets. Ask the dealers what they like about the event and what they would change. Question them about what's selling well and what price ranges attract buyers. Decide whether your merchandise will fit in at a particular market. Inquire about other flea markets the dealers use, as well as the ones they like to shop. Don't forget to find out how and where the flea market is advertised. The greater the number of people who hear about the market, the more customers you will likely have.

Next, study the environment. Are there plenty of shoppers? Are the facilities well kept? Are there affordable concessions and clean restrooms? All of these are important considerations for keeping shoppers happy. As a dealer, you'll quickly learn that an unhappy customer is less likely to make a purchase.

Calculating costs: It's important to know how much you'll have to spend to get started in the flea market business, whether you're interested in selling only once or want to set up every weekend. Talk to the promoter about rates and the availability of booth space. Do the dealers also rent tables for displaying their goodies, or will you need to bring some from home? Of course, don't overlook the incidental expenses, such as gas for travel, meals while away from home, and the cost of a motel if you're traveling any distance. All those things can quickly cut into your profit.

Factoring time: If you are retired, you might have unlimited time to devote to your new hobby. But if you're still holding down a 9-to-5 job, can you get away from your desk in time to get on the road and set up at your favorite flea market? Before committing to a particular market, ask the promoter about the event's set-up policy. Because dealers often arrange their booths before the show begins, you may need to spend Friday traveling to your destination and setting up, in preparation for the crowd that will spill through the gates early Saturday morning.

One other factor to consider is how early you plan to arrive at your booth during the show.

When we asked flea market dealers for tips, they repeatedly told us, "Arrive early." After only one flea market experience, you'll appreciate the need to be ready before the show opens, in order to maximize sales to early shoppers as well as other dealers.

Some dealers also mentioned that it's important to be willing to stay late at a show. Leaving too soon might get you home in time to catch that made-for-TV movie you wanted to see, but it can also mean you miss out on sales to last-minute bargain hunters.

Deciding what to take: In addition to your merchandise, you'll need the following.

Tables—Unless tables are provided by the promoter, you'll need something to display your items on. Card tables and larger folding tables are ideal.

Chair—Don't forget something to sit on during lulls in the action.

Cash box and change—A small locking cash box and adequate change, both bills and coins, will be essential.

Spending money—In addition to the money for your cash box, you'll want to take along some extra funds for any purchases you might make or to buy lunch.

Wrapping material—Newspapers, tissue, and bubble wrap will protect your customers' purchases on the trip home.

Tape—This can be used to secure the wrapping material around an item or for posting signs in your booth.

Bags and boxes—You will need paper or plastic bags to hold sold merchandise if the customer doesn't have their own carry-all. Cardboard boxes are good for packaging larger pieces or multiple items.

Receipt books—You'll want to record your sales, and your customer will appreciate a copy of the transaction.

Price tags—Pack some extra price tags for any items you purchase for resale while traveling to the flea market or while at the event. You might also discover you've forgotten to mark some merchandise, and extra tags will come in handy.

Business cards—Don't be bashful about handing out business cards to anyone who is interested in your merchandise. It may result in a sale long after you've packed up and gone home. When a shopper has time to reconsider your Wizard of Oz book he walked away from at the show, knowing how to contact you could put that one in the sold column.

Price guides—Pack a few of your favorite price guides, including one general-line guide that covers the market as a whole. (Of course, we strongly recommend this book!) They'll come in handy for determining whether an Annie lunchbox is a good buy or for showing a customer where to find information on a club for jelly glass collectors.

Showcase—Consider keeping any valuable small items in a showcase, which will discourage theft.

Sheets or tarps—You might also want to take some light, unfitted bed sheets to cover you merchandise when you're out of your booth, keeping ne'er-do-wells from being tempted by your miniature Blue Willow tea set. For outdoor shows, a light covering will also prevent dew from forming on your merchandise, while a water-resistant tarp will be more appropriate when the skies threaten rain.

Creating the display: There is no right or wrong way to display merchandise at a flea market. Some dealers achieve satisfactory results by simply placing their wares on a blanket on the ground. Others adopt a more professional approach, using tables with table covers, risers and lights. We believe the latter provides better exposure for your merchandise, and increased visibility can translate to increased sales.

One of the best things you can do to encourage sales is to price all of your merchandise. Some shoppers hesitate to ask for the price of an item that's untagged. Others may not ask out of principal, believing the dealer will quote a figure that's artificially inflated if the shopper is dressed nicely and appears to be financially fit. Don't run the risk of losing a sale because your merchandise isn't marked.

Providing customer service: The manner in which you treat your customers is the single most important factor in ensuring your success as a flea market dealer. Never underestimate the importance of greeting every individual who enters your booth. A genuine smile and polite conversation might be all it takes to win over a shopper who's debating whether to buy your hula girl nodder. Customers who are treated with courtesy will remember you, and a friend you make today might well be a customer you keep for life.

The Great American Flea Market Quiz

Test your knowledge about some of the hot items on today's market

At the races

Hot Wheels 1993 McDonald's race car.

1998 Racing Champions 1/24 scale die-cast model.

Q. Okay, so maybe you aren't Jeff Gordon. But it probably doesn't take a NASCAR superstar to get the answer to this quiz. In the race for a collector's budget, which of these HOT flea market finds will only cost you a buck, and which is more likely to have you reaching for a $20 bill?

A. Bigger is better, when it comes to these two HOT collectibles. The Racing Champions model is valued at $20, while the Hot Wheels toy will put smiles on faces of collectors for only $1.

Birds of a feather

Rooster salt and pepper shakers, 4-5/8" high.

Robin figurine, 4-1/4" high.

Q. What's that they say about birds of a feather? These collectibles never flocked together, since different makers produced them. Take a good look—a little birdwatching, so to speak—and see if you can tell which was made by Holt Howard and which carries a tag for Lefton.

A. Are you a birdbrain? The rooster salt and pepper shakers were made by Holt Howard around 1960. Standing 4-5/8" high, collectors crow when they can find them priced less than $35 a pair. The robin figurine was made by Lefton. The 4-1/4" high figurine is worth $12.

Off the wall

Abingdon #435 wall pocket.

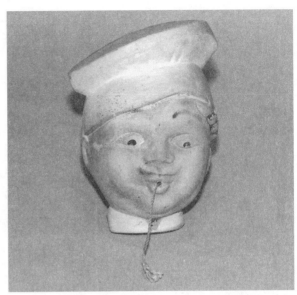

Chalkware chef string holder.

Q. Many flea market shoppers are looking for good-quality merchandise that's not recognized by the seller. For shoppers, coming home with a bargain makes the trip all the more worthwhile. If these items were tagged $10 apiece, they'd each be a steal. But, which would be the better buy?

A. String holders are still HOT at flea markets, but the Chef remains a relatively common find. This example, having some wear, is valued at $42. Wall pockets are also in demand, and this one made by Abingdon has a value of $120. Put in perspective, the choice is obvious.

Who's hungry?

Burger Chef paper cup, 5" high.

Longaberger 1993 Inaugural Basket.

Q. Working up an appetite yet? Before you give up on these quizzes and head for the drive-thru or maybe even a picnic at the park, see if you can answer this question. Are these two HOT collectibles worth A) less than $5 apiece, B) less than $100 apiece, or C) more than $100 apiece.

A. Remember how Mama Bear's porridge was too cold and Papa Bear's porridge was too hot, while Baby Bear's porridge was just right. The same principle applies here. Answer A is too low, while answer C is too high. If you chose answer B, you're just right. The Burger chef cup is worth just under $10, while the Longaberger basket has a value of $65.

A day in the sun

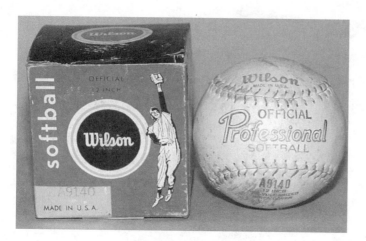

Wilson professional softball, original box.

J. Chein sand pail, some rust.

Q. When was the last time you built a sandcastle or played a game of softball? We could all certainly use more leisure time. Spending those extra hours looking for flea market bargains would be a good way to catch some sun. There's good news/bad news regarding the condition of these two HOT items, which are found in our "Sand Pails" and "Sporting Goods" categories. Do you know what it is?

A. The good news is the softball has its original box, which increases its value. The bad news is the rust on the sand pail, which takes its worth down a notch. The sand pail is valued at $48, while the softball is worth $6.

Odds and ends

Miss America pattern Depression glass divided relish.

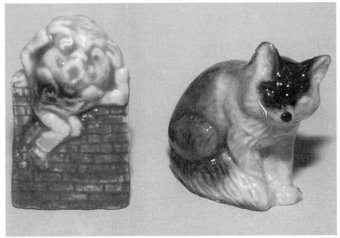

Wade Humpty Dumpty and Fox.

Scottie figural lighter.

Q. You've seen the guy at the carnival who can guess a person's age, right? (And just how does he do that?) Now here's your chance to be a sideshow superstar. Can you put these three HOT items in chronological order according to when they were made, from oldest to newest?

A. Did you rank them this way: Depression glass, Scotties, and Wade ceramics? If so, move to the head of the class, because you ranked them correctly. Want to make a guess at their value? That's okay, we'll tell you. The pink relish is worth $25, the Wade figures are valued at $8.50 each, and the Scotties lighter brings $13.50.

For exciting collecting trends and newly expanded areas look for the following symbols:

✪ Hot Topic
✮ New Warman's Listing

(May have been in another Warman's title.)

❖ ABC Items

Generations of nannies and mothers have educated children by using colorful china with letters of the alphabet, numbers, etc. Most ABC plates were imported to the United States from England. They were highly popular between 1780 and 1860, when literacy rates were low. Originally available for only a few cents, they served a practical purpose on the table while also affording an inexpensive education. Often these charming children's wares incorporated nursery rhymes or sayings meant to inspire goodness in the user.

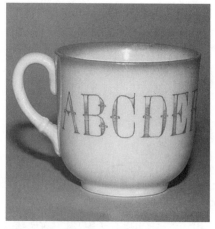

ABC cup, pink luster letters and rim, A through M, 2-5/8" high, $40.

References: Irene and Ralph Lindsay, *ABC Plates & Mugs*, Collector Books, 1998; Margaret and Kenn Whitmyer, *Collector's Encyclopedia of Children's Dishes*, Collector Books, 1993.

Collectors' Clubs: ABC Plate & Mug Collectors, 67 Stevens Ave, Old Bridge, NJ 08857.

For additional listings, see *Warman's Antiques & Collectibles* and *Warman's Country.*

Baby cup, sterling, Wm. B. Kerr & Co., nursery rhyme pictures and the alphabet, mkd "American Beauty" in the bottom, 2-1/4" h, 2-1/2" dia 250.00

Bowl, Campbell Soup Kid in chef's hat, alphabet around bottom inside of bowl, "Alicia" in center, premium...........................14.00

Cup, small, silver luster, floral sprig dec...................................135.00

Mug
    Bird perched on branch, alphabet on side, brown transfer with blue accents.........245.00
    DEF and children playing shuttlecock, pink transfer.......165.00
    Franklin's Maxim, "Slough Like Rust Consumes Faster Than Labor Wears," black transfer 165.00
    Tin, band of flowers, 1-7/8" h, 2-3/4" dia.....................175.00

Plate, carnival glass, marigold, stork and baby circled by numbers in center, alphabet around edge, 7-3/4" dia 89.00

Plate, china
    Cat and mouse, Staffordshire, Elsmore and Son, 8" dia 225.00
    Child reading, Staffordshire, black transfer, short hairline, edge flakes, 5" dia.........35.00
    Crusoe at Work, brown transfer, blue and yellow accents, brown printed alphabet border 225.00
    Elephant, Staffordshire, polychrome, Brownhills Pottery, Wild Animal Series, 7-3/8" dia 235.00
    "F's for The Fowls And The Farm...," scene of animals inside barn, blue transfer, raised alphabet border 185.00
    Girl and cottage, polychrome, 8" dia 195.00

Little Boy Blue 80.00
"Make Hay While The Sun Shines," 6" dia 175.00
"The Tulip and the Butterfly," J. & G. Meakin, 5-3/8" dia.. 265.00
"The Walk," shows gentleman riding horse, c1860, unmkd 220.00
Two boys in cart pulled by dog, Staffordshire, 7" dia 125.00
White, emb letters, beaded edge, 7" dia 50.00
Plate, ironstone, white, green letters, 6-5/8" dia 62.00
Plate, tin
    George Washington, c1890s, 6" dia...............................175.00
    Girl on swing, lithographed center, printed alphabet border 60.00
    Two kittens playing with basket of wood, 4-1/2" dia......180.00
    Who Killed Cock Robin?, 8" dia 115.00

✪ Abingdon Pottery

The Abingdon Sanitary Manufacturing Company of Abingdon, IL, was founded in 1908. Although originally created to make plumbing fixtures, an art pottery line was introduced around 1933. In 1945 the company's name was changed to Abingdon Potteries, Inc., with production of the art pottery line continuing until 1950, when fire destroyed the art pottery kiln. The company then focused its attention on plumbing fixtures, eventually, becoming Briggs Manufacturing Company.

Reference: Joe Paradis, *Abingdon Art Pottery*, Schiffer Publishing, 1996.

Collectors' Club: Abingdon Pottery Collectors' Club, 210 Knox Hwy S, Abingdon, IL 61410.

For additional listings, see *Warman's Americana & Collectibles.*

Ashtray, #456 ....36.00
Bookend
    Goose, #98, single 42.00
    Horse head, #441, black, pr 75.00

Seagull, #305, single 70.00
Candleholder, double scroll, blue, gold trim, wear to gold, pr..35.00
Compote, #568, white, 5" h, base 2" sq 25.00
Console bowl
    #377, yellow, handle continues into bowl, 3-3/4" h, 14" w 45.00
    #532, green, leaf design, 10" l 27.50
Cookie jar
    Daisy.................................45.00
    Money Bag, #588..............80.00
    Pineapple, lid repaired.......75.00
    Sunflower...........................45.00
Figure
    Goose, #571, blue 45.00
    Peacock, pink 40.00
Flower pot, #151, white, hp floral dec, 5" h 25.00
Planter
    Fan shape, light blue, 4-1/2" h, 8" l.................................32.00
    Sailing Ship, sea green glaze, rope handles 40.00
Salt and pepper shakers, Little Bo Peep, pr...........................45.00
String holder, mouse 90.00
Tray, green, 10-3/4" x 8"..........22.50
Vase
    Blue, #117, 9-3/4" h 45.00
    Boyne pattern, 2 handles, pale peach, 9" h...................35.00
    Double cornucopia, #482, white, 11" l...............................35.00
    Fan, #513, salmon color, 9" h 25.00
    Ivory, #181, 2 handles........50.00
    Orange, 2 handles, 10" h...52.00
Wall pocket
    Book...............................50.00
    Calla Lily 60.00

❖ Action Figures

Action figures are posable models with flexible joints. Generally made of plastic, the figures portray real or fictional characters and their clothing, personal equipment, vehicles, and other accessories. The earliest action figures were the hard-plastic Hartland figures that depicted popular Western television heroes of the 1950s. During the late 1950s, Louis Marx also produced action figures for a number of their playsets, but it was GI Joe, introduced in 1964, that

triggered the modern action figure craze. Mego established the link between action figures and the movies when the company issued series based on *Planet of the Apes* and *Star Trek: The Motion Picture*. Kenner jumped on the bandwagon with the production of *Star Wars* figures in 1977.

References: Elizabeth A. Stephan, *Toy Shop's Action Figure Price Guide*, Krause Publications, 2000; John Bonavita, *Mego Action Figure Toys*, Schiffer Publishing, 1996; Paris & Susan Manos, *Collectible Action Figures*, 2nd ed., Collector Books, 1996; John Marshall, *Action Figures of the 1980s*, Schiffer Publishing, 1998.

Periodicals: *Action Figure News & Review*, 556 Monroe Tpk, Monroe, CT 06468; *Tomart's Action Figure Digest*, Tomart Publications, 3300 Encrete Ln, Dayton, OH 45439.

Collectors' Clubs: Captain Action Collectors Club, P.O. Box 2095, Halesite, NY 11743; Captain Action Society of Pittsburgh, 516 Cubbage St, Carnegie, PA 15106.

Alien, Slasher, Spider-Man, loose 7.50
AT-AT Commander 40.00
Banzai...................................10.00
Bedrock, Spawn, loose...........15.00
Bespin Guard Black, 3" h 12.00
Betty Mustin, Mask, Kenner, MOC 20.00
Boba Fett, Star Wars, 2 circles, MIP 25.00
Brett Hull, Starting Lineup, 1994 ....10.00
Carcass 25.00
Clear Iceman, X-Men...............25.00
Deadproof, #1, X-Men 25.00
Death Star Commander, Star Wars 10.00
Dorian, Mask, Kenner, MOC....20.00
Dream Team, 1996 Basketball, Starting Lineup, set 1 of 2..30.00
Eric Lindros, Starting Lineup, 1996, MOC 24.00
Hannibal, A-Team, Galoob, MOC 20.00
Heads Up, Mask, Kenner, MOC 20.00
Human Torch, Fantastic Four 7.50
Jim Carey, Starting Lineup, 1996 ....15.00
Joker, Legends of Batman,......15.00

Leia Organa, Star Wars, ...20.00
Low-Light, GI Joe, 1989, loose, 3-3/4" h 14.00
Luke Skywalker, Star Wars, 1st issue, 12" h, MIP..............38.00
Luke, X-Wing, 3" 12.00
Mystique, Marvel, loose, 10" h 15.00
Peter Parker, Spider-Man, loose 10.00
Phantasm, Batman, animated, foreign card 24.00
Picard, Star Trek, loose 10.00
Power Droid, loose, 3" h 8.00
Quick Draw, Mask, Kenner, MOC 20.00
Rogue, Marvel, loose, 10" h....12.00
Sabretooth #1, X-Men.............10.00
Spider-Man, super-posable, 10" h 10.00
Steve Bono, Starting Lineup, MOC 12.00
Tornado, Mask, Kenner, MOC 20.00
Tremor, Spawn, loose 12.00
Troll, Spawn 15.00
Vampire, Spawn, loose 17.50
Werewolf, Spawn, loose 20.00
Wild Wolf, Mask, Kenner, MOC 18.00
Willie Mays, Starting Lineup ...20.00
Wolfman, vinyl clothes, 1960s, 3-1/2" h 90.00
World War I Aviator Ace, GI Joe mail-in 60.00

❖ Adams

For collectors, the name Adams denotes quality English pottery. Since the company's inception in 1770, Adams potteries have been located in seven locations. Various marks have been used over the years, ranging from a simple "Adams" to more complex variations of the name. Some pieces were not marked.

Creamer, scene of three people in front of English buildings, dark blue transfer, wishbone handle, imp "Adams" 165.00
Cup and saucer, handleless, Adams Rose pattern, imp "Adams" 225.00
Dish, Cries of London-Ten Bunches A Penny Primrose, rect.....50.00
Mush mug, The Farmers Arms 90.00
Pitcher, Adams Rose pattern, scalloped rim 110.00

Plate
   Adams Rose pattern, early 95.00
   English scene, dark blue trans-
      fer, imp "Adams"..........270.00
   Shakespeare Series, Sir John
      Falstaff, black transfer, blue
      and green accents, orange
      border...........................35.00

❖ Advertising

Advertisers of the 19th and early 20th centuries understood the necessity of catching the attention of potential customers. Colorful graphics were an important feature of mass-produced advertising items beginning in the late 1800s. Not only did bright, creative packaging attract attention, it also helped customers identify and locate particular brands during an era in which many people could not read. Those same colorful designs serve as head-turners for today's collectors, just as they did for buyers of a bygone era.

References: Ted Hake, *Hake's Guide to Advertising Collectibles*, Wallace-Homestead, 1992; Bob and Sharon Huxford, *Huxford's Collectible Advertising,* 3rd ed., Collector Books, 1996; Don and Elizabeth Johnson, *Warman's Advertising*, Krause Publications, 2000; Patricia McDaniel, *Drugstore Collectibles,* Wallace-Homestead, 1994.

Sultana Peanut Butter pail, 1-pound, $66.

Periodicals: *Creamers*, P.O. Box 11, Lake Villa, IL 60046; *Paper Collectors' Marketplace*, P.O. Box 128, Scandinavia, WI 54917; *Advertising Collectors Express*, P.O. Box 221, Mayview, MO 64071.

Collectors' Clubs: Advertising Cup & Mug Collectors of America, P.O. Box 680, Solon, IA 52333; Antique Advertising Assoc. of America, P.O. Box 1121, Morton Grove, IL 60053, www.pastime.org; Ephemera Society of America, P.O. Box 95, Cazenovia, NY 13035; Farm Machinery Advertising Collectors, 10108 Tamarack Dr, Vienna, VA 22182; Inner Seal Collectors Club, 4585 Saron Dr, Lexington, KY 40515; National Assoc. of Paper & Advertising Collectors, P.O. Box 500, Mount Joy, PA 17552; Porcelain Advertising Collectors Club, P.O. Box 381, Marshfield Hills, MA 02151-0381. Tin Container Collectors Assoc, P.O. Box 440101, Aurora, CO 80044.

For additional listings, see *Warman's Antiques & Collectibles, Warman's Americana & Collectibles* and *Warman's Advertising* as well as specific categories in this edition.

Advertisement, Lee Overalls, fabric sample, 1920s...................20.00
Banner, Holsum Bread, illus by Howard Brown, 58" w......125.00
Billhook, Ceresota Flour..........50.00
Blotter
   Levi's, stiff cardboard, full color art, black and white imprint for local dealer, unused, 1960s, 2-3/4" x 6-1/4" 20.00
   Pan-Am Gasoline, celluloid cover with country scene and adv, Dufe W. Fling Oil Co., 3" h, 7-3/4" l....................90.00
Book, *Chase & Sanborn Coffee & Tea Importers*, 1889 ....30.00
Box, Baker's Chocolate, wood, 12-lb 25.00
Box opener, Wrigley's, 1940s ..70.00
Bowl, Bird's Eye, General Foods 27.50
Cleanser, Pow Wow, multicolor graphic of Indian in headdress 55.00
Coat hanger, San Francisco Cleaning & Drying Works, wood .10.00
Coffee cup, White Castle........35.00

Hires syrup dispenser, porcelain, 13-1/2" high, $1,485.

Coffee measure, "Coffee Satisfaction is assured by A & P Coffee Service," aluminum, 3-3/4" l 8.00
Coffee tin, H & K Coffee, 3-lb.. 55.00
Counter display, Gillette Blue Blades, cardboard, easel back, 1930s, 30" x 22"................ 85.00
Crate, Warner's Kidney Liver & Remedy, wood, holds 2 doz bottles 165.00
Emery board, Wead's Bread... 20.00
Folder, Marcelle Face Powder, samples 18.00
Jar, Horlick's Malted Milk, orig lids, set of 4 .... 125.00
Liquor jug, Fleischmann's, dark blue pottery 90.00
Lunch box, Slim Jims, Aladdin, no thermos,.......................... 20.00
Mending kit, Real Silk Hosiery .. 5.00
Pail, Picwick Peanut Butter, faded and dented, 12-oz, 3-1/2" h, 3-1/4" dia 25.00
Plate, Quick Service Laundry, tin, c1900 .... 35.00
Record buffer, Victor 40.00
Ruler, Clark Bars, wood 8.00
Salesman's brochure, Superior Matches, matchbook covers, "Glamour Girls Series" 45.00
Sample, Mavis Face Powder .. 14.00
Soap box, Rub-No-More, shows elephants 40.00
Tape measure, Fab................. 35.00
Theater slide, advertising Kingnut Oleomargarine, orig box, pr 30.00
Tip tray, Clysmic Water, woman, deer and giant bottle of product 45.00

Tray, copper, Angelus Marshmallows, shows early Angelus Chocolate Marshmallows box, mkd "Rusckheim Bros & Eckstein, Chicago," 3-3/8" w, 5" l 50.00

Tumbler, Small Grain Distilling, Louisville, etched, paneled sides, 4" h 55.00

Wallet, Rock Island Plow, cloth 24.00

Whetstone, Lavacide, For Fumigation, celluloid, Innis, Speiden & Co., N.Y., ... 35.00

Whistle, Atwater Kent Radios .. 15.00

Wrapper, Huskey Ice Cream Bar, snow dog 15.00

Yardstick, Smith's Furniture Store 10.00

❖ Advertising Characters

Just as advertisers used colorful labels to attract attention, the use of characters became quite important. When consumers didn't know what brand to buy, they often decided to trust the character or personality promoting a product. Today many of these characters generate strong collector interest. From Mr. Peanut to the Campbell Kids, there is a plethora of items available to collectors.

References: Warren Dotz, *Advertising Character Collectibles*, Collector Books, 1993; *What a Character*, Chronicle Books, 1996; Don and Elizabeth Johnson, *Warman's Advertising*, Krause Publications, 2000; Mary Jane Lamphier, *Zany Characters of the Ad World*, Collector Books, 1995; David and Micki Young, *Campbell's Soup Collectibles from A to Z*, Krause Publications, 1998.

For additional listings, see *Warman's Antiques & Collectibles*, *Warman's Americana & Collectibles* and *Warman's Advertising*, as well as specific categories in this edition.

Reproduction Alert.

Aristocrat Tomato, figure, Heinz, smiling red tomato wearing black monocle and top hat, "Heinz" in relief on front of base and "57" logo on three sides, c1950 .... 245.00

Chiquita Banana stuffed toy, 14-1/2" high, $20.

Bud Man, Budweiser Beer, flesh-colored foam rubber doll, red outfit with dark blue gloves and boots, black, white and red bow tie, "Budweiser" and "Bud Man" applied stickers on chest, late 1960s, 18" h 120.00

Charlie Tuna
Alarm Clock, wind-up, brass, Lux Time Co. 65.00
Doll, vinyl, 7-1/2" h 30.00

Dutch Boy Paint, hand puppet, vinyl head, fabric body, orig cellophane bag, 1960s, 11" h 45.00

Elsie the Cow, Borden's
Badge, white ground, blue lettering, 1-1/2" dia 10.00
Ball, West Texas State Buffaloes, white, blue lettering, 4" dia 15.00
Fountain glass, clear glass, frosted image of Elsie and name, tiny Borden Co. copyright, c1940, 6-1/4" h, pr 35.00
Postcard, Elsie and Elmer, color, traveling scene 25.00
Ring, plastic, dark gold luster, center clear plastic dome over multicolor Elsie image, 1950 .... 35.00
Salt and pepper shakers, Elsie and Elmer, china, c1940, pr 125.00

Eveready Cat, bank 10.00

Florida Orange Bird, bank, orange vinyl, green hair and wings, Hong Kong, c1960, 4-3/4" h 35.00

Hamburger Helper Helping Hand, figure, gold painted plaster, four-fingered glove, smiling face on palm, sealed in orig cellophane bag, generic box, 1-1/4" x 2" x 3" h 18.00

Hamm's Bear, cup, Hamm's Beer, blue and red artwork of trademark bear relaxing in back yard, beret and glasses on one side, running with tray of beer on other, Dixie, c1970, 5" h, set of 4 .... 16.00

Johnny, Philip Morris
Pinback button, 1930s 35.00
Sign, emb tin, worn, 12" x 14" 95.00

Johnny Walker Red, mug 15.00

Kool Cigarettes
Dr. Kool, figure, painted plaster, wearing stethoscope and carrying satchel with name on side, late 1930s, professional repair to base chip, 4-1/2" h 136.00
Willie and Millie, salt and pepper shakers, figural, black and white plastic, yellow and red accents, c1950, 3-1/2" h 35.00

Mr. Clean, figure, Procter and Gamble, painted vinyl, muscular, bald-headed figure with green earring in one ear, c1961, 8" h 135.00

Nipper, RCA Victor
Coffee mug, plastic 8.00
Snow dome 40.00

Oscar Mayer, Weinermobile, bank, plastic.................................. 30.00

Pillsbury Doughboy, Pillsbury Co.
Doll, vinyl, smiling full figure boy, blue accent eyes, button on cap, copyright 1971 Pillsbury Co., Minneapolis, 7-1/4" h 18.00
Salt and pepper shakers, 4" h Poppin Fresh, 3-1/4" h Poppie, names on bases, copyright 1974 .... 28.00

Reddy Kilowatt
Figure, plastic, white head and translucent pink body on black base, hands and boots glow after exposure to bright light, mid-1930s, 5" h, base 1/4" x 1-1/2" x 3" 300.00
Magic Gripper, textured yellow rubber disk, image of Reddy the Chef, c1950, 4-3/4" dia, orig red and white paper envelope 5-1/4" sq 20.00

Magnepad, quilted hot pad with
    magnet, white with red image
    of Reddy, gray fabric reverse,
    unopened clear cellophane
    bag, c1950, 5-3/4" sq 30.00
Pin, brass and red enamel figure,
    c1950, 1" h, orig diecut card
    2-1/4" x 2-3/4" 40.00
Tony the Tiger, spoon, silverplate,
    emb "Kellogg's" 10.00

❖ Air Guns

"You'll shoot your eye out!" That
admonition is uttered by mothers
everywhere, yet kids continue their
love affair with BB guns and pellet
guns. Air guns trace their roots to
the time of Napoleon, but most collectors set their sights on examples
manufactured since the late 19th
century. Air guns made in the 1800s
command premium prices, while
models from the 20th century are
kinder to the bank account. Collectors also search for go-withs such as
ammunition containers.
Benjamin 30-30 carbine, rust-blis-
    tered barrel 42.00

Book
    The American BB Gun by Arni
        Dunathan.......................71.00
    *The Complete Book of the Air
        Gun* by George C. Nonte,
        Stackpole Books, 1970
        ....100.00
History of the Daisy BB Gun by Cass
    S. Hough, 1976.................58.00
Daisy
    Model 21 double barrel BB gun
        ....425.00
    Model 25 commemorative BB
        gun, c1986, MIB 250.00
    Model 89 ....90.00
    Model 1894 ....65.00
Postcard, depicts American Youth's
    Bill of Rights poster, c1947, 5" x
    7" 31.00
Red Ryder
    1983, sundial, large compass,
        orig box noting "A Christmas
        Story"............................395.00
    1998, 60th anniversary BB gun,
        retail production model, MIB
        ....40.00
Shot tube, shoots cork ball instead
    of BBs, for Model 21/25/99
    ....95.00

**Daisy Bulls-Eye BB Target Pis-
tol, Model 177, original box,
$50.**

Target, Daisy, metal, targets spin
    when hit, 6" h, 8" w 62.00
Token, depicts Red Ryder and
    Beave, brass, 2" dia.......... 15.00
Upton, Model 40, 1,000-shot, nickel-
    plated, c1921 .... 350.00

❖ Airline Collectibles (Commercial)

Come fly with me! The friendly
skies continue beckoning collectors
today. As airlines merge, change
names, or even go out of business,
interest in related memorabilia will
increase.

Periodical: *Airliners*, P.O. Box
52-1238, Miami, FL 33152.

Collectors' Clubs: Aeronautic & Air
Label Collectors Club, P.O. Box
1239, Elgin, IL, 60121; C.A.L./N-X-
211 Collectors Society, 226 Tioga
Ave, Bensenville, IL 60106; Gay Air-
line Club, P.O. Box 69A04, West
Hollywood, CA 90069; World Airline
Historical Society, 3381 Apple Tree
Ln, Erlanger, KY 41018.
For additional listings, see *Warman's
    Americana & Collectibles.*
Cup and saucer, Delta Airlines, for
    VIP International flights, Mayer
    China 25.00
Dinner plate, Delta Airlines, for VIP
    International flights, Mayer
    China 20.00
Cigar cutter, pocket, Pan Am, 1901
    .... 70.00
Napkin holder, American Airlines,
    open-ended metal clasp, center
    with "AA" soaring eagle symbol,
    c1930 .... 15.00

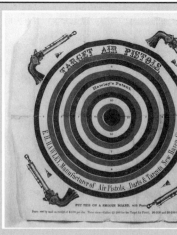
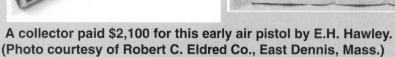

**A collector paid $2,100 for this early air pistol by E.H. Hawley.
(Photo courtesy of Robert C. Eldred Co., East Dennis, Mass.)**

An early find. Think your Daisy BB gun is old? Think again!
While Daisy is still the big name when it comes to airguns, examples
that predate the company are always in demand. That was the case for
this 22-100 caliber air pistol made by E.H. Hawley. Circa 1860, this
unusual prize was found in an attic in Massachusetts. Housed in a
japanned box, the gun had a 5-inch barrel and came with a target sheet,
instruction and 10 broadsheets. It was auctioned by Robert C. Eldred Co.
of East Dennis, Mass., selling for $2,100.

Place setting, United Airlines, china 42.00

Playing cards, c1960-80, box 3/4" x 2-1/4" x 3-1/2"

American Airlines, US mail plane 10.00

Delta Airlines, white pyramid 8.00

Eastern/Ryder, text with logo 8.00

Ozark, snow-covered Rockies 10.00

TWA Collectors Series, Douglas DC-9, 1966....................12.00

Postcard, unused

Aerolineas Argentinas, Carrasco Airport, Montevideo Uruguay, black and white, 1950s, 10.00

Air Canada, preparing for take-off, oversized...................6.00

Air Transat, Lockheed L1011, color, oversized...............6.00

Alitalia, Caravelle III S.E. 210, radio print on back 8.00

KLM, Douglas DC-6B, airline issued, slight crease 7.00

Lufthansa DC-10, airline issued 5.00

Pan American, Super 6 Clipper, color 8.00

Piedmont Airlines, Boeing 737-300 series, color, oversized 6.00

Pluna, Uruguay, Boeing 737 ....6.00

Old Taylor whiskey bottle, glass, "Bottled Especially for Delta," 4-7/8" high, $4.50.

Trans-Canada Airlines, airline issued, Viscount at Windsor Airport, Windsor, Ontario, Canada...........................8.00

Statuette, Air-India, painted plastic, turbaned man on green flying carpet, orig label "Ameya Industries/Bombay, India," c1970, 4-1/2" h 35.00

Stewardess wings, United Airlines, silver accent wings, red, white and blue center logo, orig black and white card, c1960, unused, 2" w....................................20.00

Toy car, TWA Airlines, airport service car, tin friction, 11" l..........120.00

Toy plane

Corvair Inter-Continental Jet, friction, 14" l, MIB 145.00

Pan Am Boeing 747, battery op, automatic stop and go action, flashing jet engines, realistic sound, 13" l, MIB.........225.00

Pan Am Boeing 747, friction, 7" l, MIB..............................225.00

Royal Dutch Airlines, KLM Corvair jet, friction, 14" l......95.00

Travel bag, Pan Am World.......10.00

❖ Akro Agate

Akro Agate began producing marbles in 1911. The company moved from Ohio to Clarksburg, W.Va. in 1914. By the 1930s, competition in the marble industry was fierce, and the company chose to diversify its product line. Floral dinnerware and children's play dishes were among their most successful products.

Reference: Gene Florence, *Collectors Encyclopedia of Akro Agate Glassware,* rev ed, Collector Books, 1975 (1992 value update).

Collectors' Clubs: Akro Agate Art Assoc, P.O. Box 758, Salem, NH 03079; Akro Agate Collector's Club, 10 Bailey St, Clarksburg, WV 26301.

For additional listings, see *Warman's Americana & Collectibles.*

Reproduction Alert.

Children's play dishes

Cereal bowl, large

Interior Panel, transparent blue 40.00

Interior Panel, transparent green 15.00

Yellow Akro Agate vase, $15.

Stacked Disk, transparent blue 40.00

Creamer

Chiquita, cobalt blue.......... 10.00

Interior Panel, transparent topaz 20.00

Stacked Disk, pink............. 25.00

Stippled Band, large, green 30.00

Cup and saucer

Chiquita, opaque green....... 8.00

Interior Panel, turquoise 42.00

Stippled Band, green......... 30.00

Pitcher

Stacked Disk, opaque green 12.00

Stippled Band, transparent green 18.00

Plate

Concentric Rib, yellow......... 8.00

Interior Panel, opaque blue 15.00

Interior Panel, transparent topaz 10.00

Octagonal, large, green....... 8.00

Stacked Disk, blue 6.00

Stippled Band, large, topaz 10.00

Set

Interior Panel, transparent topaz, cups, saucers, plates, creamer and sugar, teapot with lid, service for 4... 215.00

Octagonal, green cups and plates, white saucers and lids, yellow creamer and sugar, blue teapot, closed handles, 17-pc set.................... 125.00

Sugar, cov

Chiquita, opaque green or transparent cobalt.................. 8.00

Stacked Disc, pink 50.00
Teapot, cov
  Chiquita, opaque green 18.00
  Interior Panel, large, green, white
    lid 45.00
  Octagonal, open handle,
    medium blue, green lid..24.00
  Stippled Band, small, green
    ....35.00
Tumbler, Stacked Disk and Interior
  Panel, transparent green, 2" h
    ....12.00
Water set, octagonal, open handle,
  blue pitcher, 2 dark and 2 light
  green tumblers 70.00

Other

Ashtray, hexagon, blue and white,
  4-1/2" w 30.00
Cornucopia, orange and white ..8.00
Flowerpot
  Scalloped top, blue, 5-1/2" h
    ....30.00
  Stacked Disk, green and white,
    2-1/2" h 12.00
Lamp, brown and blue marble, black
  octagonal top, Globe Spec. Co.,
  top 4" dia, 12" h 75.00
Marbles, Chinese checkers, orig
  box, set of 60....................130.00
Mexicalli jar, covered, orange and
  white...................................40.00
Planter, wire cart holder, orange and
  white, rect..........................38.00
Powder jar, Colonial Lady, white
  ....65.00
Vase
  3-3/4" h, green and white marble
    ....15.00
  6-1/4" h, blue and white marble
    ....35.00

❖ Aladdin Lamps

Many collectors use the term Aladdin to refer to items produced by the Mantle Lamp Company of America. Founded in Chicago in 1908, the company was known for its lamps. Vintage Aladdin lamps were made of metal and glass, and Alacite was the name given to their popular creamy, translucent glass. Collectors insist that lamps possess all the correct parts, including original shades, which can be difficult to find.

References: J. W. Courter, *Aladdin Collectors Manual & Price Guide #19*, self-published (3935 Kelley Rd, Kevil, KY 42053), 1996; —, *Aladdin, The Magic Name In Lamps*, rev ed, self-published, 1997.

Collectors' Club: Aladdin Knights of the Mystic Light, 3935 Kelley Rd, Kevil, KY 42053.

Electric
  Alacite table lamp, ivory,
    embossed leaf design, cut-
    through scalloped base,
    wreath-shaped Alacite finial,
    22-1/4" h........................92.00
  Alacite wall lamp, white, U-
    shaped arm, 8-1/2" h.....93.50
  G-217 table lamp, ivory Alacite,
    gold metal base, vase design
    with leaf spray in high relief,
    c1940 ....75.00
  Hopalong Cassidy bullet lamp,
    Alacite, worn decal, no shade,
    10" h............................325.00
  M-123, lady figural, metal, orig
    fleur-de-lis finial 405.00
Kerosene
  B-26 Simplicity "Decalmania"
    lamp, pink Alacite, c1948-53
    ....325.00
  Beehive, ruby, complete with B
    burner, wick, chimney, insect
    screen and shade, c1937
    ....795.00
  Model 8, 401 shade..........256.00
  Moonstone Quilt, green, B
    burner,wick, chimney, c1937
    ....335.00

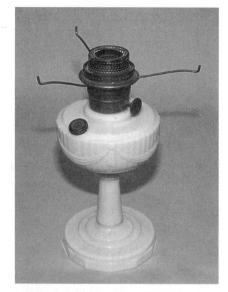

Tall Lincoln Drape oil lamp, Alacite, $275.

Moonstone Quilt, white, B
  burner, wick, chimney, c1937
  ....350.00
Tall Lincoln Drape, ruby flashed,
  1940s shade...............861.00
Tall Lincoln Drape, cobalt
  ....1,100.00
Washington Drape, amber, plain
  stem, B burner, wick, chimney, shade, c1940 ......195.00

❖ Albums

Albums consist of a grouping of pages that are bound together and used for a similar purpose. Albums can range in size from small examples used for autographs to larger, more ornate types for storing photographs. They offer a unique glimpse into the life of their owner. An autograph album might show one's friends and their sentiments of a bygone era. Photograph albums filled with images of unidentified people are often found at flea markets. Usually the value of these individual "instant relatives" is minimal, but if the photographs happen to include a famous person, an interesting pose, or an unusual setting, the value the album is enhanced.

Autograph
  Leather cover, N.Y., 1877, 2" x 5"
    ....100.00
  Velvet cover, "Autograph" emb
    on front, faded red, filled with
    autographs, some including
    caricatures....................75.00
  Daguerreotype, gutta percha,
    scrolling motif, dark brown
    ....50.00
Photograph
  Celluloid cover, swans, trees and
    couple in Victorian dress on
    bridge, fleur-de-lis border,
    front cover shades from cel-
    ery to lime to orange, back
    cover ivory celluloid, spine is
    cut velvet, 26 5-1/2" x 3-3/4"
    openings and 16 2" x 3-1/2"
    openings, pages bordered in
    gold leaf, orig clasp, unused
    ....165.00
  Celluloid cover, floral motif
    ....85.00

Photograph album, wooden cover with Scottie illustration, dated 1937, 7" x 9-1/2", $12.

Leather cover, brass closure, photos of Hoover family of New York, worn 110.00

Leather cover, hand-painted accents, inside script reads December 1st, 1886, 5-3/4" l, 4-3/8" w 35.00

Olympic logo, 1984, large format, MIB 10.00

Velvet cover, maroon, "Our Friends" in nickel plate metal, c1890-1900, filled with old photos, 11" x 9" 140.00

Wood, "Our Honeymoon" in relief, Silver Springs, Fla., hp flamingo motif, unused, 9" x 6" 36.00

Scrapbook, made by Everett S. Pratt, Amherst College, class of 1897, details of campus activities glued in, pages fragile 750.00

Tintype, leather cover, holds 24 tintypes, 1-1/2" x 1-1/4" 225.00

✪ Aliens, Space-Related

From little green creatures to Martians, collectors are fascinated by science fiction and aliens. As you can see from this sampling, space-related items encompass a wide variety of collectibles, from scary and spooky to just plain fun. Any alien collection is sure to be out of this world!

References: Dana Cain, *UFO & Alien Collectibles Price Guide*, Krause Publications, 1998; Rex Miller, *The Investor's Guide to Vintage Character Collectibles*, Krause Publications, 1999; Frank M. Robinson, *Science Fiction of the Twentieth Century, An Illustrated History*, Collectors Press, 1999; Stuart W. Wells, III, *Science Fiction Collectibles*, Krause Publications, 1999.

Periodicals: *Starlog Magazine*, 275 Park Ave S, New York, NY 10016; *Strange New Worlds*, P.O. Box 223, Tallevast, FL 34270.

Collectors' Clubs: Galaxy Patrol, 22 Colton St, Worcester, MA 01610; Lost in Space Fan Club, 550 Trinity, Westfield, NJ 07090; Society for the Advancement of Space Activities, P.O. Box 192, Kent Hills, ME 04349. For additional listings, see *Warman's Americana & Collectibles.*

Action figure, Space Marine Drake, Kenner, 1992, MIP 16.00

Book, *The Great Book of Movie Monsters*, Jan Stacy and Ryder Syverson, Contemporary Books, 1983, 351 pgs 15.00

Cap, from movie *Alien*, 1992, black, neon green writing, adjustable strap, officially licensed by Universal Industries, Inc 10.00

Christmas ornament, Kringles Bumper Cars, Santa, reindeer and space alien, Hallmark, 1991, MIB 50.00

Keychain, Toy Story, Pizza Planet vending machine, antennae light, orig Basic Fun blister pack 4.75

Model, from movie *Alien*, Aurora, MIB 125.00

Toy, Liddle Kiddles Kozmic Space Ship, red with lime green wheels, clear dome, Mattel, c1969-70, 5-1/2" h 80.00

Magazine
   Cinemacabre #2, George Stover, includes film characters, *Alien, Superman* and *Dawn of the Dead*, late 1970s 15.00
   Famous Monsters of Filmland #143, *Close Encounters, Alien,* and *Star Wars* 8.00
   Famous Monsters of Filmland #159, *Time After Time* and *Alien* 12.50

Puppet, Alf, red shirt and cap, Alien Productions, 1988, played with 10.00

Toy, Rocket Racer #8, Yonezawa, 11-1/2" l 775.00

❖ Almanacs

While few of us today rely on almanacs for forecasting the weather, it wasn't too long ago that many folks did. They got much more than weather information from these charming little booklets. Beauty tips, household hints, and exercise regimens were also included.

Agricultural Almanac, 1922, John Baer's Sons, Inc., Lancaster, Pa. 15.00

Angler's Almanac for Fresh & Salt Water, 1949, ed by Jason G. Clark, 128 pgs 7.00

Dr. Miles Almanac, 1932, red, white and blue cover, 32 pgs, cover loose, worn, 6" x 9-1/2" 7.50

Healthway Products Almanac, 1940, Illinois Herb Co. 12.00

Hostetter's Illustrated United States Almanac, 1876, Pittsburgh, Pa., missing back cover, 7-3/4" x 5" 20.00

Maine Farmer's Almanac, 1916, wear and stains 15.00

MacDonald's Farmer's Almanac, 1922, Binghamton, N.Y. 5.00

Old Farmer's Almanac, 1857, wear and stains 12.00

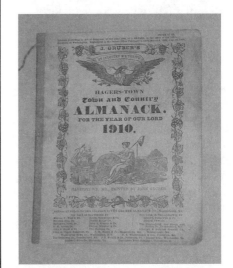

Hagers-Town Town and Country Almanack, 1910, $5.

Rawleigh's Almanac & Catalog,
    1936, 6-1/2" x 9-1/2" 10.00
The Herbalist Almanac, 1942, Meyer
    trademark, cover shows Indians
    bringing in herbs to dry, 5-5/8" x
    8-3/8" 9.00
The Ladies Birthday Almanac, 1937,
    Medlock's Drug Store, Roscoe,
    Texas 12.00
*The Tribune Almanac and Political
    Register,* 1860, Horace Greeley
    & Co. 35.00
Uncle Sam's Almanac, 1941, com-
    piled by Frederic J. Haskin, 64
    pgs, small tear on spine 7.50
Weather Almanac and Handbook,
    1940, Miles Laboratories,
    Elkhart, Ind., 6" x 9-1/2" 10.00

❖ Aluminum, Hand-Wrought

The aluminum giftware market began in the 1920s, providing consumers with an interesting new medium to replace fancy silver and silver-plate items. In order to remain competitive, many silver manufacturers added aluminum articles to their product lines during the Depression. Many well-known metalsmiths contributed their skills to the production of hammered aluminum. With the advent of mass-production and the accompanying wider distribution of aluminum giftware, there was less demand for individually-produced items. Only a few producers continue turning out quality work using the age-old and time-tested methods of metal crafting.

References: Everett Grist, *Collectible Aluminum,* Collector Books, 1994; Dannie A. Woodard, *Hammered Aluminum Hand-Wrought Collectibles,* Book 2, Aluminum Collectors' Books, 1993; Dannie Woodard and Billie Wood, *Hammered Aluminum,* self-published, 1983.

Periodical: *Aluminist,* P.O. Box 1346, Weatherford, TX 76086.

Collectors' Clubs: Aluminum Collectors, P.O. Box 1346, Weatherford, TX 76086; Wendell August Collectors Guild, P.O. Box 107, Grove City, PA 16127.
For additional listings, see *Warman's Americana & Collectibles.*
Basket, pie-crust edges, dimpled handle, mkd on back "The Beauty Line, Designed Aluminum" with rose, 14" x 10-1/2" 18.00
Bowl
    Hammered, handles are flowers and ribbons, 8-3/8" excluding handles 12.00
    Pine Cone pattern, Wendell August Forge, 8" d 45.00
Candlestick, Farberware, floral dec on holder, mkd on bottom, 3-3/4" h, pr 17.50
Casserole carrier, holds Fire-King casserole, moving the handle lifts the metal lid 35.00
Coaster, Stanhome, shows house, 4 imp legs, set of 4 .... 14.00
Compote, ftd, fluted edges, emb fruit motif, 6" h, 6-1/2" dia 10.00
Desk set, Bali Bamboo pattern, Everlast Forge, 3-pc set 48.00
Ice bucket
    Hammered, aqua porcelain liner, 1950s, 12" h excluding handle, 8-3/4" dia 100.00
    Hammered, rosette as knob, wear, 6" h excluding handle, 8" dia 20.00
Lazy Susan, Everlast, Art Deco leaping stag in relief, mkd on bottom 30.00
Nut bowl, footed, floral dec, 4" h, 9" l 20.00
Pitcher
    Hammered, handle knotted and riveted to pitcher, mkd with globe logo and "World, Hand Forged," wear, 8-1/2" h.. 35.00
    Regal, red, black handle 15.00
Plate, flying ducks and cattails, 5" d 6.00
Salad set, tulip dec, matching serving utensils, Buenilum Hand Wrought 24.00
Serving dish, 3-part, Colonial, applied flower in center, 1 section with flower dec 14.00
Tidbit tray, 3 tiers, Dogwood pattern, mkd "Wilson Specialties Co., Inc., Brooklyn, N.Y.," 10" h, 13" dia 30.00

Hand-wrought aluminum handbag, swing handles, pressed floral pattern, $95.

Tray
    Art Deco geometric pattern, sgd Canterbury Arts, 19" x 11" including handles 18.00
    Fruit and floral dec, pie-crust edge, curved handles, 18-1/2" x 11-1/2" 23.00
    Paisley pattern, Keystone, emb floral dec, 20" dia including handles 25.00
    Rose design, scalloped and pierced open-work edge, 12-1/2" x 7" 14.50
Tray with 6 cordials, cordials with cutout floral dec and glass inserts, tray 12" x 3-1/2", cordials 3" h, set 75.00
Wastebasket, painted emb rose on front 20.00

❖ American Bisque

The American Bisque Company was founded in Williamstown, West Virginia, in 1919. Although the pottery originally produced china-head dolls, it quickly expanded its inventory to include serving dishes, cookie jars, ashtrays, and other decorative ceramic pieces. B.E. Allen, founder of the Sterling China Company, invested heavily in American Bisque and eventually purchased its remaining stock. In 1982 the plant was sold and operated briefly under the name American China Company. The business closed in 1983.

Spotted pig pitcher, American Bisque, 7-3/4" high, $77.50.

Trademarks used by American Bisque included Sequoia Ware and Berkeley, the former used on items sold in gift shops, and the latter found on products sold through chain stores. Their cookie jars are marked with "ABC" inside blocks.

For additional listings, see *Warman's Americana & Collectibles* and *Warman's American Pottery & Porcelain*.

Bank, Popeye, small chip on collar, pipe not orig 375.00
Clothes sprinkler, figural, cat, marbles for eyes 145.00
Cookie jar
   Baby Elephant, bonnet 165.00
   Bear with Cookie, mkd "USA"
   .... 80.00
   Beehive, mkd "USA," 11-3/4" h
   .... 165.00
   Candy Cane Babies 200.00
   Coffee Pot, mkd "USA," 9-1/2" h
   .... 110.00
   Cookie Truck, mkd "USA 744,"
   11-1/2" h 195.00
   Donald Duck, standing 385.00
   Jack-in-the-Box, imp "USA" on
   back, 12" h 195.00
   Kitten, mkd "USA," 11-3/4" h
   .... 165.00
   Milk Wagon, mkd "USA 740,"
   11-3/4" h 165.00
   Toy Soldier, mkd "USA 743,"
   11-1/4" h 225.00
   Yogi Bear 510.00
Food mold, fish, white, red trim, incised "ABC," ring for hanging, 10" l 15.00
Pitcher, chick, gold trim 48.00

Planter
   Flamingo, 7-1/4" h x 10" l ...65.00
   Lamb, 4-3/4" h, 6-1/2" l 8.00
Teapot, Red Rose, gold trim, 6-1/2" h 55.00
Vase
   6" h, white heart, blue bow
   .... 28.00
   7-1/4" h, green, fern frond handles 20.00

❖ Amusement Parks

Whhheeee!! What fun a trip to an amusement park can be. Doesn't everybody bring home some sort of souvenir? Today's collectors scout flea markets for these treasures, keeping the excitement of that vacation trip alive a little longer.

Ashtray, Coney Island, metal, parachute jump in full relief, several rides and general views also emb, early 1940s, 5-1/2" h, 3-1/2" w 65.00
Charm bracelet, Disneyland, six charms, copyright Walt Disney Productions, MIB 40.00
Desk calendar, mechanical, metal, Great Adventure Amusement Park, N.J., shows Ferris wheel and other rides, paper label "Made in Japan," 3" h 24.00
Pennant, felt, "Storyland, Asbury Park, N.J.," red ground, shows King Arthur's Court with knight on horseback, 26" l 22.00
Pin, goldtone sailboat with Coney Island, NY plaque, attached by chain to numerals 41 (1941) 39.00
Plate, Freedomland Amusement Park, pottery, 1960s, 5-1/4" dia 45.00
Postcard
   Coney Island, postmarked Brooklyn/Coney Island 1939 .... 3.00
   Coney Island, emb "Souvenir of Coney Island" surrounded by detailed shells, pre-1920, unused 7.00
   Disneyland, 1969 .... 3.00
   Heinz Ocean Pier, Atlantic City, unused 10.00
   Palisade Amusement Park, postmarked June 12, 1911 ..... 4.00

Postcard purse, leather, fringed bottom, woman and red rose on one side, scorpion and hearts on other, bought at Coney Island, mailed from N.C. to Colo., 1907, red drawstring unstrung, tear 20.00
Tumbler, Nathan's Famous Hot Dogs (Coney Island, Long Island and Yonkers) painted logo, 4-5/8" h 4.00
Wallet, child's, Asbury Park, NJ, surfing and sailing scenes 20.00

❖ Anchor Hocking

Founded in 1905, Hocking Glass Company was located in Lancaster, Ohio. In 1937 the company merged with Anchor Cap & Closure Company, forming the highly successful Anchor Hocking Corp. The company's primary output consisted of glass items for household use, including several Depression-era patterns. Much of their kitchenware and tableware is marked, enabling collectors to identify these pieces.

References: Gene Florence, *Anchor Hocking's Fire King & More*, 2nd ed, Collector Books, 2000; ——, *Collectible Glassware from the 40's, 50's, 60's*, 5th ed, Collector Books, 2000; ——, *Kitchen Glassware of the Depression Years*, 5th ed, Collector Books, 1995 (1997 value update); Joe Keller and David Ross, *Jadite: An Identification and Price Guide*, 2nd ed, Schiffer Publishing, 2000; Gary & Dale Kilgo and Jerry & Gail Wilkins, *Collectors Guide to Anchor Hocking's Fire-King Glassware*, K & W Collectibles, 1991; ——, *Collectors Guide to Anchor Hocking's Fire-King Glassware, Volume II*, K & W Collectibles, 1998; April M. Tvorak, *Fire-King*, 5th ed, self-published, 1997.

Periodicals: *Fire-King Monthly*, P.O. Box 70594, Tuscaloosa, AL 35407; *Fire-King News*, K & W Collectibles, Inc., P.O. Box 374, Addison, AL 35540.

Collectors' Club: Fire-King Collectors Club, 1161 Woodrow St, #3, Redwood City, CA 94061.

For additional listings, see *Warman's Glass*, as well as specific categories in this edition.

Batter bowl, set of nested bowls, transparent green, 7", 8", 9", and 10" dia 95.00

Berry bowl, Coronation pattern, handle, ruby, 8" dia 15.00

Bowl, Desert Gold pattern, amber, orig sticker 8.00

Condiment set, cruet and salt and pepper shakers, blue trim .. 25.00

Covered animal dish, fish, clear glass 20.00

Egg cup, Jade-ite 47.50

Food chopper, red tin top, mkd "Anchor Hocking, Federal Tool Corp." 18.00

Iced tea tumbler, Boopie, set of 6 .... 70.00

Mayonnaise dish with underplate, Jubilee pattern 150.00

Mixing bowl, Vitrock, 8-1/2" dia 18.00

Mug, Bo Peep 12.00

Punch set, Early American Prescut, bowl, stand, 12 cups, plastic hangers, plastic ladle 50.00

Range salt and pepper shakers, opaque Delphite blue, some corrosion on salt lid, pr 25.00

Salad set, hp salad bowl, two cruets, salt and pepper shakers, all marked "AH" on bottom, c1950 .... 25.00

Salt and pepper shakers, Early American Prescut, individual size, pr 75.00

Forest Green vase, Anchor Hocking, 6-3/8" high, $4.

Syrup pitcher, red top, mkd "Anchor Hocking, Federal Tool Corp.," 5-1/2" h 15.00

Tom and Jerry set, large bowl with 5 matching cups, white ground, red decor 12.00

Tumbler, Manhattan pattern, pink, 10 oz, set of 6 .... 150.00

Turkey platter, milk glass, raised center turkey, fruit border, oval, 11-3/4" x 15-1/2" 60.00

Vase
   Moonstone, ruffled, 5-1/2" h 60.00
   Royal Ruby, 4" h 12.00

Water Pitcher, Early American Prescut, 60 oz 45.00

❖ Angels

Many flea market shoppers are searching for angels to add to their collections. Perhaps they believe in guardian angels. In any event, they are finding them on all manner of objects, from figurines to artwork.

Collectors' Clubs: Angel Collector Club, 14 Parkview Ct, Crystal Lake, IL 60012-3540; Angels Collectors' Club of America, 12225 S Potomac, Phoenix, AZ 85044.

Advertising mirror "Angelus Marshmallows," angel holding box of marshmallows 80.00

Candleholders, Clay Art, 4" x 3," pr 12.00

Christmas ornament, wax over composition, human hair wig, spun glass wings, cloth dress, Germany 55.00

Christmas tree topper
   Papier-mâché, blue dress, silver cardboard wings and crown, kneeling on silver sphere, silver tube 45.00
   Spun glass and cardboard, 6" h 24.00
   Chromolithograph, diecut 7" h, tinsel trim, German 18.00
   8" h, tinsel and lametta trim 10.00

Cookie cutter, aluminum, 5" h 5.00

Cookie jar, sgd Rick Wisecarver, #65 of 250, 1993 .... 245.00

Figurine
   Angel playing a harp, ceramic, gold label on bottom "Handmade in Japan" and "MY," 3-1/2" h 5.00

Josef Originals, birthday angel 11, sewing, imp mark and paper label, 5" h 17.50

Lefton, December, blue stone in center of pink flower, 1960-1983, 4-1/2" h 26.00

Pair of hands with pink angel nestled in them, gold trim, applied roses, 5-1/4" h.. 35.00

Young boy playing ball with angel 7.00

Illuminated, GLO-rious Angel by Glolite, Chicago, IL, hard plastic, silver, angel near mint cond, box fair cond 24.00

Light switch cover, angel dec, Bernat 5.00

Matchsafe, celluloid 145.00

Ornament, hard plastic, silver with gold hair and halo, white wings, 4-1/4" h 12.00

Perfume bottle, Avon, Angel Song with Lyre, Here's My Heart perfume, frosted glass, orig contents 8.00

Pin, goldtone, small rhinestone accents 5.00

Planter, Lefton China, angel on cloud 40.00

Plate
   Goebel, Heavenly Angel, 1st in a series, 1971, orig box . 400.00
   Hummel, Herald Angel, 1977 Christmas plate, Schmid Bros., 7-3/4" dia 32.00

Salt and pepper shakers, porcelain, 3-3/4" h, pr 25.00

Snow dome, Josef, porcelain base, 5-3/4" h, glass ball 4" dia .. 35.00

Tie tac, angel head, brasstone, mkd "HNS" 12.00

Wall pocket, Royal Copley, 6" h 80.00

❖ Animal Dishes, Covered

These clever covered dishes were first popular during the Victorian era, when they were used to hold foods and sweets on elaborate sideboards. China manufacturers produced some examples, but most were made of glass, representing many of the major glass companies. They can be found in colored and white milk glass, clear glass, and many colors of translucent glass.

Amber glass hen-on-nest, 7-1/2" long, $10.

Bird on nest, white milk glass, West-
   moreland, 7" x 6" 65.00
Dolphin, chocolate glass, Green-
   town, chip on tail 195.00
Eagle, milk glass, eggs and nest on
   base, front emb "The American
   Hen," mkd 75.00
Fish, white milk glass, red glass
   eyes 195.00
Frog, dark brown slag, base emb
   "Schepps," 5-1/2" l, 4-1/2" w,
   4-1/2" h 45.00
Hen on nest
   Marbleized, head turned to left,
     white and deep blue, Atter-
     bury 185.00
   Mirage (pale orchid), Boyd,
     5-1/2" l, 4-1/4" w, 5-3/4" h
     .... 20.00
   Transparent blue, Kemple Glass,
     mkd "K" 35.00
Lovebirds, pink irid, "M" in shield for
   Mosser, 6-1/2" l, 5" w, 5-1/4" h
   .... 25.00
Owl, green slag, Imperial Glass, mkd
   "IG" 60.00
Rabbit
   Amber, Greentown 250.00
   Frosted, white, Vallerystahl
     .... 65.00
Setter, white milk glass, sgd "Flac-
   cus," repair to lid 150.00
Turtle, vaseline, Boyd, lid mkd
   "NMGCS," base mkd "B" in dia-
   mond, 5-1/2" l, 4-1/2" w, 3-3/4" h
   .... 29.00

❖ Animation Art

A "cel" is an animation drawing on celluloid, a technique attributed to Earl Hurd. Although the process was perfected under animation giants Walt Disney and Max Fleischer, individual artists such as Ub Iwerks, Walter Lantz, and Paul Terry—along with studios such as Columbia, MGM, Paramount/Famous Studios, and Warner Brothers—did pioneering work.

One second of film requires over 20 animation cels. The approximate number of cels used to make a cartoon can be determined by multiplying the length of the cartoon in minutes by 60 seconds by 24.

References: Jeff Lotman, *Animation Art: The Early Years*, Schiffer Publishing, 1995; ——, *Animation Art: The Later Years*, Schiffer Publishing, 1996; ——, *Animation Art at Auction: Since 1994*, Schiffer Publishing, 1998.

Periodicals: *Animation Film Art*, P.O. Box 25547, Los Angeles, CA 90025; *Animation Magazine*, 4676 Admiralty Way, Suite 210, Marina Del Ray, CA 90292; *Animato!*, P.O. Box 1240, Cambridge, MA 02238; *In Toon!*, P.O. Box 217, Gracie Station, New York, NY, 10028; *Storyboard/The Art of Laughter*, 80 Main St, Nashua, NH 03060.

Collectors' Club: Greater Washington Animation Collectors Club, 12423 Hedges Run Dr #184, Lake Ridge, VA 22192.

For additional listings, see *Warman's Americana & Collectibles.*
101 Dalmatians, The Colonel, 8" x
   6-3/4", frame 13" x 13-1/2" 425.00
Flintstones, Fred & Wilma with Barney and Betty Rubble, orig production cel, multi-cel setup,
   mounted on full celluloid,
   framed, glazed, 16" x 19"
   .... 425.00
Jungle Book, Baloo, Walt Disney,
   1967, gouache on celluloid, cel
   trimmed, unframed, 6-1/2" x 4"
   .... 925.00
Scooby Doo, sgd "246/11 #60!
   SC36," 14-3/4" x 11-3/4"
   .... 150.00

Smurf, #240 21 65 F-17, matted, 11"
   x 14" 95.00
Sylvester, orig production cel,
   gouache on full celluloid, accom-
   panied by orig layout drawing,
   c1960, mounted, framed,
   glazed, 17" x 32" 450.00
Teenage Mutant Ninja Turtles, certificate of authenticity, copyright
   dates 1985 to 1991, matted, 11"
   x 14" 85.00
Winnie the Pooh with Rabbit and
   Piglet, 1960s orig film 350.00

❖ Anri

This Italian ceramics manufacturer has had quite an impact on the market for limited-edition collectibles. Items by Anri can be found in various forms, with the work of several different artists featured.

Periodical: *Collector's Mart Magazine*, 700 E State St, Iola, WI 54990.

Collectors' Club: Club Anri, 55 Parcella Park Dr, Randolph MA 02368.
Egg, J. Ferrandiz, baby coming out
   of egg, dated, 1980s, firing
   check 18.00
Figure
   Baker Sugar Heart, 1969, 3" h
     .... 485.00
   Camel Driver, mkd "Anri Italy,"
     orig paper sticker, 3" h
     .... 450.00
   Inspector, 6-1/2" h 375.00
   Mickey and Minnie Mouse,
     stamped "Walt Disney Com-
     pany", 4" h, pr 690.00
   Morning Chores, Sarah Kay,
     1983 .... 465.00
   Riding through the Rain, children
     and donkey under umbrella,
     ink stamp mark "Anri Italy"
     .... 450.00
   Spreading the Word, 6-3/8" h
     .... 450.00
   Stolen Kiss, ink stamp, 3" h
     .... 400.00
   Talking to the Animals, 1969, 3"
     h 155.00
   The Bouquet, 5-3/4" h 300.00
   The Quintet, 1969, 3" h ... 190.00
   Wanderlust, 5-7/8" h 425.00
Limited edition plate
   Disney Four Star Collection,
     Maestro Mickey, 1989, MIB
     .... 75.00

J. Ferrandiz, Heavenly Strings,
1989, MIB.................... 175.00
Music box, Ave Marie De Lour-
des by Ferrandiz 275.00

★✪ Anthropo-morphic Collectibles

Even before the creation of Veggie Tales, tomatoes and cucumbers had a life of their own. Merchants discovered years ago they could attract a customer's attention by giving human characteristics to inanimate objects. Flea markets are a great place to find anthropomorphic collectibles. Don't hesitate if you see something you like, since this area of collecting is heating up.

Condiment jar, banana boy, green
bowtie and brown hat, slotted lid
to insert spoon, worn, 5-1/2" h
.... 55.00
Covered jar, crying onion, lid labeled
"Onions," 3-1/2" h, 4-3/4" dia
.... 40.00
Embroidery pattern, 6 motifs of smiling vegetables, Alice Brooks
#7059, unused, fading 3.00
Head vase, apple, illegible incised
mark and 97608, orig chenille
bee insert 29.00
Rolling pin set, toothpick holder and
salt and pepper shakers sit in
rolling pin, 4-pc set 23.00
Salt and pepper shakers
Apples, full-figure, green-and-black dresses, applied black
bead eyes, 1 with 2 holes, 1
with 3, cork stoppers, 2-1/2"
h, pr 24.00
Cucumbers, green suits, 1 with 4
holes, 1 with 3, missing stoppers 4-1/4" h, pr 43.00
Lunchbox or picnic basket
heads, mkd PY with an N
inside a C, Japan, one missing stopper, one orig rubber
stopper, pr 150.00
Mushrooms, Napco, pr 36.00
Pear and orange, 1-pc, Japan,
2-1/2" h, 3-1/4" w 20.00
Shaker, onion, 1 crying, 1 holding
head, GNCO, cork stoppers,
3" h, pr 22.00

Chalkware fruit plaques, grapes, blueberries cherries and banana, set of 4, $50.

Soap dish, Alice in Wonderland
among anthropomorphic flowers,
bottom stamped "Soap Dish, Not
for Tableware," copyright Walt
Disney Productions, 6-1/4" x 5"
.... 59.00
Teapot with salt and pepper shakers,
1 boy and 1 girl shaker in teapot
form, orig corks, unmkd, teapot
5" h, shakers 2-1/2" h, set .76.00
Toothpick holder, corn, based on
animated character from Walt
Disney World's "The Land,"
copyright 1981 .... 39.00
Transfer patterns, The Vitamin Ball,
24 characters include 10 couples, 12-pc orchestra, conductor
and singer, Joseph Walker Co.,
orig packet with split along top
.... 32.00

❖ Appliances

Appliances of all types fascinate collectors, with the most common question being, "Does it work?" Please exercise caution when attempting to see if an item functions. Damaged cords and frayed wiring can lead to unpleasant results. When considering a purchase, remember that original instructions, parts, and boxes add greatly to the value of vintage appliances.

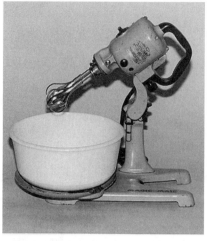

Fitzgerald Magic Maid electric mixer, green, $115.

References: Linda Campbell Franklin, *300 Years of Kitchen Collectibles,* 4th ed, Krause Publications, 1998; Helen Greguire, *Collector's Guide to Toasters & Accessories,* Collector Books, 1997; Gary Miller and K.M. Scotty Mitchell, *Price Guide to Collectible Kitchen Appliances*, Wallace-Homestead, 1991.

Collectors' Club: Electric Breakfast Club, P.O. Box 306, White Mills, PA 18473.

For additional listings, see *Warman's Americana & Collectibles.*

Blender, Osterizer, Model #10, 1-qt
Kerr jar for the top, small chips to
enamel, repair to switch.... 40.00
Chafing dish, Manning Bowman,
1930s, bright chrome Art Deco
design, two part top, hot plate
base, black Bakelite knob and
handles 75.00
Drink mixer, Weining Made Rite Co.,
lightweight metal, cream and
green motor, single shaft, 1930s
.... 25.00
Egg cooker, Hankscraft Co., yellow
china base, instructions on metal
plate on bottom, 1930s 35.00
Flour sifter, Miracle Flour Sifter, electric, cream body, blue wood handle, 1934 .... 35.00
Grill, Sunbeam, model FP, 12" x
12" x 4" 45.00
Hot plate, Blue Line by Montgomery
Ward, stainless steel frame,
brass nameplate, orig blue
painted wood handles, cloth
cord, 9" x 5" 50.00

Juicer/Mixer, Sunbeam Mixmaster, jade-ite bowls 150.00
Milk shake mixer, A.C. Gilbert Co., missing metal cup for mixing 60.00
Mixer, Montgomery Ward, electric beater with glass jar, green handle on beater 65.00
Toaster
  General Mills, 2 slice, chrome body, wheat decor on side, black Bakelite base, early 1940s 35.00
  Landers, Frary & Clarke, #E-947, electric, swing-out doors, 1915 .... 75.00
Waffle iron
  Griswold, electric, 1920-1930, orig box 120.00
  Toastmaster, model 2D2, makes 8" waffles....................... 45.00
  Universal, electric, porcelain top, replaced cord 65.00

❖ Art Deco

The term Art Deco is derived from the French name for the Paris Exhibition of 1927, *L'Exposition International des Arts Décorative et Industriels Mondernes.* The style became quite popular, with its sleek, angular forms and simple lines reflected in everything from artwork to skyscrapers of the period.

References: Jean L. Druesedow, *Authentic Art Deco Interiors and Furniture in Full*, Dover Publications, 1997; Mary Gaston, *Collector's Guide to Art Deco*, 2nd ed, Collector Books, 1997.

Periodical: Echoes Report, P.O. Box 2321, Maaspee, MA 02649.

Collectors' Clubs: Canadian Art Deco Society, #302 884 Bute St, Vancouver, British Columbia, V6E 1YA, Canada; International Coalition of Art Deco Societies, One Murdock Terrace, Brighton, MA 02135; Miami Design Preservation League, PO Bin L, Miami Beach, FL 33119.
For additional listings, see *Warman's Antiques & Collectibles*.
Brush, pearlized pink, matching comb, Fuller, 1925............. 65.00

Art Deco silver-plated creamer and sugar, 4-1/4" high, pair, $25.

Chair, side, chromed metal rod frame, triangular back over triangular upholstered seat, 32" h, pr 100.00
Clock, desk, General Electric, rect black glass clock face with chrome numerals, etched leaf and scallop dec on chrome center, imp marks on back, 5-5/8" h, 7-1/2" l 175.00
Demitasse cup and saucer, cream ground, multicolor floral dec, stamped on base, Honiton Pottery, Devon, England 90.00
Figure
  Rearing horse in upright horseshoe, carved and polished black granite, scratches, minor chips, 5-1/2" h ...190.00
  Dancer, bronze, ivory dec, brass inlaid malachite box base, French, c1920-25, 11" h 275.00
Fruit bowl, Lotus Fan dec, silver plate, Rogers, c1923-25, 2-1/2" h, 11" dia............................ 90.00
Magazine rack, bronze, upright circular sides with openwork design of greyhound in stride, scrolling leaf border, c1930, 4-1/2" w, 11-7/8" l, 12" h ..375.00
Salad servers, fork and spoon, Swedish, c1930-35, 11-3/4" l 50.00
Tile, 8" sq, rust, tan, off-white and purple design of lady, 4 short feet, mkd "Longwy, France, Primavera" with shield and crown 415.00
Vase, ball shape, mottled blue, #601, mkd "Rumrill," 6" dia 125.00

❖ Art Nouveau

Sensuous female forms with flowing lines are the signature motif of this style. The Art Nouveau period started during the 1890s and continued for the next 40 years, popular in both Europe and America. Leading designers of the time introduced the style's sweeping lines into their works. Florals, insects and other forms from nature were popular motifs.

References: Fiona Gallagher, *Christie's Art Nouveau*, Watsun-Guptill Publications, 2000; Paul Greenhalgh, *Art Nouveau 1890-1914*, Harry N. Abrams, 2000; Constance M. Greiff, *Art Nouveau*, Abbeville Press, 1995.
For additional listings, see *Warman's Antiques & Collectibles*.
Ashtray, molded, clear glass, reverse relief of Leda and Swan, c1925, ground spot at base, nicks to bottom edge, 3-3/8" w, 5-1/4" l, 7/8" h 175.00
Belt buckle, polychrome enamel, silver mount, minor enamel loss 245.00
Bird cage, beechwood, onion domed body, wirework sides, scrolled feet, 33" h 800.00
Box, domed cov, paneled box of rust brown shaded to colorless cased glass, acid-etched dec with textured surface, gilt highlights, bottom mkd "H 57," Continental, early 20th C, 4" h 350.00
Brush, silver-plate
  Nude woman on back, 7-1/4" l 50.00
  Scrolls, initials, dated 1916, 7-1/4" l 50.00
  Woman's face, 5" l 75.00
Bud vase, Vaseline, metal circle of nudes supporting vase.... 190.00
Candlesticks, tricorn, raised stylized floral and leaf motifs, bronze patina, pr....................... 150.00
Clock, green bisque, gold and pink highlights, gilt metal, imp Charenton marks, France, c1900, hand missing, nicks 825.00
Desk set, onyx, two inkwells, blotter, note pad, card holder and pen holder, inlaid lapis lazuli band, imp hallmarks, London, c1921, 6-pc set 300.00

Dinner gong, mahogany, five graduated bronze bells, exotic wood
floral marquetry on sides, bells
restrung, 12" w, 10-1/2" d, 10" h
....450.00

Figure, Fame, gilt-spelter, on marble
base, figure after E. Villianis,
French, 17" h...................275.00

Inkstand, brass, two-tiered letter
holder, hinged lid on inkwell,
etched floral decor, base imp
"D.R.G.M. 237670 Ges Gesch,"
3-7/8" h............................120.00

Lamp, polychromed, three lights with
frosted shades issuing from foliate standard, classical maidens
and child below on sq base, hoof
feet, 40" h.........................300.00

Mirror, cast bronze, Rococo, kidney
shape, 19-1/2" h..............250.00

Picture frame, silver, English hallmarks, 4-3/4" h x 6-1/2".....90.00

Umbrella stand, cast iron, emb floral
dec, old green repaint, 28-1/2" h
....150.00

❖ Art Pottery

The art pottery movement in
America lasted from about 1880 until
the first World War. During that time,
more than 200 companies produced
decorative ceramics ranging from
borderline production ware to intricately decorated, labor-intensive artware. The latter would help establish
America as a decorative arts power-
house. When buying art pottery,
remember that condition is critical in
determining price. Chips, cracks, or
damage of any kind can drastically
reduce the price of an item.

References: Susan and Al
Bagdade, *Warman's American Pot-
tery and Porcelain*, 2nd ed, Krause
Publications, 2000; Paul Evans, *Art
Pottery of the United States*, 2nd ed,
Feingold & Lewis Publishing, 1987;
Lucile Henzke, *Art Pottery of Amer-
ica*, rev ed, Schiffer Publishing,
1996; Ralph and Terry Kovel, *Kov-
els' American Art Pottery*, Crown
Publishers, 1993; David Rago,
American Art Pottery, Knicker-
bocker Press, 1997.

Periodical: *Style 1900*, 17 S Main
St, Lambertville, NJ 08530.

Collectors' Clubs: American Art
Pottery Assoc, P.O. Box 1226, Westport, MA 02790; Pottery Lovers
Reunion, 4969 Hudson Dr, Stow, OH
44224.

For additional listings, see *Warman's
Antiques & Collectibles*, as well
as specific categories in this
edition.

Bowl
Hampshire, leaf tooling, curdled
blue glaze, 3" h, 5-3/4" dia
...................................302.50
Teco, 3 feet, green matte glaze,
minor rust stains on interior,
3-3/4" h.........................330.00

Candlestick, Walley Pottery, bulbous
top, flared base, striated brown-
yellow high glaze, smooth green
ground, looped handle, imp
mark, 10" h......................290.00

Creamer, Owens Pottery, Aqua
Verdi, green matte, imp mark,
3-1/2" h.............................75.00

Figurine, Overbeck, woman with
basket, chip on hat repaired,
2-5/8" h...........................770.00

Inkwell, Owens Pottery, lime leaves,
brown ground, sgd, 3-3/4" dia
....110.00

Lamp, Muncie Pottery, Art Deco
design, green and pink matte
glaze, mkd "C. Brown Pottery
Co. Cin. & Lou. Pike Cincinnati,"
10-1/2" h (excluding fixture)
....660.00

Mug, Walrath Pottery, reddish-brown
foliate dec, brown ground, imp
mark, 4-1/2" h, pr..............435.00

Paperweight, Owens Majolica, stag
head and "Edmiston Horney
Company, Zanesville, Ohio,"
green glaze, 2-3/8" h, 3-7/8" w
....82.50

Perfume jug, Owens Utopian,
orange coronation decor by
Edith Bell, #967, 5-1/2" h
....247.50

Pitcher, Merrimac Pottery, matte
green glaze, restoration to rim
chip, stamped mark, 6-3/4" h
....300.00

Tile, Walley Pottery, relief turtle dec,
thick crackle matte green glaze,
imp mark, 7-1/2" dia........460.00

Tankard, Hampshire, green matte
glaze, 11-1/4" h.................275.00

Trivet, Newcomb College, moss-
covered tree decor by Henrietta
Bailey, 1923, 4" dia.......1,870.00

**Bybee art pottery vase, blue-
and-white mottled glaze, 6"
high, $45.**

Umbrella stand, unknown maker,
Arts & Crafts design, green
matte glaze, minor glaze skips,
20-1/4" h..........................110.00

Vase
Avon Faience, flowers and stylized leaves, minor chips,
5-3/4" h...................... 522.50
Clewell, crusty green over brown
patina, #407-2-6, minor
scuffs, hole in bottom, 8-1/2" h
.... 440.00
Gladding McBean, Oxblood, oval
decal, 4" h................... 247.50
Hampshire, embossed leaves,
mottled yellow and green
matte glaze, 6-3/4" h .. 660.00
Muncie Pottery, Ruba Rhombic
vase, shape 312-5, white over
blue matte glaze, 4-1/8" h
.... 467.50
Pewabic, hand-thrown, mottled
blue luster glaze, 5-5/8" h
.... 467.50
Seldon Bybee, 2 flat handles,
embossed floral pattern,
metallic green and brown
glaze, 1927, 5-1/2" h 82.50
Teco, green matte glaze, 4-3/4" h
.... 385.00
Norwetta, green matte glaze,
10-1/8" h..................... 165.00
Owens Utopian, English ivy
decor by Harry Larzelere,
square, 3" h, glaze nick
.... 88.00

✵ Arts and Crafts

Decorative arts in America took on an entirely new look during the Arts and Crafts movement. This period, from 1895 to 1920, was greatly influenced by leading proponents Elbert Hubbard and his Roycrofters, the brothers Stickley, Frank Lloyd Wright, Charles and Henry Greene, George Niedecken, and Lucia and Arthur Mathews. Individualistic design and a re-emphasis on handcraftsmanship were important features of their work. Most Arts & Crafts furniture was made of oak. The market for good-quality furniture and accessories remains extremely strong.

References: Bruce Johnson, *Pegged Joint*, Knock on Wood Publications, 1995; Thomas K. Maher, *The Jarvie Shop: The Candlesticks and Metalwork of Robert R. Jarvie*, Turn of the Century Editions, 1997; James Massey and Shirley Maxwell, *Arts & Crafts Design in America: A State-By-State Guide*, Chronicle Books, 1998; Richard and Hilary Myers, *William Morris Tiles*, Antique Collectors' Club, 1996; David Rago, *American Art Pottery*, Knickerbocker Press, 1997; Paul Royka, *Mission Furniture from the American Arts & Crafts Movement*, Schiffer Publishing, 1997.

Periodicals: *American Bungalow*, P.O. Box 756, Sierra Madre, CA 91204; *Style 1900*, 333 N Main St, Lambertville, NJ 08530

Collectors' Clubs: Foundation for the Study of the Arts & Crafts Movement, Roycroft Campus, 31 S. Grove St., East Aurora, NY 14052; Roycrofters-At-Large Assoc, P.O. Box 417, East Aurora, NY 14052; William Morris Society of Canada, 1942 Delaney Dr, Mississaugua, Ontario, L5J 3L1, Canada.

For additional listings, see *Warman's Antiques & Collectibles*.

Bowl, pottery, Clewell, copper color with applied brass plaque, "The Ffowler Simpson Co. Advertising Cleveland," 1-3/8" h, 3-3/4" dia 247.50

Candlestick, Karl Kipp, hammered copper, orig patina, 6-1/2" h, pr 2,645.00
Child's chair, Gustav Stickley, #342, 2-slat back, worn orig leather seat, orig finish, 23" h 460.00
Clock, mantle, Hampshire Pottery, green matte glaze, Seth Thomas movement, 14-3/4" h 1,320.00
Desk lamp, Handel, etched shade in brown with green highlights, bronzed metal base, 12" h 1,840.00
Dresser, L&JG Stickley, #101, Prairie School influence, 3 short drawers over 2 long drawers, orig mirror supported by tapered posts, orig finish, 68" h, 54" w 2,875.00
Hall tree, L&JG Stickley, #89, single pole, copper hooks, corbelled base, 72" h 1,380.00
High chair, Gustav Stickley, #388, ladderback, orig leather seat, 37" h 3,450.00
Jardiniere, hammered copper, corset shape, handles, orig patina, 12" h, 18" dia 430.00
Magazine stand, mahogany, 4 shelves over arched toe board, orig finish, 38" h, 18" w 345.00
Mirror, attributed to Stickley Brothers, rectangular oak frame with peg and thru-tenon construction, refinished, 25" h, 39" w 1,035.00
Plaque, pottery, American Encaustic Tile, snow scene with trees, mkd A.E.T. Co., framed, 9-1/8" h, 4-5/8" w 1,045.00
Plate, Dedham Pottery, mushroom pattern, blue and white, 8-1/2" dia..................................690.00
Rocking chair, Gustav Stickley arm rocker, #311-1/2, mahogany, V-back, 5 vertical slats, orig worn leather cushion, 34" h......920.00
Rug, Gustav Stickley, drugget style, Greek key border, unusual organic design, brown and oatmeal, 101" x 117"..........5,175.00
Stool, Limbert cricket stool, #2001/2, canted legs, orig leather cover and tacks, orig finish, 7" h, 18" w, 10" d 632.50
Umbrella stand, Gustav Stickley, #54, 4 tapered posts, orig copper drip pan, recent finish, unsigned, 34" h, 12" sq....575.00

Vase
Hammered copper, Roycroft, American Beauty form, orig patina, 21-1/2" h 4,025.00
Pottery, California Faience, matte green glaze with silver crystalline, 9-3/4" h .. 1,320.00
Waste basket, mahogany, orig finish, 16" h, 11" sq................... 490.00

❖ Ashtrays

Now that smoking is unfashionable in certain circles, ashtray collectors are finding more choices to pick from at their favorite flea markets. To narrow the field, many collectors specialize in a particular type of ashtray, whether advertising, souvenir, or figural.

References: Art Anderson, *Casinos and Their Ashtrays*, 1994, self-published; Nancy Wanvig, *Collector's Guide to Ashtrays*, 2nd ed, Collector Books, 1999.

Amber, glass, molded eagle in center, 9-1/4" 8.00
Capitol Metals Co., emb brass 10.00
Carnation Ice Cream, glass 5.00
Cigar wrapper, made with orig wrappers incl King Edwards S&S, Dutch Masters and Robt. Burns de Luxe, wrappers under clear glass, 3 cigar slots, 4-1/4" dia 35.00
Coal bucket, glass, amethyst, metal handle, 2-3/4" h (excluding handle), 5" w at widest point... 12.00
Collie, chalkware, ashtray with 3 cigarette holders, 3-1/2" dia, dog 8-3/4" h, 7-1/2" w 22.00

Aluminum ashtray advertising Bowmar Instrument Corp., 3-5/8" x 4-7/8", $2.

Coors, ceramic, company logo and advertising, 6" dia 8.00
Coronation of Queen Elizabeth II, ceramic, 1953, gold trim, 3-1/2" sq 15.00
Courtyard, New Orleans, porcelain 8.00
Disneyland, mkd "Walt Disney Productions Japan," some fading, 5" 8.00
Esso, clear glass, blue and red dealer inscription, c1950, 4-1/4" x 4-1/4" x 1" h 35.00
Grand Canyon, silvertone metal, emb with attractions, 5-1/2" 12.00
Harvard University, glass, 3-1/2" sq 3.00
Hawaii, Aloha, pot metal, emb, 1939 .... 20.00
Lion, chalkware, a few paint chips, ash mark in ashtray, 10-1/2" h, 9" w 30.00
Penske Racing, 1984 Indy 500 Winner, helmet shape 15.00
Pool table shape, with Joe Camel shooting pool, 7-1/4" x 4-1/2" 8.00
Reddy Kilowatt, clear glass, red and white reverse-painted image on bottom, c1950, 4" dia 38.00
Ryan's Wharf, glass 8.00
Tournament of Roses, ceramic .. 9.00
White Horse Whiskey, glass 10.00

Aunt Jemima and Uncle Mose creamer and sugar, F.&F. Mold & Die Works, pair, $20.

❖ Aunt Jemima

The Pearl Milling Company first used the image of Aunt Jemima in 1889. The firm's owner, Charles G. Underwood, had been searching for a symbol his company could use for a new self-rising pancake mix. Reportedly, a team of blackface comedians performing a cakewalk to a song called "Aunt Jemima" served as his inspiration.

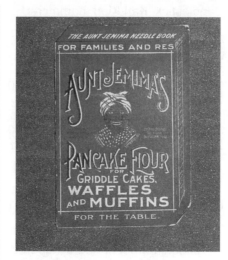

Aunt Jemima advertising needle book, 5-1/4" high, $250.

References: Patiki Gibbs, *Black Collectibles Sold in America*, Collector Books, 1987 (1996 value update); Dawn Reno, *Encyclopedia of Black Collectibles*, Wallace-Homestead/Krause, 1996; J.P. Thompson, *Collecting Black Memorabilia*, L-W Book Sales, 1996; Jean Williams Turner, *Collectible Aunt Jemima*, Schiffer Publishing, 1994.

Collectors' Club: Black Memorabilia Collector's Assoc, 2482 Devoe Terrace, Bronx, NY 10468.

Button, "Aunt Jemima Breakfast Club," tin litho, color image of smiling Jemima, red ground, black text "Eat a Better Breakfast," c1960, 4" dia 35.00
Cookbook, *Aunt Jemima Magical Recipes*, 1954, 26 pgs, softcover, booklet form, spine split at top, 4-1/4" x 6" 45.00
Cookie jar, hard plastic, F&F Mold & Die Works, Dayton, Ohio . 450.00
Creamer and sugar, plastic, Aunt Jemima and Uncle Mose, F&F Mold & Die Works, Dayton, Ohio 150.00
Doll, stuffed vinyl, 1940s, 12" h 165.00
Hat, Aunt Jemima's Breakfast Club, paper, fold-out style 20.00
Magazine tear sheet, Aunt Jemima Pancakes, 1949, 13" x 5" .. 15.00
Nelson family with Aunt Jemima pancakes, 1956, full-page . 25.00
Pancake mold, round with 4 animal shapes, aluminum, 1950s, 8-1/2" dia 125.00

Paper plate, c1950, 9-1/4" dia 30.00
Place mat, paper, Aunt Jemima's Kitchen, full-color, unused. 20.00
Pot holder, "There's Love in every Bite—Aunt Jemima," soiled, 6" sq 20.00
Salt and pepper shakers, Aunt Jemima and Uncle Mose, plastic, mkd "F&F Mold & Die Works, Dayton, Ohio, Made in USA," 3-1/4" h, pr 45.00
Shaker, hard plastic, mail-away premium, "Perfect Pancakes in 10 Shakes," emb image of Aunt Jemima on lid, 8-3/4" h 90.00
Sheet music, Aunt Jemima's Picnic Day, 1914 .... 25.00
String holder, chalkware, 1940s-1950s, orig paint 395.00
Syrup pitcher, Made in U.S.A., 5-1/2" h 65.00
Thimble, porcelain, Aunt Jemima and Uncle Mose, c1980, 1-1/8" h 12.50

❖ Autographs

Folks have been asking, "May I have your autograph?" for decades. Most celebrities will gladly oblige, but because many items have been signed with autopens and other mechanical devices, it's sometimes tough to know if a particular signature is authentic. Doing business with reputable dealers, asking questions, and conducting your own research will go a long way toward making your purchases good ones.

References: Mark Allen Baker, *All-Sport Autographs*, Krause Publications, 1995; ——, *Advanced Autograph Collecting*, Krause Publications, 2000; ——, *Collector's Guide to Celebrity Autographs*, 2nd ed, Krause Publications, 2000; *Standard Guide to Collecting Autographs*, Krause Publications, 1999; Kevin Keating and Michael Kolleth, *The Negro Leagues Autograph Guide*, Tuff Stuff Books, 1999; Kevin Martin, *Signatures of the Stars*, Antique Trader Books, 1998; Tom Mortenson, *Standard Catalog of Sports Autographs*, Krause Publications, 2000; George Sanders, Helen Sanders and Ralph Roberts, *Sand-*

ers Price Guide to Sports Autographs, 2nd ed, Alexander Books, 1997; ——, Sanders Price Guide to Autographs, 5th ed, Alexander Books, 2000.

Periodicals: Autograph Collector, 510-A S Corona Mall, Corona, CA 91720-1420; Autograph Review, 305 Carlton Rd, Syracuse, NY 13207; Autograph Times, 1125 W Baseline Rd, #2-153-M, Mesa, AZ 85210-9501; Autographs & Memorabilia, P.O. Box 224, Coffeyville, KS 67337.

Collectors' Clubs: International Autograph Collectors Club & Dealers Alliance, 4575 Sheriden St, Suite 111, Hollywood, FL 33021-3575; Manuscript Society, 350 N Niagara St, Burbank, CA 95105-3648; Universal Autograph Collectors Club, P.O. Box 6181, Washington, DC 20044; Washington Historical Autograph & Certificate Organization, P.O. Box 2428, Springfield, VA 22152-2428.

For additional listings, see Warman's Antiques & Collectibles and Warman's Americana & Collectibles.

❖ Abbreviations

Dealers use the following abbreviations to describe autographed materials and their sizes.

Materials:
ADS—Autograph Document Signed
ALS—Autograph Letter Signed
AQS—Autograph Quotation Signed
CS—Card Signed
DS—Document Signed
FDC—First Day Cover
LS—Letter Signed
PS—Photograph Signed
TLS—Typed Letter Signed

Sizes (approximate):
Folio—12 x 16 inches
4to—8 x 10 inches
8vo—7 x 7 inches
12mo—3 x 5 inches

Aaron, Hank, baseball bat 135.00
Belson, Louie, real photo postcard, autographed 1948, several other signatures 65.00
Berra, Ford and Rizzuto, sepia photo, 11" x 14" 90.00
Bush, Barbara, First Lady, Blair House stationery, 3" x 2" ...60.00
Campbell, Earl, football 125.00
Conick, Harry, Jr., black-and-white glossy photo, 8" x 10" 35.00
Crawford, Cindy, black-and-white glossy photo, 8" x 10" 60.00
Day, Doris, letter 45.00
Dawson, Andre, baseball.........25.00
DeNiro, Robert, black-and-white glossy photo, 8" x 10" 60.00
DiMaggio, Joe, black-and-white glossy photo, 11" x 14" 175.00
Elkington, Steve, U.S. Open golf cap 35.00
Fields, W.C., as Poppy playing cigar box cello, promotional photo, 10" x 13" 90.00
Foreman, George, black-and-white glossy photo, 8" x 10" 40.00
Gill, Vince, black-and-white glossy photo, 8" x 10" 35.00
Griebling, Otto, first day cover, hp watercolor cachet of clown, sgd on back 45.00
Houston, Whitney, black-and-white glossy photo, 8" x 10" 60.00
Ives, Burl, letter.......................38.00
Jones, Spike, radio photo 75.00
Kemp, Jack, black-and-white glossy photo, 16" x 20" 60.00
Leigh, Vivien, letter, personal stationery, 1959 ....650.00
Parton, Dolly, black-and-white glossy photo, 8" x 10" 35.00
Rogers, Ginger, black-and-white photo, 8" x 10" 70.00
Roland, Ruth, silent film queen, wedding photo, inscription .45.00
Ryan, Nolan, Legends Magazine cover...............................150.00
Sellers, Peter, letter, personal stationery, 1959 ....125.00
Sousa, John Philip, card mounted to album page.....................125.00
Yeager, Chuck and Scott Crossfield, first day cover honoring Glenn Curtiss, canceled NY, 1980 ....60.00
West, Mae, theater playbill, for stage production of Kenley Players "Come On Up, Ring Twice," July 7, 1952, 12 pgs, 6" x 9" 75.00

Whitehouse, Eula, book, Texas Flowers in Natural Colors, 1st ed, 1936............................ 48.00
Woods, Tiger, black-and-white photo, 8" x 10" 65.00

❖ Automobilia

People have always had love affairs with their cars, and automobilia represents one of the biggest collecting areas in today's market. Flea markets are excellent sources for all types of materials relating to automobiles—parts, accessories, advertising, etc. Specialized flea markets held in conjunction with car shows offer the best opportunities for finding automobilia, but general flea markets can also hold some choice items for collectors.

Reference: Gordon Gardner and Alistair Morris, Automobilia, 20th Century International Reference with Price Guide, 3rd ed, Antique Collectors' Club, 1999.

Periodicals: Automobile Quarterly, 15040 Kutztown Rd, P.O. Box 348, Kutztown, PA 19530; Cars & Parts, P.O. Box 482, Sydney, OH 45365; Classic Car Source, www.classic-car.com; Hemmings Motor News, P.O. Box 256, Bennington, VT 05201; Old Cars Price Guide, 700 E State St, Iola, WI 54990; Old Cars Weekly, News & Marketplace, 700 E State St, Iola, WI 54990.

Collectors' Clubs: Classic Gauge & Oiler Hounds, Rte 1, Box 9, Farview, SD 57027; Hubcap Collectors Club, P.O. Box 54, Buckley, MI 49620; International Petroliana Collectors Assoc, P.O. Box 937, Powell, OH 43065; Spark Plug Collectors of America, 14018 NE 85th St, Elk River, MN 55330.

For additional listings, see Warman's Antiques & Collectibles.

Ashtray, Chrysler, 1933........... 45.00
Book, Edison Spark Plugs 15.00
Cartoon book, Volkswagen, 1960s 25.00
Clock, electric, neon, "Chevrolet Genuine Parts," Chevy logo in center, 19" dia................. 375.00

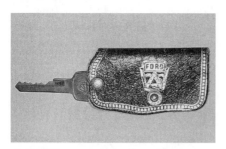

Ford key holder, blue leather, $7.50.

Dealer brochure, Ford, 1954, shows all models, staple hole, unfolded 21" x 24" 30.00

Folder, advertising

Buick, 1950, 8 color pgs, shows models, 7-3/4" x 10-3/4" 25.00

Oldsmobile, 1963, color, 6 models, 10-1/2" x 10-1/2".......5.00

Opel Manta, 1974, specs on last pg, 7-1/2" sq....................4.00

Hubcap emblem, LaSalle, "LAS" design, some paint loss, slight bend, 3" dia 60.00

Lapel pin, Ford logo, cloissoné, 1-1/2" l 4.00

Model kit, Mazda Rotary Engine, 1972 ....25.00

Owner's manual, Ford Thunderbird, 1959, near mint cond 40.00

Pinback button

Chevrolet, "Harrisburg Zone Salesmen's Jamboree, Bloomsburg-1937," Chevrolet logo in center, 2-1/8" dia 20.00

Hudson, 1939 ....35.00

Promo car, Mustang, 1964, hardtop 55.00

Showroom catalogue

Chevrolet, 1946, 29 pgs, sun fading on back, shelf wear along bottom, 11-1/4" x 9" 275.00

Chevrolet, 1952, 31 pgs, contains paint chips and upholstery samples, 9"x 12-1/4" 225.00

Souvenir book, *Blackhawk Automotive Museum*, 1988, softcover, 8" x 11" 4.00

❖ Autry, Gene

One of the famous singing cowboys most Baby Boomers remember, Gene Autry spawned a wide range of items for collectors to enjoy. Since he delighted us on the movie screen, radio, and television, an interesting variety of collectibles can be found at today's flea markets. A visit to the Gene Autry Western Heritage Museum in Los Angeles is a must for all dedicated Gene Autry collectors.

Periodicals: *Cowboy Collector Newsletter*, P.O. Box 7496, Long Beach, CA 90807; *Gene Autry Star Telegram*, Gene Autry Museum, P.O. Box 67, Gene Autry, OK 73436; *Spur*, Gene Autry Western Heritage Museum, 4700 Western Heritage Way, Los Angeles, CA 90027-1462; *Westerner*, Box 5232-32, Vienna, WV 26105; *Westerns & Serials*, Route 1, Box 103, Vernon Center, MN 56090.

Collectors' Clubs: Gene Autry Fan Club, 4322 Heidelberg Ave, St Louis, MO 63123-6812; Gene Autry International Fan Club, 20 Cranleigh Gardens, Stoke Bishop, Bristol B59 1HD, UK.

Arcade card, 4-on-1, also shows Buffalo Bill Jr., Elton Britt and Roy Rogers........................20.00

Book

Gene Autry and the Golden Stallion, Cole Fannin, 1954, 282 pages, hardcover, wear...7.50

Gene Autry and the Bandits of Silver Tip, Better Little Book, 1949, worn, $15.

Gene Autry and the Thief River Outlaws, Whitman, 1944, 249 pgs, hardcover, dj 30.00

Cap pistol, silvered metal, simulated pearl handle, c1950, 8" l ... 35.00

Comic book, Gene Autry, Dell

#5, 1947 ....50.00

#40, 1950 ....20.00

#78, 1953 ....20.00

#94, 1954 ....12.00

Cookie jar, McMee Productions, signature across back, copyright 1955 Autry Museum of Western Heritage, 15" h 225.00

Guitar, Emenee, orig box 75.00

Handout, Sunbeam Bread, color photo of Gene and Champion, 1950s, 8" x 10"....................5.00

Little Golden Book, Gene Autry and Champion, 1956 ....25.00

Pennant, large 55.00

Record, *Merry Christmas with Gene Autry*, 45 rpm, 1950, orig box, 4-record set......................40.00

Gene Autry's Western Classics, Columbia, 78 rpm, 1947, 4-record set 45.00

Sheet music, *Mister and Mississippi*, 1951 ....22.50

Songbook, *Sgt. Gene Autry Presents his Favorite Patriotic and Hillbilly Songs*, 48 pgs, 1993, cover detached 45.00

Suspenders, clips with horses, straps with sliding metal guns, 18-1/2" l 195.00

Toy pistol, metal, emb "Gene Autry" on both sides, orange plastic inserts on sides of grips, trigger not functioning, rust 55.00

View-Master, with 2 reels and sleeves, 1950s, orig box, some loose frames 39.00

Watch.....................................110.00

Writing pad, full-color cover, 9" x 5-1/2" 32.00

❖ Autumn Leaf

A premium for the Jewel Tea Company, this dinnerware pattern was produced from 1933 until 1978. Autumn Leaf became so popular with American housewives that other companies began making accessories to complement the pattern.

Reference: Jim and Lynn Salko, *Hall's Autumn Leaf China and Jewel Tea Collectibles*, self-published, 1996.

Collectors' Clubs: Autumn Leaf Reissues Assoc, 19238 Dorchester Circle, Strongsville, OH 44136; National Autumn Leaf Collectors Club, 7346 Shamrock Drive, Indianapolis, IN 46217.

For additional listings, see *Warman's Americana & Collectibles*.

Bean pot, one handle, 1930s, 190.00
Berry bowl, 5-1/2" dia 5.00
Bread and butter plate 8.00
Butter dish, covered, 1-lb 190.00
Cake plate, gold trim, 9-1/2" dia
.... 30.00
Canister, metal, plastic lid........ 25.00
Coasters, set of 8 .... 48.00
Coffeepot, metal infuser, mkd "Hall's Superior...Mary Dunbar," used condition, lid missing, 11" h
.... 40.00
Creamer and sugar, cov, ruffled
.... 35.00
Cream soup bowl 20.00
Cup and saucer 17.50
Dinner plate 18.00
Drippings jar 40.00
Flour sifter, metal, 1930s, light rust, worn 250.00
Fruit bowl, stamp marked "Superior Hall Quality Dinnerware," 5-1/2" dia 14.00
Jug, ball form, gold circle mark "Hall's Superior, Tested and Approved by Mary Dunbar, Jewel Homemaking Institute, Superior Ware," 7" h 70.00
Mixing bowl, small rim chip, worn gold, 6-1/4" dia 5.00

Autumn Leaf Aladdin teapot, 10-1/2" long, $75.

Pie plate, dark spots from use, 9-1/2" dia 18.00
Pitcher, gold trim worn, 7" h 40.00
Range set 42.00
Salad plate 12.00
Teapot, Aladdin, infuser, finial with 3 gold stripes, gold mark "Hall's Superior Quality Kitchenware"
.... 120.00
Tidbit server, 3 tiers 100.00
Tumbler, 6" h 35.00
Vegetable, cov 165.00

❖ Aviation Collectibles

Flying machines continue to fascinate us, and aviation collectibles are soaring at flea markets around the country. Collectors can find material related to hot air balloons, dirigibles and zeppelins, early flight, and modern planes. From paper items to toys, the sky's the limit in this category.

Periodical: *Airliners*, P.O. Box 52-1238, Miami, FL 33152.

Collectors' Club: World Airline Historical Society, 3381 Apple Tree Ln, Erlanger, KY 41048.

For additional listings, see *Warman's Americana & Collectibles*. Also see Airlines, Lindbergh, and other related categories in this edition.

Album, desk top, Pluna, Primeras Lineas Uruguayas de Navegacion Aerea, 7" x 4-1/4" 55.00
Ashtray, Aerolineas Argentinas, porcelain, 3-3/4" x 3-3/4" 14.50
Book, *Official Guide of Commercial Aviation*, in Spanish, shows schedules of all companies operating in South America, Nov 1957 .... 25.00
Cigarette lighter, desk type, chrome plated, lighter compartment in wing, c1937 .... 95.00
Comic book, *Jim Ray's Aviation Sketchbook*, #2, 1946, ink stain on front, wear, yellowing, 64 pgs
.... 18.00
Dish, Lineas Aereas Paraguayas, inscribed "LAP," semi-porcelain, 6-1/4" x 4" 15.00
Game, Wings: The Air Mail Game, Parker Brothers, set of 99 cards, orig instruction sheet, copyright 1928, 4" x 5-1/2" 25.00

The American Clipper postcard, unused, $3.

Magazine tear sheet, Bendix Aviation Corp, 1947, *Saturday Evening Post* 2.00
Gum cards, Aviation Pioneers, includes Hugo Junkers, Otto Lilienthal and Orville Wright, biographies in German, set of 3
.... 15.00
Model, diecast
    KLM 747, Matchbox, 1988, orig bubble pack, 3-3/4" wingspan, 4-3/8" l 35.00
    Korean Airlines Airbus, Matchbox, 1988, orig bubble pack, 3-1/2" wingspan, 4-1/4" l
    .... 35.00
    Lufthansa 747, Matchbox, 1988, orig bubble pack, 3-3/4" wingspan, 4-3/8" l 35.00
    Pan Am 747, Matchbox, 1988, orig bubble pack, 3-3/4" wingspan, 4-3/8" l 35.00
    TWA 767-300, Herpa, German, scale 1:500, MIP 35.00
Palm puzzle, Vosin box aircraft in flight, silvered rim, plastic cover, full color paper playing surface, inscription "1908 80 Kahen/Frankreich," German, c1970 .... 35.00
Pin, Aerolineas Argentinas, enameled metal, 1" l 15.00
Plate, Martin Aviation, Vernon Kilns, brown illus of 5 aircraft, c1940, 10-1/2" dia 55.00
Postcard, Friendship Airport, Baltimore, Md., textured paper, tinted art, C.T. Art-Colortone, mid-1950s, 3-1/2" x 5-1/2", unused, set of 4 .... 18.00

Teaspoon, Aviation Building, N.Y.
World's Fair, 1939 .... 15.00
Toy truck, Trans World Air Lines,
Japan, 1980s, 3-1/2" l 25.00

❖ Avon

Ding, dong...Avon calling! After years of producing fine cosmetics in interesting containers, Avon has branched out, producing a wide variety of items that collectors look for. Expect to find items that are well-marked, and remember that original contents and packaging will increase values.

References: Bud Hastin, *Bud Hastin's Avon Products & California Perfume Co. Collector's Encyclopedia*, 16th ed., self-published, 2000, P.O. 9868, Kansas City, MO 64134.

Periodical: *Avon Times*, P.O. Box 9868, Kansas City, MO 64134.

Collectors' Clubs: National Assoc of Avon Collectors, P.O. Box 7006, Kansas City, MO 64113; Shawnee Avon Bottle Collectors Club, 1418 32nd NE, Canton, OH 44714; Sooner Avon Bottle Collectors Club, 6119 S Hudson, Tulsa, OK 74136; Western World Avon Collectors Club, P.O. Box 23785, Pleasant Hills, CA 94523.

For additional listings, see *Warman's Americana & Collectibles.* Also see Cape Cod in this edition for information on Avon's glassware line.

Avon Sterling Six aftershave, original box, $10.

Barbie, Avon Spring Blossom Barbie, first in series 40.00
Bell, frosted, orig box, 3-1/2" h .. 9.00
Bottle, figural
Boot, empty 5.00
Ford car, 1936 model, box in fair condition 20.00
Liberty Bell, full 10.00
Shoe, empty 5.00
Steam locomotive, The General 4-4-0, full, box end torn . 40.00
Toby mug, empty 5.00
Chamberstick, pewter, mkd "Avon American Heirlooms" 10.00
Collector's plate, Freedom, 1974 .... 35.00
Cologne bottle, Moodwind, dogwood flower design, paper label, 3" h 15.00
Decanter, totem pole 7.00
Goblet, Mount Vernon series, cobalt
George Washington 3.00
Martha Washington 5.00

Jewelry
Locket, faux pearls around edge, blue and lavender violets in center, space for 2 photos, 1-1/2" l 12.00
Pin, leaf shape, 50th anniversary 40.00
Stick pin, key, goldtone, 2" l 15.00
Suite, bracelet, clip earrings and ring, imitation amethyst 15.00
Magazine tear sheet, Avon for Men, 1967 .... 5.00
Perfume bottle
Elusive, clear, silver top, 3" h 9.00
Owl, frosted glass, 4-1/2" h . 9.00
Plate
For Avon Representatives Only, 1977 .... 5.00
Strawberry, 1978, 7-1/2" dia 12.00
Wildflowers of the Eastern States, Wedgwood, 8" dia 15.00
Wildflowers of the Southern States, Wedgwood, 8" dia 15.00
Potpourri, figural pig, orig sticker 5.00
Soaky
Mickey Mouse, 1969, orig bubble bath and box, 7" h 25.00
Pluto, empty, 6" h 20.00
Soap
Aristocat Kitten, 1970s, orig box 65.00
Christmas Children, girl holds doll, boy holds toy rocking horse, 1983 .... 9.00
Statue, Mother's Love, 1982, 6" h 15.00
Stein
Train, 1982, 8" h 25.00
Western, 1980, 8" h 25.00
Thimble, porcelain, blue and red flowers, mkd "Avon" 6.00

TIAS Top 10

The following list ranks the most highly sought collectibles on the Internet during 2000.

1. **Avon**
2. China
3. Cookie jars
4. Roseville
5. Furniture

6. Noritake
7. Lamps
8. McCoy
9. Clocks
10. Books

Source: www.tias.com

B

For exciting collecting trends
and newly expanded areas look
for the following symbols:

⊛ Hot Topic

✮ New Warman's Listing

(May have been in another Warman's title.)

❖ Baby-Related Collectibles

Grandmas and politicians love them, and now more and more collectors are seeking items related to them. Perhaps it's nostalgia, perhaps it's the delightful colorful images. Whatever the reason, items related to babies and their care are quite popular.

Reference: Joan Stryker Grubaugh, *A Collector's Guide to the Gerber Baby*, self-published, 1998.

Baby bottle, emb "Baby" and emb image of infant, bottom mkd Keystone, 6-3/4" h 29.00
Baby powder tin
   Stork, graphic of stork, 3-oz. 70.00
   ZBT, Sterling Drugs Inc., blue ground, front shows baby in tub of water, sides show baby playing with toys, 5-1/4" h 28.00
Baby ring, 12k yellow gold, 4mm ruby, size 3-1/2 .... 80.00
Baby scale, metal, good working cond 65.00
Baby spoon, sterling silver, monogrammed "F," marked GHF Sterling (G.H. French Co., Mass.), some wear, 3" l 12.50
Blanket, 38" x 45", light blue and white, jointed teddy bears in various poses, 1940s 100.00
Bowl, Libby's baby food premium, plastic, green, emb "Libby's Baby Food" and smiling baby 8.00

Feeding bottle, clear glass, 8-ounce, 6" long, $10.

Calendar, 1941, Mennen, baby products illus 15.00
Rattle, sterling silver, 6-1/2" l ... 70.00
Safety pin box, "My Baby Lamb," cover shows baby with lamb, top lifts to show selection of pins (included), sides missing ... 65.00
Sweater, hand-knitted, cream wool with satin ribbon trim, newborn to 3 months 35.00
Talcum tin
   Bauer & Black, oval, 4-1/2" x 3-1/2" 80.00
   California Perfume Co., toy soldier graphic, 2 small areas of paint loss, oval, 4" h 78.00
   Vision d'Eden, American Co., Memphis TN, shows baby on a pillow with angel watching, removable cap and shaker top, a few tiny paint chips, 3-1/2" h 48.00

❖ Baccarat Glass

This French glassware manufacturer is still producing lovely wares, and their paperweights are well known to collectors. Vintage Baccarat glass commands high prices, but contemporary pieces can be found at flea markets for reasonable amounts.

Box, cov, white airplane design on sides, etched mark, 2-1/4" h, 2-3/4" dia 125.00
Cologne bottle, Rose Tiente, pinwheel swirled body, 5" h 90.00
Figure
   Baker, MIB 95.00
   Bull 190.00

Finger bowl, with underplate, ruby ground, gold medallions, and floral decor 350.00
Ice bucket, two reeded bands, swing handle, silvered metal mounts, ball finial on lid 200.00
Paperweight, Pisces, sulphide, c1955 .... 150.00
Toothpick holder, Rose Tiente 110.00
Wine decanter, Rose Tiente, Zipper pattern, matching stopper, 10" h 225.00

❖ Badges

Name tags and identification badges have become quite popular with collectors, and each provides a brief glimpse into history. Examples found with photographs and other pertinent information about the original user are especially prized.

Captain, Boy's State, American Legion logo 38.00
Chauffeur's
   Illinois, 1951, 1-3/4" x 1-1/4" 25.00
   New York, 1926-27, screw-type back, light wear 35.00
   Oklahoma, 1938, pin-type back 35.00
Dick Tracy Detective Club, brass, Dick Tracy in center with star on each side 26.00
Employee, National Cash Register Co., Dayton, OH, emb metal, 1-5/8" h, 2" l 90.00
Fire Department, Inspector, U.S. Naval Air Station, fire truck in center of shield 50.00

25-year badge, International Order of Odd Fellows, 1899 patent date, 1-1/2" diameter, $15.

Junior Police, Brattleboro, VT, 1950s
....35.00
Lone Ranger, masked cowboy, sheriff and gun, metal, orig package, 1960s, mkd "Made in Japan"
....8.00
Police, "Special Officer," brasstone, 1-3/4" x 2-1/2"....................30.00
Hunting, fishing, trapping license badge, New York, 1930, 1-3/4"
....55.00
Service station attendant
    Conoco, nickel over brass, cloisonné porcelain lettering, 1-5/8" h, 2-1/4" l..........170.00
    Standard Oil, nickel over brass, cloisonné porcelain lettering, 1-5/8" h, 2-1/4" l..........325.00
    Texaco, bronze finish, cloisonné porcelain logo, 1-3/4" h, 2" l
    ....275.00
"Town of Islip, Town Attorney, Asst. T.A. #262," brasstone, 2" x 2-1/4"....................................58.00
Toy, "Special Police," 1950s, on orig card, 3-1/2" x 2-3/4"...........17.00

❖ Bakelite

Bakelite is an early form of plastic that was first produced in 1907. A registered trade name, Bakelite was derived from the name of its inventor, Leo H. Baekeland. Items made of Bakelite were formed in molds, subjected to heat and pressure, and then cooled.

Reference: Karima Parry, *Bakelite Bangles*, Krause Publications, 1999. For additional listings, see *Warman's Americana & Collectibles* and *Warman's Jewelry.*

Ashtray, black and white, 8" dia
....45.00
Box, cov, amber and brown swirl
....20.00
Bracelet, bangle, octagon, chocolate marble with butterscotch swirls, some wear, 2-1/2"............50.00
Bracelet, stretch, lemon slices, brown cylinder shapes....100.00
Buckle, carved flower on each end, dark blue, rect..................20.00
Button, translucent amber and brown swirl, orig card, set of 5
....15.00
Cake server, green handle......12.00

Bakelite poker chip set, $395.

Corn cob holder, diamond shape, 2 prongs, red or green, pr.....15.00
Desk set, Art Deco, butterscotch, ink tray, two note pad holders
....225.00
Napkin ring, chick....................30.00
Pie crimper, marbleized butterscotch handle..................................4.50
Salt and pepper shakers, gear shape, marbleized caramel, chrome lids, 2" h, pr............85.00
Stationery box, Art Deco winged horse design, brown, American Stationery Co......................75.00
Toothpick holder, figural dachshund, green.................................95.00

❖ Ballerinas

Swirling images of dancing ladies grace many types of objects, all to the delight of ballerina collectors.

Barbie outfit, #989, leotard, paper tiara and skirt, 1965.........150.00
Doll, Madame Alexander, 1970s, unplayed-with cond, 17" h
....200.00
Figure, porcelain
    Lefton China, 5-3/4" h........36.00
    Royal Doulton, NH 2116, 1952, 7-1/2" h........................400.00
    Royal Dux, adjusting shoe, raised pink triangle mark, 6-1/2" h..........................95.00
Jewelry
    Charm bracelet, silvertone, 9 charms, mkd "Monet," 1950s, 8" l................................55.00
Pin, figural, rhinestones, silver setting, 2-1/2" l......................95.00
Music box
    Bisque figure with glass eyes, cylinder base, French, 9" h
    ....300.00

"Tina the Ballerina" 45 rpm record, Peter Pan Players & Orchestra, $5.

Jewelry box type, ballerina twirls in front of mirror on opened lid, divided jewelry box int, c1960............................10.00
Paper dolls, *Little Ballerina*, Whitman #1951, c1959, uncut . 28.00

❖ Banks, Still

The golden age of still banks was ushered in with the advent of the cast-iron bank. Usually in the form of animals or humans, they were often painted to increase their appeal, and many businesses and banks used them as a means of advertising. Tin-lithographed still banks were often used as premiums, being popular from 1930 to 1955.

Still banks, as listed below, are those with no moving parts. Mechanical banks, with some type of action, are thoroughly covered in *Warman's Antiques & Collectibles.*

References: Don Duer, *A Penny Saved: Still and Mechanical Banks*, Schiffer Publishing, 1993; —, *Penny Banks Around the World*, Schiffer Publishing, 1997; Earnest Ida and Jane Pitman, *Dictionary of Still Banks*, Long's Americana, 1980; Beverly and Jim Mangus, *Collector's Guide to Banks*, Collector Books, 1998; Andy and Susan Moore, *The Penny Bank Book: Collecting Still Banks*, 3rd ed, Schiffer Publishing, 2000; Tom and Loretta Stoddard, *Ceramic Coin Banks*, Collector Books, 1997.

Periodicals: *Glass Bank Collector*, P.O. Box 155, Poland, NY 13431; *Heuser's Quarterly Collectible Bank Newsletter*, P.O. Box 300, West Winfield, NY 13491.

Collectors' Clubs: Mechanical Bank Collectors of America, P.O. Box 128, Allegan, MI 49010, www.mechanicalbanks.org; Still Bank Collector's Club of America, 4175 Millersville Rd, Indianapolis, IN 46205, www.stillbankclub.com.

For additional listings, see *Warman's Antiques & Collectibles* and *Warman's Americana & Collectibles*.

Reproduction Alert.

Big Boy, vinyl, smiling figure, black lettered name on chest, dark-blue eye accents, base stamped "Niagara Plastics, Erie, Pa.," c1960, 8" h 75.00

Book, cover opens, made for Encyclopedia Americana, with key to open 65.00

Church, tin litho, U.S. Metal Co. 18.00

Cookie Monster, sgd Jim Henson, orig Sesame Street box 24.00

Cylinder, litho tin, black, white, red, yellow and blue designs of young children, white top with smiling sun as coin slot, late 1930s, 3" dia, 3-1/2" h 35.00

Elsie the Cow, chalk, c. 1950s, 6-5/8" h 395.00

Glass, buffalo on one side, Indian on other, round, 7" h 22.50

Globe, "As you save so you prosper" on pedestal, Ohio Art Co., 4-1/2" h 35.00

Conoco Super Motor Oil still bank, $20.

Howard Johnson's restaurant, plastic, building shape, 1960s 28.00

Hubert the Lion, Lefton 40.00

Log Cabin Bank for Lincoln Pennies, red plastic stopper, mkd Japan, 5" x 3-1/4" x 3-3/4" 20.00

London tour bus, Warner Bros 35.00

Pabst Blue Ribbon Beer, miniature beer can, 1936-37 patent date, coin slot in top, 2-3/4" h 38.00

Peter Rabbit, Wedgwood, 6 sides, 3-1/2" h 30.00

Pinocchio on whale, musical, Schmid 35.00

Snappy Service, smiling figure, blue and white outfit, red and white company label on chest, name in relief in white letters on red base, c1970 .... 60.00

Snoopy and Woodstock, lying on jack-o-lantern, Whitman Candies, 4-1/2" h 10.00

Squirrel, Goebel 35.00

The Jetsons, spaceship, licensed by Hanna-Barbera 375.00

Uncle Sam
   Figural, glazed ceramic, red, white, blue and fleshtones 55.00
   Register bank, 3-coin register opens at $10, will hold up to $50, Ohio Art Co. 35.00

❖ Barber Bottles

At the turn of the century, barbershops used decorated bottles to hold oils and other liquids that were used on a daily basis. These colorful glass bottles included examples made of art glass, pattern glass, and milk glass, as well as a variety of commercially prepared and labeled bottles.

References: *Barbershop Collectibles*, L-W Book Sales, 1996; Keith E. Estep, *Shaving Mug & Barber Bottle Book*, Schiffer Publishing, 1995; Richard Holiner, *Collecting Barber Bottles*, Collector Books, 1986.

For additional listings, see *Warman's Antiques & Collectibles.*

Reproduction Alert.

Amber, Hobnail, 3-ring neck, curled lip, bulbous base, 1 knob broken, 6-3/4" h 200.00

Amethyst, middle has matte finish with orange enameled deco, top and bottom are white and gold enameled deco, wear, 6-3/4" h 200.00

Aqua, Inverted Thumbprint, enameled deco of 18th C gentleman, 2 panels satin finish, 2 panels clear, metal top, 9-1/2" h 280.00

Clear
   Hazel Atlas, double plastic cap possibly Bakelite, 7" h, pr 45.00
   Paper label, Empire Quinine Hair Tonic, Empire Barber and Beauty Supply Co., screw cap, contents, 1-gal, 12" h 25.00

Coin Spot, blue opalescent, orig stopper 300.00

Cut glass, clear, bulbous base, unpolished pontil, chips at neck, 7" h 225.00

F. W. Fitch, emb, dug 15.00

Green, all-over pattern of white enameled flowers with orange centers, white stopper, 9" h 250.00

Light green, enameled floral deco, missing stopper, 7-1/2" h 145.00

Milk glass
   Witch Hazel, painted letters and flower dec, 9" h 115.00
   Hobnail, Imperial Glass, bottom mkd IG, 7-1/4" h 28.00

Purple, white enameled floral dec, missing stopper, 8-1/2" h 150.00

White, orange letters, "Bay Rum," 7" h 95.00

❖ Barbershop and Beauty Shop Collectibles

Flea markets are great places to search for items related to barbershops and beauty shops. Following the decline of the barbershop as an important social institution and with the advent of uni-sex regional chains, early barbering and beauty products are becoming increasingly popular. Attractive advertising and interesting examples of barbering equipment add color and style to collections.

Koken salesman's sample, $51,750. (Photo courtesy of James D. Julia, Inc., Fairfield, Maine)

It's a record

A little off the top?

Actually, the buyer of this salesman's sample Koken barber chair was more than a few hairs lighter after purchasing this rarity. The 1895 hydraulic chair was made of carved mahogany. It set a record price for a salesman's sample when it realized $51,750 during a James D. Julia auction in 1999.

Reference: *Barbershop Collectibles*, L-W Book Sales, 1996.

Collectors' Club: Safety Razor Collectors' Guild, P.O. Box 885, Crescent City, CA 95531.

For additional listings, see *Warman's Americana & Collectibles* and Shaving Mugs in this edition.

Barber brush
    Half doll porcelain handle .. 20.00
    Penguin handle, wood, paint chipped, 1940s 35.00
Beer mug, Barber Shop Whistle Stop, "For Good Cheer, Whistle for Your Beer," applied googly eyes, barber pole handle with whistle, mkd "G. C....Japan," 5-1/4" h 50.00
Counter map, Wardonia Razor Blades, rubber, 9" x 8" 18.00
Display case, West Hair Nets, tiered display case, tin litho picture of flapper in touring car inside lid, 15" h, 6" w, 5" dia 60.00
Facial kit, Revlon, Moondrops at Home, orig packaging 45.00
Hair net, blond, orig envelope
    .... 3.00

Modern Service porcelain sign, Bob White Sign Co., Milwaukee, 48-1/8" high, $300.

Magazine tear sheet, adv
    Eversharp Schick Safety Razor, 1958 .... 8.00
    Lady Schick, 1956 .... 6.00
    Norelco Speedshaver, 1957
        .... 6.00
    Remington 60 electric shaver, 1962 .... 6.00
    Remington Princess, 1959 ... 5.00
    Remington Rollectric, 1958
        .... 6.00
    Sunbeam Blade Electric Shavemaster Razor, 1957 .... 6.00
Match book cover, Norman's Modern Barber Shop 6.00
Newspaper, *Barber's Journal,* 1881
    .... 12.00
Poster, Packer's Tar Soap, scene of barber shaving customer, 1900, 9" x 12" 40.00
Razor tin, Yankee Blades, tin litho, eagles and center image of man shaving, red ground, 1-1/4" w, 2-1/4" l 200.00

Record, "Famous Barber Shop Ballads," Mills Brothers, 45 rpm, 1948, 3-record set 45.00
Safety razor, Burham, razor with 3 blades in orig envelope, tin litho safety razor tin, red ground, black lettering, unused 160.00
Shaving brush, Ever Ready, black celluloid handle, dark bristles, orig box 15.00
Sign, Beauty Shoppe, two-sided flange sign, porcelain, Art Deco lady with finger wave hairdo, 12" h, 24" l 275.00
Tin
    Bouquet Talcum Powder ... 25.00
    Magic Shaving Powder 25.00
Towel steamer, nickel-plated copper, porcelain-over-steel base
    .... 325.00

✪ Barbie

Mattel patented the Barbie fashion doll in 1958, with the first versions reaching store shelves in 1959. Her friends, including Ken and Skipper, joined the ranks in subsequent years. Accessories, clothes, room settings, and all types of related merchandise soon followed. A plethora of books cover Barbie, and her life is well documented. Her appeal is widespread, and she is the most collected doll ever created.

References: J. Michael Augustyniak, *Collector's Encyclopedia of Barbie Doll Exclusives and More*, 2nd ed, Collector Books, 2000; Stefanie Deutsch, *Barbie, the First 30 Years*, Collector Books, 2001; Sibyl DeWein and Joan Ashabraner, *Collector's Encyclopedia of Barbie Dolls and Collectibles*, Collector Books, 2000; Connie Craig Kaplan, *Collector's Guide to Barbie Doll Vinyl Cases*, Collector Books, 1999; Patricia Long, *Barbie's Closet: Price Guide for Barbie & Friends Fashions and Accessories, 1959-1973*, Krause Publications, 1999; Maria Martinez-Esguerra, *Collector's Guide to 1990s Barbie Dolls*, Collector Books, 1999; Marcie Melillo, *Ultimate Barbie Doll Book*, Krause

Publications, 1996; Lorraine Mieszala, *Collector's Guide to Barbie Doll Paper Dolls*, Collector Books, 2000; Kitturah B. Westenhouser, *The Story of Barbie*, 2nd ed, Collector Books, 2000.

Periodicals: *Barbie Bazaar*, 5617 6th Ave, Kenosha, WI 53140; *Barbie Fashions*, 387 Park Ave S, New York, NY 10016; *Barbie Talks Some More*, 19 Jamestown Dr, Cincinnati, OH 45241.

For additional listings, see *Warman's Americana & Collectibles*.

Accessories
    Dog N' Duds, #1613, 1964 10.00
    Swimming pool, inflatable, no box 20.00
Activity book, *Skipper and Scott Beauty Sticker Fun*, 1980 ....5.00
Book, *Portrait of Skipper*, 1964..5.00
Camera, Super Star Cameramatic Flash Camera, 1978..........20.00
Car, Hot Rod, #1460, 1963....195.00
Carrying case, Barbie and Midge, pink, 1964..........................30.00
Clothing
    Dreamy Pink, nightgown and robe, slippers missing, 1968 ....40.00
    Faux Fur, skirt and jacket...80.00
    Garden Party, #931, 1963 ....155.00
    Icebreaker, #942, 1964....140.00
    Pajama Fun 8.00
Doll
    Barbie, brunette, bubble cut 125.00
    Barbie, ponytail, curly bangs, red hair, 1958 ....200.00
    FAO Schwarz, Silver Screen 265.00
    Holiday, 1989 ....275.00
    Ken 25.00
    Ken, 1960, plaid pants, turtleneck, blue coat............150.00
    Midge, #1080, 1964.........675.00
    Oriental Barbie, #3262.....155.00
    Ricky..................................25.00
    Scott, #1019, 1979.............70.00
    Skipper, #950, 1963.........120.00
    Winter Fantasy.................250.00
Lunch box
    Barbie and Francie, vinyl, multicolor graphics, copyright 1965 Mattel, King-Seeley Thermos Co., 6-1/4" x 9" x 4" 55.00

The World of Barbie, vinyl, blue, multicolor images of Barbie, copyright 1971 Mattel, King-Seeley, used, 6-3/4" x 8-3/4" x 4" dia 50.00
Pencil case, Skipper and Skooter, Standard Plastic, 1966 ......15.00
Playset, Fashion Plaza, 1976..80.00
Record, 33-1/3 rpm, sealed, 12-1/2" x 12-1/2"
    Birthday Album.....................6.50
    Sing-Along 6.00
Western dress-up set, child's, display box with vest, wrist cuffs, rope tie, belt, spats and western hat, copyright 1981 Mattel, H-G Industries, unused, 5" x 14-1/2" x 19" 35.00

❖ Bar Ware

Back in the days when recreation rooms were popular in homes, bars were often an important component of that scene. Of course, a well-equipped bar was a necessity. Novelty items and functional equipment from bars are now making their way to flea markets.

Reference: Stephen Visakay, *Vintage Bar Ware*, Collector Books, 1997.
For additional listings, see Cocktail Shakers in this edition.
Bar guide, *Esquire's Liquor Intelligencer*, 1938, wear, few pages loose, 5-1/2" x 7" 28.00

Glass with directions for mixing drinks, 6" high, $2.

Cocktail glasses, ruby, 2-1/2" h, set of 8................................ 125.00
Cordial set, six glass cordials with cut floral dec, 1-1/2" x 3", matching 12" x 3-1/2" aluminum tray 95.00
Ice bucket, glass, hp horse and riding crops on both sides, hammered aluminum handle, gold band at top and bottom..... 10.00
Jigger, frosted glass, Indian motif, Canada on back, 4-oz......... 4.00
Mixer, clear glass, black lettering, recipes on side, 5-3/4" h ... 14.00
Paper napkins, Ed Nofziger's Mad-Nagerie Sip 'n Snack, different animal illus, orig box, 6-1/2" x 6-1/2" 14.00
Pitcher, sterling overlay of golfer on both sides 100.00
Seltzer bottle, blue glass, "Babad's Miami Seltzer Co.," bottle made in Czechoslovakia........... 100.00
Shot glass, Lucite, clear and black, glass magnifies female nude in bottom when held to light.. 50.00
Sipper/stirrer, sterling, fashioned to resemble bamboo, orig box, 8-1/2" l, set of 4................. 50.00
Soda siphon, stainless steel, Sparklets Corp., N.Y., 1940s 80.00
Tray and coasters, wood, tray shows man sleeping and "Silence, Genius at Work," coasters with humorous sayings, Canada, 1950s, tray 12" x 8", 6 coasters 3" dia............................... 88.00

❖ Baseball Cards

Baseball cards were first printed in the late 19th century. By 1900 the most common cards were those made by tobacco companies, including American Tobacco Company. Most of the tobacco-related cards (identified as T cards) were produced between 1909 and 1915. During the 1920s, American Caramel, National Caramel, and York Caramel candy companies issued cards identified in lists as E cards.

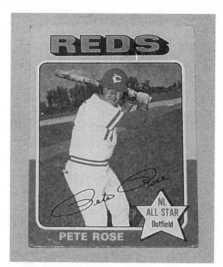

Pete Rose, NL All-Star Outfield, #320, Topps, 1975, $15.

During the 1930s, Goudey Gum Company of Boston, and Gum, Inc., were the primary producers of baseball cards. Following World War II, Bowman Gum of Philadelphia, the successor to Gum, Inc., led the way. Topps, Inc., of Brooklyn, NY, bought Bowman in 1956, and Fleer of Philadelphia and Donruss of Memphis joined the competitive ranks in the early 1980s.

References: *All Sport Alphabetical Price Guide,* Krause Publications, 1995; *Baseball's Top 500,* Krause Publications, 1999; *Standard Catalog of Baseball Cards,* 10th ed, Krause Publications, 2000.

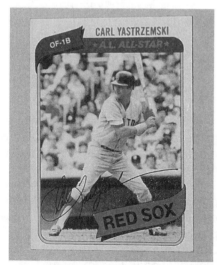

Carl Yastrzemski, Red Sox, A.L. All-Star, #720, Topps, 1980, $5.

Periodicals: *Baseball Update,* 220 Sunrise Hwy, Suite 284, Rockville Centre, NY 11570; *Beckett Baseball Card Monthly,* 4887 Alpha Rd, Suite 200, Dallas, TX 75244; *Card Trade,* 700 E State St, Iola, WI 54990; *Diamond Angle,* P.O. Box 409, Kaunakakai, HI 96748; *Sports Cards Magazine & Price Guide,* 700 E State St, Iola, WI 54990; *Sports Collectors Digest,* 700 E State St, Iola, WI 54990; *Your Season Ticket,* 106 Liberty Rd, Woodsburg, MD 21790.

Collectors' Clubs: There are many local clubs for card collectors, but there is not a national organization at this time.

Reproduction Alert.

The following listings are merely a sampling of the thousands of baseball cards available. For detailed listings, see *2001 Standard Catalog of Baseball Cards,* 10th ed, by Bob Lemke, Krause Publications, 2000.

1970 Topps, VG cond.
    Complete set, 720 cards ..350.00
    Common player, 1-271.......30.00
    Common player, 272-546...40.00
    Common player, 547-633.....1.00
    Common player, 634-720.....4.75
1984 Donruss
    Complete set, 660 cards ..180.00
    Common player.................15.00
1995 Bowman
    Complete set, 439 cards ..240.00
    Common player.................10.00
1998 Fleer Update
    Complete set, 100 cards 50.00
    Common player.................10.00

❖ Baseball Memorabilia

"Play ball!" How those words excite fans and collectors alike. America's fascination with this popular national pastime guarantees a wide range of collectibles to choose from at flea markets.

References: Mark Allen Baker, *All Sport Autograph Guide,* Krause Publications, 1994; ——, *Sports Collectors Digest Baseball Autograph Handbook,* 2nd ed, Krause Publications, 1991; ——, *Team Baseballs,*

Krause Publications, 1992; Mark Larson, *Complete Guide to Baseball Memorabilia,* 3rd ed, Krause Publications, 1996; Mark Larson, Rick Hines, and Dave Platta, *Mickey Mantle Memorabilia,* Krause Publications, 1993.

Cincinnati Reds 1984 Yearbook Magazine, 56 pages, 10-7/8" x 8-1/2", $15.

Periodicals: *Baseball Hobby News,* 4540 Kearney Villa Rd, San Diego, CA 92123; *John L. Raybin's Baseball Autograph News,* 527 3rd Ave, #294-A, New York, NY 10016; *Sports Cards Magazine & Price Guide,* 700 E State St, Iola, WI 54990; *Sports Collectors Digest,* 700 E State St, Iola, WI 54990; *Tuff Stuff,* P.O. Box 1637, Glen Allen, VA 23060.

Collectors' Clubs: Glove Collector, 14057 Rolling Hills Ln, Dallas, TX 75210; Society for American Baseball Research, P.O. Box 93183, Cleveland, OH 44101

Reproduction Alert.

Autograph
    Mel Allen, on Yankee Stadium
        postcard....................... 26.00
    Don Clendenon, Tug McGraw
        and Ron Swoboda on 1969
        New York Mets pennant
        .... 60.00
Baseball, autographed
    Bench, Johnny 50.00
    Carew, Rod 50.00
    Mays, Willie.................... 100.00
    Reese, PeeWee 125.00

A swing and a hit

Hillerich & Bradsby, Louisville Slugger Co. produces special black ebony bats to commemorate World Series games. The bats have gold facsimile signatures of the team members, and they are awarded to participating players and league dignitaries. Because they are produced in limited numbers, collector interest tends to drive the marketplace.

1965, Minnesota Twins .600.00
1992, Atlanta Braves.....500.00
1993, Toronto Blue Jays
...............................500.00

Baseball, team-signed
   All-Star Game, American
      League, 1967, faded ...100.00
   Minnesota Twins, 1991, 13 sig-
      natures........................100.00
Book
   Baseball Personalities, Jimmy
      Powers, 1949, 320 pgs, tat-
      tered dustjacket.............15.00
   *Throwing Heat: The Autobiogra-
   phy of Nolan Ryan*, Nolan
      Ryan and Harvey Frommer,
      1988.............................25.00
   A Whole Different Game, Marvin
      Miller, Birch Lane Press, 1991
      ....10.00
Brochure, season ticket plans,
   Washington Senators, 1963
   ....15.00
Charm, plastic, green weiner, "Pitts-
   burgh Pirates Official Green
   Weenie," copyright 1966, 1-1/2"
   x 8-1/2" l 10.00
Cocktail napkin, San Diego All-Star
   Game, July 14, 1992...........2.00
Coffee cup, plastic, Detroit Tigers
   ....25.00
Game, Baseball Golden Trivia Game
   - Major League Edition 1984,
   trivia card packs unopened, MIB
   ....30.00
Mug, figural, comic batter handle
   ....70.00
Patch, New York Giants, 1950s,
   flocking on vinyl, 3-1/2" dia
   ....50.00

Pennant
   Cincinnati Redlegs, red with pink
      and white detailing, one tassle
      missing, 29" l.................55.00
   National Baseball Hall of Fame
      and Museum, Cooperstown,
      N.Y., 12" l.......................18.00
   Schedule, Pittsburgh Pirates,
      1936.............................50.00
   New York Mets, 1969, team-
      signed...........................60.00
Place mat, paper, scalloped edge,
   photo showing aerial view of
   Yankee Stadium, "Yankee Sta-
   dium Baseball's Proud Heritage,"
   early 1960s, 9-1/2" x 14-1/2"
   ....7.50
Postcard, Yankee Stadium, auto-
   graphed by Mel Allen, Babe
   Ruth stamp with first-day cancel-
   lation...................................26.00
Press guide, Minnesota Twins, 1963
   ....40.00
Record, *Hank Aaron The Life Of A
   Legend*, 33-1/3 rpm, single
   record on Fleetwood label, interviews and career highlights, mid
   1970s, unopened...............10.00
Salt and pepper shakers, bisque,
   batter and umpire 95.00
Schedule, Pittsburgh Pirates, 1936,
   back stamped "Kennedy Hardware Co., Sportsman's Headquarters"............................50.00
Toothbrush, bat shape, beige plastic,
   Cincinnati Reds, Oracare, early
   1970s, 6" l............................8.00
Trade card, "Struck Out," comical
   baseball player, "W.M. Elder,
   Dealer in Drugs and Medicines",
   late 1800s, removed from scrapbook, 3-1/4" x 5-1/4"..........35.00
Whiffle ball, white vinyl ball 2-1/4"
   dia, black-and-white box 2-1/2"
   sq, photo of Tim McCarver on
   lid, c1960 ....10.00
World Series pins
   1966, Dodgers 100.00
   1974, Oakland A's............375.00
   1982, St. Louis Cardinals...50.00
   1984, San Diego Padres....75.00
   1995, Atlanta Braves........100.00
World Series program
   1948, Indians v Braves, no writ-
      ing, some cover wear 85.00
   1996, Yankees v Braves 10.00

❖ Basketball Cards

This relatively new collecting area is growing quickly. As with baseball cards, it's important to know your subject in order to spot unusual and valuable cards.

Reference: *Standard Catalog of Basketball Cards*, 4th ed, Krause Publications, 2000.

Periodicals: *Sports Cards Magazine & Price Guide*, 700 E State St, Iola, WI 54990; *Sports Collectors Digest*, 700 E State St, Iola, WI 54990; *Beckett Basketball Card Monthly*, Beckett Publications, P.O. Box 7652, Red Oak, IA 51591-0652 The following listings are merely a sampling of the thousands of basketball cards available.

Fleer
   1985 Series, 90 cards, with stick-
      ers 30.00
   1998, #1 ....15.00
Johnson, Larry, stadium club ..10.00
Olympics Dream Team, 1992, orig
   collector's album, includes Larry
   Bird, Charles Barkley, Michael
   Jordan, Scottie Pippen, Karl Mal-
   one, coaches, set of 25 cards
   ....15.00
SkyBox Series, 15 cards per pack,
   series of 36 factory sealed
   packs, 1990 ....18.50
Topps
   1995, complete #1 set.......35.00
   1997, factory set...............25.00
Upper Deck, 10 cards per pack,
   series of 30 packs, 1995...15.00

❖ Basketball Memorabilia

Since its introduction in 1891, players and spectators have enjoyed the game of basketball. So popular is the sport that phrases such as "Hoosier Hysteria" and "March Madness" have been added to the lexicon. The NBA is working hard to promote collecting among its fans, and the WNBA has created a whole new field of collectibles.

Periodical: *Sports Collectors Digest*, 700 E State St, Iola, WI 54990.

Action Figure, MOC

Barkley, Charles, Headliners NBA.............................. 10.00

Drexler, Clyde, Rockets, Headliners NBA 5.00

Frazier, Will, Starting Line-Up, 1997 .... 15.00

Hill, Grant, Detroit Pistons, Headliners NBA 7.50

Autograph, 8" x 10" photo

Bird, Larry 34.00

Johnson, Magic.................. 36.00

Mercer, Ron 15.00

Van Horn, K 25.00

Autographed Jersey

Bryant, Kobe.................... 340.00

Jones, Eddie.................... 185.00

Christmas Ornament, Hallmark Treasury series

Hill, Grant, 1998, includes Fleer SkyBox trading card, 4-1/4" h 12.00

Johnson, Magic, 1997, includes Fleer SkyBox trading card, 5-1/2" h 14.00

New York Nicks, 1997, ceramic, orig box 8.00

Seattle Sonics, 1997, ceramic, orig box 8.00

Doll, Dennis Rodman, extra outfit, wig, vinyl, 12" h 40.00

Dribbler, Knicks, black, 1959, Japan 35.00

Game, Cadaco, #165, 1973, unused, MIB 30.00

Hallmark Magic Johnson ornament, original box, $14.

Photograph

Grove City, OH, early 1930s, 5" x 7".................................... 30.00

Petrovic Drazen, wire service photo of young Yugoslav player, 1989..................... 3.50

Plaque, David Robinson, photo of him wearing Spurs jersey, copyrighted 1990 NBA, and cards, matted, display frame, 8" x 10" 35.00

Seals and Diecuts, Dennison, package of 4 pcs, unused, orig cellophane packaging 7.50

Tie tack with chain, male basketball player 12.00

For exciting collecting trends and newly expanded areas look for the following symbols:

✪ Hot Topic

✳ New Warman's Listing

(May have been in another Warman's edition.)

❖ Baskets

Wonderful examples of all types of baskets can be found at flea markets. Check carefully for wear and damage, and make sure they are priced accordingly.

Baby basket, wicker, hood formed at one end, handles, some damage and splits 75.00

Banana, large, two handles woven into sides, loosely woven, damage...................................... 45.00

Cheese basket, woven splint, old patina, some damage, string wrapped repair at rims, 21" dia 115.00

Gathering, rye straw, oval, wear and damage, 15" x 21" 85.00

Market, woven splint handle 90.00

Melon shape, woven splint, bentwood handle, 15" dia 85.00

Nantucket, pocketbook type, whalebone plaque on lid, imperfections, 6" h........................ 175.00

Peach, wide slats, wooden base, 11-1/2" h 2.00

Picnic, woven splint, two folding lids attached to sides with leather loops, c1950 .... 25.00

Porcupine, woven splint, cov, contemporary, labeled "Edith Bonde," 9" h...................... 75.00

Sewing, cov, round, ring-type handles, slight wear................ 45.00

Buttocks basket, 14" x 11", $95.

❖ Batman

"Holy cow, Batman! Why is everyone staring at us?" This famous super hero and his cast of cohorts can be found in abundance at local flea markets. Watch for examples related to contemporary movies as well as items with tie-ins to the television series and the comic characters.

References: Bill Bruegman, *Superhero Collectibles*, Toy Scouts, 1996; Joe Desris, *Golden Age of Batman*, Artabras, 1994.

Collectors' Club: Batman TV Series Fan Club, P.O. Box 107, Venice, CA 90291.

Action figure, Penguin, 1992, 9" h 100.00

Batmobile, Corgi, #267, diecast, copyright 1983, MIB........ 190.00

Batphone Hot-Line................ 575.00

Bubble Bath, 1990s, unused, 8-3/4" h 25.00

Escape Gun, black or red, 1966, sealed in orig blister.......... 45.00

Figure

Batman, Ertl, cast metal, 1990, sealed in orig blister pack with collector card, 2" h........ 15.00

Penguin, Batman Returns, Applause tag, plastic, 1992, 9" h 25.00

Inflatable figure, plastic, 1989, 13" h 40.00

Thermos brand plastic lunch box and thermos, $20.

Kite, Batman & Robin, plastic, 1982, sealed in orig package 20.00
Notebook, spiral bound, Michael Keaton, unused 1.50
Pen set, Batman & Robin, DC Comics, 1978 .... 30.00
PEZ, Batman, #5, 1985, used 35.00
Pin, plastic, 1989, pack of 12 assorted figures 12.00
Plastic bag, 1989, unused, 7-1/2" x 4-1/2" 1.00
Puzzle, Batman & Robin, 1981, 130 pcs, unused, 10-3/4" x 8-1/2" 12.00
Robot, tin wind-up, Biliken, Japan, MIB 175.00
Scale model, Bat Car, Valtoys, 3-3/4" l, MOC 25.00
Schoolbook cover, 1966, 20" x 13" 15.00
Straw, figural, 18 assorted figures in box 9.00
Toy
    Bat Cave, 1960s, orig box 85.00
    Pix-A-Go-Go, featuring the Penguin, National Periodical Publications, 1966, sealed in orig shrink wrap 75.00

❖ Battery-Operated Toys

Battery-operated toys have amused children for decades. Originally inexpensive, these toys were made in large quantities, and many still exist today. Values increase quickly for examples in good working condition and for those playthings with interesting actions or with the original box.

References: Sharon Korbeck & Elizabeth A. Stephan, *2001 Toys & Prices*, 8th ed, Krause Publications, 2000; Richard O'Brien, *Collecting Toys*, 8th ed, Krause Publications, 1997.

Big Top Champ Circus Clown, MIB 95.00
BMW 3.5 CSL turbo car, tin, Dunlop and Bosch Electric advertising, MIB 120.00
Brave Eagle, beating drum, raising war hoop, MIB 145.00
Bubble Blowing Monkey, raises hand from pan on lap to mouth, MIB 195.00
Button the Pup, MIB 375.00
Captain Blushwell, vinyl head, Japan, 1970s, MIB 85.00
Carnival Choo Choo, plastic, Hong Kong, 1970s, MIB 55.00
Comical Clara, MIB 495.00
Fighter Plane Bombardier, orig box 395.00
Happy Miner, MIB 1,075.00
Knock-Out Boxers, orig box... 295.00
Lamborghini Countach car, red, MIB 120.00
Love-Love Volkswagen Beetle, tin, orange, blinking light in back window, advertising for Mobil, Champion and Goodyear, MIB 145.00
McGregor, Scotsman smoking cigar, moves up and down from treasure chest, MIB 195.00
My Fair Dancer, litho tin, dancer in naval outfit, seahorse graphics on base, MIB, 11" h 225.00
Picnic Bear, orig box 125.00
Roller Coaster, plastic, Hong Kong, 1970s, MIB 55.00
Rosko, bartender, shakes, pours and drinks, smoke rises from ears, MIB 75.00
Santa Claus, orig box 225.00
School Bus, tin litho, switch opens doors, headlights light 175.00
Smoking Grandpa, smokes, but pipe doesn't light, Japan 85.00
Sniffy Dog with Bee, Modern Toys, Japan, 1970s, MIB 55.00
Space Explorer, turn-over action, Gakken, Japan, MIB 100.00
Traffic Policeman, MIB 490.00

Battery-operated red Volkswagen Beetle, metal, 10" long, $40.

Tumbles the Bear, Yanoman, 1970s, MIB 85.00
US Army Helicopter, C-7 .... 90.00
Walking Gorilla, MIB 1,275.00
Waltzing Matilda, MIB 875.00

❖ Bauer Pottery

Many people think of brightly colored California pottery when they hear the name Bauer, but the company actually produced utilitarian earthenware and stoneware for many years before expanding their product line. John Bauer founded the company in 1885 in Paducah, Kentucky, but the plant was moved to Los Angeles in 1909. Artware, dinnerware, and kitchenware became mainstays of the company until a strike in 1961 forced them out of business the following year.

Reference: Jeffrey B. Snyder, *Beautiful Bauer*, Schiffer Publishing, 2000.

Butter pat tray
    Black, scratches in center, 4-1/2" dia 75.00
    Red orange, a few scratches, 4-1/2" dia 50.00
Coffee cup, green-gray, 4" d... 14.00
Dog dish, large, cobalt 150.00
Flower pot, Pinnacle, pink, glazed-over crease in clay, 7-1/4" h 50.00
Gravy boat, bright yellow, imp mark, 10" w, 4" h 30.00
Ice pitcher, ringware, 2-qt, 2 small chips to handle 175.00
Pitcher, squat form, yellow, 2-qt, hairline to ice lip 55.00

Plate

Ringware, jade green, 9" dia 45.00

Plainware, black, imp mark, 1930s, 2 small nicks, 9-1/2" dia 20.00

Relish, speckled white, 15-3/4" x 7-1/2" 30.00

Rose bowl, Fred Johnson, hand-thrown, 8-1/2" dia 90.00

Vegetable bowl, ringware, yellow, oval, 9" 125.00

Water jug, Brusche, speckled pink 65.00

❖ Bavarian China

Flea markets are wonderful places to find examples of this colorful china. Several china manufacturers in the Bavarian porcelain center of southern Germany produced a wide variety of items that are collectively referred to as Bavarian china.

For additional listings, see *Warman's Antiques & Collectibles*.

Bowl, large orange poppies, green leaves 85.00

Creamer and sugar, purple and white pansy dec, mkd "Meschendorf, Bavaria" 65.00

Cup and saucer, roses and leaves, gold handle 25.00

Hair receiver, apple blossom dec, mkd "T S. & Co." 60.00

Portrait plate, elaborate portrait of lady, sgd "L. B. Chaffee, R. C. Bavaria," 100.00

Ramekin and underplate, ruffled, small red roses and green leaves, gold trim 45.00

"An Irish Jaunting Car" dish, Bavaria Schumann, 4-1/2" x 6-3/4", $10.

Salt and pepper shakers, pink apple blossom sprays, white ground, reticulated gold tops, pr 35.00

Shaving mug, pink carnations, mkd "Royal Bavaria"...................65.00

Sugar shaker, hp, pastel pansies 60.00

Teapot, yellow, colorful iris dec 60.00

❖ Beanie Babies

The original set of nine Beanie Babies was released in 1993. The resulting collector enthusiasm and speculation quickly priced many children out of the market. Intended as simple, inexpensive playthings, these bean-stuffed personalities took on a life of their own, with some examples commanding exorbitant prices. The current market has returned to a level more consistent with the fun factor of these toys.

References: Shawn Brecka, *The Beanie Family Album and Collectors Guide*, Antique Trader Books, 1998; Les and Sue Fox, *The Beanie Baby Handbook*, West Highland Publishing, 1997; Rosie Wells, *Rosie's Price Guide for Ty's Beanie Babies*, Rosie Wells Enterprises, 1997.

Ants the anteater 6.00
Baldy the eagle........................10.00
Bernie the St. Bernard...............6.00
Bessie the cow 60.00
Bruno the terrier.......................6.00
Cubbie the bear......................20.00

Congo, $5.

Daisy the cow 6.00
Ears the bunny....................... 12.00
Flash the dolphin 95.00
Flip the cat 24.00
Goldie the goldfish 55.00
Gracie the swan....................... 7.00
Hoot the owl.......................... 39.00
Lizzy the lizard 19.00
Manny the manatee 150.00
Patti the platypus 15.00
Quackers the duck................... 8.00
Rover the dog 16.00
Sly the fox 6.00
Snort the bull........................... 6.00
Sting the ray......................... 150.00
Tank the armadillo.................. 70.00
Weenie the dog....................... 18.00
Ziggy the zebra 10.00
Zip the cat 20.00

❖ Beatles

The Fab Four created quite a sensation with their music during the 1960s. Beatlemania fueled the creation of a plethora of items paying tribute to the group and bearing the singers' likenesses. Record albums, concert ephemera, and even dolls can be found at local flea markets.

Reference: Jeff Augsburger, Marty Eck and Rick Rann, *Beatles Memorabilia Price Guide*, 3rd ed, Antique Trader Books, 1997.

Periodicals: *Beatlefan*, P.O. Box 33515, Decatur, GA 30033; *Instant Karma*, P.O. Box 256, Sault Ste. Marie, MI 39783.

Collectors Clubs: Beatles Connection, P.O. Box 1066, Pinealls Park, FL 34665; Beatles Fan Club, 397 Edgewood Ave, New Haven, CT 06511; Beatles Fan Club of Great Britain, Superstore Productions, 123 Marina, St. Leonards on Sea, East Sussex, England TN38 OBN; Working Class Hero Club, 3311 Niagara St, Pittsburgh, PA 15213.

For additional listings, see *Warman's Americana & Collectibles*.

Reproduction Alert.

Arcade card, shows all 4 men, black-and-white, cream reverse with write-up on the group, 1965, major crease to 1 corner..... 5.00

Remco Beatles nodders, each 5" high, original box, set of four, $500.

Collector plate
  The Beatles Live in Concert, 1st issue in the Beatles Collection, 1991, issued by Delphi (a division of The Bradley Exchange), #13108L, with paperwork, orig box 65.00
  The Beatles Sgt. Pepper, 25th anniversary, 1992, issued by Delphi (a division of The Bradley Exchange), #9374A, with all paperwork, orig box .. 75.00
Game, Flip Your Wig, Milton Bradley, 1964 .... 95.00
Glass, pictures Beatles with instruments, insulating coating around middle, 1960s, 5-1/4" h ... 185.00
Halloween costume, child's, orig costume, mask and box .. 700.00
Jigsaw puzzle, official Beatles fan club puzzle, black-and-white, shows band with instruments, 1964, 8-1/4" x 10-3/4"........ 46.00
Lunch box, few scratches and dents, vacuum bottle missing..... 625.00
Magazine
  Accoustic Guitar, vol. 2 #1 (July/August 1991), Beatles cover, includes transcriptions for 3 Beatles songs 6.00
  Pop Weekly, #17 U.K. issue, December 1963, Beatles cover, inside articles and photos of Elvis and Billy Fury, 7-1/8" x 9-1/2" 24.00

Saturday Evening Post, August 27, 1966, Beatles cover, illus 6-page article on the group, loose cover, 11" x 14" 20.00
The Beatles Book Monthly #16, Nov. 1964, U.K. fan magazine, Paul and Ringo on cover, 6" x 8-1/2" 18.00
TV Guide, commemorative ed, 1995, includes story on Beatles....................................5.00
Postcard, shows Beatles with printed autographs, 1964, unused, 2 pinholes 10.00
Souvenir song album, features words and music to early recordings, biographical sketches and guitar chords, early 1960s, 32 pgs, small tears 25.00
Sheet music, *Day Tripper*, 1964 ....20.00
Wallet, red and white, imprinted autographs and photo of the group, clasp missing, 4-3/8" x 7-1/2" 95.00

✪ Beatrix Potter

Collectors are hot on the trail of this lovable English hare, and flea markets are a good place to spot him. Peter and the rest of the Beatrix Potter family are frequently sighted, since many of the items are in current production and, thus, readily available.

Baby cup, silver plate, "The World of Peter Rabbit by Beatrix Potter," F. Warne & Co. Ltd. 39.00
Book
  Ginger and Pickles, F. Warne & Co. Ltd., copyright renewed 1937, pictorial endpapers, paste-on picture on cover, owner's name inside cover 25.00
  Histoire de Jeannot Lapin, French, translated by Victorine Ballon and Julienne Profichet, F. Warne & Co. Ltd., color illus and endpapers, hardcover, slight wear to edges 50.00
  The Tale of Squirrel Nutkin, F. Warne & Co. Ltd., copyright renewed 1931, 27 full-page color plates and endpapers, hardcover, 84 pgs, owner's name inside cover 45.00

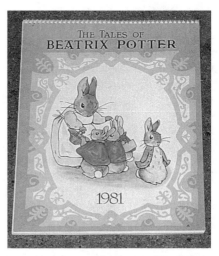

The Tales of Beatrix Potter 1981 calendar, $1.

The Tale of Two Bad Mice, F. Warne & Co. Ltd., copyright renewed 1932, hardcover, paste-on picture on cover 25.00
Cookie tin, Peter Rabbit, 3" h, 7-1/2" dia 8.00
Figure
  Anna Maria, F. Warne & Co. Ltd., stamped "Beswick, England" and "Beatrix Potter's Anna Maria" on bottom, 3" h 350.00
  Benjamin Bunny, Beswick, 1st version gold mark BP-2 .... 480.00
  Benjamin Bunny, stamped "Beswick, England" on bottom, 4-1/8" h 70.00
  Flopsy, Mopsy and Cottontail, Beswick, 1st version gold mark BP-2 .... 330.00
  Lady Mouse, Beswick, gold mark, BP-2 .... 300.00
  Peter Rabbit, Beswick, 1st version gold mark BP-2 ... 240.00
  Squirrel Nutkin, stamped "Beswick, Made in England" on bottom, copyright 1989 Royal Doulton, 3-1/2" h 56.00
  Tailor of Gloucester, Beswick, 1st version gold mark BP-2 .... 270.00
  Timmy Willie, F. Warne & Co. Ltd., stamped "Beswick, England" on bottom, copyright 1949, 3" h 50.00

❖ Beer Cans

Prior to Prohibition, beer was stored and shipped in kegs. After the Prohibition Act was repealed in 1933, many breweries did not resume business. Those that did start up again wanted to expand their distribution areas, and brewers found themselves in need of an inexpensive alternative for holding their product. Cans fit the bill nicely. The first patent for a lined can was issued to the American Can Company in 1934. The rest, as they say, is history.

Reference: Thomas Toepfer, *Beer Cans*, L-W Book Sales, 1976 (1995 value update).

Collectors' Club: Beer Can Collectors of America, 747 Merus Ct, Fenton, MO 63026, www.bcca.com.

Acme Beer, flat top, faded , 12-oz 5.00
Bad Frog Malt Liquor, stay tab top, aluminum, 16-oz..................3.00
Budweiser, tab top, 10-oz..........5.50
Colorado Gold Label, tab top, steel, 12-oz 6.00
Coors, flat top, aluminum, full, 7-oz 11.00
Fyfe & Drum, tab top, steel, 12-oz 4.00
GB, Brace Bros., flat top, 1 side faded, 12-oz 25.00
Hudepohl, 1975 Cincinnati Reds, tab top, steel, 12-oz..................4.00
King Snedley's, tab top, 12-oz. 10.00
Lucky Lager, flat top, 7-oz 15.00
Ortel's '92, tab top, 12-oz 2.00

Croft Champagne Ale, Crown Brewing Co., $75; Genesee Ale, Genessee Brewing Co., $50.

Piels Real Draft, "New Aluminum Can," air-sealed, 12-oz 4.00
Schmidt's Bicentennial, Cornwallis, tab top, 12-oz.......................1.50
Topper, tab top, 12-oz 5.00
Zodiac Malt Liquor, tab top, 12-oz 2.00

❖ Belleek

There's an old Irish saying that newlyweds who receive a wedding gift of Belleek will have their marriage blessed with lasting happiness. It's a great sentiment, and Belleek certainly does make a nice wedding gift. A thin, ivory-colored porcelain with an almost iridescent look, Belleek traces its roots to Fermanagh, Ireland, in 1857. The approximate age of a piece can be determined by looking at the mark. From 1863 to 1946 black marks were used; green marks were introduced in 1946.

Collectors' Club: The Belleek Collectors' Society, 9893 Georgetown Pk, Suite 525, Great Falls, VA 22066.

For additional listings, see *Warman's Antiques & Collectibles* and *Warman's English & Continental Pottery & Porcelain.*

Biscuit barrel, Basketweave pattern, cov, 6th green mark, 1965-80 ....100.00
Cake plate, cream and gold, 6th green mark, 1965-80, 10-1/2" dia..................................90.00
Creamer
    Cleary pattern, 3rd green mark 60.00
    Pastel yellow ribbon and bow accents, green mark......60.00
Creamer and sugar
    Clover pattern, 6th green mark, 1965-80 ....100.00
    Shamrock pattern, married pair, green marks, 1945-55 ....120.00
Cream jug, Lily of the Valley pattern, 2nd black mark, 1891-1926 ....195.00
Cup and saucer, Shell pattern, 2nd black mark, 1891-1926 ....195.00
Demitasse cup and saucer, green mark on cup, gold mark on saucer, c1956 ....50.00

Dish, Shamrock pattern, 3rd green mark................................. 60.00
Dresser vase, detailed rose and leaves, green mark, 3-3/4" h 185.00
Figure
    Pig, 2" h, 3" l...................... 90.00
    Terrier, green mark, 3-1/2" h 45.00
Honey pot, barrel type, clover leaves dec, 7th gold-brown mark, 1980-93............................ 80.00
Mustache cup, Tridacna pattern, first black mark 125.00
Nut bowl set, Shell pattern, white ext, yellow int, black mark, 9 pcs 700.00
Plate, Harp and Shamrock pattern, 5th mark, 9" dia................. 60.00
Potpourri vase, Basketweave pattern, 6th green mark, 1965-80, 4-1/2" h 100.00
Salt, open, star, 3rd black mark 60.00
Sugar bowl, open, yellow ribbon and box accents, green mark .. 45.00
Tea set, Basketweave pattern, 6th green mark, 1965-80, repair to spout 275.00

❖ Bells

From the tinkle of a silver bell to the clanging of a ship's bell, the music of bells has enchanted collectors for decades. When considering a purchase, check for stress fractures and other signs of use, and also look to see if the clapper is original.

Collectors' Clubs: American Bell Assoc, Alter Rd, Box 386, Natrona Heights, PA 15065; American Bell Assoc International, Inc, 7210 Bellbrook Dr, San Antonio, TX 78227.

Ceramic
    Aunt Jemima, Japan, 1940s, 3-1/2" h 75.00
    Hawaiian Hula Girl, mkd "Made in Japan," 4-1/2" h 36.00
    Mermaid, 4-1/2" h.............. 24.00
Church, cast brass, wrought iron clapper, suspended from chain, Reading, PA, late 18th C, 20" h 990.00
Desk, bronze, iron base, ornate mechanism, Victorian, 3" w, 5" h 135.00

Metal novelty Liberty Bell, 2-1/2" high, $2.50.

Door-mounted, brass, filigree mounting 45.00
Glass
    Daisy and Button, satin vaseline, 6-1/2" h 75.00
    Fenton, Statue of Liberty, hand painted dec 35.00
    Murano, gold wash, orig sticker, 4" h 65.00
    Princess House, cut design, 6-3/4" h 10.00
Porcelain, Danbury Mint, Mother's Day, pink flowers 18.00

❖ Belt Buckles

A collection of belt buckles consists of items that are small and easy to store, and which represent a variety of materials. What more could one want in a collection? Some of the more ornate examples are elaborately cast or set with precious and semi-precious stones.
Reproduction Alert.
Bakelite
    O-shaped, red, silvertone knobs, 2-1/2" dia 29.00
    Round, carved, front is black, back is yellow, 3" dia 55.00
    Round, with cross bar, arrows and other shapes, carved, apple juice color, 1930s, 3" dia 60.00
Boy Scouts, 1977 National Jamboree 15.00
Hockey, brass 10.00

Chicago World's Fair belt buckle, $25.

Iron Maiden, "Number of the Beast," shows album cover, made in England, numbered, mint cond 41.00
Lion Oil Co., silvertone, mountain lion and company name, owner's name and 1993 on back, 2-1/4" x 3-1/4" 35.00
Marlboro, brass, oval, star and steer, copyright 1987, 2-1/2" x 3-1/2" 20.00
Masonic emblem, 2" x 2-7/8" ... 12.00
National Finals Rodeo, Hesston
    1977, bull riding 42.00
    1985, calf roping 10.50
Piedmont Airlines, goldtone, orig plastic wrap and box, 2-7/8" x 2-3/8" 150.00
Schlitz Light, brass and pewter, light blue enamel inlay, 1976 ..... 25.00
Shriner emblem, silvertone 20.00
Steam shovel, brass 12.00
Sterling silver, 3 turquoise-colored stones, leaf appliqué, 1970s 145.00
Western, Wil-Aren Originals, 2-1/2" h, 3-3/4" w 20.00

❖ Bennington Pottery

Although the company has been in existence for a century and a half, only their more contemporary items are included here.
Bowl, black and gray speckled, oval, 15" l 90.00
Mug, frog in bottom, white, 1977 .... 10.00
Plate
    Abstract fish dec, 10" dia ... 70.00
    Bread, 6" dia 6.00
Wall plaque, owl, 8-3/4" x 7" 65.00

❖ Beswick

Beswick characters are well known to collectors and include figures from children's literature as well as animals and other subjects. James Wright Beswick and his son, John, organized the firm in the 1890s. By 1969, the company was sold to Royal Doulton Tableware, Ltd., which still produces many Beswick animals.

References: Diana Callow et al., *The Charlton Standard Catalogue of Beswick Animals*, 2nd ed, Charlton Press, 1996; Diana and John Callow, *The Charlton Standard Catalogue of Beswick Pottery*, Charlton Press, 1997; Harvey May, *The Beswick Price Guide*, 3rd ed, Francis Joseph Publications, 1995, distributed by Krause Publications.
Child's feeding dish, Mickey and Donald on bicycle 140.00
Decanter, monk, underplate and four mugs 250.00
Figure
    Barnaby Rudge 60.00
    Chippy Hackee, Beatrix Potter, copyright 1979 .... 55.00
    Grooming Kittens, two tabbies 135.00
    Hereford Bull, 6" h 225.00
    Horse, wooden base, 7-1/2" h 1600.00
    Jemima Puddleduck, Beatrix Potter, 1947 .... 95.00
    Johnny Town Mouse, Beatrix Potter, 1954, 3-1/2" h 65.00
    King of Hearts, 4" h 150.00
    Mrs. Ribby, Beatrix Potter, 1951, 3-1/2" h 75.00
    Palamino Horse, #1261, 6-3/4" h 165.00
    Peddler, mkd #1347, sgd "Susie Jamaica," 7" h 265.00
    Samuel Whiskers, BP2 ... 250.00
    Scottie, white, ladybug on nose, HN804, 1940-69 .... 225.00
    Siamese Cat Standing, #1896, 1963-80, oval mark, 6-1/2" h 100.00
    Swish Tail Horse, #1182, orig Beswick sticker, 8-1/2" h 225.00
    Tony Weller 85.00
    Trout, #1390, 4" h 150.00

Mug

    Falstaff, inscribed "Pistol with Wit or Steel, Merry Wives of Windsor," #1127, 1948-73, 4" h.................................85.00

    Hamlet, inscribed "To Be or Not To Be," #1147, 4-1/4" h .85.00

Modelle jug, shape #694, floral deco and rabbit, stamped "Made in England, 694, Beswick Ware," 1939-62, 9-1/4" h, 6" w....135.00

Plate, Disney characters, 7" dia 95.00

Shoe, old woman seated inside, Beatrix Potter, gold stamped mark, 3-3/4" w, 2-1/2" h...175.00

Tankard, A Christmas Carol, 1971 ....50.00

Tulip vase, shape #843, semi-gloss white, 1940-43, 4" h 50.00

❖ Bibles

Bibles are only occasionally found at flea markets, since most families either keep those that belonged to their loved ones, or donate them to a local church. From time to time, old large family Bibles do surface at flea markets and book sales. Prices can range from a few dollars to several hundred, depending on the illustrations, date, type of Bible, condition, etc. Potential buyers are often more interested in the genealogical information that might be contained therein. Before selling a family Bible, consider sharing its historical or genealogical information with family members. Additionally, historical societies and libraries are generally grateful for such information.

Family Bible, dates start 1825, many engravings, 11" x 9-1/2" ..250.00

Family Worship Edition, King James Version, 1948, many color pictures, Nashville Bible House, Nashville, Tenn., ink spots on some pages........................35.00

Gilt engraved tooled leather, 1867, American Bible Society, N.Y., trace gilt to page edges, a few minor tears, 5-3/4" x 4-1/4" 60.00

New Testament Bible ABC Book, full-color illus, The Book Concern, Columbus, Ohio, name on front cover, 16 pgs, 8-1/4" x 10-1/2"..............................8.00

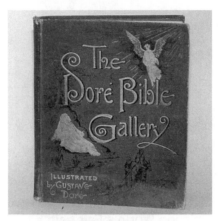

***The Dore Bible Gallery* by Gustave Dore, Henry Altemus, Philadelphia, $50.**

Presentation Bible, Masonic Edition, Masonic emblem on cover, copyright 1932, never inscribed 395.00

Service testament and prayer book, U.S. Military issue, 1943, leather case imprinted with gold name of orig owner, tear to case at snap 80.00

Soldier's pocket Bible, New Testament and Psalms, 1862, inscribed 1864/Lowell, Mass. 275.00

❖ Bicentennial

Remember all that hoopla surrounding 1976? How many of you have stashed away some bit of Bicentennial memorabilia? These items are becoming more common at flea markets, and historically minded individuals are adding them to their collections. Perhaps these pieces of the past will turn into treasures.

Beer can, "Narragansett Salutes the Bicentennial," tab top, aluminum, 12-oz...................................2.00

Commemorative bottle, Liberty Bell, clear, Lejion Brandy, Lejion Champagne Cellars, Cloverdale, Calif., 4/5-qt 16.00

Decanter, Royal Halburton China for the F.O.E., "Eagles are People Helping People…," 7" h 25.00

Dolls, Campbell Soup, hard plastic, Colonial clothes, 10-1/2" h, pr 150.00

Indiana Glass Bicentennial plate, Liberty Bell design, original box, $5.

Drinking glass, Elsie Family, Spirit of '76, red, white and blue patriotic dec, family in colonial garb, Elsie playing drum, Elmer playing fife, Beauregard playing small drum, 5-1/2" h, pr 28.00

Guidebook, Washington: *The Official Bicentennial Guidebook*, ed by Nancy Love, 1976, softcover, 213 pgs 5.00

Paperweight, eagle, brown slag-type glass, Fenton, 3-1/2" h......30.00

Pinback button, Spirit of '76, America's Bicentennial, 1776-1976, 3-1/2" dia 20.00

Plate

    Avon, clear glass, bald eagle holding shield and arrows, "United States of America Bicentennial 1776-1976," 9-1/8" l, 6-3/4" w 5.00

    Bing & Grondahl, bald eagle in center, 13 colonies around edge, blue, gold trim, orig box 50.00

    Fenton, powder blue, George Washington at Valley Forge, 3rd in a series of 4, 8-1/4" dia 35.00

    Frankoma, Patriots/Leaders, white sand glaze, 8-1/2" dia 30.00

    Schmid, Mickey Mouse, orig box 45.00

    St. Clair, Joe, carnival glass, blue, 5-1/2" dia 40.00

    Viletta, Liberty Bell center, scenic border, 10-1/2" dia 7.50

Tray, anodized aluminum, mkd "The United States of America 1776-1976" and "Pepsi 1898-1976," 10-7/8" dia 25.00

Tumbler, black and metallic gold deco, White House on one side, Capitol on other, "United States Bicentennial 1776-1976" 5.00

U.S. mint set, silver, 1976, San Francisco, uncirculated............. 30.00

❖ Bicycles

"Look, Ma! No hands!" Gee, haven't we all shouted that once or twice? And how many of us wish we still had those really nifty old bikes, banana seats and all?

References: Fermo Galbiati and Nino Ciravegna, *Bicycle*, Chronicle Books, 1994; Jim Hurd, *Bicycle Blue Book*, Memory Lane Classics, 1997; Jay Pridmore and Jim Hurd, *The American Bicycle*, Motorbooks International, 1996; Neil S. Wood, *Evolution of the Bicycle*, vol. 1 (1991, 1994 value update), vol. 2 (1994), L-W Book Sales.

Periodicals: *Antique/Classic Bicycle News*, P.O. Box 1049, Ann Arbor, MI 48106; *Bicycle Trader*, P.O. Box 3324, Ashland, OR 97520; *Classic & Antique Bicycle Exchange*, 325 W Hornbeam Dr, Longwood, FL 32779; *Classic Bike News*, 5046 E Wilson Rd, Clio, MI, 48420; *National Antique & Classic Bicycle*, P.O. Box 5600, Pittsburgh, PA 15207.

Collectors' Clubs: Cascade Classic Cycle Club, 7935 SE Market St, Portland, OR 97215; Classic Bicycle and Whizzer Club, 35769 Simon, Clinton Twp, MI 48035; International Veteran Cycle Assoc, 248 Highland Dr, Findlay, OH 45840; The Wheelmen, 55 Bucknell Ave, Trenton, NJ 08619.

For additional listings, see *Warman's Americana & Collectibles.*

Badge, L.A.W. 18th Annual Meet, Philadelphia, Aug 4-7, 1897, diecut brass 65.00

Bicycle
   Ace Clyde and Motor Works, metal label, as found cond 150.00
   Columbia, Fire Arrow 300.00
   Columbia, Twinbar 3,200.00
   Huffy, Radiobike........... 2,000.00
   Monark, Silver King, hexagonal tube 900.00

   Roadmaster, Luxury Liner, restored 620.00
   Schwinn, Corvette 300.00
   Schwinn, Hornet............... 425.00
   Schwinn, Mark II Jaguar .. 750.00
   Sears, Elgin, Skylark, very good orig cond 2,250.00
Bicycle ornament, Bambi, celluloid, 1940s, 4" h 125.00
Book, *Riding High*, A. Judson Palmer, autographed 65.00
Catalog
   Eclipse, Elmira, N.Y............ 48.00
   Indian Bicycle 90.00
   Rollfast 70.00
Handle bar grips, wooden, for high wheeler, unused 65.00
Limited edition collectible, Bicycle Shop, Village Series, Princeton Galleries, porcelain, 1-1/4" h 15.00
Magazine tear sheet
   Murray Bicycles, Strato-Flite, LeMans and Wildcat, *Boys' Life*, 1966 .... 3.00
   Raleigh, Chopper, *Boys' Life*, 1970 .... 3.00
   Roadmaster, half sheet, *Saturday Evening Post*, 1951 .. 2.00
   Schwinn Bicycles, from back cover, reverse slightly scuffed 2.00
   Schwinn Christmas, Orange Krate, Lemon Peeler, Apple Krate, and Pea Picker 3.00
   Sears, The Screamer Bicycle 3.00
Pin, bicycle shape
   Goldtone, front wheel turns, faux pearls, 2-1/4" x 2-5/8" 8.50
   Silvertone, clear stones in center, 2" x 1-1/4" 15.00
Pinback button, Schwinn, 7/8" dia 28.00
Print, Donald Duck riding bicycle, glow-in-the-dark, Walt Disney Productions, orig frame, 9" x 11" 38.00
Stickpin, United States Tire Co., brass stickpin of happy bug wearing hat and peddling bicycle, c1920, card with imprint of company 1-1/4" x 3" 25.00

For exciting collecting trends and newly expanded areas look for the following symbols:

⊙ Hot Topic

✯ New Warman's Listing

(May have been in another Warman's title.)

❖ Big Little Books

The Whitman Publishing Company first trademarked these books in the 1930s, but the term is also used to describe similar books published by a number of other companies. Several advertisers contracted to use Big Little Books as premiums, including Cocomalt and Kool-Aid. Television characters were introduced to the format in the 1950s.

References: Bill Borden, *The Big Book of Big Little Books*, Chronicle Books, 1997; Larry Jacobs, *Big Little Books*, Collector Books, 1996; Lawrence Lowery, *Lowery's Collector's Guide to Big Little Books and Similar Books*, privately printed, 1981; *Price Guide to Big Little Books & Better Little, Jumbo, Tiny Tales, A Fast-Action Story*, etc., L-W Book Sales, 1995.

Collectors' Club: Big Little Book Collector Club of America, P.O. Box 1242, Danville, CA 94526.

Brer Rabbit from Song of the South, #1426, 1947 .... 70.00
Buck Rogers, Moons of Saturn 35.00
Don Winslow of the Navy........ 32.00
Flash Gordon 55.00
G-Men Breaking the Gambling Ring, #1482, 1942 .... 60.00
Little Orphan Annie in the Den of the Thieves, 1948 .... 25.00
Little Women........................... 20.00

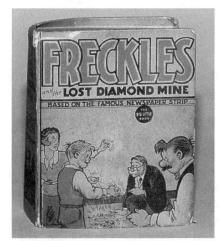

Freckles and the Lost Diamond Mine, **Big Little Book, $25.**

Mickey Mouse and Bobo the Elephant, #1160, 1935............85.00
Mickey Mouse Runs His Own Newspaper, #1409, 1937...........40.00
Skeezix at the Military Academy, #1408, 1938......................35.00
Snow White and the Seven Dwarfs, #1460, 1938......................60.00
Treasure Island, #1141, Jackie Cooper, Wallace Berry...........110.00

❖ Billiards

"Rack 'em up, boys!" was the resounding cry heard in many pool halls. Today collectors enjoy poking around flea markets looking for vintage pool equipment as well as decorating accessories with a billiards theme.

Ashtray, Joe Camel shooting pool, 6-1/4" x 4-1/2"....................20.00
Balls, Catalin, complete set.....50.00
Bridge, brass mounted standard cue 70.00
Cue case, wall-mounted, ornate Victorian type, painted and ebonized wooden frame..........200.00
Cue chalk, Electric Billiards, red and white box, mkd "Oliver L. Briggs & Son, Boston, MA," 7/8" sq 25.00
Magazine tear sheet, The Irish Skirmishers Blind Pool, from *Puck*, Sept, 1882.........................25.00
Mirror, celluloid, advertising "The Wonders Pool Parlors," Scranton, PA, multicolor graphics of topless women surrounded by cherubs, American Art Works, some light surface scratching, 1-3/4" x 2-3/4"..................575.00
Pool cue, Budweiser, Pabst.....30.00

❖ Bing and Grondahl

This Danish company has produced fine-quality Christmas plates for decades. However, many collectors have chosen to branch out and also include some of the company's other products, such as bells and figurines, in their collections.

Reference: Pat Owen, *Bing & Grondahl Christmas Plates,* Landfall Press, 1995.

Periodical: *Collector's Mart Magazine*, 700 E State St, Iola, WI 54990.

Bell
    1976, Old North Church, Boston, Mass., 5" h.............25.00
    1978, Notre Dame Cathedral 55.00
    1991, Independence Hall, 4" h, MIB................................30.00

Figurine
    Boy with accordion, #1991, boy seated on barrel, 9" h..225.00
    Fish woman, #2233, old woman sitting on bench, box of eels on one side, basket of flounder and other fish in front, old pail with scales, Axel Locher, 8" l, 7" w......................500.00
    Girl with doll, #1721, 8" h 110.00
    Girl with flowers, #2298, 6" h 140.00
    Girl with puppy, #2316, 5-1/4" h 125.00
    Penguin, #1821, 3-1/8" h .150.00
    Skier, 8-1/2" h 130.00
    Youthful Boldness, #2162, 7-1/2" h........................175.00

Limited-edition collector plate
    Christmas at Home, 1971, #8000/9071, green backstamp 27.00
    Christmas in Greenland, 1972, green backstamp...........22.00
    Christmas in the Village, 1974, #8000/9074, green backstamp 26.00

Bing & Grondahl vase, 7-1/4" high, $40.

    Christmas Peace, 1981.....35.00
    Christmas Tree, 1982........35.00
    Country Christmas, 1973 .. 20.00
    Fox and Cubs, 1979, Mother's Day, 6" dia 35.00
    Hare and Young, 1971, Mother's Day, 6" dia 40.00
    Lion and Cubs, 1982, Mother's Day, 6" dia 55.00
    Raccoon and Young, 1983, Mother's Day, 6" dia 55.00
    Stork and Nestling, 1984, Mother's Day, 6" dia 50.00
    Woodpecker and Young, 1980, Mother's Day, 6" dia 35.00
Planter, Dutch shoe 275.00
Thimble, soaring seagull, mkd "B & G 4831, Made in Denmark" 20.00
Vase, Pomegranate, painted fruit, leafy branches and butterfly in relief, shades of blue, mustard, orange and green, gilt highlights, B&G stamp in brown on base, 4" h 275.00

❖ Birdcages

Birds of a feather flock together, particularly when kept behind bars. Birdcages have long been used for the rather mundane and practical purpose of keeping winged creatures confined. Now, however, designers are using them for their decorative appeal.

Brass
    Domed, round, ball finial, wooden bottom, 1 glass waterer, 13"h, 12" dia ... 55.00
    Hendryx, pagoda style, doors slide up, 1 attached glass feeder, wood swing, pull-out tray, sgd on bottom, 14"h, 12-1/2" sq 145.00
Plastic, rectangular, pale green, engraved floral dec on front and on top around handle, metal bottom, 2 doors, with feeders, ladder and perches, 10-1/2" h, 11" w, 7-1/2" d..................85.00
Wire
    Black and gold, round, japanned tin, ship motifs on sides, orig swings, perch and hanging pottery feeders, 3 scalloped legs, 18-1/2" h, 10" dia 150.00

Domed, round, painted white, arched cutout-work door with orig brass screen and orig brass handle, 3 cast iron owls clip to hold bottom to top, orig perches and glass feeders, 14-1/2" h, 12" dia 125.00

Hendryx, round, domed top, attached pedestal, 19" h, 11" dia 40.00

❖ Birdhouses

Due to their folk art nature, many vintage birdhouses can be found in collector's living rooms, as opposed to their usual places in pine trees and on fence posts. Vintage birdhouses in good original condition are in demand, but don't overlook some of the high-quality contemporary examples on today's market.

Metal

Contemporary, made from 5 Colorado license plates, 9" h, 5" l, 5" w 18.00

Vintage, made from 2-qt tin can, orig gray paint, some rust 22.50

Pottery, cottage design in blues, greens and reds, Louisville Stoneware, 10" h 55.00

Wood

Martin house, 20-hole 60.00

Vintage, traditional form, metal roof, orig red paint, 7" h 65.00

Wayne Sims, contemporary, church design, rough cedar siding, 10" h 20.00

Uhl Pottery Co. birdhouse, chipped ledge, $200.

❖ Bisque

Bisque is a rather generic term used for china wares that have been fired, but that have not been glazed. Pieces usually have a slightly rough texture, and they are highly susceptible to chips.

Doll

Black, articulated arms and legs, hp facial features, new dress, 4-1/2" h, ...20.00

German, 1-pc body and head, sleep eyes, closed mouth, glued wig, no clothing, 2-1/2" h..........................65.00

Figure

Bashful (Snow White figure), worn paint, mkd "Walt Disney," 4-1/4" h 37.50

Blue Boy, Colonial-style dress, 14-3/4" h......................125.00

Colonial Boy, Occupied Japan, mkd "Paulux," 1 finger missing, 6-1/4" h...................18.00

Elephant, 4" h 9.00

Fiddler, Occupied Japan, 3" h 9.00

Mickey Mouse with walking stick, 1930s, Walt Disney, mkd "Made in Japan," 4" h 75.00

Stopper, clown figure, removable hat, mkd "Germany 6325," 3-3/4" h 25.00

Toothbrush holder

3 Little Pigs, Walt Disney, mkd "Made in Japan," 1930s 100.00

Bisque figurine of a child leaning against a stump, 17" high, $60.

Mickey and Minnie Mouse, copyright Walt Disney, mkd "Made in Japan," worn paint, 4-1/2" h 245.00

✪ Black Memorabilia

Black memorabilia is a term used to describe a very broad field of collectibles. It encompasses Black history and ethnic issues, as well as those items that have impacted our lives from a cultural standpoint. America's flea markets are great sources for Black memorabilia now that more dealers are recognizing the increased popularity of these items.

References: Douglas Congdon-Martin, *Images in Black: 150 Years of Black Collectibles,* 2nd ed, Schiffer, 1999; Kevin Keating and Michael Kolleth, *The Negro Leagues Autograph Guide,* Tuff Stuff Books, 1999; J.L. Mashburn, *Black Postcard Price Guide,* 2nd ed, Colonial House, 1999.

Periodicals: *Blackin,* 559 22nd Ave, Rock Island, IL 61201; *Lookin Back at Black,* 6087 Glen Harbor Dr, San Jose CA 95123.

Collectors' Clubs: Black Memorabilia Collector's Assoc, 2482 Devoe Terrace, Bronx, NY 10468; International Golliwogg Collectors Club, P.O. Box 612, Woodstock, NY 12498.

Reproduction Alert.

For additional listings, see *Warman's Antiques & Collectibles* and *Warman's Americana & Collectibles.*

Advertising tin, Durham's Cocoanut 175.00

Bank, Mammy, cast iron, 4-1/2" h 95.00

Carry-out box, Coon Chicken Inn 200.00

Cigar box, Old Plantation Brand, emb, 11" l 60.00

Clock, luncheon type, black women dec, 1950s 45.00

Comics page, Kemple Duke of Dahomey, 1911 .... 45.00

Cookbook, *Dixie Southern Cookbook* 50.00

Dart board, tin over cardboard, Sambo, name on straw hat, Wyandotte Toy Mfg., dents and scratch, 23" h, 14" w..........80.00

Dice, multicolor, spring activated, mkd "Alco Britain HK"........90.00

Doll, Golliwogg, black face and jacket, white shirt and gloves, red tie and pants, mkd "Made in England"..........185.00

Game, The Game of Hitch Hiker, Whitman, 1937..................75.00

Humidor, majolica, boy sitting on large melon, pipe in hand, small chip on foot and top, 10-1/2" h 875.00

Lunch box, Dixie Kid Cut Plug, litho tin 290.00

Magazine, Life, Dec 8, 1972, featuring Diana Ross on cover ...18.00

Nodder, girl, hp, porcelain, mkd "Japan"..........300.00

Notepad and pencil holder, painted hard plastic, Mammy, insert pencil as broomstick in one hand, orig paper label, 1950s....150.00

Photograph, unidentified subject
  Little boy in front of train 75.00
  Man in formal dress, graduation, 1910..........45.00

Pitcher, Mandy, Omnibus 160.00

Poster
  Paper, black man saying goodbye to wife and going off to war, colored regiment marching by, 1918, framed, 19-1/2" h, 15-1/2" w..........75.00
  Cardboard, "Ragtime Jubilee, Big Time Minstrel Review," 22" h, 14" w..........25.00

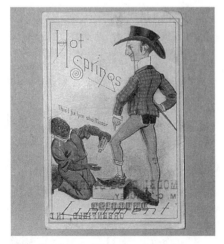

Hot Springs Liniment trade card, $30.

Pot hanger, chalkware, black boy and girl, wire hook, 7-1/2" x 5-1/2"..........125.00

Ramp walker, multicolor, USA, c1920..........65.00

Recipe holder, Mammy, wood 45.00

Reservation card, Coon Chicken Inn 100.00

Salt and pepper shakers, pr
  Jemima & Uncle Mose, F & F, damaged..........35.00
  Mammy & Chef, 5" h..........55.00
  Mammy & Chef, ceramic, 8" h, Japan, 1940s..........115.00

Sign, diecut cardboard
  Gold Dust Washing Powder, Gold Dust Twins shown on package, large letter "L" on top, formerly part of larger hanging sign, 13-1/2" h, 9-1/2" w..........60.00
  Hambone Sweets, color graphics on both sides, black caricature aviator smiling and puffing on cigar while seated in aircraft, titled "Going Over," orig string loop handle, late 1920s, 7" dia..........38.00

Soda bottle, emb "Mammy".....70.00

Souvenir spoon, Summerville, S.C., double-sided full-figured black holding melon, engraved bowl 110.00

Tea towel, boy and girl eating watermelon, pr..........25.00

Toy
  Dancing Dan, in front of lamp post on stage, microphone remote attached to stage, 13" h, MIB..........375.00
  Strutting Sam, tap dancer on pedestal, tin, battery op, 11" h, MIB..........475.00

Wall plaque, head, chalk, pr 125.00

❖ Blenko

Blenko handcrafted glass was made in Milton, West Virginia. Interesting crackle glass items and a reliance on strong colors have earned the company a place in the hearts of many. Original labels read "Blenko Handcraft" and are shaped like a hand.

Beaker, crackle, crystal body, applied blue rosettes, 9-1/2" h 135.00

Bottle, amberina, style 64B, orig silver label, 10" h..........40.00

Paperweight, crab, orange, orig label, 4-1/8" dia..........10.00

Pitcher, crackle, turquoise, long applied handle..........110.00

Sculpture, owl, dark amber, orig label, 6-7/8" h..........75.00

Vase
  4" h, double neck, turquoise 50.00
  8" h, ruby red, crimped, ftd, 1950s..........150.00
  9" h, crackle, avocado green 115.00
  9-1/4" h, emerald green, fluted, pontil scar..........95.00
  9-1/2" h, crystal, four applied blue rosettes, orig label 135.00
  9-3/4" h, crackle, clear body, applied blue-green leaves 135.00
  10-1/2" h, crackle, reddish-orange body, crimped top 135.00
  11-1/2" h, blue, three applied blue berries..........115.00
  17" h, crackle, orange 135.00

❖ Blue & White Pottery/ Stoneware

Although termed blue-and-white, this category also includes blue-and-gray pottery and stoneware. Widely produced from the late 19th century through the 1930s, these items were originally marketed as inexpensive wares for everyday household use. Butter crocks, pitchers, and saltboxes are among the most commonly found pieces. Many examples feature a white or gray body with an embossed geometric, floral, or fruit pattern. The piece was then highlighted with bands and splashes of blue to accentuate the molded pattern.

Reference: Kathryn McNerney, *Blue & White Stoneware*, Collector Books, 1995.

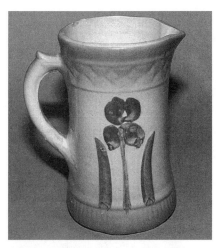

Pitcher, Iris design, rim chip, 8-3/4" high, $220.

Collectors' Club: Blue & White Pottery Club, 224 12th St NW, Cedar Rapids, IA 52405.

Reproduction Alert.

Bowl
  Apricot pattern, milk bowl, 4" h, 9-1/2" dia.........................80.00
  Flying Birds, berry bowl ...125.00
Butter crock
  "Butter" in oval, blue sponging, 9" dia 275.00
  Colonial, with lid, 4-1/4" h 375.00
  Cows, minor base flakes, lid missing large piece 225.00
  Daisy & Trellis, with lid, minor glaze flake at bail 80.00
Canister
  "Cereal," Basketweave, no lid 383.00
  "Coffee," Basketweave, inner rim chips, mended lid 75.00
  "Raisins," Basketweave, with lid, mint cond. 350.00

Soap dish, scrolled design, unmarked, 4-7/8" diameter, $125.

Meat tenderizer
  Wildflower, crazed, replaced handle 375.00
  Windmill 80.00
Pitcher
  Avenue of Trees...............275.00
  Basketweave, water pitcher 125.00
  Dainty Fruit.......................400.00
  Dutch Boy & Girl 125.00
  Leaping Deer 347.50

❖ Blue Ridge Pottery

Erwin, TN, was home to Southern Potteries, Inc., chartered in 1920. By 1938 the company was producing Blue Ridge dinnerware, marketing the items as "Hand Painted Under the Glaze." Most of their competitors used decals to create designs, and Southern Potteries was able to capitalize on this difference. The colorful, cheery floral patterns made Blue Ridge dinnerware a favorite with consumers. However, inexpensive imports and a move toward plastic dinnerware forced the company out of business in 1957.

References: Betty and Bill Newbound, *Collector's Encyclopedia of Blue Ridge Dinnerware*, Collector Books, 1994; —, *Southern Potteries, Inc.*, 3rd ed, Collector Books, 1989 (1995 value update); Frances and John Ruffin, *Blue Ridge China Today*, Schiffer Publishing, 1997.

Periodicals: *Blue Ridge Beacon Magazine*, P.O. Box 629, Mountain City, GA 30562; *National Blue Ridge Newsletter*, 144 Highland Dr, Blountville, TN 37617.

Collectors' Club: Blue Ridge Collectors Club, 208 Harris St, Erwin, TN 37650.

For additional listings, see *Warman's Americana & Collectibles* and *Warman's American Pottery & Porcelain*.

Ashtray, Chintz 35.00
Bonbon
  Easter Parade, flat 150.00
  Iris, center handle, 4-section 150.00
  Cake plate, Maple Leaf Easter Parade.................115.00

Blue Ridge platter, 11-3/4" diameter, $25.

  Verna...............................115.00
Cigarette box
  Ships 100.00
  Seaside 175.00
  Rose Marie.....................115.00
Covered box, Rose Marie, round 160.00
Cream and sugar, footed
  Easter Parade, sugar only. 58.00
  Rose Marie.....................140.00
  Rose of Sharon 140.00
Pitcher
  Sculptured Fruit, 7" h.......125.00
  Trailee Rose, spiral, 6-1/2" h 135.00
Plate, dinner, 10" dia
  Freedom...........................22.00
  Red Velvet........................25.00
  Sweet Clover....................22.00
Plate, salad
  Country Fair, green edge .. 30.00
  Duff, set of 8....................225.00
  Flower bowl 30.00
  Honolulu 30.00
  Salad bowl, Candlewick 85.00
Shaker, footed
  Dog Tooth Violet, pr..........115.00
  Floral Blossom, pr 125.00
  Nova Leda, pr 89.00
  Rose of Marie, pr..............95.00
  Rose of Sharon, pr 35.00
Snack set, Colonial, plate and cup 48.00

❖ Blue Willow

This intricate pattern features a weeping willow along the banks of a river by a Japanese village. More than 200 manufacturers have produced items with variations of this pattern, generally blue on a white background. Josiah Spode first introduced the pattern in 1810, and it is still being used today.

References: Mary Frank Gaston, *Blue Willow*, 2nd ed, Collector Books, 1990 (2000 value update); Jennifer A. Lindbeck, *A Collector's Guide to Willow Ware*, Schiffer Publishing, 2000.

Periodicals: *American Willow Report*, P.O. Box 900, Oakridge, OR 97463; *The Willow Transfer Quarterly, Willow Word*, P.O. Box 13382, Arlington, TX 76094.

Collectors' Clubs: International Willow Collectors, P.O. Box 13382, Arlington, TX 76094-0382; Willow Society, 39 Medhurst Rd, Toronto, Ontario M4B 1B2 Canada.

Berry bowl, Homer Laughlin, small 6.50
Bouillon and underplate, Ridgway 85.00
Cake plate, tab handles, Royal China Co. 24.00
Cereal bowl, unmarked 8.00
Creamer and sugar, Allerton . 125.00
Cup, mkd "USA" 3.00
Cup and saucer
    Buffalo Pottery 25.00
    Shenango 15.00
Demitasse cup and saucer, mkd "Allerton" 15.00
Dessert plate, unmarked 5.00
Funnel 85.00
Gravy boat, mkd "Willow, Woods Ware, Woods & Sons, England," 8-1/4" l 100.00
Grill plate, mkd "Moriyama," 10-1/2" dia 45.00
Mustard pot, cov, unmarked, rough edges, 3" h 110.00
Oil lamp, blue and white ceramic base, 1950s 85.00
Pie plate, 10" dia 50.00
Plate, dinner
    Booth's 65.00
    Buffalo Pottery 20.00

Blue Willow cup and saucer, unmarked, $5.

Dudson, Wilcox & Till Ltd., Hanley, England, 10" dia, set of 10 .... 325.00
Unmarked 8.00
Platter, mkd "J. J. & Co.," hairlines, 17-3/4" l 60.00
Pudding mold, 5-3/4" dia 60.00
Saucer, unmarked 3.00
Soup bowl, unmarked 10.00
Teapot, cov, emb "Sadler, England" 165.00
Tray, metal, wear 15.00
Vegetable bowl, open, round, mkd "J. & G. Meakin" 65.00

❖ Boehm Porcelain

From humble beginnings in a studio in Trenton, New Jersey, Edward Marshall Boehm has created exquisite porcelain sculptures. A second production site, Boehm Studios, was opened in Malvern, England, in the early 1970s and is still in business today.

Collectors' Club: Boehm Porcelain Society, P.O. Box 5051, Trenton, NJ 08638.

Limited-edition plate
    American Redstart, 1975, based on designs of Edward Marshall Boehm, made by Lenox China, 24 kt gold edge, orig box, certificate 70.00
    Lion, Great Animals of the World, World Wildlife Fund, 1978, orig round walnut frame, 10-1/2" dia 48.00
    Mountain Bluebirds, 1972, based on designs of Edward Marshall Boehm, made by Lenox China, 24 kt gold edge, orig box, certificate 100.00
Sculpture
    American Eagle 1,000.00
    Blue Jay, #436, 4-1/2" h ... 150.00
    Bob White Quail, #407, minor damage 750.00
    Cardinal, female, #425, 15" h 700.00
    Crocus, 5" h 210.00
    Daisies, #3002 .... 800.00
    Hummingbird, 6-1/4" h 220.00
    Madonna La Pieta, c. 1958, 4-1/2" h 110.00

Pelican, #4016 .... 1,000.00
Saw Whet Owl, #20078, Made in England, 5-1/2" h 250.00
Screech Owl, #20079, Made in England, 5-1/4" h 250.00

Brass squirrel bookends, 5-1/4" high, pair, $45.

❖ Bookends

These useful objects can be found in almost every medium and range from purely functional to extraordinarily whimsical.

Arts & Crafts, hammered copper with deer cutout design, wrought-iron trim, 5-1/2" h, 4" w 55.00
Cocker spaniels, chalkware, 5-1/2" h 30.00
Elephant, Rookwood Pottery, ivory color, 1936, 5-1/2" h, 6" l 225.00
Gardenia, Roseville Pottery, gray and white, pr 200.00
Horse, rearing, L.E. Smith, emerald green glass, 8" h 55.00
Indian brave, chiseled face of native American, metal, green felt back, 6-1/2" h, 4-1/4" w, 2-1/8" d 75.00
Indian chief bust, leather headdress 130.00
Liberty Bell, bronze, 5" h 35.00
Scottie, Frankart, bronze-tone brass, 1 repaired, 5" h, 5" l, pr 59.00
Stagecoach, pulled by 2 teams of horses, "Old Coaching Days" on base, bronze-finish metal, 4-1/4" h, pr 45.00

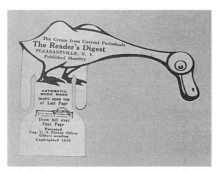

Reader's Digest paper bookmark, 1933, 3-1/2" high, 4-1/2" long, $15.

❖ Bookmarks

Ranging from delicate filagreed clips to intricately embroidered fabric to simple cardboard shapes, bookmarks have assisted readers for decades. Interesting examples can be found at flea markets if one looks carefully.

Periodical: *Bookmark Collector*, 1002 W 25th St, Erie, PA 16502.

Collectors' Club: Antique Bookmark Collector's Assoc, 2224 Cherokee St, St. Louis, MO 63118.
Advertising
   Kirk Johnson & Co., Lebanon, Pa., pianos and organs, Victorian girl in pink dress with bouquet of roses, edges worn, 1 corner torn, 6" x 2" 15.00
   Poll Parrot shoes, die-cut cardboard, "They Speak for Themselves," 3-3/4" x 1-1/2"..12.00
Snickers, 1987, 4-1/4" x 3" ..2.50
Cloth, Abraham Lincoln, oval silhouette, quote from Gettysburg Address, black on cream, with orig sales card, c1935, 5-1/2" h 20.00
Cross stitch on punched paper, "Love," beige, salmon and green dec, 6-1/4" l 9.00
Embroidered, "Week of Birthdays," flowers in metallic red thread, poem, 8-1/2" x 2"...............75.00
Photograph on paper, young woman 5.00
Plastic
   Donald Duck figural, "Book Mark, Disneyland," hand-painted 26.00

Lord's Prayer, die-cut cross, page-holder type, 4-3/4" x 1-1/4"...............................6.00
World's Fair, 1964-65 New York World's Fair, celluloid.........35.00

☸ Books

All types of books can be found flea markets. A book's value can be increased by a great binding, an early copyright, a first printing, interesting illustrations, an original dust jacket, or a famous author. At flea markets, prices for books can range from a dime to thousands of dollars.

Many book collectors are turning to their computers and using the Internet to find books. There are several sites devoted to antique books and also several ways to search for titles.

To remove a musty smell from a book, sprinkle baking soda onto several pages, close, and let it rest for a few days. When you remove the baking soda, the smell should disappear. Avoid books with mold, or you might be bringing home a big problem.

References: *American Book Prices Current*, Bancroft Parkman, published annually; Sharon and Bob Huxford, *Huxford's Old Book Value Guide*, 11th ed, Collector Books, 1999.

Periodicals: *AB Bookman's Weekly*, P.O. Box AB, Clifton, NJ 07015; *Biblio Magazine*, 845 Wilamette St, P.O. Box 10603, Eugene, OR 97401;

Book Source Monthly, 2007 Syosett Dr, P.O. Box 567, Cazenovia, NY 13035; *Rare Book Bulletin*, P.O. Box 201, Peoria, IL 61650; *The Book Collector's Magazine*, P.O. Box 65166, Tucson, AZ 85728.

Collectors' Club: Antiquarian Booksellers Assoc of America, 20 West 44th St, 4th Floor, New York, NY 10036.

The following listings are a mere sampling of the many books that may be found at flea markets.
A Guest At Ludlow & Other Stories, E.W. Nye, Bowen, Merill, 1897 .... 10.00
An Old Sweetheart of Mine, James W. Riley, Bobbs Merrill, illus by H. Christy, dec front cover 18.00
Caesar and Christ, the Story of Civilization, Will Durant, Simon & Schuster, 1944, color maps 14.00
Fannie Kemble, A Passionate Victorian, Margaret Armstrong, MacMillan, 1938, shelf-worn edges, 382 pgs 9.00
Fifteen Flags, Ric Hardman, Little Brown, 1968, 1st ed, history of 27th Inf. Reg. 50.00
Grapes and Wines from Home Vineyards, U. P. Hedrick, Oxford Univ Press, 1945, 2nd printing, 24 plates, drawings, dj 9.00
Great Women, Beacon Lights of History, John Lord, Ford-Howard, N.Y., 1886, worn, 522 pgs... 8.00
Homespun Tales, Kate Douglas Wiggin, Grosset & Dunlap, N.Y., 1920, 344 pgs 18.00

Hoosier Zion, Presbyterians in Early Indiana, L. C. Rudolph, Yale Univ. Press, 1963, 218 pgs 10.00

John G. Johnson, Lawyer & Art Collector, 1841-1917, Barrie F. Winkleman, Univ. of Pennsylvania Press, 1942, 315 pgs 10.00

Journey Through A Century, Biography of Alice Young Lindley, 1853-1951, Ethlyn Walkington, 1966, 119 pgs 10.00

My Garden of Hearts, A New Book of Stories and Human Life, Love & Experience, Margaret E. Sangster, Christian Herald, 1913, 439 pgs 13.00

Navy Yearbook, Andrews & Engel, 1944, 1st ed, 376 pgs, illus 105.00

Pennsylvania, Guide to Keystone State, WPA Writers Program, Univ. of Pennsylvania, 1940, 660 pgs, ex-library.................... 16.00

Remembered Laughter, The Life of Noel Coward, Cole Lesley, Knopf, 1977, 481 pgs, dj 8.50

Singin' Fiddler of Lost Hope Hollow, Jean Thomas, Dutton & Co., 1938, 1st ed, ex-library...... 20.00

Tar Heels, A Portrait of North Carolina, Jonathon Daniels, Dodd & Mead, 1941 .... 15.00

The Adventures of Snooki and Snak, Lillian Elizabeth Roy, 1928, hardcover, some pgs colored ... 35.00

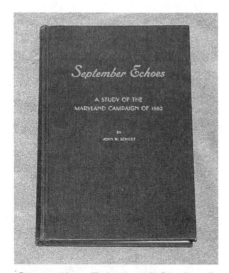

September Echoes: A Study of the Maryland Campaign of 1862 by John W. Schildt, The Valley Register, 1960, historical Civil War book, $30.

The Art of Egypt Through The Ages, Sir E. Densin Ross, Edwin Rudge, 1931, 6 color plates, 410 black-and-white illus, cloth binding.......................................75.00

The House of Pride, Tales of Hawaii, Jack London, MacMillan, 1912 ....9.00

The Lonely Lady of San Clemente: The Story of Pat Nixon, Lester David, Crowell, 1947, 224 pgs, dj..7.50

The Mammoth Hunters, Jean Auel, Crown, 1985, 1st ed, 645 pgs, maps, dj.............................12.00

The Treasures of Louis Comfort Tiffany, Doubleday, 1980, 304 pgs, color and black-and-white illus, dj..75.00

The Wise Garden Encyclopedia, A Complete & Convenient Guide To Every Detail of Gardening, Wise & Co., 1951, color and black-and-white illus, 1,380 pgs 14.50

The Writings of Abraham Lincoln, 8-vol set, Centennial edition, 1905, illus 55.00

Tree and Toadstools, M. C. Rayner, Rodale Press, 1947, illus, dj 9.00

❖ Books, Children's

Flea markets are great places to look for children's books, and examples with interesting illustrations are particularly sought. Because condition is critical in determining price, check carefully for crayon illustrations by budding young artists. Likewise, make sure all the pages are there.

References: E. Lee Baumgarten, *Price Guide for Children's & Illustrated Books for the Years 1880–1960*, self-published, 1996; David & Virginia Brown, *Whitman Juvenile Books*, Collector Books, 1997; Diane McClure Jones and Rosemary Jones, *Collector's Guide to Children's Books, 1850 to 1950*, Collector Books, 1997; —, *Collector's Guide to Children's Books, 1950-1975*, Collector Books, 2000; E. Christian Mattson and Thomas B. Davis, *A Collector's Guide to Hardcover Boys' Series Books*, self-published, 1996.

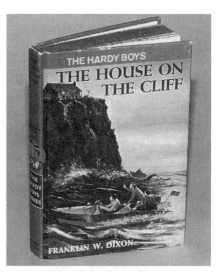

Hardy Boys, *The House on the Cliff*, 1959, Grosset & Dunlap, $5.

Periodicals: *Book Source Monthly*, 2007 Syossett Dr, P.O. Box 567, Cazenovia, NY 13035; *Martha's KidLit Newsletter*, P.O. Box 1488, Ames, IA 50010; *Mystery & Adventure Series Review*, P.O. Box 3488, Tucson, AZ 85722; *The Authorized Edition Newsletter*, RR1, Box 73, Machias, ME 04654; *Yellowback Library*, P.O. Box 36172, Des Moines, IA 50315.

Collectors' Clubs: Many specialized collector clubs exist.

A Child's Garden of Verses, Marla Kirt, 1919, 4th imprint........ 17.50

Children's Praise & Worship for Sunday School, A. L. Byers, Anderson College, IN, 1928 .... 6.50

Elsie's Girlhood, Martha Finley, Dodd, Mead & Co., 1872, emb pansies on cover............... 20.00

Guess Who, Dick & Jane, Scott Foresman, 1951................ 45.00

How the Grinch Stole Christmas, Dr. Seuss, 1957, red and green cover 25.00

Jo's Boys, Louisa May Alcott, 1918, 10 plates, top edges gold 10.00

Joyful Poems for Children, James W. Riley, 1946, 1st ed 28.00

Mattie's Home, S.W. Partridge & Co., London, red cover 25.00

Mother Goose In Silhouettes, Katherine Buffum, 1907, 1st ed, few minor tears 37.50

Pollyana Grows Up, E.H. Porter, H.W. Taylor illus, 1915, 1st ed 22.00

Raggedy Ann in the Snow White Castle, Johnny Gruelle, Bobbs-Merrill, 1960, 95 pgs..........21.50
Stories from Hans Andersen, Edward Dulac, 15 color pictures 135.00
The Big Book of Burgess Nature Stories, T. Burgess, illus by H. Cady, 1945, 370 pgs 24.00
The Password To Larkspur Lane, Nancy Drew, 1933, blue and orange cover, dj.................25.00
Treasure Island, Robert Louis Stevenson, illus by Paul Frame, Whitman, 1955 ....5.00
Uncle Arthur's Bedtime Stories, 1976, Arthur S. Maxwell, 5 vol set 25.00
Wooden Willie, Johnny Gruelle, M. A. Donohue & Co., 1927, Colland Co., cover illus by Gruelle 70.00

❖ Bootjacks

Designed to ease the removal of boots, bootjacks were primarily made of cast iron or wood. The heel of a boot is placed in the U-shaped opening at the front of the jack, the other foot is placed on the rear of the jack, and the boot is pried off the front foot. Examples range from crude, one-of-a-kind versions to examples with elaborate, artistic castings and carvings.

In 1852 the United States Patent Office awarded its first patent for a bootjack to Saris Thomson of Hartsville, Massachusetts.

Reproduction Alert.
Beetle, cast iron, mkd "Depose," French, 10-1/2" l.................50.00
Double pistol, cast iron, mkd "From Younder E Bros." 205.00
Lee Riders, wooden, small pc of rubber missing, 12" l...............35.00
Naughty Nellie
  Antique, cast iron, 9-1/2" l. 80.00
  Reproduction, cast iron, 9" l 10.00
Scrolled design with horseshoe end, Victorian, cast iron, 11" l...195.00
Scrolled design with V-shaped end, openwork design of intertwined stems, cast iron, 12" l........45.00
Wooden, homemade
  Tiger maple, 10" l...............30.00
  Pine, oval ends, sq nails, 25" l 30.00
  Walnut, carved heart and openwork, 22" l 45.00

❖ Bottle Openers

Back in the dark ages before pull tops and twist off tops, folks actually used these wonderful bottle openers. Today collectors seek them out at flea markets. Some collectors prefer the figural types and try to find interesting examples with good paint. Other collectors concentrate on finding interesting advertising bottle openers.

Collectors' Clubs: Figural Bottle Opener Collectors Club, 3 Ave A, Latrobe, PA 15650; Just for Openers, 3712 Sunningdale Way, Durham, NC 22707.
For additional listings, see *Warman's Americana & Collectibles.*

Reproduction Alert
4-eyed man, Wilton, wear, 3-1/2" x 3-1/2" 55.00
Atlanta 1996 Centennial Olympic Games, shows American flag, 4-1/2" l 12.00
Bell Telephone hard hat, cast iron, MIB 50.00
Benson & Hedges 100's, bottle opener and keychain, metal, 1-1/2" x 3-1/2" 10.00
Black boy and alligator, figural, cast iron, 2-3/4" h 145.00
Canada Dry, metal, 3-1/8" l........3.50

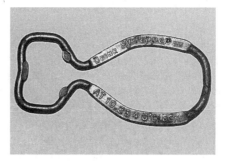
Dr. Pepper bottle opener, $30.

Coca-Cola, wall-mount, Starr X type, cast iron, some rust 22.00
Drunk on a lamp post, cast iron, paint chips, 4-3/8" h 15.00
Edelweiss Beer, A Case of Good Judgement, metal, 4-3/4" l.. 3.00
Face painted on wooden handle, metal opener, Japan, 4-3/4" h 4.50
Falstaff Beer, wall-mount, Starr X type, orig box 24.00
Guitar-shaped bottle opener and nodder, opener sticks to magnet on front of nodder figure ... 25.00
Miller Brewing Co., metal, some rust 3.00
Pabst, metal, some rust 2.00
Parrot on stand, cast iron, mkd "JW" (John Wright), 5-1/4" h...... 95.00
Singing cowboy, cast iron, 4-3/4" h 95.00
Walt Disney World, 4-1/2" l 5.00

Starr "X" Coca-Cola opener with original box, $22.50.

I'll drink to that!

Raymond Brown's name might not be a familiar one, but you've probably seen one of his best-known inventions—a cast-iron, wall-mount bottle opener. In 1925, when soda was sold in glass bottles, Brown, the owner of several bottling plants, developed an opener that didn't damage the bottle when the cap was pried off. To make the new opener, Brown Manufacturing in Newport News, VA, was founded. Brown's opener consisted of a slanted, curved lip that attached to the wall with two screws. By adding a space for advertising, Brown greatly expanded the market for his device. The most famous advertiser was Coca-Cola.

Brown's design, the Starr "X" bottle opener, is still produced for bottlers, breweries, wholesalers, distributors, and retailers. For a list of advertising that has appeared on the openers over the years, see the Starr Web site at www.bottleopener.com.

❖ Bottles

Many types of bottles are found at flea markets. Prices vary according to rarity, condition, and color. Several excellent reference books are available to assist collectors.

References: Ralph & Terry Kovel, *Kovels' Bottles Price List*, 10th ed, Crown Publishers, 1996; Michael Polak, *Bottles*, 2nd ed, Avon Books, 1997; Carlo and Dorothy Sellari, *The Standard Old Bottle Price Guide*, 1989 (1997 value update), Collector Books.

Periodicals: *Antique Bottle and Glass Collector*, P.O. Box 187, East Greenville, PA 18041; *Canadian Bottle and Stoneware Collector*, 179D Woodridge Crescent, Nepean, Ontario K2B 7T2 Canada.

Collectors' Clubs: American Collectors of Infant Feeders, 5161 W 59th St, Indianapolis, IN 46254; Federation of Historical Bottle Collectors, Inc; 1485 Buck Hill Dr, Southampton, PA 18966; Midwest Antique Fruit Jar & Bottle Club, P.O. Box 38, Flat Rock, IN 47234; New England Antique Bottle Club, 120 Commonwealth Rd, Lynn, MA 01904.

For additional listings, see *Warman's Antiques & Collectibles Price Guide* and *Warman's Glass*. The following listings are a mere sampling of the bottles that may be found at flea markets.

Hutchison-type bottle, "Jumbo Bottling Works, Cincinnati, O.," aqua, embossed letters, chipped lip, 7" high, $65.

Acme Nursing Bottle, clear, laydown type, emb 70.00
Bull Dog Brand Liquid Glue, aqua, ring collar 6.50
Calla Nurser, oval, clear, emb, ring on neck 8.50
Cole & Southey, Washington, D.C., soda water, aquamarine .. 110.00
Empire Nursing Bottle, bent neck 50.00
Everett & Barron Co. Shoe Polish, oval, clear 5.00
Kranks Cold Cream, milk glass .6.50
Lysol, cylindrical, amber, emb "Not to be Taken".......................12.00
Missiquoi Springs, apricot-amber, applied sloping collared mouth with ring, smooth base, 1 qt 150.00
Mother's Comfort, clear, turtle type 25.00
Neamand's Drug Store, clear ..30.00
Owl Drug Co., owl sitting on mortar, cobalt blue 70.00
Pre Cream Rye, bartender's type 35.00
Sloan's Liniment, castor oil 20.00
Violet Dulce Vanishing Cream, eight panels, 2-1/2" h 7.50

❖ Boxes

Collectors love boxes of all kinds. Interior decorators also scout flea markets for useful boxes. The colorful labels of these vintage packages are delightful to display. Locked boxes offer the mystery of a treasure inside, but don't be lured into paying too much.

Apple, pine, old red paint, conical feet, 9-3/4" x 10" x 4" h....310.00
Baker's Chocolate, wood, 12-lb size 25.00
Book shape, green onyx, brass and wood trim, wear and chips, 5" l 165.00
Candle, hanging, pine and hardwood, old worn gray paint, 10-1/4" w 330.00
Candy box, Whitman's Pleasure Island Chocolates, cardboard, pirate scenes on 5 sides, map on bottom, 1924......................28.00
Collar box, gold paper ground, pink, green and yellow flowers, clear celluloid overlay, pretty woman in center...........................175.00

Frank's bottle crate, wooden, $8.

Dome top, cast brass, relief eagle and crowns, English, 19th C., 4" l................................... 175.00
Dresser, white ground, small pink flowers and green leaves, mkd "Nippon," rect.................... 35.00
Fairies Bath Perfume, unopened, 1920s............................... 12.00
Heart shape, silver-plated, small gold bow trim, velvet lining 35.00
King Brand Rolled Oats 45.00
Ladies Favorite Polish, paper label 10.00
National Lead Co., paint chip samples 25.00
Pine, worn orig brown graining, yellow ground, machine dovetails, 16-1/4" l 200.00
Regal Underwear, cardboard.. 20.00
Snuff, shoe shaped, curved toe, worn black lacquer, inlaid pewter trim, 3" l............................ 225.00
Ward Baking Co., wood 100.00

❖ Boy Scouts

The Boy Scout pledge has been recited by millions of youngsters throughout the years. Collectibles relating to scouting troops, jamborees, etc., are eagerly sought and readily found at flea markets.

Reference: George Cuhaj, *Standard Price Guide to U.S. Scouting Collectibles*, Krause Publications, 1998.

Periodicals: *Fleur-de-Lis*, 5 Dawes Ct, Novato, CA, 94947; *Scout Memorabilia*, P.O. Box 1121, Manchester, NH 03105.

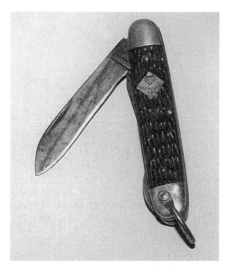

Camillus 3-blade knife, Cub Scouts BSA, 6" with blade extended, $18.

Collectors' Clubs: American Scouting Traders Assoc, P.O. Box 210013, San Francisco, CA 94121; National Scouting Collectors Soc, 803 E Scott St, Tuscola, IL 61953; World Scout Dealers, 509-1 Margaret Ave, Kitchener, Ontario N2H 6M4 Canada.

For additional listings, see *Warman's Americana & Collectibles.*

Axe, mkd Collins, oak handle, dated 1916, 12" l 85.00
Birthday card, "Happy Scout Birthday," recruitment nature, c1960s, unused with orig mailing envelope, card 5-3/8" x 4-1/4" 5.00
Bugle, Lexcraft, 17" l 250.00
Canteen, Diamond Brand, canvas cover, c1950s 12.00
Card, 25-year veteran card, dated 1949, toning 8.50
Coffee mug, "Blackhawk Area Council" and "Appreciation 72" .. 12.00
Drum, all tin, litho scenes on sides, 5-1/4" h, 11" dia 245.00
Handbook, March 1963, Norman Rockwell cover, tears, binding loose 15.00
Hat
    Scoutmasters, Boy Scouts of America insignia, felt, c1950s 125.00
    Stetson, mkd "John B. Stetson Co. #1," leather chin strap, c1930s 65.00

Mask, wolf head, tears, 7-1/2" w, 9-1/2" l 55.00
Necktie, black tie with gold Boy Scout shields, orig box shows Boy Scout wearing tie, "Boy Scouts Of America Supply Division, New Brunswick, NJ Melrose Park, San Francisco," worn and stained box 70.00
Patch
    15-year, c1930s-40s, 2" dia 35.00
    1974 Third Jumpin' Joe Jamboree, Eastern Arkansas Area Council, 3" dia 13.00
    Diamond Jubilee, 3" dia 18.00
    St. Louis Council 1941 Camporee, 3-1/2" x 2" 34.00
Pin, dated 1911 .... 27.50
Triple-signal set, orig box, 1933 .... 125.00
Trophy, round plastic base, copper-colored metal Boy Scout figure, 8-1/2" h 35.00
Woody's Slide Carving Combination Pack, carving knife and 7 pre-printed basswood carving blanks, orig box, yellowed . 45.00

❖ Boyd Crystal Art Glass

The Boyd Family of Cambridge, Ohio, has made some interesting colored glassware over the years. Many of their molds were purchased from leading glass companies, such as Imperial.

Reference: Boyd's Crystal Art Glass, *Boyd Crystal Art Glass: The Tradition Continues,* published by author.

Periodical: *Boyd's Crystal Art Glass Newsletter,* 1203 Morton Ave, P.O. Box 127, Cambridge, OH 43725.

Collectors' Club: Boyd Art Glass Collectors Guild, P.O. Box 52, Hatboro, PA 19040.

Doll, Louise, yellow slag 25.00
Duckling, periwinkle, 1-1/2" h .. 10.00
Elephant, Zack, Mardi Gras, red and gold slag, 3-1/2" 35.00
Hand, rubina, 4" l 20.00
Horse, Joey, 4" h
    Amethyst, 1st logo 30.00

Delphinum 21.00
Furr Green 20.00
Mardi Gras, orange slag.... 20.00
Horse, Rocky, Black Beauty, 4" l 20.00
Pickle dish, orange and yellow slag, yellow hob trim, sides emb "Love's request is Pickles," 9" l 45.00
Pie vent, duck, yellow or blue . 35.00
Pig, Candyland, purple, 2" h ... 15.00
Salt
    Bird, orange and gold slag, 3" l 26.00
    Chick, Spring Surprise, red and gold slag, 2" 10.00
Shoe, Daisy and Button, bow on front, ribbed bottom, mkd, 5-1/2"
    Light blue......................... 40.00
    Vaseline............................ 20.00
Tomahawk, cobalt, 7" l 26.00
Tractor, 1 blue irid, 1 carnival irid, 1 orange/red slag, 1 red carnival irid and 1 blue slag, each mkd "Boyd" on front, each 2-3/4" l, set of 5 .... 125.00
Wine glass, chocolate slag, 1st logo, 4" h 20.00

✪ Boyd's Bears & Friends

What's better than a teddy bear? How about collectible teddy bears with personality? Plus, Boyd's bears have companion figurines, magnets, and accessories, making them a popular collectible for the new millennium.

Alissa Witebred, white, yellow jumper, matching bow and flowers, 12" h 25.00
Gary Bearenthal, bean bag construction, 16" h 50.00
Hemingway, fishing vest and hat, 14" h 32.00
Lincoln B. Bearrington, golden brown mohair, 16" h 85.00
Miss Prissy Fussybuns, long haired white cat, dark blue hat with flowers, 16" h 25.00
Mrs. Mertz, hand knit pink and white checked sweater, pink accented hat, 10" h 25.00

Mrs. Trumball, fully jointed, hand-knit green sweater, matching hat, 10" h 28.00
Mr. Trumball, mocha colored, dark brown sweater, plaid bowtie, 10" h 25.00
Petula P. Fallsbeary, 9" h 10.00
Regena Haresford, white rabbit, blue checked dress, matching bow, 13" h 25.00
Sally Quignapple & Annie, bear 10" h, doll 5" h 22.00
Uncle Leo, hand-knit sweater, ball cap, 10" h 32.00

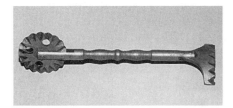

Brass pie crimper with coggle wheel, $10.

❖ Brass

An alloy of copper and zinc, brass is an extremely durable yet malleable metal. It has long been favored for creating decorative and functional objects. Because it is so durable, many brass items can be found at flea markets. Avoid pieces with unusual wear, those that are broken, or examples that are poorly polished.

References: Mary Frank Gaston, *Antique Brass & Copper*, Collector Books, 1992 (1994 value update); Henry J. Kaufmann, *Early American Copper, Tin & Brass*, Astragal Press, 1995.

Reproduction Alert.

Ashtray, rope design on rim, 5" dia 12.00
Bed warmer, pierced brass pan, long wooden handle 135.00
Blowtorch, metal handle, discoloration, dent, 5-1/2" h 22.00
Bridal rosette, heart shape 38.50
Candlesticks, mkd "Wainberg," made in Jerusalem, 8-1/2" h, pr 40.00
Chestnut roaster, heart-shaped, pierced lid, decorative handle, English, 19-1/2" l 300.00

Cigar cutter, pocket type 40.00
Door slot, mkd "Letters" on hinged flap, 2-3/4" h, 6-1/2" w 25.00
Mortar and pestle, 4-1/2" h 65.00
Pail, iron bail with rat-tail ends, 8" h, 12" dia 45.00
Sleigh bells, set of 6, graduated, on leather hame strap, 24" l 137.50
Spittoon, 3-3/4" h, 9-1/2" dia.... 34.00
Teapot, floral design on 1 side, Oriental lettering on other, swing handle, 9" x 7" 28.00
Tray, stamped with Holland scenes, attached handles, 17" x 10" 45.00

❖ Brastoff, Sascha

This internationally known designer and artist began producing ceramic artware in 1953. If a piece is marked with his full name, it was made by him. Pieces marked "Sascha B" indicate he supervised the production, but didn't necessarily make the item himself.

Ashtray
    Abstract pattern, 8" l 39.00
    Alaska pattern hooded ashtray, Eskimo face design, 5" h, 5" w 65.00
    Igloo design, 4-1/2" h, 6" dia 55.00
Ashtray and cigarette set, Rooftops pattern, c1958, ashtray 13-1/2" x 5", lighter 3-3/4" h, cigarette container 2-5/8" w, 3 pcs 150.00
Bowl
    Mosaic pattern, 3 feet, minor paint chips, 14-1/2" l, 12" w 145.00
    Star Steed pattern, sunfish design, 3 feet, 9-3/4" l, 8-1/2" w 110.00
Cigarette lighter, Aztec or Mayan pattern, floral design, 1-1/4" h, 4-1/4" w 45.00
Dish
    Alaska pattern, shell form, 11-1/2" l 85.00
    Jewel Bird pattern, 10" dia . 85.00
    Star Steed pattern, sq 65.00
Figure
    Horse, blue with silver trim, 10-1/4" h, pr 600.00
    Polar bear, 9" l 195.00
Lamp, full signature 695.00
Plate, ChiChi Bird pattern, 8-1/2" dia 100.00

Small dish with pear decoration, Sascha B., 3-3/4" square, $25.

Platter, Alaska pattern, seal on white ground with blue sky, painted by Matt Adams, 13-3/4" x 8-1/4" 130.00
Tobacco jar, Abstract pattern, stainless steel lid, rust stains, glaze flaws, 6-1/2" h 65.00
Vase
    Aztec or Mayan pattern, gold horse design, rooster mark, 5-1/2" h, 8-1/2" w 125.00
    Elk design, 8" h 75.00
    Fruit design, 15" h 145.00
    Gold leaves design, white and speckled yellow ground, rooster mark, 9-1/4" h, pr 265.00
    Orange and Gold pattern, 12" h 155.00
    Rooftops pattern, cylindrical, matte finish, 8-1/2" h.... 115.00
    Totem Pole pattern, 8" h.... 75.00
    Vanity Fair pattern, rooster mark, 10" h 155.00
Wall plaque, stylized fish, 1 turquoise, 1 maroon, 12" l, pr 110.00
Wall pocket, Provincial Rooster pattern, 4" h, 5" w 95.00

❖ Brayton Laguna Ceramics

Brayton Laguna Ceramics was founded by Durline E. Brayton, a potter who produced his wares in his home in South Laguna Beach, California. Following Brayton's death in 1951, employees operated the company until it closed in 1963.

Candleholders, Blackamoor, 4-3/4"
  h, pr 125.00
Cookie jar, teal ground, golden
  brown partridges, black
  branches, #V-11, incised mark
  .... 260.00
Creamer and sugar, Calico Cat and
  Gingham Dog 90.00
Figure
  Gay Nineties Bar, three men
    posing, glaze flake on one
    shoe, 8-1/2" h, 7-1/2" l
    .... 110.00
  Lady with Wolfhounds, powder
    blue dress, yellow hair, 1943,
    11" h 115.00
  Petunia, black girl, 6-1/4" h
    .... 175.00
  Purple Cow, 9" l 195.00
  Sambo, black boy, repaired chip
    on back of hat, 7-3/4" h
    .... 140.00
  Snow White's Deer, 6-1/2" h
    .... 125.00
Flower ring 35.00
Oak bucket, glazed dec 45.00
Planter
  Kneeling Blackamoor, slight
    paint wear 125.00
  Matilda, holding two planter bas-
    kets held by strap across her
    shoulders, yellow vest with
    wine and green accents, wine
    colored skirt, incised mark,
    c1930-37, 7-5/8" h 90.00
Salt and pepper shakers, Mammy
  and Chef, c1940, 5" h, pr
  .... 195.00

❖ Breadboxes

Breadboxes were once a necessary item in all well-equipped kitchens. Today these boxes are finding
their way to flea markets. Make
sure the interior is clean and free of
rust if you're going to use this flea
market treasure.
Chrome, black Bakelite handle, rect
  .... 15.00
Graniteware, gray, raised red han-
  dles and letters "Bread," sq
  .... 35.00
Metal
  Enameled white, light blue Art
    Deco design, mkd "Germany,"
    16" l, 9" d, 6" h 85.00
  Painted green, scene of lady with
    watering can, 13" l, 9" h
    .... 65.00

Painted white, 1950s, 10-1/2" l,
  17" w 30.00
Plastic, turquoise, clear top, rounded
  corners, 1940s, 11-3/4" l, 4-3/4"
  w, 5-1/4" h 24.00
Porcelain, Blue Willow, roof-shaped
  lid, 13-1/2" l 80.00

❖ Breweriana

Collectors have always enjoyed
finding new examples of breweriana
at their favorite flea markets. Some
specialize in items from a particular
brewery, while others collect only
one type of item, such as beer
trays. Whatever they enjoy, their
collections are bound to be colorful.

Reference: Herb and Helen Hay-
dock, *World of Beer Memorabilia*,
Collector Books, 1997.

Periodicals: *All About Beer*, 1627
Marion Ave, Durham, NC 27705;
Barley Corn News, P.O. Box 2328,
Falls Church, VA 22042; *Suds 'n'
Stuff*, 4765 Galacia Way, Oceanside,
CA 92056.

Collectors' Clubs: American Brew-
eriana Assoc, P.O. Box 11157,
Pueblo, CO 81001; East Coast
Breweriana Assoc, P.O. Box 64,
Chapel Hill, NC 27514; National
Assoc of Breweriana Advertising,
2343 Met-To-Wee Lane, Wauwa-
tosa, WI 53226.

Reproduction Alert.
Bottle opener
  Blatz Milwaukee Beer 8.00
  Wagner Lockheed International,
    plastic handle 8.00
Clock
  Budweiser, pocket watch form,
    electric, "Budweiser 1876,
    King of Beers," 15-1/2" dia
    .... 55.00
  Fort Pitt Special Beer, light-up,
    convex glass, 15" dia .. 105.00

**Metal bottle opener, "Carling,
Not For Sale," 3-5/8" long, $2.**

Schlitz glass, 5-1/4" high, $3.

Pabst Blue Ribbon, plastic, 17"
  dia 90.00
Dexterity puzzle, Miller High Life,
  can-shape, in orig plastic wrap-
  per, 5" h 20.00
Door push, Pabst Blue Ribbon Beer,
  7-1/4" h, 4-1/4" w 125.00
Inflatable football, Coors 13.00
Mug, features Vermont, made in
  Japan, rim chip 12.00
Playing cards, Miller High Life, "The
  Champagne of Bottle Beer," Girl
  on Moon logo, 1950s, orig box,
  used 16.50
Score pad, Falstaff Beer, for gin
  rummy, eight sheets, 8-3/4" x
  7-5/8" 13.00
Sign
  Budweiser, cardboard, "Custer's
    Last Stand," shows Battle of
    Little Big Horn, 20" h, 41" w
    .... 125.00
  Genesee Beer, doubled-sided
    window sign, late 1950s, 11"
    dia 18.00
  O'Keefe Canadian Ale, hard
    plastic, wooden easel for
    countertop display, 16" x 11"
    .... 14.00
  Pabst, red neon, blue ribbon bor-
    der, plastic protector, 19" h,
    21" w 90.00
Stein, Miller, 1988, Great American
  Achievements, 3rd in a series
  .... 22.50
Stock certificate, Falstaff Brewing
  Corp., 1970 .... 13.00
Tap, Schlitz, wood and ceramic
  .... 25.00
Tray
  Budweiser, tin, "St. Louis Levee
    In Early Seventies," shows
    paddlewheeler at busy dock,
    1914 copyright 140.00

Coors Light, gray and white, dated 1982, wear, 13" dia 10.00

Schlitz, "The beer that made Milwaukee famous," 13" dia 75.00

Tumbler, Budweiser, Christmas theme, 1940s-50s, with orig box 8.50

❖ Breyer

Founded in 1943, the Breyer Molding Company of Chicago has created some interesting radio and television cases. However, the company is best known for its animals, which were started as a sideline but had gained great popularity by 1958. The facility continued to develop new techniques, creating interesting new figures, primarily horses. The production operation was moved to New Jersey after the firm was acquired by Reeves International.

References: Felicia Browell, *Breyer Animal Collector's Guide,* 2nd ed, Collector Books; Nancy Atkinson Young, *Breyer Molds and Models: Horses, Riders and Animals*, rev and updated 5th ed, Schiffer Publishing.

Periodicals: *The Hobby Horse News*, 2053 Dryehaven Drive, Tallahassee, FL 32311; *The Model Horse Trader*, 143 Mercer Way, Upland, CA 91720; *TRR Pony Express*, 71 Aloha Circle, North Little Rock, AR 72120.

Collectors' Clubs: Breyer Collectors Club, 14 Industrial Rd, Pequannock, NJ 07440; North American Model Horse Show Association, P.O. Box 50508, Denton, TX 76206.
Web Site: www.breyerhorses.com

Accessories
Bucket, MIB 3.00
Crop 8.00
Hobbles, MIB 4.00
Horse barn, pine, MIB 270.00
Leather saddlebag, MIB 16.00
McClellan military saddle set, MIB 30.00
Nylon halter with cotton lead rope, MIB 12.00
Stable blanket, quilted, blue and yellow, MIB 7.00
Tack box, blue, MIB 10.00

Animals
Alpine Goat, 1999, MIB 6.00
Black Bear, 1967-1974 .... 50.00
Collie, Honey, 1995-1996, MIB 55.00
Elephant, re-release, 1992-1993, MIB 45.00
Hawk, black, 1991-1992 .... 25.00
Kitten, Cleopatra, 1994-1996 ... 65.00
Moose, 1966-1996 .... 35.00
Texas Longhorn Bull, 1963-1990 .... 30.00

Horses
Arabian foal, black, 1999, MIB 15.00
Black Stallion Returns set, 1983-1993 .... 65.00
Bucking Bronco, rose-grey, 1999, MIB 30.00
Dan Patch, limited edition, 1990, MIB 90.00
Fighting Stallion
   Alabaster, matte, 1973-1985 .... 40.00
   Bay, Toys R Us, 1993, MIB 50.00
Little Bits scale (approx 4-1/2" to 5" h)
   Appaloosa, 1985-1988 .... 15.00
   Clydesdale, 1984-1988 ...... 20.00
   Morgan, black, star face, 1965-1987 .... 50.00
Palomino
   Grazing foal, 1965-1971 .... 25.00
   Rearing stallion, 1965-1981 .... 35.00
Polo Pony, 1976-1981, damaged box 50.00
Running mare, chestnut, 1963-1974 .... 35.00
Secretariat, 1987-1996, MIB 50.00
Shetland Pony, alabaster, 1963-1973 .... 25.00
Stablemate scale (approx 2-3/4" h)
   Citation, 1975-1990 .... 10.00
   Morgan stallion, chestnut, 1989-1994 .... 15.00
   Thoroughbred mare, bay, 1989-1994 .... 15.00

Breyer donkey, 8-1/2" long, $65.

❖ Bride's Baskets

The term *bride's basket* usually refers to a decorative glass bowl in a fancy silver or silver-plate holder. This traditional gift to brides was meant as a showpiece for the young couple's sideboard. Over time, bowls would be damaged, so it is not uncommon to find a bowl that is mismatched with a base.

Blue, ruffled, leaves, blossom, gold dec, no frame 150.00
Cranberry, applied glass trim, SP holder, 6" dia 195.00
Cranberry opalescent, no frame 140.00
Fenton, maize, amber and crystal crest, hp roses on int, white ext, SP holder, 10-1/2" dia 275.00
Overshot, ruby crimped edging, polished pontil, 10" dia 350.00
Satin glass, shaded purple, white underside, purple and white enameled flowers, lacy foliage dec, 10-3/4" dia 225.00
Silver plate, mkd "Middletown Plate Co., Quadruple Plate 1857," 9-1/2" dia, 5-1/2" h excluding handle 140.00
Tiffany, Favrile, #516, art glass insert with opalescent swirl, amethyst tint, bronze base, sgd .. 1,450.00
Vasa Murrhina, outer amber layer, center layer with cream colored spots, random toffee colored spots, dark veins, gold mica flakes, mulberry pink lining, crossed thorn handles, 10" dia 635.00

❖ British Royalty

Generations of collectors have been fascinated by the British Royal family, having saved memorabilia associated with the king's clan. Quite an assortment survives from the past, in addition to the plethora of items associated with present-day royal weddings, births, and state visits.

"Coronation, June 2nd, 1953, H.M. Queen Elizabeth II, 4-1/8" high, crazed, $30.

Periodical: *British Royalty Commemorative Collectors Newsletter,* P.O. Box 294, Lititz, PA 17543.

Collectors' Club: Commemorative Collector's Society, Lumless House, Gainsborough Rd, Winthrope, New Newark, Nottingham NG24 1NR UK. For additional listings, see *Warman's Antiques & Collectibles,* as well as Princess Diana Collectibles in this edition.

Bell, Queen Elizabeth Coronation, 1953 .... 30.00

Book, *The Princess Elizabeth Gift Book,* Cynthia Asquith and Eileen Bigland, four illus of fruit, worn 10.00

Box, cov, Elizabeth, the Queen Mother, 1980, 80th Birthday, color portrait, Crown Staffordshire, 4" dia 75.00

Cup and saucer, Elizabeth II, portrait flanked by flags, coronation, pairs of flags inside cup and saucer 45.00

Goblet, Royal Wedding Commemorative, 6" h, MIB 70.00

Invitation, crossed American and British flags at top, "The Honorable Fiorello H. LaGuardia, Mayor of the City of New York, invites you to participate in the city's welcome to Their Majesties King George VI and Queen Elizabeth," June, 1939 .... 45.00

Lithophane cup, Alexandra, 1902 .... 195.00

Loving cup, Elizabeth II and Philip, 1972 Silver Wedding Anniversary, Paragon, 3" h 175.00

Magic Lantern slide, Victoria and Albert 25.00

Matchbook cover, Their Most Gracious Majesties, Canada, May 15-June 15, 1939 .... 18.00

Mug, Queen Elizabeth Coronation, 1953 .... 24.00

Plaque, Queen Elizabeth Coronation, incised "Canada," 7" dia 35.00

Plate, Queen Victoria, Jubilee Year, Royal Worcester, 10-1/2" dia 275.00

Tin, Queen Elizabeth, Coronation, June, 1953, slight discoloration top, rust inside 8.00

❖ Bronze

An alloy of copper and tin, bronze is a sturdy metal that has been used to create functional and decorative objects for centuries. Collectors should be aware that some objects merely have a bronze coating and are not solid bronze. Those pieces are valued considerably less than if they were solid bronze.

Ashtray, round, leaf form, applied salamander, c1910, 7-1/2" dia 120.00

Bookends, baby shoes, dated 1948 .... 25.00

Calling card tray, nude sitting with lioness 130.00

Figure
Horse with reins, made in Japan, 2" h, 2-1/4" l 5.00
Donkey with gear, "Souvenir of Las Vegas, Nev.," made in Japan, 2-1/4" h, 2-1/4" l ... 5.00

Bronze wall plaque, bust of Washington with crossed flags and eagle, embossed "1789 1889 Centennial," 7-1/2" x 13", $80.

Inkwell, Tiffany Studios, Zodiac pattern, orig insert with 1 rim chip 635.00

Sewing clamp, figural, hand clenching a hook, 3-3/4" h 575.00

Wall plaque, American Telephone and Telegraph Co., 9" dia 250.00

❖ Bubblegum & Non-Sport Trading Cards

Bubblegum trading cards were big business in the late 1930s, especially for the Goudey Gum Company and National Chicle Company. They produced several series that had collectors clamoring for more. Bowman, Donruss, Topps, and Fleer eventually joined the marketplace also. Today, some companies omit the gum, concentrating solely on the trading cards.

Periodicals: *Non-Sport Update,* 4019 Green St, P.O. Box 5858, Harrisburg, PA 17110; *Non-Sports Illustrated,* P.O. Box 126, Lincoln, MA 01773; *Wrapper,* P.O. Box 227, Geneva, IL 60134.

Collectors' Club: United States Cartophilic Society, P.O. Box 4020, St. Augustine, FL 32085.

The following listings are merely a sampling of the many bubblegum cards available. Prices are for complete sets in excellent condition.

Andy Griffith Show, 1990, set of 110 cards, mint 25.00

Batman trading card, "What Tim Burton Wants," #238, Second Series, 25 cents.

Batman, Topps, 1966, Riddle-Back series, 38-card set........... 250.00
Battlestar Galactica, Topps, 132 cards and 22 stickers to a set 40.00
Beanie Babies, Series 2
    Caw.................................... 35.00
    Princess............................ 35.00
Beatles, B-11 of 16, Revolver, lyrics of Eleanor Rigby on back 3.00
Combat, Series 2, Donruss, 1964, 66-card set 250.00
Elvis Presley, Boxcar Enterprises, Inc., 1978, complete set .. 135.00
Fabian, Topps, 1959, 115-card set 120.00
Good Guys & Bad Guys, Leaf, 1966, 72-card set 275.00
Green Hornet, #29, 1966.......... 5.00
Gremlins, 1984 .... 10.00
Mars Attacks, Topps, 1962, 55-card set 1,650.00
Movie Stars, Bowman, 1948, 36-card set 360.00
Mickey Mouse, #3 .... 30.00
Rock Stars, Donruss, 1979, 66-card set 48.00
Simpsons, Radioactive Man, #412 .... 5.00
Tarzan, 1966, Philadelphia Chewing Gum Co., 66-card set...... 185.00
Wild Man, Bowman, 1950, 72-card set 1,250.00

❖ Bunnykins

These charming bunny characters have delighted children for many years. But, did you know that they were created by a nun? Barbara Vernon Bailey submitted her designs from the convent. Many of her designs were inspired by stories she remembered her father telling. The Bunnykins line was introduced in 1934. A new series of figures was modeled by Albert Hallam in the 1970s.

Baby plate, letter box, Barbara Vernon Bailey 75.00
Baby set, plate and 2-handled mug, Royal Doulton.................... 55.00
Bowl, Royal Doulton, Barbara Vernon 95.00
Coupe, slight use scratches, 3-1/2" dia 30.00
Child's cup, two handles, mkd "English Fine Bone China, Bunnykins, Royal Doulton Tableware Ltd, 1936" 55.00

Bunnykins child's dish, 6-1/4" diameter, $40.

Child's plate, mkd "English Fine Bone China, Bunnykins, Royal Doulton Tableware Ltd, 1936" 50.00
Christmas plate, 8" dia............. 18.00
Figure
    Bridesmaid, DB173, 3-3/4" 40.00
    Buntie Bunnykins helping Mother, DB2 .... 85.00
    Doctor Bunnykins, 4-1/2" h 40.00
    Easter Greetings 55.00
    Fisherman Bunny, DB170, 4" h 50.00
    Fortune Teller 60.00
    Jack and Jill Bunnykins, 4-1/2" h 120.00
    Little Bo Peep, 4-1/2" h 60.00
    Little Jack Horner, 3-1/2" h 60.00
    Mother and Baby Bunnykins, DB167, 1997 .... 45.00
    Nurse 45.00
    Policeman, DB64 .... 45.00
    Reginald Up To No Good, cold cast, discontinued 20.00
    Sailor Bunny, 1997, discontinued 55.00
    Seaside, 1998 .... 55.00
    Sundial, Warren Platt 50.00
    Uncle Sam, brown backstamp, 1985, 4-1/2" h................ 45.00

❖ Business & Office Machines

Folks who collect have always been fascinated with objects that are no longer in style or that technology has deemed obsolete. Early business and office machines fall into that category. Future generations will have fun pondering over some of these gadgets.

Zenith office stamp, 6" high, $5.

Collectors' Club: Early Typewriters Collectors Assoc, 2591 Military Ave, Los Angeles, CA 90064.
Adding machine
    Burroughs.......................... 17.50
    Star.................................... 15.00
    Victor 10.00
Advertising pencil, "H.G. Bancroft, Typewriters, Office Equipment and Supplies," shows manual typewriter 7.00
Checkwriter, SafeGuard.......... 25.00
Dictaphone, Model 10 .... 50.00
Notary seal, Stark County, Ohio, wear 90.00
Typewriter
    American Index, Model 2, 1893 .... 870.00
    L.C. Smith & Corona, Comet model............................. 65.00
    Royal, bookkeeper's model, wide platen............................. 40.00
    Underwood No. 5, 1930s 225.00
Typewriter ribbon tin
    McGregor, shows man playing bagpipes, black and silver, 2-1/2" w 65.00
    Pure Silk, woman in red dress, 2-1/2" dia 30.00
    Silhouette, woman typing at desk, 2-1/2" dia............. 30.00

❖ Buster Brown

R.F. (Richard Felton) Outcault first introduced the mischievous Buster Brown and his dog Tige in a *New York Herald* comic strip in 1902. During the St. Louis World's Fair Exposition of 1904, the characters were sold to merchants for use as trademarks. Outcault's idea to license rights to his comic figures was particularly innovative for the early 1900s. Subsequently, more than 50 different products incorporated the Buster Brown names and likenesses in their advertising and packaging.

Bank, cast iron, Buster Brown and Tige, orig gold paint, 5-1/4" h 200.00
Booklet, *Quick Meal Gasoline Stoves*, Buster Brown cover 135.00
Box, Buster Brown Shoes, empty 15.00
Camera.....................................65.00
Clicker, celluloid, Buster Brown Shoes, 1-1/4" dia.............225.00
Display, plaster Buster Brown and Tige, mkd "Buena Park Calif. 1972," 17-1/2" h, 11" w....395.00
Hot plate, ceramic, wear, scratches to design........................... 105.00
Lapel stud, 1-1/4" dia 45.00
Fob, Buster Brown Blue Ribbon Shoes, oval, silver, shows Buster Brown and Tige 28.00
Mask, die-cut paper, shows Buster Brown, 8-1/2" h...................13.00
Pencil holder, wood and cardboard, tin top, orig label, 10-1/2" l 85.00
Pocket mirror, celluloid, Buster Brown Vacation Days Carnival, 2-1/4" dia...........................45.00
Ring, flicker ring, plastic 8.00
Shaving mug, shows Buster Brown with blue and white teapot, Tige holds blue cup, scalloped edge, Germany, 2-1/2" h 295.00
Teacup, white with pink trim 72.50
Toy, Buster Brown Brownbilt Shoes cardboard gun and bullet disk, unpunched 45.00

❖ Busts

Decorative busts immortalized heroes and other special people. Made of durable materials such as marble, bronze, or alabaster, they are particularly long-lived. At one time, it was considered a sign of wealth to display a popular bust as part of your home decor. Values increase for examples with a plaque that identifies the subject, foundry or maker, and date.

Benjamin Franklin, carved oak, old brown alligatored finish, black carved base, sgd "Harris," 15" h 800.00
Cavalier, porcelain, sepia colors, mkd "Teplitz," c1910, 8-1/2" h 185.00
Child, bronze, gilt, green onyx base, mkd "S. Klaber & Co. Foundry N.Y.," 6-3/4" h 85.00
George Washington, cast plaster, orig bronze finish, 35" h...125.00
John Locke, black basalt, raised base, imp title and mark, Wedgwood, c1865, 7-3/4" h......525.00
Smiling Gypsy girl, plaster, Continental, 21-1/4" h 450.00
Virgin Mary, bronze, two tone finish, black granite base, sgd "F. de Luca," 18-1/2" h...............120.00
Young woman, marble, head piece, cowl neck, 7-1/2" h 250.00
Woman in hat, spelter, inscribed title, Victorian, 14-3/4" h..........375.00

Frosted glass bust of Christopher Columbus, pedestal marked "World's Fair 1893," 5-1/4" high, $145.

❖ Buttonhooks

Originally used for hooking tiny buttons on gloves, dresses, and shoes, these long narrow hooks are sometimes found hiding in vintage sewing baskets.

Bone handle, folding, 3-3/4" l.. 20.00
Celluloid handle
    6-1/8" l, mkd "Parisian Ivory," Loonen France trademark 25.00
    7-1/8" l, black etched floral design........................... 12.50
Sterling
    6" l, floral and leaf design, mkd "Tiffany & Co. Pat'd '98" 800.00
    6-1/8" l, feather paisley design 35.00
    6-1/4" l, swirling design, mkd "Tiffany & Co." 100.00
    7-1/4" l, Art Nouveau design 45.00
    7-1/4" l, shield shaped handle, hallmark for Birmingham, England, 1907 .... 25.00

Buttonhook, plastic handle, 7-1/2" long, $3.

❖ Buttons

Buttons are collected according to age, material, and subject matter. The National Button Society, founded in 1939, has designated 1918 as the dividing line between old and modern buttons. Shanks and backmarks are important elements to consider when determining age.

References: There are many excellent button books available to collectors. Some of the standard reference books include Fink & Ditzler, *Buttons: The Collector's Guide To Selecting, Restoring and Enjoying New & Vintage Buttons,* 1993; Elizabeth Hughes and Marion Lester, *The*

Big Book of Buttons, reprinted by New Leaf Publishers, 1981; Sally C. Luscomb, *The Collector's Encyclopedia of Buttons*, 4th ed, Schiffer Publishing, 1999; Florence Zacharie Nicholls, *Button Handbook, with three supplements*, 1943-1949, reprinted by New Leaf Publishers.

Periodical: *Button Bytes*, www.tias.com/articles/buttons (an internet magazine devoted to buttons).

Collectors' Clubs: National Button Society, 2733 Juno Place, Apt 4, Akron, OH 44313-4137; Pioneer Button Club, 102 Frederick St, Oshawa, Ontario L1G 2B3 Canada; The Button Club, P.O. Box 2274, Seal Beach, CA 90740.

Bakelite
    Brass center......................15.00
    Log, carved, red...................2.50
    Tortoiseshell, large disc, 2-1/8"
       dia 5.00

Black glass
    Gold luster, fabric-look, self
      shank, mkd "Le Mode,"
      1950s, 7/8" l 4.00
    Silver luster, petal look, self
      shank with threaded groove,
      mkd "Le Chic," 1950s, 13/16"
      ....4.00
Carnival glass, purple
    Buckle & Scrolls, 5/8" dia...10.00
    Frog....................................12.00
    Lazy Wheel, 5/8" dia 12.00
    Windmill, 5/8" dia 14.00
Czechoslovakian glass, diminutive
    Cobalt, inlaid ribbons of light
      green glass, multicolor foil,
      metal box shank, 3/8" dia
      ....5.00
    Floral bouquet, set of 12 ......2.00
Figural, plastic
    Apple, realistic coloring, metal
      shank.............................1.25
    Flower basket, pastels, metal
      shank.............................1.50
    Mickey Mouse, 6 figural buttons
      on orig card, mkd "W. D. Ent.,"
      Mickey, Pluto, and Donald
      Duck on corners, unused
      .... 110.00

Mouse, small, blue, self shank
    .... 3.00
Jade, green floral, Qing Dynasty,
    1-1/4" dia 70.00
Moonglow (glass)
    Black with red, colorless glass
      molded with plants and flow-
      ers, back mark is straight line
      with angled line at both ends,
      self shank, 1/2" dia 5.00
    Green flower, gold trim, 1/2" dia
      .... 2.00
    White, gold trim, four lobed, self
      shank, 1/2" dia................ 2.00
Paperweight, complicated millefiori
    by John Gooderham, white
    base, 8 flower canes, center
    small red, white, and blue cane,
    brass wire shank, sgd with "J"
    cane on back, 5/8" dia, 1/2" h
    .... 20.00
Stenciled china
    Black and white zebra stripes
      .... 1.00
    Blue and white flower 2.00

C

For exciting collecting trends and newly expanded areas look for the following symbols:

⚙ Hot Topic

✭ New Warman's Listing

(May have been in another Warman's title.)

❖ Cake Collectibles

Here's a sweet collectible for you. In our recent trips to flea markets, we've seen more and more of these items. Doesn't anyone bake anymore? It certainly seems as if there are a lot of cake pans for sale!

Cake cutting set, Fagley Junior Card Party Cake Cutters, deck of cards, heart, diamond, spade and club, orig 3-1/2" x 3-1/2" box 15.00

Cake plate, white and orange poppies, green luster ground, mkd "RS Germany" 90.00

Candle holders for birthday cake, 101 Dalmatians, three puppies, red, yellow, white and black plastic 4.00

Cookie board, wood, metal top, 12 impressions 35.00

Cupcake spike, baker with hat, Yeakel's Bakery 5.00

Pan

Bird shape, old 30.00

Child's building block shape 10.00

Icing knife, "Swans Down Cake Flour Makes Better Cakes," 12-3/8" long, $5.

Garfield shape 15.00

Santa shape 10.00

Topper

Bells, pink satin 25.00

Bride and groom, tulle on base, orig flowers, c1945 .... 65.00

Bugs Bunny, six matching birthday candle holders, Wilton, 1978 .... 24.00

Comic character 24.00

Disney 24.00

Mickey & Minnie Mouse 24.00

Snoopy 24.00

Snow White 24.00

❖ Calculators

What would we do without pocket calculators? Some of the first models are beginning to command steep prices; however, as with most other collectibles, condition is important. Collectors also want the original box and instruction sheet. Don't overlook examples with advertising.

References: Bruce Flamm and Guy Ball, *Collector's Guide to Pocket Calculators*, Wilson/Barnett Publishing, 1997; Thomas F. Haddock, *Collector's Guide to Personal Computers and Pocket Calculators*, Books Americana, 1993.

Collectors' Club: International Assoc. of Calculator Collectors, P.O. Box 70513, Riverside, CA 92513.

Addiator Duplex, brass 25.00

Belltown Antique Car Club Show, 30th Anniversary, August 4, 1996, "A World of Thanks," 2-1/4" x 3-1/2" 5.00

Bohn Instant 30.00

Bowmar 901B 70.00

Burger King/Nickelodeon, 1999, 3-1/2" l 5.00

Casio HL-809, 2-3/4" x 4-1/2", MIB 25.00

Commodore MM1 .... 75.00

Craig 4502 .... 55.00

Crown CL 130 .... 150.00

Donald Duck Calculator, Happy Birthday Donald Duck, 1934-84, Bradley Quartz Calculator, clock, 12" ruler, made in Hong Kong, mint in orig mailing box 35.00

Keystone 390 .... 55.00

Lloyds 303 .... 20.00

National 25.00

Radio Shack EC 425 .... 50.00

Royal Digital 3 .... 110.00

Wendy's, pen, pencil, and calculator set 6.00

❖ Calendar Plates

Many of these interesting plates were made as giveaways for local merchants. They were often produced by popular manufacturers of the day, such as Homer Laughlin and Royal China. Many have fanciful gold trim and interesting scenes. Expect to pay more for a plate that is sold in the area where it originated.

Periodical: *The Calendar*, 710 N Lake Shore Dr, Barrington, IL 60010.

1908, tiger kitten, "Souvenir of Weston, Vt.," scalloped edge, chip, 9" dia 43.00

1909, flying bird with 1909 sash, "Souvenir of Centralia, Ill.," 8-1/4" dia 58.00

1910, man fishing in stream, horseshoe design, "Compliments of The Parker-Hildebrand Co., Boscobel, Wis.," wear, 7-1/4" dia 35.00

1911, Abraham Lincoln portrait, "Compliments of Chas. Seepe & Sons, Peru, Ill.," 9" dia. 95.00

1911, "Three of Us," wishbone design with girl pushing baby buggy, boy walking beside her, "Compliments of H. F. Roehrich, Wausau, Wis.," hairline, 8-3/4" dia 65.00

1913, floral and holly designs, "Compliments of H. E. Yorks, Oriole, Pa.," cracks, 8-1/2" dia 32.00

1913, scene of Rainbow Falls, Yosemite Valley, "Compliments of M.J. Wiley, Bellwood, Pa.," scalloped gold rim, mkd "Carnation McNicol," 9-3/8" dia 88.00

1953, horses holding up a shield, woman with child, zodiac figures, "1953 Por Excellente 1953," Homer Laughlin, 10-1/8" dia 28.00

1955, floral wreath, Simplicity, Canonsburg, 10" dia 15.00

1960, zodiac figures, edge chip, 9-1/2" dia 6.50

1961 calendar plate, Royal China, $15.

1961, English cottage and bridge, "God Bless This House Through All This Year," Royal Staffordshire, 9" dia 18.50

1964, montage of New Jersey map, capitol dome, state seal and Revolutionary War soldier, "The State of New Jersey 1664 Tercentenary 1964," Kettlesprings Kilns, Alliance, OH, 10-1/8" dia 28.00

1969, Currier & Ives, green, Royal China 40.00

1971, cherubs playing and working, Wedgwood, 9-7/8" dia 32.00

1973, Gaston's Mill, Beaver Creek State Park (Columbiana County, OH), history of mill on back, 10-1/4" dia 25.00

1973, tin, scenes of bowling, football, water skiing and tennis, 10" dia 17.50

1980, Memory Plate by Alton Tobey, mural of memorable people and events, limited edition of 1,980 plates, Fairmont China, 12-1/4" dia 68.00

1984, Columbia space shuttle, "Hail Columbia," Spencer 28.00

1996, Wedgwood Peter Rabbit, 8" dia 32.50

❖ Calendars

With a brand new century, what better thing to collect than calendars? They often contain artwork by the best illustrators of the day, in addition to advertising, household hints, and necessary telephone numbers.

1910 calendar, Fike Brothers, Eglan Roller Mills, Eglan, W.Va., 22-1/4" x 14", $35.

Periodical: *The Calendar,* 710 N Lake Shore Dr, Barrington, IL 60010.

Collectors' Club: Calendar Collector Society, (send SASE to) American Resources, 18222 Flower Hill Way #299, Gaithersburg, MD 20879, www.collectors.org/ccs.

1901, Colgate, miniature, flower 20.00

1918, World War I, Swift's Premium, "The Girl I Leave Behind Me," soldier saying goodbye, illus by Haskell Coffin, sheets for January to March, pc missing, 15" x 8-1/4" 100.00

1928, Hartney Machine & Motor Works, titled "Discovered," two dogs pointing at prey in forest scene, 16-1/2" h, 10-1/2" w, full pad....................................55.00

1937, "Liberty, A Weekly for Everybody," 12 separate calendar prints, advertises Penna Refrigeration Co., Philadelphia, Pa., 12-1/2" x 7" 18.00

1952, "Myers Truck Lines, Knox City, Mo.," cowgirl and horse, unused, 20-3/4" x 12" 22.50

1963, "Seattle World's Fair," linen towel, 30" x 15-1/4"............38.00

1969, "Brothers United" by Alton S. Tobey, thumbtack holes in corners, 1 corner missing, some notes, 12" x 14" 20.00

1976, "Mischief Makers," 3 puppies and a basket, full calendar pad, Leo's Shoe Store, Rehrersburg, Pa., 16-1/2" x 10".............. 12.00

1977, hunting scenes, advertises Weaver & Son Food Market, Merriam, Kansas, unused. 12.00

1983, Chicago Cubs, by Jim Langford...................................... 9.50

1995, NBA Jam Session, 16-month, fair cond 3.00

❖ California Potteries

This catchall category includes small studio potteries located in California.

Will & George Climes
   Bluebird figurine, "Will & George, California" paper label, 3-1/4" h 40.00
   Robin figurine, "Will & George, California" paper label, 3" h 40.00

Freeman & McFarlin, elephant figurine, orig foil sticker, chips on ear and trunk, 6" h, 7-1/2" l 55.00

Hollydale, chop plate, gold-yellow, swirled edges, 11-1/2" dia. 22.00

Madeline Original, vase 35.00

Maurice of California, covered cigarette and 2 ashtrays, white with gold trim, 3 pcs 23.00

Santa Rosa, L.A. Potteries, plate, hp plums, 10-1/8" dia............. 18.00

TAE Artist's Barn, Fillmore, Calif., scouring pad, nest with red bird at side 15.00

Treasure Craft, ashtray 12.00

"Artist California" Gouder vase, 5" high, 9-1/2" wide, cracked, $12.

California Raisins figure, $3.

❖ California Raisins

Savvy collectors began stashing California Raisins as soon as they appeared. So far, their investments haven't paid off, but hopefully they are enjoying their collections.

Bank, 1987 6-3/4" h...................8.00
Figure
   Alotta Stile, purple boom box and pink boots, Hardee's 4th promotion, 1991, 2" h.........10.00
   Bass player with gray slippers, 2nd promotion, 1988, MIP, 3" h................. 11.00
   Drummer with black hat and yellow feather, 2nd commercial issue, 1988, 3" h 10.00
   F.F. Strings, blue guitar and orange sneakers, Hardee's 2nd promotion, 1988, 2" h
   ....7.00
   Hands, hands touching head with fingers pointed up, Hardee's 1st promotion, 1987, 2" h..................................7.00
   Hands, left hand up, right hand down, Post Raisin Bran issue, 1987, 3" h........................7.00
   Rollin' Rollo, yellow roller skates and hat marked H, Hardee's 2nd promotion, 1988, 2" h
   ....7.00

Saxophone, gold sax, no hat, Hardee's 1st promotion, 1987, 2" h.................7.00
Sunglasses, orange sunglasses with index fingers touching face, Hardee's 4th promotion, 1991, 2" h.......................10.00
Lunch box and thermos, "The California Raisins," plastic, blue ground 24.00
Pinback button, The California Raisins, 1-1/2" dia.....................4.00
Valentines, pack of 38 cards and teacher card, 1988, MIB 6.00

❖ Camark Pottery

Based in Camden, Arkansas, Camark Pottery was founded by Samuel Jack Carnes in 1926. The factory produced earthenware, art pottery, and decorative accessories. Several of the head potters had originally worked for Weller Pottery. The company remained in business until 1966.

Reference: David Edwin Gifford, *Collector's Guide to Camark Pottery*, Collector Books, 1997.

Collectors' Club: Arkansas Pottery Collectors Soc, P.O. Box 7617, Little Rock, AR 72217.

Basket, Iris pattern, hp in blue and green pastels, 9-1/2" h 185.00
Ewer, spiral design, #134, pastel blue, 6-3/4" h 39.00
Jam pot, black, 4-1/2" h............12.00
Pitcher, miniature, 3-1/2" h 19.00
Seal, black, with glass bowl that fits onto seal's nose, 11" h.....135.00
Strawberry planter, hanging, ribbed design, white, mkd N-50, 7" h
   ....45.00
Vase
   Dark green overflow glaze, 4-1/2" h..........................45.00
   Trophy-shape, black, 2-handle, 7-1/4" h..........................35.00
   Fan-shape, light blue, crack, 12-1/4" h, 16-1/2" w.......65.00
   Water Lily pattern, mkd A10K, orig paper label, 7-1/2" h
   ....195.00
Window box, green matte glaze, 2-3/4" h, 8" w 18.00

Heliotrope console bowl, Cambridge Glass, 10" diameter, $90.

❖ Cambridge Glass

Cambridge Glass Company of Cambridge, Ohio, was incorporated in 1901. Initially, the company made clear tableware, but they later expanded into colored, etched, and engraved glass. Over 40 different hues were produced in blown and pressed glass. Cambridge used five different marks, but not every piece was marked. The plant closed in 1954, with some of the molds being sold to the Imperial Glass Company in Bellaire, Ohio.

References: Gene Florence, *Elegant Glassware of the Depression Era*, 9th ed, Collector Books, 2000; National Cambridge Collectors, *Cambridge Glass Co.*, Cambridge, Ohio (reprint of 1930 catalog and supplements through 1934), Collector Books, 1976 (1996 value update); ——, *Cambridge Glass Co., Cambridge, Ohio, 1949 thru 1953* (catalog reprint), Collector Books, 1976 (1996 value update); ——, *Colors in Cambridge Glass*, Collector Books, 1984 (1993 value update); Bill and Phyllis Smith, *Cambridge Glass 1927–1929* (1986) and *Identification Guide to Cambridge Glass 1927–1929* (updated prices 1996).

Collectors' Club: National Cambridge Collectors, P.O. Box 416, Cambridge, OH 43725.

Cambridge pottery two-handled vase, yellow, green and brown high-gloss glaze, 8" high, $300.

For additional listings, see *Warman's Antiques & Collectibles* and *Warman's Glass.*

Bell, Blossom Time, crystal 95.00
Bowl and underplate, Wildflower, crystal, gold trim 385.00
Butter dish, cov, Gadroon, crystal 45.00
Candy dish, cov, Wildflower, crystal, 3 parts 20.00
Champagne, Wildflower, crystal 24.00
Cocktail
    Caprice, blue......................48.00
    Diane, crystal.....................15.00
    Cordial, Caprice, blue 124.00
Creamer and sugar
    Caprice, crystal..................35.00
    Cascade, emerald green ...35.00
Cup and saucer
    Decagon, pink....................10.00
    Martha Washington............45.00
Finger bowl, Adam, yellow 25.00
Flower frog, Draped Lady, amber 200.00
Goblet, Diane, crystal..............25.00
Iced tea tumbler, Lexington 18.00
Lemon plate, Caprice, blue, 5" dia 15.00
Mustard, cov, Farber Brothers, cobalt..................................50.00
Plate, Crown Tuscan, 7" dia 45.00

Relish, Mt. Vernon, 5 part, crystal 35.00
Server, center handle, Decagon, blue....................................20.00
Swan, crystal, sgd, 7" 35.00
Tumbler
    Adam, yellow, ftd................25.00
    Caprice, blue, 12-oz, ftd.....40.00
Vase, Songbird and Butterfly, #402, blue, 12" h 395.00
Wine, Caprice, crystal..............25.00

❖ Cameo Glass

Antique cameo glass is actually several layers of glass that have been cut in a cameo technique. Look for examples that are aesthetically pleasing, free of damage, and have a signature or paper label.

For additional listings, see *Warman's Antiques & Collectibles* and *Warman's Glass.*

Reproduction Alert.

Candy dish, heavy walled sq dish, mottled yellow and red, layered in dark green, etched trees by lake, cameo sgd "Daum Nancy," rim nick, central burst bubble 635.00
Salt, bucket form, two upright handles, frosted clear ground, cameo etched and enameled black tree-lined shore, distant ruins, gilt rim, sgd "Daum (cross) Nancy" in gilt on base, small rim chips, 1-3/8" h..................575.00
Vase
    3" h, miniature, oval body, frosted pink with opal amber, layered in olive green, cameo etched nasturtium blossoms, bud and leafy vines, sgd "Galle" at side..............500.00
    5" h, flared, pink mottled yellow overlaid ground, green layer etched as blossoms, buds and leafy stems, sgd "Arsall" in design.....................325.00
    5-1/4" h, quatraform body, pink and colorless, overlaid in maroon, etched berry and leaf dec, sgd "Legras" at side, rim nick..............................200.00
    6" h, shaped body, frosted pink, fiery amber and colorless, overlaid in butterscotch yellow, blossoming nasturtiums and leafy vines, sgd "Galle" at side..............................575.00

    6-3/4" h, transparent topaz, footed urn shape, faceted scalloped rim, deeply recessed etched panels of six repeating vertical units, base inscribed "Schneider LeVerre Francais" 250.00
    8" h, swelled pink oval body, overlaid in red, burgundy-black, cameo etched riverside scene, church and mountains on far shore, cameo sgd "Richard" at edge........600.00
    9-3/4" h, flared oval body, pink, white and colorless, overlaid in white, green and yellow, cameo etched seed clusters hanging from leafy branches, Asian-style "Galle" mark on side.............................950.00
    12" h, colorless oval body, overlaid in bright cobalt, faceted and etched, wide medial band, classical chariot scene, European....................750.00

❖ Cameos

Most jewelry collectors include a few cameos in their treasures. These carved beauties enchant buyers. When purchasing a shell-carved cameo, check that the settings are secure and original to the cameo. Hold the piece up to the light. If light passes through the carved layers, you're in luck, for if you can't see the image when held this way, it's probably a modern copy.

Bracelet, carved lava, various colored cameos, Victorian, 14k yg mounting.....................1,500.00

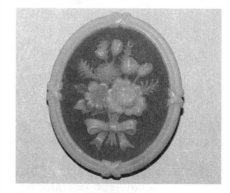

Avon plastic cameo brooch, 1-1/2" high, $5.

Brooch
　Rose, marquisette setting 125.00
　Scenic, house in center of oval
　　plaque, white gold setting
　　.....................................900.00
　Woman, flapper style hair-do, off-
　　shoulder dress, white gold
　　setting 600.00
　Woman, head and shoulders,
　　flowers in hair, Victorian,
　　carved agate, gold beadwork
　　frame, 18k yg setting...850.00
Compact, onyx cameo, marcasite
　ring, yellow enamel 425.00
Pendant
　Diamond shaped frame, cameo
　　with dancing figure, flowing
　　dress and scarf, 14k yg set-
　　ting 850.00
　Oval, woman's profile, flowers in
　　her hair, 14k gold setting
　　.....................................250.00
Ring, small woman's profile, dia-
　mond necklace ornament, white
　gold basket setting 1,250.00
Stickpin, carved shell with woman's
　profile, 14k yg mounting and pin
　...400.00

❖ Cameras and Accessories

Many cameras and their accessories and ephemera find their way to
flea markets. Carefully check com-
pleteness and condition. To some
extent, the type of lens or the special
features available on a particular
model determines value.

For additional listings, see *Warman's
Antiques & Collectibles* and *Warman's Americana & Collectibles*.

Zeiss Icon folding camera, $50.

Reference: James and Joan McKeown, *McKeown's Price Guide to
Antique & Classic Cameras, 1997-
1998*, 10th ed, Centennial Photo
Service, 1997.

Periodicals: *Camera Shopper*, P.O.
Box 1086, New Cannan, CT 06840;
Classic Camera, P.O. Box 1270,
New York, NY 10157-2078; *Shutter-
bug*, 5211 S Washington Ave, Titus-
ville, FL 32780.

Collectors' Clubs: American Photographic Historical Soc, 1150 Avenue
of the Americas, New York, NY
10036; American Society of Camera Collectors, 7952 Genesta Ave,
Van Nuys, CA 91406; International
Kodak Historical Soc, P.O. Box 21,
Flourtown, PA 19301; Leica Histori-
cal Soc of America, 7611 Dornoch
Ln, Dallas, TX 75248; Nikon Histori-
cal Soc, P.O. Box 3213, Munster, IN
46321; Zeiss Historical Soc, 300
Waxwing Dr, Cranbury, NJ 08512.
Accessories, Kodak Kodachrome
　box, bag and metal film can,
　1959...................................12.00
Beaker, clear glass, footed, "Use
　Only Kodak For Photography,"
　4" h...................................20.00
Camera
　Agfa Isolette 30.00
　Argus A3 ....20.00
　Argus Argoflex 75 ....10.00
　Canon Canonette...............45.00
　Kodak Box 620...................12.00
　Kodak Brownie Hawkeye.....5.00
　Kodak Brownie No. 2A, Model C
　　.....................................27.00
　Kodak Duoflex...................15.00
　Kodak Hawkeye No. 2C.......5.00
　Kodak Pocket Type 102, Model
　　96 ....135.00
　Kodak Tourist II 15.00
　Voigtlander Avus 60.00
　Wards AM 450 ....45.00
Watch, Kodak/Olympic souvenir
　watch, Kodak and Olympic logos
　on face, synthetic leather band
　..6.00

**For exciting collecting trends
and newly expanded areas look
for the following symbols:**

✪ Hot Topic

✫ New Warman's Listing

(May have been in another Warman's title.)

❖ Campbell's Soup

Joseph Campbell and Abram
Anderson started a canning plant in
Camden, New Jersey, in 1869, but it
wasn't until 1897 that the facility
began producing soup. The red-and-
white Campbell's label was introduced in 1898, and the gold medallion that graced the company's cans
until just recently was awarded in
1900. The pudgy, round-faced
Campbell Kids were introduced in
1904, but their contemporary phy-
siques are slimmer and trimmer.

Reference: David and Micki Young,
*Campbell's Soup Collectibles from A
to Z*, Krause Publications, 1998.

Collectors' Clubs: Campbell Kids
Collectors, 649 Bayview Dr., Akron,
OH 44319; Campbell's Soup Collec-
tor Club, 414 Country Lane Ct.,
Wauconda, IL 60084.
Baby dish, shows Campbell's Kids,
　7-1/2" dia 55.00
Bank
　Tin, contains 6" plastic doll,
　　1998, MIP, 7-3/8" h 15.00
　Tin, 125th anniversary, Tomato
　　Soup, 4" h...................... 5.00
Book, *The Campbell's Kids at Home*
　by Alma S. Lach, Rand McNally
　Elf Book, 1954, story by Alma S.
　Lach, minor wear 35.00
Clock, wall, schoolhouse type, boy
　and girl holding soup can, 1983
　..................................... 120.00
Cookbook, *Easy Ways to Good
　Meals*, softcover, 1951...... 18.00
Novelty radio, tomato soup can
　shape, orig box 45.00

**Metal Campbell's tray, 9" x 14",
$15.**

Pennant, felt, "Campbell's Soups," white text, red ground, 1 shows child in rocker, 1 shows child with pail, 21" h, 8" w, pr ...253.00

Poster, Campbell's Kids behind board promoting weekly grocer's specials, can of soup in lower-left corner, tears, framed, 30" h, 23" w 121.00

Watch, Campbell's Kid in green dress with hat and mirror, adult size, dated 1982................61.00

❖ Candlesticks

Designed to keep a burning candle upright, candlesticks can be found in all shapes and sizes at flea markets.

Reference: Gene Florence, *Glass Candlesticks of the Depression Era*, Collector Books, 2000.

Brass

　　Chamberstick, side pushup, saucer handle, English, dents, 4-1/2" h 88.00

　　Queen Anne, ring-turned base, boldly turned column, orig pushup, 12" h, pr.........275.00

　　Ring-turned, stepped base, baluster stem, polished, 8-1/2'" h.......................247.50

　　Victorian, beehive, pushup, mkd England, 6" h, pr 165.00

Glass

　　Black, 2-handle, round base, 3-1/2" h, pr 35.00

　　Crystal, L.E. Smith, 4-1/2" h, pr 32.50

Green Vaseline glass, 3" h, pr 45.00

Milk glass, twisting form, square base, 6-1/2" high, pair, $25.

Milk glass, Dolphin pattern, Westmoreland, 4-1/2" h, pr 45.00

Porcelain, ivory, gold accents, single flower in middle, French, pr 175.00

Pottery

　　Fulper chamberstick, Wisteria glaze, 7-1/4" h 176.00

　　Rookwood, cactus flower form, mottled gray over pink matte glaze, 1927, 3-3/4" h, pr 209.00

Sheet iron, hog scraper, round base, tubular shaft, ejector mechanism on side, ejector knob stamped "HYD," minor rust, 6-1/2" h 190.00

Tin, Tindeco, orig stenciling, 6-3/4" h, pr.........................65.00

✿ Candlewick

Imperial pattern No. 400, known as Candlewick, was introduced in 1936 and was an instant hit with American consumers. The line was continuously produced until 1982. After Imperial declared bankruptcy, several of the molds were sold, and other companies began producing this pattern, often in different colors.

References: Gene Florence, *Elegant Glassware of the Depression Era*, 8th ed, Collector Books, 1999; National Imperial Glass Collector's Soc, *Imperial Glass Encyclopedia, Vol. I: A–Cane*, The Glass Press, 1995; —, *Imperial Glass Catalog Reprint*, Antique Publications, 1991; Virginia R. Scott, *Collector's Guide to Imperial Candlewick*, 4th ed, self-published, no date; Mary M. Wetzel-Tomalka, *Candlewick: The Jewel of Imperial, Book I*, and *Book II*, 1995; —, *Candlewick, The Jewel of Imperial, Price Guide '99 and More*, 1998, self-published.

Periodicals: *Glasszette*, National Imperial Glass Collector's Soc, P.O. Box 534, Bellaire, OH 43528; *The Candlewick Collector Newsletter*, National Candlewick Collector's Club, 275 Milledge Terrace, Athens, GA 30606.

Oval Candlewick relish dish, 4-5/8" x 8-1/2", $15.

Collectors' Clubs: National Candlewick Collector's Club, 275 Milledge Terrace, Athens, GA 30606; National Imperial Glass Collector's Soc, P.O. Box 534, Bellaire, OH 43528. Check with these organizations for local clubs in your area.

Reproduction Alert.

For additional listings, see *Warman's Americana & Collectibles* and *Warman's Glass*.

Ashtray, 6" dia........................... 8.00

Basket, turned-up sides, applied handle, 6-1/2" 35.00

Bonbon, #51H, heart shape, handle, 6"............................... 35.00

Bowl, #106B, belled, 12" dia... 70.00

Bud vase, 87F, fan, floral cutting, 8-1/2" h 90.00

Butter dish, 1/4-pound 25.00

Cake plate, sterling silver pedestal 65.00

Canape plate, #36 .... 12.00

Candy dish, cov, 5-1/2" dia 35.00

Celery tray, #105, 13" 40.00

Champagne, saucer 20.00

Cigarette holder, eagle........... 95.00

Coaster 12.00

Compote, 4 bead stem, 8" dia 65.00

Creamer and sugar, matching tray 25.00

Cup and saucer, #37, coffee... 14.00

Deviled egg tray, 11-1/2" dia ... 95.00

Jelly server, 1 bead stem, 2 bead cover 50.00

Marmalade jar, cov 60.00

Pastry tray, #68D, floral cutting, 11-1/2" l............................ 80.00

Plate, beaded edge

　　6" dia 6.50

　　8-1/2" dia 12.00

　　10-1/4" dia 32.00

Relish, #55, 4 part.................. 30.00

Salt and pepper shakers, #247, pr 45.00

Sherbet, low, #19, 5-oz............ 18.00
Tidbit server, 2 tiers 55.00
Tumbler, water......................... 30.00
Vase, #87C, crimped, plain top, 8" h
.... 50.00

❖ Candy Containers

Figural glass candy containers have been a part of childhood since 1876, when they were first introduced at the Centennial Exposition in Philadelphia. These interesting glass containers often commemorated historical events. Candy containers were also made of papier-mache, cardboard, and tin. All are highly collectible and eagerly sought at flea markets.

References: *Candy Containers*, L-W Book Sales, 1996; Douglas M. Dezso, J. Lion Poirier & Rose D. Poirier, *Collector's Guide to Candy Containers*, Collector Books, 1997; George Eikelberner and Serge Agadjanian, *Complete American Glass Candy Containers Handbook*, revised and published by Adele L. Bowden, 1986; Jennie Long, *Album of Candy Containers*, vol. I (1978), vol. II (1983), self-published.

Collectors' Club: Candy Container Collectors of America, P.O. Box 352, Chelmsford, MA 01824-0352.

For additional listings, see *Warman's Antiques & Collectibles* and *Warman's Americana & Collectibles*.

Lantern candy container, J.C. Crosetti Co., glass with metal closure, $25

Reproduction Alert.
Battleship, glass, orig cardboard closure, printed "Victory Glass Inc."
.... 48.00
Black cat, with pumpkin, papier-mache, German 75.00
Boat, clear glass, 5-1/4" l 35.00
Boot, papier-mache, red and white
.... 24.00
Bulldog, glass, orig paint 90.00
Candyland Express, pull toy train, Loft's Candy, N.Y., diecut litho and cardboard train, orig string, 9" l 60.00
Disney Rocketeer, plastic, full, MIB
.... 8.00
Dog, glass, blue 15.00
Duck, cardboard, nodding head
.... 18.50
Fire hydrant, Fleer Co., Philadelphia, 3" h 5.00
Football, tin, German 18.00
Hat, milk glass, screw-on tin brim, 2-7/8" w 35.00
Hen on nest, glass, 2-pc, Millstein
.... 15.00
Lantern, large, glass and metal
.... 35.00
Locomotive #888, clear glass, 4" l
.... 35.00
Model T, glass 24.00
Owl, glass, stylized feathers, painted, screw-on cap 90.00
Pistol, glass 30.00
Pumpkin man, bisque 45.00
Rabbit, papier-mache, pulling basket, pasteboard wheels 55.00
Rooster, glass, screw-on cap
.... 125.00
Suitcase
    Cardboard, The Leader Novelty Candy Co., 2-1/2" h, 2-3/4" w
    .... 35.00
    Cardboard, Round the World Candy and Toy Novelty, Confectioners Trading Corp., Brooklyn, 1936, 2-3/4" h
    .... 38.00
    Glass with wire handle, 2-3/8" h, 3-5/8" w 79.00
Telephone, glass, candlestick type
.... 50.00
Turkey, chalk, metal feet, German
.... 35.00
Uncle Sam, Fanny Farmer, some wear, 9-1/4" h 90.00
Witch, bisque 40.00

❖ Cap Guns

"Bang! Bang!" was the cry of many a youngster playing Cowboys and Indians. Whether you were the good guy or the bad guy, you needed a reliable six-shooter. The first toy cap gun was produced in the 1870s and was made of cast iron. It remained the material of choice until around World War II, when paper, rubber, glass, steel, tin, wood and even zinc were used. By the 1950s, diecast metal and plastic were being used.

References: Rudy D'Angelo, *Cowboy Hero Cap Pistols*, Antique Trader Books, 1997; James L. Dundas, *Cap Guns with Values*, Schiffer Publishing, 1996; Jerrell Little, *Price Guide to Cowboy Cap Guns and Guitars*, L-W Book Sales, 1996; Jim Schlever, *Backyard Buckaroos: Collecting Western Toy Guns*, Books Americana/Krause Publications, 1996.

Periodical: *Toy Gun Collectors of America Newsletter*, 312 Sterling Way, Anaheim, CA 92807.

Collectors' Club: Toy Gun Collectors of America, 3009 Oleander Ave., San Marcos, CA 92069.
Buck'n Bronc......................... 115.00
Buffalo Bill, J.&E. Stevens, repeating, 1920s, orig box 320.00
Champion, Kilgore, brown grips, 1960s, 11" l 70.00
Cheyenne Shooter, Hamilton .. 70.00
Cowboy, Hubley, dull nickel, 1950s, 11-1/2" l 90.00
Fanner 50, Mattel
    Impala grips, c1962, 10-1/2" l
    .... 55.00

Hubley cap gun, plastic grips, $55.

Stag grips, c1959, 10-1/2" l
................................210.00
Flintlock, double barrel, Hubley,
amber color, 9" l 25.00
Gene Autry .44, Leslie-Hentry,
1950s, 11" l.....................165.00
Invincible, Kilgore, cast iron, c1938,
5" l....................................35.00
Maverick
Long barrel, black and white
grips, 1960s, 11" l........280.00
Short barrel, nickel finish, new
white grips, 1960s, 9" l..55.00
Roy Rogers, Classy, gold grips, 10" l
....435.00
Texan, Hubley, 1940s, black grips,
9-1/2" l............................130.00
Wagon Trail, white grips, 9" l
................................175.00

❖ Cape Cod by Avon

This ruby red pattern was an instant hit with Avon lovers. Today, many pieces can be found at flea markets. Remember that this is a mass-produced pattern and examples in very good condition are available.

Bread and butter set, orig box
................................25.00
Candlesticks, pr
2-1/4" h, grooved pattern ...20.00
8-3/4" h, one with Bird of Para-
dise, one with Patchwork
Cologne.........................25.00
Creamer and sugar 22.00
Cruet, 5-3/4" h 12.50
Dessert plate 8.00
Goblet..8.00
Luncheon plate........................10.00

Cape Cod salt and pepper shakers, 4-1/2" high, pair, $15.

Napkin rings, 1-3/4" d, set of 4
................................45.00
Salad plate.................................7.00
Salt and pepper shakers, 4-1/2" h, pr
................................18.00
Sauce boat, 8" l.......................55.00
Vase, ftd, 8" h 22.00
Water pitcher, 48-oz, 7-1/2" h
................................40.00
Wine goblet...............................8.00
Wine set, 10" decanter, 4 matching
wine tumblers 35.00

❖ Care Bears

Some people wear their hearts on their sleeves. Care Bears wear them (and other symbols representing personality traits) on their tummies. Kids of all ages have welcomed these lovable creatures into their homes—and their collections—since American Greetings Corp. first introduced them in 1982.

Bank, plush Love-A-Lot Bear, miss-
ing plug, wear 2.50
Book
Caring is What Counts, hard-
cover, worn.......................1.50
*Bedtime Bears Book of Bedtime
Poems*, hardcover, loose
binding.............................0.50
Card game, Which Bear's Where,
bends................................2.50
Comb, folding, Tenderheart, MIP
................................3.00
Dolls, plush
Baby Tugs Bear #2 ....10.00
Bedtime Bear, 18" 12.50
Birthday Bear, worn, 18" 6.00
Braveheart Lion, 13" 9.00
Champ Bear #1, wear, 13".15.00
Champ Bear #2, 13" 22.00
Champ Bear, tag removed, 6"
................................7.00
Cheer Bear, 13" 7.00
Cheer Bear Cub 18.00
Friend Bear, wear, 13" 5.00
Love-A-Lot Bear, 13"............6.50
Dolls, poseable
Baby Hugs #2 ....4.25
Goodluck Bear 2.50
Glass, Tenderheart Bear, Pizza Hut
................................8.00
Mug, plastic, Cheer Bear with pink
"hat" lid................................3.25
Rattle, clear ball with Tenderheart
inside 3.50

Sticker book
Brio, 28 stickers, dated 1994,
marker on cover 3.00
Caring and Sharing #1, Pizza
Hut, stickers in place, some
coloring.......................... 2.00
Panini, 3 stickers missing.... 5.00
Swim ring, Coleco, "Splash Into Fun"
.... 4.50

❖ Carlton Ware

Wiltshow and Robinson first manufactured this brightly colored pottery at their Charlton Works, Stoke-on-Trent, factory around 1890. In 1957, the company's name was changed to Carlton Ware, Ltd.

Collectors' Club: Carlton Ware Collectors International, P.O. Box 161, Sevenoaks, Kent TN15 6GA England.

Basket, Waterlily, green, 3-1/2" h
.... 125.00
Bowl
Muffin bowl, Buttercup, yellow
.... 25.00
Hydrangea, blue, 9-3/4" dia
.... 125.00
Condiment set, Crinoline Lady
.... 225.00
Cruet egg set, Apple Blossom, yel-
low, 7 pcs 150.00
Cream and sugar, Foxglove, green
.... 65.00
Cup and saucer, Foxglove, green
.... 80.00
Honey pot with lid, Wild Rose, yellow
.... 89.00
Jam dish with knife, Buttercup, pink,
orig box, knife glued........ 125.00
Knife, Wild Rose, green 55.00
Plate
Buttercup, pink, chip, 6-1/2" dia
.... 110.00
Buttercup, yellow, 7" x 6-1/2"
.... 85.00
Hydrangea, green, 11-1/4" dia
.... 165.00
Reamer, Buttercup, yellow.... 195.00
Sauceboat and stand, Buttercup,
yellow.............................. 150.00
Spoon
Raspberry.......................... 60.00
Wild Rose, green.............. 60.00
Teapot
Foxglove, green, small chip
.... 425.00
Waterlily, green, 2-cup..... 395.00

❖ Carnival Chalkware

Brightly painted plaster-of-Paris figures given away as prizes at carnivals continue to capture the eye of collectors. Most of these figures date from the 1920s through the 1960s.

Ashtray
    Collie, 8-3/4" h, ashtray 3-1/2"
        dia 22.00
    German shepherd, dated 1936,
        paint loss, 8-1/2" h 20.00
Bank, dog, long ears, yellow bow tie,
    wear, 12" h 32.00
Figure
    Cocker spaniel, reclining.... 15.00
    Cocker spaniel, sitting, some glitter, 11" h 43.00
    Collie, black and white, some glitter, base chips, 11-1/2" h
        .... 40.00
    Elephant by tree stump, 3 chips, 6" h 15.00
    Horse, flat back side, 5-1/2" h
        .... 15.00
    Poodle, sitting, 3-1/2" h...... 10.00
    Scottie, 2 dogs side by side, chips, 9-1/4" h 85.00
    Tex, cowboy, 11" h 19.00

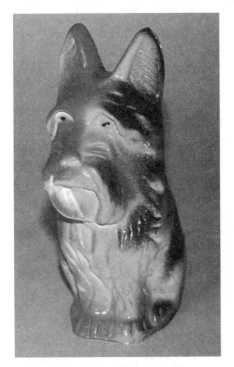

Chalkware dog, 6-1/2" high, $15.

Blackberry Wreath carnival glass dish, 7" diameter, $80.

⊛ Carnival Glass

Carnival glass can be found in many different colors, including marigold, purples, greens, blues, reds, and pastels, all with a metallic-looking sheen or iridescence. Many different manufacturers created the hundreds of patterns

References: Carl O. Burns, *Collector's Guide to Northwood Carnival Glass*, L-W Book Sales, 1994; —, *Dugan and Diamond Carnival Glass, 1909-1931*, Collector Books, 1998; —, *Imperial Carnival Glass*, Collector Books, 1996 (1999 value update); Dave Doty, *A Field Guide to Carnival Glass*, Antique Trader Publications, 1998; Bill Edwards and Mike Carwile, *Standard Encyclopedia of Carnival Glass*, 7th ed, Collector Books, 2000; —, *Standard Encyclopedia of Carnival Glass Price Guide*, 12th ed, Collector Books, 2000; Diane C. Rosington, *Carnival Glass Club Commemoratives, 1964-1999*, self-published, 2000; Glen and Steven Thistlewood, *Carnival Glass, The Magic & The Mystery*, Schiffer Publishing, 1998; Margaret and Ken Whitmyer, *Fenton Art Glass: 1907-1939*, Collector Books, 1996 (1999 value update).

Periodical: *Network, PageWorks*, P.O. Box 2385, Mt. Pleasant, SC 29465.

Collectors' Clubs: American Carnival Glass Assoc, 9621 Springwater Ln, Miamisburg, OH 45342; Canadian Carnival Glass Assoc, 107 Montcalm Dr., Kitchner, Ontario N2B 2R4 Canada; Collectible Carnival Glass Assoc, 3103 Brentwood Circle, Grand Island, NE 68801; Heart of America Carnival Glass Assoc, 43-5 W 78th St, Prairie Village, KS 66208; International Carnival Glass Assoc, P.O. Box 306, Mentone, IN 46539. Many clubs have regional chapters. Contact the national organization for information about a club in your area.

For additional listings, see *Warman's Antiques & Collectibles* and *Warman's Glass*.

Reproduction Alert.

Bonbon
    Fruits & Flowers, purple 85.00
    Grape & Cable, blue.......... 90.00
Bowl
    Fruits & Flowers, amethyst, 7-1/4" dia 70.00
    Grape & Cable, ftd, pastel, 7-1/2" dia................................ 70.00
    Holly & Berry, peach opalescent
        ....110.00
    Peacock & Grape, marigold, 9" dia................................ 50.00
    Peacock at Urn, green, 10-1/2" dia............................ 250.00
    Raindrops, peach opalescent, 8-3/4" dia 85.00
    Strawberry, amethyst, 8-3/4" dia
        .... 85.00
    Vintage Leaf, green, 7-1/2" dia
        .... 72.00
Bushel basket, white, Northwood
    .... 120.00
Calling card tray, Pond Lily, white
    .... 25.00
Candy dish, Drapery, white ... 125.00
Compote, Petals, amethyst, 7-1/2" x 3-3/4" 45.00
Hat, Luster Flute, amethyst..... 32.00
Ice cream bowl, Trout Fly, marigold, satin finish...................... 525.00
Miniature compote, Blackberry, marigold.................................. 40.00
Mug, 3-1/2" h
    Orange Tree, aqua 60.00
    Singing Birds, amethyst .. 215.00
Pickle dish, Poppy, blue.......... 45.00
Pitcher, 9" h, Butterfly & Berry, marigold 265.00
Plate, Vintage, green, 7-1/2" dia
    .... 140.00
Punch cup, Fashion, marigold 24.00

Rose bowl
Double Stem, domed foot, peach opalescent..................160.00
Grape Delight, white..........95.00
Sauce, Windmill, purple...........55.00
Tankard pitcher, Paneled Dandelion, marigold..................400.00
Tumble-up, Smooth Rays, marigold..................60.00
Tumbler
Butterfly & Berry, marigold..................30.00
Concave Diamond, Celeste blue..................30.00
Paneled Dandelion, marigold..................48.00
Raspberries, amethyst.......75.00
Vase
Fine Rib, powder blue, 10" h..................60.00
Ripple, amethyst, 11" h....110.00

❖ Cartoon Characters

They've entertained generations for decades and now collectors seek them out at flea markets. The charm and humor of cartoon characters light up collections across the country.

References: Ted Hake, *Hake's Price Guide To Character Toys,* Gemstone Publishing, 2000; Jim Harmon, *Radio & TV Premiums,* Krause Publications, 1997.

Periodical: *Frostbite Falls Far-Flung Flier* (Rocky & Bullwinkle), P.O. Box 39, Macedonia, OH 44056.

Collectors' Clubs: Betty Boop Fan Club, 6025 Fullerton Ave, Apt 2, Buena Park, CA 90621; Peanuts Collector Club, 539 Sudden Valley, Bellingham, WA 98226; Pogo Fan Club, 6908 Wentworth Ave S, Richfield, MN 55423; Popeye Fan Club, Ste 151, 5995 Stage Rd, Barlette, TN 38184; R.F. Outcault Soc, 103 Doubloon Dr, Slidell, LA 70461.

Airplane, Quick Draw McGraw..................365.00
Bank, Felix the Cat, tin...........55.00
Big Little Book, *Andy Panda and The Mad Dog Mystery,* Whitman #1431..................40.00
Birthday card, Ziggy, unused.....1.00
Box, Andy Gump Sunshine Biscuits, cardboard, 5" x 3" x 2".....425.00

Plastic Bugs Bunny mug, $12.50.

Bubble gum wrapper, Popeye, 1981, 5-1/2" x 5-1/2"..................45.00
Charm, Shmoo, bright silver-colored plastic, 1940s..................18.00
Colorforms, Huckleberry Hound, 1960, MIB..................75.00
Coloring set, Felix the Cat, Color By Number Pictures, orig colored pencils, Hasbro, unopened pack..................100.00
Comic book, *Popeye,* large size format, 1972, 14" x 11"..........15.00
Cookie jar
Bugs Bunny..................40.00
Felix the Cat..................50.00
Doll
Archie, cloth, 16" h.............30.00
Felix the Cat..................8.00
Snuffy Smith, stuffed felt, 17" h..................175.00
Figure
Archie, Sirocco, painted brown military uniform and hat, 1944..................24.00
Popeye, jointed wood, 4-1/2" h, copyright K.F.S...........145.00
Game
Barney Google an' Snuffy Smith, Milton Bradley, 1963, orig box..................42.00
Underdog, 1964, missing one decal..................65.00
Harmonica, Underdog.............35.00
Music box, Betty Boop as cowgirl..................45.00
Napkin holder, Popeye, ceramic..................15.00
Nodder, Moon Mullins, mkd "Made in Germany"..................65.00

Pencil holder, plastic, figural, Garfield..................2.00
Perfume set, Little Lulu..........85.00
Pinback button
High Admiral Cigarettes, Yellow Kid..................35.00
Member Archie Club, 1-1/2" dia..................20.00
New Funnies, Andy Panda, black, white, red and bright yellow..................25.00
Ring, Little Lulu..................40.00
Salt and pepper shakers, pr
Betty Boop..................15.00
Bugs Bunny and Taz.........15.00
Felix the Cat..................20.00
Sparkler, Yellow Kid........275.00
Talking doll
Beanie (Beanie & Cecil), 8-1/2" h, orig box..................415.00
Bugs Bunny, Mattel, seven phrases, 1971............155.00
Target set, Felix the Cat, 2-in-1, gun and orig stoppers, orig box..................175.00
Teapot, Betty Boop.................35.00
Thermos, Casper the Friendly Ghost..................75.00
Vase, Betty Boop..................30.00
Wristwatch, Smitty, gray aged dial, black, white, red and green figure, New Haven Clock Co., orig case, c1935..................250.00

❖ Cash Registers

One of the necessities of any store is a good cash register. However, with today's electronic gadgets, the large styles of yesterday have been cast aside. Collectors gather up these units, restore them, and then enjoy their purchase.

Collectors' Club: Cash Register Collectors Club of America, P.O. Box 20534, Dayton, OH 45420

National, candy store size
Ornate cast detail, milk glass shelf on front, 21-1/4" x 10-1/4" x 16"..................675.00
Polished brass, cast detail, milk glass shelf, oak base has 1" chip on corner, minor edge chips on glass, top banner missing, 17" x 10-1/4" x 16"..................715.00

National
    Model 5 .... 2,200.00
    Model 313, small, emb brass,
        marble ledge, 17" h, missing
        "Amount Purchased" mar-
        quee, restored............. 750.00
Wooden, loose money in back
    .... 125.00

❖ Cassidy, Hopalong

Hopalong Cassidy was a cowboy hero who successfully made the leap from movies to radio to television. Hoppy was also a master at self-promotion and did a lot of advertising, as did many other early cowboy heroes.

Collectors' Clubs: Friends of Hopalong Cassidy Fan Club, 6310 Friendship Dr, New Concord, OH 43762; Westerns & Serials Fan Club, Route 1, Box 103, Vernon Center, MN 56090-9744.

Reference: Joseph J. Caro, *Hopalong Cassidy Collectibles*, Cowboy Collector Publications, 1997.

Bank, figural, blue plastic, 4-1/2" h
    .... 330.00
Bicycle, Rollfast Hopalong Cassidy
    bicycle 1,100.00
Boots, rubber, with spurs, black with
    white trim, Goodyear Rubber
    Co., size 3 .... 250.00
Bread label, Bond Bread 100.00
Cap gun, Schmidt, black grips, gold
    plating.............................. 425.00
Cookie jar, Hopalong and Topper,
    Happy Memories Collectibles
    .... 275.00
Director's chair, Bar 20, child's, small
    tear on seat 275.00
Paper dolls, Hopalong Cassidy
    Paper Dolls and Punch Out
    Ranch Set, uncut............. 305.00

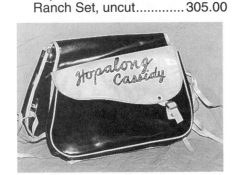

Hopalong Cassidy vinyl saddle-bags, $1,300.

Play set, Hopalong Cassidy Western
    Frontier Set, MIB 550.00
Photograph, autographed, 5" x 7"
    .... 90.00
Radio, Arvin, Model 441T, red, orig
    lariat-like antenna 1,225.00
Sweater, child's, green cardigan,
    1955, repair 75.00
Wristwatch, orig box with saddle,
    U.S. Time......................... 260.00

❖ Cast Iron

Cast iron has long been a favorite metal for creating durable goods, such as cooking utensils, farm implements, and tools.

Periodicals: *Cast Iron Cookware News*, 28 Angela Ave, San Anselmo, CA 94960; *Kettles n' Cookware*, Drawer B, Perrysburg, NY 14129.

Collectors' Club: Griswold & Cast Iron Cookware Assoc, 54 Macon Ave, Asheville, NC 28801.

Boot scraper, scroll ends, green
    granite base..................... 110.00
Christmas tree stand, openwork
    base with trees and stars, orig
    green paint, 2-1/2" h, 7-3/4" sq
    .... 75.00

Cast-iron boot scraper, lyre design, 13-1/2" x 9", $75.

Curling iron, 10-1/4" l 22.00
Dutch oven, #8, Griswold, painted
    black 55.00
Egg beater, Dover, wooden knob,
    10-1/4" l 25.00
Lemon squeezer, porcelain insert,
    1868 patent date............... 58.00
Muffin tin, hearts motif, 8 cups
    .... 110.00
Match safe, double holders, 4" h,
    4" w................................. 125.00
Skillet, #8, Griswold 38.00
Snow bird, 6" wingspan 40.00
Trivet, horseshoe shape, "Good
    Luck To All Who Use This
    Stand," 1870 patent date,
    repainted, 8" l, 4-1/2" w..... 20.00

Reproduction cast-iron building stars.

Buyer Beware!

A lot of people are seeing stars these days. That's not a good thing!

Folks haven't been bonking their noggins more than usual, causing the cartoon-like stars that are associated with being rendered half-unconscious. Instead, they're seeing reproduction cast-iron building stars.

It seems these architectural midgets are everywhere. It only took a few showing up in illustrations in decorator magazines for people to go crazy for the things. Trouble is, many are being offered on the secondary market, where they're being represented as old. Your socks are probably older than these things.

The original building stars were used on the outside of 19th-century structures, tying off the ends of metal supports that helped stabilize the structure.

There's nothing wrong with buying the newer versions, providing you know what you're getting and the price is reasonable. How do you tell the new from the old? Most of the contemporary examples have been intentionally rusted. New rust has a bright-orange color, compared to the darker rust found on an object that has aged slowly over a long period of time.

❖ Catalina Pottery

Catalina Pottery is one of the California potteries that has begun attracting collector interest in recent years. The company was founded in 1927 on Santa Catalina Island. Dinnerware production was added in 1931. In 1937, Gladding, McBean & Co. bought the firm and closed the island plant.

Ashtray, fish, blue 60.00
Bowl, low bowl, light orange exterior, turquoise interior, 10" x 6"
.... 25.00
Cigarette box, covered, horse's head, ivory 475.00
Cup and saucer, green 60.00
Head vase, terra cotta and turquoise
.... 185.00
Vase
    Fan-shape, tan and green, 9" h
    .... 125.00
    Fluted design, white, 10" h
    .... 225.00
    Shell design, white exterior, light-blue interior, 7-1/4" h 75.00

❖ Catalogs

Old trade and merchandise catalogs are sought by collectors. They are sometimes the best source of information about what a company produced.

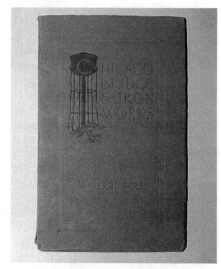

1912 catalog, *Chicago Bridge & Iron Works: Water Towers*, $20.

Reference: Ron Barlow and Ray Reynolds, *Insider's Guide To Old Books, Magazines, Newspapers and Trade Catalogs*, Windmill Publishing, 1996.

For additional listings, see *Warman's Antiques & Collectibles* and *Warman's Americana & Collectibles.*

Avon, spiral-bound, 169 pgs, 1950s
.... 30.00
Baker Furniture Co., Holland, Mich., 48 pgs, 1947 .... 38.00
Bausch & Lomb Optical Co., Rochester, N.Y., 122 pgs, 1919
.... 55.00
Boggs & Clarke Mfgrs., Syracuse, N.Y., 16 pgs, 1889 .... 15.00
Boston Lightning Rod Co., Boston, Mass., 22 pgs, 1915 .... 38.00
Buffalo Manufacturing Co., Buffalo, N.Y., 24 pgs, 1901 .... 19.00
Burgess Plant & Seed Co., Galesburg, Wis., 82 pgs, 1944 .... 10.00
Butler Brothers, St. Louis, 50th anniversary catalog, May 1927, 420 pgs 40.00
Century Furniture Co., Grand Rapids, Mich., 40 pgs, 1931 ..... 50.00
Diamond Dyes, Burlington, Vt., 83 pgs, 1931 .... 18.00
Fisher Price, 27 pgs, 1963 .... 50.00
Geneva Wagon Co., Geneva, N.Y., 44 pgs, 1905, worn 75.00
George Delker Co., Henderson, Ky., buggies catalog, 40 pgs, 1926
.... 75.00
Hartz Mountain Products, 32 pgs, 1933 .... 18.00
Henry Field Seed & Nursery Co., spring catalog, 126 pgs, 1973
.... 10.00
John Deere Co., Chicago, Ill., 24 pgs, 1970 .... 14.00
Jordan, Marsh & Co., Boston, Mass., 254 pgs, 1895 .... 33.00
Kirsch Manufacturing Co., Diturgis, Mich., 18 pgs, 1922 .... 13.00
Milton Bradley Co., Boston, Mass., 124 pgs, 1923 .... 22.00
Montgomery Ward & Co., Fall & Winter, 1,144 pgs, 1956 ..... 32.00
New England Power Assoc., Boston, Mass., 38 pgs, 1927 .... 40.00
Oakes Poultry and Hog Equipment Catalog, Tipton, Ind., 60 pgs, 1957 .... 7.50
Reliable Incubators, Quincy, Ill., 1896 .... 27.00

Union Furniture Co., Rockford, Ill., 28 pgs, 1921 .... 45.00
Winchester Western, 31 pgs, 1962
.... 15.00
F. H. Woodruff & Sons, Milford, Conn., garden vegetables, 44 pgs, 1927 .... 10.00

❖ Cat Collectibles

It's purrfectly obvious—cat collectors love their cats, whether they are live and furry or an inanimate collectible. More often than not, collectors purchase objects that resemble their favorite furry friends.

Collectors' Clubs: Cat Collectors, 33161 Wendy Dr, Sterling Heights, MI 48310; Cat's Meow Collectors' Club, 2163 Great Trails Dr, Wooster, OH 44691, www. catsmeow.com.

Reproduction Alert.

For additional listings, see *Warman's Americana & Collectibles.*

Avon bottle, Kitten's Hideaway, white kitten in brown basket, 1974 8.00
Bookends, ceramic, black cats, gold trim, mkd "Japan," c1950 .. 30.00
Bookmark, figural cat face, celluloid, reverse mkd "don't kiss me," 22" l green cord, c1920, 1-3/4" w x 1-3/4" h 65.00
Comic book, *Felix the Cat*, All Pictures Comics, 1945 .... 50.00
Cup and saucer, child size, cat on pussy willow twig, mkd "Made in Japan" 12.00
Figure
    Cat Band, ceramic, 6 white cats in blue jackets, gold instruments, Japan 60.00

M.A. Hadley pottery cat, 5" high, $25.

Country Christmas, cats among presents, Lowell Davis, 1984 ......525.00
Pitcher, figural, tail forms handle, clear glass, incised "WMF Germany," 8-1/4" h 25.00
Planter, brown and white cat, blue bow, standing upright, one paw raised 12.00
Print, French artist, H. Gobin, titled "Le Tigre," 1840.................80.00
Record album, Classical Cats, London Records, 78 RPM, 1982 ....20.00
Salt and pepper shakers, black and white figures, blue bows, porcelain, mkd "Czechoslovakia," pr 18.50
Teapot, figural, Norcrest..........40.00
Tea towel, linen.......................10.00
Thermometer, hammered aluminum, white metal cat on base 45.00
Toy, tin, yellow and red cat, red ball and wheels, mkd "MAR Toys Made in USA," 6" l...........115.00
Wall plaque, Kitty Kat Family, Miller Studios, chalkware, orig box, unused 30.00

❖ Celluloid

The first commercially successful form of plastic, celluloid has been a part of our world since the 1870s. Modern plastics have proved to be safer and easier to manufacture, so items made from celluloid are becoming quite collectible.

For additional information, see *Warman's Antiques & Collectibles,* and *Warman's Americana & Collectibles.*

Animal, horse, 7" l, cream, brown highlights, hp eyes, marked with VCO intertwined mark 48.00
Bar pin, ivory-grained, orange and brown layered pearlescence, hp rose motif 15.00
Bookmark, cream colored, diecut, poinsettia motif, Psalm 22 printed on front.................15.00
Brush and comb set, child's, orig box 20.00
Doll, 6-1/2" l, crepe paper cone-shaped body....................100.00
Doll, blue glass eyes, moveable arms and legs, dressed in fabric skirt, crochet top, bandana around head, earrings, 9" h 90.00

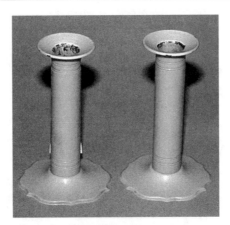

Celluloid candlesticks, 5-1/2" high, pair, $75.

Dresser tray, imitation tortoiseshell rim, glass and lace center 35.00
Necklace, red chain, berries 50.00
Picture frame, oval, ivory grained, easel back, 8" x 10" 20.00
Pocket mirror, oval, souvenir of Niagara Falls, printed colored drawing of falls, 2-1/2" h............20.00
Rattle, blue and white, egg shape, white handle 18.50
Roly poly, chicken, weighted base, 2-1/2" dia 38.00

❖ Central Glass

In 1863, Central Glass Works of Wheeling, West Virginia, was established as a cooperative. A group of workmen from J. H. Hobbs, Brockunier and Company undertook the venture. It failed shortly thereafter and was reorganized as a stock company in 1867. Production continued until 1939, consisting of tableware and barware for commercial and domestic use.

Bowl, Frances, green, crimped, 11" dia....................................40.00
Butter dish, cov, Chippendale pattern, colorless 20.00
Candlestick, ribbed deep blue, silver trim, 9" h 42.00
Cocktail, Balda, lavender.........30.00
Compote, Optic ribbing, amethyst, 12" dia, 8-1/2" h...............250.00
Creamer and sugar, Chippendale, 1909...................................50.00
Decanter, Brazen Shield, pattern #98, 1905, 10" h 45.00

Fruit bowl, Frances, 3 toes, green, 10" dia.............................35.00
Goblet, water
    Acorn, colorless.................15.00
    Balda, lavender 30.00
    Veninga, colorless............15.00
Hair receiver, cov, Chippendale, colorless 15.00
Jug, Yodel, lotus etch, pink and crystal, 64-oz......................300.00
Mayonnaise, Morgan, ftd, 2 handles, matching ladle, rose........165.00
Tumbler, Yodel, lotus etch, pink and crystal
    2-3/4-oz, ftd 40.00
    7-oz, ftd 30.00
    12-oz, ftd 35.00
Water pitcher, Acorn, colorless 35.00
Water set, Greek, pitcher and six 7-oz tumblers, pink and crystal 500.00

❖ Ceramic Arts Studio

Located in Madison, Wisconsin, Ceramic Arts Studio produced wheel-thrown ceramics. Founded in 1941 by Lawrence Rabbett and Ruben Sand, the studio turned out interesting ceramics until 1955.

Collectors' Club: Ceramic Art Studio Collectors Assoc, P.O. Box 46, Madison, WI 53701.
Aladdin's Lamp, 3" l 56.00
Bank, Tony the Barber 125.00
Creamer, kitten, head removes to fill, 5-1/2" h 25.00
Figure
    Black boy on crocodile, mkd crocodile 4-5/8" l, unmkd boy 2-1/2" h, 2 pcs 220.00
    Cocker spaniel, sitting, black, 2-3/4" h........................27.00
    Dutch children, kissing 75.00
    Harry and Lilibeth, gay nineties couple, green clothing, both mkd, male 6-1/2" h, female 6-3/4" h, pr..................90.00
    Lamb, 3-1/2" h...................35.00
    Little Bo Peep, green clothing, 5-1/4" h 40.00
    Polish Couple, unmkd, 6-1/4" h and 6-1/2" h, pr.............98.00
    Sultan on pillow, part of the Harem Group, 4-3/4" h . 80.00

Shelf sitter, boy with dog, girl with kitten, pr 90.00
Pitcher, miniature, emb bust of Washington circled by stars, 3" h 55.00
Salt and pepper shakers
Brown bear and cub, nested, pr 85.00
Cow and calf, snugglers, both mkd, 5-1/4" h and 2-1/4" h, pr 190.00
Elephant, male 3-3/4" h, female 3-1/4" h, both mkd with CAS logo, pr 70.00
Gingham Dog and Calico Cat, cat 2-7/8" h, dog 2-3/4" h, both mkd, pr 95.00
Gorilla and baby, nested, pr 100.00
Mouse and cheese, pr 37.00

❖ Cereal Boxes

Cereal boxes have incorporated clever advertising, premiums, and activities for years. Early boxes were designed to appeal to the cook in the household, but as children began requesting their favorite brands and saving box tops to get a specific premium, the whole industry refocused on that group. By the 1970s, special promotional boxes were created, giving collectors even more opportunities to expand their collections.

Collectors' Club: Sugar-Charged Cereal Collectors, 5400 Cheshire Meadows Way, Fairfax, VA 22032.
Batman, Ralston, hologram t-shirt offer, 1989 ....9.00
Corn Kix, Rocket Space O-Gauge, 1950s 90.00
Corn Pops, Kellogg's, Batman Forever with Batman, #1 in series of 4, copyright 1995...............10.00
Froot Loops, Kellogg's, Mattel Fun on Wheels contest, 1970...30.00
Kaboom, flat/proof, no die-cut or scoring, border-signed by printers, stamped "Oct 9, 1979," 1 sheet 80.00
Puffa Puffa Rice, Kellogg's, H.R. Pufnstuf patch, 1970, unopened, 8-oz, 6-1/4" x 8-3/4".........750.00
Rice Chex, red check design, 1950s 65.00

Spoonsize Shredded Wheat, Nabisco, Spoonmen on front, Tobor robot offer on back, flat 450.00
Sugar Smacks, seal balancing bowl of cereal on nose, Exploding Battleship offer on back, 1958, 9-oz, hole in bottom front, 7-1/2" x 9-1/2" 36.00
Wheaties
Muhammad Ali, 1960s picture, 1998 ....10.00
Baseball pitcher on front, Illustrated Classics Comic Books offer on back, 1960, 12-oz, split along top edge, 10-3/4" x 7-1/2" 450.00
Lou Gehrig, flat 8.50
Minnesota Vikings, NFC Central Division Champions, regional issue, 1992, 18-oz.........28.50
Babe Ruth, flat 8.50
Chris Spielman in high school football uniform, Search for Champions, 12-oz 81.00
Shirley Temple's The Bowery Princess on back, 1936, 8-oz, top and bottom cut, replaced bottom flap, 8-1/2" x 6-1/4" 200.00

❖ Cereal Premiums

This category includes all of those fun things we saved after eating all that cereal. Sometimes these goodies were tucked into the box. Other premiums were things that you earned, through saving box tops, coupons, etc. Whatever the method, the treasure was the premium, and, at today's prices, collectors are having the most fun now.
Bowl sitter/pencil topper, Pinocchio 10.00
Cereal bowl, Tom Mix, "Hot Ralston Cereal for Straight Shooters," white china, illus, copyright 1982, Ralston Purina.........35.00
Delivery truck, 1921 Model T, Matchbox, copyright 1989, Kellogg's Apple Jacks 8.00
Figures, Snap, Crackle, and Pop, wood and fabric, mkd, dated, Kellogg's 1972 ....55.00

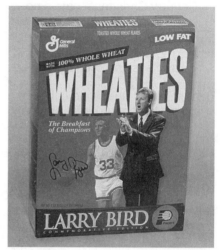

Larry Bird commemorative Wheaties box, unopened, $6.50.

Flashlight, Lurch, attached by cellophane to box of Addams Family Cereal, Ralston, copyright 1991 .... 8.00
Flicker ring, Frankenberry playing drums, early 1970s 100.00
Magnet, Trix, Arjon Manufacturing Corp., MOC......................... 8.00
Ornament, Sugar Bear, spins inside glow-in-the-dark holder, MIP, 4" h, 2" w.............................. 10.00
Wacky Wobbler, Count Chocula, bobbing head, made by Funko Inc., orig box, 7" h............. 10.00
Waste can, Twinkles and his Friends, General Mills, metal, 1961, some dents 300.00

❖ Character and Promotional Drinking Glasses

Everybody's got one or two of these in the cupboard. However, there are also dedicated collectors who find flea markets are good hunting ground for the newer additions. Thanks to modern advertisers, such as Coca-Cola and McDonald's, there are many examples to find.

Periodical: Collector Glass News, P.O. Box 308, Slippery Rock, PA 16057.

Lord-Kruge, Star Trek III, Taco Bell, 5-3/4" high, $4.

Collectors' Club: Promotional Glass Collectors Assoc, 3001 Bethel Rd, New Wilmington, PA 16142.

Annie and Sandy, Swenson's, 1982 .... 8.00
Aquaman, DC Comics, Pepsi, 1978 .... 17.50
Batman, Pepsi, 16-oz, 1978 .... 18.00
BC Ice Age, riding on wheel, Arby's, 1981 .... 9.00
Beaky Buzzard, Warner Bros., Pepsi, 1973 .... 17.50
Betty, Coca-Cola 12.00
Bugs Bunny, Pepsi, 1973, copyright Warner Bros. Inc. 9.00
Bullwinkle, Crossing the Delaware, Arby's, 1976 .... 12.00
Charlie Chaplin, Movie Star series, Arby's 9.00
Charlie Tuna, 3-3/4" h, 3" dia, clear, single image of Charlie in white, no inscription, heavily fluted base, c1970, pr 25.00
Daffy Duck, Pepsi, Warner Bros., 1976 .... 18.00
Empire Strikes Back, Luke Sky-walker, Burger King, 1980 .... 17.50
Endangered Species, Bengal Tiger, Burger Chef, 1978 .... 7.50
Flash, Pepsi, 1976 .... 18.00
Little Bamm-Bamm, Flintstones, Hardee's, 1991 .... 6.00
Mayor McCheese taking pictures, McDonald's 5.00
Noid, beach chair, Domino's Pizza, 1988 .... 2.50
Rocky, In the Dawn's Early Light, Arby's, 1975 .... 10.00

Santa and Elves, Coca-Cola 9.00
Superman, Pepsi, 1976 .... 18.00
Superman In Action, National Periodical Publications, 1966, 4-1/4" h 35.00
Underdog, Brockway Glass Co., Pepsi, 16-oz, small logo 25.00
Wendy, Brockway Glass Co., 16-oz 15.00

❖ Character Banks

Banks that depict characters, whether they are cartoon, fictional, or real, are popular with collectors. Because so many of them are figural, they create a colorful scene when displayed.

Batman, glazed ceramic, 1966, 7" h 24.00
Betty Boop 20.00
Bugs Bunny, pot metal 60.00
Buster Brown and Tige, cast iron, c1910 .... 165.00
Captain Marvel, dime register type, litho tin, Fawcett Publications, 1948 .... 85.00
Fred Flintstone, vinyl, 12-1/2" h 20.00
Lucy, Peppermint Patty and Linus, baseball uniforms, 1973 .... 50.00
Laurel and Hardy, plastic, 14" h 45.00
Old Dutch Cleanser, litho tin 25.00
Peanuts, on dog house, Bank of America, 1970s 50.00
Popeye, multicolor litho metal, mkd "Popeye Daily Quarter Bank," Kalon Co., 1950s 115.00
Woodsey Owl, pottery 45.00

Humpty Dumpty character bank, pottery, 3-5/8" high, $65.

❖ Character Clocks and Watches

Telling time is more fun when your favorite character gives you a hand. Condition is important when collecting clocks and watches. Examples with original bands, boxes, stands, and works will bring a higher price.

Betty Boop
    Clock 45.00
    Watch 35.00
Charlie Tuna, wristwatch, full-color image of Charlie on silver ground, copyright 1971 Star-Kist Foods, grained purple leather band 75.00
Flintstones, wall clock, battery op 15.00
Gene Autry, wristwatch 135.00
Jetsons, watch, lunch-box type, Fossil, MIB 80.00
Lone Ranger, wristwatch, metal case, Lone Ranger on galloping Silver, orig tan strap, c1940 .... 165.00
Roy Rogers, alarm clock, color dial, c1970 .... 30.00
Smitty, wristwatch, gray aged dial, white, red, and green figure, New Haven Clock Co., 1935, orig case 250.00
Snoopy, alarm clock 30.00
Star Wars, alarm clock, talking 35.00

✪ Character Collectibles

Some characters got their start on early radio programs, some were popular advertising spokesmen, and some were permanent fixtures on the newspaper comic page. As collectors become younger and younger, so do the ages of the characters they search for. Foxy Grandpa is giving way to Gumby and now even Rugrats.

References: Bill Bruegman, *Cartoon Friends of the Baby Boom Era,*

Cap'n Penny Productions, 1993; ——, *Superhero Collectibles*, Toy Scouts, 1996; *Cartoon & Character Toys of the 50s, 60s, & 70s*, L-W Book Sales, 1995; Ted Hake, *Hake's Guide to Cowboy Character Collectibles*, Wallace-Homestead, 1994; ——, *Hake's Price Guide to Character Toys*, Gemstone Publishing, 1998; Jim Harmon, *Radio & TV Premiums*, Krause Publications, 1997; Jack Koch, *Howdy Doody*, Collector Books, 1996; Cynthia Boris Liljeblad, *TV Toys and the Shows That Inspired Them*, Krause Publications, 1996; David Longest, *Character Toys and Collectibles* (1984, 1992 value update), 2nd Series (1987, 1990 value update), Collector Books; Rex Miller, *The Investor's Guide To Vintage Collectibles*, Krause Publications, 1998; Richard O'Brien, *Collecting Toys*, 8th ed, Krause Publications, 1997; David and Micki Young, *Campbell's Soup Collectibles from A to Z*, Krause Publications, 1998.

Collectors' Clubs: Charlie Tuna Collectors Club, 7812 NW Hampton Rd, Kansas City, MO 64152; Dick Tracy Fan Club, P.O. Box 632, Manitou Springs, CO 80829; Howdy Doody Memorabilia Collectors Club, 8 Hunt Ct, Flemington, NJ 08822; Official Popeye Fan Club, 1001 State St, Chester, IL 62233.

For additional listings, see *Warman's Antiques & Collectibles* and *Warman's Americana & Collectibles*, as well as specific categories in this edition.

Alf, coloring book, 30 pages, Spanish text, 1989, unused 12.00

Borden ceramic mugs, Elsie and Elmer, Universal Pottery, 3-1/8" high, $50 each.

Bullwinkle, coloring book, *Bullwinkle & Dudley Do Right*, Saalfield, copyright 1971, unused 30.00
Charlie Tuna, doll, vinyl 30.00
Dennis the Menace
    Book, *Dennis The Menace*, Hank Ketchum, Holt & Co., 1952, 1st ed, hardcover 35.00
    Lamp, figural 50.00
Dick Tracy
    Candy bar wrapper, premium offer, 1950s 10.00
    Toy, two-way radio set, 1950, MIB..............................40.00
Garfield, telephone, figural 48.00
Jetsons
    Colorforms Set, copyright Colorforms and Hanna-Barbera, 1963 ....40.00
    Record, "The Jetsons, First Family on the Moon," 33 rpm, 1977 ....60.00
Kayo and Moon Mullins
    Pinback button, black and white, Los Angeles Evening Express contest, 1-1/4" dia 45.00
    Salt and pepper shakers, chalkware, 3" h, flakes, pr......60.00
Ozark Ike, Christmas card, 1951, unused..............................12.00
Pogo, mug, plastic, full-color illus 75.00
Popeye, flashlight, figural, King Features..................................30.00
Tillie the Toiler, 4-puzzle set, diecut cardboard, Saalfield Publishing, 1935..................................65.00
Tom and Jerry, pinback button, Tom and Jerry Go For Stroehmann's Bread, black, red and white litho, 1950s..............................25.00

❖ Chase Chrome and Brass

This American firm produced many interesting chrome and brass items. Their pieces are well marked and quite stylish.

Ashtray with matchbox holder, round, 2 cigarette holders, sq clip for matchbox 18.00
Box, round, copper, leafy design around base, mkd, lid with shell-shaped handle, wear, 4-3/4" x 2" 8.00

Candle snuffer, Puritan, MIB... 85.00
Cigarette urn, sq base, round container, mkd, 2-3/8" h, base 2-1/2" sq 45.00
Cocktail ball, chromium, tray 6-1/4" dia, ball 3-1/4" dia 45.00
Cordial cup............................. 85.00
Desk lamp, Half Moon, Art Deco, sgnd, replaced shade, ding on base 225.00
Humidor, round, mkd, large knob on lid, 6" dia, 6" h.................. 95.00
Serving dish, polished chrome, 2 compartments, glass liner, stationary handle, with some wear 45.00

Chein tin wind-up Ferris wheel, $150.

❖ Chein Toys

An American toy company, Chein produced quality toys from the 1930s through the 1950s. Many of their playthings were lithographed on tin, and they are clearly marked.

Cabin Cruiser motor boat, litho tin, 15" l, 4" w, sgnd "Princess Pat," 1940s, MIB..................... 275.00
Carousel, litho tin wind-up 60.00
Disneyland Roller Coaster, one car 640.00
Donald Duck, litho tin wind-up 65.00
Hook and ladder, replaced ladders 750.00
Motor boat, litho tin, sgnd "Peggy Jane," 14" l, 3" w, 1930s, MIB 225.00

Penguin, wind-up, played-with condition 75.00
Playland Merry Go Round 575.00
Roller Coaster, 2 cars, MIB ... 590.00
Roly poly, monkey, 1930s 365.00
Sand pail, litho tin, fish dec 35.00
Sand shovel, litho tin 25.00
Waddling duck, litho tin wind-up, c1935 .... 75.00

❖ Chess Set

This game of kings has been played for centuries. Be certain that all of the playing pieces are present and that the age of the board matches the age of the pieces.
Bakelite, 1930s-1940s, box rough and hinge damaged 380.00
Carved marble pieces, fitted case, no playing board 40.00
Civil War, Franklin Mint 345.00
Football, hard plastic figures, green and white board, 1967, with *Official Football Chess Rule Book*, 22 pgs, unplayed, figures 3" h, box 24" x 19" 78.00
Lord of the Rings 200.00
Plastic, molded, black and white, cardboard board 15.00
Porcelain, blue and white, bases mkd "Royal Dux, Made in Czechoslovakia," early 20th C 995.00
Revolutionary War, Franklin Mint, issued 1986 .... 280.00
Star Trek, 25th Anniversary Edition, authorized by Paramount Pictures 300.00
Wood, hand carved, c1920 ..... 80.00

❖ Children's Collectibles

This category is a bit of a catchall, including things that children played with, as well as articles they used in their rooms.
Bib clips, sterling silver, clothespin type 75.00
Blocks, wood, bright colors, c1950, some wear 20.00
Cloth book, handmade, buttons, zipper, etc. to teach children hand skills 10.00
Diaper holder, fabric, clown face, striped body 10.00

Child's drum, lithographed tin, Ohio Art Co., 5-3/8" high, 13" diameter, $70.

Kitchen cupboard, some old paint, some restoration 400.00
Lamp, clown in rocking chair, music box base, orig shade 40.00
Night light, plug-in type, figural teddy bear, plastic 5.00
Piano, "Concert," baby grand 110.00
Print, Asleep & Awake, Bessie Gutmann, double matted, orig frame 150.00
Rattle with whistle, bone, 3-3/4" l 95.00
Scooter, steel frame and wheels, wooden platform and handle, worn orig red paint, black and yellow striping, partial label "...Arrow Deluxe" 150.00
Sewing machine, Singer, cast iron and nickeled steel, 6-3/4" h 150.00
Wagon, Roller Bearing Coaster, wood, metal fittings, black stenciled label, old red and brown paint, some touch-up to paint 385.00
Wall plaques, plaster of Paris, Jack and Jill on one, Humpty Dumpty on other, self-framed, pr 20.00
Wastebasket, tin, yellow ground, hp teddy bear on side, wear and dents 15.00

❖ Children's Dishes

We've all made mud pies and other goodies. What better way to serve them to our dolls and teddies than on pretty, child-size dishes?

Collectors' Club: Toy Dish Collectors, P.O. Box 159, Bethlehem, CT 06751.
Baking set, tin, cookie tin, canister, bowl, pie pan, cake pans, angel food pan, muffin pan, etc. 25.00
Bundt pan, aluminum, 3-3/4" w 4.00
Chocolate pot, china, decal with Model T and passengers .. 90.00
Cup and saucer
    Blue Willow pattern 15.00
    Holly, Napco, Japan, 2-1/4" dia saucer 7.00
    Luster ware, Japan, floral dec 4.50
    Moss Rose pattern 7.50
    Peach Luster, Fire-King 25.00
Dinnerware set
    China, pink transferware Punch dec, mkd "Allerton & Sons," cup, saucer and three 5-1/2" dia plates 150.00
    Depression glass, Diana, crystal, gold trim, rack, 12-pc set 125.00
    Plastic, Tinkerbell, Walt Disney, 9 pcs 25.00
Mug, Little Bo Peep, 3-1/2" h .. 22.00
Plate
    Hey Diddle Diddle, blue and white, 6-1/2" dia 30.00
    Moss Rose pattern, 2-1/2" dia 3.00
Silverware set, aluminum, 4 spoons, 4 forks, knife, and pie server 15.00
Strainer and meat grinder, Little Homemaker, Wirecraft Corp., NYC, MOC 18.00
Sugar bowl, luster ware, Japan, 1-1/2" h 3.00
Teapot
    Aluminum, black wood knob, swing handle 25.00
    China, Occupied Japan 85.00
    Plastic, mkd "Eagle Toys, Made in Canada," 4" x 6" 3.00
Tea set
    Akro Agate, orig box mkd "The Little American Maid, No. 3000" 300.00
    Magic Mountain, mkd "Made in Japan," MIB 20.00

❖ Chintz Ware

Chintz ware is the general term for brightly-colored, multi-flower china patterns made primarily in England. These popular patterns resemble chintz fabrics and were produced by many manufacturers. After declining in popularity for years following World War II, chintz has enjoyed a lively comeback over the past several years.

References: Eileen Busby, *Royal Winton Porcelain*, The Glass Press Inc.,1998; Linda Eberle and Susan Scott, *Charlton Standard Catalogue of Chintz*, 3rd ed, Charlton Press, 1999; Muriel Miller, *Collecting Royal Winton Chintz*, Francis Joseph Publications, 1996, Jo Anne Welch, *Chintz Ceramics*, 3rd ed, Schiffer Publishing, 2000.

Collectors' Clubs: Chintz Collectors Club, P.O. Box 50888, Pasadena, CA 91115, www. chintznet.com; Chintz Connection, P.O. Box 222, Riverdale, MD 20738; Royal Winton International Collectors' Club, Dancer's End, Northall, Bedfordshire LU6 2EU, England; Royal Winton Collectors' Club, 2 Kareela Road, Baulkham Hills, Australia 2153.

For additional listings, see *Warman's Antiques & Collectibles* and *Warman's English & Continental Pottery & Porcelain*.

Reproduction Alert.

Biscuit barrel, Erphila, Czech 225.00
Bowl, Marguerite, Royal Winton,
    9-1/2" x 10"......................265.00
Bread tray, Old Cottage, Royal Winton 200.00

Handled dish, Japan, 5-5/8" square, $25.

Breakfast set, Rosebud Iridescent,
    green 250.00
Cake tray, 2 tiers, Midwinter, mkd "Stylecraft, Fashion Tableware by Midwinter, Staffordshire, England" 190.00
Condiment set, salt and pepper shakers, mustard pot, chromed metal handle 245.00
Creamer and sugar, Queen Anne, Royal Winton 285.00
Cup, #12586, Shelley 50.00
Cup and saucer
    Marguerite, Shelley, cup damaged 50.00
    Rosina.............................20.00
Dish, Dubarry, Kent 125.00
Mustard, cov, Summertime, Royal Winton 175.00
Plate
    Dubarry, Kent, 8-1/2" dia..165.00
    Melody, Royal Crown, 9" dia 195.00
    Old Cottage, Royal Winton, 8" dia 50.00
    Sweet Pea, Royal Winton, 5" sq 100.00
Soup bowl, two handles, underplate, Old Cottage, Royal Winton 145.00
Teapot, cov, Marina, Lord Nelson 325.00
Toast rack, mkd "Green & Co. Ltd., Gresley, made in England" 20.00
Tray
    Old Cottage, Royal Winton 150.00
    Summertime......................95.00

❖ Chocolate Related

Many collectors suffer from a sweet tooth. Happily there are wonderful examples of items relating to chocolate that can satisfy those cravings.

Box, Hershey's Milk Chocolate Candy Bars, held 24 bars, cover has torn corners, partial factory seal attached, 5" x 7".........15.00
Can
    Cocomalt, food/drink powder, sample size, orig contents 50.00
    Donald Duck Chocolate Syrup, Walt Disney Productions, mint cond, 4-1/2" h, 2-5/8" dia 190.00

Hershey's Sweet Milk Chocolate box, worn, $15.

Comic book, *Major Inapak Space Ace*, #1, 1951, Magazine Enterprises, N.Y., giveaway for "Inapak-The Best Chocolate Drink in the World" 10.00
Cup, restaurant china, Inca Ware, Shenango China, tan with red "Nestle's".......................... 16.00
Cup and saucer, Johnston's Hot Chocolate, mkd "Salem China" 35.00
Milk shake glass, hard plastic, soda fountain style, premium, Quik rabbit and blue "Nestle's Quik," 16-oz, 6-3/4" h, pr 12.00
Mold
    Clown, metal, 10-1/2" x 4-1/2" 62.00
    Egg, with divider.............. 150.00
    Santa, #427, 2 small holes, 4-1/2" h...................... 125.00
Mug, plastic, Nestle's Quik Bunny, 2 handles, 4" h.................... 12.00
Pitcher, hard plastic, Nestle's Quik rabbit, 9" h 22.00
Toy truck, plastic, Hershey's Milk Chocolate, two removable Hershey Kisses, Buddy L, 1982, mkd "Made in Japan"........ 15.00

❖ Christmas and Easter Seals

The National Tuberculosis Association issued seals, pinback buttons, and other items in order to educate the public and raise funds for their work. The American Lung Association also issued seals.

Booklet, Christmas Seals, 200, thin paper between each sheet, 1939 .... 22.00

Uncut sheet of 1977 Christmas Seals, $3.

Bottle, commemorative, Coca-Cola, Easter Seals, 1997 .... 11.50
Figurine, girl holding potted flower, "His Love will Shine on You," Easter Seals Limited Edition 11.50
Full sheet, 100
American Lung Assoc, Christmas, 1976 .... 5.00
Christmas Seals, 1927 .... 8.00
Christmas Seals, 1943 .... 5.00
Easter Seals, 1957 .... 2.00
Poster
"Fight the Big Bad Wolf 'Tuberculosis,' Buy Christmas Seals," paper, shows wolf and pigs, 1934, pinholes, 1" tear, 15" x 10-1/2" 160.00
"Holiday Greetings, Sold Here, Christmas Seals, Protect your Home from Tuberculosis," hardstock, Santa Claus art by Walter Sasse, Official Post Office Dept. stamps, 1936, some soiling, 11" x 14" 45.00

❖ Christmas

One of the most celebrated holidays of the year has provided us with many collectibles. Some collectors specialize in only one type of object or one character, such as Santa. Others just love Christmas and collect a wide variety of objects.

References: Beth Dees, *Santa's Guide to Contemporary Christmas Collectibles*, Krause Publications, 1997; George Johnson, *Christmas Ornaments, Lights & Decorations* (1987, 1998 value update), Vol. II (1996), Vol. III (1996), Collector Books; Clara Johnson Scroggins, *Silver Christmas Ornaments*, Krause Publications, 1997; Lissa and Dick Smith, *Holiday Collectibles*, Krause Publications, 1998.

Collectors' Club: Golden Glow of Christmas Past, 6401 Winsdale St, Golden Valley, MN 55427.

For additional listings, see *Warman's Antiques & Collectibles* and *Warman's Americana & Collectibles*.

Bell, Mickey Mouse in sleigh with Dumbo, Schmid, limited edition, 1978, orig box 50.00
Book
The Bird's Christmas Carol, Kate Douglas Wiggin, 1912, color plates 35.00
The Romance of a Christmas Card, Kate Douglas Wiggin, 4 color plates, black-and-white drawings by Alice Hunt, 1916, 1st ed 35.00
Candy container
Belsnickle style, faded felt outfit, 7" h 275.00
Santa wearing snow shoes and holding Christmas tree, hard plastic, sack with opening for candy, Rosbro Plastics, 4-1/2" h 40.00

Postcard, St. Nicholas in green robe, $10.

"Twas the Night Before Christmas" tin with Santa on rooftop, 2-1/4" high (excluding handle), 4-3/4" long, $357.50.

Waving Santa in sleigh, hard plastic, yellow, hole in 1 arm for candy cane, 4" h, 5" l 44.00
Chocolate mold, Santa, #427, 2 small holes in body, 4-1/2" h 125.00
Display, Rudolph the Red-Nosed Reindeer, with feed sack, Annalee, orig 1971 tag, 36" h .. 450.00
Lantern, Santa Claus, battery op, head is glass, surface rust on chromed parts, works 75.00
Light bulb
Cluster of grapes, purple, mkd "15V Japan" on cap, minor paint loss, 2-3/4" h 9.00
Lantern shape, hp, late 1940s-early 1950s, filaments good, 2-1/2" x 4-1/2" 22.50
Snowman, milk glass, mkd "120V Japan" on cap, working cond, minor paint loss, 3-1/2" h 12.50
Little Golden Book, *Rudolph the Red-Nosed Reindeer*, #331, 1958.................................... 5.00
Nativity set, Precious Moments, "Prepare Ye The Way Of The Lord," #E-0508, angels preparing manger, 1983, from 1" to 6-1/2" h, 6 pcs 120.00
Nodder, Santa with tree, 4-1/2" h 33.00
Ornament
Campbell Soup Kids, 1988, MIB 12.50

Mickey Mouse's 50th Birthday, Schmid, limited edition, 1978, orig box 15.00

Santa Claus, red plastic, painted white trim, black eyes, 1940s-1950s, 3-1/4" h 16.00

Turkey, Great Gobbles, Christopher Radko, retired, hang tag attached, 6" h 60.00

Pinback button, celluloid cover, metal back, Santa, "Merry Christmas & Happy New Year," 1-1/4" dia 35.00

Plate

Cherubs surrounding Nativity scene, Wedgwood, 1997 .... 19.00

Mickey Mouse as Santa, Schmid, limited edition, 5th in a series, 1977 .... 60.00

Sheet music, *Rudolph the Red-Nosed Reindeer* by Johnny Mark, copyright 1949, with lyrics and music as recorded by Gene Autry, some foxing 6.00

Snow Dome, Nativity scene, #833, made in Hong Kong, 2-1/4" h 10.00

Stocking Mr. & Mrs. Frosty, red flannel, white flannel top cuff, "Wes" written in glitter box on cuff, 1950s 12.00

Santa, Shenango Fine China, early 1950s, 8" dia 25.00

Santa with sack of toys and reindeer, "Merry Christmas," felt with red trim, 17" l 6.00

Tree stand, cast iron, Christmas scenes, 3 diamond-shape screws, sgnd "Gesetzl-Gesch," 6" h, 11-1/2" sq 100.00

❖ Cigar Collectibles

The late 1990s certainly revived the fine art of cigar smoking. And, along with this newfound interest, collectors are enjoying an increase in the number cigar-related collectibles to add to their collections.

Periodicals: *The Cigar Label Gazette*, P.O. Box 3, Lake Forest, CA 92630; *Tobacco Antiques and Collectibles Market*, Box 11652, Houston, TX 77293.

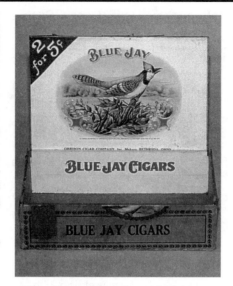

Blue Jay Cigars box, $40.

Collectors' Clubs: Cigar Label Collectors International, P.O. Box 66, Sharon Center, OH 44274; International Lighter Collectors, P.O. Box 536, Quitman, TX 75783; International Seal, Label and Cigar Band Soc, 8915 E. Bellevue St, Tucson, AZ 85715; Pocket Lighter Preservation Guild, P.O. Box 1054, Addison, IL 60101.

Bowl, small, glass, covered with cigar bands 35.00

Can, El Paxo, litho tin, Indian princess, 5" dia 187.00

Cigar case, silver color, holds 3 cigars, 5-1/2" 11.00

Counter display, litho tin, "Kennebec" in silver oval over portrait of Indian flanked by tomahawks, image repeated inside lid, 2-1/4" h, 8-1/2" w, 5" dia 28.50

Jar, amber glass, fired-on text, tin lid, "Mercantile Cigars, 5 Cents," 5-1/2" h, 4-1/2" dia 16.50

Label

Our Kitties, white cat and black cat 10.00

Joe Cannon, emb, 6" x 10" 10.00

Quaker Cigar 7.00

Premium coupon, United Cigar Stores Company of America, set of 4 .... 8.00

Sign, cardboard, "Smoke Jennie Lind, Hand Made Havana, 5 Cents," 8-1/4" x 14-1/2" ... 132.00

Sign, paper, "Golden's Blue Ribbon Cigars," blue and white, mint cond, 5-1/2" x 10" 8.00

War Eagle Cigars tin, 5-1/4" high, 5" diameter, $130.

Sign, tin Baxter's Cigars, "Drum 5 Cent Cigar, Beat All, How Good They Are" on drumhead, red and white, 13-3/4" h, 9-1/2" w 88.00

Tin, Between The Acts, little cigars, full, 1920s 20.00

❖ Cigarette Collectibles

During the 1990s, the cigarette industry took a beating in regards to its product and its advertising methods. However, collecting interest in the topic is hot! Whether this politically incorrect habit will be snuffed out is anyone's guess.

Periodical: *Tobacco Antiques and Collectibles Market*, Box 11652, Houston, TX 77293.

Collectors' Clubs: Ashtray Collectors Club, P.O. Box 11652, Houston, TX 77293; Camel Joe & Friends, 2205 Hess Drive, Cresthill, IL 60435; Cigarette Pack Collectors Assoc, 61 Searle St, Georgetown, MA 01833; International Lighter Collectors, P.O. Box 536, Quitman, TX 75783; International Seal, Label & Cigar Band Soc, 8915 E. Bellevue St, Tuscon, AZ 85715; Pocket Lighter Preservation Guild, P.O. Box 1054, Addison, IL 60101.

Winston sign, tin, $40.

Ashtray, metal, figural, Mt. Rushmore, made in Japan 17.50
Box, cardboard, flat 50, cardboard case shows 3 guards holding cards saying "Season's Greetings" 92.50
Cigarette case, made of folded and woven Winston cigarette packs 35.00
Cigarette silk
    Duckbill, New South Wales, yellowed, 2" x 3" 7.50
    Goat, Italy, slight fraying, 2" x 3" 9.00
    Gorilla, French Congo, 2" x 3" 9.00
Display, litho tin, "They're so Refreshing! Kool Cigarettes," 8" h, 7-1/8" w, 4-1/8" dia 25.00
Sign, tin, "Smoke Kools," emb penguin with pack of Kools, 16-3/4" x 8-1/2" 83.00
Thermometer, litho tin, "Chesterfield, More Than Ever, They Satisfy," emb cigarette pack, 13-1/2" h, 5-3/4" w 121.00
Tin
    Vertical box, litho tin, "Cinco Londres Cigars," oval medallion of a couple and ostrich, yellow ground, 5-1/4" h, 3" sq .. 44.00
    Vertical pocket, litho tin, hinged lid, "Ardath Cigarettes Splendo, Mild Natural Egyptian Blend," held 25 cigarettes, 3-1/4" h, 4" w, 1" dia 37.50

❖ Circus Collectibles

Whether it's the allure of the big tent or the dazzling acts, circuses have delighted kids of all ages since the 18th century. Of course this has helped to generate lots of collectibles, advertising, schedules, etc.

Overland Circus cast-iron toy wagon, reproduction with some age, $20.

Periodical: *Circus Report*, 525 Oak St., El Cerrito, CA 94530.

Collectors' Clubs: Circus Fans Assoc of America, P.O. Box 59710, Potomac, MD 20859; Circus Historical Soc, 3477 Vienna Court, Westerville, OH 43081; Circus Model Builders International, 347 Lonsdale Ave, Dayton, OH 45419.

Circus pass, Circus Hall of Fame, Sarasota, Fla. 3.50
Clown, celluloid figure riding fuzzy horse, mkd "M. M.," orig box 75.00
Cookie jar, white glass clown, red circus motif 25.00
Doll, clown, cloth body, painted plaster head, celluloid hand (1 missing), Ringling Bros., 1936, crazing and flaking to head, stain and hole to fabric 175.00
Little Golden Book, *Howdy Doody's Circus*, 1st ed, 1950 .... 16.00
Magazine/program, Ringling Bros. and Barnum & Bailey Circus, 1949, cover illus by E. McKnight Kauffer, water stains 30.00
Pinback button, "Souvenir of the Circus," shows clown, 1-3/4" dia 9.50
Pop-Up Book, *Circus*, 1979 ..... 15.00
Poster
    Al G. Kelly & Miller Bros. giraffe, 28" h, 21" w 60.00
    Hunt Bros. Circus, shows saber tooth tiger 95.00
Press-out book, *Tiny Circus*, Whitman, 1972, 8" x 11-1/2" 9.00
Ring, grey metal, circus giant Al Tomaini 35.00

Stuffed elephant, King Tusk, gold blanket with silver trim, plastic tusks 5" l, Ringling Bros. Barnum and Bailey Combined Shows, made in Korea, 11" h, 21" l 48.00
Wade figurine, circus elephant, sitting, 1-1/4" h 8.00

❖ Civil War

This sad time in American history has led to an interesting range of collectibles, including weapons, uniforms, flags, and ephemera.

Periodicals: *Military Collector Magazine*, PO Box 245, Lyon Station, PA 19536; *Military Collector News*, P.O. Box 702073, Tulsa, OK 74170; *North South Trader's Civil War*, PO Drawer 631, Orange, VA 22960.

Collectors' Clubs: American Soc of Military Insignia Collectors, 526 Lafayette Ave, Palmerton, PA 18071; Assoc of Military Uniform Collectors, P.O. Box 1876, Elyria, OH 44036; Company of Military Historians, North Main St, Westbrook, CT 06498; Military Collectors Soc, 137 S Almar Dr, Fort Lauderdale, FL 33334; Orders and Medals Soc of America, P.O. Box 484, Glassboro, NJ 08028.

Reproduction Alert.

Badge, Daughters of the Union, Veterans Encampment, red, white and blue striped ribbon, oval brass hanger bar with covered wagon drawn by 6 horses, cello pendant of Gen. John F. Reynolds, ribbon inscribed "19th Annual Encampment, Lancaster, Pa., 1931," 1-1/4" x 4" 25.00

Civil War cartridge box, marked "R. Dingee, New York," $200.

Belt, enlisted man's, black leather, brass retaining clips, oval brass "U.S." buckle 175.00
Button, brass, U.S. eagle imprint 10.00
Cartridge box plate, lead filled die-struck brass, iron wire fasteners, Maryland, mkd "E. Gaylord" on back......................... 3,600.00
Frock coat, swallowtail, boy's, inked "Robert Beecher" on inner pocket label, dark blue with 2 rows of U.S. Army staff officer's buttons, post-war button maker 950.00
Print, *Battles of the Rebellion*, 1863, Charles Magnus lithographer, hand-colored, framed 400.00
Recruiting broadside, woodcut, "One More Rally, Boys!" and eagle with "The Union Forever" ribbon, New York, matted, verso repaired with archival tape, 2 light stains, 17" x 11" 2,250.00
Tintype, unidentified Union soldier 30.00

❖ Clarice Cliff

To some collectors the name Clarice Cliff means Art Deco. To others, it's the bright ceramics created by this talented English woman. Cliff's work is becoming very popular and very expensive.

Collectors' Club: Clarice Cliff Collector's Club, Fantasque House, Tennis Dr, The Park, Nottingham, NG7 1AE, England.

Reproduction Alert.
For additional information and listings, see *Warman's Antique & Collectibles* and *Warman's English & Continental Pottery & Porcelain.*
Biscuit barrel, Celtic Harvest, hp floral dec, 6-1/2" h 395.00
Bowl, Bizarre, Blue Chintz, 4" h, 8" dia 750.00
Fruit bowl, Lily Pad, blues and greens, 5" h, 8" l 300.00
Honey pot, Bizarre, floral design, 4" h 295.00
Jam/honey pot, Autumn Crocus, 3" h 500.00
Plate, Crocus, center scratched, 8-3/4" dia 185.00

Salt and pepper shakers, Bizarre, Blue Chintz, pepper 3" h, salt 3-1/4" h, pr......................550.00
Sugar sifter, conical, Autumn Crocus, 5-1/2" h 600.00
Teapot, Cotswold, slight crazing, 5" h 145.00
Vegetable dish, cov, Duvivier...75.00
Wall vase, cloud shape with flying swallow 200.00

❖ Cleminson Pottery

This California pottery is known for its hand-decorated pieces. Started by Betty Cleminson in her El Monte, California, home, the business grew to the point of expansion in 1943.

Reproduction Alert.
Child's cup, clown head, conical hat cover, rough spots 80.00
Clothes sprinkler, Chinese man, 8" h 90.00
Creamer and sugar, figural, King and Queen......................... 85.00
"Gram's" bowl, cov, bowl 2-1/2" h 27.00
Hors d'oeuvre set, 7 dishes and wooden lazy Susan base, 16" dia................................. 72.00
Ring holder, bulldog, white and peach, tail holds rings........27.00
Salt and pepper shakers
    Pixies, 1 with 5 holes, 1 with 7 holes, orig corks, crazing, wear to bottoms, pr 75.00
    Sailors, male "Old Salt" and female "Hot Stuff," 5-1/4" h............ 75.00
Sprinkler bottle, hand-painted, crazing, 8-3/4" h 75.00

String holder, ceramic, heart shape, lid lettered "You'll Always Have Pull with Me," 5" h............ 110.00
Wall pocket, clock.............. 24.00

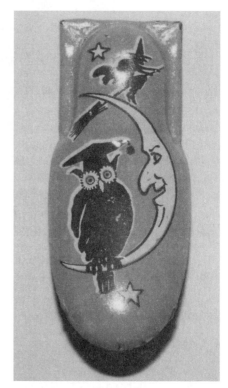

Halloween clicker, Kirchhof, Newark, N.J., 1-3/4" long, $17.50.

❖ Clickers

These little giveaways were popular with early advertisers and children, too.
Buster Brown Shoes, round, "Extra Wear in Every Pair," shows Buster and Tige, 1-1/4" dia 225.00

A piece of history

Clickers, also known as crickets, have long been an inexpensive child's toy that became popular with merchants who emblazoned the small metal items with graphics and advertising. One type of clicker, however, was of a much more serious nature.

Plain-looking clickers were issued to paratroopers before the D-Day invasion during World War II. The crickets were used to identify friendly troops in the dark or behind obstacles.

Reproductions exist, so be careful when buying a clicker said to have been used on D-Day. The best course of action is to purchase such historical items from a well-established militaria dealer who offers a written money-back guarantee of authenticity.

Cowboy playing guitar, Japan . 13.00
Frog, frog-shaped, Life of the Party
Products, Kirchhof, 1-1/2" x 3" x
1" 38.00
Golliwogg, with clown, 4" l 320.00
Halloween, frog-shaped, shows
witch on broom, haunted house
and flying bats, T. Cohn, 1940s,
tin, 3" l 30.00
OshKosh, "Clicks Everywhere with
Everyone, Buy 'em at Arm-
strong's" 65.00
Poll Parrot Shoes, shows parrot on
tree limb, 4-1/4" x 1-3/4" 90.00
Quaker State, 1-7/8" l 68.00
Red Goose Shoes
Goose head form, 1-7/8" x 5/8"
.... 165.00
Standing goose, dark blue
ground, image off-center,
1-7/8" x 7/8" 110.00
Smile, "Drink Smile, It's So Good"
.... 54.00
Sohio, 2-3/8" x 1-1/4" 80.00
WeatherBird Shoes
"They're Weatherized, For Boys,
For Girls" 26.00
"All Leather For All Weather"
.... 55.00

❖ Clocks

Tick-tock. Most clock collectors specialize and seek particular manufacturers or certain types of clocks. Buyers should carefully examine a clock to determine if it's in working order. Missing parts may result in considerable expense after the sale when it's time to pay for repairs.

Celluloid clock, 3" high, $30.

TIAS Top 10

The following list ranks the most highly sought collectibles on the Internet during 2000.

1. Avon
2. China
3. Cookie jars
4. Roseville
5. Furniture

6. Noritake
7. Lamps
8. McCoy
9. Clocks
10. Books

Source: www.tias.com

References: Robert W.D. Ball, *American Shelf & Wall Clocks*, 2nd ed, Schiffer Publishing, 1999; Robert and Harriet Swedberg, *Price Guide to Antique Clocks*, Krause Publications, 1998.

Periodical: *Clocks,* 4314 W 238th St, Torrance, CA 90505.

Collectors' Club: National Association of Watch and Clock Collectors, Inc, 514 Poplar St, Columbia, PA 17512.

For additional listings, see *Warman's Antiques & Collectibles* and *Warman's Americana & Collectibles*.

Advertising
Purina Poultry Chows, electric, 3
dials, red, white and blue
checkered bag style, alarm
.... 45.00
Rexall, wooden Seth Thomas
clock, 1954 Rexall Award of
Merit, small mortar and pestle
at top, 23" h 50.00
Alarm, Champion, 30-hour movement, metal frame, 9" h 75.00
Animated
Ballerina, music box, United
.... 150.00
Fireplace, Mastercrafter's
.... 125.00
Grandmother, rocking chair,
Haddon 190.00
Spinning Wheel, Lux 85.00
Ansonia, shelf, gingerbread, carved
and pressed walnut case, paper
on zinc dial, silver dec glass, 8-
day time and strike movement
with pendulum, 22" h 185.00

Electric, Cincinnati Reds logo, wood
frame, 1940s 65.00
Empire, shelf, mahogany veneer,
ebonized and stencil gilded
pilasters and crest, wooden
works with weights, key and
pendulum, worn paper label
"William Orion & Co.," door with
mirror in base, replaced reverse-
painted panel, finials missing,
some veneer damage and repair
.... 350.00
Marshall Fields, mantle 65.00
Seth Thomas, Cambridge, textured
oak case, 8-day movement,
23-3/4" h, 15" w 315.00
Weatherstation, L.L. Bean, clock,
thermometer, hygrometer and
moonphase, oak jointed round
case, 11-3/4" dia, bezel..... 75.00

❖ Cloisonné

Cloisonné is an interesting decorative technique in which small wires are adhered to a metal surface, and then the design is filled in with enamel, creating a very colorful pattern. The more intricate the design and the enameling, or the older the piece, the higher the price can be.

Collectors' Club: Cloisonné Collectors Club, P.O. Box 96, Rockport, MA 01966.

Reproduction Alert.

For additional listings, see *Warman's Antiques & Collectibles Price Guide.*

Box, 2" x 3" 100.00
Button, red ground, multicolor
design, 1-1/4" dia 25.00

Cloisonné covered jar, green and white, 9" high, $45.

Charger, roosters and floral dec, black ground, Chinese, late 19th C, surface scratches, 14" dia 190.00

Cigarette case, green, 3 dragons, Chinese 175.00

Cross pendant, blue ground, rose and white dec, Russian hallmarks 150.00

Desk set, brush pot, pen, pen tray, blotter and paper holder, Japan 130.00

Planter, classical symbol and scroll dec, blue ground, Chinese, 11" dia 100.00

Tea kettle, multicolor scrolling lotus flowers, medium blue ground, double handles, Chinese, 19th C 690.00

Vase, 6-sided, each side with shield below floral band, alternating dragon and phoenix motif, flecked blue ground, Japan, early 20th C, 6" h............. 145.00

❖ Clothes Sprinklers

Here's a part of the flea market world that has taken off. Who would have ever thought that Grandma's way of preparing ironing would become so popular with collectors? Because many of these handy sprinklers are figural, they make great display pieces.

Chinese Man, ceramic, 8-1/4" h 120.00

Dutch boy, ceramic, 8-1/4" h 295.00

Elephant, ceramic
Pink and gray 165.00
White..............................110.00

Glass, clear recycled bottle, black rubber and tin stopper top ...5.00

Iron shape, white ceramic, green ivy dec...................................125.00

Mammy, ceramic, white dress, 7" h 495.00

Merry Maid, plastic, mkd "Made in USA" 15.00

Rooster, ceramic, some paint missing, 10" h 165.00

Siamese cat, ceramic, 8-1/4" h 195.00

Sprinkle Plenty, 8" h.................85.00

Sprinkle Plenty ceramic clothes sprinkler, yellow and green, $65.

❖ Clothing

As fashions change from year to year, collecting vintage clothing never seems to go out of style. Many clothing collectors look for prestigious labels as well as garments that are in good condition.

References: Blanche Cirker (ed.), *1920s Fashions From B. Altman & Company*, Dover, 1999; Paula Jean Darnell, *Victorian to Vamp, Women's Clothing 1900-1929*, Fabric Fancies, 2000; Carol Belanger Grafton, *Fashions of the Thirties*, Dover Publications, 1993; —, *Shoes, Hats and Fashion Accessories*, Dover Publications, 1998; —, *Victorian Fashion: A Pictorial Archive*, Dover Publications, 1999; Kristina Harris, *Authentic Victorian Dressmaking Techniques*, Dover Publications, 1999; —, *Collector's Guide to Vintage Fashions*, Collector Books, 1999; —, *Victorian & Edwardian Fashions for Women*, Schiffer Publishing, 1995; —, *Vintage Fashions for Women*, Schiffer Publishing, 1996; Erhard Klepper, *Costume Through The Ages*, Dover Publications, 1999; Elizabeth Kurella, *The Complete Guide to Vintage Textiles*, Krause Publications, 1999; Ellie Laubner, *Fashions of the Roaring '20s*, Schiffer Publishing, 1996; —, *Fashions of the Turbulent 1930s*, Schiffer Publishing, 2000; Mary Brooks Picken, *A Dictionary of Costume and Fashion: Historic and Modern,* Dover Publications, 1999.

Periodicals: *Glass Slipper*, 653 S Orange Ave, Sarasota, FL 34236; *Lady's Gallery*, P.O. Box 1761, Independence, MO 64055; *Lill's Vintage Clothing Newsletter*, 19 Jamestown Dr, Cincinnati, OH 45241; *Vintage Clothing Newsletter*, P.O. Box 88892, Seattle, WA 98138; *Vintage Connection*, 904 N 65th St, Springfield, OR 97478; *Vintage Gazette*, 194 Amity St, Amherst, MA 01002.

Collectors' Clubs: The Costume Soc of America, P.O. Box 73, Earleville, MD 21919; Vintage Fashion and Costume Jewelry Club, P.O. Box 265, Glen Oaks, NY 11004.

For additional listings, see *Warman's Antiques & Collectibles* and *Warman's Americana & Collectibles*.

Bathing suit, girl's, cotton print, ruffles, 1950s 15.00

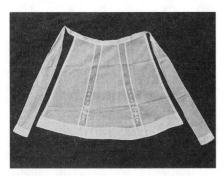

Apron, white cotton, embroidered florals, $45.

Bed jacket, satin, pink, ecru lace trim, labeled "B. Altman & Co. NY," 1930s 35.00

Blouse
    Beaded taffeta, black, black glass beads at yoke, hand sewn.............................90.00
    Cotton, white, Victorian cutwork 25.00

Bridesmaid's gown, pink chiffon, satin ribbon trim, size 10 ...50.00

Cape, mohair, black, ankle length, c1930 ....90.00

Christening gown, cotton, white, lace trim, matching bonnet, 47" l 115.00

Coat
    Boy's, linen, hand stitched, dec cuffs 35.00
    Lady's, Persian Lamp, black, matching hat and muff ..95.00

Dress
    Girl's, georgette and chiffon, pink, c1920....................75.00
    Lady's, black satin, 1920s..90.00
    Lady's, cotton, flowered, large organdy collar, waist tie 85.00

Pajamas, lady's, silk, red, 1920s 75.00

Pant suit, top and palazzo pants, Andrea Gayle, bright green, orange, yellow, pink, gray and purple satiny material, 2 pcs 65.00

Riding habit, sidesaddle style, skirt buttons to create back bustle, black, Victorian................450.00

Skirt, lady's, black wool, Victorian 45.00

Suit
    Boy's, navy wool blazer, short pants, orig Tom Sawyer brand 45.00

Lady's, linen, straight skirt, jacket with shoulder pads and fitted waist, English 70.00

Man's, black gabardine, jacket, vest, trousers, size 42, c1940 ....50.00

Waistcoat, gentleman's, English, 18th C, embroidered on front with feather and boat motif, floral and dotted border, buttons embroidered with floral sprigs 550.00

Wedding gown, satin, ivory, padded shoulders, sweetheart neckline, waist swag, self train, c1940 ....140.00

❖ Clothing Accessories

Clothing accents and accessories are even more collectible than vintage clothing. Perhaps this is because many of these accessories are just as fun to use today as when they were originally created. And, as with vintage clothing, with proper care and handling, it's perfectly acceptable to use these collectibles.

References: LaRue Johnson Bruton, *Ladies' Vintage Accessories*, Collector Books, 2000; Roseann Ettinger, *Handbags*, 3rd ed, Schiffer Publishing, 1999; Roselyn Gerson, *Vintage & Contemporary Purse Accessories*, Collector Books, 1997; —, *Vintage & Vogue Ladies Compacts*, 2nd ed, Collector Books, 2000; —, *Vintage Vanity Bags and Purses*, Collector Books, 1994 (1997 value update); Michael Jay Goldberg, *The Ties That Blind*, Schiffer Publishing, 1997; Richard Holiner, *Antique Purses*, Collector Books, 1999; Susan Langley, *Vintage Hats & Bonnets, 1770-1970*, Collector Books, 1997 (1999 value update); Rosanna Mihalick, *Collecting Handkerchiefs*, Schiffer Publishing, 2000; Laura M. Mueller, *Collector's Encyclopedia of Compacts, Carryalls & Face Powder Boxes*, Collector Books, Vol. I (1999 values), Vol. II (1997 values); Leslie Piña, Lorita Winfield, and Constance Korosec, *Beads in Fashion, 1900-2000*, Schiffer Publishing, 1999; Maureen

Reilly, *Hot Shoes, 100 Years*, Schiffer Publishing, 1998; Desire Smith, *Fashion Footwear, 1800-1970*, Schiffer Publishing, 2000; —, *Hats*, Schiffer Publishing, 1996; —, *Vintage Styles: 1920-1960*, Schiffer Publishing, 1997; Jeffrey B. Snyder, *Stetson Hats & The John B. Stetson Company 1865-1970*, Schiffer Publishing, 1997; Lorita Winfield, Leslie Pina, and Constance Korosec, *Beads on Bags, 1880s to 2000*, Schiffer Publishing, 2000.

Periodicals: *Glass Slipper*, 653 S Orange Ave, Sarasota, FL 34236; *Lady's Gallery*, P.O. Box 1761, Independence, MO 64055; *Lill's Vintage Clothing Newsletter*, 19 Jamestown Dr, Cincinnati, OH 45241; *The Vintage Connection*, 904 N 65th St, Springfield, OR 97478; *Vintage Clothing Newsletter*, P.O. Box 88892, Seattle, WA 98138; *Vintage Gazette*, 194 Amity St, Amherst, MA 01002.

Collectors' Clubs: The Costume Society of America, P.O. Box 73, Earleville, MD 21919; Vintage Fashion and Costume Jewelry Club, P.O. Box 265, Glen Oaks, NY 11004.

For additional listings, see *Warman's Antiques & Collectibles* and *Warman's Americana & Collectibles*.

Apron, child's, pink, lace and silk ribbons, 24" x 14"................. 70.00

Baby bonnet, white cotton, pink ribbon ties, c1960 .... 10.00

Collar, beaded and fur, white, early 1950s............................... 10.00

Beaded handbag, floral design, crocheted top, $60.

Gloves, lady's, satin, long, white 20.00
Handkerchief, 26" x 28-1/2", printed cotton, scene of Continental political satire, red, blue and brown, tan ground, 19th C, minor fabric loss 260.00
Hat
Beanie (Beanie & Cecil), propeller top 55.00
Indiana Jones, "Official," size XL 50.00
Muff
Child's, white rabbit fur 25.00
Lady's, dark brown sable fur, hand crocheted liner 35.00
Shawl, paisley, dark ground, long fringe, small holes 70.00
Stole, marabou, white.............. 50.00
Sweater, child's, hand-knit, train on back.................................. 30.00
Teddy, yellow, pink emb trim on bodice, 1920s........................... 25.00
Tie, hp scene of New York harbor, 1940s 12.00
Yoke, crocheted, ribbon trim.... 15.00

❖ Cobalt Blue Glassware Items

Blue has always been a favorite color for interior decorating. There has been a resurgence in the popularity of cobalt blue glassware items. A quick tip for telling the age of cobalt glass is the "greasy fingers test"—try rubbing your fingertips over the surface of a piece. If you get a slightly greasy feeling or leave streaks on the glass, it's a modern creation.

Animal dish, cov, hen on nest, Kemple Glass.................... 15.00
Barber bottle, 7" h 85.00
Basket, applied clear handle, 4" h 40.00
Bell, figural handle of man, 6" h 18.00
Bottle, violin shape 12.00
Paperweight, apple shape, cobalt blue crackle glass body, hand-blown, hand-applied crystal stem and leaf, Blenko Glass Co., 6" h, 3-1/2" w 65.00
Plate, 3 bunnies at top, Westmoreland Glass Co................... 15.00

Cobalt glass with silver-plated holder, grapes design, marked Japan, 3-1/8" high, $10.

Rose bowl, white stripes and white edging................................ 20.00
Salt and pepper shakers, range size, 6" h, pr 80.00
Tumbler, 5" h, "Atlantic City," white frosted design with skyline, ocean and hotels 45.00
Vase, cone, applied glass flower, clear pedestal base, 8-1/4" h 45.00

✪ Coca-Cola

An Atlanta pharmacist, John S. Pemberton, is credited with first developing the syrup base used for Coca-Cola. He was attempting to formulate a patent medicine for those experiencing headaches, nervousness, or stomach upsets. In 1887, Willis E. Venable mixed the syrup with carbonated water, and the rest was history. The Atlanta Journal carried the first print ad for Coca-Cola on May 29, 1886. In 1893, a trademark was granted for Coca-Cola written in script, and in 1945, the term Coke was registered.

References: Bob and Debra Henrich, *Cola-Cola Commemorative Bottles*, Collector Books, 1998; Allan Petretti, *Petretti's Coca-Cola Collectibles Price Guide*, 10th ed, Antique Trader Books, 1997; Allan Petretti and Chris Beyer, *Classic Coca-Cola Calendars*, Antique Trader Books, 1999; —, *Classic Coca-Cola Serving Trays*, Antique Trader Books, 1998; B. J. Summers, *B. J. Summers' Guide to Coca-Cola*, Collector Books, 1996; Al and Helen Wilson, *Wilson's Coca-Cola Guide*, Schiffer Publishing, 1997.

Collectors' Club: Cavanagh's Coca-Cola Christmas Collector's Soc, 1000 Holcomb Woods Parkway, Suite 440B, Roswell, GA 30076; Coca-Cola Collectors Club, 400 Monemar Ave, Baltimore, MD 21228-5213; Coca-Cola Collectors Club International, P.O. Box 49166, Atlanta, GA 30359-1166.

It's a record

The record price for a Coca-Cola sign sold at auction is $83,375, for this example sold in 1997 by James D. Julia, Inc.

Coca-Cola sign, $83,375. (Photo courtesy of James D. Julia, Inc., Fairfield, Maine)

Reproduction Alert.
For additional listings, see *Warman's Advertising, Warman's Antiques & Collectibles* and *Warman's Americana & Collectibles.*

Badge, hat, bronze, circa 1940s, "Drink Coca-Cola," cond. 8.5+, 3-1/2" 38.50

Banner, silk, white with gold fringe, "things go better with Coke" in red text, 1960s, light soiling, 46" h, 23-1/2" w 55.00

Baseball scorekeeper, perpetual counter 121.00

Blotter, paper
    1929, "The pause that refreshes," man and woman with Cokes, framed 121.00
    1935, "The drink that keeps you feeling fit for duty ahead" 38.50
    1940, "The greatest pause on earth," clown 55.00

Calendar, paper
    1937, boy with dog and fishing pole, full pad, framed, cover sheet in poor condition 440.00
    1946, Sprite boy on cover, complete 825.00
    1958 .... 143.00
    1960 .... 22.00

Card table, 1930s, bottle logos in corners, Coke tag on back 55.00

Carrier, 6-pack
    Aluminum, 1940s, embossed "Coca-Cola" 66.00

Coca-Cola can, large diamond, circa 1960, $175.

Wooden, early 1940s, lift handle, "Drink Coca-Cola in Bottles, Pause ... Go refreshed" logo with wings, mkd "new consumer case," red on yellow ground 231.00

Clock, light-up, metal and glass, rectangular, "Drink Coca-Cola," clock face over red text, white ground, 11" h, 12" w 165.00

Coasters, colored aluminum, 1950s, boxed set of 8, orig box 66.00

Cooler, Cavalier picnic cooler, 1950s, "Drink Coca-Cola in Bottles," orig box, 18" h, 18" w, 13" dia 440.00

Dish, pretzel, circa 1935, 3 miniature Coke bottles hold central round dish 187.00

Dispenser, syrup, countertop, metal, 1940s, "Drink Coca-Cola, Ice Cold" in oval, end has "Have A Coke" in circle, with glass stand/mounting hardware, 14" h, 8" w, 18" dia 110.00

Doll, Santa Claus
    White Santa, 1950s-1960s, stuffed body, black boots, 18" h 110.00
    Black Santa, white boots .. 154.00

Glass, clear glass, modified flare style, 1910s-1920s, "Coca-Cola" 71.50

Kickplate, tin, 1942, man and woman with bottle, "Drink Coca-Cola," red ground, NOS 962.50

Kite, paper, Hi-Flier, "Coca-Cola" above bottle, orig support/strings/sticks, circa 1930s 550.00

Magazine advertisement
    1914, "Delicious Coca-Cola, Pure and Wholesome," portrait of woman drinking glass of Coke, back cover of *The National Sunday Magazine,* framed 38.50
    1936, "Thru 50 Years...the pause that refreshes," color image of 2 women in bathing suits 44.00

Menu sign, tin, 1960s, "Enjoy Coca-Cola" in red circle logo beside "things go better with Coke" slogan, red/white top over green board, 28" h, 20" w 330.00

Music box, plastic, cooler shape, circa 1950s 143.00

Night light, 1950s, plastic, bottle cap shape, orig box 49.50

Sign, cardboard cutout
    1951, "Be refreshed" in banner by button sign, 3 women at table drinking glasses of Coke 16" h, 24" w 165.00
    1954, "Stock up Now...Take Some Home," bottle through ring of food, 4 hangers, 4' h, 3' w 302.50

Sign, celluloid
    Circa 1940s, "Coca-Cola, Delicious, Refreshing," orig envelope, 9" dia 330.00
    1940s-1950s, "Coca-Cola" in script over hobbleskirt bottle, 9" dia 275.00

Sign, paper
    "Sweetwater Clifton," pro basketball player in New York outfit, framed, 13" h, 11-1/2" w 440.00
    "Take Along Coke in 12 oz. Cans, Buy a Case," large-diamond can and dock scene, framed, 20" h, 36" w ... 352.00

Sign, tin, embossed, 1961, "Drink Coca-Cola, Enjoy That Refreshing New Feeling," white text on red fish tail ground on white, clean-cut ends, rolled top/bottom border, 24" h, 36" w 143.00

Thermometer, tin
    1930s, rounded top/bottom, gold hobbleskirt bottle, red ground, cond. 6, 16" h 143.00
    1940, "Drink Coca-Cola, Delicious and Refreshing," silhouette of girl drinking bottle of Coke, cond. 7, 16" h, 6-1/2" w 231.00

Toy
    Car, litho tin, Ford taxi, friction, made by Taiyo (Japanese), 1960s, orig box, 3" h, 10-1/2" w 302.50
    Truck, Buddy L, model 5426, pressed steel, yellow with 5 cases and 2 hand trucks, orig box cond. 7, truck cond. 9-9.25+, 15" l 550.00
    Truck, Marx, plastic, cardboard side panels picture cases, 6 plastic cases on top, 1956, orig box 605.00

Tray

1907, large oval, "Drink Coca-
Cola, Relieves Fatigue, 5¢,"
woman in green dress with
white trim, glass in right hand,
gold border, cond. 7.5-7.75,
16-1/2" h, 13-1/2" w .5,060.00

1908, topless, semi-nude
woman, "Wherever Ginger
Ale, Seltzer or Soda is Good,
Coca-Cola is Better - Try It,"
few shallow dents/bends, rim
with scratches/chips, cond.
8.25-8.5................. 11,000.00

1914, Betty, woman in white
shawl and bonnet, "Drink
Coca-Cola, Delicious and
Refreshing," "Ward Gayden"
engraved above bonnet, possibly a presentation tray,
chips, cond. 8.5-8.75...550.00

1922, Summer Girl, woman in
wide-brim hat, cond. 8.5
.....................................935.00

1928, Soda Jerk...............367.50

1931, The Barefoot Boy, boy in
straw hat sitting on ground
eating lunch, puppy at his feet
.... 1,045.00

1940, Sailor Girl, girl in sailor outfit sitting on dock 605.00

1941, Skater Girl, woman in
skates sitting on log 412.50

❖ Cocktail Shakers

"Make mine a dry martini" was the
plea of many well-heeled party
guests we gazed at in the movies.
To make that perfect drink, a clever
device called the cocktail shaker
was used. Today these shakers are
finding their way to flea markets and
collectors.

Reference: Stephen Visakay, *Vintage Bar Ware*, Collector Books,
1997.

Aluminum, gold color, shaker top
has insert with holes, Mirro,
1950s, 8-1/2" h 18.00

Chrome, Farberware, incised bands,
13-1/2" h...........................50.00

Farber Bros., Bakelite handle,
12-1/2" h...........................85.00

Glass

Cobalt, barbell, 3-pc chrome top
.....................................595.00

**Art Deco cocktail shaker, ruby
glass, chrome top, 12-1/2" long,
$55.**

Clear, silver-plate top, 9" h
.....................................48.00

Clear with images of dogs, metal
lid, 1950s-1960s, 8" h....45.00

Clear with yellow circles of varying sizes, chrome pour top
with removable lid, 11-1/4" h
.....................................22.00

Ruby, gold rooster on side, 2
gold bands, chrome strainer
and top, bands worn, dent in
lid, 11" h.........................85.00

Plastic and metal, traffic light shape,
battery op, orig swizzle stick,
1950s................................50.00

Pottery, green, Rookwood, mkd on
base, 1951, 12" h 700.00

Set, clear glass, ribbed, chrome top,
six matching glasses 60.00

Silverplate, 3 engraved golf scenes,
Meriden Silverplate Co., early
1900s, wear to plating on the lid,
10" h 295.00

❖ Coffee Mills

The secret to a really great cup of
coffee has always been freshly
ground coffee beans. Today's collectors are discovering this is still the
case. With the current popularity of
coffee, perhaps we'll see an
increase in coffee mills.

Collectors' Club: Assoc of Coffee
Mill Enthusiasts, 657 Old Mountain
Road, Marietta, GA 30064.

Arcade, wall style, top jar emb "Crystal," tin twist lid mkd Arcade,
lower glass container on adjustable platform, overall 17" h
....185.00

Elma, tin, orig brown and green
paint, wear 85.00

Enterprise #0 ....100.00

John Chatillon & Sons, cast iron,
drawer, single handle, worn,
12-3/4" h 850.00

Kitchen Aid, electric, white metal
base with glass jar, 14" h
....145.00

Olde Thompson, wooden, drawer,
handle with wooden knob, 6-3/4"
sq 95.00

Parker's Union Coffee Mill, wood,
label on front, 9-1/4" h..... 145.00

Rossenhaus, wooden, German or
Dutch, 3-3/4" x 4-1/4", 8" h
....48.00

Wood, drawer, metal cup to hold
beans, iron handle, 7-1/4" sq
....125.00

**Coffee mill, wooden dovetailed
case, cast iron top and handle,
8-1/2" high, 6" square, $110.**

Campbell Brand Coffee pail, 4-pound, $120.

Old Reliable Coffee tin, 1-pound, keywind, $20.

❖ Coffee Tins

Here's an advertising category that has only gotten hotter over the past few years. Collected for their colorful labels, these tins are found in many sizes and shapes.

Anchor Coffee, 1-lb 25.00
Bowers Bros. Coffee, Richmond, Va., round, large, emb top 50.00
Breakfast Call Coffee, round slip top, 3-lb 125.00
Del Monte Coffee, key lid 45.00
Folger's Coffee, 5-lb, keywind 50.00
Gold Bond Coffee, 1-lb, screw top 35.00
Hersh's Best............................70.00
King Cole.................................70.00
Luzianne Coffee, small size, Mammy illus 95.00
Mammy Coffee, 4-lb size, Mammy illus 500.00
National's Best Blend, 1-lb, screw top 60.00
Red Rose, 1-lb, keywind 45.00
Sears Coffee Pail 200.00
Society Brand, tin litho, 2" h ..325.00
White House Coffee, 1-lb, tin vacuum pack, keywind..........400.00

❖ Coin Ops & Trade Stimulators

Because many of these machines have seen a lot of use, expect to find wear and maybe even a repair or two.

References: Richard M. Bueschel, *Collector's Guide to Vintage Coin Machines*, Schiffer Publishing, 1995; ——, *Guide to Vintage Trade Stimulators & Counter Games*, Schiffer Publishing, 1997; ——, *Lemons, Cherries and Bell-Fruit-Gum*, Royal Bell Books, 1995; ——, *Pinball 1*, Hoflin Publishing, 1988; ——, *Slots 1*, Hoflin Publishing, 1989.

Periodicals: *Always Jukin'*, 221 Yesler Way, Seattle, WA 98104; *Antique Amusements Slot Machines & Jukebox Gazette*, 909 26th St NW, Washington, DC 20037; *Around the Vending Wheel*, 5417 Castana Ave, Lakewood, CA 90712; *Coin Drop International*, 5815 W 52nd Ave, Denver, CO 80212; *Coin Machine Trader*, 569 Kansas SE, P.O. Box 602, Huron, SD 57350; *Coin-Op Classics*, 17844 Toiyabe St, Fountain Valley, CA 92708; *Coin Slot*, 4401 Zephyr St, Wheat Ridge, CO 80033; *Gameroom Magazine*, 1014 Mt Tabor Rd, New Albany, IN 47150; *Jukebox Collector*, 2545 SE 60th Street, Des Moines, IA 50317; *Loose Change*, 1515 S Commerce St, Las Vegas, NV 89102; *Pin Game Journal*, 31937 Olde Franklin Dr, Farmington, MI, 48334; *Scopitone Newsletter*, 810 Courtland Dr, Ballwin, MO 63021.

Collectors' Club: Coin Operated Collectors Assoc, 1511 Holliston Trail, Ft. Wayne, IN 46825.

Duck Hunter, 1¢, arcade, shoots penny at target for gum ball, ABT Silver King, c1949 .... 250.00
Fortune Telling, Waitling, scale, #400, 1948 .... 400.00
Marklin Phillies, cigars, 1930s 150.00
Marvel, 1 cent, cigarette/gumball/ 3-reel trade simulator slot machine, Bakelite knob, paper cigarette labels on reels, 11" h, 8" w, 11" d 550.00
Mercury, 1 cent, cigarette trade stimulator slot machine, blue-green color, wear, paint chipped along top, 11" h, 9" w, 10-1/2" dia 550.00
Pete's Penny Ante trade stimulator, 1920s............................. 400.00
Skill Game, Kicker/Catcher, 5¢, 3 balls, Baker Mfg., c1940 .... 400.00
Stamp Machine, Shipman, 1960 .... 35.00
Tally-Ho, 5¢, wood rail pinball machine 250.00
Zeno Gum, 1¢, wooden case dispensed sticks of gum, c1910 .... 600.00

❖ Coins, American and Foreign

Coin collecting has been a favorite pastime for generations. Coin collectors are very particular about the grading of their coins, and they have established very specific guidelines. Many coin collectors find treasures at flea markets, partly because they are dedicated lookers, but also because they are usually very knowledgeable about their field.

For more information about this fascinating hobby, check the following references and periodicals.

1906 Liberty Head nickel, $1.

References: Krause Publications is the country's premier publisher of books on coins. The following are all excellent references by this publisher. Colin Bruce and George Cuhaj, *Standard Catalog of World Coins, 1601-1700*; Richard Doty, *America's Money-America's Story*; Dave Harper, *1999 North American Coins & Prices*, 8th ed; Chester Krause and Clifford Mishler, ed by Colin Bruce, *Standard Catalog of World Coins, 1801-1900*; Richard Lobel, Mark Davidson, Alan Hallistone and Eleni Caligas, *Coincraft's 1998 Standard Catalog of English & UK Coins, 1066 to Date*; N. Douglas Nicol, ed by Colin Bruce, *Standard Catalog of German Coins, 1601-Present*, 2nd ed; Jules Reiver, *The United States Early Silver Dollars, 1794 to 1804*; Wayne G. Sayles, *Ancient Coin Collecting V*; Bob Wilhite, *1998 Auction Prices Realized*, 17th ed.

Periodicals: *Coin Prices, Numismatic News, Coins,* and *World Coin News* are all published by Krause Publications, 700 E State St, Iola, WI 54990.

❖ College Collectibles

Flea markets are great places to look for college items. Most collectors concentrate on memorabilia from their alma mater.

Book, *The College Book of Verse*, ed by R. M. Gay, 1927, Riverside Press, Cambridge, Mass., 4" x 6-1/2" 20.00

Coloring book, Univ. of Florida

Gators, 1982, unused 15.00

Cuff links, Vassar, gold colored, pr 50.00

Etching, interior of Chapel at Univ. of Chicago, by Leon R. Pescheret, framed 60.00

Handbook, Harbrace College, 1951, hardcover............................4.00

Lunch box, oval, graphics of colorful college pennants 16.00

Mascot, Baylor Univ., bear, hard rubber, 1950s.........................20.00

Pennant
    Indiana Univ., red and white, 30" l 12.00
    Iowa State, maroon and gold felt, 23" l 12.00

Photograph, Colorado Agricultural College, black-and-white photo of track team, 1904............65.00

Pinback button, Texas Bowl, 1960s, red and white 4.00

Plate
    Alma College, Alma, Mich., Vernon Kilns 30.00
    Robinson Hall, Albion College, Albion, Mich., Wedgwood, 10-1/4" dia 45.00
    Susanna Wesley Hall, Albion College, Albion, Mich., Wedgwood, 10-1/4" dia 45.00

Postcard
    A and M College, campus scene, unused 1.00
    Bruce Hall, Central College, Conway, Ark., unused 3.00
    Campus, Univ. of Chicago, Ill., 1926, unused 2.50

Main Hall, Rutgers Univ., N.J., 1946, unused.................. 2.00

Meridian Senior High School-Junior College, Meridian, Miss., unused 4.00

The Student Center, Douglass College, New Brunswick, N.J., used............................ 2.00

Program, Rice Univ. vs Univ. of Houston, Sept. 11, 1971 . 100.00

Souvenir plate, Alma College, Mich., Vernon Kilns..................... 30.00

Souvenir spoon, St. Mary's College 35.00

Textbook, *Food for the Family*, Wilmot and Batter, hardcover, 1938, some writing inside 30.00

Yearbook, Oregon Agricultural College, 1920 .... 50.00

❂ Coloring & Activity Books

This is another area that is hot. Coloring and paint books were introduced in the early 1900s, but they didn't really catch on until the 1930s, when manufacturers began printing coloring books based on child stars, such as Shirley Temple. Most collectors look for uncolored books, but some will buy books with neatly executed work.

Michigan State University stein, $20.

Zoo Animals to Color, Whitman, 1953, unused, $10.

Africa, A Missionary Color Book for Children, Paul Hubartt, 10-3/4" x 7-1/2," few pgs colored......12.00

A-Team New Adventures Coloring and Activity Book, Modern Promotions, 1984, 24 pgs, binding tears and activities completed 5.00

Christmas Cut-Out and Coloring Book, illus by Florence Sarah Winship, flocked hat on cover Santa, 1954, 15" x 11", unused 35.00

Dumbo Press-Out Book 6.00

Elsie's My Family and Friends, 10 pgs, 4" x 6" 22.00

The Tiger in the Tank, Esso/Humble, 7-1/2" x 8-1/2," giveaway booklet, 16 pgs, tiger-related cartoon style coloring pages, full color cover art, early 1970s, unused 35.00

E. T. Coloring Book, Wanderer Book, Simon & Schuster, Universal Studios, 1982, 8" x 11" 15.00

GI Joe, 16 pgs, Spanish text, 1990, unused 12.00

Henry, 1956, one page colored30.00

Huckleberry Finn, Treasure Books, 1960s, 30 pgs, used, some damage 5.00

Lady and the Tramp Sticker Activity Book, unused 6.00

Monkey Shines, 1953, 8-1/4" x 11-3/8", few pages colored, some yellowing..................12.00

Pinocchio................................20.00

Planet of the Apes, Artcraft, authorized ed, Apjac Productions, Twentieth Century Fox Film Corp., some pages colored 20.00

Oh Susanna, Children's Musical Pack O' Fun, coloring book, punch-out toys, story book, unbreakable record, caricatures of black family, 1950s 95.00

Sambo's Restaurant Family Funbook Activity Book, 1978, unused..............................42.00

School Days Coloring Book, 1956, 6 pgs colored 9.50

Sound and Say Phonics Coloring Book, 1948, unused...........18.50

Spider-Man, 16 pgs 12.00

The Love Bug, Hunt's Food promotional, 1969, full page promo on back cover, unused............20.00

Thundercats, red cover, printed in Mexico, 1989, unused 15.00

Winnie Winkle, copyright 1953 ....75.00

Wizard of Oz, Waldman Publishing Corp., N.Y., 1966, 8" x 11", unused..............................10.00

❖ Comedian Collectibles

Those who can make us laugh seem to find their way into our hearts. Some collectors are now choosing to concentrate on these folks and are having a great time doing it.

Also see Autographs, Character Collectibles, and Movie Collectibles in this edition.

Book, *Don't Shoot, It's Only Me: Bob Hope's Comedy History of the United States*, Bob Hope, Putnam, 1990, 315 pgs, used...7.50

Colorforms set, Three Stooges, 1959, MIB 270.00

Coloring book, *Bob Hope*, Saalfield, unused..............................18.00

Comic book

    Jackie Gleason & The Honeymooners, #2 ....35.00

    Laurel & Hardy 3-D Comic Book, #2, 1987 ....7.00

Cookie jar, I Love Lucy 100.00

Game, Laurel and Hardy, Transogram, 1962 copyright 42.50

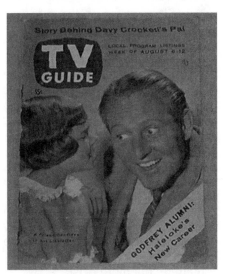

TV Guide, Art Linkletter cover, Aug. 6-12, 1955, $7.50.

Magazine

    Life, Feb. 4, 1946, Bob Hope and Bing Crosby cover 10.00

    Pet Milk Magazine, 1958, Red Skelton cover................ 15.00

    Song Hits, 1948, Bob Hope cover............................ 16.00

    Time, April 7, 1947, Fred Allen cover story.................... 25.00

    TV Guide, Feb. 25-March 3, ·1967, Phyllis Diller cover 15.00

Matchbook, Comedian Series, 1975

    Fields, W.C. 5.00

    Lewis, Jerry 5.00

    Marx, Groucho 21.00

Notebook binder, Laugh-In, 1969 .... 20.00

Photo, sgd, Benny Hill, 3-1/4" x 5-1/2" 255.00

Photo, sgd, 8" x 10"

    Hope, Bob 35.00

    Jones, Spike..................... 25.00

    Seinfeld, Jerry 20.00

    Skelton, Red..................... 45.00

Photo and clipped signature, Bud Abbott 100.00

Poster, Scrooged, Bill Murray and Robert Mitchum, rolled, 41" x 27" 7.00

Press kit, George Carlin, 1977 .... 10.00

Puppet, Jerry Lewis, 9" h, fabric, soft vinyl head, c1950.............. 55.00

Salt and pepper shakers, Three Stooges, pr 20.00

Tobacco card, Jimmy Durante, 1930s............................... 10.00

T-shirt, Carrot Top, black, XL .. 10.00

Waste basket, Laugh-In, litho show characters 45.00

❖ Comic Books

Comic books date back to the 1890s when newspapers started to print their popular funny-strips in book form. By the late 1930s, comic book manufacturers were producing all kinds of tales to delight young readers. Through the years, the artwork found in comic books has gotten more and more sophisticated, and many collectors now specialize in a particular artist or maker.

This is one of those areas in which collectors have learned to rely on good reference books. We've listed a few of the current publications here, but more exist.

References: *Comic Buyer's Guide Annual*, Krause Publications, issued annually; Dick Lupoff and Don Thompson (eds.), *All in Color for a Dime*, Krause Publications, 1997; Alex G. Malloy, *Comics Values Annual 2001*, Antique Trader Books, 2001; Robert M. Overstreet, *Overstreet Comic Book Price Guide*, 31st ed. Harper Resource, 2001; Peter Bickford, Brent Frankenhoff, and Maggie Thompson, *Comic Book Checklist & Price Guide*, 7th ed, Krause Publications, 2001.

Periodical: *Comics Buyer's Guide*, 700 E State St, Iola, WI 54990.

Collectors' Clubs: American Comics Exchange, 351-T Baldwin Rd, Hempstead, NY 11550; Fawcett Collectors of America & Magazine Enterprise, too!, 301 E Buena Vista Ave, North Augusta, SC 29841.

Reproduction Alert.

Battlestar Galactica, 1978, 10" x
   13-1/2" 15.00
Bewitched, #8 .... 3.75
Blondie, 1972, 14" x 11" 15.00
Crime Reporter, #2 .... 68.00
Daredevil, Oct, #114 .... 10.00
Fightin' Marines, #15 .... 5.00
Frankenstein, Classics Illustrated,
   #6 .... 4.50
Get Smart, #5 .... 5.00
Henry, 1971, 14" x 11" 15.00
Jungle Adventures, #3 .... 2.00
Katy Keene, #45 .... 12.50
Mister Miracle, June, #2 .... 9.00
Oliver Twist, Classics Illustrated, #17
   .... 2.00

Walt Disney's Man in Space, Dell, #716, 1956, $30.

Red Ryder, Frame-Up, Dell, #133,
   August, 1954, slight wear
   .... 18.00
Sherlock Holmes, Classics Illus-
   trated, #2 .... 40.00
Sleeping Beauty, Walt Disney, #1
   .... 20.00
Spider-Man, 1974, 14" x 11" 15.00
Star Wars Galaxy, Dark Horse Spe-
   cial, Fall, 1944, premier issue,
   factory sealed, cards and comic
   book 12.50
Super Heroes, #4 .... 2.50
Terry and the Pirates and the
   Dragon Lady, Dell, #6, 1936,
   oversized, C-8 .... 150.00
The Ghost in the Lady's Boudoir,
   Consolidated Book Publishers,
   1945 .... 38.00
The Phantom, Feature Book #20,
   1939, large size 290.00
Woody Woodpecker, #194, copy-
   right 1981, some wear 4.00
Zebra Jungle Empress, #1 ..... 22.00

❖ Commemorative Glasses

Decorative drinking glasses have always been a popular way to commemorate a special event or place.

Airplane, single propeller, green
   images of early planes, 1940s
   .... 16.00

Pro Football Champions glass, lists winning teams from 1948-1959, 5-3/4" high, $15.

Florida, hard plastic, hand-painted,
   c1950
   2-1/2" h, flamingo dec 10.00
   3-1/2" h, flamingo dec, mkd
     "ACM Rogers Plastic,
     Warren, Mass." 15.00
Gettysburg Address, etched on clear
   glass 20.00
Lord's Prayer, etched on clear glass
   .... 20.00
Midwinter Fair, 1894, ruby stained,
   etched "Edward Doyle" 110.00
Niagara Falls, Prospect Point, gold
   rim 20.00
The Alamo, San Antonio, Tx., three
   portraits 18.00
Whittier's Birthplace, etched,
   waisted tumbler 60.00

❖ Commemorative Medals

Commemorative medals are collected according to type, subject matter, and maker. Collectors look for unusual examples and prefer those in very good condition. Information on medal collecting is often found in coin reference books, and many coin dealers also handle medals.

American Legion
Circular, bronze and enamel,
1-1/4" dia........................8.00
With attached pinback button,
"12th Grand Promenade,
Camden, N.J., 1932".....12.00
Junior Baseball District Champs,
American Legion, 1-1/4" dia
....35.00
Knights of Pythias, medal with bar
pin, "Conn. Lodge 37," name on
back..................................38.00
Kodak Movie Awards, bronze, by
Medallic Art Co., N.Y., "Spon-
sored in Cooperation with
UFF/UFPA and CINE," 3" dia
....19.00
Military
Armed Forces Reserve, ribbon
bar and pin, 1-1/4" dia medal,
MOC..............................28.00
Canada, 1939-45 Victory Medal,
ribbon............................38.00
Cross with eagle, "1917-1918
United States Forces," back
reads "Presented by the people of Williamsburg, Mass. to
(blank for name) in grateful
recognition of patriotic service in the World War 1917-
1918," 1-1/4" x 1-1/4"....35.00
Drill Corps 1944 on bar pin,
medal reads "York Comy,
New York, S. J. Ecker," ster-
ling 28.00
Efficiency, Honor, Fidelity, back
reads "For Good Conduct,"
name inscribed..............16.00
For Merit, Army Air Forces, bar
pin with medal, sterling
....35.00
For Merit, 500 Hours, Army Air
Forces, bar pin with medal,
sterling 38.00
For Merit, 1000 Hours, Army Air
Forces, bar pin with medal,
sterling 38.00
Heroic or Meritorious Achieve-
ment, no name, ribbon..12.00
Merit Cross, 1st Class, Nazi, orig
box 165.00
Nazi Police Service, 18 years
....150.00
Waffen SS Army Infantry Assault
Badge............................50.00

❖ Compacts & Purse Accessories

Ladies have been powdering their noses for years and using interesting compacts to perform this task. Today's collectors have a variety of shapes, materials, and makers to search for at flea markets.

References: Roselyn Gerson, *Ladies Compacts*, Wallace-Homestead, 1996; ——, *Vintage and Contemporary Purse Accessories, Solid Perfumes, Lipsticks, & Mirrors*, Collector Books, 1997; ——, *Vintage Ladies Compacts*, Collector Books, 1996; ——, *Vintage Vanity Bags and Purses: An Identification and Value Guide*, 1994, 1997 value update, Collector Books; Laura M. Mueller, *Collector's Encyclopedia of Compacts, Carryalls & Face Powder Boxes* (1994, 1999 value update), vol. II (1997), Collector Books.

Collectors' Club: Compact Collectors Club, P.O. Box 40, Lynbrook, NY 11563.
For additional listings, see *Warman's Antiques & Collectibles* and *Warman's Americana & Collectibles*.
Avon, oval, lid dec with blue and
green checkerboard pattern
....35.00
Coty, #405, envelope box........65.00
Djer Kiss, with fairy.................95.00
Dorset, 3-1/8" sq, white, gold birds,
flowers, and leaves, mkd "Dorset, Fifth Avenue," slight discoloration around edges.........15.00
Dunhill, Mary, rouge.................28.00
Elgin, I Love You in different lan-
guages, cupids and hearts on
front 48.00
Elp Talcum, blue plastic box, unused
....24.00
Evans, goldtone and mother-of-
pearl, compact and lipstick combination 45.00
German, 2-7/8" dia, double mirror,
couple in colonial dress, mkd
"Made in West Germany", slight
discoloration 10.00
Halston, silver plated, name on puff,
used.................................150.00

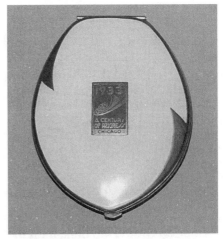
1933 Chicago World's Fair compact, $65.

Mondane Beauty Box, goldtone,
rhinestone basket, 3 reservoirs
....125.00
Norida, emb lady, silvertone....75.00
Petit Point, 2-1/4" x 2-3/4", gold
metal edge, red and yellow
roses, blue flowers, green
leaves, plain black petit point on
back 15.00
Princess Pat, rouge and large puff,
orig package 20.00
Rowanta, brown enamel, oval petit-
point compact 65.00
Souvenir, Atlantic City, NJ, rouge
compartment and puff.......48.00
Timepact, enamel, black, elongated
horseshoe shape, case and
watch 190.00
V8, clear rhinestone perimeter, black
enameled metal hinged lid,
raised V8 symbol accented with
rhinestones, some orig powder,
puff, little wear to case 95.00
Volupte, Adam and Eve under apple
tree...................................55.00
Whiting & Davis, vanity bag, silvered
mesh, etched and engraved lid,
braided carrying chain, 1920s
....425.00

❖ Computers & Computer Games

Technology is improving so rapidly that your computer is almost outdated before you've even had a chance to remove it from the box. With our increasing reliance on computers and our continual quest for

America Online 4.0 disk, mint in package, $1.

the biggest and the fastest, it's a sure bet that more computers will find their way to flea markets. Make sure you've got all the parts and as many original documents as possible when buying a computer on the secondary market. Because this is a relatively new segment of the flea market scene for many dealers, firm pricing is not yet established.

Apple

    Macintosh, 128K, 1st ed, standard keyboard and mouse 325.00

    Macintosh Plus, 1MB, beige 50.00

    IIc, 128K RAM, 1st "portable" computer made by Apple, includes power supply ... 65.00

Atari XL 800, additional modem 125.00

Compaq, typical PC, heavily used 50.00

Epson HX-40, laptop, 4MB RAM, 1987 .... 125.00

IBM, typical PC, 5-1/4" floppy drive, heavily used 75.00

Packard Bell, typical PC, 3-1/4" disc drive, moderate use 75.00

Zenith, PC, 5-1/4" floppy drive, 28K hard drive, working condition 25.00

❖ Condiment Sets

Condiment or castor sets are useful tableware containers. Usually they contain salt and pepper shakers as well as mustard pots, and perhaps bottles for vinegar, oil, etc.

Early castor sets are found with pressed or cut glass bottles held in a silver frame with matching tops and stoppers. China condiment sets have a more whimsical flavor.

Chintz, James Kent, salt and pepper, jam with spoon, matching tray 100.00

Chrome plated base metal, tray, salt and pepper, sugar bowl, all with cobalt glass liners visible through metal openwork, celluloid handles on tray, Occupied Japan, wear to plating 25.00

Condiment dish, cobalt, silverplate holder, 5" h, 8-1/8" x 3-1/4" 116.00

Hobnail, white milk glass, salt and pepper shakers, creamer, sugar and mustard, matching round tray with chrome loop handle 95.00

Pixieware, Holt Howard

    Mayonnaise 60.00

    Relish 55.00

Plastic, 4 red pots with yellow lids, relish, mustard, jam and 1 unlabeled, mkd Aladdin, each 3-1/2" h 38.00

Pickle castor, E.G. Webster & Bro., N.Y., polished silver-plate, some brass trim, 12" high, $225.

Pressed glass, clear

    2 glass cruets, dry mustard with spoon, salt and pepper, metal holder, 1 stopper damaged, silverplating worn 125.00

    Salt and pepper shakers, mustard, silverplate holder   125.00

Porcelain, Strawberry pattern, 8 pcs (plate, 3 triangular bowls, 3 spoons, lid) 45.00

Wedgwood, tray and covered pots 42.00

❖ Consolidated Glass Co.

Formed in 1893, Consolidated Glass produced interesting glassware and lamps until 1964, when a fire destroyed the plant. Some of the Consolidated patterns, such as Ruba Rombic and Dancing Nymph, are highly sought by collectors. However, don't overlook some of the other interesting color combinations and shapes produced by this firm.

Collectors' Club: Phoenix and Consolidated Glass Collectors, P.O. Box 81974, Chicago, IL 60681.

For additional listings, see *Warman's Antiques & Collectibles* and *Warman's Glass.*

Berry bowl, master, Cone, pink, glossy, SP rim 115.00

Bowl, Catalonian, yellow, 9-1/2" dia 48.00

Butter dish, cov, Cosmos pattern, pink bands 200.00

Cosmos pitcher, Consolidated Glass Co., 9" high, $265.

Candlestick, Five Fruits, Martele, green 32.00
Cigarette box, Catalonian, ruby flashed lid, crystal base 65.00
Cup and saucer, Catalonian, green 265.00
Goblet, Dancing Nymph, French Crystal 90.00
Lamp, Dogwood, brown and white 140.00
Night light, blown-out floral shade, silvered base, 10" h.........660.00
Nut dish, Ruba Rombic, smoky topaz 350.00
Pitcher, Cosmos pattern, 9" h 265.00
Plate, Catalonian, green, 7" dia 25.00
Puff box, cov, Lovebirds, blue 115.00
Toothpick holder, Florette, cased pink....................................75.00
Tumbler, Catalonian, ftd, green, 5-1/4" h..............................30.00
Vase
    Dancing Nymph, crimped, ruby stained, reverse French Crystal highlights, 5" h........125.00
    Poppy, green cased 550.00

❖ Construction Toys

Building toys have delighted children for many years. Today's collectors look for sets in original boxes with all the tools, vehicles, instructions, etc.
A.C. Gilbert
    Chemistry Experiment Lab, 3 pc metal box 35.00
    Erector Set, No. 4, complete, orig instructions...........285.00
    Erector Set No. 10181, Action Helicopter......................80.00
American National Building Box, The White House, wood pieces, landscaping, orig wood box ...120.00
Auburn Rubber, Building Bricks, 1940s 25.00
Embossing Company, No. 408, Jonnyville Blocks, deluxe edition, blocks, trees, hook and ladder, village plan 65.00
Halsman, American Plastic Bricks, #717 ....45.00
Lego, Main Street Set, orig box and pcs, unused.....................120.00

Lincoln Logs, #25 ....75.00
Tinkertoy, box with odd parts and pieces 10.00

❖ Cookbooks and Recipe Leaflets

Whether you're whipping up a cake or a gourmet meal, you just might need a cookbook. Collectors have long treasured these books and leaflets promoting different household products. Collectors are eager to find those with advertising or displays that show Depression glass, etc.

Periodicals: *Cook Book*, P.O. Box 88, Steuben, ME 04680; *Cookbook Collector Exchange*, P.O. Box 32369, San Jose, CA 95152-2369; *Cook Book Gossip*, P.O. Box 56, St. James, MO 65559; *Old Cookbook News & Views*, 4756 Terrace Dr, San Diego, CA 92116-2514.

Collectors' Club: Cook Book Collectors Club of America, P.O. Box 56, St. James, MO 65559.
A General's Diary of Treasured Recipes, Brigadier General Frank Dorn, 1953.........................10.00

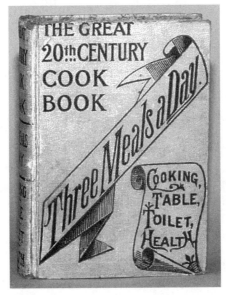

The Great 20th Century Cook Book by Maud C. Cooke, The L.W. Walter Co., Chicago, 1902, worn, $12.

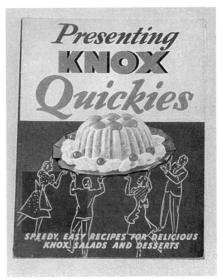

Knox Quickies, **1938, 23 pages, $10.**

Any One Can Bake, Royal Baking Powder, 1929, 100 pgs 10.00
Baker's Chocolate Cookbook, 1926, 64 pgs 15.00
Betty Crocker's Picture Cook Book, McGraw-Hill, 1950, 1st ed, 9th printing, 463 pgs 18.50
Carnation Cookbook, Mary Blake, 1943, softcover 10.00
Frigidaire Recipe Book, 1931, softcover, 48 pgs 5.00
From Amish and Mennonite Kitchens, Phyllis Pell, Good & Rachel Pellman, 1984, 420 pgs 10.00
Hershey's Index Recipe Book, 1934 ....12.00
Holiday Food Fun: Creative Ideas for Halloween, Thanksgiving, Christmas, and More, Pub. Int., Ltd., 1993, 4th ed, 96 pgs ... 8.00
Knox Gelatin Cookbook, 1933, 71 pgs 12.00
Louisiana Kitchen, Chef Paul Prudhomme, 1984, 351 pgs 11.00
Marvelous Meals with Minute Tapioca, 1938, 24 pgs 4.00
McCormack Cookbook, 1924, 32 pgs 34.00
Monarch Range Cook Book, shows gas and electric ranges, 72 pgs 10.00
My Hundred Favorite Recipes, Carnation Milk, 1927...............15.00
Philadelphia Cook Book of Town and Country, Anna Wetherill Reed, Branhall House, 1963, 346 pgs 15.00

Pillsbury Family Cookbook, 1863 .... 12.00
Rawleigh's Good Health Guide Almanac Cookbook, 1951, 31 pgs 12.00
Royal Cookbook, 1939, 64 pgs 10.00
Ryzon Baking Powder Cookbook, Marion Harris Neil, 1916, hardcover, 81 pgs 25.00
Shumway's Canning Recipes, booklet form 5.00
Southern Pacific Company Cookbook, 1940 .... 40.00
The Cookbook of the Stars, 1941, hardcover, 394 pgs 35.00
The Cooking of China, Food of the World, Emily Hawn, 1968, Time-Life Books 9.50
The Soup and Sandwich Handbook, Campbell Soups, thermal mug on cover, 1971 .... 12.00
Your Frigidaire Recipes, 1937 ... 3.50

❖ Cookie Cutters

Cookie cutters are found in various metals and plastics. Look for cutters in good condition and that are free of rust and crumbs.

Periodicals: *Around Ohio*, 508 N Clinton, Defiance, OH 43512; *Cookie Crumbs*, 1167 Teal Rd SW, Dellroy, OH 44620; *Cookies*, 9610 Greenview Ln, Manassas, VA 20109-3320.

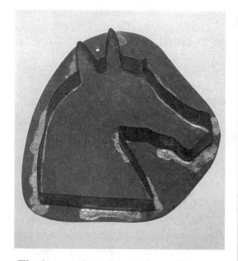

Tin horse head cookie cutter, $15.

Collectors' Club: Cookie Cutters Club, 1167 Teal Rd SW, Dellroy, OH 44620.
The following are tin or aluminum figural cookie cutters.
Bird, hand-made, 3-1/2" x 4" ...15.00
Biscuit, red wood handle, 2-3/4" dia 10.50
Bunny, rolled edge, spot soldered, 5" h 3.50
Chicken, 2" w, 2" h, 1920s 22.50
Club, green wood handle 7.50
Cowboy, gingerbread type, 6" h, stamped design, aluminum 15.00
Elephant, orig box mkd "Campaign Cookie Cutter-Vote Republican" 50.00
Flower, red wood handle, 2-1/2" dia 10.00
Gingerbread man, rolled edge, spot soldered, 5" h 4.00
Horse, aluminum, 1-3/4" 10.00
Lion, aluminum, 1-3/4" 10.00
Rabbit, green wood handle, 4" l 12.50
Reindeer, tin, 3" 12.00
Santa, hard red plastic 4.00
Set
    Alumode, stainless steel, reindeer, lamp, star, Christmas tree, Santa and snowman, orig box 15.00
    Aunt Chick Flower Garden Cookie Cutters, red plastic, strawberry, morning glory, daisy, crocus, wild rose, tulip, holly and poinsettia, 1950s, orig box, cutters show slight use 32.00
    Hallmark, Peanuts Gang, Christmas Cutters, four plastic cutters, orig box 35.00
Squirrel, soldered handle, used 10.00

Star, tin, 2" 6.50
Turkey, tin, 2" 8.50

❖ Cookie Jars

Cookie jars have been a highly desirable collectible for years. Today more and more cookie jars are appearing at flea markets, some new, some vintage. If you're looking for new jars, check for a signature by the artist or company's mark and the original box will add to the value. If vintage jars are more your style, check carefully for signs of use and damage.

McCoy coffee grinder cookie jar, 10" high, $48.

TIAS Top 10

The following list ranks the most highly sought collectibles on the Internet during 2000.

1. Avon
2. China
3. **Cookie jars**
4. Roseville
5. Furniture

6. Noritake
7. Lamps
8. McCoy
9. Clocks
10. Books

Source: www.tias.com

Periodicals: *Cookie Jar Collectors Express*, P.O. Box 221, Mayview, MO 64071-0221; *Cookie Jarrin'*, RR2, Box 504, Walterboro, SC 29488-9278; *Crazed Over Cookie Jars*, P.O. Box 254, Savanna, IL 61074.

Collectors' Club: Cookie Jar Club, P.O. Box 451005, Miami, FL 33245-1005.

For additional listings, see *Warman's Americana & Collectibles*.

Animaniacs 80.00
Basket, brown, lemons 20.00
Bear, roller skating, Metlox, 13" h
.... 75.00
Blue Bonnet Sue 40.00
Bugs Bunny 40.00
Buzz Lightyear, Treasure Craft
.... 225.00
Cactus, wearing bandana and cowboy hat, Treasure Craft 50.00
Cathy, Papel 75.00
Chef, American Bisque 90.00
Cookie Jug, brown stoneware, 11" h
.... 30.00
Curious George 50.00
Elvis, in car 100.00
Felix 50.00
Flintstones 50.00
Foghorn Leghorn 50.00
Handy Harry, Pfaltzgraff 185.00
I Love Lucy 100.00
King Corn, Shawnee, 10-1/2" h
.... 355.00
Magilla Gorilla, Twin Winton .. 275.00
Marilyn Monroe 50.00
Marvin Martian 50.00
Maxine 60.00
Mickey Mouse, mkd "Walt Disney Productions" 250.00
Mrs. Potts 35.00
Nanna, Mammy-type, Treasure Craft, USA, 1989 .... 95.00
Olympics, Warner Bros., 1996, 75.00
101 Dalmatians 40.00
Quaker Oats, 120th Anniversary
.... 70.00
Pillsbury Funfetti 45.00
Pink Panther, Treasure Craft
.... 125.00

Ranger Bear with Badge, Twin Winton, mkd "Code #84" 60.00
Sailor Boy, Shawnee Commemorative, limited to 100 jars, designed by S.A. Corl, produced by Mark Supnick, 1992, black hair
.... 495.00
Socks, Whitehouse Cat 40.00
Smokey Bear, 50th Anniversary
.... 275.00
Superman 85.00
Sylvester and Tweety, Applause
.... 55.00
Television Set, young Indian and teepee image on front 120.00
Troll, Norlin 55.00
Uncle Sam, American Cookie Jar Co. 150.00
Yosemite Sam 40.00
Wile E. Coyote 40.00

❖ Cooper, Susie

This English designer founded her own pottery in 1932. Her designs were bright and innovative.

Collectors' Club: Susie Cooper Collectors Group, P.O. Box 7436, London, N12 7GF, UK.

For additional listings, see *Warman's English & Continental Pottery & Porcelain*.

Bowl, Longleaf, 7-1/2" dia 60.00
Coffeepot
   Patricia Rose pattern, Kestrel shape, light green with pink rose, 7-1/2" h 550.00
   Nosegay pattern, Kestrel shape, 7" h 450.00
Cup and saucer, Orchid 85.00
Cup, saucer and plate
   Romance Pink, rim wear 45.00
   Tigerlily 80.00
Demitasse cup and saucer
   Endon 60.00
   Swansea Spray, pink 50.00
Gravy pitcher and plate, Floral Spray, crazing 70.00
Pitcher
   Crescent Sgraffito, inner lip damage, 7" h 300.00
   Dresden Spray, 4-1/2" h 95.00
   Susan's Red, 4" h 80.00
Plate, Apple 42.00
Soup Bowl, Dresden Spray 18.00

❖ Coors Pottery

Founded in Golden, Colorado, Coors Pottery produced industrial, chemical, and scientific porcelain wares. They then developed a household cooking ware and, later, six dinnerware lines. The company went out of business in the early 1940s, having lasted only 30 years.

Periodical: *Coors Pottery Newsletter*, 3808 Carr Place, N Seattle, WA 98103.

Ashtray
   Dark-brown, 6" l 15.00
   Green 15.00
Bowl, cov, Rosebud 60.00
Cake knife, Rosebud, maroon, yellow rosebud, green leaves
.... 37.50
Cup and saucer, Rosebud
   Blue 35.00
   White 50.00
Mortar and pestle, white, 3" h, 5" w
.... 110.00
Pitcher, Rosebud, chip, 6-1/2" h, 7-1/2" w 115.00
Platter, Mello-Tone, oval, canary yellow 24.00
Teapot, Rosebud 80.00
Vase
   Urn shape, 2 handles, green ext, white int, 5-3/4" h, 7" w
.... 55.00
   Round body, matte blue ext, white int, 10" h 100.00

❖ Copper

Copper has long been a favored metal with craftsmen as it is relatively easy to work with and is durable. Copper culinary items are lined with a thin protective coating of tin to prevent poisoning. It is not uncommon to find these items relined. Care should be taken to make sure the protective lining is intact before using any copper pots, etc. for domestic use.

References: Mary Frank Gaston, *Antique Brass & Copper*, Collector Books, 1992 (1994 value update); Henry J. Kaufmann, *Early American Copper, Tin & Brass*, Astragal Press, 1995.

Copper pan with wooden handle, $10.

Ashtray, sombrero shape, painted design of trees and water, 4" dia 12.00
Blowtorch, Bernz, red wood handle, 10" h 30.00
Colander, punched star design, 10-3/4" dia 80.00
Funnel, 4" h 12.00
Ladle, 6" dia copper bowl with rounded bottom, wrought-iron handle, 20-3/8" l 45.00
Lighter, cowboy boot form, 5-1/2" h 12.00
Measure, round with flat bottom, straight sides, broad flared tapering spout, C-shaped handle, wear, dents, 10" h, 6-5/8" dia 25.00
Pan
    Frying, metal handle, 5-1/4" dia, 9-1/4" l 35.00
    I. Young & Co., East Boston, Mass., brass handle, copper pan 1-3/4" h, 3-1/4" dia 25.00
Teakettle, dovetailed, hinged cover on spout, scrolled finial, stamped initials, 10" h 165.00
Teapot, Paul Revereware, wooden grip on handle 30.00
Vacuum washer, conical copper head, wooden handle, British Vacuum Washer Co., 1921 patent date, 24" l 95.00
Wash tub 75.00

❖ Costumes

Playing dress-up has always been fun for children. Collectors today enjoy finding vintage Halloween and other type of costumes. It's possible to find some very interesting costumes and accessories at flea markets.

Collectors' Club: The Costume Soc of America, P.O. Box 73, Earleville, MD 21919.

Banana Splits, orig costume, mask, box 80.00
Barnabas Collins, orig costume, mask, box 990.00
Bat Masterson, orig box 140.00
Batman, display bag, vinyl cape, mask, cuffs and badge, copyright 1966 National Periodical Publications 120.00
Captain Action, cloth outfit, mask, knife, 2 pistols, skull, brass knuckles, holster, belt, rifle and boots, orig box, copyright 1966 Ideal Toy Corp. 225.00
Captain Kangaroo, orig costume, mask, box 85.00
Cowboy, child size
    Boots, Acme 85.00
    Chaps 90.00
    Outfit, 4 pcs, 1960s 200.00
    Vest and chaps, hide rosettes 150.00
E.T., orig costume, mask, box 15.00
Fred Flintstone, vinyl mask and outfit, Ben Cooper, copyright 1973 Hanna-Barbera, orig box ... 40.00
Jaws, orig costume, mask, box 45.00
Little House on the Prairie, Laura, orig costume, mask, box 7.50
Matador, adult size, heavily embroidered, sequins and gold metallic thread, minor wear 120.00
Miss Piggy, orig costume, mask, box 15.00
Red Riding Hood, red cotton cape and skirt, yellow yarn braids sewn on hood, homemade, c1950 .... 35.00
Rosey the Robot, orig costume, mask, box 350.00
Star Wars, R2-D2, plastic mask, vinyl costume, Ben Cooper, copyright 1977, orig box 40.00
Thunderbirds, orig costume, mask, box 325.00
Winky Dink, orig costume, mask, box 200.00
Zorro, orig costume, mask, box 90.00

Cottage Ware covered butter dish, 4-1/2" high, 6-1/2" long, 5-1/2" wide, $55.

❖ Cottage Ware

Cottage Ware is the name given to charming English tea items that are shaped like a cottage. It is possible to complete a set of all the pieces necessary for serving a proper tea.

Biscuit jar, wicker handle, Price Bros., 7-1/2" h 95.00
Butter dish, cov, Fox and Hounds pattern, Kensington Cottage Ware 165.00
Creamer and sugar, brown, yellow, green and pink
    Keele Street Potteries 45.00
    Ye Old Cottage, Made in England, ink stamp in wreath "Price Bros. Made in England, Cottage Ware, Reg. No. 845007" 120.00
Cup and saucer, Price Bros. ... 35.00
Jam jar, cov, mkd "Kensington, England" 35.00
Milk pitcher, mkd "Price Brothers, England," 7-1/4" h 75.00
Set, creamer, cov sugar, cov jam jar, mkd "Keele Street Potteries" 95.00
Teapot, brown, yellow, green and pink, Ye Old Cottage, ink stamp in wreath "Price Bros. Made in England, Cottage Ware, Reg. No. 845007"
    8" w, 5-1/2" h 100.00
    8-1/2" w, 6" h, slight crazing to glaze 90.00

❖ Counter Culture

"Cool, man!" Whether you lived through the 1960s or just fantasize about that era of hippies and beatniks, you should know that collectors are actively seeking those love beads and psychedelic things.

Bolo tie medallion, star design, pink star, circles and checks shading from gray to light tan in background, Peter Max 15.00
Book, *Psychedelic Pscounds*, Alan Vorde, interviews with psychedelic bands 30.00
Bumper sticker, Save the Whales 1.00
Cigarette holder, Beatnik, figural man or woman, orig cardboard and plastic pkg, Hong Kong, 1950s 40.00
Medallion, peace sign, bronzed metal 10.00

Mood ring, adjustable band 12.00
Pet rock, MIB 35.00
Pinback button
    Feed Twiggy, black-and-white
        center photo, mkd "1967
        Design Unlimited 1896
        Pacific, S.F." 20.00
    Go Mod, white lettering, deep
        pink background, 1970s,
        2-1/4" dia 10.00
    Jerry Garcia for President, 1980,
        2-1/8" sq, black-and white
        photo, yellow lettering ... 15.00

❖ Country Store Collectibles

Today we tend to think of old time
store items as "Country Store." In
reality, much of the memorabilia we
collect was from small stores located
in cities as well as country locales.
These stores offered people a place
to meet, stock up on supplies, and
catch up on the latest gossip. They
were filled with advertising, cases,
cabinets, and all kinds of consumer
goods.

Reference: Richard A. Penn, *Mom
and Pop Stores*, R.S. Pennyfield's,
1998.

Broom display, hanging, metal,
    round with ring for holding
    brooms by handles 100.00
Coffee barrel, BAR Special Blend,
    R.A. Railton Co., Chicago, 75
    lbs, 25-1/2" h, 17-1/2" dia
    .... 175.00
Coffee grinder, double wheel, Enter-
    prise, cast iron, old red and blue
    repaint, yellow details, finial
    replaced 357.50
Cracker box lid, tin with glass insert
    "Purity Pretzel Co., Stuber &
        Kuck Co., Peoria, Ill." 27.00
    "Uneeda Bakers" 30.00
Crate, Rumford Baking Powder, held
    1 dozen cans, 5-3/4" h, 13" w,
    10" dia 25.00

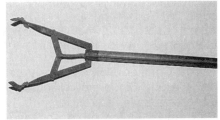

**Can grabber, metal grips on
wooden shaft, 54-1/2" long, $45.**

Display
    Beechnut Gum, tin, 27-1/2" x
        15-1/2", c1950, 3 tiers
        .... 130.00
    Yeast Foam, tin, wall mounted,
        "Eat Yeast Foam" 27-1/2" h,
        2-1/2" dia 60.00
Scoop, 5", tin, wood handle 28.00
Seed box
    "Choice Flower Seeds From
        D.M. Ferry & Co., Detroit,
        Mich.," shows 3 children in
        flower garden, oak, litho
        paper label under lid, 6-3/4" h,
        11-1/2" w, 9-3/4" dia 440.00
    "Reliable Seeds, From the Sioux
        City Nursery & Seed Co.
        Sioux City, Iowa," wood,
        machine dovetails, paper
        labels on front and inside lid,
        chipping to labels, ... 187.00
Seed packet, Ruppert's Seeds,
    Washington, D.C., orig 10 cents,
    color picture of the vegetable or
    fruit 1.00
Spool cabinet, "Clark's Mile-End
    Spool," wood, 5 drawers with
    reverse-painted glass fronts
    advertising product, paint loss to
    glass, 19" h, 30" w 495.00
Store jar
    Clear, swirl lid with ground stop-
        per, 11" h, 4-1/2" dia 125.00
    Necco Candies, clear, orig lid,
        10-1/2" h 55.00
String holder, cast iron
    Beehive form, 6" h, 7-1/4" dia
        .... 150.00
    Inverted J-shaped arm, 11" h
        .... 45.00
Tobacco cutter, cast iron, "Griffin
    Goodner Grocer Co., Tulsa,
    Okla," 1914 patent date, 8-1/2"
    h, 12-3/4" l 195.00

❖ Country Western

Even if you've never been to
Nashville, you've probably tapped
your foot to a few country western
tunes. Country Western collectors
know their favorite stars and eagerly
search for memorabilia, autographs,
records, and other items related to
their singing careers.

Periodical: *Goldmine*, 700 E State
St, Iola, WI 54990.
Book
    Johnny Cash: Man in Black,
        Johnny Cash, Zondervan
        Books, 1975, 1st ed, 244 pgs,
        edges nicked 8.75

Kentucky Stand, Jere Wheel-
        wright, 1951, 279 pgs 6.00
Photo, Dolly Parton, sgd, black-and-
    white, 8" x10" 35.00
Ring, cowboy hat form, sterling sil-
    ver, c1940 .... 85.00
Sheet music, How's The World
    Treating You?, Boudleaux Bryant
    and Chet Atkins, recorded by
    Eddie Arnold, 1952 .... 13.00
Straw hat, Dale Evans model
    .... 180.00
T-shirt, Garth Brooks, "The Hits,"
    promo, face image and "Garth"
    on front 35.00

❖ Cowan Pottery

Cowan Pottery encompasses
both utilitarian ware and artistic
ware. R. Guy Cowan began making
pottery in Ohio around 1915 and
continued until 1931. Most pieces
are marked with an incised name.
Later a black stamp mark and initials
were used.

Bookends, Sunbonnet Girl, yellow
    glaze, pr 245.00
Candlestick, pearlized blue, 4" h, pr
    .... 150.00
Card holder, green, chip, 3-1/2" h
    .... 50.00
Cigarette holder, sea horse, aqua
    .... 42.00
Compote, diamond shape, tan ext,
    green int, 2" h 38.00
Console set, oval bowl, 2 short can-
    dlesticks, white 200.00
Match holder, cream color, 3-1/2" h
    .... 60.00
Trivet, scalloped rim, bust of young
    girl framed by flowers 325.00
Vase, fan shape, apple green, gold
    specks, 5" h 90.00

❖ Cowboy Heroes

Although most cowboy heroes
were matinee idols, there were some
cowboy heroes who were popular
radio and/or television personalities.
Many of today's collectors specialize
in one character or show, but some
are fascinated with all kinds of cowboy memorabilia.

Periodicals: *Collecting Hollywood*,
American Collectors Exchange,
2401 Broad St, Chattanooga, TN

Cowan Jazz bowl, $121,000. (Photo courtesy of Cincinnati Art Galleries, Cincinnati, Ohio)

It's a record

Here's a bowl that gives a whole new meaning to the term "All that jazz."

Made by Cowan, this Jazz bowl set a record price when it was sold for $121,000 by Cincinnati Art Gallery during 2000.

The work of Viktor Schreckengost, the large Jazz bowl had incised Art Deco motifs representing entertainment, commerce and day-to-day life in New York. On the interior were stars and planets. Made circa 1930 in two shades of blue, the bowl was 11-1/4 inches high and 16-1/4 inches in diameter. A 1-inch chip on the foot had been professionally repaired. It's believed that fewer than 50 large Jazz bowls were made.

The bowl was purchased by the Cleveland Museum of Art.

37408; *Cowboy Collector Newsletter*, P.O. Box 7486, Long Beach, CA 90807; *Westerner*, Box 5232-32, Vienna, WV 26105; *Westerns & Serials*, Route 1, Box 103, Vernon Center, MN 56090.

Collectors' Clubs: Cowboy Collector Network, P.O. Box 7486, Long Beach, CA 90807, www.hopalong.com; Cowboy Collector Soc, 4248 Burningtown Rd, Franklin, NC 28734

For additional listings, see *Warman's Americana & Collectibles* and categories covering specific cowboys in this edition.

Arcade card
    Bob Baker, on rearing horse, black-and-white 12.00
    John Mack Brown, green tones 12.00
    Sunset Carson, red tones .. 12.00
    Fred MacMurray, gun drawn, black-and-white 10.00
    Charles Starrett, full color .. 15.00
Big Little Book, *Bobby Benson on the H-Bar-O Ranch*, Whitman, 1934 .... 42.00
Comic book, *Red Ryder Comics*, #102, Dell, 1952 .... 18.50
Guitar, Buck Jones, 37" l 250.00
Movie, *Zane Gray Adventure Stories Action-Packed Thrillers*, 16mm, orig box 40.00
Movie poster, McLintock, John Wayne spanking Maureen O'Hara, 1963 .... 250.00
Photograph, William S. Hart, 1980s re-release 5.50
Sheet music, *You Two-Timed Me One Time Too Often* by Jenny Lou Carson, recorded by Tex Ritter, 1945, Ritter on cover 13.00

Red Ryder Lucky Coin, $10.

Target game, Straight Arrow, litho tin board, 3 magnetic feather-tipped arrows, National Biscuit Co., c1950 .... 75.00

❖ Cow Collectibles

Cows have been a part of the folk art and country decorating schemes for years. But cow collectors will be the first to tell you that they are also popular themes for advertising and even children's items.

Periodical: *Moosletter*, 240 Wahl Ave, Evans City, PA 16033.
Blotter, Cow Brand Baking Soda, 4" x 9-1/4" 15.00
Butter crock, ink stamp of cows, large chip on lid 225.00
Butter mold, 2-pc, rectangular, cow motif, ornamental designs along outer edge, 3-1/2" x 4-7/8" 192.50
Butter stamp, 1-pc
    Cow feeding from trough, small floral design and cluster of 4 diamonds, spool-shaped handle, 4" dia 350.00

Cow with tree, 3-5/8" dia . 170.00
Cookie jar
    Brush-McCoy, mouse on cow, early 1950s 200.00
    Elsie the Cow in barrel, 11-1/2" h 400.00
Creamer
    "Fairway, Made in Japan," 1950s, 4-1/2" h, 6-1/2" l 38.00
    Royal Bayreuth, unmkd, c1920, 6-1/2" h, 10" l 395.00
    Souvenir of Washington, D.C., mkd "Hand Painted, Japan," 1940s, 3-1/4" h, 5-1/4" l 45.00
Pitcher, blue & white pottery, Cows pattern............................ 170.00
Sign, flange "Slow, Cattle Crossing," porcelain, 2-sided, 18" h, 14" w 115.00
Toy, ramp walker, plastic, brown and white, 1950s, mkd "Made in Hong Kong," orig sealed cellophane 18.00

M.A. Hadley pottery cow plate, 11" diameter, $20.

❖ Cracker Jack

When Frederick William Rueckheim added molasses to popcorn in 1896, the concoction became known as Cracker Jack. Beginning in 1910, each box contained a coupon that could be redeemed for a prize. It wasn't until 1912 that the prizes themselves were placed in the boxes.

The Cracker Jack sailor boy and his little dog Bingo first appeared in the company's advertisements in 1916 and debuted on the boxes in 1919. Early toy prizes were made of paper, wood, and even lead, with plastic toys introduced after 1948.

References: Alex Jaramillo, *Cracker Jack Prizes*, Abbeville Press, 1989; Larry White, *Cracker Jack Toys: The Complete Unofficial Guide for Collectors*, Schiffer Publishing, 1997.

Collectors' Club: Cracker Jack Collectors Assoc, 5469 S Dorchester Ave, Chicago, IL 60616.

Activity book, *Cracker Jack Painting & Drawing Book*, Saalfield, 1917, 24 pgs 45.00

Booklet, *Cracker Jack Riddles*, red, white and blue cover, 42 pgs, 1920s 60.00

Bowl and cup, plastic, roughness to rims, bowl 5-1/2" dia, cup 3-1/2" h............................. 12.50

Doll, Cracker Jack boy, fabric, 8" h 16.00

Flat whistle, advertises Cracker Jack, 1" x 2-5/8" 110.00

Prize

    Auto Race spin toy, one crease 13.00

    Clown with poodle, plastic, pale green, 1-3/4" h 2.00

    Horse & wagon, tin, red, white and blue, 1930's, 2-1/4" l 65.00

    Spinner, blue and white, "Always on Top" 95.00

    Spoon and fork, tin, 1930s, 2" l 10.00

    Watch, litho, 1940s 85.00

Cracker Jack Cocoanut Corn Crisp tin, 8-1/2" high, 5-1/2" diameter, $225.

❖ Crackle Glass

Crackle glass can be identified by the web-like system of light cracks that cover the surface of the glass. These cracks are an intentional part of the design, but because they are random, no two pieces are alike. From the late 1930s to the early 1970s, crackle glass was quite popular in the West Virginia glass houses, including Pilgrim, Blenko, Kanawha, and Viking.

References: Judy Alford, *Collecting Crackle Glass with Values*, Schiffer, 1997; Stan and Arlene Weiman, *Crackle Glass Identification and Value Guide, Book I (1996), Book II (1998)*, Collector Books.

Collectors' Club: Collectors of Crackle Glass, P.O. Box 1186, N. Massapequa, NY 11758.

For additional listings, see *Warman's Glass*.

Beaker, 7" h, 5" w, hand-blown crystal, hand-applied mint green leaves, Blenko Glass 75.00

Bottle, figural, fish, amber, orig paper label "Imported by St. Julian Wine Company, Detroit, Mich.," applied mouth, fins, and eyes, 15-1/2" l...................275.00

Bowl, 8-1/4" h, 5-1/4" dia, crystal bowl, amethyst foot, Blenko Glass 85.00

Bud vase, amberina, Kanawha, orig label, 7-1/4" h 60.00

Candy dish, cov, amberina, Kanawha, 3" h 45.00

Creamer, emerald green body, clear handle, Pilgrim...................35.00

Ladle, amethyst handle, crystal bowl, Blenko Glass, 15" l.160.00

Lemonade set, 8-1/4" h pitcher, applied reeded handle, 6 glasses 4-3/4" h, topaz 295.00

Nappy, 5" x 5-1/4" x 2" h, heart shaped, amberina, hand-blown, pontil scar, Blenko Glass ...65.00

Crackle glass rose bowl, aqua, 3" high, 4" diameter, $12.

Paperweight, 6" h, apple, amethyst, applied crystal stem and leaf, Blenko Glass 55.00

Punch bowl set, large punch bowl with clear cover, four glasses, clear, orig German manufacturer's stickers, 9-3/4" h .. 500.00

Punch cup, emerald green body, clear handle, Pilgrim 20.00

Rose bowl, blue, 6" h, 9" w, Blenko Glass, c1950 .... 75.00

Vase

    4" h, 4" w, double neck, Blenko Glass 35.00

    5-1/2" h, smoke gray 65.00

Cranberry glass vase, enameled fern-like decoration, ormolu stand, 4-1/4" high, $75.

❖ Cranberry Glass

When a glassmaker mixes a small amount of powdered gold in a warm blob of molten glass, the glass changes to a rich cranberry color, hence the name. Because glassmakers used slightly different formulas, there are slight differences in shade between examples of cranberry glass.

For additional listings, see *Warman's Antiques & Collectibles* and *Warman's Glass*.

Reproduction Alert.

Basket, Hobnail, clear twisted thorn handle, Fenton.................. 20.00

Bottle, Inverted Thumbprint pattern, white enameled dot flowers and bands, gold trim, clear faceted ball stopper, 8-1/2" h 150.00

Box, 4", crystal rigaree 140.00
Candlestick, applied yellow eel dec, 10-1/2" h.......................... 125.00
Creamer, Optic pattern, fluted top, applied clear handle 90.00
Pitcher, Ripple and Thumbprint pattern, bulbous, round mouth, applied clear handle, 6-1/2" h 125.00
Sauce dish, Hobb's Hobnail pattern 45.00
Toothpick holder, crystal prunts 48.00
Tumble-up, Inverted Thumbprint pattern 75.00
Vase, 8-7/8" h, bulbous, white enameled lilies of the valley dec, cylindrical neck 125.00

❖ Credit Cards and Tokens

Some people use credit cards to shop and others shop for credit cards. Plastic charge cards became big business in the 1950s. Before that, folks used charge plates, coins, and tokens. Some stores issued paper cards before plastic became the material of choice with card vendors.

Periodical: *Credit Cards and Phone Cards News*, P.O. Box 8481, St Petersburg, FL 33738.

Collectors' Clubs: Active Token Collectors Organization, P.O. Box 1573, Sioux Falls, SD 57101; American Credit Card Collectors Society, P.O. Box 1992, Midlothian, VA 23112; American Numismatic Association, 818 N. Cascade Ave., Colorado Springs, CO 80903; American Vecturist Assoc, P.O. Box 1204, Boston, MA 02104; Token & Medal Society, 9230 SW 59th St, Miami, FL 33173.

Charge coin, Hotel LaSalle, Chicago, 21209 on the back . 100.00
Charge plate, Charga-Plate Stores, Cleveland, Ohio, unsigned 10.00
Credit cards
    ABC Credit Inc., 1955 .... 3.00
    American Express, April 1959, paper 1,060.00
    American Express, October 1959, plastic................ 160.00
    Diner's Club, 1966, colored blocks, blue top 50.00
    Chase Visa, 1987, gold card, plastic............................ 8.00
    Hertz, 1960 .... 22.50

Hotels Statler, 1931, cardboard 35.00
Saks Fifth Avenue, paperboard 24.00
Socony-Vacuum Oil Co., 1937, paper......................20.00
Standard Oil Co. of California, 1939, paper 14.00
Sunoco, 1968, plastic 16.50
TWA, Getaway Card, couple in swim suits, 1974 .... 15.00
Tokens
    Bamberger & Co., celluloid 225.00
Plotkin Bros., Boston, white metal, lion's head over shield, PB logo, rect...................................18.00

Davy Crockett handkerchief, $40.

❖ Crockett, Davy

"King of the Wild Frontier" described Walt Disney's version of this popular American character.
Carrying case, paper covering with snakeskin pattern, felt likeness of Davy Crockett glued to side 55.00
Comic book, *Davy Crockett, Indian Fighter*, #631, Dell, 1955 ...35.00
Cookie jar, Brush, unmkd, 1956, 10-1/4" h 425.00
Friction toy, stagecoach, rubber tires off wheels, 5-1/4" l, 3-1/4" h 250.00
Fringe jacket, 1950s, some stains 55.00
Moccasins, suede leather, child's size 3, imprinted with Davy Crockett insignia, slight wear 32.00
Mug, white milk glass, green image 28.00
Paper plate, "Walt Disney's Official Davy Crockett Indian Fighter," shows 4 movie scenes in each corner, c1955, 6-1/4" sq 18.00
Record and book, *Disneyland Davy Crockett Record Story Book*, 24-pg book and long-playing

record, Walt Disney Productions, 1971, 7-1/4" sq 29.00
Ring, plastic 60.00
Tie clip, coppertone metal, 1950s, mint cond 18.00

❖ Crooksville Pottery

Crooksville Pottery in Crooksville, Ohio made semi-porcelain dinnerware and housewares from 1902 until 1959. Some pieces were marked.
Cup and saucer
    Iva Lure 25.00
    Sun Lure........................... 22.00
Gravy boat, Iva Lure 35.00
Pitcher and cover, Petit Point House, 6" h 90.00
Plate, bread and butter
    Iva Lure 9.00
    Petit Point House 6.50
Plate, dinner
    Apple Blossom 12.00
    Dinner Rose 18.00
    Flamingo 15.00
    Iva Lure 30.00
    Sun Lure........................... 22.00
Plate, salad, Iva Lure.............. 15.00
Platter
    Petit Point House, 13-1/4" dia 40.00
    Wildflowers, oval, 13" l 25.00
Sugar, cov, Petit Point House 25.00
Vegetable, open, oval
    Bittersweet 30.00
    Iva Lure 35.00
Vegetable, Wildflowers, 8-3/4" dia 25.00

❖ Crown Devon

Crown Devon is an English pottery dating from 1870 to 1982. The factory was located at Stoke-on-Trent and produced a wide range of pottery, from majolica, luster wares, figurines, souvenir wares, etc.
For additional listings, see *Warman's English & Continental Pottery & Porcelain.*
Ashtray, Hot Scent 25.00
Bowl, oval, pedestal base, painted green, orange and black, geometric banding, gilt accents, paper label, 11" l 90.00
Cheese dish, Spring pattern, red and blue flowers and urn, scattered ivy, tan shaded ground, slant top 85.00

Condiment set, silver-plated holder 160.00
Jug, musical
   Auld Lang Syne, dec of men in tavern, 4-1/2" h 85.00
   Here's A Health Unto Her Majesty, raised tinted portraits of Queen Elizabeth II, colored bands, gold trim 145.00
Saucer, Coaching Days, 5" dia..3.00
Tidbit, floral form, orange enameled highlights, 6" l, 4-1/2" w, 1" h 25.00
Toby jug
   Chelsea Pensioner, 1950s, 4" h 60.00
   Guardsman, 1960s, 8-1/4" h 90.00
Vase, two geese in flight, patch of cat-o-nine tails, mkd with crown over "Crown Devon, Fieldings, Made in England 5785," impressed 1183, 11" h 95.00

❖ Cuff Links

Certain fashion styles dictated long sleeves that needed to be fastened with a decorative cuff link. These little jewelry treasures have been making colorful statements for years. Look for backs and closures in different styles.

References: Most jewelry books will contain information about cuff links, including Christie Romero's *Warman's Jewelry.*

Collectors' Club: National Cuff Link Society, P.O. Box 346, Prospect Heights, IL 60070.
Brushed and textured goldtone metal, smoky black center stone, 1970s 6.00
Cameo, hematite-type stone, silver-tone setting........................... 8.00
Gold filled, yellow and white gold, dumb bell style, swivel back, marquise cut, engine turned design on top, plain back, sgd "S & W" (Sturtevant and Whiting Co.) 30.00
Gold filled, yellow and white gold, dumb bell style, swivel back, octagon shape, machine and hand engraved design on top, plain back, sgd "S & S" 45.00
Gold, 10k yellow, hexagon shape, engine turned engraved design on front, sgd "NJSC" in four leaf clover, c1920 .... 125.00
Gold, 14k rose, cushion shape top, inlaid turquoise, crescent shape back, late 19th C, wear and some cracking to turquoise 175.00

Green stones, gold finish, pair, $1.

Gold, 14k yellow, round, engine turned design on front and back, sgd "C" in arrowhead, c1920 .... 225.00
Gold, 14k yellow, two rubies set in each, c1960 .... 395.00
Gold, 18k yellow, Art Deco style, little diamonds in center of MOP plaques, set in platinum bezels 350.00
Goldtone, pink cabochon stone 10.00
Silver colored, prong-set yellow stones 12.00
Silverplated, mkd "Correct Links" 4.00
Silvertone, knight riding horse ...8.00
Silvertone, mother-of-pearl disks 10.00
Silvertone, textured and polished metal, dark blue stone, mkd "Pat 2874,381" 10.00
Silvertone, white around smoky gray center, Victorian 18.00
Snappers, enameled black and white, 1/2" dia 15.00

❖ Cupids

Cute little cupids have been charming our hearts since Victorian times. They can be found on many types of objects, just watch out for those arrows. They might be pointing at you.

Collectors' Club: Cupid Collectors Club, 2116 Lincoln St, Cedar Falls, IA 50613, www.net-ins.net/showcase/cupidclub/.
Bookends, cast iron, 8" h, some damage, pr 75.00
Box, cov, porcelain, yellow glazed ground, cupids on base and top, flower finial, green "Hand Painted, Made in Japan" mark, 4-1/4" l 30.00
Bud vase, amber shading to clear, white enameled cupid, in the style of Mary Gregory, 8-5/8" h, some wear, slight gold loss at top rim.............................. 175.00

Dresser box, ceramic, heart shaped, cupids on top, bow pattern on base 35.00
Dresser set, beveled mirror with red cupids, brass handles with filigree................................. 250.00
Easter card, postcard type, pair of Cupids with Easter Egg, unused 5.00
Figure, bisque, 4-1/2" h........... 20.00
Jar, cov, porcelain, orange and gold, center scene of Victorian woman and cupid, 4-1/2" dia......... 35.00
Limited edition plate, Wedgwood, Mother's Day, 1984, musical cupids under tree 40.00
Pin, shooting arrow
   Brass, Coro, lavender and white rhinestones, c1940, 2" x 2" 42.00
   Sterling silver, intent expression, stamped "Sterling" on back, c1940, 2" l, 2-1/2" w.....110.00
Pitcher, ceramic, beige ground, cupid on each side, black wreath and "Japan" on bottom, 7-3/4" h 45.00
Postcard, Cupid sharpening arrow, holding bow, unused 5.00
Print, orig frame
   Cupid Asleep....................115.00
   Cupid Awake 115.00
Valentine, postcard type
   Biplane with cupid, "To My Valentine, Cupid's stolen my heart which he is bringing to you" 15.00
   Cupid with heart in wheelbarrow, "It's all for You," leather postcard, postmarked Indianapolis 6.00
   Man and woman in floral heart wreath with cupid, "A Token of My True Love," used....... 7.50
   Two small children playing peek-a-boo with Cupid, postmarked 1919 .... 8.00
Vase, Bristol Glass, transfer dec of woman and cupids, English, c1880, 8" h.... 295.00

❖ Cups and Saucers

Cup and saucer collecting is a hobby that many different generations have enjoyed. Some porcelain makers have created special cups and saucers for collectors. Other collectors prefer collecting cups and saucers that were made as dinnerware or even Depression glass patterns.

Demitasse cup with petal-shaped saucer, pink, gold and white, unmarked, 2-1/8" high, $5.

Apple dec, natural colors, green foliage, white ground..............25.00
Bavaria, blue luster ext, MOP int, black handle and rim, mkd "Bavaria"..........................10.00
Belleek, Limpet pattern, 3rd black mark 100.00
Beswick, Benjamin Bunny, Royal Albert mark........................17.50
Bone china, purple thistles, green leaves and pods, brown stems, gold trim 17.50
Coronation, George and Elizabeth, sepia portraits, multicolor royal crest on saucer, gold trim, Aynsley......................................95.00
Deldare Ware, street scene, Buffalo Pottery.............................225.00
Flow Blue, Hamilton pattern 45.00
Forget Me Not, white shaded to cobalt blue ground, gold int, gold striped handle and rim, mkd "Made in Germany" 12.00
Moss Rose, gold trim, mkd "H & Co. Limoges" 30.00
Remember Me, brown and pink flowers, scalloped saucer, mustache guard in cup 35.00
Roses dec, gold handle, mkd "Germany" 30.00
White, thin gold trim, unmkd....20.00

❖ Cuspidors

Called cuspidors or spittoons, these functional items can be found in metal or ceramic. They were common elements in bars, on trains, and even in homes.
Cast iron, turtle form, copper shell and bowl, mkd "Golden Novelty Co., Chicago, Ill.," 1901 patent date, orig paint, 13-1/2" l
....485.00
Graniteware
Cobalt/white swirl, white int, 4-1/4" h, 7-1/2" dia 300.00

Carnival glass cuspidor, soda gold, Imperial Glass, 7" diameter, $42.

Columbian, 1-pc...............275.00
Gray, lady's spit cup, 3" h, 4-1/4" dia 85.00
Ironstone, warrior and lion transfer, copper luster....................265.00
Pewter, bulbous body, flared rim, handle, unmkd, 4-3/4" h 82.50
Pottery/stoneware
Albany glaze, incised "L.J. Underwood. Barberton, Ohio. July 24, '09" and "L.J.U., 7-24-1909," 4-1/2" dia............93.50
Blue and white, butterfly and shield pattern, 6" h, 7-1/2" dia 85.00
Brown glaze, embossed vines 35.00
Green and cream, stylized floral design............................85.00
McCoy, green.....................75.00
Romantic Staffordshire, blue transfer, molded basketweave pattern 260.00
Spongeware, circular sponged dabs around body, blue bands at rim and shoulder, 4-1/2" h 99.00
Yellowware, green, blue and tan sponging, 7-1/2" dia...........80.00

❖ Custard Glass

Custard glass is a yellowish opaque glass. Its color is derived from the uranium salts that are added to the hot molten glass. Because different manufacturers used slightly different formulas, you can expect variations in color from maker to maker.

Collectors' Club: Custard Glass Collectors Soc, 14312 SE 111th St, Oklahoma City, OK 73165.
For additional listings, see *Warman's Antiques & Collectibles* and *Warman's Glass.*

Berry bowl, master, Louis XV, good gold 110.00
Butter dish, cov, Georgia Gem, enamel dec 300.00
Celery, Ring Band................ 300.00
Compote, Argonaut Shell........ 80.00
Creamer, Jackson.................. 70.00
Goblet, Grape and Gothic Arches, nutmeg stain 75.00
Napkin ring, Diamond with Peg 150.00
Plate, Grape and Cable 55.00
Punch cup, Northwood Grape 50.00
Sauce, ftd, Intaglio 90.00
Spooner, Intaglio..................... 95.00
Sugar, cov, Georgia Gem, pink floral dec 185.00
Table set, cov butter, creamer, cov sugar and spooner, Argonaut Shell............................... 425.00
Toothpick holder, Louis XV ... 200.00
Tumbler, Vermont................... 90.00

Custard glass tumbler, "Souvenir of Cedar Point, Ohio," $65.

❖ Cut Glass

Cut glass should sparkle and feel sharp to the touch. It has been made by American and European companies for many years. Most companies didn't sign their work, but collectors can identify different makers by their intricate patterns.

Collectors' Club: American Cut Glass Assoc, P.O. Box 482, Ramona, CA 92065.

For additional listings, see *Warman's Antiques & Collectibles* and *Warman's Glass*.

Basket, diamond miters, diamond points, small stars, 6" x 4-1/4" x 6" h, pinhead nick 55.00

Bowl
    Brilliant cut pinwheels, hobstars, and miters, 8" x 3-3/4" 145.00
    Heavy blank, serrated rim, two rows of vertical rays, star bottom, 8-1/4" dia 45.00

Carafe, 2-1/2" floral leaf band, star, file, fan, and criss-cross cutting, molded neck, 8" h 70.00

Creamer and sugar, hobstar, American Brilliant Period, 3" h 50.00

Decanter, stopper, large hobstars, deep miters, fan, file, hallmarked silver neck and rim, 11" h, 3" sq 130.00

Dish, heart shaped, handle, American Brilliant Period, 5" 45.00

Goblet, strawberry diamond, pinwheel, and fan, notched stem, 7-pc set 350.00

Nappy, hobstar center, intaglio floral, strawberry diamond button border, 6" dia 45.00

Perfume bottle, 6-sided, alternating panels of Harvard pattern and engraved florals, rayed base, matching faceted stopper, American Brilliant Period 175.00

Pickle tray, checkerboard, hobstar, 7" x 3" 45.00

Plate, alternating hobstars and, large graduated circles and fans, notched miters, hobstars, 15-3/4" h, Higgins & Seiter 250.00

Water pitcher, Keystone Rose pattern, 10" h 190.00

❖ Cybis

Opened as an artists' studio by Polish immigrants, Boleslaw Cybis and his wife Marja, this enterprise turned out porcelain sculptures. Cybis porcelains are exquisitely detailed.

Bear, 1968 .... 400.00
Bluebirds, nesting, 1978 .... 250.00
Buffalo, 1968 .... 200.00
Dandy Dancing Dog, 1977 .... 300.00

Easter Egg Hunt, 1972 .... 220.00
Independence Celebration, 1972 .... 210.00
Kitten Chantilly, 1984 .... 215.00
Lullaby Pink, 1986 .... 195.00
Madonna, with bird, damage to bird's tail 100.00
Merry Christmas, 1982 .... 315.00
Pinto, 1972 .... 225.00
Raccoon, with berries, 8-3/4" 170.00
Recital, 1985 .... 300.00
Sebastian Seal, 1976 .... 250.00
Snail, 1968, 4" l, 2-3/4" h 125.00
Summer, 1982 .... 210.00
Windy Day, 1972 .... 215.00

❖ Czechoslovakian Collectibles

Finding an object marked "Made in Czechoslovakia" assures you that it was made after 1918, when the country proclaimed its independence. Marks that also include other names, such as Bohemia or Austria, indicate that the piece pre-dates the country's independence. Expect to find good quality workmanship and bright colors.

Periodical: *New Glass Review*, Bardounova 2140 149 00 Praha 4, Prague, Czech Republic.

Collectors' Club: Czechoslovakian Collectors Guild International, P.O. Box 901395, Kansas City, MO 64190.

For additional listings, see *Warman's Antiques & Collectibles* and *Warman's Glass*.

Belt buckle, metal, 4 amber rhinestones, mkd "Czechoslovakia 81-Ges Gesch" 18.00

Bowl, brightly colored dec, incised mark, 9" dia 60.00

Box, cov, blue glass, sterling rosary 120.00

Flower frog, bird on stump, pottery 35.00

Lemonade set, 13" h blown glass pitcher, 4 matching glasses, bright orange, black silhouettes of children at play, trees, birds and animals, applied handle 225.00

Necklace
    Fringed, multicolor, 2 baroque pearls, 4" w, 20" l 110.00

Glass, red center pendant, brass setting, red glass and brass filigree beads, 13" l, mkd on "O" ring 95.00

Marbleized green stone, set in brass, small green spacer beads, clear rhinestones set at top 80.00

Perfume bottle, small, heavily cut Amethyst 125.00

Crystal, large faceted stopper 60.00

Pink 125.00

Smoky topaz, enameled dec, large stopper 90.00

Pitcher, cream, blue stripes, stamp mark, 4-1/4" h 45.00

Place card holders, glass, set of 6, orig box 80.00

Powder box, cov, yellow glass, black knob finial on lid 75.00

Vase
    6-1/4" h, glass, cylindrical, mottled white and purple, cased to clear, enameled stylized vignette of woman fishing, silver mounted rim with English hallmarks, c1930 .... 275.00
    9-1/4" h, 4" w, pottery, 6 sides, 3 legs, glaze flake 225.00
    10" h, pottery, brightly painted, incised numbers 118.00

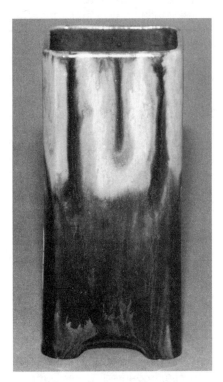

Multi-color Czechoslovakian square vase, 4-5/8" high, $14.

D

For exciting collecting trends and newly expanded areas look for the following symbols:

⊛ Hot Topic

★ New Warman's Listing

(May have been in another Warman's title.)

❖ Dairy Collectibles

Collecting items pertaining to dairies is a popular segment of the antiques and collectibles marketplace. Some collectors specialize in examples from local dairies, while others concentrate on specific items such as milk bottles or milk bottle caps.

Periodicals: *Creamers*, P.O. Box 11, Lake Villa, IL 60046; *Cream Separator and Dairy Collectors Newsletter*, Route 3, P.O. Box 488, Arcadia, WI 54612; *Fiz Biz*, P.O. Box 115, Omaha, NE, 68101; *The Milk Route*, 4 Ox Bow Rd, Westport, CT 06880.

Collectors' Clubs: Cream Separator and Dairy Collectors, Rt 3, P.O. Box 488, Arcadia, WI, 54612; National Assoc of Milk Bottle Collectors, 4 Ox Bow Rd, Westport, CT 06880.

Cookbook
  300 Dairy Tasty, Healthful Dishes, softcover, 1940, 42 pgs, 6" x 8-3/4".................. 4.00
  1001 Dairy Dishes from the Sealtest Kitchens, softcover, 1963, 288 pgs 5.00
  Dairy-Best Desserts, softcover, 1960s, 18 pg, 5-1/4" x 7-1/2" 2.00
Dairy bucket, miniature, tin and brass, imprinted "Dairy Outfit Co., Limited Makers," 2" h 45.00

The Milk Your Milkman Brings educational booklet, $9.

Drinking glass
  King Quality Dairy, St. Louis, red text, 5-1/4" h 45.00
  Little pig playing fiddle, red image, copyright Walt Disney, 2nd Dairy Series, 1936-37, 4-1/4" h 70.00
Milk box, galvanized
  "Property of Homestead Dairy," painted white, insulated, 10" x 11" x 13-1/2" 20.00
  "Hedlins Richer Milk," 10" x 10" x 12-1/2" 45.00
Model train car, HO scale, Dairymen's League billboard refrigerator car, missing brake wheel 10.00
Paperweight, white-veined marble, embedded emblem, Dixie Dairy 75th Anniversary 25.00
Spinner, plastic with paper inlay, Dellwood Milk & Dairy Products 30.00
Thermometer, silhouette image of baby in highchair, "Compliments of Barry's Dairy Products, Phone 1062, New Ulm, Minn.," 4" x 5" 45.00
Toy, dairy wagon, tin, wind-up, yellow and red wagon, pulled by black horse, Marx, orig box 450.00
Trade card, diecut, Borden milk wagon pulled by horse 25.00
Whistle, plastic, bugle shape, red and white, Foremost Dairy, 1950s, 5" l 32.00

❖ Dakin

Dakin collectibles are cuddly and fun to collect. Look for original tags to help identify genuine Dakin.
Coca-Cola polar bear, white, red scarf, 1993, no tag, 14" h .. 20.00
Doll, cloth, three faces 55.00

Donald Duck, articulated, orig string tag, 1972, 9" h 37.50
Garfield the College Cat, United Feature Syndicate, Inc., Dakin, Inc. San Francisco, Calif. tags, 1981 .... 18.00
Lassie, 10", jointed, 1978...... 100.00
Mouse, tagged "Dream Pets, R. Dakin Company, Japan" ... 10.00
Polar bear, Jelly Roll Oldetyme Bear, white plush, 12" h.............. 15.00
Rooster, bright yellow plumage, red jersey, Denver, Colo. radio station promotional piece, 1980, tush tag 7.50
Smokey Bear, orig tags, c1970, 8" h 40.00

❖ Decorative Accessories

Call it "kitsch" or "bric-a-brac," but decorative accessories make a statement about who we are as we decorate our living spaces. Decorators have been using objects d'art for years. Now that many of these objects are coming onto the flea market scene, collectors get a second chance to add some of these decorative objects to their domain.
Bird house, snow covered, DeForest 110.00
Bust, Sheherazade, chalkware painted to resemble bronze 250.00
Cigar store Indian, chief, 70-1/4" h, pine, carved and painted, red, white and blue feathered headdress, gold and red gown, holding dagger in right hand, tobacco and cigars in other, black painted base, 19th C 2,750.00
Cornucopia vase, pierced rim, painted floral motif, four feet with fish scales, stamped and imp mark, 1913, orig paper label reads "Fisher, Budapest" 300.00
Cricket cage, brass 35.00
Crocus pot, ceramic, white ground, purple floral design, unmkd 2.00
Figure
  Charging elephant, brass, antique bronze finish, 29" h, 30" l 300.00

Gooney bird, 6-5/8" h, chip carved wings, black and orange paint, blue and yellow details, long legs, rect base, Pa. origin, early 20th C 525.00

Rooster, 5-1/4" h, pine, cross-hatched wing detail, orange, red, yellow, pink and green, standing on grassy mound, Carl Snavely, Lititz, PA, 20th C 400.00

Fruit, alabaster, apple, pear or orange, each 45.00

Inkwell
Figural, rose, brass, color wash, pink and red petals, green stem 250.00
Paperweight, multicolor concentric millefiori base, dated 1848 cane, Whitefriars 190.00

Lamp, traffic meter base, cloth shade 50.00

Magnifier, 8" l, silver-plated bronze, Faux Bamboo, c1960-65, made for and retailed by Bonwit Teller, N.Y., mkd as such, also "Made in Italy" 100.00

Mantel ornaments, 12-1/2" h, fruit and foliage design, chalkware, American, made in 19th C, some paint wear, pr...................475.00

Rug, hooked, "Home Is Where The Heart Is," log cabin center, pine trees and fence 1,000.00

Theorem, watercolor on velvet, basket of fruit, unidentified maker, framed 200.00

Urn, Capo-di-Monte, ovoid, central molded frieze with figures and cupids, molded floral garlands, multicolor dec, pedestal base 450.00

Wall plaque
Basket shape, chalkware, paint dec 45.00
Masks, Comedy and Tragedy, white ceramic, unmkd ...70.00

❖ Decoys

Designed to coax waterfowl into target range, decoys have been made of wood, papier-mache, canvas, and metal. These hand-carved and even machine-made decoys have been recognized as an indigenous American art form. Signed examples are quite desirable, as are decoys made by noted regional artists.

References: Loy S. Harrell Jr., *Decoys: North America's One Hundred Greatest*, Krause Publications, 2000; Bob and Sharon Huxford, *The Collector's Guide to Decoys,* vol. I (1990), vol. II (1992), Collector Books; Carl F. Luckey, *Collecting Antique Bird Decoys and Duck Calls,* 2nd ed, Books Americana, 1992; Donald J. Peterson, *Folk Art Fish Decoys*, Schiffer Publishing, 1996.

Periodicals: *Decoy Magazine*, P.O. Box 787, Lewes, DE, 19558; *North America Decoys*, P.O. Box 246, Spanish Fork, UT 84660; *Wildfowl Carving & Collecting*, 500 Vaughn St, Harrisburg, PA 17110.

Collectors' Clubs: Midwest Decoy Collectors Assoc, P.O. Box 4110, St. Charles, IL 60174; Minnesota Decoy Collectors Assoc, P.O. Box 130084, St. Paul, MN 55113; Ohio Decoy Collectors and Carvers Assoc, P.O. Box 499, Richfield, OH 44286. For additional listings, see *Warman's Antiques & Collectibles.*

Reproduction Alert.
Bluebill hen, factory carved, 14-1/2" l 75.00
Canada Goose, folding, waterproof wax-coated graphics, W.R. Johnson Co., Seattle, Wash., 1940s................................75.00
Canvasback, iron keel in bottom for ballast, Chesapeake Bay area of Maryland, working repaint, early 1900s, 14-1/2" l 155.00
Canvasback drake, painted eyes, solid body, original hand-made lead weight, old black alligatored repaint, late 1800s, 12-1/2" l 210.00
Maryland, early 1900s, re-headed, 14-1/2" l 155.00
Dove, papier mache, clothespin on bottom to hold decoy in place, 9" l 35.00

Bluebill Drake decoy, Rozell Bliss, circa 1910, $290.

Ear of corn
Papier mache, Carry-Lite Decoy Co., Milwaukee, Wisc., 1940s, unused..........................45.00
Wooden, painted yellow, 9" l 25.00

Goldeneye drake, tack eyes, lead weight inset in bottom, hollow construction held together with pegs, by Stanley Grant, Barnegat Bay, N.J., c1880, old repaint, bill repaired 225.00

Merganser, red breast, carved late 20th C, Maine or Nova Scotia, 19" l................................335.00

Red Head, Eastern Shore of Maryland, 13" l.......................135.00

❖ Deeds and Documents

Collectors seek out interesting vintage deeds and other documents from which to glean historical information. When purchasing a deed, check for authentic signatures, revenue stamps, seals, etc. Prices for deeds vary according to age, size, and location. Expect to pay $10 and upward for a common deed, more if a famous person's name appears. Documents also vary in price, with value being determined by content, date, signature, etc.

Help Wanted Poster, W. R. Parsons, Chicago, Ill., c1900, "Agents Wanted by Manufacturers of the Daisy Stair Corner" 18.00

Land indenture, Pennsylvania
Bucks County, signed by John Penn, sale of 1,000 acres, seal with some chipping, 15" h, 32" w........................ 220.00
Lancaster County, 24-1/4" h, 29-5/8" w 330.00
Northern Liberties, splits 23" h, 24" w............................ 82.50

Land transfer, "Lot four in block two in the town of Heppner, Oregon," July 20, 1882, slight staining 5.00

Letterhead
Arkansas State Penitentiary, 1949, discusses purchase of fishing equipment 10.00

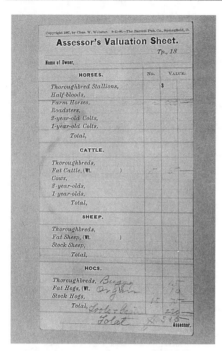

Assessor's Valuation Sheet, lists horses, cattle, sheep and hogs, late 1800s, 8-3/8" x 4-1/4", $3.

The Bennett House, Augustine, Fla., c1915, 2 pages both with letterhead, 6" x 9-1/2" 6.00

Geo. Spalt Soda Fountains & Drug Store Fixtures, 1911 ....5.50

United States Senate, letter from Robert F. Kennedy to constituent, Sept 20, 1966, with envelope with printed postal facsimile signature of RFK 135.00

Jimmy Carter, letter to constituent, March 1980, sgd Jimmy (Not authentic) but Walter Mondale autograph across bottom 48.00

New Tifft House, John Hood & Co., Pan American Exposition, Buffalo 1901, writing both sides, May 4, 1900, 6" x 9-1/2" 15.00

Warranty deed, The Red Man Land Company, Anadarko, Okla., 1954, grants for the sum of 1 dollar, 2 sq. inches of an orig Indian reservation, edges rough 40.00

❖ Degenhart Glass

Operating from 1947 until 1978, John and Elizabeth Degenhart created glass novelties under the name of Crystal Art Glass. They created some unusual colors. When Crystal Art Glass went out of business, many of the molds were purchased by Boyd Crystal Art Glass, also located in Cambridge, Ohio.

Collectors' Club: Friends of Degenhart, Degenhart Paperweight and Glass Museum, Inc, 65323 Highland Hills Rd, P.O. Box 186, Cambridge, OH 43725.

Reproduction Alert.

Animal covered dish
  Hen, mint green, 3" 22.00
  Turkey, custard...................60.00
Bell, bicentennial, amethyst.......7.50
Candy dish, cov, wildflower, twilight blue....................................32.00
Cup plate, heart and lyre, mulberry 15.00
Hand, tomato red......................30.00
Hat, daisy and button, milk blue 10.00
Owl
  Antique blue 45.00
  Emerald green 45.00
  Midnight sun.......................30.00
Paperweight
  Multicolor floral bouquet, 3-1/2" dia 250.00
  Single blue flower, 3" dia..250.00
Salt, bird, amber 12.00
Toothpick holder, basket, milk white 20.00
Vase, Forget-Me-Not, crystal...20.00

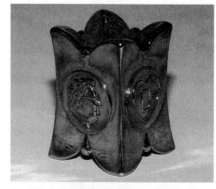

Red toothpick holder, marked "Degenhart Museum," 3" high, $15.

Delft planter, made in Holland, 4-3/4" high, 5" diameter, $10.

❖ Delftware

Traditional Dutch motifs of windmills and tulips often decorate these wares, which are white with blue decorations.

For additional listings, see *Warman's Antiques & Collectibles* and *Warman's English & Continental Pottery & Porcelain*.

Reproduction Alert.

Ashtray, windmill scene, applied Dutch shoes on rim, mkd, 4-1/4" dia 15.00
Coffee grinder, wall mount, orig decal "Made in Holland, DEVE, 1921," 13" l 305.00
Creamer, cow shape, windmill on one side, floral deco on the other, 3-1/4" h, 5-1/2" l 25.00
Decanter, windmill scene, bottom mkd "Delft, Ram, made in Holland," missing cork............ 68.00
Figurine, Dutch girl, Japan, 4-1/4" h 18.00
Pin, floral, sterling framing and clasp, mkd, 1-1/8" dia 90.00
Urn
  3-1/4" h, windmill on front, bottom mkd "4107, Delft Blue, Holland" 25.00
  4-5/8" h, mkd "Delft Blaun Handpainted, Made in Holland" 68.00
Wall pocket, Dutch shoe, windmill scene, mkd, hole in heel to hang, 8" l.................................... 18.00

❖ Depression Glass

Depression glass was made from 1920 to 1940. It was inexpensive machine-made glass and was produced by numerous companies in various patterns and colors.

References: There are many excellent reference books on Depression glass. Gene Florence, Carl Luckey, Kent G. Washburn and others have all authored books on Depression glass. Hazel Marie Weatherman wrote the first and most referred to editions, titled *Colored Glassware of the Depression Era*, Books 1 and 2, plus several supplements.

Periodicals: *The Daze*, P.O. Box 57, Otisville, MI 48463; *Depression Glass Shopper On-Line Magazine*, www.dgshopper.com.

Collectors' Clubs: Canadian Depression Glass Club, 1026 Forestwood Dr, Mississauga, Ontario L5C 1G8, Canada; National Depression Glass Assoc, Inc, P.O. Box 8264, Wichita, KS 67209; 20-30-40 Society, Inc, P.O. Box 856, LaGrange, IL 60525.

For additional listings, see *Warman's Depression Glass*.

The following listings are a mere sampling of the current Depression glass market.

Reproduction Alert.

Ashtray
Adam, Jeannette Glass Co., green, 4-1/2" dia 25.00

Aunt Polly blue sherbet, $15.

Mayfair amber plate, 9-1/2" diameter, $14.

Diana, Federal Glass Co., pink 4.00
Early American Prescut (Anchor Hocking), crystal, 4" dia...3.00
Forest Green, Anchor Hocking Glass Co., 4-5/8" sq 5.50
Harp, Jeannette Glass Co., crystal 4.50
Manhattan (Horizontal Ribbed), Anchor Hocking Glass Co., crystal............................11.00
Moroccan Amethyst, Hazel Ware, 3-1/2" dia 5.75
Windsor (Windsor Diamond), Jeannette Glass Co., pink, 5-3/4" dia 35.00
Berry bowl, individual
Anniversary, Jeannette Glass Co., irid, 4-7/8" dia...........4.50
Bowknot, green 16.00
Colonial Fluted (Rope), Federal Glass Co., green 11.00
Fortune, Hocking Glass Co., pink 6.00
Normandie (Bouquet and Lattice), Federal Glass Co., irid, 5" dia 5.00
Old Cafe, Hocking Glass Co., ruby 6.00
Patrician (Spoke), Federal Glass Co., amber 12.00
Sharon (Cabbage Rose), Federal Glass Co., pink.......10.00
Berry bowl, master
Aunt Polly, U.S. Glass Co., blue 45.00
Cameo (Ballerina, Dancing Girl), Hocking Glass Co., pink 150.00
Heritage, Federal Glass Co., pink..............................42.00

Indiana Custard, (Flower and Leaf Band), Indiana Glass Co., French Ivory 32.00
Pretzel, Indiana Glass Co., crystal..................................18.00
Raindrops (Optic Design), Federal Glass Co., green ... 45.00
Ribbon, Hazel Atlas Glass Co., green 30.00
Strawberry, U.S. Glass Co., green or pink 20.00
Bowl
American Pioneer, Liberty Works, crystal, 9" dia.... 24.00
Bamboo Optic, Liberty, green, 4-1/4" dia 6.00
Carolyn, Lancaster, 11" dia, topaz...........................36.00
Early American Prescut, (Anchor Hocking), crystal, ruffled, 8-3/4" dia 9.00
Iris (Iris and Herringbone) Jeannette Glass Co., irid, 9-1/2" dia...............................10.00
Jody, Lancaster, oval, topaz, 12" l 35.00
Jubilee, Lancaster Glass Co., pink, 8" dia..................265.00
Moonstone, Anchor Hocking Glass Co., cloverleaf, opal 13.00
Oyster and Pearl, Anchor Hocking Glass Co., heart shape, ruby, 5-1/4" w...............15.00
Roxana, Hazel Atlas Glass Co., golden topaz................12.00
Butter dish, cov
Anniversary, Jeannette Glass Co., pink 60.00
Block Optic (Block), Hocking Glass Co., green 50.00
Doric, Jeannette Glass Co., green 90.00
Floral (Poinsettia), Jeannette Glass Co., green 90.00

Petal Swirl salad bowl, ultra marine, 9" diameter, $25.

Moderntone, Hazel Atlas, cobalt, metal cov.................... 100.00
Royal Lace, Hazel Atlas, pink 150.00
U.S. Swirl, U.S. Glass Co., green or pink 115.00
Windsor (Windsor Diamond), Jeannette Glass Co., pink 60.00

Butter dish top, Colonial Knife & Fork, Hocking, green 20.00

Cake plate
    Adam, Jeannette Glass Co., green............................ 32.00
    Anniversary, Jeannette Glass Co., crystal, round........... 7.50
    Block Optic (Block), Hocking Glass Co., crystal.......... 18.00
    Cameo (Ballerina, Dancing Girl), Hocking Glass Co., green, 10" dia 22.00
    Holiday (Buttons and Bows), Jeannette Glass Co., pink, 10-1/2" dia................... 100.00
    Miss America, (Diamond Pattern), Hocking Glass Co. 25.00
    Primo (Paneled Aster), U.S. Glass Co., green or yellow 23.50
    Thistle, Macbeth-Evans, green 150.00

Cake stand, Harp, Jeannette Glass Co., crystal 25.00

Candy dish, cov
    Cloverleaf, Hazel Atlas, green 45.00
    Floragold, Jeannette Glass Co., irid 15.00
    Moroccan Amethyst, Hazel Ware, tall...................... 32.00
    Ribbon, Hazel Atlas, black 38.00

Celery tray, Pretzel, Indiana Glass Co., crystal 8.00

Cereal bowl
    Aurora, Hazel Atlas, pink ... 14.00
    Cherry Blossom, Jeannette Glass Co., green........... 35.00
    Daisy (No. 620), Indiana Glass Co., fired-on red............ 25.00
    Horseshoe (No. 612), Indiana Glass Co., green or yellow 25.00
    Old Cafe, Hocking Glass Co., crystal or pink.................. 8.00
    Ribbon, Hazel Atlas Glass Co., green...................... 25.00
    Royal Ruby, Anchor Hocking Glass Co. 12.00

Coaster
    Adam, Jeannette Glass Co., pink 32.00
    Cherry Blossom, Jeannette Glass Co., green or pink 15.00
    Miss America, (Diamond Pattern), Hocking Glass Co., crystal........................20.00

Cocktail, Royal Ruby, Anchor Hocking Glass Co. 8.50

Compote
    Anniversary, Jeannette Glass Co., crystal, ruffled 6.50
    Floragold, Jeannette Glass Co., irid, ruffled, 5-1/4" dia ..695.00
    Manhattan (Horizontal Ribbed), Anchor Hocking Glass Co., crystal, 5-3/4" h 32.00
    Windsor (Windsor Diamond), Jeannette Glass Co., crystal 6.00

Console set, Block Optic (Block), Hocking Glass Co., amber, bowl 11-3/4" dia, 2 candlesticks 1-3/4" h, 3-pc set........................160.00

Cookie jar, cov
    Manhattan (Horizontal Ribbed), Anchor Hocking Glass Co., crystal...........................35.00
    Mayfair (Open Rose), Hocking Glass Co., green 575.00
    Princess, Hocking Glass Co., blue 875.00

Creamer
    Adam, Jeannette Glass Co., green 22.00
    Bamboo Optic, Liberty, ftd, green 10.00
    Christmas Candy (No. 624), Indiana Glass Co., crystal ...12.00
    Colonial Knife & Fork, Hocking, crystal...........................18.00
    Cube (Cubist), Jeannette Glass Co., green 10.00
    Holiday (Buttons and Bows), Jeannette Glass Co., pink 12.50
    Newport (Hairpin), Hazel Atlas, cobalt...........................20.00
    Ovide, Hazel Atlas, black 7.00
    Raindrops (Optic Design), Federal Glass Co. 8.00
    Royal Ruby, Anchor Hocking Glass Co., flat.................8.00
    Sunflower, Jeannette Glass Co., green or pink 20.00

Cream soup
    American Sweetheart, Macbeth-Evans, monax 120.00

Mayfair, Federal Glass Co., amber 18.00
Moderntone, Hazel Atlas, amethyst, ruffled, 5" dia....... 30.00
Patrician (Spoke), Federal Glass Co., amber.................... 16.00

Cup and saucer
    Cameo (Ballerina, Dancing Girl), Hocking Glass Co., crystal 14.00
    Dogwood, Macbeth-Evans, green 40.00
    Doric & Pansy, Jeannette Glass Co., ultramarine........... 21.00
    Lorain, Indiana Glass Co., crystal or green 15.00
    Madrid, Federal Glass Co., amber 9.00
    Parrot (Sylvan), Federal Glass Co., green.................... 55.00
    Pretzel, Indiana Glass Co., crystal.................................. 8.00

Fruit bowl
    Bubble (Bullseye Provincial), Hocking Glass Co., crystal, 4-1/2" dia 5.00
    Floragold, Jeannette Glass Co., irid................................ 8.50
    Heritage, Federal Glass Co., crystal 15.00
    Iris (Iris and Herringbone) Jeannette Glass Co., ruffled, 11-1/2" dia 15.00
    Oyster and Pearls, Anchor Hocking Glass Co., pink 10.00
    Raindrops (Optic Design), Federal Glass Co., green 11.00

Goblet
    Block Optic (Block), Hocking Glass Co., green 24.00
    Bubble (Bullseye Provincial), Hocking Glass Co., forest green 15.00
    Colonial Block, Hazel Atlas, crystal................................ 9.00
    Colonial Knife & Fork, Hocking, crystal, slight chip on one rib, 5-3/4" h........................ 18.00
    Diamond Point, ruby stained, 7-1/2" h........................ 35.00
    Moroccan Amethyst, Hazel Ware 10.00
    Old English (Threading), Indiana Glass Co., amber, green, or pink.............................. 30.00
    Ring, (Banded Rings), Hocking Glass Co., crystal 7.00

Iced tea tumbler, ftd, 12-oz
    Circle, Hocking Glass Co., green or pink......................... 17.50

Dewdrop, Jeannette Glass Co., crystal............17.50
Diamond Quilted, (Flat Diamond), Imperial Glass Co., green or pink.............10.00
Hobnail, Hocking Glass Co., crystal............8.50
Homespun (Fine Rib), Jeannette Glass Co., crystal or pink............32.00
Ships (Sailboat, Sportsman Series), Hazel Atlas, cobalt blue............18.00
Juice tumbler, ftd
Fortune, Hocking Glass Co., crystal............8.00
Old Cafe, Hocking Glass Co., crystal or pink............10.00
Peanut butter, unknown maker, crystal............9.00
Royal Ruby, Anchor Hocking, ruby............5.00
Mayonnaise set, underplate, orig ladle
Christmas Candy (No. 624), Indiana Glass Co., crystal...24.00
Diamond Quilted, (Flat Diamond), Imperial Glass Co., blue............65.00
Patrick, Lancaster Glass Co., yellow............80.00
Mug
Block Optic (Block), Hocking Glass Co., green...........35.00
Moderntone, Hazel Atlas, white............8.50
Parfait, Harp, Jeannette Glass Co., crystal............18.00
Pitcher
Adam, Jeannette Glass Co., pink, 32-oz............125.00
Crystal Leaf, Macbeth-Evans, pink............45.00
Floragold, Jeannette Glass Co., irid............40.00
Forest Green, Anchor Hocking Glass Co., 22-oz............22.50
Fruits, Hazel Atlas, green..85.00
New Century, Hazel Atlas, ice lip, 80-oz, cobalt............45.00
Ring, (Banded Rings), Hocking Glass Co., decorated or green, 60-oz............25.00
Plate
American Pioneer, Liberty Works, crystal, 6" dia....12.50
American Sweetheart, Macbeth-Evans, monax, 9" dia....10.00
Aurora, Hazel Atlas, cobalt, 6-1/2" dia............12.00

Bowknot, green, 7" dia.......12.50
Bubble (Bullseye Provincial), Hocking Glass Co., crystal, 6-3/4" dia............3.50
Cameo (Ballerina, Dancing Girl), Hocking Glass Co., green, 8" dia............12.00
Cherry Blossom, Jeannette Glass Co., grill, green or pink, 9" dia............22.00
Circle, Hocking Glass Co., green or pink, 8-1/4" dia..........11.00
Colonial Knife & Fork, Hocking, pink, slight wear, 6" dia....4.00
Columbia, Federal Glass Co., pink, 9-1/2" dia............32.00
Doric, green or pink, 6" dia..6.50
Doric & Pansy, Jeannette Glass Co., dinner, ultramarine............35.00
Early American Prescut, (Anchor Hocking), crystal, 11" dia............10.00
Egg Harbor, Liberty, luncheon, green or pink............9.00
Floragold, Jeannette Glass Co., dinner, irid, 8-1/2" dia....35.00
Floral, (Poinsettia), Jeannette Glass Co., salad, pink, 8" dia............15.00
Floral and Diamond Band, (Poinsettia), Jeannette Glass Co., luncheon, green or pink, 8" dia............40.00
Florentine No. 1 (Old Florentine, Poppy No. 1), Hazel Atlas, dinner, green, 10" dia....16.00
Florentine No. 2 (Poppy No. 2), Hazel Atlas, dinner, yellow, 10" dia............15.00
Fortune, Hocking Glass Co., luncheon, crystal or pink, 8" dia............17.50
Georgian (Lovebirds), Federal Glass Co., luncheon, green, 8" dia............10.00
Hobnail, Hocking Glass Co., luncheon, crystal, 8-1/2" dia............5.50
Holiday (Buttons and Bows), Jeannette Glass Co., sherbet, pink, 6" dia............6.00
Homespun (Fine Rib), Jeannette Glass Co., dinner, crystal or pink, 9-1/2" dia............17.00
Horseshoe (No. 612), Indiana Glass Co., salad, green or yellow, 8-3/8" dia...........10.00
Iris (Iris and Herringbone) Jeannette Glass Co., dinner, irid, 9" dia............45.00

Jubilee, Lancaster Glass Co., luncheon, 9-3/4" dia......16.50
Lace Edge (Katy Blue), Imperial Glass Co., blue, 10" dia............90.00
Madrid, Federal Glass Co., amber, 8-7/8" dia............8.00
Manhattan (Horizontal Ribbed), Anchor Hocking Glass Co., crystal, 7" dia............6.00
Mayfair (Open Rose), Hocking Glass Co., pink, 8-1/2" dia............25.00
Miss America, (Diamond Pattern), Hocking Glass Co., dinner, crystal............15.00
Moderntone, Hazel Atlas, cobalt, 7-3/4" dia............12.50
Moroccan Amethyst, Hazel Ware, dinner, amethyst, 9-3/4" dia............7.00
Newport (Hairpin), Hazel Atlas, dinner, fired-on color, 8-1/2" dia............15.00
Normandie (Bouquet and Lattice), Federal Glass Co., irid, 6" dia............3.00
Old Cafe, Hocking Glass Co., crystal or pink, sherbet, 6" dia............4.00
Old Colony (Lace Edge, Open Lace), Hocking Glass Co., dinner, crystal............33.00
Parrot (Sylvan), Federal Glass Co., dinner, green, 9" dia............38.00
Patrician (Spoke), Federal Glass Co., amber, 7-1/2" dia...15.00
Patrick, Lancaster Glass Co., luncheon, pink, 8" dia...45.00
Peanut Butter, unknown maker, luncheon, crystal, 8" dia.5.00
Petalware, Macbeth-Evans, dinner, monax, 9" dia........10.00
Pineapple & Floral (No. 618), Indiana Glass Co., sherbet, amber, 6" dia............6.00
Pretzel (No. 622), Indiana Glass Co., dinner, crystal, 9-3/4" dia............10.00
Primo (Paneled Aster), U.S. Glass Co., dinner, green, 10" dia............22.50
Princess, Hocking Glass Co., grill, green or pink, 9-1/2" dia............15.00
Queen Mary (Prismatic Line, Vertical Ribbed), Hocking Glass Co., crystal, 6" dia............4.00

Romansque, octagonal, gold, 8" dia 8.00

Rose Cameo, Belmont Tumbler Co., salad, green, 7" dia 16.00

Rosemary (Dutch Rose), Federal Glass Co., dinner, green, 9-1/2" dia......................15.00

Roulette (Many Windows), Hocking Glass Co., luncheon, crystal, 8-1/2" dia...................7.00

Round Robin, sherbet, irid or green, 6" dia...................7.00

Roxana, Hazel Atlas, sherbet, crystal, 6" dia 4.00

Royal Lace, Hazel Atlas, luncheon, cobalt, 8-1/2" dia 30.00

Royal Ruby, Anchor Hocking, salad, ruby, 7" dia............3.00

Sandwich, Anchor Hocking, crystal, 9" dia 20.00

Ships (Sailboat, Sportsman Series), Hazel Atlas, dinner, cobalt, 9" dia 32.00

Sierra Pinwheel, Jeannette Glass Co., dinner, green, 9" dia 18.00

Starlight, Hazel Atlas, dinner, crystal, 9-1/2" dia 7.00

Tea Room, Indiana Glass Co., luncheon, green, 8-1/4" dia 37.50

Thistle, Macbeth-Evans, luncheon, green, 8" dia......22.00

Vernon (No. 616), Indiana Glass Co., luncheon, green or yellow, 8" dia......................10.00

Waterford (Waffle), Hocking Glass Co., dinner, crystal 10.00

Windsor (Windsor Diamond), Jeannette Glass Co., dinner, green or pink, 9" dia......25.00

Platter

Cherry Blossom, Jeannette Glass Co., green...........48.00

Georgian (Lovebirds), Federal Glass Co., green...........70.00

Indiana Custard, (Flower and Leaf Band), Indiana Glass Co., French ivory...........30.00

Lace Edge (Katy Blue), Imperial Glass Co., blue, 13" l ..165.00

Royal Lace, Hazel Atlas, pink 40.00

Windsor (Windsor Diamond), Jeannette Glass Co., green, oval, 11-1/2" l 25.00

Punch bowl set, Royal Ruby, Anchor Hocking, bowl, 12 cups....110.00

Relish

Doric, Jeannette Glass Co., green 32.00

Early American Prescut, (Anchor Hocking), crystal, 4-part, 11" dia 10.00

Lorain, Indiana Glass Co., 4-part, crystal or green, 8" dia ..17.50

Miss America (Diamond Pattern), Hocking Glass Co., 4-part, crystal 11.00

Pretzel (No. 622), Indiana Glass Co., 3-part, crystal...........9.00

Princess, Hocking Glass Co., 4-part, apricot 100.00

Tea Room, Indiana Glass Co., divided, green................30.00

Salt and pepper shakers, pr

Adam, Jeannette Glass Co., green 100.00

American Sweetheart, Macbeth-Evans, monax 325.00

Florentine No. 2 (Poppy No. 2), Hazel Atlas, green.........40.00

Hex Optic (Honeycomb), Jeannette Glass Co., green or pink 30.00

Manhattan (Horizontal Ribbed), Anchor Hocking Glass Co., crystal...........................50.00

Ribbon, Hazel Atlas, green 25.00

Waterford (Waffle), Hocking Glass Co., crystal, tall 7.00

Sandwich server, center handle

Daisy (No. 620), Indiana Glass Co., amber 14.50

Landrum, Lancaster, topaz 55.00

Old English (Threading), Indiana Glass Co., amber 60.00

Ring, (Banded Rings), Hocking Glass Co., decorated or green 15.00

Spiral, Hocking Glass Co., green 30.00

Twisted Optic, Imperial, canary 35.00

Sherbet

Adam, Jeannette Glass Co., green 40.00

April, Macbeth-Evans, ftd, pink, 4" h................................15.00

Bowknot, unknown maker, green 24.00

Cherry Blossom, Jeannette Glass Co., pink..............17.00

Florentine No. 1 (Old Florentine, Poppy No. 1), Hazel Atlas, yellow 16.00

Florentine No. 2 (Poppy No. 2), Hazel Atlas, yellow 8.00

Forest Green, Anchor Hocking Glass Co., Boopie, green 7.00

Fruits, Hazel Atlas, pink 7.50

Hex Optic (Honeycomb), Jeannette Glass Co., green or pink 5.00

Iris (Iris and Herringbone) Jeannette Glass Co., irid, 2-1/2" h 15.50

Old English (Threading), Indiana Glass Co., green 20.00

Parrot (Sylvan), Federal Glass Co., cone shape, green 24.00

Peanut Butter, unknown maker, crystal 4.00

Raindrops (Optic Design), Federal Glass Co., crystal 4.50

Sunflower, Jeannette Glass Co., green 13.50

Thumbprint, Federal Glass Co., green 7.00

Windsor (Windsor Diamond), Jeannette Glass Co., pink 13.00

Snack set, Harp, Jeannette Glass Co., crystal.................... 48.00

Sugar, cov

Bamboo Optic, Liberty, ftd, green 10.00

Cameo (Ballerina, Dancing Girl), Hocking Glass Co., pink, 3-1/4" h 100.00

Cube (Cubist), Jeannette Glass Co., green or pink, 3".... 25.00

Holiday (Buttons and Bows), Jeannette Glass Co., pink 25.00

Madrid, Federal Glass Co., amber 7.00

Ring, (Banded Rings), Hocking Glass Co., dec............. 10.00

Sierra Pinwheel, Jeannette Glass Co., pink 20.00

Tulip, Dell Glass Co., blue 20.00

Vernon (No. 616), Indiana Glass Co., crystal 12.00

Tumbler

Bamboo Optic, Liberty, ftd, pink, 8-oz, 5-1/2" h............... 15.00

Bubble (Bullseye Provincial), Hocking Glass Co., crystal 5.00

Cherryberry, U.S. Glass Co., irid, 3-5/8" h 20.00
Columbia, Federal Glass Co., crystal, 4-oz 30.00
Fortune, Hocking Glass Co., pink 10.00
Forest Green, Anchor Hocking Glass Co., green, 9-oz 7.00
Hex Optic (Honeycomb), Jeannette Glass Co., green or pink, 7-oz, 4-3/4" h 8.00
Horseshoe (No. 612), Indiana Glass Co., green, 9-oz, ftd 22.00
Madrid, Federal Glass Co., amber, 5-1/2" h 18.00
Mayfair (Open Rose), Hocking Glass Co., ftd, pink, 6-1/2" h 40.00
Moderntone, Hazel Atlas, cone, white 4.00
Peanut Butter, unknown maker, crystal 7.00
Princess, Hocking Glass Co., green, 9-oz 28.00
Pyramid (No. 610), Indiana Glass Co., ftd, crystal or pink, 8-oz 50.00
Rose Cameo, Belmont Tumbler Co., green 22.50
Ships (Sailboat, Sportsman Series), Hazel Atlas, cobalt, 9-oz 14.00
Vernon (No. 616), Indiana Glass Co., yellow 35.00
Vegetable, open
Cameo (Ballerina, Dancing Girl), Hocking Glass Co., green 30.00
Daisy (No. 620), Indiana Glass Co., dark green 10.00
Doric, Jeannette Glass Co., pink 30.00
Florentine No. 2 (Poppy No. 2), Hazel Atlas, cov, yellow 55.00
Horseshoe (No. 612), Indiana Glass Co., green or yellow, 8-1/2" dia 30.00
Pineapple & Floral (No. 618), Indiana Glass Co., amber or crystal 30.00
Rosemary (Dutch Rose), Federal Glass Co., green 37.00
Sharon (Cabbage Rose), Federal Glass Co., oval, amber 20.00
Star, Federal Glass Co., amber 10.00

Tea Room, Indiana Glass Co., green 75.00
Whiskey
Diamond Quilted, (Flat Diamond), Imperial Glass Co., pink 12.00
Hex Optic (Honeycomb), Jeannette Glass Co., green or pink 8.50
Hobnail, Hocking Glass Co., crystal 5.00
Raindrops (Optic Design), Federal Glass Co., green 9.00

❖ Desert Storm

Collectibles from this historical event are making their way to flea markets. Because these items are relatively new, expect to find them in very good condition.
Comic book, *Desert Storm Journal, #1*, 1991 .... 5.00
Keychain, "Operation Desert Storm, Come Home," with yellow ribbon, 2" 8.00
Lighter, butane, "Desert Storm" 5.00
Pin, "Support Our Troops, Desert Storm," shows yellow ribbon and American flag 3.00
Pinback button
Color photo of George Bush in military jacket, 2" sq 3.50
"I Support the Troops in Desert Storm," blue ground with white stars, wavy red and white stripes, 2-1/4" dia ... 5.00
"Operation Desert Storm, Support Our Troops," stars & stripes shield and planes, 2-1/4" dia 7.50
"Support Desert Storm, Free Kuwait," flags of Kuwait and the U.S., 1-3/4" dia 8.50

POW/MIA bracelet, "Maj Thomas F Koritz USAF 01-27-91 Iraq," aluminum, $2.50.

Santa Claus dexterity puzzle, 2-1/4" diameter, $30.

❖ Dexterity Puzzles

Small enough to hold in the palm of your hand, these little puzzles have provided hours of enjoyment for kids and collectors alike. From inauspicious beginnings as premiums or giveaways, these tiny playthings have certainly increased in value over the years.
Harlequin Puzzle, cardboard, paper and glass, by Journet, directions on bottom, 3-1/4" x 4-1/4" . 30.00
Hungry Pup, cardboard and glass, A.C. Gilbert Co., c1940, 3-1/4" x 4-1/4" 40.00
Indian, tin and glass, "Nabisco Shredded Wheat Juniors" on back, 1-1/4" dia 15.00
Lucky Horseshoe, cardboard and glass, A.C. Gilbert Co., c1940, 3-1/4" x 4-1/4" 40.00
New York-Paris Aero Race 65.00
Pin U Ring It, cardboard, paper and glass, by Journet, directions on bottom, 3-1/4" x 4-1/4" 20.00
Quints, 1930s 90.00
Sgt. Biff O'Hara, "Nabisco Shredded Wheat Juniors" on back, 1-1/4" dia 30.00
Smurfs/PEZ, graphics show Smurf girl shooting PEZ into Papa Smurf's mouth, green case, European, 1980s 10.00

Turnstyle Puzzle, cardboard, paper and glass, by Journet, directions on bottom, 5" x 4" 25.00

Two-sided, cardboard and glass, standing clown with detached head on one side, clown riding in locomotive on other, Japan, 2-3/4" dia 40.00

❖ Dick Tracy

Here's a comic strip character that made it to the big-time—movies! He and his pals generated some great collectibles along the way.

Badge, brass, pinback, Dick Tracy Detective Club 35.00

Bop bag, inflatable, Imperial Toys, 1990, orig box 40.00

Coloring book, *Dick Tracy Movie Coloring Book,* collector card photos on back cover, 1990, unused 5.00

Comic book, Motorola Presents *Dick Tracy Comics,* 1953 .... 15.00

Film, 8mm, "Brain Game," black-and-white, silent, Republic Pictures, orig box 5-1/4" sq 28.00

Game, Dick Tracy Crime Stopper, Ideal, 1963, unopened, water stain on box, 19" x 13" 70.00

Little Golden Book, *Dick Tracy,* 1962, minor wear to cover 15.00

Lunch box, metal, Crime Stoppers, Aladdin Industries, 1967, 1/2-pint Aladdin thermos 250.00

Ring, metal, adjustable, enameled deco, mkd "Copyright Wendy Gell, Disney Co." 49.00

Aladdin plastic lunch box and thermos, $20.

Squad Car No. 1, friction, tin litho characters in windows, Marx, 1950s, friction drive needs repair, 6" l 175.00

Trading cards, Willard's Chocolates, 56 cards, 1930s, complete set 90.00

Water pistol, Luger style, 1971 .... 40.00

❖ Dinnerware

Complete sets of dinnerware frequently appear at flea markets. They are usually priced considerably less than what you'd expect to pay for a comparable new set, unless, of course, it's manufactured by one of the more desirable names in dinnerware, such as Royal or Stangl. It's not unusual for a few pieces to be missing or damaged, but they are easily replaced with today's replacement services.

❖ Dionne Quints

Born in Ontario, Canada, on May 28, 1934, these 5 little girls excited everyone. They led an interesting yet sheltered life, attracting attention from around the world. Of course, all of this adoration resulted in a wide variety of collectibles and souvenirs.

Collectors' Club: Dionne Quint Collectors, P.O. Box 2527, Woburn, MA 01888.

Booklet

The Dionne Quintuplets: We're Two Years Old, Willis Thornton, Whitman Publishing Co., 1936, softcover, 40 pgs .50.00

The Story of the Dionne Quintuplets, Whitman Publishing Co., 1935, authorized edition, 40 pgs, 9-1/2" x 10" 40.00

Calendar, 1945, Armstrong Lumber, features Dionne Quints, 8-1/2" x 11" 35.00

Fan, cardboard, wooden handle, sepia-tone picture of young Quints in chairs, back lettered "Use Linco Gasoline Motor Oil," small tear 30.00

Figurines, 3 with baskets, 1 with basket of flowers, 1 with Scottie dog, bottoms mkd "Dresden," 2 chips, each 5-1/2" h, set of 5 .... 850.00

Magazine cover, *Woman's World,* Feb, 1937 .... 12.00

Paper dolls, *Let's Play House with the Dionne Quints,* unused 55.00

Photo, News Colorfoto, Dionne Quints visit New York, 1950 .... 5.00

Postcard, Dr. Dafoe and babies 18.00

⚙ Disneyana

Walt Disney was the impetus for a wonderful cast of characters that still delights children of all ages. Through the many Disney movies and television shows, many collectibles are available. Check for the official "Walt Disney Enterprises" logo.

References: Ted Hake, *Hake's Guide to Character Toys,* 3rd ed, Gemstone Publishing, 2000; Rex Miller, *The Investor's Guide to Vintage Character Collectibles,* Krause Publications, 1999.

Periodicals: *Mouse Rap Monthly,* P.O. Box 1064, Ojai, CA 93024; *Tomart's Disneyana Digest,* 3300 Encrete Ln, Dayton, OH 45439; *Tomart's Disneyana Update,* 3300 Encrete Ln, Dayton, OH 45439.

Child's dish, Mickey Mouse and Clarabelle, wear, $250.

Collectors' Clubs: Imagination Guild, P.O. Box 907, Boulder Creek, CA 95006; Mouse Club East, P.O. Box 3195, Wakefield, MA 01880; National Fantasy Fan Club for Disneyana Collectors and Enthusiasts, P.O. Box 19212, Irvine, CA 92713.

Bank, Cinderella 35.00
Bell, Tinkerbell handle, bronze colored metal, emb "Copyright Walt Disney Productions," 3-1/4" h 55.00
Book
   Mickey Never Fails, DC Heath, 1939, hardcover, school reader 32.00
   Thumper, Grosset & Dunlap, 1942, 32 pgs 30.00
Bookends, Donald Duck carrying school books, chalkware, pr 25.00
Bubble gum card, Mickey Mouse, #23 .... 8.00
Canasta cards, Elmer the Elephant, factory sealed, 1930s 50.00
Car, Donald's Nephew, tin and celluloid wind-up, 5-1/2" l, dated 1966 .... 215.00
Christmas light set, 1930s 135.00
Doll, Pollyanna, 30" h 100.00
Drinking glass, Donald Duck, "Full, Going, Going, Gone!," 1940s, 4-3/4" h 40.00
Earrings, clip-on, Mickey Mouse 35.00
Figure
   Donald Duck's nephew, reading book, bisque, 1950s 85.00
   Dumbo 35.00

Donald Duck Drummer tin wind-up toy, Linemar, 6-1/2" high, $150.

Pinocchio, bisque, 1940s, 3" h 110.00
Thumper, painted and glazed ceramic, tan, brown and pink, Hagen-Renaker, 1940s 50.00
Film, Donald the Skater, 1935, black-and-white, 16mm, orig box 24.00
Flasher pin, I Like Disneyland/Mickey Mouse, 1950s 40.00
Hair brush, Mickey Mouse, Walt Disney Enterprises, 1930, orig box 45.00
Iron-on patch, 3 images of Mickey, dated 1946, orig package .. 24.00
Labels, stick-on, English, 1940s, full sheet 85.00
Magic Movie Palette, Mickey and Minnie, 1935 store giveaway 210.00
Music box, Happy, figural 30.00
Napkin holder with salt and pepper shakers, Snow White, Enesco, copyright Walt Disney Productions 1964, 6" h, set 400.00
Paper dolls, Mary Poppins Cut-Out Book, Watkins-Strathmore Co., 1964, Jane and Michael on front, 8 pgs, uncut 40.00
Pinback button
   Mickey Mouse Club, copyright 1928, 1-1/4", some wear and rust 40.00
   Official Mickey Mouse Store, Kay Kamen Ltd., yellowed paper insert, 1937 .... 35.00
Rug, Uncle Scrooge McDuck, woven, 1950s, slight wear, 34" x 21" 175.00
Salt and pepper shakers, Ludwig Von Drake, 1961, MIP, pr 285.00
Scuffy shoe polish bottle, Mickey Mouse, 1950s, hard black contents 20.00
Stamp, Mickey Mouse, Walt Disney Enterprises 40.00
Teapot, cov, large, Mickey Mouse 95.00

Television, Build Your Own TV, 6 Walt Disney full-color films, punched out parts, Tower Press Product, Made in England, 1950s, 9-1/2" x 7" 125.00
Thermos, Disney's Wonderful World, Aladdin, 6-1/2" h 10.00
Tile, 6" sq, by Kemper Thomas
   Mickey 125.00
   Pluto, attached 1944 calendar 95.00
Toy, Mickey Mouse Train, battery op 100.00
Tray, Mickey and Minnie, Ohio Art, 1930s, tin, 7-1/2" l, shows wear 95.00
Valentine, Jiminy Cricket, diecut, movable arms, 1939 .... 27.50
Wall plaque, Mickey Mouse as band leader, mkd "Ceramica De Cuernavaca," 1970s 95.00
Wristwatch, silvered metal case, white dial, Mickey with red gloves, c1970, working 50.00

❖ Disneyland and Disney World

From celebrities to kids of all ages, lots of folks enjoy Disneyland and Disney World. Collectibles from these wonderful amusement parks are eagerly sought.

References: Ted Hake, *Hake's Guide to Character Toys*, 3rd ed, Gemstone Publishing, 2000; Rex Miller, *The Investor's Guide to Vintage Character Collectibles*, Krause Publications, 1999.

Periodicals: *Mouse Rap Monthly*, P.O. Box 1064, Ojai, CA 93024; *Tomart's Disneyana Digest*, 3300 Encrete Ln, Dayton, OH 45439; *Tomart's Disneyana Update*, 3300 Encrete Ln, Dayton, OH 45439.

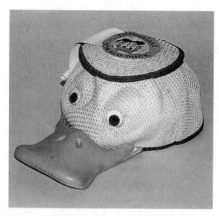

Donald Duck Disneyland hat, Walt Disney Productions label, 9-1/2" long, $20.

Collectors' Clubs: Imagination Guild, P.O. Box 907, Boulder Creek, CA 95006; Mouse Club East, P.O. Box 3195, Wakefield, MA 01880; National Fantasy Fan Club for Disneyana Collectors and Enthusiasts, P.O. Box 19212, Irvine, CA 92713.

Book, *Disneyland*, hardcover, 1969, 9-1/2" x 11" 40.00
Coke cans, Toon Town, 6-pack, Mickey, Roger Rabbit, Donald, Goofy 20.00
Guide book, 32 pgs, 1965 .... 65.00
Little Golden Book, *Donald Duck in Disneyland*, 1955 .... 15.00
Locket, brass, heart shape, raised castle on front, pink and blue accents, late 1950s 28.00
Map, Welcome to Disneyland, fold-out, 1958, 12" x 8-1/2" 80.00
Pinback button, Main Street Commemorative, blue text, 3000th Performance, Sept 4, 1991, color photo 37.50
Plate, Disneyland, lace edge, multi-color center design, 7-1/4" dia 6.00
Poster, Family Fun Night, 1971, copyright Walt Disney Productions, 9" x 12" 45.00
Puzzle, Walt Disney Disneyland, Fantasy Land, 1955 .... 45.00
Salt and pepper shakers, one shows Main Street, other shows Sleeping Beauty castle, pr.......... 40.00
Tray, metal, white designs around rim, 1960s 15.00
Wrist watch, 35 Years of Magic-Disneyland, Mickey's face, band with relief of Fantasy Land Castle, the Matterhorn and Ferris wheel, Japan, MIB............. 25.00

❖ Dog Collectibles

Collecting dog-related items is a fun sport for many collectors. Some specialize in collectibles showing a certain breed; others look for items with canines that resemble a favorite pet. Those who are celebrity-minded search for famous dog characters, such as Tige, Rin Tin Tin, and Lassie.

Collectors' Clubs: Canine Collectors Club, 736 N Western Ave, Suite 314, Lake Forest, IL 60045; Wee Scots, P.O. Box 1597, Winchester, VA 22604.

Bank, Rival Dog Food, early version with 8-dog graphic, 2-3/4" h 38.00
Book, *The Rin Tin Tin Book of Dog Care*, Lee Duncan, Prentice Hall, 1958, dj.............................40.00
Bottle opener, wall-mount, cast iron, bulldog, 4" h, 3-1/2" w........75.00
Chalkware, cocker spaniel, standing, 6" h 38.00
Christmas ornament, milk glass, painted red, doesn't light, 4" h 45.00
Clothes brush, bulldog, porcelain head for handle, paint worn, 7" l 69.00
Cookie jar, McCoy, Mac Dog, mkd "208 USA".......................160.00
Costume jewelry
   Brooch, poodle, Trifari, sits begging, goldtone metal, grey rhinestone accents, mother-of-pearl body, collar with 3 gray baguettes, red cabachon eye, 2-1/4" h, 7/8" w 45.00

Dog pincushion with tape measure (tongue) and thimble holder (tail), 4" high, $25.

Watch brooch, goldtone poodle with watch attached to its feet, green rhinestone eyes, pearl earrings and collar, watch mkd "Sovereign," works, 2-1/2" h, 1-7/8" w 85.00
Figure, ceramic, German shepherd, standing, 1935 State Fair, chips 80.00
Jar, ceramic, Dan the Dog, Alpo advertising, 8" h 65.00
Magazine ad, Gaines dog food, shows Rin Tin Tin, 1947 ..... 9.00
Salt and pepper shakers
   Collie, reclining and standing, 4-1/2" h (standing), pr... 25.00
   Dog and black boy, Regal China, 3-3/4" h, pr.................. 175.00
   Fido and Fifi, Ken-L-Ration advertising, yellow plastic dog, black plastic cat, F&F Mold & Die Works, Dayton, Ohio, 3-1/4" h, pr 25.00
   Puppies, Occupied Japan, 3 pcs, puppy's heads insert into base, 2-1/2" h, 3" w, pr . 29.00
String holder, chalkware, terrier, 8-1/2" h, pr 195.00
Toothbrush holder, dog holds toothbrush in mouth, Japan, 5-1/8" h 95.00

❖ Dollhouse Furniture

Dollhouse furnishings are those tiny articles used to finish and accessorize a dollhouse. Materials and methods of production range from fine handmade wooden pieces to molded plastic items. Several toy manufacturers, such as Tootsietoy, Petite Princess, and Renwal, made dollhouse furnishings.

References: Nora Earnshaw, *Collecting Dolls' Houses and Miniatures*, Pincushion Press, 1993; Herbert F. Schiffer and Peter B. Schiffer, *Miniature Antique Furniture: Doll House and Children's Furniture from the United States and Europe*, Schiffer Publishing, 1995; Margaret Towner, *Dollhouse Furniture*, Running Press, 1993; Dian Zillner and Patty Cooper, *Antique and Collectible Dollhouses and their Furnishings*, Schiffer Publishing, 1998; Dian Zillner with Patty Cooper, *Furnished Dollhouses 1880s-1980s*, Schiffer Publishing, 2001.

Periodicals: *Doll Castle News*, P.O. Box 247, Washington, NJ 07882; *Miniature Collector*, 30595 Eight Mile, Livonia, MI 48152; *Nutshell News*, P.O. Box 1612, Waukesha, WI 53187.

Collectors' Clubs: Dollhouse & Miniature Collectors, P.O. Box 16, Bellaire, MI 49615; National Assoc of Miniature Enthusiasts, P.O. Box 69, Carmel, IN 46032.

Arm chair, Petite Princess, matching ottoman 27.50
Bathroom set, Tootsietoy, 10 pcs, orig box 85.00
Bear rug, white, purple velvet lining, glass eyes 35.00
Bed, Renwal, twin size 9.00
Bedroom suite, Tootsietoy, 6 pcs, orig box 65.00
Candelabra, Petite Princess, MOC 12.00
Chaise lounge, Petite Princess, one pillow missing 10.00
Chest of drawers, walnut, handmade 65.00
Coffee maker, Bodo Hennig, red and black 11.50
Cradle, Renwal, turquoise 16.00
Desk, maple, hinged front, royal blue and black int 115.00
Fireplace, Renwal, brown plastic 37.50
Garbage can, cylindrical, lid lifts with foot pedal, red body, yellow pedal and lid, Renwal 15.00
Kitchen set, Allied, hard plastic, orig box 30.00
Lamp, floor, Petite Princess 1.50

Jaydon 9-piece set of plastic dollhouse furniture, original box, $35.

Lamp, table, Petite Princess 1.00
Living room chair, plastic, uphol- stered look, Petite Princess, one cushion missing 8.00
Living room suite
  Arcade, cast iron, sofa and chair 185.00
  Tootsietoy, sofa, two chairs, library table, 2 lamps, phono- graph stand, 7 pcs 90.00
Piano, Ideal, plastic, litho, mirror 30.00
Plant stand, Petite Princess 1.00
Server, woodtone plastic, Renwal, one drawer opens 5.00
Slide, silver and blue, Renwal .20.00
Wing chair, Petite Princess, MIB 15.00

❖ Dollhouses

Early dollhouses were reserved for the wealthy and were designed primarily as display cabinets for collections of valuable miniatures rather than as playthings for children. The first American doll houses were made in the late 18th century, but it wasn't until 1860, with the development of chromolithography, that they were mass-produced.

References: Nora Earnshaw, *Collecting Dolls' Houses and Miniatures*, Pincushion Press, 1993; Constance Eileen King, *Dolls and Dolls' Houses*, Hamlyn, 1989; Dian Zillner and Patty Cooper, *Antique and Collectible Dollhouses and their Furnishings*, Schiffer Publishing, 1998; Dian Zillner with Patty Cooper, *Furnished Dollhouses 1880s-1980s*, Schiffer Publishing, 2001.

Periodical: *Doll Castle News*, P.O. Box 247, Washington, NJ 07882.

Collectors' Club: Dollhouse & Miniature Collectors, P.O. Box 16, Bellaire, MI 49615.

Bing, Germany, garage, litho tin, double doors, complete with 2 orig cars 600.00
Bliss, chromolith on wood
  Stable, 2-story, red shingle roof, painted green and red cupola, painted red base, single opening door on 2nd floor, brown papier-mache horse, mkd "R. Bliss" 900.00

  Victorian, 2 rooms, 2-story, high steeple roof, dormer windows, spindled porch railing, sec- ond floor balcony 1,400.00
Converse, cottage, red and green litho on redwood, printed bay windows, roof dormer 550.00
Handmade, 2-story, working front door, porch with columns and porch swing, orig yellow, green and red paint, int carpets, wall- paper, remnants of curtains, c1900 .... 750.00
Ideal, colonial style, 3 rooms up, 3 rooms down, balcony, back open 300.00
McLoughlin, folding, 2 rooms, dec int, orig box 925.00
Schoenhut, mansion, 2-story, 8 rooms, attic, large dormer, 20 glass windows, orig decal, 1923 .... 1,850.00
Tootsietoy, printed Masonite, half timbered style, 4 rooms, remov- able roof 200.00

❖ Doll Accessories

Collectors are just finding out what little girls have always known— you can't really play dolls unless you also have the beds, cribs, bassinets, and other necessary items found in a real nursery. Barbie has her own furniture and accessories, plus an extensive wardrobe. But, she wasn't the first doll to be so fortunate. Many early dolls came complete with trunks of clothes, shoes, and other fine accessories.

References: Charles F. Donovan, Jr., *Renwal: World's Finest Toys, Dollhouse Furniture*, L-W Book Sales, 1999; Jean Mahan, *Doll Furniture, 1950s-1980s*, Hobby House Press, 1997.

Bassinet, fold-up type, holds water 65.00
Blanket chest, pine, old worn repaint, 6-board type 450.00
Bunk beds, wood, orig bedding, c1960 .... 80.00
Chest of drawers, Empire style, mahogany and mahogany veneer, 3 dovetailed drawers, scrolled feet, some veneer dam- age 500.00

Cupboard, 2 open shelves over 2 cupboard doors, Strawberry Shortcake dec, litho tin, wear 10.00
Doll bed
Folding, hickory and maple, Mystic, Conn., c1900 .... 50.00
Wood, wheels, 25-1/2" l, 14" w, 22" h 150.00
Fainting couch, professionally restored 130.00
Kitchen set, metal, sink, stove and refrigerator, colorful litho dec 175.00
Outfit, Crissy, orange and white polka dot blouse, matching bell bottom pants 10.00
Stroller, red plaid seat, white metal frame, c1960, played-with condition 20.00
Trunk, dome-top, lined with wallpaper, orig handles................ 75.00
Wash tub, aluminum, 5" dia..... 15.00

✪ Dolls

Made from a wide variety of materials, dolls have always been favorite playthings of the young and the young at heart. Doll collectors are a very dedicated group. Some specialize in a particular style of doll or company, while others simply love them all. There are hundreds of examples for collectors to consider. Condition, age, markings, and original clothing all help to determine a doll's value.

Cabbage Patch Kids doll, $35.

References: Jan Foulke, *14th Blue Book Dolls and Values*, Hobby House Press, 2000; Dawn Herlocher, *Antique Trader's Doll Makers & Marks*, Antique Trader Books, 1999; —, *200 Years of Dolls*, Antique Trader Books, 1996; R. Lane Herron, *Warman's Dolls*, Krause Publications, 1998; Michele Karl, *Composition & Wood Dolls and Toys: A Collector's Reference Guide*, Antique Trader Books, 1998; Constance King, *Collecting Dolls Reference and Price Guide*, Antique Collectors' Club, 1999; Ursula R. Mertz, *Collector's Encyclopedia of American Composition Dolls, 1900 to 1950*, Collector Books, 1999; Patsy Moyer, *Doll Values, Antique to Modern*, 4th ed, Collector Books, 2000; —, *Modern Collectible Dolls*, Vol. IV, Collector Books, 2000; Cindy Cabulis, *Collector's Guide to Dolls of the 1960s and 1970s,* Collector Books, 2000.

Periodicals: *Antique & Collectible Dolls*, 218 W Woodin Blvd, Dallas, TX 75224; *Antique Doll Collector*, 6 Woodside Ave, Suite 300, Northport, NY 11768; *Doll Collector's Price Guide*, 306 E Parr Rd, Berne, IN 46711; *Doll-E-Gram*, P.O. Box 1212, Bellevue, WA 98009-1212; *Doll Life*, 243 Newton-Sparta Rd, Newton, NJ 07860; *Doll Reader*, 741 Miller Drive SE, Harrisburg, PA 20175; *Doll Times*, 218 W Woodin Blvd, Dallas, TX 75224; *Doll World*, 306 East Parr Rd, Berne, IN 46711; *Dollmasters*, P.O. Box 151, Annapolis, MD 21404; *Dolls: The Collector's Magazine*, 170 Fifth Ave, 12th Floor, New York, NY 10010.

Collectors' Clubs: Annalee Doll Society, P.O. Box 708, Meredith, NH 03253; Doll Collector International, P.O. Box 2761, Oshkosh, WI 54903; Doll Costumers Guild, 7112 W Grovers Ave, Glendale, AZ 85308; Doll Doctor's Assoc, 6204 Ocean Front Ave, Virginia Beach, VA 23451; Ginny Doll Club, P.O. Box 338, Oakdale, CA 95361; Madame Alexander Doll Fan Club, P.O. Box 330, Mundelein, IL 60060; United Federation of Doll Clubs, 10920 N Ambassador Dr, Suite 130, Kansas City, MO 64153.

Cinderella storybook doll, Madame Alexander, with original box (not shown), $1,200.

Artist type
Yollanda Bell, Picture Perfect, Baby Sarah, pink nightgown, teddy bear, bunny slippers, 14" h 125.00
Dianna Effner, Sweetness, christening dress, 1988 ...... 125.00
Kay McKee, Ryan, holding frog, retired 1997, MIB........ 195.00
Annie Wahl for Richard Simmons, Sister Mary Margaret, hallmarked, cloth tag, developed with L.L. Knickerbocker Co., 11" h 80.00
Bed doll, silk face, painted bangs, gray wig, sewn shoes, undressed...................... 100.00
Boudoir type, French, cloth face 160.00
Celebrity or character
Angie Dickinson, Police Woman, Horsman, mint doll, box fair 65.00
Brooke Shields, suntan, MIB 65.00
Buffy and Mrs. Beasley, vinyl head, plastic body, Mattel, Inc., MIB 125.00
Fannie Brice, composition head, painted features, Ideal, 1938 .... 185.00
Girl Scout, Effanbee, hat missing, 8" h 25.00
Kate Jackson, Mattel, 12" h 70.00
Liberty Boy, World War I Soldier, composition head, Ideal, 1917 .... 200.00

Mary Poppins, vinyl head and arms, plastic body and legs, Horsman, 1964 .... 55.00

Cloth

Heather, Knickerbocker, painted features, calico dress and hat, MIB.................................. 20.00

Raggedy Ann, Christmas box 35.00

Composition

Anne Shirley, Effanbee, orig clothes, 18" h 195.00

Deanna Durbin, orig box, 15" h 245.00

Dream Baby, Arranbee, redressed, 20" h.......... 115.00

Judy Garland, Wizard of Oz costume, Ideal, 18" h........ 675.00

Nancy, Arranbee, orig outfit, 21" h............................ 410.00

Plastic

Bonnie Walker, Ideal, redressed, 17" h.............................. 90.00

Mary Ellen, Madame Alexander, orig clothes, 31" h 225.00

Penny Brite, orig clothes.... 45.00

Tammy, Ideal, orig clothes 45.00

Tiny Terri Lee, 10" h, Terri Lee Dolls, trunk with 6 orig outfits 450.00

Souvenir, Beefeater, GR symbol on hat, painted features, hand sculpted papier-mâché face, felt clothing, 1950, 9" h . 95.00

Vinyl

Butterball, Effanbee, all orig 65.00

Ginny, Girl Scout outfit, 8" h 115.00

Mary Poppins, Horsman, extra clothes........................... 70.00

Truly Scrumptious, Mattel, 11-1/2" h......................... 95.00

Vinyl and hard plastic

Andy, Eegee, 12" h 25.00

Brenda Star, Madame Alexander, played with, 12" h 450.00

Chatty Cathy, Mattel, talking, MIB............................... 85.00

Littlest Angel, Arranbee, 11" h 45.00

Brass Victorian doorknob set, $22.50.

❖ Doorknobs

If a man's home is his castle, it's no wonder that collectors have latched on to the idea of collecting ornamental doorknobs and other types of hardware. A special doorknob can give a house personality and a bit of pizzazz.

Reference: Web Wilson, *Antique Hardware Price Guide*, Krause Publications, 1999.

Collectors' Club: Antique Doorknob Collectors of America, P.O. Box 126, Eola, IL 60519.

Doorknob

Arts and Crafts, stamped metal, rose motif, 1 nickel-plated, 1 copper-plated, knobs 2" dia, matching plates 9" h x 1-1/2" w, pr 50.00

Brass, emb, with plate, pr ..45.00

Eastlake style, brass..........40.00

Glass, clear, pr 25.00

Glass, mercury, 2-1/4" dia, pr 80.00

Porcelain, hp, fixed brass rosette, mkd "H & S Pitts Patent," 19th C, 2-1/2" dia 275.00

Porcelain, Limoges, floral deco, gold accents, pr...........150.00

Doorknob plate, china, oval, rose pattern, 6-3/8" h, 3-1/2" w, set of 4...55.00

Door knocker, dog, cast iron, old tan paint..................................235.00

Mail slot cover, brass, emb "Letters," Victorian............................48.00

❖ Doorstops

Functional figural doorstops became popular in the late 19th century. Examples could be either flat-backed or three-dimensional. The doorstop's condition is critical to determining value, and collectors prefer doorstops with as much original paint as possible. The following listings are for examples that retain at least 80% of their original paint

Collectors' Club: Doorstop Collectors of America, 1881-G Spring Rd, Vineland, NJ 08630.

Reproduction Alert.

All listings are cast iron unless otherwise noted.

Boston terrier, 9-1/2" h 85.00

Cape Cod, house shape, mkd "Albany Fdy," 5-3/4" h, 8-3/4" w 225.00

Clipper ship, mkd "Copyright Creation Co. 1930," 10-1/2" h, 11-1/4" w 75.00

Fireside Cat 150.00

Flower basket

Marigolds, Hubley, mkd "Made in USA" and "315," 7-1/2" x 8" 175.00

Petunias & Daisies, Hubley 115.00

5-3/4" h, 4-3/4" w............. 100.00

Golfer, 10" h 475.00

Parrot...................................... 65.00

Pointer dog, 8" h, 14" w 495.00

Show horse, Chestnut, Hubley, slight retouch to nose...... 150.00

Cast-iron oversized jack, 6-1/2" x 7-1/2", $35.

❖ Dr. Seuss

Remember reading *Green Eggs and Ham* and *The Cat In The Hat?* Both of those titles are dear to Dr. Seuss collectors. This is a field in which collectors are still establishing fair market values, primarily because so many of the items are just now entering the secondary market. Adding to the thrill of the hunt is the fact that this favorite author also wrote under several pseudonyms.

Books

The 500 Hats of Bartholomew Cubbins, 1938, Vanguard Press, orig dj 95.00
Happy Birthday To You!, 1959 ....26.00
You're Only Old Once, 1986 ....20.00

Cereal bowl, plastic, "The Wubbulous World of Dr. Seuss"......6.00
Drinking glass, High Seuss Navy, Esso Oil premium, 1950s, 5-1/4" h..............................70.00
Growth chart, The Cat in the Hat Growth Chart, paper, orig packaging 17.50
Jelly glass, No. 1, The Cat In The Hat and the Zubbie Wump, "The Wubbulous World of Dr Seuss," 1996, 4" h...........................2.00
Lunch box, metal, Aladdin, 1970, matching plastic thermos 200.00
Pin, pewter, figural, Cat in the Hat 12.00

Cat in the Hat centerpiece, Hallmark, original envelope, $45.

Pinback button, "The PAT in the HAT, Pat Buchanan for President," white lettering on blue/gray ground, caricature of Buchanan in giant red and white hat, 3" dia 5.50

Libbey drinking glass, red, yellow and blue tulips, 6-1/2" high, $2.

❖ Drinking Glasses

Many drinking glasses start out life as part of a set, but due to breakage and other tragedies, they are sometimes orphaned and end up at flea markets, just waiting for a new home.

Bohemian glass, ruby flashed, cut design, gold dec, 4-pc set 150.00
Carnival glass
    Grape pattern, pastel 30.00
    Orange Tree, blue..............60.00
    Peacock at Fountain, amethyst 25.00
Cut glass
    Clear Button Russian pattern 95.00
    Hobstars...........................40.00
Depression era
    American Sweetheart, monax 95.00
    Flowers, yellow and green 12.00
    Stars, white 10.00
    Sunbonnet Girl, red, white and blue 15.00
Early American glass, blown
    Cobalt, paneled, pinpoint flakes on foot, 3-1/8" h...........125.00

Olive green, old paper label, broken blisters, Midwestern, 4" h 700.00
Fenton Glass, Diamond Optic, Aqua 6.00
Fiesta Ware, cobalt 75.00
Heisey, Rose Etch, 12-oz, ftd . 50.00
Libbey Glass, green, slight swirl pattern, mkd, set of 5.............72.00
Northwood, blue, 1" opalescent white band at top, mkd......10.00
Pattern glass, clear
    Colorado pattern 15.00
    Kokomo pattern.................25.00
    Yale pattern 25.00

❖ Drug Store Collectibles

Aacchhoo! Here is another collecting field where the collectors are beginning to really specialize. Whether they collect paper ephemera relating to drug stores, or perhaps collect items related to a favorite local drug store, or perhaps bottles or old packaging, this is a fun category. However, please don't try any of the remedies you might find. Those old compounds might not be stable any more.

Periodical: *The Drug Store Collector*, 3851 Gable Lane Drive, #513, Indianapolis, IN 46208.

For additional listings, see *Warman's Americana & Collectibles*.

Apothecary jar, Tr. Nuc. Vom., glass stopper, 9-1/4" high, $65.

Almanac, 1937, *The Ladies Birthday Almanac*, Medlock's Drug Store, Roscoe, Texas................... 12.00

Bottle

Bromo-Seltzer, The Emerson Company, Baltimore cobalt, 2-1/2" dia....................... 10.00

Sodium Phosphate, United Drug Company, corked, aluminum screw-top, 4-oz 30.00

Calendar, Ramon's Pills, merchant from Gerrardstown, W.Va., 1963, January-June on 1 side, July-December on other, folded 15.00

Fan, cardboard with wooden handle, Burke Drug Co., The Real Drug Store, Morganton, N.C., 14-3/4" h, 9-1/2" w16.00

Glass, ice cream soda

Clear, ribbed stems, 8" h, set of 5 ....30.00

Light amber, 7" h, set of 6.. 55.00

Jar, glass, Ramon's, countertop, blue metal lid, Ramon's character in 2 places.................. 150.00

Matchbook, "Humphrey Drug Store, Home Store of Vice President Hubert H. Humphrey," shows Liberty Bell 7.50

Needle book, Rexall - Make A Point of Saving At Our Rexall Drug Store, 3 needle packets and threader........................... 16.00

Ornament, Hallmark, Neighborhood Drugstore, Nostalgic Houses and Shops series, MIB, 1994 ....25.00

Paper ephemera, order form for opium, Crawford's Drug Store, Atlantic City, NJ, 1920, 10-1/2" h, 8-1/2" w 20.00

Scale, chemist's, General Scientific Co., milk glass platforms, 2 weights, 8" h, 13" w 150.00

Tin

Doan's, tin and cardboard, 40-count.......................... 7.00

Dr. Scholl's Foot Powder, cylindrical, green, black and gold, 6-1/4" h..........................20.00

Men-Tho-Lo, Leighton Supply Co., orig box and instruction sheet, 2-1/2" dia 12.50

Nyal Cold Capsules, Nyal Co., Detroit, black and orange, 3" x 2" x 1/2" 12.50

Trade card, Hood's Latest Tooth Powder, Emlet's Drug Store, Hanover, PA, shows woman's face breaking through newspaper 15.00

❖ Duncan and Miller Glassware

The glass company known as Duncan & Sons and later as Duncan and Miller, was founded in 1865 and continued through 1956. Their slogan was "The Loveliest Glassware in America," and many collectors will certainly agree with that sentiment.

Collectors Club: National Duncan Glass Soc, P.O. Box 965, Washington, PA 15301.

For additional listings, see *Warman's Antiques & Collectibles* and *Warman's Glass*.

Animal

Goose, fat 280.00

Heron 100.00

Swan, red bowl, 7-1/2" h....45.00

Ashtray, Terrace, red, sq..........35.00

Bowl, First Love, crystal, 9" dia 75.00

Candelabra, First Love, crystal, 2-light, pr..........................75.00

Candy jar, cov, Sandwich, chartreuse, 8-1/2" h 95.00

Champagne, Terrace, red........95.00

Coaster, Sandwich, crystal 15.00

Cocktail glass, Caribbean, blue, 3-3/4 oz............................. 48.00

Creamer and sugar, Passion Flower, crystal 42.00

Cup and saucer, Radiance, light blue................................... 24.00

Goblet

Caribbean, blue................. 40.00

Festival of Flowers, crystal 30.00

Plaza, cobalt..................... 40.00

Ice cream dish, Sandwich, crystal, ftd...................................... 12.00

Oyster cocktail, First Love, crystal 24.00

Plate

Radiance, light blue, 8-1/2" dia 12.00

Sandwich, green, 8" dia 24.00

Spiral Flute, crystal, 10-3/8" dia 15.00

Relish dish, divided, Caribbean, blue 30.00

Sherbet, Sandwich, green 12.00

Tumbler, Terrace, red.............. 40.00

Whiskey, Seahorse, etch #502, red and crystal 48.00

Wine glass, Sandwich, crystal 20.00

Caribbean candleholders, sapphire blue, Duncan and Miller, pair, $300.

❖ Earp, Wyatt

Hugh O'Brian starred when Wyatt Earp's character got his own television show. Western collectors search for this cowboy hero at many flea markets.

Bowl, cereal, Hazel Atlas, set of 5 ....200.00
Color and stencil set, Hugh O'Brian, MIB..................................145.00
Comic book, Wyatt Earp, #21, 1958 ....10.00
Gun set, Hubley, black and white leather double holster, "Marshal Wyatt Earp" logo, 2 No. 247 Wyatt Earp Buntline Specials, purple swirl grips, 10-3/4" l, set 175.00
Mug, Wild West Collection, mkd "D6711," 1985-89, handle is a gun and sheriff's badge, 5-1/2" h 200.00
Puzzle, frame tray, full-color portrait, Whitman, 1958 ....25.00
Statue, Hartland 125.00

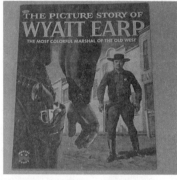

The Picture Story of Wyatt Earp, **Wonder Books, 1956, $8.**

❖ Easter Collectibles

Here's a holiday that's always hoppy to be collected. From chicks to bunnies, this one is fun and whimsical, in addition to having a serious, religious side.

Barbie, Easter Party Barbie, orig box 37.00
Book, *The Easter Story*, 1904 ....32.50
Candy container, cardboard rabbit and cart, yellow, red and purple, 4 red wooden wheels, wear, 9" l 65.00
Cottage cheese container
  Continental Can Co., Newark, N.J., blue rabbit face, pink ground, 1-lb. 8.00
  Dixie Cup Div. of American Co. 12.00
Easter egg, papier-mâché, 2 baby chicks on front, Easter basket filled with lily of the valley flowers, flowered paper int, 3" w, 4-1/2" l 75.00
Lollipop holder, bunny form, yellow plastic, green trim, holes in bunny's hand for sticks, 4" h 12.00
Plate
  Ceramic, Easter Morning Visitor, Recco, from the "Hearts & Flowers" collection by Sandra Kuck, 2 girls with bunny and basket of flowers, #2474A, 7th in series, 1992, 8-1/2" dia 25.00
  Paper, Easter bunny, eggs, and spring flowers, 8-3/4" sq..4.00
  Sterling silver, "Easter Christ," Salvador Dali, Lincoln Mint, 1972, 1st ed, orig box, 9" dia 225.00
Postcard
  Angel theme, printed in Germany 4.00
  "Best Easter Wishes," 2 roosters, April 1908 postmark 6.00
  "Easter Joys Attend Thee," rabbits and flowers, Gibson Art Co., Cincinnati.................3.00
Sheet music, "Easter Dawn" by A. Fieldhouse, 1904, edges rough 15.00
Snowbunnies figures, Dept. 56 Counting the Days Til Easter, 1997, MIB....................24.00

Easter cottage cheese container, made to double as a small basket, 2-7/8" high, 4-1/4" diameter, $14.

I'll Color the Easter Egg, MIB 18.00
Wishing You a Happy Easter, MIB 32.50

❖ Eggbeaters

Before modern kitchens were outfitted with electric appliances, eggbeaters were powered by hand. More than 1,000 patents were issued for items designed to beat eggs, and most of them were granted prior to the 1900s.

References: Linda Campbell Franklin, *300 Years of Kitchen Collectibles,* 4th ed, Krause Publications, 1997; Don Thornton, *Beat This: The Eggbeater Chronicles,* Off Beat Books, 1994.

A&J High Speed Beater, red handle, wooden knob, some finish loss, 12" l................................. 10.00
Androck, red handle, red wooden knob, mkd "Another Androck Product, Made In The United States of America" 15.00
Dover, cast iron, 10-1/4" l........ 25.00
Ekco Best, 2 arrowheads mark, turquoise plastic handle and knob, 12" l................................. 8.00
Ladd, blue handle, 11" l 18.00
One-Hand Whip, Eagle Precision Mfg Corp., chip, 12-1/2" l.. 59.00
Taplin Light Running Eggbeater, metal, 1908 patent date.... 18.00
Turbine Egg Beater, metal, wooden knob, Cassady-Fairbank Mfg. Co., Chicago, 1912 patent date, 10-1/2" l 32.50

Keystone Egg and Cream Beater, metal top, $75.

Ullman, wooden handle, 11" l
....18.00
Unmarked, child-size, red wooden
    handle, 4-1/4" l 9.50

❖ Eggcups

Delicate eggcups make a wonderful collection, both useful and pretty to look at. Some were made as part of dinner services, and others were simply novelty items.

Collectors' Club: Eggcup Collectors' Corner, 67 Stevens Ave, Old Bridge, NJ 08857.
Ceramic or porcelain
    Cactus scene on yellow ground,
        mkd "Japan," minor crack,
        2-1/2" h 2.00
    Child's, Indian motif, gold trim,
        blue Japan stamp, 2-1/4" h
        ....18.00
    Figural, chick, milk glass, mkd
        "Made in France/Opalex"
        ....18.00
    Figural, lady with hat, salt shaker
        in red hat, mkd "Italy C22,"
        5-1/2" h 65.00
    Hand-painted, mkd "Japan,"
        1950s, 4" h 12.00
    Hen on nest, mkd "Worcester
        Royal Porcelain Co., Ltd.,
        Worcester, England," 4-5/8" h
        ....30.00
    Limoges, white, gold trim ... 30.00
    Mickey Mouse, mkd "Walt Disney
        Productions," 3-3/4" h ...85.00
    Organdie, Vernon Kilns......15.00
    Rabbit leaning against eggshell
        house, incised "Germany
        6458" on back, red stamped
        "69" on bottom, 3-1/4" h,
        2-1/2" w........................50.00

Stangl eggcup, 3-1/4" high, $25.

Rabbit with cane, incised "Germany 6450" on back, red
    stamped "76" on base,
    3-1/4" h, 2-1/2" w..........50.00
Turquoise ground, tree limb,
    leaves and acorns dec 8.00
Jasper, blue, white dec, Wedgwood,
    Portland base mark, 1910 .85.00
Silverplate, holds 4 eggs, ftd base
    with swags, mkd "C & Co, E.P.,"
    castle mark 235.00
Sterling silver, small bird-type feet,
    mkd "Paris" 150.00
Wood, hand-painted leaves and
    flowers, mkd "Wien," 2-1/2" h,
    1-1/4" dia 5.00

❖ Egg Timers

Figural egg timers are really catching on with collectors. They are colorful, cute, and useful, too.
Bellhop, kneeling, earthenware, 3" h,
    worn...................................85.00
Building, emb details, plastic, glass
    timer, emb "Casdon" 4" h...40.00
Chef, porcelain, red "Germany"
    mark, incised numbers on back,
    3-3/4" h 110.00
Chef, standing, porcelain, mkd
    "Made in Germany," 3-1/2" h
    ....85.00
Chick, wooden diecut, paper label
    "Lorri Design," 3-3/4" h 50.00
Dutch girl, porcelain, mkd "Germany
    2," 3-1/4" h.........................80.00
Elf with mushroom, plastic, back
    emb "A. Casdon Product, Made
    in England," 3" h, 5" w 50.00

Hour glass shape, wood and glass,
    4" h 3.00
Housemaid with towel, earthenware,
    Japan, 4" h.........................70.00
Humpty Dumpty, hard plastic, mkd
    "A. Casdon Product, Made in
    England," 4" h 95.00
Isle of Man, hard plastic, unused
    ....32.00
Jenny Jones, hard plastic, apron
    emb "Jenny Jones," back emb
    "A. Casdon Product, Made in
    England," 4-1/4" h.............65.00
Kitchen Pixie, Enesco, recipe clip on
    back, 5-1/2" h...................45.00
Milk bottle shape, People Dairy Co.,
    5-1/8" x 2-1/4", orig box 85.00
Mr. Micawber, ceramic, mkd "Made
    in Germany," 4" h..............65.00
Peasant woman, porcelain, script
    sgd "Germany," 4-1/2" h....80.00
Pine bark, pinecone decal dec,
    3-1/4" h 30.00
Sailor boy, white suit, blue details,
    stamped "Germany," 3-1/4" h
    ....110.00
Sea captain, 5-1/2" h 25.00
Telephone, candlestick-type,
    wooden, mkd "Cornwall Wood
    Products, Paris, Maine," 5" h
    ....35.00
Windmill with bird, earthenware,
    mkd "Germany" and incised
    "Germany 825," 3-3/4" h .. 95.00
Woman with shawl, porcelain,
    incised lettering on front "Cymru
    am byth," stamped "Foreign" in
    red ink on bottom, incised "Germany" and numbers on back,
    4-1/4" h 110.00

❖ Elephant Collectibles

Many folks consider elephants to be a symbol of luck. Particularly lucky are those elephants with their trunks raised. Whether due to their size or the fact that they are exotic, people just seem to enjoy them.

Periodical: *Jumbo Jargon*, 1002 W 25th St, Erie, PA 16502.
Ashtray, elephant foot, silver-plate,
    3-1/2" dia 25.00
Bank, cast iron, painted gold, A. Williams, USA, some wear to orig
    paint.................................110.00

Bottle opener, figural, cast iron, sitting, trunk raised
  Brown, pink eyes and tongue, 3-1/2" h 55.00
  Pink, "GOP" on base, 3-1/4" h 55.00
Cigarette dispenser, cast iron 95.00
Creamer and sugar, lusterware, red blankets, black riding on sugar, mkd "Made in Japan," c1940 .... 190.00
Figure
  Crystal, Orrefors, 4" h 85.00
  Porcelain, acrobat, pastel blue, white and beige, triangular gold "Royal Dux" sticker, oval "Made in Czech Republic" sticker, 4-1/4" h 55.00
  Maple, child riding on back of elephant with raised trunk, ink stamp "Anri Italy Ferrandiz," 4-1/2" h 450.00
  Teak, carved adult and baby, 20th C, one tusk missing, 23-1/2" h 140.00
Lamp, elephant with girl, hand painted, Japan, 14" h 45.00
Napkin ring, Bakelite, navy blue, c1940 .... 65.00
Pie bird, mkd "Nutbrown Pie Funnel, Made in England," c1940 185.00
Pin, gold tone, figural............... 25.00
Pitcher, Shawnee, 2-cup, hairline 40.00
Planter, figural, pottery, unmkd
  5" h, glossy finish............... 18.00
  8" x 5-1/2" 20.00
Postcard, Elephant Hotel, Margate City, NJ, 1953...................... 7.50
Salt and pepper shakers, figural, mkd "Japan," pr 24.00
Toy, Elmer Elephant, gray, bow tie and hat, rubber, Sieberling, 5" h 165.00

Cast-iron elephant cigarette dispenser, decal for 1933 Chicago World's Fair, 5" high, 8" long, $165.

Enesco "Pals" figurine, circa 1982, with box (not shown), 3-3/4" high, $10.

❖ Enesco

Enesco has made quality limited editions for years. Some are marked with a stamp, while others have foil labels or paper tags. The company's Precious Moments line is a favorite of collectors.

Also see Precious Moments in this edition.

Bank, Garfield, arms folded, 6" h 60.00
Dealer sign, "The Rose O'Neill Kewpie Collection by Enesco," 3-3/4" h, 1991 .... 45.00
Figure
  Betsy Ross and Friend, 4-1/2" h 18.00
  Blot, Dalmatian, 1960s, 3-3/4" h 125.00
  Irish Mouse, hard plastic, 2-1/2" h.......................... 5.00
  Penny Whistler Lane, Mummy & Weeney, 1-1/4" h............. 4.00
  Pluto, 1960s, copyright Walt Disney Productions, 6-1/4" h 60.00
  Shaggy Dog, copyright Walt Disney Productions, orig paper tag, foil sticker, 5" h 65.00
  Snow White and Seven Dwarfs, Walt Disney Productions Japan, 1960s............... 275.00
Mug, Mouseketeers, emb Mickey Mouse face, foil label, c1960 .... 50.00

Music box, Love Story, Mickey and Minnie Mouse, plays "Love Makes The World Go Round," 6" h, orig paper label........ 75.00
Powder shaker, winking cat 15.00
Salt and pepper shakers, pr
  Blue Birds, orig paper labels, 4" h 24.00
  Christmas Presents, white, green dots, red ribbon, paper label, 2-1/2" h 14.00
  Colonial America, orig box, 4" h 24.00
  Goofy and Teepee, copyright Disney, 1990s............... 20.00
  Piggy Chef, yellow base, clear plastic pig, white plastic chef hat, paper label, orig box 18.00
  Pixies, orig foil labels, 4" h 24.00
  Squirrels, holding large green acorn, orig gold foil labels 22.00
Snow dome, Nag's Head, NC, mouse on skis, oval 15.00

❖ Ertl

Although Ertl has produced a wide range of toys and figures, the company is perhaps best known as a manufacturer of farm toys. Ertl also specializes in promotional and commemorative trucks and banks, the sale of which has most certainly assisted a number of volunteer fire companies and other civic groups.

Collectors' Club: Ertl Collectors Club, PO Box 500, Dyersville, IA 52040.

Airplane
  American Airlines 40.00
  Shell Oil, tri-motor 50.00
  US Navy Air Express......... 30.00
Bank
  Ford Mustang, 1996, Goal Line Classic, MIB 30.00
  Jewel Tea, 1905 truck, orig packaging............................ 65.00
  Kodak, replica of Ford's first delivery car, MIB........... 75.00
Car
  Batmobile, 1989, paint worn, 3-3/4" l 5.00
  Corvette Coupe, 1967, green 25.00

Dick Tracy, Microsize set, 1990, crayons and cars, MIB 8.50

Donald Duck and Goofy in roadster, "Yankee Doodle Donald," MIB, 4" h, 6-1/2" l 50.00

Figure, diecast
Daffy Duck, driving fire engine, Looney Tunes, 1980s, MOC 40.00
Wondergirl, 1990, MOC, 2" h 15.00

Pedal tractor, International Harvester, rip in metal seat, metal emblems painted red, chaindriven 750.00

Semi-trailer, Jewel Tea, orig box 100.00

Tractor
International, paint chips, 2-3/4" h, 4-3/4" l 15.00
John Deere, utility tractor, 1993, 1/16th scale.................... 36.00

Tractor and wagon set, "Campbell's" on tractor, "Campbell's Harvest of Good Foods" on wagon, box mkd "September-October 1985" 300.00

Trailer, farm, movable tailgate, paint chips, 3-3/4" h, 12" l 12.00

✭ Ethnic Collectibles

All men were created equal, but they haven't always been treated that way. Many of today's collectibles reflect the stereotypes of a bygone era.

Bank, Indian chief, porcelain, Japan, 4" h 87.50

Brooch, Chinaman, holding pole with 7 beads, enameled, C-clasp, 3" h 65.00

Chinaman postcard, 1911 copyright, $30.

Figurine, Polish couple, unmkd Ceramic Arts Studio, 6-1/2" h, pr 98.00

Lamp, sleeping Mexican, pink glass, no shade, 7-3/4" h 65.00

Nodder
Chinaman, composition, Japan, 6-1/2" h...........................65.00
Chinaman, papier-mâché on wooden base, 1920s ...135.00

Perfume bottle, sleeping Mexican, chip on hat, 1-1/4" h 45.00

Salt and pepper shakers, Indian chief and brave, 3-1/4" h, pr 30.00

String holder, Indian chief, chalkware, 1950s, 8-3/4" h 275.00

Toothbrush holder, sleeping Mexican, Japan, 6" h...............120.00

Trade card, Chinaman, "New Process Starch, Firmenich Mfg. Co., Peoria, Ill.," 2-3/4" x 4".......20.00

❖ Eyeglasses

Some collectors are always on the lookout for vintage eyeglasses. Spectacles are great decorator accents. Other flea market buyers look for period eyeglasses that they can use for theatrical purposes or that can be worn during historical reenactments.

Reference: Nancy N. Schiffer, *Eyeglass Retrospective*, Schiffer Publishing, 2000.

Jewelry, scarf holder, eyeglasses design, rhinestone-studded, 1" dia 4.50

Monocle, gold frame 25.00

Plastic
8-sided lenses 20.00
Mauritius, red with rhinestones and leopard 32.00
Miniature cat's-eye, champagne color, accented with rhinestones on the eye piece and temples 105.00
Swank, black with glitter.... 32.00
Vogue, cat's-eye, gold and taupe, silver and gold accents 32.00

Premium, cardboard glasses, Checkers Popcorn Confection, "When I go out to Play, I always shout Hurray! For with these specs, I can see the Checks, On Checkers a mile away," toning 19.00

Wire rim, gold, case mkd "Henderson Jeweler and Optometrist, Delhi, N.Y.".......................... 35.00

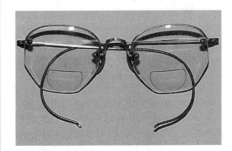

Gold-rimmed spectacles, $20.

F

❖ 4-H

Pledging head, heart, hands, and health, 4-H club members have been awarded (and have made) a multitude of 4-H collectibles since the organization's inception around 1902. Expect renewed interest in this field as the centennial of the 4-H Youth Development Program is 2002. While pins, ribbons, and trophies are the traditional finds, don't overlook 4-H projects themselves. Entomology collections—those small display boxes filled with bugs and butterflies—are especially attracting attention for their folk art nature.

Calendar, 1957, front shows boy and prize pig, black-and-white photos, F.W. Bosworth Co., Plymouth, IN, 7" x 9-1/2" 8.00

Cookbook, *Prize Winning Recipes: 4-H and F.H.A. Favorite Food Shows*, Suburban Propane Gas, 1957, paperback, 62 pages, worn spine, 8-1/2" x 5-1/2" .. 2.00

"Souvenir State Fair" pin, $5.

Fruit jar rings, full box, mkd "4-H" 5.00

Magazine, *National Geographic*, November 1948, feature on 4-H clubs, worn spine.................6.50

Paperweight, gold plated metal, round base, clover finial, 2 1/2" h 9.00

Pin
   1st Year, 1950s 2.50
   3rd Year, mkd "Presented by N.Y. State Bankers Assn," 3.00
   4th Year, green, black and silver, clover logo, mkd "sterling," orig card 5.00
   1987 Ohio State Fair Participant, shaped like state of Ohio................................3.50
   Junior Leadership, gold, enameled clover logo, 1960s ...4.25
   Swine, gold, enameled clover, pig's head in relief, mkd "County Honor Swine Ribbon, First Premium, Breeders Division, Marshall County 4-H Fair, Argos, 1939," blue...4.50

Songbook, *National 4-H Club Songbook*, 1954, softcover, 65 pgs 6.00

Tie tac, gold, green enamel clover logo......................................3.25

U.S. postage stamps, SC1005, 4-H club issue, 1952, full sheet of 50, unused.............................14.50

❖ Farber Brothers/ Krome Kraft

Farber Brothers was located in New York City, from 1919 to 1965. Their principal business derived from the sale of fine table accessories. Some of these items had ceramic or glass inserts by such quality manufacturers as Lenox and Cambridge. The bases were of chrome, silver plate, or mosaic gold. Most of their output was marked Farber Brothers, and they did use some paper labels with the Krome Kraft name.

Candlesticks, Cambridge nude stem, one with cracked base, 8-1/2" h, pr.......................125.00

Cocktail shaker, Bakelite handle, 12-1/2" h...........................85.00

Farberware Art Deco creamer and sugar, wooden handles, 4" high, pair, $30.

Compote, Cambridge amber bowl, chrome holder, 7-1/4" h..... 50.00

Cordial set, figural woman center, 6 different colored 2-1/8" h glasses, chrome tray....... 125.00

Decanter, Cambridge, Duchess, filigree, amber, 12" h 75.00

Goblet, amber glass bowl, chrome stem, 5-7/8" h, set of 4.... 125.00

Mustard, cov, cobalt Cambridge bowl, chrome lid................ 50.00

Percolator set, hammered chrome, Bakelite handles, electric percolator, creamer, sugar and tray 45.00

Salt and pepper shakers, Cambridge, amber, 2-1/2" h, pr 30.00

Shaker, textured surface, Bakelite handle, stamped "Krome Kraft by Farber Bros.".............. 45.00

Tray, crystal and chrome, 9-1/2" l 42.00

Tumbler, 12-oz, varied colors, Cambridge #5633, set of 6..... 150.00

Wine, Cambridge, amethyst, 6-1/2" h, set of 6 .... 150.00

❖ Fans, Electric

Summer heat often melts other collectors, but such is not the case for those who specialize in electric fans. Almost every manufacturer has made electric fans, and there are many varieties to collect. Look for clever designs, well-made fans, and well-known names. Visually check the wiring and other mechanics before plugging in any electrical appliance. Then sit back and enjoy the breeze!

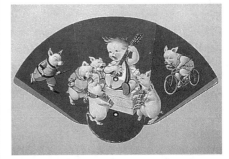

Paper advertising fan, Charles Twelvetrees illustration, 7" high, 10" wide, $15.

M-F-A, Mutual Insurance Co., Little Rock, Ark., cardboard, wooden handle, creases, tear, 12" h 7.00
Moxie, Eileen Perry, copyright 1925, all paper, edge wear, 8-3/8" x 5-1/4" 95.00
Southern belles in cypress garden, 3 panels, funeral home adv on back 15.00
Tums for the Tummy, hand screen type, young boy beckons to girl leaving drugstore 35.00

References: John M. Witt, *Collector's Guide to Electric Fans*, Collector Books, 1997; ——, *Witt's Field Guide to Electric Desk Fans*, self-published, 1993.

Collectors' Club: American Fan Collector Assoc, P.O. Box 5473, Sarasota, FL 34277.

Ceiling
Emerson CF28, 2-blade, restored 3,000.00
Emerson CF30, 5-blade, good orig condition 4,000.00
Desk, oscillating, brass cage and blades, orig tags 125.00
Floor model, Westinghouse, adjustable, quatrefoil metal standard, cast iron base, metal "Westinghouse" tag, mid 20th C, 58" h 175.00
Tabletop
Emerson, #444A, black, gold painted blades, 2-speed, 1926, 8" 35.00
General Electric, #2364327, Whiz, polished brass blades, glossy hunter green finish, 1924, 9" 40.00
Knapp-Monarch, brown finish, 1940, 9" 18.00
Polar Cub, black metal base, mkd "A. C. Gilbert, New Haven, Conn.," 8-1/2" dia, 11" h 65.00
Robbins & Meyers, 4 blades, oscillating, cast iron base 150.00

Westinghouse, mkd "USA Cat. N 12LAH, Part No. Y-35258" 28.00

❖ Fans, Hand-Held

Today we tend to think of fans as decorative accessories, but for our ancestors, they were the primary means of cooling themselves. Collectors can find a wide range of advertising fans, practical fans, and highly decorative fans. Care needs to be taken when handling some of the more delicate examples, as they may be made of feathers, ivory, mother of pearl, or even very fine kid.

Collectors' Club: FANA, Fan Assoc of North America, Suite 128, 1409 N Cedar Crest Blvd, Allentown, PA 18104.
For additional listings, see *Warman's Antiques & Collectibles.*
Advertising
"666 Quartette" laxative, Hill's Pharmacy, Tampa, Fla., cardboard, chipped wooden handle, creases, 11-1/4" h...16.00
Independent Life and Accident Insurance Co., Jacksonville, Fla., "Cooling Off," shows naked child walking toward river, Scheer, #3183, cardboard, wooden handle.....8.00

❖ Farm Collectibles

Farm collectors are saving an important part of our American heritage. Collecting and protecting the items related to or used on a farm will give future generations insights into the amount of work farming entailed.

References: C.H. Wendel, *Encyclopedia of American Farm Implements & Antiques*, Krause Publications, 1997; ——, *Unusual Vintage Tractors*, Krause Publications, 1996.

Periodicals: *Antique Power*, P.O. Box 1000, Westerville, OH 43081; *Belt Pulley*, P.O. Box 83, Nokomis, IL 62075; *Country Wagon Journal*, P.O. Box 331, W Milford, NJ 07480; *Farm Antiques News*, 812 N 3rd St, Tarkio, MO 64491; *Farm Collector*, 1503 SW 42nd St, Topeka, KS 66609; *Rusty Iron Monthly*, P.O. Box 342, Sandwich, IL 60548; *Tractor Classics*, P.O. Box 191, Listowel, Ontario N4H 3HE Canada; *Turtle River Toy News & Oliver Collector's News*, RR1, Box 44, Manvel, ND 58256.

Collectors' Clubs: Antique Engine, Tractor & Toy Club, 5731 Paradise Rd, Slatington, PA 18080; Cast Iron Seat Collectors Assoc, P.O. Box 14, Ionia, MO 65335; Early American Steam Engine & Old Equipment Soc, P.O. Box 652, Red Lion, PA 17356; Farm Machinery Advertising Collectors, 10108 Tamarack Dr, Vienna, VA 22182; The Feedsack Club, 25 S Starr Ave, Apt. 16, Pittsburgh, PA 15202-3424; International Harvester Collectibles, 310 Busse Hwy, Suite 250, Park Ridge, IL 60068-3251.

Advertisement, 1948 Oliver Model 88 industrial tractor, black-and-white, 10-1/4" x 7-1/2" 20.00

Book, *Farm Life on The South Plains Of Texas* 18.50

Booklet, International Harvester, *Make Soil Productive*, 64 pgs, 1931 .... 8.50

Bridle rosette, heart shape 38.50

Cider press, oak and other hardwoods, old refinish, mortised and pegged, base with 4 legs, threaded wooden shaft missing its handle, 44" h, 26" w, 15" d 220.00

Feed chest, smoke-decor, white ground with black smoke, slant-lid, 3 interior compartments, turned legs with ball feet, wear, mouse holes, 35-1/2" h, 53-1/4" w, 24" d 375.00

Flour sack, printed paper
"Harvest Queen Improved Roller Flour, Red Mills," shows woman in bonnet, Centre Hill, Pa., framed, soiled, stains, 20" h, 14" w 50.00
"Snow Flake, Pine Creek Mills, 48 lbs.," shows snow scene of a mill, framed, soiled, stains, 20" h, 14" w 80.00

Goat yoke, single, wood, bentwood bow................................. 60.00

"Ford Farming" tin sign, 11" x 22", $30.

Hay fork, wooden, 4-prong, 3 wooden prongs on front with 4th mounted on handle with iron bracket, 84" l 60.00

Hay hook, cast iron with wood handle, 14" l 15.00

Hummel, Farm Boy, #66, stylized bee mark, 5-3/4" h 350.00

Magazine
Farm Journal, May 1937, faded, folds.............................. 6.00
Farm Journal, June 1958, tear 5.00
Farm Journal, Feb. 1963, chickens on cover.................... 4.00

Medallion, John Deere, front shows bust of John Deere and "He gave the world the steel plow," back shows wagon train and plow with "John Deere Quality Farm Equipment, since 1837" 35.00

Memo book, Agrico Fertilizer, 1947 calendar............................. 3.50

Milking stool, wooden, crescent-shaped seat, 3 round splayed stake legs, primitive, refinished, 8" h, 17" w, 7" d 35.00

Operator's manual
Allis-Chalmers, model B front-mounted planter, 600 series, soiling 8.25
Ford, model 8N tractor, 1948 .... 50.00
John Deere, horse-drawn cultivator, 7 pgs, stains, folds 40.00
John Deere, model "E" and "ET" manure spreaders, February 1940, 28 pgs, soiled, folded, pages loose................... 30.00
John Deere, sweep-type planting and fertilizing attachments for tractor cultivators, light soiling 5.25

Pinback button, celluloid
Lamb Wire Fence Co., red and white, black accents, early 1900s 15.00
Purina Chicken Chowder, red and white checkered feed sack, blue ground, white slogan "If Chicken Chowder Won't Make Your Hens Lay They Must Be Roosters," 1920s 10.00

Plate, 1982 National Farm Toy Show, 5th anniversary, Fenton, hp deco, limited to 500 ....155.00

Sickle, 21" l, wooden frame, iron blade 25.00

Sign, paper
"Buckeye, Our New Low Down Drills, They Are Endorsed And Demanded," central scene of man driving 2-horse team pulling drill, 4 smaller images of horse-drawn equipment, 30" h, 21-1/4" w 715.00
"Compliments of Ohio Rake Co., Dayton, O.," Statue of Liberty in center, images of ship at sea, Civil War battle, farmer using horse-drawn rake, framed, 28-1/2" h, 34-1/2" w 2,310.00
"Deere Vehicles Are All Right," shows stag pulling buckboard, orig frame, light stains, small pinhole spots of litho loss, 23-1/2" h, 31-1/2" w . 1,771.00

Tape measure, metal, Kent Feeds, Nichols (Iowa) Grain and Feed, 2-digit phone number, scratches, 2" dia................................. 25.00

❖ Farm Toys

Toy and farm machinery manufacturers have provided young farmers with wonderfully detailed farm toys. Today's collectors are eager to find good examples and can find additions to their collections ranging from toys from the 1920s to the present.

Reference: —, *Standard Catalog of Farm Toys: An Identification and Price Guide,* (Fall 2001) Krause Publications, 700 E State St, Iola, WI 54990.

Periodicals: *Toy Tractor Times,* P.O. Box 156, Osage, IA 50461; *Turtle River Toy News & Oliver Collector's News,* RR1, Box 44, Manvel, ND 58256.

Collectors' Clubs: Antique Engine, Tractor & Toy Club, 5731 Paradise Rd, Slatington, PA 18080; CTM Farm Toy & Collectors Club, P.O. Box 489, Rocanville, Saskatchewan S0A 3L0 Canada; Ertl Replicas Collectors' Club, Hwys 136 and 20, Dyersville, IA 52040; Farm Toy Collectors Club, P.O. Box 38, Boxholm, IA 50040.

Combine

Claas, Matchbox, #65C, red body, yellow head, 1967, orig box with wear 9.50
Co-op, litho tin, friction, Marx, 6" l 30.00
Matchbox, #51, 1978, MIB ... 8.00
Corn picker, John Deere, steel, Ertl 55.00
Harrow, tandem disc, Corgi, 1967 .... 15.00
Hay rack, Arcade, 7" l 85.00
Manure spreader, McCormick-Deering, team of horses, Arcade 65.00
Plow, Case, Ertl 10.00
Steam engine, Mamod, English, c1965, 6-3/4" h, 10" l 275.00

Tractor

Auburn Rubber, blue, 1930s, 1 tire losing rubber, 4-3/4" l 45.00
Farmall, 1991 National Farm Toy Show, Ertl, 9" l 40.00
Fordson, Hubley, cast iron, 5-1/2" l 150.00
International, Tootsietoy 10.00
John Deere 630, 1988 National Farm Toy Show, 1/43rd scale, Ertl, orig box 30.00
John Deere, Matchbox, #50, green body, 1964 .... 15.00
Tru-Scale, 4-1/2" h, 8" l 125.00

Truck

Chevrolet livestock truck, Smith-Miller, unpainted cab and trailer, 1946 .... 175.00
Farm stake truck, Tonka, #0404, 1963 .... 60.00
Farm truck, battery-op, litho tin, Japan, 1950s, 9-1/4" l . 150.00

❖ Fast Food Collectibles

The hamburger has long been a popular American food, and fast food restaurants have certainly done their best to convince us that they hold the secret to the perfect sandwich. And, in an effort to increase sales and generate future purchases, they've added toys and premiums. These special extras have become an interesting part of the collectibles marketplace.

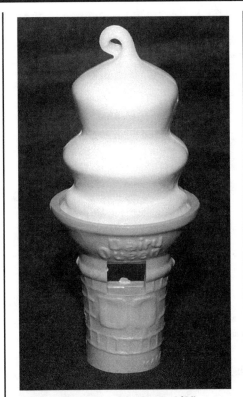

Dairy Queen whistle, 3-1/8" high, $10.

References: Alex G. Malloy and Robert J. Sodaro, *Kiddie Meal Collectibles*, Krause Publications, February, 2001; Elizabeth A. Stephan, *Ultimate Price Guide to Fast Food Collectibles*, Krause Publications, 1999; Gail Pope and Keith Hammond, *Fast Food Toys*, 2nd ed, Schiffer Publishing, 1998.

Periodical: *The Fast Food Collectors Express*, P.O. Box 221, Mayview, MO 64071-0221.

For additional listings, see *Warman's Americana & Collectibles* and McDonald's in this edition.

Ashtray, Howard Johnson's, clear glass, shows stylized building, post-1966, 4-1/2" w 6.00
Bank, figural, Big Boy, rubber, copyright 1973, 9-1/4" h 28.00
Bowl, plastic, Dairy Queen, yellow, Schroeder Paper Co., Cincinnati 9.00

Building

Bob's Big Boy Restaurant, Lefton, NRFB, 6" h, 8" w 45.00
KFC Kentucky Fried Chicken Restaurant, Lefton, NRFB, 6" h, 8" w 45.00

Calendar, Burger King, Olympic games theme, 1980 .... 4.00
Doll, Burger King, molded plastic head and hands, 1980, 22" h 35.00
Glider, King Glider, Burger King, Styrofoam, 1978 .... 2.50

Mug

Hardee's Breakfast Club, 1993 .... 3.00
Hardee's Rise and Shine Homemade Biscuits, ceramic, 1984 .... 6.00
Lendy's Hamburgers, ftd, ceramic, shows character in Lendy's hat carrying a double hamburger 44.00

Paperweight, Wendy's, "Decade II," metal and celluloid 29.00
Pen, pencil and calculator set, Wendy's 6.00
Pinback button, Vote for Col. Sanders, KFC, blue and white, 1972, 1-1/2" dia 24.00
Salt shaker, Dairy Queen, chocolate dip ice cream cone, 4-1/4" h 22.00
Teddy bear, Burger King, Crayola blue bear, 1986, 7" h 8.00
Tray, plastic, Snuffy's Shanty's, shows Snuffy Smith and gang, mkd Camtray Cambro Mfg. Co., 13-1/2" x 10-1/2" 28.00

✪ Fenton Glass

Founded by Frank L. Fenton in 1905 in Martin's Ferry, Ohio, Fenton first decorated glassware for other makers. By 1907, the company was making its own glass and had relocated to Williamstown, West Virginia. Today the company is still producing quality glass, and collectors are encouraged to visit the factory site and museum in Williamstown.

References: There are several very good older reference books about Fenton Glass.

Periodicals: *Butterfly Net,* 302 Pheasant Run, Kaukauna, WI 54130; *Glass Messenger*, 700 Elizabeth St, Williamstown, WV 26187.

Collectors' Clubs: Fenton Art Glass Collectors of America, P.O. Box 384, Williamstown, WV 26187; National Fenton Glass Soc, P.O. Box 4008, Marietta, OH 45750.

For additional listings and a detailed list of reference books, see *Warman's Antiques & Collectibles* and *Warman's Glass*.

Ashtray, ruby 20.00
Basket, Cranberry Opal, Hobnail
....95.00
Bell, Christmas Morn...............45.00
Bon bon, Rosalene Butterfly, 2 handles..35.00
Bowl
   Gold Crest, 8" dia 40.00
   Peach Crest, shell shape, 10" dia
....75.00
   Rosalene, basketweave.....32.00
Cake dish, Silver Crest, white, 13"
   dia 65.00
Candlesticks, Ming, cornucopia,
   5" h, pr...............................50.00
Candy dish, cov
   Custard, hp pink daffodils, sgd
     "Louise Piper".............. 165.00
   Lamb's Tongue, turquoise..35.00
   Teardrop, white 55.00
Compote, Waterlily, Rosalene .30.00
Condiment set, Teardrop, white
....55.00
Creamer, Diamond Optic, ruby
....30.00
Cruet, #418 Coin Dot, cranberry
   opalescent...................... 120.00
Epergne, Petite French Opal, 4" h
....40.00
Fairy Light, Colonial Amber, Hobnail,
   3 pcs..................................25.00
Float bowl, Silver Crest, 13" dia
....45.00
Flower frog, Nymph, blue opalescent, 6-3/4" h, 2-3/4" w......48.00
Goblet, Lincoln Inn, red 24.00

Fenton white hobnail vase, ruffled lip, paper label, 10-1/2" high, $55.

Hat, Swirl Optic, French opalescent,
   #1922.............................. 115.00
Hurricane Lamp, five petal blue dogwood dec 75.00
Pitcher, Coin Dot, cranberry opalescent....................................65.00
Plate
   Fenton Rose, dolphin handles,
     #1621, 6" dia 27.50
   Ming Rose, #107, 8" dia.....32.00
Salt and pepper shakers, Hobnail,
   cranberry opalescent, flat,
   #3806, pr 50.00
Sherbet, Lincoln Inn, pink........15.00
Tumbler, ftd, Lincoln Inn, red, 5-oz
....25.00
Vase
   5-3/4" h, fan shape, Hobnail, ruffled rim, white milk glass
....18.00
   7" h, Burmese, roses, sgd "Sue
     Foster"..........................120.00
   10" h, Apple Tree, milk glass
....95.00
   11" h, cranberry Snow Crest,
     swirl 60.00
Wine Goblet, Lincoln Inn, red ..25.00

❖ Fiesta

Frederick Rhead designed this popular Homer Laughlin pattern. It was first introduced in 1936 and became a real hit after a vigorous marketing campaign in the early 1940s. Original colors were red, dark blue, light green, brilliant yellow, and ivory. Turquoise was added in 1937. Red was removed in 1943, but brought back in 1959. Light green, dark blue, and ivory were retired in 1951 and replaced by forest green, rose, chartreuse, and gray. Medium green was added in the late 1950s. By 1969, the popular pattern was redesigned and finally discontinued in 1972. However, by 1986, Homer Laughlin had reintroduced the pattern, but in a new formula and with new colors, including a darker blue, black, white, apricot, rose, and even pastels some years later.

Collectors' Clubs: Fiesta Club of America, P.O. Box 15383, Loves Park, IL 61132; Fiesta Collectors Club, 19238 Dorchester Circle, Strongsville, OH 44136.

Fiesta turquoise disk pitcher, $125.

Reproduction Alert.

For additional listings, see *Warman's Antiques & Collectibles, Warman's Americana & Collectibles,* and *Warman's American Pottery & Porcelain.*

Ashtray
   Forest green..................... 60.00
   Gray 77.00
   Red................................... 60.00
   Light green 44.00
   Turquoise 50.00
   Yellow.............................. 50.00
Candleholder
   Bulb, cobalt, pr 165.00
   Bulb, yellow, pr................110.00
   Tripod, red, pr.................. 357.50
   Tripod, light green, pr 330.00
Carafe
   Cobalt........................... 220.00
   Ivory 1998.00
   Red................................. 275.00
   Turquoise 247.50
Casserole
   Cobalt........................... 154.00
   Gray 176.00
   Ivory 88.00
   Yellow 143.00
   Turquoise 137.50
Cream soup
   Chartreuse 68.50
   Cobalt............................110.00
   Red................................. 55.00
   Turquoise 165.00
   Yellow 100.00
Cup and saucer, pair
   Cobalt............................ 155.00
   Medium green 255.00
   Red................................. 100.00
   Turquoise 155.00

Egg cup
  Cobalt 88.00
  Forest green 105.00
  Gray 121.00
  Red 143.00
  Rose 110.00
Fruit bowl, 11-3/4" dia
  Cobalt 275.00
  Ivory 247.50
  Red 330.00
  Yellow 192.50
Mug
  Chartreuse 77.00
  Cobalt 55.00
  Gray 71.50
  Ivory 71.50
  Medium green 137.50
  Red 71.50
Nappy, 8-1/2" dia
  Cobalt 33.00
  Medium green 121.00
  Red 33.00
Nappy, 9-1/2" dia
  Cobalt 44.00
  Light green 38.50
  Turquoise 22.00
Plate, 6" dia
  Ivory 33.00
  Medium green 137.50
  Turquoise 38.50
Plate, 9" dia
  Gray 33.00
  Medium green 100.00
  Red 55.00
  Turquoise 59.50
  Yellow 44.00
Platter
  Medium green 165.00
  Turquoise 22.00
  Red 50.00
  Rose 38.50
Teapot, medium
  Cobalt 143.00
  Medium green 1,485.00
  Red 100.00
  Yellow 100.00
Teapot, large
  Light green 176.00
  Red 187.00
Tumbler, juice
  Cobalt 44.00
  Ivory 52.50
  Red 93.50
  Turquoise 66.00
  Yellow 33.00
Tumbler, water
  Cobalt 77.50
  Ivory 71.50
  Red 75.00

Vase, 8" h
  Cobalt 467.50
  Ivory 440.00
  Light green 467.50
  Turquoise 412.50
  Yellow 467.50
Vase, 10" h
  Light green 522.50
  Red 660.00
  Yellow 632.50
Vase, 12" h
  Ivory 660.00
  Light green 742.50
  Red, minor nick 825.00
  Yellow 770.00
Water pitcher, disk
  Chartreuse 165.00
  Cobalt 143.00
  Forest green 154.00
  Light green 100.00
  Red 121.00
  Turquoise 77.00

❖ Figurines

Collectors will usually find an assortment of figurines to pick from while browsing at their favorite flea market. Some specialize in certain types of figurines, while others concentrate on specific makers.
Aloha, Treasure Craft, 1959 .... 45.00
Angel Fish, green "Japan" mark, 2" h
  .... 7.00
Blue jar, mkd "Homco" 25.00
Dove, Artesania Rinconada, retired
  1987 .... 90.00
Eagle, Artesania Rinconada, retired
  1987 .... 250.00

Occupied Japan figurine, reclining Oriental girl, 4-1/2" long, $12.

Friar, holding sausages, pewter and
  ceramic, 3-1/4" h 50.00
Girl with watering can, Japan
  .... 35.00
Graduate, Pen Delflin, hp stonecraft
  .... 85.00
Lion and child, porcelain, mkd
  "Japan" on bottom, 5" w, 4" h
  .... 38.00
Man, glass, blue head, hands, and
  shows applied bushy hair, 4" h
  .... 12.00
Oriental girl, 6" h 15.00
Parrot, chip on tail 15.00
Polar Pal, paddling kayak, with Mal-
  amute puppy, icy blue pool base,
  Westland Resin, retired 35.00
Ram, small chip on base, 6-1/4" h
  .... 10.00
Rottweiler, Beswick, 5-3/4" h .. 95.00
Snowbunny, "I'll Love You Forever,"
  Dept 56, 4-3/4" h 15.00
Wild Rabbit, Artesania Rinconada,
  retired 1995 .... 100.00
Woman, wearing evening gown,
  holding feather fan 12.00

❖ Finch, Kay

Kay Finch started her pottery in her California home around 1935. She was eventually joined by her husband, Braden, and son, George—artists and sculptors in their own right. Together, they produced interesting figures and tableware until 1963.
Angel, white and blue, 4-1/2" h
  .... 95.00
Bank, Sassy Pig 165.00
Bowl, egg shape, daisies at top, pink
  ext, Kay Finch pink int, mkd,
  5-1/2" l, 3-3/4" h 95.00
Candleholder, white flower, 14" h
  .... 35.00
Dish, shell, chartreuse, mkd, 12" x
  10", slight crazing 40.00
Figure
  Ambrosia Persian Cat, flake on
    ear, 10-3/4" h 600.00
  Bunny, 3" h 160.00
  Cherub 160.00
  Lamb, pink, 2-1/4" h 50.00
  Muff the Cat, 3-1/2" h 75.00
  Owl, slight blemish on beak, 4" h
    .... 60.00
  Peep the Duck 45.00
  Smiley Pig, sgd, slight paint loss,
    6-3/4" h, 8" l 350.00

Vicki, as is.........................350.00
Mug, Santa, #4950................145.00
Planter
    Baby block and bear........100.00
    Cat, 7" l, 6" h....................185.00
Soup tureen, turkey...............500.00
Wall pocket, Santa 90.00

❖ Firearms Accessories

Collectors of firearm accessories and related memorabilia have found that flea markets are great sources for adding to their collections. Collectors of firearms are well advised to ask to see any required licenses on the part of vendors they are dealing with. Some states are getting strict about this collecting area. For that reason, we've decided not to include firearms prices in this edition, as fewer quality dealers are choosing to use flea markets to sell guns. Memorabilia, advertising, and related items are still sold at general flea markets, and those items are covered here.

References: Ned Schwing, *Standard Catalog of Firearms*, 11th ed, Krause Publications, 2001; John Ogle, *Colt Memorabilia Price Guide,* Krause Publications, 1998; John Walter, *Rifles of the World*, 2nd ed. Krause Publications, 1998.

Periodicals: *Gun List,* 700 E State St, Iola, WI 54990; *Military Trader,* P.O. Box 1050, Dubuque, IA 52004; *The Gun Report*, P.O. Box 38, Aledo, IL 61231.

Collectors' Club: The Winchester Arms Collectors Assoc, P.O. Box 6754, Great Falls, MT 59406.
Box
    Federal Hi-Power Rifled Slugs, shotgun shells, 5-count . 22.00
    Hoppe's Gun Cleaning Patches, 1940, wear 22.00
    Monark, 16-gauge shotgun shells, Federal Cartridge Corp., Minneapolis........45.00
    Wards Red Head, 12-gauge shotgun shells, shows goose 25.00
Bullet mold, Winchester, cast iron with wooden handle 65.00

Check
    Colt firearms founder Sam Colt, Phoenix Bank, Hartford 125.00
    Sharps Rifle Co., Bridgeport, CT, 1878 ....75.00
Folder, diecut, shotgun shape, Winchester New Rival Shells, blue, yellow and red stiff paper, 1930s, 2" x 6-1/4"..........................85.00
Pinback button
    Peters Ammunition, red, white and blue, gold letters, c1910 ....50.00
    Shoot Peters Shells, brass and red shell on white ground, Pulver Co., early 1900s 40.00
    Winchester Products, red and white "W" on blue and silver design, early 1900s.......40.00
Tin, Dupont Superfine Gun Powder, paper label shows animals, 6" h 79.00
Trophy cup, Pennsylvania Gun Club, 1902, wood, pewter trim and handle, mkd "Smith Patterson & Co., Boston"....................150.00

❖ Firefighters

Hats off to firefighters, those brave men and women who help others in time of need. Many of them also collect fire memorabilia.

Periodical: *Fire Apparatus Journal*, P.O. Box 121205, Staten Island, NY 10314.

Collectors' Clubs: Antique Fire Apparatus Club of America, 5420 S Kedvale Ave, Chicago, IL 60632; Fire Collectors Club, P.O. Box 992, Milwaukee, WI 53201; Fire Mark Circle of the Americas, 2859 Marlin Dr, Chamblee, GA 30341; Great Lakes International Antique Fire Apparatus Assoc, 4457 285th St, Toledo, OH 43611; International Fire Buff Associates, 7509 Chesapeake Ave, Baltimore, MD 21219; Society for the Preservation & Appreciation of Motor Fire Apparatus in America, P.O. Box 2005, Syracuse, NY 13320.
Advertisement, 1926 Deluge Master Fire Fighter fire truck, Prospect Fire Engine Co., Prospect, Ohio, black-and-white, 9" x 6" 19.00

Badge
    Mineola Fire Dept, relief image of fire hydrant on one side, hook and ladder on other, c1950, 2" x 2" 10.00
    Western Pennsylvania Fireman's Assoc., Sharpsburg Delegate, 22nd annual convention, 1915................85.00
Book
    Five Little Firemen, Golden Press, 1949 ....4.00
    Jiminy Cricket Fire Fighter, Mickey Mouse Club Books, 1956 ....17.50
Bucket, galvanized tin, red lettering, "Fire Only".........................35.00
Comic book, *Smokey Bear*, firefighter motif, 1969 ....10.00
Doll, Firefighter Barbie, Mattel, 1995, MIB 40.00
Figurine, Real Heroes Top Jake Firefighter, firefighter in full gear, Ertl, 1998, 12" h, NRFB...........31.00
Fire extinguisher, Fyr Fyter Fire Fighter Model A, brass......45.00
Helmet, Quakertown Fire Dept, No. 1, black, leather shield, orig liner 75.00
Hose nozzle, brass 50.00
Movie, "Chimp the Fireman," Castle Films, box worn, end flaps missing......................................28.00
Pinback button, celluloid, "Firemen's Celebration," on ribbon, shows fireman, 1958, 1-1/4" dia, 3-3/4" l 18.00
Stein, Tribute to American Firefighters, Avon, 1989, 8" h 40.00
Toy
    Chief's car, litho tin, battery op, Linemar, Japan, 1950s, MIB 225.00
    Helmet, Emergency 51, wear 40.00
    Rampwalker, fireman with hose, Marx 110.00
Wrench, brass, 7-function, polished, lacquered, 12-3/4" x 3-1/4" 98.00

✪ Fire-King

Made by Anchor Hocking Glass Co., Fire-King is currently one of the hottest segments of the glass market. Production of ovenproof Fire-King glass began in 1942 and continued until 1972. Dinnerware was made in several patterns, and a variety of colors, including azurite, forest green, gray, ivory, jade-ite, peach luster, pink, ruby red, sapphire blue, opaque turquoise, and white. Some pieces were also decorated with decals. Jade-ite items, a light green opaque color, are currently the most popular and command high prices. Fire-King also manufactured utilitarian kitchenware that is also quite popular with collectors.

References: Gene Florence, *Anchor Hocking's Fire King & More*, 2nd ed, Collector Books, 2000; ——, *Collectible Glassware from the 40's, 50's, 60's*, 5th ed, Collector Books, 2000; ——, *Kitchen Glassware of the Depression Years*, 5th ed, Collector Books, 1995 (1997 value update); Joe Keller and David Ross, *Jade-ite*, 2nd ed, Schiffer Publishing, 2000; Gary & Dale Kilgo and Jerry & Gail Wilkins, *Collectors Guide to Anchor Hocking's Fire-King Glassware*, K&W Collectibles Publisher, 1991; ——, *Collectors Guide to Anchor Hocking's Fire-King Glassware*, vol 2, K&W Collectibles Publisher, 1998.

Periodicals: *Fire-King Monthly*, P.O. Box 70594, Tuscaloosa, AL 35407; *Fire-King News*, K&W Collectibles, P.O. Box 374, Addison, AL 35540.

Collectors' Club: Fire-King Collectors Club, 1161 Woodrow St, #3, Redwood City, CA 94061.

For additional listings, see *Warman's Americana & Collectibles*, *Warman's Glass*, and *Warman's Depression Glass*.

Dinnerware

Alice, Jade-ite
    Cup and saucer 12.00
    Dinner plate 70.00
Salad plate 14.00

Fire-King snack set, turquoise blue, $10.

Charm, Azurite
    Bowl, 4-3/4" dia 5.00
    Cereal bowl, 6" dia 18.00
    Cup and saucer....................4.00
    Luncheon plate 5.00
    Salad plate 15.00
Jane Ray
    Berry bowl, ivory 55.00
    Cup and saucer.................15.00
    Demitasse cup and saucer,
        jade-ite 85.00
    Dinner plate, 9" dia, ivory ...55.00
    Soup bowl, 7-5/8" dia 30.00
Laurel Gray
    Bowl, 4-1/2" dia 6.00
    Creamer and sugar 7.00
    Cup and saucer....................5.00
    Dinner plate.........................8.00
    Serving plate, 11" 40.00
Peach Luster, child's cup, 2" h,
    2-1/2" w 22.00
Restaurant ware, Jade-ite, heavy
    Bowl, 4-3/4" dia 15.00
    Cereal bowl, 5" dia 35.00
    Chili bowl...........................15.00
    Creamer and sugar, cov.....35.00
    Cup and saucer.................18.00
    Dinner plate, 9" dia 32.00
    Grill plate...........................35.00
    Luncheon plate 85.00
    Mug...................................15.00
    Platter, 9-1/4" l 60.00
    Platter, 11-1/2" l.................65.00
    Salad plate 15.00
Swirl, Azurite
    Cup and saucer....................8.00
    Dinner plate.........................8.50
    Platter, oval 20.00
    Salad plate 7.00
Swirl, Ivory
    Cup and saucer....................7.00
    Dinner plate, orig label 11.00
    Soup, flat, orig label 12.00
    Starter set, orig pictorial box,
        4 dinner plates, 4 cups and
        saucers..........................60.00
Turquoise
    Child's plate, divided, 7-1/2" dia
        ....40.00
    Starter set, orig box............75.00

Kitchenware

Red Dots
    Grease jar, white 35.00
    Mixing bowl set, white, 7", 8" and
        9" dia 70.00
    Salt and pepper shakers,
        white, pr........................45.00
Stripes
    Grease jar 35.00

    Salt and pepper shakers, pr
        ....37.50
Swirl
    Pie pan, orig label 15.00
    Range shaker, orig tulip top
        ....24.00
Tulip
    Bowl, 9-1/2" dia 35.00
    Grease jar, ivory 35.00
    Grease jar, white 35.00
    Turquoise, bowl, splashproof,
        3-qt 25.00

Ovenware

Baker, Sapphire Blue, individual
    serving size........................ 4.50
Casserole, cov, Sapphire Blue,
    1-pint 14.00
Custard cup, crystal, orig label . 3.00
Loaf pan, Sapphire Blue 17.50
Pie plate, crystal, 10-oz 4.00
Utility bowl, Sapphire Blue, 7" dia
    .... 14.00

❖ Fireplace Collectibles

In addition to providing a place to hang your stocking at Christmas, fireplaces also serve as important decorative and functional elements. And, as such, they need to be accessorized. Flea markets are wonderful places to find interesting objects to accomplish this goal.

Andiron
    Bulldog, cast iron, 16" h, pr
        .... 880.00
    Woman, cast iron, 14" h, pr
        .... 165.00
Bellows, fruit and foliage decor, yellow paint, green banding, 18" l
    .... 330.00
Broom, wooden handle, 49-1/4" l
    .... 35.00
Coal hod, hammered brass, emb tavern scenes, 25" h 90.00
Fender, brass, reticulated front
    .... 245.00
Fireback, cast iron, figures in relief, floral garland border, floral basket cartouche flanked by sphinx, dated 1963, cracked, 26" x 16-1/2" 110.00
Fire lighter, gun shape, Dunhill
    .... 90.00
Fireplace, artificial, cast iron, electric, Arts & Crafts style, 2 bulbs with porcelain sockets, 21" w
    .... 375.00

Fire screen
   Oak, medallion decor, beadwork
      molding, 27" h, 20" w 90.00
   Fabric, courting couple, wooden
      frame, Victorian, 34-1/2" h,
      24" w 325.00
Log fork, wrought iron, long round
   handle, cast-brass ovoid finial,
   some rust, 44" l 25.00
Mantlepiece
   Cast iron, late 19th C., 40" h,
      43" w 1,200.00
   Oak, full columns, beveled mir-
      ror, 82" h, 60" w........ 1,400.00
   Slate, 19th C., 43" h, 44-1/2" w
      .... 535.00
Shovel and tongs, wrought iron,
   brass finials, 30" l, pr 55.00

❖ Fishbowl Ornaments

Perhaps you want to give Goldie a little company or a place to play hide and seek with her friends. Imaginative collectors can find an interesting assortment of aquatic ornaments to brighten their aquariums. Check that the paint is nontoxic and the item is waterproof.

Aquarium background panel, blues,
   greens 2.00
Castle, ceramic
   4" h, 3-3/4" w, white and brown
      .... 16.00
   4" h, 4-1/4" w, mkd Zenith, 1968
      .... 12.00

Redware aquarium castle, greenish glaze, 3-1/2" high, $15.

Ferns, flowers, vines, plastic, each
   .... .50
Figure
   Deep Sea Diver 2.00
   Goldfish, ceramic, 3-1/2" l, pr
      .... 22.00
   Mermaid, seated 3.00
Pagoda, ceramic, blue, yellow, bur-
   gundy and green, 3-1/4" h,
   3-1/2" w, Japan 16.00

❖ Fisher, Harrison

Harrison Fisher was a well-known illustrator and portraitist of the 19th century. Many collectors search for illustrations that bear his signature.

Magazine cover
   Cosmopolitan, May 1919, Salva-
      tion Army Girl 30.00
   Ladies Home Journal, Oct, 1909,
      American Girls Abroad series,
      footer reads "The American
      Girl in the Netherlands, 9-1/2"
      x 14-3/4" 25.00
Postcard, typical view of American
   Girl series 15.00
Poster, "I Summon You to Comrade-
   ship in the Red Cross," WWI,
   heavy edge wear, 40" x 28"
   .... 335.00
Print, framed
   "Fair Exhibitor", lady with bull-
      dog, collie and Pekingese,
      copyright 1910, Crowell Pub-
      lishing, 8-1/2" x 11-3/4"
      .... 220.00
   "In Suspense," woman having
      tea, seated gentleman, copy-
      right Charles Scribner &
      Sons, 12" x 17-1/2" 295.00
   "The Sport," lady with 3 dogs and
      horse, copyright Charles
      Scribner & Sons, 12-3/4" x
      16-3/4", faint watermark
      .... 220.00
   Woman holding locket, c1910, 8"
      x 10" 115.00
Watercolor, "Moonlit Romance," sgd,
   dated 1910, 9-1/2" x 14-1/2"
   .... 1,500.00

Play Family School, plastic, $15.

❖ Fisher-Price Toys

What kid didn't play with Fisher-Price toys as a child? Founded in East Aurora, New York, in 1930, the company eventually became one of the leading producers of children's toys. Collectors still search for, and sometimes play with, all types of Fisher-Price items. Flea markets are prime hunting ground for both old and new examples.

Reference: Brad Cassity, *Fisher-Price Toys,* Collector Books, 2000; John J. Murray and Bruce Fox, *Fisher-Price,* 1931-1963, 2nd ed, Books Americana/Krause Publications, 1991.

Collectors' Club: Fisher-Price Collector's Club, 1442 N Ogden, Mesa, AZ 85205.

Bunny Cart, #311, mint 100.00
Circus Train set, 4 pcs, 30" l ... 48.00
Dollhouse, furniture, 1969, orig box
   .... 225.00
Little People Farm Play Set, #2501,
   1986, played-with cond, orig box
   .... 55.00
Mickey Puddle Jumper, played-with
   cond 95.00
Peek-A-Boo TV, plays Hey Diddle
   Diddle, paper labels removed
   .... 75.00
Play Family Village, #997, 1973,
   most pcs included, played-with
   cond 65.00

Huffy Puffy Train, wooden, worn, 2 pieces, $30.

School House, 1971, played-with cond 15.00
Windup Clock, #998, played-with cond 75.00
Woodsey Squirrel 50.00
Xylophone, #798, Walt Disney Productions, 1942, some wear 350.00

❖ Fishing

Perhaps the only thing better than meandering through a flea market on a lazy summer afternoon is going to the waterhole to do a little fishing. Recently, several auction houses have established record-setting prices for lures, ephemera, and other related fishing items.

References: Carl F. Luckey, *Old Fishing Lures & Tackle*, 5th ed. Krause Publications, 2000; Arlan Carter, *19th Century Fishing Lures*, Collector Books, 2000; Dudley Murphy and Rick Edmisten, *Fishing Lure Collectibles*, 2nd ed, Collector Books, 2001.

Periodicals: *American Fly Fisher*, P.O. Box 42, Manchester, VT 05254; *Antique Angler Newsletter*, P.O. Box K, Stockton, NJ 08559; *Fishing Collectibles Magazine*, 2005 Tree House Ln, Plano, TX 75023; *The Fisherman's Trader*, P.O. Box 203, Gillette, NJ 07933.

Collectors' Clubs: American Fish Decoy Assoc, 624 Merritt St, Fife Lake, MI 49633; National Fishing Lure Collectors Club, Box 4012, Reed Spring, MO 65737; Old Reel Collectors Assoc, 849 NE 70th Ave, Portland, OR 97213.

Bobber
    Panfish float, hp, black, red and white stripes, 5" l 12.00
    Pike float, hp, yellow, green and red stripes, 12" l 27.50
Creel, wicker, center lid hole, early 1900, used 65.00
Decoy, Ice King, perch, wood, painted, Bear Creek Co., 7" l 70.00
Lure
    Carters Bestever, 3" l, white and red, pressed eyes 9.00
    Creek Chub Co., Baby Beetle, yellow and green wings 40.00
    Heddon, King Bassor, red, gold spot, glass eyes 35.00
    Meadow Brook, rainbow, 1-1/4" l, orig box 120.00
    Paw Paw, underwater minnow, green, and black, tack eyes, 3 hooks 18.00
    Pfleuger, polished nickel minnow, glass eyes, 5 hooks, 3-5/8" l 250.00
    Shakespeare, mouse, white and red, thin body, glass eyes, 3-5/8" l 30.00
    South Bend, Panatella, green crackleback finish, glass eyes, orig box 50.00
    Strike-It, green, yellow and red spots, glass eyes 40.00
Reel
    Hardy, Perfect Fly Reel, English, 3-3/8" x 1-1/4" 150.00
    Horton, #3, suede bag 425.00
    Meek 33, Bluegrass, suede bag 425.00
    Pflueger 1420 templar lightly scratched owner's name 175.00

Weber Floataline tin, 2-1/2" square, $5.

Shakespeare, tournament 110.00
Union Hardware Co., raised pillar type, nickel and brass ... 30.00
Rod
    Hardy, split-bamboo fly, English, 2-pc, 1 tip, 7' l 250.00
    Heddon Co., casting, nickel silver fittings, split-bamboo fly, fish decal brown wraps, bag and tube, 5-1/2' l 50.00
    Shakespeare Co., premier model, 3-pc, 2 tips, split-bamboo fly, dark brown wraps, 7-1/2' l 35.00
    Unknown maker, bamboo, fly fishing, rod and reel 125.00
Tackle box, leather 470.00
Trophy, large mouth bass, mounted on 13" x 9" wood 115.00

❖ Fitz & Floyd

Fitz & Floyd is a true American success story. In the late 1950s the company served as a distributor for other company's products. After Pat Fitzpatrick died, Bob Floyd went on to establish a colorful niche in the dinnerware and table accessories business by introducing the mix-and-match philosophy. Most Fitz & Floyd is sold through the company's own stores. Some items are marked "Fitz & Floyd," while others bear the "OCI" mark of their Omnibus subsidiary.

Caddy, Sockhoppers 275.00
Candy jar and candle holder, Old World Santa, incised "Copyright F, 1993," 9-1/2" h 95.00
Coffee pot
    Montpelier, blue and gold 130.00
    Roanoke, gold encrusted border 165.00
Cookie jar
    Daisy the Cow, sgd OCI .. 125.00
    German Santa, incised "copyright OCI, 1989," 11-1/2" h 155.00
    Hampshire Pig, incised "Copyright F & F 1992" 195.00
    Mama Bear, 1991, 11" h.. 165.00
    Pig Waiter, incised "Copyright FF 1987" 165.00
    Prunella Pig, orig paper label 150.00
    Queen of Hearts, incised "Copyright F & F 1992," 10-1/2" h 245.00

Rio Rita, designed by Vicki Balcou, 10-3/4" h.............195.00
Russian Santa, incised "Copyright OCI, 1991," 10-1/4" h
.....................................145.00
The Cookie Factory, copyright 1987, removable sign for "Cookies" and "No Cookies Today"........................125.00
Dish, cov, figural, pumpkin, few flakes on leaves, 5" h........18.00
Figure
　Cinderella and Godmother
　.....................................75.00
　Giraffe..................................45.00
　Night Before Christmas....175.00
　Rio Rita.................................85.00
Gravy boat
　Christmas Wonderland....140.00
　Renaissance, cinnabar....140.00
Platter
　Holly, medium..................190.00
　Platine D'Or, medium.......160.00
　Renaissance, large..........165.00
Rabbit series figure
　Ballooning Bunnies............85.00
　Bustles & Beaus................85.00
　Busy Bunnies....................85.00
　Floral Rabbit.....................60.00
　Hat Box.............................85.00
　Mayfair.............................85.00
　Mother..............................65.00
Salt and pepper shakers, pr
　Cat and Ball of Twine, 3-3/4" h
　.....................................25.00
　Ham & Eggs, 4" h..............30.00
　Kittens, 3-1/2" h.................27.50
　Mama Bunny and Baby Bunny, 4" h...............................22.50
　Policeman and Patrol Car, 4-5/8" h..........................22.50
Teapot, Renaissance, cinnabar
　.....................................150.00
Vase, white and green, black details, 8" h..................................48.00

❖ Flag-Related

It's a grand old flag, indeed. Not only are flags collectible, but so are countless items having a flag motif.

Collectors' Club: North American Vexillological Assoc, Suite 225, 1977 N Olden Ave, Trenton, NJ 08618.
Lapel pin, plastic flag with 50 stars, Reddy Kilowatt, "Reddy Says Thanks for Voting," orig card, set of 5...........................22.00
Booklet, *Our Flag*, Department of Defense, 1960, 24 pgs........7.50

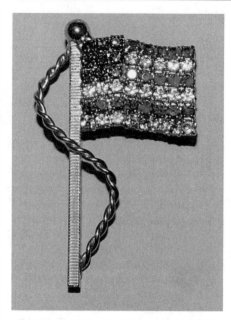

Costume jewelry flag pin, 1-7/8" high, $5.

Cigar felt, American flag, 48 stars, 10-1/2" x 8-1/2"...................4.00
Flag
　36-star, 1908-12, stars sewn on, 4" x 5"..........................70.00
　38-star, coarse muslin, mounted on stick, 12-1/2" x 22"...50.00
　44-star, tacked to 50" wooden pole, stains, tears, 19-3/4" x 34-1/2".......................145.00
　45-star, painted stars, tear, 11" x 16"................................85.00
Flag pole stand, lion-paw feet, mkd "Loyalty," "Fraternity," "Charity" and "1883," 3-1/2" h, 8" sq
　...175.00
Jewelry, costume, flag pin
　Ciner, enameled stripes, raised gold lines, 50 stars, 1-1/2" x 1-3/4"...........................32.00
　Coro, red, white and blue enameling, clear rhinestones, 1-1/4" x 1-1/2"...............88.00
　Unmarked, rhinestones, 2" h
　...14.00
License plate attachment, 48-star flag, 6" x 5 1/2".................35.00
Pinback button, celluloid, shows American flag, 7/8" dia......18.00
Postcard, flag and poem, "Our country stands for Humanity...," unused, 1920s....................8.00
Trivet, Frankoma, sand glaze, America's Stars & Stripes, Flag of Freedom, 1776-1976, commemorative backstamp, 6-1/2" dia
　...20.00

Poster, "Give It Your Best," World War II, shows 48-star flag, 1942 office of War Information, fold lines, 28-1/2" x 20"...........60.00

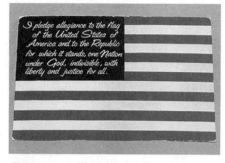

Postcard, flag motif, Dexter Press, 25 cents.

❖ Flamingos

Long-legged and bright pink, these feathered friends bring smiles to the faces of collectors. Pink flamingos as yard ornaments have passed their golden anniversary, attesting to the lasting appeal of these birds.
Cookie jar, copyright "Lotus, China," pink and green.................115.00
Cup and saucer, miniature, Florida scene with pink flamingo, gold trim, 1-1/2" h.....................7.00
Desk calendar, metal, shows month, day and date, Japan.......145.00
Figurine
　Ceramic, unmkd, probably Lefton, 5-1/2" h.............87.50
　Ceramic, Will George, 7-3/4" h
　.....................................245.00
　Plastic, souvenir of Sunken Gardens, Fla., 1 flamingo with head down, 1 with head up, 4-1/2" h........................15.00
　Glass, "Wesley Johnson's Club Flamingo, 1836 Fillmore St., San Francisco, The Texas Playhouse," 4-3/4" h................15.00
Jewelry, costume
　Plastic flamingo pin, "Hialeah, 1967," 3" h......................5.00
　Enamel and rhinestone flying flamingo, Coro, 3" x 4-1/2"
　.....................................525.00
Lawn ornament, plastic, white, orig legs...................................35.00
Napkin ring, c1980, 3" h, set of 4
　.....................................20.00

Nodder, Standing Ovations, 1987,
7" h 39.00
Paperweight, bronze, "The Lakeeny
Malleable Co., Cleveland, Ohio,"
5-3/4" h 68.00
Photograph album, wooden, "Our
Honeymoon" cut in relief, Silver
Springs, Fla., 9" x 6" 36.00
Planter
10-1/2" h, unmkd, probably Mad-
dux of California 195.00
7-1/4" h x 10" l, attributed to
American Bisque 65.00
Thermometer
Ceramic, "Souvenir of Florida,"
6" h 57.50
Wooden, embossed wall plaque,
"Silver Springs, Fla." 5" dia
.... 19.00
Tray, plastic, 2 flamingos flying
across inlet at Marineland, Fla.,
11-3/4" dia 42.00
TV lamp/planter combination, Lane
& Co., Van Nuys, Calif., 1957,
14-1/2" h, 16" w 495.00
Vase
Double, "Souvenir of Florida,"
unmkd, probably Maddux of
California, 5" h 75.00
Sunglow, Hull, 8-3/4" h 75.00

❖ Flashlights

Shall we shed a little light on an
interesting collectible topic? Flash-
lights actually evolved from early
bicycle lights. Conrad Hubert
invented the first tubular hand-held
flashlight in 1899.

Collectors' Club: Flashlight Collectors of America, P.O. Box 4095, Tus-
tin, CA 92781.
Candle, Eveready, #1643, cast
metal base, cream-colored
painted candle, 1932 .... 40.00
Lantern
Delta Lantern, Buddy model,
1919 .... 15.00
Eveready, #4707, nickel-plated
case, large bull's eye lens,
1912 .... 25.00
Novelty
Flintstones, 1975, MOC, 3" h
.... 15.00
Frankenstein, c1960, 9-1/2" l
.... 48.00
Hulk Hogan, WWF Wrestling,
1991 .... 12.00
Peter Pan, McDonald's premium,
MIB 4.00

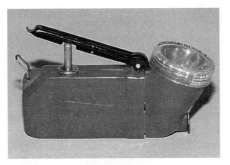

**Daco-Lite flashlight, Dayton
Acme Co., hand-powered, red
plastic case, black metal pump
handle, 5-3/4" long, $10.**

Ultimate Warrior, WWF Wres-
tling, 1991 .... 10.00
Railroad, Jenks, brass, patent
July 25, 1911 .... 90.00
Tubular
Aurora, all nickel case 20.00
Bond Electric Co., Jersey City,
NJ, 1940s, 5-1/4" l 10.00
Homart, all metal, 1930s,
10-1/2" l 35.00
Jack Armstrong, 1-1/2" dia,
4-1/2" h 85.00
Ray-O-Vac, Space Patrol ... 40.00
Winchester, marble lens, gold-
colored body, 1919-26,
5-1/2" l 100.00
Yale, #3302, double-ended, flood
lens and spot lens 30.00
Vest pocket
Eveready, Masterlight, #6662,
nickel-plated, ruby push-but-
ton switch, 1904 .... 30.00
Franco, glass button switch
.... 25.00

❖ Flatware

Whether you're setting an elegant
table or striving for an informal look,
great looking flatware is a must.
There are many, many patterns to
choose from, and the price range
reflects the age, maker, and composition of the service being considered. In addition to a number of
excellent reference books, there are
many matching services that can
help you complete a flatware set.
But, many of us enjoy the hunt and
prefer to scout flea markets for those
additional place settings and unique
serving pieces.

References: Frances M. Bones and
Lee Roy Fisher, *Standard Encyclo-
pedia of American Silverplate*, Col-
lector Books, 1998; Tere Hagan,
Silverplated Flatware, rev 4th ed,
Collector Books, 1990 (1998 value
update). Maryanne Dolan, *Ameri-
can Sterling Silver Flatware 1830s-
1990s*, Krause Publications.
Bacon server, Old Maryland, Kirk-
Steiff 90.00
Bonbon, Princess Patricia, Gorham
.... 18.50
Butter knife
Bridal Rose, Alvin 30.00
Fleetwood, Manchester 15.00
Silver Wheat, Reed & Barton
.... 15.00
Carving set, Cactus, Jensen . 325.00
Cheese knife, Allure, Rogers, 1939
.... 8.00
Cocktail fork
Contour, Towle 24.00
Empress, International 10.00
Cold meat fork
Moselle, American Silver Co.
.... 60.00
Silver Spray, Towle 32.00
Cream soup spoon
Bridal Rose, Alvin 65.00
Fleetwood, Manchester 30.00
Demitasse spoon, Virginia Carvel,
Towle 12.00
Dessert spoon, Bridal Rose, Alvin
.... 60.00
Dinner fork
Bridal Rose, Alvin 55.00
Concord, Whiting 25.00
Fleetwood, Manchester 30.00
Trianon, Dominick & Haff,
pierced, sterling silver, set of 6
.... 150.00
Dinner knife
Colonial Fiddle, Tuttle 25.00
King George, Gorham 40.00
Lily of the Valley, Gorham .. 27.50
Fish knife, Acorn, Jensen 38.00
Grapefruit spoon, Fleetwood,
Manchester 20.00

**Sterling silver knife, English
hallmarks, grapes pattern, $10.**

Gravy ladle
Continental, Tuttle..............70.00
Horizon, Easterling 40.00
Silver Spray, Towle 34.00
Iced tea spoon
Lily of the Valley, Gorham ..30.00
Romansque, Alvin..............20.00
Lemon fork
Princess Patricia, Gorham
....17.50
Silver Spray, Towle 16.00
Luncheon fork
King Albert, Whiting 20.00
Silver Wheat, Reed & Barton
....24.00
Luncheon knife, King George,
Gorham 35.00
Meat fork, DuBarry, International
....90.00
Olive fork, Chippendale, Alvin .25.00
Pasta scoop, Beauvoir, Tuttle.. 25.00
Pickle fork, Silver Spray, Towle
....17.00
Pie server, Acorn, Jensen 135.00
Place setting
Contour, Towle...................95.00
Prelude, International.........60.00
Salad fork
Chapel Bells, Alvin.............20.00
Horizon, Easterling 20.00
Salt spoon, Old Master, Towle
.... 11.00
Sardine fork, Cambridge, Gorham
....50.00
Steak knife, King George, Gorham
....40.00
Sugar spoon
Copenhagen, Manchester .24.00
Fairfax, Dugan 28.00
Windsor, Towle...................12.00
Sugar tongs, Bridal Rose, Alvin,
large 90.00
Tablespoon
Colonial Fiddle, Tuttle, pierced
....55.00
King Albert, Whiting 30.00
Rambler Rose, Towle.........30.00
Teaspoon
Bridal Rose, Alvin 24.00
Fairfax, Dugan 18.00
Old Master, Towle 17.00
Old Mirror, Towle................24.00
Princess Patricia, Gorham
....15.00
Rambler Rose, Towle.........15.00
Rose Solitaire, Towle 10.00

❖ Florence Ceramics

Florence Ward began producing decorative ceramic items in her Pasadena, California, workshop in 1939. By 1946 her business had grown to the point that it occupied a full-size plant, and her husband and son joined the company to help keep up with demand. Semi-porcelain figurines and other decorative accessories were produced until 1977 when operations ceased.

Collectors' Club: Florence Collector's Club, P.O. Box 122, Richland, WA 99352.

Bust, white, 9-1/2" h
Choir Boy 75.00
Pamela and David............300.00
Cigarette box, cov
Lady's head, green, cameo
....125.00
Winter...............................245.00
Dealer sign 395.00
Figure
Abigail 160.00
Bea...................................150.00
Blue Boy............................295.00
Camille..............................245.00
Choir Boy 45.00
Douglas.............................240.00
Irene.................................55.00
Jim 75.00
Melanie 100.00
Rhett 300.00
Sarah 115.00
Scarlett..............................175.00
Sue Ellen..........................225.00

Flow Blue Copeland covered soup tureen, $650.

❖ Flow Blue

The name of this pretty china is derived from the blue design that is flowed or blurred on a white background to create a distinctive look. Flow blue china was first produced in 1830 in the Staffordshire district of England. Many potteries manufactured flow blue, including some American firms.

References: Susan and Al Bagdade, *Warman's English & Continental Pottery & Porcelain*, 3rd ed, Krause Publications, 1998; Mary F. Gaston, *Collector's Encyclopedia of Flow Blue China*, Collector Books, 1983 (1993 value update); Jeffrey B. Snyder, *Fascinating Flow Blue*, Schiffer Publishing, 1997; —, *Flow Blue: A Closer Look*, Schiffer Publishing, 2000; —, *Flow Blue: A Collector's Guide to Pattern, History, and Values*, Schiffer Publishing, 1992; —, *Historic Flow Blue*, Schiffer Publishing, 1994; Petra Williams, *Flow Blue China and Mulberry Ware: Similarity and Value Guide*, rev ed, Fountain House East, 1993.

Collectors' Club: Flow Blue International Collectors' Club, 1048 Llano, Pasadena, TX 77504.
Reproduction Alert.
For additional listings, see *Warman's Antiques & Collectibles, Warman's Americana & Collectibles,* and *Warman's English & Continental Pottery & Porcelain.*
Bacon platter, Touraine, 10" l 245.00
Bone dish, Albany................... 50.00
Butter dish, cov, insert, Chapoo,
Wedgwood...................... 525.00
Butter pat, 3" dia
Argyle, Grindley................. 50.00
Delph, Sebring 35.00
La Francaise 28.00
Cake plate, Cracked Ice, International Pottery.................. 120.00
Coffee cup and saucer, Arcadia,
large................................. 85.00
Creamer, Fairy Villas, 5" h 275.00
Cup, handleless, Amoy......... 250.00
Cup and saucer
Astoria 120.00
Colonial, Homer Laughlin .. 85.00
Touraine 90.00
Winona, French China Co. 65.00
Dessert bowl, Poppy, Warwick
.... 30.00

Gravy boat, Chapoo, Wedgwood 275.00
Milk pitcher, Argyle, J & E Mayer 145.00
Plate
    Colonial, Homer Laughlin, 10" dia 65.00
    Dundee, Ridgways, 10" dia 125.00
    Eclipse, Johnson Bros., 7" dia 65.00
    Fairy Villas, 10-1/2" dia 135.00
    Iris, 10" dia 75.00
    Royal Blue, Burgess & Campbell, 9-7/8" dia 75.00
    Touraine, Stanley Pottery, 8-3/4" dia 60.00
Platter, Gothic, c1850 ....700.00
Sauce tureen, underplate, Wedgwood................................400.00
Serving bowl, Conway, 9" dia 135.00
Soup plate
    Alaska, Grindley.................75.00
    Royal Blue, Burgess & Campbell 55.00
    Touraine, Stanley Pottery, 7-1/2" dia 75.00
Teapot, cov, Strawberry.........200.00
Toothbrush holder, Alaska, Grindley 145.00

❖ Flower Frogs

Flower frogs are those neat holders that were sometimes designed to complement a bowl or vase. Others were made to be purely functional and had holes to insert flower stems, making flower arranging a little easier.

Art Deco lady
    6" h, white porcelain, dancing nude..............................90.00
    7-1/2" h, mkd "3941 Germany," c1930 ....195.00
Bird, figural, bright colors, mkd "Made in Japan," 5-1/2" h, chipped..............................50.00
California Pottery, candle holder type, made to hold fresh flowers around candle, mkd "Calif USA V17," 3-1/2" h, 4" w 20.00
Cambridge Glass
    Draped Lady, amber, 8-1/2" h 200.00

Rose Lady, green.............250.00
Two Kids, crystal 155.00
German, nude, lavender scarf, porcelain, 9-1/2" h................135.00
Muncie, green, 3-1/2" w...........35.00
Rookwood, figural nude, porcelain glaze, c1930 ....325.00
Ruby glass, 3" d 12.00
Silver deposit glass, clear glass frog with candleholder, 4" dia....45.00
Van Briggle, light blue, mkd "Van Briggle/Colo. Spgs," 4-1/2" dia 82.00
Weller, Brighton Woodpecker, 6" h, 3-1/2" w, 3" l....................520.00

❖ Flygsfors Glass

This might be a new name to glass collectors. This Swedish glass was created in the 1950s and is quite unique, having a flowing appearance. Items are usually brightly colored and encased in colorless crystal. Most pieces are signed on the base by creator Paul Kedelv. The glassworks was taken over by Orrefors in the 1970s and subsequently closed in 1980.

Console bowl
    Deep blue changing to dark pink to crystal, sgd "Coquille Flygsfors," 10" l, 4-1/2" w, 6" h 85.00
    Light cranberry cased to crystal, 14" l, 8-1/2" w, 3-1/2" h..75.00
Dish, oval
    Clear to orange to deep peach center, sgd "Flygsfors 53 Kedelv," 14" l, 8-1/2" w, 4" h 250.00
    Cranberry with white threading, 4-1/2" w, 3-1/2" h.........100.00
Vase
    3-1/2" h, 3" dia, internally dec with pink and green stripes, sgd "Flygsfors, 61" 120.00
    6" h, clear, orange dec, floral top, etched signature on base "Flygsfors, Coquille, 1959" 350.00
    12" h, 6-1/4" dia at top, sculptural type, clear to peach, sgd "Flygsfors Coquille," narrow base 400.00

⊛ Folk Art

Folk art remains one area of collecting that doesn't have clearly defined boundaries. Some people confine folk art to non-academic, handmade objects. Others include manufactured material. When referring to artwork, the term encompasses everything from crude drawings by untalented children to works by academically trained artists that depict common people and scenery. The following listings illustrate the diversity of this category.

References: Wendy Lavitt, *Animals in American Folk Art*, Knopf, 1990; George H. Meyer, *American Folk Art Canes*, Sandringham Press, 1992; Donald J. Petersen, *Folk Art Fish Decoys*, Schiffer Publishing, 1996; Beatrix Rumford and Carolyn Weekly, *Treasures in American Folk Art from the Abby Aldrich Rockefeller Folk Art Center*, Little, Brown Co., 1989.

Periodicals: *Folk Art Finder*, One River, Essex, CT 06426; *Folk Art Illustrated*, P.O. Box 906, Marietta, OH 45750.

Collectors' Club: Folk Art Society of America, P.O. Box 17041, Richmond, VA 23226.

Museums: Abby Aldrich Rockefeller Folk Art Center, Williamsburg, VA; Museum of American Folk Art, New York, NY; Museum of Early Southern Decorative Arts, Winston-Salem, NC.

Bar of Procter and Gamble soap carved into the shape of a rabbit, 4-3/8" by 2-3/4", $20.

Cane, wooden
  Dog handle, dark-brown paint, root-carved, worn 165.00
  Lion's head, glass eyes, gold metal band with presentation engraving dated 1924, Malacca shaft, horn ferrule 467.50
  Snake, 1 spiraling snake, black bead eyes, salmon repair, mushroom cap handle, 31-1/2" l 357.50
Carving
  Hat, smoke-deco, mustard-painted carved walnut burl, stars around band and top, 19th C, minor wear, 4-1/2" h, 12-1/4" dia 920.00
  Grouping, painted wood 2-story house and carved and painted figures celebrating the 4th of July, includes band members and croquet players, 14 figures, house 10" h, base 14" sq 1,430.00
Face jug
  Burlon Craig, glossy black-brown Albany slip, large ears, pop-eyed, 1-pc eyebrow, china plate teeth, pierced nostrils, mkd "B.B. Craig, Vale, N.C.," c1980-82, 6" h 247.50
  Marie Rogers, glossy Albany slip with multicolor drippings, tongue sticking out, white teeth, blue pupils, incised beard and eyelashes, script and impressed marks, early 1980s, 9-1/8" h 143.00
Fruit, papier-mache and painted cloth, old polychrome, 12 pcs 137.50
Indian club, red and black grained, 18" h, pr 181.50
Painting, watercolor on paper, flowers and heart, yellow roses and snowdrops in corners, heart formed of multicolor vining flowers, "Forget Me Not" with verse, name and 1866, molded wooden frame, glued down, foxing, edge damage, 11" h, 12-1/4" w 110.00
Sculpture, limestone
  Bust, Indian, mkd "E.R." (Popeye Reed), 9-1/2" h 275.00
  Indian in canoe, mkd "E. Reed 1976 A.D.," 5-1/2" h, 7-3/4" l 660.00

Sculpture, sandstone
  Bookends, seated figures of Adam and Eve, mkd "E. Reed 1976 A.D.," 11" h, pr 495.00
  Catfish, raised eyes, mouth and fins, attributed to Popeye Reed , 32-1/2" l 247.50
  Straight razor, walnut, red finish on handle, gray on blade, mkd "WIK," 20" l 330.00

❖ Food Molds

Flea markets are great places to find food molds. Originally intended for creating cakes, ice cream, chocolate, etc. in interesting shapes, many of these molds are now collected for their decorative appeal.

Cast iron
  Pig head, 9" dia 302.50
  Sheep, 14-1/2" l 110.00
Graniteware
  Rabbit, blue/white, 3-3/4" l, 3" w 130.00
  Strawberry, gray, 1-3/4" h, 5" l, 4" w 235.00
  Turk's head, blue/white swirl 115.00
Ironstone, pineapple, oval with flat bottom, rounded fluted sides, discolored, 2-3/4" h, 4-1/4" x 5-1/2" 250.00
Pewter, ice cream mold
  Floral wreath, "E.&Co., 1142," 3-3/4" dia 40.00
  Heart, mkd "E.&Co., N.Y., 902," 4-1/8" h 38.50

Pewter ice cream mold, stork with bag, marked "E.&Co. N.Y. 1151," 5-1/4" high, $85.

Santa Claus, full-figure, "E.&Co.," 4-5/8" h 247.50
Redware, Turk's head, scalloped and fluted, hairlines, small chips, 11" dia 71.50
Yellowware, pudding mold
  Ear of corn, scalloped designs on interior sides, simple gallery-like foot, oval, 4-3/8" h, 7-3/8" x 9-1/4" 170.00
  Pear, deep bowl shape, ribbed sides, dark-brown glaze, roughness on rim, hairline, 4" h, 7" dia 49.50
  Sheath of wheat, minor rim chips, 3-1/4" h, 7-5/8" l 110.00
Tin, fish pudding mold, minor rust, 2-3/4" h, 10" l, 5-5/8" w 70.00

❖ Football Cards

Trading cards for this sport are readily found at flea markets. As with baseball cards and other sports trading cards, it is relatively easy for collectors to check values and scarcity.

Reference: *Standard Catalog of Football Cards*, 4th ed, Krause Publications, 2001.

Periodicals: *Sports Cards Magazine & Price Guide*, 700 E State St, Iola, WI 54990; *Sports Collectors Digest*, 700 E State St, Iola, WI 54990; *Beckett Football Card Monthly*, Beckett Publications, P.O. Box 7652, Red Oak, IA 51591-0652.

Note: The following listings are merely a sampling of the thousands of cards readily available to collectors. For detailed information, we recommend the *Standard Catalog of Football Cards* by the editors of *Sports Collectors Digest*, Krause Publications.

Bowman, complete set
  1992, 573 cards 160.00
  1995, 357 cards 125.00
  1998, 220 cards 100.00
Bowman, individual cards
  1995, Kordell Stewart, #105 .... 20.00
  1995, Curtis Martin, #301 .. 10.00
  1998, Peyton Manning, #1 .... 15.00
  1998, Randy Moss, #182 .. 30.00
Topps, complete set
  1980, 528 cards 65.00

1985, 396 cards 80.00
1990, 528 cards 10.00
1995, 468 cards 45.00
1998, 360 cards 70.00
Topps, individual cards
    1984, John Elway, #63 ..... 125.00
    1984, Dan Marino, #123 .. 130.00
    1989, Chris Carter, #121 ...... 2.00
    1993, Drew Bledsoe, #130 .. 3.00
    1998, Troy Aikman, #75 .... 1.00

❖ Football Memorabilia

Every collector has a favorite team or player. Most can tell you more about their collection and the game of football than you'll ever need to know. This dedicated fan truly enjoys the sport and the collectibles it generates every year.

Reference: John Carpenter, *Price Guide to Packers Memorabilia*, Krause Publications, 1998.

Periodical: *Sports Collectors Digest*, 700 E State St, Iola, WI 54990.
Autographed photo, 8" x 10"
    Jim Brown 30.00
    Red Grange 150.00
Book, *Out of Their League*, 1971
    .... 5.00
Comic book, *Football Thrills*, #2, 1951 .... 35.00

Plastic cup, Hardee's ABC Monday Night Football, 7" high, $1.

Cup, Super Bowl XXIX, 1995, Tupperware 5.00
Doll, rubber face, plush body, Charm Toy Co., 1960s 35.00
Figurine, Sports Impressions
    Boomer Esiason, Cincinnati Bengals 40.00
    Art Monk, 1993, MIB, 5" h .. 30.00
Football, Wilson, "Official Intercollegiate Wilson TD," some lacings broken, labels faded 95.00
Game
    TV Football, Coleco, 1974 .... 30.00
    Football Bag-A-Telle, orig box, 6" x 11" 20.00
Key chain, Super Bowl XXX, NRFP 6.00
Pajama bottoms, football print, cotton 15.00
Pennant, felt
    Chicago Bears, black background, orange "Bears," orange, green and red football art, orange felt trim, late 1940s 25.00
    Philadelphia Eagles, 1940s-1950s, 28" l 35.00
Program
    Notre Dame v USC, Nov 21, 1931 .... 100.00
    Super Bowl XXII, 1988 .... 20.00
Salt and pepper shakers, Football Hall of Fame, porcelain, 2-3/4" h 19.00
TV Guide, Super Bowl Preview, Jan 28-Feb 3, 1995 .... 6.00
Yearbook, Green Bay Packers, 1974, autographed by coaches and players 40.00

❖ Fostoria Glass

The Fostoria Glass Company was initially located in Fostoria, Ohio, but in 1891 it was relocated to Moundsville, West Virginia. Their fine glass tableware included delicate engraved patterns and also pressed patterns. Like many other American glass manufacturers of that era, several of their lines were also produced in various colors.

Collectors' Clubs: Fostoria Glass Collectors, P.O. Box 1625 Orange, CA 92856; Fostoria Glass Soc of America, P.O. Box 826, Moundsville, WV 26041.

Colonial Mirror goblet, Fostoria, circa 1930, $45.

Reproduction Alert.
For additional listings and a detailed list of reference books, see *Warman's Antiques & Collectibles* and *Warman's Glass.*
Ashtray, Century, individual size 12.00
Berry bowl, June, blue 50.00
Bookends, Lyre, pr 145.00
Bowl, Baroque, blue, 4" dia 22.00
Butter, cov, America, round ... 125.00
Cake salver, Corsage 32.00
Candy dish, cov, Coin, amber, round 35.00
Celery vase, Double Greek Key 140.00
Champagne flute, Kimberly 2990 .... 15.00
Cheese and cracker, Chintz 70.00
Cigarette holder with ashtray, Two Tone, #5092, amethyst and crystal 75.00
Claret, June, blue 95.00
Creamer and sugar
    Alexis, hotel size, cut dec 115.00
    Fairfax, green, ftd 35.00
Cream soup, American 47.50
Cruet, Coin, olive green 50.00
Demitasse cup and saucer, June, topaz 60.00

Goblet, water
    American, 7" h 17.50
    Baroque, blue 25.00
    Chintz 25.00
    Colonial Dame, 11-oz 15.00
Ice tub, American, 6-1/2" dia ... 60.00
Juice tumbler, Navarre 24.00
Mayonnaise, underplate, Colony
    .... 25.00
Nut cup, Fairfax, amber 15.00
Pitcher
    Beverly, amber 125.00
    Jamestown, green 115.00
    Meadow Rose 195.00
Plate
    Baroque, blue, salad 14.00
    Colony, dinner 35.00
    Fairfax, green, salad 6.50
    Lafayette, luncheon 24.00
Platter, American, 12" l 60.00
Relish
    American, 2-part 18.00
    Chintz, 2-part 30.00
    Silver Spruce, 3-part 35.00
    Salad bowl, Fairfax, green
    .... 27.50
Sherbet
    Colonial Dame, 6-1/2 oz 10.00
    Fairfax, yellow 12.00
    Jamestown, medium blue .. 15.00
    Versailles, topaz 18.00
Sugar, cov, Coin, olive green ... 30.00
Syrup, glass lid, American 135.00
Top Hat, American, 4" h 50.00
Tumbler
    Chintz, ftd 24.00
    Vernon, etched 17.50
Tumbler, old-fashioned (cocktail),
    Coin, crystal 30.00
Vase
    American, flared, 9-1/2" h
    .... 200.00
    Two Tone, #2470, red and crys-
    tal, 10" h 150.00
Water pitcher, Coin, olive green
    .... 55.00
Wedding bowl, Coin, red 65.00
Whiskey, American 17.50
Wine
    American 15.00
    Chintz 38.00
    Jamestown, green 20.00

❖ Franciscan Ware

Gladding, McBean and Co., of Los Angeles, California, first produced this popular dinnerware around 1934. Their use of primary colors and simple shapes was met with much enthusiasm. Production was finally halted in 1986.

Collectors' Club: Franciscan Collectors Club, 8412 5th Ave NE, Seattle, WA 98115.

For additional listings, see *Warman's Americana & Collectibles* and *Warman's American Pottery & Porcelain.*

Ashtray, Starburst 25.00
Bowl
    Apple, ftd 22.00
    Coronado, turquoise, 7-1/2" dia
    .... 17.50
Bread and butter plate, Apple .. 14.00
Butter dish, cov, Starburst 42.00
Cereal bowl, Meadow Rose 22.00
Coffeepot
    Denmark, blue 100.00
    Heritage 80.00
Chop plate
    Apple, 14" dia 125.00
    Starburst 62.00
Creamer and sugar
    Apple 60.00
    Magnolia 75.00
Cup and saucer
    Apple 16.00
    Poppy 32.00
Demitasse cup and saucer
    Desert Rose 48.00
    Rosemore 45.00
Dinner plate
    Apple 20.00
    Poppy 37.50

Franciscan butter dish, 7-1/2" long, $50.

Eggcup, Desert Rose 35.00
Fruit bowl, Poppy 30.00
Gravy boat
    Arcadia, green, gold trim . 145.00
    Del Monte 140.00
    Fremont 145.00
    Granville 120.00
    Mesa, gold trim 110.00
    Woodside 140.00
Grill plate, Apple 140.00
Jam jar, Apple 135.00
Mixing bowl, Apple, 9" dia 90.00
Platter
    Fremont, large 175.00
    Olympic, white, violets, gold trim,
    large 165.00
    Renaissance, gray border, gold
    trim, medium 150.00
Relish
    Coronado, 12" l 70.00
    Ivy, 11" l 60.00
Salad plate, Apple 18.00
Salt and pepper shakers, pr
    Apple, small 36.00
    Mariposa 98.00
Side salad plate, Starburst, crescent shape 27.50
Snack plate, Meadow Rose .. 170.00
Soup bowl, Desert Rose 18.00
Sugar bowl, cov
    Canton, gray, black and rose floral, cream ground 75.00
    Del Monte 82.00
    Olympic, white, violets, gold trim
    .... 90.00
Teapot, cov
    Apple 65.00
    Mariposa 165.00
    Meadow Rose 200.00
Turkey platter, Apple 320.00
Tumbler, ivy 30.00
Vegetable bowl, cov, Palomar, Jasper 190.00
Vegetable bowl, oval
    Carmel, platinum trim 86.00
    Fremont 98.00
    Olympic, white, violets, gold trim
    .... 88.00
    Woodside 90.00
Water pitcher, Coronado 45.00

❖ Frankart

Frankart is the name used by artist Arthur Von Frankenberg, who achieved his goal of mass producing "art objects" in the mid 1920s. Most of his creations were stylized forms, particularly ashtrays, bookends, lamps, vases, etc. The pieces were cast in white metal, and one of several popular metallic finishes was then applied. Finishes ranged in color from copper to gold to gunmetal gray, in addition to several iridescent pastel colors.

Note: The following listings have a bronzoid finish (bronze colored).
Ashtray
    Duck, outstretched wings support green glass ash receiver 145.00
    Nude, kneeling on cushions, holding 3" dia removable pottery ashtray 250.00
    Scottie, black enamel base, mkd 275.00
Bookends, pr
    Cocker Spaniels, c1934, 6-1/4" h 165.00
    Gazelles, 7-1/4" l, 6-1/4" h 225.00
    Owls, 6" h 225.00
    Scotties, 5" l, 5" h, one repaired 60.00
Cigarette box, back-to-back nudes supporting green glass box 475.00
Lamp, standing nude holding 6" round crackle glass globe shade 450.00

❖ Frankoma Pottery

John N. Frank founded Frankoma Pottery in Oklahoma in 1933. Prior to 1954, the pottery used a honey-tan colored clay from Ada, Oklahoma. Brick-red clay from Sapulpa has also been used, and pink clay is in use currently. The plant has suffered several disastrous fires over the years, including one that destroyed all of the molds that had been used prior to 1983.

Reference: Phyllis and Tom Bess, *Frankoma and Other Oklahoma Potteries*, Schiffer Publishing, 2000.

Collectors' Club: Frankoma Family Collectors Assoc, P.O. Box 32571, Oklahoma City, OK 73123.
For additional listings, see *Warman's Antiques & Collectibles* and *Warman's American Pottery & Porcelain*.

Yellow GOP elephant mug, Frankoma, $20.

Ashtray, Texas shape, pink, mkd 459, 6-1/4" l 17.50
Butter dish, cov, Aztec, green..25.00
Casserole, Aztec, #7W, 10" w 40.00
Deviled egg tray, green glaze, mkd "Frankoma #819," 12" dia..35.00
Dish, leaf-shape, green and brown, mkd 225, 9-1/4" x 4 1/2" 18.00
Figurine
    Indian chief, desert gold, 8-1/2" h 32.00
    Woman, brown, 14-1/2" h ..45.00
Mug
    Republican elephant, maroon, 1984, 4" h....................20.00
    U.S. Postal Service, "National Maintenance Training Center, Norman, Okla.," black, 4" h 24.00
Pitcher, Wagon Wheel, prairie green, #94D, 6-1/2" h 64.00
Planter, duck, brown, 4-3/4" h 39.00
Plate
    1974 Battles for Independence, 3rd in series of 5, sand color, 8-1/4" dia......................40.00
    Kansas Centennial, 1861-1961, 9" dia 25.00
    Laid in a Manger, gray, 1969 ....15.00
    Teenagers of the Bible, Ruth the Devoted, browns, 1980, 8th in series of 10....................32.00
Teapot, brown glaze, 6-3/4" h..50.00
Trivet
    2 birds in a tree, brown, leaf pattern around edge............25.00
    Oklahoma, Prairie Green, 6-1/2" dia 28.00
Wall pocket
    Boot, brown, mkd 133, slight chip, 7" h 35.00
    Phoebe head, white, 1973-1975 re-issue, 7" h, 5" w 75.00

❖ Fraternal and Service Collectibles

Folks have often saved family items relating to benevolent societies and service clubs. Today, many of these articles are entering the flea market scene. These items tell interesting stories about how past generations spent some of their leisure time.
Belt Buckle, Shriner emblem, silvertone.................................. 20.00
Cream and sugar, Eastern Star, Lefton............................... 50.00
Cufflinks, Shriner, red and goldtone, slight damage 25.00
Cufflinks and tie clip, Masonic, cameo-type carving 150.00
Fez, Knights of Columbus....... 20.00
Letter opener, Masonic, "Jordan Lodge No. 247, F&AM, Robert Rogove-WN. 1967," in plastic case, worn lettering........... 20.00
Medal
    Loyal Order of Moose, heavily oxidized (green), 3-1/2" dia 13.00

International Order of Odd Fellows ribbon and badge, Salina, Kansas, $30.

Salvation Army, "With Heart to God and Hand to Man 1880-1955," 1-1/4" dia 18.00

Shriner, Amarillo, Texas 90.00

Medal with bar pin, Knights of Pythias, "Conn Lodge 37," name on back.................... 38.00

Nodding head, Mason character, plaster head with damage to chin, 6" h 41.50

Pinback button, BPOE, celluloid, "Dedication, New Home, Dunellen Lodge No. 1488, October 27, 1927" on torn ribbon, 1-1/2" dia, 2-1/2" l.............. 38.00

Plate, Masonic, Shenango China 85.00

Ring, Osiris, sterling silver, synthetic ruby, sides show horses and chariot, Chicago 75.00

Salt & pepper shakers, Lions International, "Iowa" in blue, Milford Pottery by KlayKraft, 1-3/4" h 12.00

Shaving mug, Odd Fellows, traditional IOOF symbols, with owner's name, 3-3/4" h 80.00

Watch fob, Osiris, sterling silver, enameled in red-brown, green and yellow, "Osiris Temple Boosters Club," back mkd "Robbins Co., Attleboro, Mass.," 1-3/8" dia 75.00

❖ Frog Collectibles

Ribbit, ribbit! From Kermit to Frogger, frogs have been popular advertising characters in our culture.

Collectors' Club: The Frog Pond, P.O. Box 193, Beach Grove, IN 46107.

Advertising trade card, Pond's Extract 7.50

Band, Lefton Pottery trio, saxophone, accordion and banjo players, 3" h 75.00

Bank, porcelain, mkd "Made in Japan," 3-3/4" h 110.00

Beanie Baby
    Legs the Frog, retired Oct 97, protector........................ 55.00
    Smoochy the Frog, protector 16.00

Candy mold, tin 48.00

Clicker, Life of the Party Products, Kirchhof, Newark, N.J. 18.00

Pewter ice cream mold, frog on a mushroom, $55.

Condiment set, figural salt and pepper shakers on tray, stamped "Hand Decorated, Shafford, Japan"................................48.00

Cookie jar, green frog with yellow bow tie 55.00

Figure
    Bisque, German, 1" h.........15.00
    Ceramic, Josef, 5-3/4" x 4" 40.00

Netsuke, ivory, sgd, silver stand with turquoise lady bug, 1-1/4" h 145.00

Pin, figural
    Enamel, black, green eyes, Ciner, 1-1/2" x 2" 200.00
    Gold-plate, 8 pearls on back, emerald green rhinestone legs, red rhinestone eyes, sgd "Trifari Pat Pending," 1-1/2" h 110.00
    Goldtone, clear rhinestones, emerald green cabochon eyes, 2" h 45.00
    Rhinestones, 43 clear stones, green stones for eyes, 3" l 50.00
    Sterling silver, amethyst colored glass eyes, Taxco, 1-1/2" h 45.00
    Sterling silver, green agate frog, sterling silver lily pad, prong set, mkd "Hand Wrought Sterling NHE," 2-1/2" h 225.00

Planter, Niloak, dark brown swirls, 4-1/2" h 55.00

Sculpture, The Frog Prince, Franklin Mint, 1986.........................40.00

Stein, Budweiser, frog posing with bottle, another on handle, mkd "Handcrafted by Ceramate," 6" h 28.00

Toothbrush holder, frog playing mandolin, mkd "Goldcastle, Made in Japan," 6" h 145.00

❖ Fruit Jars

People in some areas of the country refer to these utilitarian glass jars as "canning jars," while others refer to them as "fruit jars" or "preserving jars." In any event, the first machine-made jar of this type was promoted by Thomas W. Dyott in 1829, and the screw-lid jar was patented in November of 1858.

Reference: Bill Schroeder, *1000 Fruit Jars Priced and Illustrated*, 5th ed, Collector Books, 1987 (1996 value update).

Periodical: *Fruit Jar Newsletter*, 364 Gregory Ave, West Orange, NJ 07052.

Collectors' Clubs: Ball Collectors Club, 22203 Doncaster, Riverview, MI 48192; Midwest Antique Fruit Jar & Bottle Club, P.O. Box 38, Flat Rock, IN 47234; Northwest Fruit Jar Collectors' Club, 12713 142nd Ave, Puyllalup, WA 98374.

Amazon Swift Seal, clear, glass lid, wire bail, quart 6.00

Atlas E-Z Seal, green, pint...... 15.00

Atlas E-Z Seal, quart, bail top, $5.

Atlas Mason's Patent
  Apple green, pint.................25.00
  Apple green, quart.............35.00
Ball Ideal, aqua, pint, glass lid, wire
  bail.......................................3.00
Ball Mason
  Apple green, quart.............25.00
  Apple green, 1/2-gal..........30.00
Bosco Double Seat, clear, quart
  ....43.00
Brighton, clear, 1/2-gal..........145.00
Commonwealth Fruit Jar, clear,
  quart...................................98.00
Everlasting Jar, light green, quart
  ....30.00
Fruit Keeper, GCC Co. monogram,
  aqua, quart..........................50.00
The Gem on front, HGW monogram
  on reverse, whittled aqua,
  1/2-gal.................................50.00
Gimball's Brothers Pure Food Store
  Philadelphia, clear, pint.....48.00
Hamilton, clear, 1/2-gal............90.00
Hero over a cross, aqua, quart
  ....38.00
The Ideal Imperial, aqua, quart
  ....35.00
Mason Fruit Jar (2 lines), amber, pint
  ....125.00
Mason Improved, 2 dots below
  Mason, apple green, quart
  ....30.00
Mason's Improved, with CFJCo.
  logo, amber, 1/2-gal........235.00
Mason's Patent, teal, 1/2-gal...25.00
Mason's Patent, Nov. 30th 1858
  Amber, quart....................325.00
  Apple green, 1/2-gal..........50.00
Mason's Patent, Nov. 30th 1858,
  CFJCo logo
  Apple green, quart.............55.00
  Light olive green, 1/2-gal
  ....100.00
Mason's 20 Patent, Nov. 30th 1858,
  aqua, quart..........................30.00
Michigan Mason, beaded neck seal,
  clear, pint............................30.00
Presto Wide Mouth, clear, glass lid,
  wire bail, 1/2-pint.................3.50
Trademark Lightning Putnam (on
  base)
  Amber, 24 oz....................135.00
  Aqua, tall quart.................100.00

❖ Fry Glass

The H.C. Fry Glass Co. of Rochester, Pennsylvania, is a sterling example of how a company must adapt in order to stay alive. Fry first produced brilliant cut glass, but by the Depression they had switched to making patented heat-resistant ovenware known as Pearl Oven Glass. In 1926 and 1927, the company also produced an art glass line known as Foval.

Reference: The H.C. Fry Glass Soc, *The Collector's Encyclopedia of Fry Glassware*, Collector Books, 1990 (1998 value update).

Collectors' Club: The H.C. Fry Glass Society, P.O. Box 41, Beaver, PA 15009.

Reproduction Alert.

For additional listings, see *Warman's Antiques & Collectibles* and *Warman's Glass*.

Butter dish, cov, Pearl Oven Ware
  ....80.00
Canape plate, Foval, cobalt center
  handle...............................175.00
Cup and saucer, Foval, cobalt handles
  ....68.00
Hot water server, cov, Foval, green
  handle and finial..............275.00
Nappy, brilliant period cut glass, pinwheel and fan with hobstar center, sgd..............................65.00
Platter, Pearl Oven Ware, 17" l
  ....65.00
Trivet, Pearl Oven Ware, 8" dia
  ....24.00
Tumbler, cut glass, pinwheel, zipper and fan motifs....................20.00
Vase, 7-1/2", Foval, jade green
  ....210.00

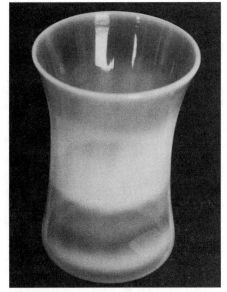

Foval waisted tumbler, Fry Glass, 3-7/8" high, $40.

❖ Fulper

Fulper Pottery, located in Flemington, New Jersey, manufactured stoneware and pottery from the early 1800s until 1935. Their pieces are usually well-marked.

Collectors' Club: Stangl/Fulper Collectors Club, P.O. Box 583, Flemington, NJ 08822.

For additional listings, see *Warman's Antiques & Collectibles* and *Warman's American Pottery & Porcelain*.

Bowl
  Chinese style, ftd, dark-green leopard-skin glaze, shape #447, flared, 7-1/2" dia
  ....525.00
  Low bowl, blue with brown drip glaze, 11" dia.............250.00
  Scalloped rim, shades of tan, green, gray, blue and rust, 3-1/2" h, 8" dia............345.00
Candleholder, butterscotch flambe, 2-1/4" h, 7-1/4" l, pr.........285.00
Flower frog
  Lily pad, matte green, 4" dia
  ....135.00
  Mushroom form, wisteria, 1-1/2" h, 2-1/2" dia........75.00
Mug, Prang, green crystalline over brown, 4" x 5"..................225.00
Pitcher, blended, ringed, 6-1/2" h, 5-1/2" w.........................135.00
Plate, Oriental style, oatmeal color with blue freckles, 9-1/8" dia
  ....185.00
Trivet, lavender blue, 6-1/2" dia
  ....145.00
Vase
  Blue crystalline glaze over blue-gray, 8-1/2" h, 5" dia...625.00
  Blue with brown, green and dark-blue, 2 handles, 5" h, 6" w
  ....400.00
  Famille rose, base chip, 5-3/4" h, 9" dia.........................575.00

❖ Funeral

Morbid as it may seem, death- and funeral-related items are popular collectibles with some people. Postmortem photographs and casket hardware are a few of the items they look for.

Bottle, Frigid embalming fluid, emb, full, 8-1/2" h......................90.00

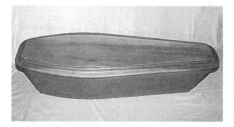

Child's wooden coffin, 43" long, 14" wide, $200.

Casket, child's, cypress, Birmingham Casket Co., Birmingham, Ala., 1930s, 46" l 115.00
Casket plate, "Our Darling" in banner over lamb, Victorian........... 20.00
Casket stands, sawhorse-type, turned wood, painted black, pr
.... 70.00
Fan, cardboard, 3-section, shows family in church, "Presented for your comfort by Wm. J. Schlup Funeral Home, The Home of Sincerity in Service, Akron, Ohio" 15.00
Hand truck, used for moving caskets, brass plate for "C.W. Price, Greenfield, Ohio," 1897 patent, brass-plated steel, spoked wheels in 2 sizes, rubber tires, 19-1/2" h, 45" l, 20-1/2" w, collapses to 8" h................... 200.00
Photograph
    Cabinet card, memorial floral arrangements, imprint of Clifford & Son, Muscatine, Iowa
    .... 6.00
    Memorial, 1890s, man's portrait in gilded frame sitting on a stool surrounded by funeral sprays, mounted, image size 7-1/2" x 9-1/2" 18.50
    Military funeral, postcard size
    .... 12.00
Lighter, Loretto Casket Co., enameled on both sides, Japan
.... 88.00

✪ Furniture

Flea markets are great places to look for furniture. And, you can expect to find furniture from almost every time period and in all kinds of condition. When shopping for furniture, make sure you take a measuring tape, know your room sizes, and have a way to get your treasures home.

References: There are many excellent reference books available. Please contact a bookseller or library.
For additional listings and a detailed list of reference books, see *Warman's American Furniture* and *Warman's Antiques & Collectibles.*
Bed, rope, spool dec on headboard and footboard, repainted
.... 200.00
Blanket chest, 47-1/2" w, 21-1/2" d, 26" h, country, pine, old mellow refinishing, dovetailed case, turned feet, base and edge moldings, walnut till and lid, wear and some edge damage..475.00
Bookcase, barrister type, stacking, glass front, 4 sections, removable top and base 395.00
Bureau, molded crest over rect mirror, candle holders at side, 2 lidded boxes, 3 drawers, orig dark brown paint, gold striping, floral dec................................... 500.00
Chair
    Oak, pressed back 100.00
    Windsor, high comb back, 1920s
    .... 95.00
Chest of drawers
    Chippendale style, walnut with inlay, molded cornice arched to accommodate 3 arched top drawers, 3 long drawers with stringing. 3 overlapping drawers in base, cabriole legs, small feet, shaped apron, refinished, base later construction, 67-3/4" h ...1,750.00
    Country style, solid cherry, 4 large drawers, scrolled front piece, scrolled feet, refinished, old glass knobs
    .... 750.00

Chair, Quaint Furniture, Stickley Bros. Co., Grand Rapids, Mich., oak, $300.

Church bench
    23" l, oak 135.00
    61" l, primitive, solid ends
    .... 165.00
Clothes tree, oak, sq center posts, all orig hooks.................. 150.00

Oak plant stand, $225.

Desk, 36" x 72-1/2" x 29-1/2" h, oak, light natural finish, traces of white, carved horseshoe detail, plate glass top, matching desk chair with cowhide back, Brandt Company 500.00

Desk chair, Arts & Crafts, Charles Limbert, horizontal H-back, orig leather seat, branded mark, c1912, 35" h 550.00

Dining room chairs, Chippendale-style, 1 arm chair, 5 side chairs, veneered, pierced splat, slip seat, cabriole legs, paw feet 950.00

Filing cabinet, oak, 4 drawers, worn finish 400.00

Hall bench, Colonial Revival, Baroque-style, cherry, shell carved crest over cartouche and griffin carved panel back, lift seat, high arms, mask carved base, paw feet, c1910, 51" h 700.00

Jelly cupboard, 2 doors, stripped 350.00

Drop-front secretary, oak veneer, $1,200.

Kitchen cabinet, painted surface, agateware sliding work surface, some wear 350.00

Music cabinet, Art Nouveau, hardwood, cherry finish, crest with beveled glass, paneled door, applied decoration, 49" h 200.00

Night stand, sq top, slightly splayed legs, small drawer, refinished 200.00

Pewter cupboard, stepback, poplar, open top with perimeter molding, 4 shelves, base with 2 raised panel doors, cutout feet, imperfections, 79" h 900.00

Pie safe, poplar and white pine, light brown paint dec, 2 drawers over 2 paneled doors, 2 circular vents on each side, 54-1/2" h 600.00

Plant stand, cast iron, worn orig gilding with red and green dec, onyx inset top, bottom shelf, 14" x 14" x 30" h 165.00

Morris chair, as found cond, very worn orig cushions 200.00

Rocking chair
  Boston style, maple seat, worn 250.00

Cane seat and back, newly caned 300.00

Wicker, painted white, sq back, basket weave pattern over openwork base, rect armrests with wrapped braces, openwork sides, braided edge trim, basket weave seat and skirt, X-form stretcher, 33" h 200.00

Table
  Coffee table, blue glass top, curving sides, lower shelf 120.00

  Dining, rect, extra leaves, mahogany colored, c1940 .... 115.00

  Drop leaf, cherry, refinished, burn mark on one leaf 400.00

  Kitchen, oak, drop leaf, some wear, c1890 .... 200.00

  Side, wrought iron, demilune, gray stone top, 28-1/4" w, 15-1/4" d 31-3/4" h 525.00

Wash stand, painted, new brasses, no back 125.00

Marble-top walnut washstand, $650.

For exciting collecting trends and newly expanded areas look for the following symbols:

✪ Hot Topic

✫ New Warman's Listing

(May have been in another Warman's title.)

❖ Gambling

Some of us buy lottery tickets, chances, etc. and are willing to take a chance on "winning it big." Others prefer to seek out memorabilia that is related to gambling, lotteries, and other games of chance.

Collectors' Club: Casino Chips & Gaming Tokens Collectors Club, P.O. Box 63, Brick, NJ 08723.

Advertisement, 2-sided card, promotes Rol-A-Top Bell Twin Jack Pot from Watling Mfg Co., Chicago, 1941 ....45.00

Ashtray

Fabulous Las Vegas, copper-coated with glass bottom with working roulette wheel, embossed scenes, lever spins wheel and ball, 1950s, 5" dia 27.50

"Night Scene, Las Vegas" souvenir plate showing Golden Nugget Gambling Hall and Hotel Apache, made in Japan, $17.50.

Golden Nugget Gambling Hall, peach carnival glass......13.00

Certificate, U.S. Internal Revenue Service Special tax stamp certificate for gaming devices, Ramona Hotel, Nevada, 1950s-1960s................................20.00

Chip

Crest and seal, Choctaw Club, Louisiana.....................175.00

Crest and seal, Green Mill Inn, Arabi, LA, 1-1/2" dia 250.00

New Southport Club of New Orleans, terra cotta and ivory 20.00

Top hat design, burgundy, 1-1/2" dia 14.00

Chuck-a-luck, red Bakelite.......75.00

Roulette wheel, wood and metal, single and double zero decals, 4-prong spinner 45.00

❖ Games

Kids of all ages have enjoyed games for decades. Some played hard, but those who carefully preserved the pieces and the instructions, and who took very good care of the box, have vintage games loved by today's collectors. Flea markets are great sources for vintage games as well as for those that feature popular television and movie characters.

References: Alex G. Malloy, *American Games Comprehensive Collector's Guide*, Antique Trader Books, 2000; Desi Scarpone, *More Board Games,* Schiffer Publishing, 2000.

Periodicals: *The Games Annual*, 5575 Arapahoe Rd, Suite D, Boulder, CO 80303; *Toy Shop*, 700 E State St, Iola, WI 54990; *Toy Trader*, P.O. Box 1050, Dubuque, IA 52004.

Collectors' Clubs: American Game Collectors Assoc, P.O. Box 44, Dresler, PA, 19025; Gamers Alliance, P.O. Box 197, East Meadow, NY 11554.

10 Commandments Game, Cadaco, 1966...................................15.00

Air Raid Target Game, Rosebud Art Co. 145.00

All Star Hockey, metal figures, 1960s 90.00

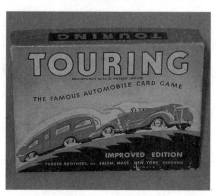

Touring: The Famous Automobile Game, Improved Edition, Parker Bros., $20.

Ally Oop Game, cylinder-shaped container 75.00

Anagrams Game, Milton Bradley, 1930s 35.00

Candyland, Milton Bradley, 1960s 10.00

Captain Video 125.00

Charlie Brown's All-Star Baseball Game, Parker Brothers, 1965 .... 30.00

Dukes of Hazzard, Ideal, 1981 10.00

Elsie and Her Family Board Game, 1941................................. 245.00

Finance and Fortune, Parker Bros., 1930s 45.00

Giggles Game, Rosebud Art Co., 1950s 45.00

Harlem Globetrotters Game, Milton Bradley, 1971 .... 95.00

The Ice Cube Game, Milton Bradley, 1972................................. 60.00

The Munsters Card Game, Milton Bradley, 1964.................... 65.00

Mystery Date........................ 75.00

Password, Milton Bradley, 1963 .... 15.00

The Real Ghostbusters, Milton Bradley, 1986 .... 6.00

Star Trek Game, Milton Bradley, 1979................................. 26.00

Stocks and Bonds, 3M Brand Bookshelf Game 8.00

✪ Gardening

There's something therapeutic about gardening. And, when the weather is bad, why not collect gardening items to soothe your spirit? Many landscapers use antique elements to enhance garden areas, so dig around flea markets for interesting gates, garden benches, etc.

Fountain with bronze nymph figure, 30" x 26" green stained-glass surround, copper base, $1,800.

Bird bath, concrete, 2-pc 35.00
Cigarette card, issued by W.D. & H.O. Wills, Ltd., Great Britain, titled "Gardening Hints," set of 10 framed together, 9-3/4" x 11-1/2" 45.00
Flowerpot, clay, typical 1.00
Garden bench, precast concrete 45.00
Gardening gloves, well worn 2.00
Harvester, R.C. Kingmaker, Carlisle, KY, orig red and black paint, handle shows some wear, 16" h, 10-1/2" w 165.00
Hoe, heart shaped blade, worn wooden handle 20.00
Planter, cement, painted green, white Viking ship and lion dec, 1930s, 15" sq, 10" h, pr ... 155.00
Seed box, litho label, wooden box with lid 30.00
Seedling bell, glass dome, knob top 35.00
Seed packet
    Shaker 7.50
    Typical................................ 3.00
Shears, wooden handles......... 25.00
Shovel, worn wood handle 15.00
Sprayer, Gulf Space, small dent in tank, 18" l 65.00
Sundial, brass, mounted on marble base 125.00
Watering can
    Child's, litho tin, floral design, 1960s 40.00
    Tin, wide brass head.......... 25.00
Watering pot, patent April 17, 1894, mkd "Imported for R & J Farquatlar & Co., Boston, Reliable Seeds, Market Street," 22" l, 9" w, 9-1/4" h 225.00

Wheel barrow, wood wheel and body, removable sides, old green paint, 62" l, 27" h, 23" w 225.00

❖ Garfield

Who's the coolest cat around the cartoon pages these days? Garfield! Flea markets are favorite hangouts for this lasagna-loving feline and his buddies.

Reference: Robert Gipson, *The Unauthorized Collector's Guide to Garfield and the Gang*, Schiffer Publishing, 2000.

Bank
    Ceramic, bowling, mkd "Garfield Copyright 1981, United Feature Syndicate, Inc.," orig stopper 60.00
    Ceramic, mkd "Garfield Copyright 1978, 1981, United Feature Syndicate, Inc.," orig stopper 60.00
    Ceramic, wearing graduation gown and cap, 5-1/2" h, mkd "Enesco".......................60.00
    Plastic, gum ball type, "Can I Borrow A Penny," orig plastic key, 6-1/2" h 20.00
Clock, alarm, Sunbeam 45.00
Keychain, Garfield playing tennis, twistable chain, blister pack, MOC 2.25
Nodder, MIB, 7-1/2" h 27.00
PEZ..6.50
Stuffed toy, standing, 1981, United Feature Syndicate, Inc., Dakin Inc., San Francisco, Calif., 10-1/4" h 16.00

McDonald's Garfield mug, 3-1/2" high, $5.

Telephone, Tyco Industries Model #1207............................... 40.00
Trophy, Garfield leaning towards Arlene, captioned "Where have you been all my life?" 4-1/4" h 25.00
Window sticker, stuffed figure, four suction cups, faded body, 6-1/2" h 4.00

❖ Gas Station Collectibles

Whether you refer to this category as Gas Station Collectibles, Service Station Memorabilia, or Petroliana isn't important. What does matter is that there are plenty of advertising items, premiums, and related materials from those places that sell us gas so we can drive to flea markets!

References: Mark Anderton, *Encyclopedia of Petroliana*, Krause Publications, 1999; Scott Benjamin and Wayne Henderson, *Gas Globes: Pennzoil to Union and Affiliates*, Schiffer Publishing, 1999; —, *Sinclair Collectibles*, Schiffer Publishing, 1997; J. Sam McIntyre, *The Esso Collectibles Handbook: Memorabilia from Standard Oil of New Jersey*, Schiffer Publishing, 1998; Rick Pease, *Petroleum Collectibles*, Schiffer Publishing, 1997; — *A Tour with Texaco: Antique Advertising and Memorabilia*, Schiffer Publishing, 1997; Charles Whitworth, *Gulf Oil Collectibles*, Schiffer Publishing, 1998.

Periodicals: *Check the Oil!*, 30 W Olentangy St, Powell, OH 43065, www.oldgas.com/info/cto.htm; *Petroleum Collectibles Monthly*, 411 Forest St, La Grange, OH 43065, www.pcmpublishing.com.

Collectors' Clubs: International Petroliana Collectors Assoc, P.O. Box 937, Powell, OH 43065; Oil Can Collectors Club, 4213 Derby Ln, Evansville, IN 47715, www.oilcancollectors.com.
Calendar
    1930, Roy Simcoe Garage, Willys-Knight and Whippet Sales and Service, Cortland, NY 50.00

Gulf Lustertone Car Wax tin, $15.

1959, Sinclair, shows attendant cleaning windshield, slight tear, 7-1/2" x 8-1/2" 28.50

Coloring book, *Esso Happy Motoring*, unused........................25.00

Doll, Texaco cheerleader, 1960s, MIB, 11-1/2" h................125.00

Drinking glass, Phillips 66, Deem Oil Co., St. Louis, 5-1/4" h 48.00

Fireman's helmet, child's, Texaco, battery-op, built-in amplifier 135.00

Johnny Service Gas Station, Topper, 1968, orig box 60.00

License plate tag, Shell Motor Oil, 1930s, wear and rust, 5-1/4" h, 3" w 39.00

Myers and Spurlock Standard Receipt book, Shell, 1950s, West Union Shell Service, Morganton, N.C. 28.00

Pin, Mobil Oil, 1932 ....35.00

Soap, Sinclair, shape of heating oil truck, emb "Sinclair Heating Oil," orig box, 4-1/8" l 28.00

Shell milk glass gas globe, 19" high, $400.

Geisha Girl salt shaker, 3-1/4" high, $15.

❖ Geisha Girl

Geisha girl porcelain consists of over 150 different patterns. It was made during the last quarter of the 19th century and again during the 1940s, primarily for export to western markets. All of the items show at least one elaborately dressed Geisha, and they are hand-painted with many bright colors. Because over 100 different manufacturers produced Geisha Girl wares, many marks can be found.

Bowl, petal design, 7" dia 20.00

Celery set, Porch, Torii Nippon mark, 5 pcs 40.00

Chocolate pot, Child Reaching for Butterfly pattern, Japan, 9-3/8" h 65.00

Chocolate set, pot and 8 cups, Japan, pot 9-3/4" h 125.00

Creamer.................................20.00

Cup and saucer
Nippon...............................25.00
Unmarked 15.00

Eggcup, Japan, 2-1/4" h 18.00

Hatpin holder, 4" h 55.00

Mug, Bamboo Trellis................20.00

Plate, 7-1/2" dia 10.00

Salt and pepper shakers, Japan, 2-1/4" h, pr.........................14.00

Toothpick holder, Parasol Modern, 2" h 12.00

❖ GI Joe

For almost forty years, GI Joe has been a favorite of children and collectors alike. GI Joe was a soldier in the 1960s, an adventurer and superhero in the 1970s, a 3-3/4" pocket-sized "Real American Hero" in the 1980s, and returned to being a 12" soldier and adventurer in the 1990s. Collectors search for GI Joe action figures, equipment, vehicles, playsets, and uniforms. The world's first action figure offers quite a variety of items to collect.

References: Vincent Santelmo, *The Complete Encyclopedia to GI Joe*, 3rd ed. Krause Publications, 2001; Vincent Santelmo, *GI Joe Identification & Price Guide, 1964-1998*, Krause Publications, 1999.

Periodical: *GI Joe Patrol,* P.O. Box 2362, Hot Springs, AR 71914.

Collectors' Clubs: GI Joe Collectors Club, 12513 Birchfalls Dr, Raleigh, NC 27614; GI Joe: Street Brigade Club, 8362 Lornay Ave, Westminster, CA 92683.

For additional listings, see *Warman's Americana & Collectibles.*

Accessories
Ammo belt......................... 18.00
Bullet proof vest, secret agent 8.00
Heavy Artillery Laser, MIB. 45.00
Goggles, orange............... 14.00
Jet pack, Jump 25.00
Life ring 1.00
Machine gun, played-with, orig box.............................. 20.00

GI Joe Adventure Team figure, 12" high, $75.

Navy flag.............................28.00
Sand bag 5.00
Ski Patrol Set.....................95.00
Snowshoes 15.00
Sleeping bag......................24.00
Tent, poles missing 20.00
Action figure, 3-3/4"
   Armadillo, 1988, loose 12.00
   Blizzard, 1988, MOC..........35.00
   Breaker, 1982, loose..........20.00
   Buzzer, 1985, MOC 45.00
   Clutch, 1982, loose............15.00
   Cobra, 1982, loose 40.00
   Crystal Ball, 1987, loose....12.00
   Dee-Jay, 1985, MOC 12.00
   Desert Camo Savage, 1994,
     mail-in, loose..................6.00
   Grunt, 1982, loose 22.00
   Iceberg, 1986, loose 10.00
   Muskrat, 1988, loose 12.00
   Short-Fuze, 1982, MOC.....75.00
   Snow Job, 1983, loose 25.00
   Spirit, 1984, loose..............19.00
   Torch, 1985, MOC..............60.00
   Torpedo, 1983, MOC 50.00
   Tunnel Rat, 1987, orig card, bubble lifting.......................25.00
   Wild Bill, 1991, MOC..........50.00
   Windmill, 1988, loose...........7.00
   Zandar, 1986, Canadian, MOC
     ....25.00

Clothing
   Beret, green 85.00
   Boots, short, black 4.00
   Boots, tall, brown 8.00
   Hat, Army...........................28.00
   Helmet, dark blue...............18.00
   Jacket, dress, Marine.........30.00
   Jacket, Russian 12.00
   Pants, dress, Marine............6.00
   Pants, ski patrol 22.00
   Shirt, Navy, 1 pocket............4.00
   Shirt, soldier, no pockets......8.00
Coloring book, 48 pgs, Spanish text, 1989 ....15.00
Playset, Atomic Man Secret Outpost, good box...................85.00
Vehicle
   Amphibious Personnel Carrier, MIB..............................150.00
   Armored Missile Vehicle Wolverine, orig, box, card missing
     ....90.00
   Flying Submarine, orig box, card missing..........................40.00
   Tank Car, motorized, MOC
     ....12.00
Weapon
   Bayonet.............................15.00
   Flare pistol 2.00

M-16.............................30.00
Night stick 20.00

❖ Girl Scouts

It's easy to identify Girl Scouts during their cookie campaigns, but they are as dedicated to community service and education as are their male counterparts. Flea market finds might include clothing, badges, and camping equipment.

Reference: George Cuhaj, *U.S. Scouting Collectibles*, 2nd ed. Krause Publications, 2001.

Periodicals: *Scout Memorabilia*, P.O. Box 1121, Manchester, NH 03105; *Scouting Collectors Quarterly*, 806 E Scott St, Tuscola, IL 61953.

Collectors' Clubs: American Scouting Traders Assoc, P.O. Box 92, Kentfield, CA 94914; International Badgers Club, 7760 NW 50th St, Lauder Hill, FL 33351; National Scouting Collectors Soc, 806 E Scott S., Tuscola, IL 61953; Scouts on Stamps Soc International, 7406 Park Dr, Tampa, FL 33610.

Award, Gray Squirrel Award, black and gray, white ground, 1980s
   ....12.00
Belt, elasticized, 31" l 14.00
Calendar
   1947, 8" x 11".....................48.00
   1967, orig envelope, 10" x 17"
     ....22.00
Canteen, aluminum, cloth jacket, Girl Scout insignia, 7-1/4" dia
   ....25.00
Charter, tan textured paper, dated Jan 1921, dark brown inscription and design, inked signatures
   ....30.00
Doll, cloth mask face, 14" h ...115.00
Handbook, 1932, olive green cloth cover with black silhouettes on front, worn..........................15.00
Hat, Brownie, wool, orig tag.....18.00
Invitation, "Sister Scout," white and green, cartoon fishes, 1980
   ....5.00
Magazine, *The American Girl,* June, 1934..................................10.00
Mug, white ground, red insignia.7.00
Pin 10.00

Pinback button
   Boone Brownie Olympics, brown and orange, early 1980s12.00
   Brownie Day, brown and orange, cartoon clown image, 1981
     ....10.00
   Girl Scouts Audubon Project, green and white, blue lettering, 1980s.....................10.00
   Girl Scouts Meet the Challenge, green and yellow, 1980s
     ....8.00
Ring, Brownie, sterling silver, adjustable, center image of dancing Brownie, 1930s.................35.00
Sash and beanie, 1960s.........25.00
Sewing kit, Brownies, red case, 1940s..............................15.00
Shirt, size 7 ....5.00

❖ Glass Knives

Most glass knives date to the Depression, produced by many of the glass manufacturers who dominated the market at that period. They vary in color and design, and, as with most collectibles, a premium is paid for examples with the original box.

Block pattern, pink 45.00
Flower handle, pink, inscribed "Nettie," mkd "Made in USA" ...40.00
Plain, green, 9-1/8" l 42.00
Three Leaf pattern, crystal......18.00
Three Star pattern, Barry Importing Co., Broadway, N.Y.
   Blue...................................42.00
   Crystal, orig box 40.00
   Pink...................................38.00
Vitex, crystal, orig box, 9" l......40.00

❖ Goebel

Many dealers and collectors associate the name "Goebel" with Hummels, but the company has also produced many other figures, animals, and accessories. Look for Hummel-type markings and well-made porcelain.

Collectors' Clubs: Friar Tuck Collectors Club, P.O. Box 262, Oswego, NY 13827; Goebel Networkers, P.O. Box 396, Lemoyne, PA 17043.

Animal figure
   Buffalo, 6" h.......................70.00
   Ducks, pr 28.00

Goebel figurine, $60.

Fish, incised mark, 3" 45.00
Irish Setter, 10" h 90.00
Spaniel Dog, 8" h 80.00
Decanter, Friar Tuck, large 130.00
Figure
 Bellhop, Sheraton, orig suitcases 425.00
 Betsey Clark 100.00
 Dutch boy on tulip, "It's A Small World, Walt Disney Productions, orig tags and box, 5-1/2" h 90.00
 Eleanor, mkd "Made in West Germany," incised numbers, 8-3/4" h 75.00
 Elisabeth, 1601, gold trim, mkd "Made in West Germany," incised numbers, 8-3/4" h 75.00
 Woody, 6" h 350.00
Flower pot, Oriental man attached to side, crown mark 90.00
Perfume lamp, Bambi, stylized bee mark, foil paper label, 6-1/2" h 275.00
Salt and pepper shakers, pr
 Flower the Skunk, orig foil label, full bee mark, black "Germany" mark, c1940, 2-3/4" h 225.00
 Friar Tuck, full bee mark, "Made in West Germany," 4" h 145.00
 Frog and toadstool 35.00
 Peppers, one red, other green,

full bee mark, black "Germany" stamp, 2" w 30.00
Vase, Figaro the Cat 90.00

❖ Goldschneider Porcelain

Friedrich Goldschneider established a porcelain and faience factory in Vienna, Austria, in 1885. Production continued there until the early 1940s, when the family fled war-torn Europe for the United States. The Goldschneider Everlast Corporation was located in Trenton, New Jersey from 1943 until 1950, producing traditional figures and accessories.

Bust, black woman, blue hair, orange highlights, pedestal base 400.00
Figure
 Lady with parasol, 8-1/2" h 85.00
 Madonna and Child, orig label, 4-1/2" h 60.00
 Southern Belle, 10-1/2" h ... 90.00
Music box, Colonial Girl 120.00
Plate, mermaid pattern 175.00
Wall mask, Art Deco, curly brown haired girl, aqua scarf 450.00

Goldschneider covered dish with multicolor bird, 11" high, $425.

Golf award, brass, key-chain size, $12.50.

❖ Golf Collectibles

"Fore!" When you consider that the game of golf has been played since the 15th century, you begin to understand how many golf collectibles are available to collectors. Flea markets are great sources for interesting clubs, paper ephemera, and other related items.

Reference: Chuck Furjanic, *Antique Golf Collectibles*, 2nd ed, Krause Publications, 1999.

Periodicals: *Golfiana Magazine*, 222 Levette Ln #4, Edwardsville, IL 62025; *US Golf Classics & Heritage Hickories*, 5207 Pennock Point Rd, Jupiter, FL 33458.

Collectors' Clubs: Golf Collectors Soc, P.O. Box 20546, Dayton, OH 45420; Logo Golf Ball Collector's Assoc, 2552 Barclay Fairway, Lake Worth, FL 33467; The Golf Club Collectors Assoc, 640 E Liberty St, Girard, OH 44420.
Ball
 Gutta percha, made in Great Britain, c1895, 60% to 70% paint, numerous iron marks 440.00
 Lynx, rubber core 18.00

Book
  Golf My Way, Jack Nicklaus with
    Ken Bowden, Simon &
    Schuster, 1974, softcover,
    265 pgs 8.00
  The Golfers Companion, Peter
    Lawless, 1st ed, 1937, 512
    pgs 150.00
Cigarette card, A. Padgham, British
  Sporting Personalities series,
  issued by W.D. & H.O. Wills,
  1937, photo of 1936 British
  Open champion, 3" x 2".......5.00
Club, Wilson, wedge, staff model,
  1959, steel shaft................60.00
Paperweight, US Open, 1980..32.00
Plate, crossed golf clubs under "D,"
  Syracuse China, scalloped
  edge, 9-3/4" dia.................35.00
Program, Bob Hope Desert Classic,
  1967 ....20.00
Putter, The Spaulding, gooseneck
  blade, period replacement grip,
  32-3/4" l..........................140.00
Tee, wooden, 1920s, two Rite Hite, 1
  Carrot, set of 3 ....20.00
Trading cards, Golf Card Set, 1981
  ....59.00

❖ Gonder Pottery

Established in 1941 by Lawton
Gonder, this Gonder Pottery was
located in Zanesville, Ohio, until it
closed in 1957. Gonder pieces are
clearly marked and many have interesting glazes.

Collectors' Club: Gonder Collec-
tors Club, 917 Hurl Dr, Pittsburgh,
PA 15236.
Bowl, white, crackle glaze, 8" dia
  ....15.00
Bust, Chinese man, green, #541,
  11" h, 12" w 495.00
Candlestick, cornucopia-shape, light
  gray, pink accents, #552, 5" h
  ....32.00
Ewer, Shell and Star pattern, green,
  13" h.................................60.00
Pitcher, twist motif, red and white
  ....65.00
Planter
  Feather, pale blue, 12" h, 10" w
    ....90.00
  Flower-shape, yellow.........15.00
  Shell-shape, gray...............58.00
  Swan, light blue, E-44, 5-1/2" h,
    5" l 25.00

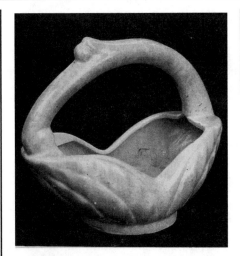

Pink and gray Gonder basket, marked "H-39," 7" high, 8-1/4" wide, $40.

Teapot, cov, brown and yellow glaze,
  mkd "Gonder USA P-31," 7" x
  11"....................................85.00
Urn, handled, gray, H-49 ....45.00
Vase, Cornucopia shape, greens,
  browns and pinks, H-14, 9" h
  ....60.00
  Peacock tail motif, minor glaze
  flaws, 12" h....................80.00

❖ Goofus Glass

Whether collectors identify it as
goofus glass, Mexican ware, or hoo-
ligan glass, there's no denying its
unique beauty. Goofus glass is actually clear pressed glass that has
been painted, usually on the back,
with a metallic gold ground and colored highlights. Because the colorful
decoration is not fired, it is very susceptible to flaking. Most goofus
glass was produced from 1890 to
about 1920.

Periodical: *Goofus Glass Gazette*,
9 Lindenwood Ct, Sterling, VA
20165.
Bowl, Roses, 8" dia 35.00
Cake plate, Dahlia and Fan, red
  flowers, gold ground 45.00
Coaster, Grapes, red grapes, gold
  ground 4.00
Dish, Chrysanthemum Sprays, red
  flowers, gold ground, scalloped
  rim, 11" dia........................85.00

Goofus glass vase, roses design, paint loss, 7" high, $20.

Plate
  Advertising, Old Rose Distilling
    Co., Chicago, 8-1/4" dia 75.00
  Apples, red fruit, gold ground,
    7-1/2" dia 28.00
  Roses, red flowers, green
    leaves, gold ground, 11" dia
    ....50.00
Vase, Cabbage Rose, gold ground,
  red roses, 7" h..................25.00

❖ Graniteware

Graniteware is the name given to
metal kitchen and dinnerwares that
have an interesting speckled or
swirled paint decoration. The first
graniteware was made in Germany
in the 1830s. By World War I, American manufacturers were taking over
the market. Common colors include
gray and white, but savvy collectors
will tell you that graniteware comes
in a variety of colors. Graniteware is
still being produced.

Adhering single or multiple layers
of enamel to metal items through the
use of high temperatures resulted in
a product with a glass-like finish that
was referred to as graniteware.
Although such pieces were advertised as quite durable, they do in fact
chip rather easily. Pattern and color
are extremely important when determining value.

Gray graniteware gill measures, 1/8-quart, $500; 1/4-quart, $165.

References: Helen Greguire, *Collector's Encyclopedia of Granite Ware: Colors, Shapes and Values, Book I* (1990, 1994 value update), *Book II* (1993, 1998 value update), Collector Books; David T. Pikul and Ellen M. Plante, *Collectible Enameled Ware: American & European*, Schiffer Publishing, 1998.

Collectors' Club: National Graniteware Society, P.O. Box 9248, Cedar Rapids, IA 52409-9248.

Reproduction Alert. Contemporary makers of graniteware produce some of the same forms and colors as those used for vintage pieces. In addition, individual pieces of vintage graniteware have been reglazed in highly desirable patterns, including Red Swirl.

Ashtray, white-speckled, "Iron Clad Manufacturing Co., New York Pan-American Exposition 1901," central design of a child holding two matches and sitting atop a pipe, 5" dia 115.00
Berry bucket
    Blue/white swirl, graniteware lid, wire handle, lid knob reattached, lid chips, 4-1/2" h, 3-3/4" dia 295.00
    Brown mottled, tin lid, wooden knob, bail handle, 4-1/4" h, 6-1/4" dia 85.00
Bucket, black/white swirl 265.00
Candlestick
    Blue/white swirl, chamberstick, chips, rust, 2-1/4" h, 5-1/4" dia 135.00
    Gray, chamberstick, 6-1/4" dia 95.00
Coffeepot
    Blue/white swirl, black handle and finial, 10-1/8" h 140.00

Gray, gooseneck spout, pewter-decor engraved Victorian design, 9-3/4" h 150.00
Colander, gray 35.00
Cream can
    Blue/white swirl, Boston cream can, tin lid, bail handle, 7-1/2" high (excluding lid) 225.00
    Gray, tin lid, wire bail, 4-1/2" high, 3-1/4" dia 225.00
Dipper, gray 40.00
Dustpan, gray mottled 35.00
Food mold, blue/white swirl, turk's head 115.00
Match safe, gray, double pockets, 5-1/8" h, 4-3/8" w 225.00
Milk pan, lava........................... 70.00
Muffin pan, 8-hole, gray, wire frame 60.00
Pie pan, cobalt/white swirl 65.00
Teapot, Snow on the Mountain, green/white, gooseneck..... 95.00
Tray, blue/white swirl, white back, 17" x 13-1/2" 90.00

❖ Greentown Glass

The term Greentown glass generally refers to items made by the Indiana Tumbler and Goblet Co., which was located in Greentown, Indiana. Starting in 1894, the company produced pressed pattern glass and bar wares. By 1900, the factory had expanded several times, and Jacob Rosenthal developed an opaque brown glass the company referred to as chocolate glass. This color innovation would save the struggling company. Rosenthal went on to develop other opaque colors, including Golden Agate and Rose Agate. The factory closed in 1903 after a fire destroyed the operation.

Collectors' Club: National Greentown Glass Assoc, 19596 Glendale Ave, South Bend, IN 46637.
Reproduction Alert.
For additional listings, see *Warman's Antiques & Collectibles* and *Warman's Glass.*
Bowl, Herringbone Buttress, green, 7-1/4" dia 135.00
Celery vase, Beaded Panel, clear 100.00
Cordial, Austria, canary yellow 125.00

Cactus pattern salt and pepper shakers, chocolate slag, Greentown Glass, $275. (Photo courtesy of Jackson's Auctioneers & Appraisers.)

Creamer
    Indian Head, opaque white 450.00
    Shuttle, chocolate, tankard style 95.00
Goblet, Overall Lattice, clear .. 45.00
Mug, 5" h, Nile Green, chip..... 35.00
Nappy, Masonic, chocolate 90.00
Salt and pepper shakers, Cactus, chocolate, pr 275.00
Tumbler, 4" h, Cactus, chocolate 30.00
Wine, Cord Drapery, amber .. 280.00

❖ Greeting Cards

From "Merry Christmas" to "Happy Birthday," we've grown up sending and receiving greeting cards. Some folks save these remembrances, and many find their way to flea markets. Some collectors look for examples with colorful images or witty sayings, while others search for interesting autographs. This is one area in which prices for the secondary market are still being established.
Birthday
    Amos & Andy, brown portraits, message includes song title "Check and Double Check," Rust Craft, inked birthday note 28.00
    Blondie, Dagwood illus, full color, Hallmark, © 1939......... 20.00

1930s birthday card, $1.

First Lady, card sgd "Mrs. Eisenhower, Nov 14, 1965, Dear Delores, May we celebrate many more mutual birthdays together," orig envelope 70.00

Golliwogg, "Say! What's Cookin?," mammy with young boy and pie 28.00

"It's Your Birthday, Well, You've Got It Coming To You, There Are Some Things You Can't Duck – So Take'em and Like'em, Here's Wishing You Luck, Many Happy Returns," front with black man peering thru fence, about to get hit with pie 30.00

Space Patrol Man, diecut, full-color, transparent green helmet, orig envelope 25.00

Christmas

"Christmas Greetings," emb holly, silver ground, The Art Lithographic Co. 9.00

"Hearty Greetings," cutout emb border, holly on front 6.50

Get Well, Amos n' Andy, black-and-white photo, Hall Bros., © 1951 .... 30.00

❖ Gregory, Mary

There is documentation that a lady named Mary Gregory did do some decorating on glassware made in the Sandwich, Massachusetts, area when the American glass industry was young. However, it is highly unlikely that Mary painted all of the items attributed to her, if she even painted any human figures at all. Myth notwithstanding, brilliantly colored glassware with white enameled painting is referred to as Mary Gregory glass.

Covered box, amethyst ground, white enameled girl in garden setting, 5-1/2" diameter, $260.

Reproduction Alert.

For additional listings, see *Warman's Antiques & Collectibles* and *Warman's Glass*.

Barber bottle, deep sapphire blue ground, white enameled child playing tennis, long neck, pontil scar 150.00

Box, cov, deep amethyst ground, white enameled boy with flowers in hand, metal fittings, 3-3/4" l 375.00

Cruet, sapphire blue, two white enameled facing girls, wear to enameling, 6-1/2" h 365.00

Goblet, electric blue ground, white enameled children, pr 275.00

Plate, cobalt ground, white enameled girl with butterfly net, 6-1/4" dia 135.00

Salt shaker, sapphire blue ground, white enameled girl in garden, brass top 195.00

Tumbler, cranberry ground, white enameled boy on one, girl on other, facing pr 120.00

Vase, cobalt ground, white enameled standing young man, gold trim 325.00

For exciting collecting trends and newly expanded areas look for the following symbols:

❂ Hot Topic

✫ New Warman's Listing

(May have been in another Warman's title.)

❖ Griswold

Here's a name that evokes thoughts of cast-iron skillets and kitchen implements. Griswold items are frequently found at flea markets. The company based in Erie, Pennsylvania, originally produced hardware. By 1914, they had begun making the cast-iron cookware that many people associate with their name. In 1946, the company was sold to a group of New York investors, and in the late 1950s the trade name Griswold was sold to their major competitor, the Wagner Manufacturing Co. Wagner continued operations, but dropped the words "Erie, Pa" from the trademark.

Reference: David G. Smith and Chuck Wafford, *The Book of Griswold & Wagner,* 2nd ed, Schiffer Publishing, 2000.

Periodical: *Kettles 'n' Cookware,* Drawer B, Perrysville, NY 14129.

Griswold No. 50 Hearts Star muffin tin, back and front, $2,000.

Collectors' Club: Griswold & Cast-Iron Cookware Assoc, Drawer B, Perrysville, NY 14129.

Note: All items cast iron unless otherwise noted.

Ashtray, #00 .... 43.00
Corn stick pan
    #28, Wheat and Corn....... 310.00
    #262, miniature 125.00
    #273 .... 50.00
Damper, mkd New American... 15.00
Dutch oven, #8 .... 55.00
Famous Patty Molds, orig box
    .... 80.00
Food mold
    Lamb, 7-3/4" h, 12" w 175.00
    Rabbit, 11" h, 8" l 355.00
Hotplate, 3-burner 145.00
Muffin pan, #808, cast aluminum
    .... 150.00
Popover pan, #10 .... 38.50
Sad iron, top mkd "Erie" and "Griswold" 135.00
Skillet
    #3 .... 22.00
    #5 .... 45.00
    #6, large logo 38.00
    #6, porcelain, red and cream
    .... 95.00
    #10 .... 60.00
Teakettle, Colonial, 5-qt 40.00
Trivet, #7, 7-1/4" dia 45.00
Waffle iron
    #8, American 50.00
    #18, Heart & Star 175.00
    Electric, orig box, 1920s .. 120.00

❖ Guardian Ware

Before aluminum came into its own as a great material for soft drink cans, it was put to use in making pots and pans. Light and versatile, aluminum became the cookware of choice for many years. Among the leading lines was Guardian Ware, with its distinctive symbol of a knight.

Cleaner, Guardian Service Cleaner, paper can, unopened, 8 oz
    .... 22.50
Coffeepot, 2-pc bottom, glass top
    .... 130.00
Cookbook, *Guardian Service Tested Recipes*, softcover, 72 pgs, shelf wear 24.00

Guardian Service Dutch oven with glass lid, 12" diameter, $45.

Fryer, glass lid
    9-1/4" dia 50.00
    12" dia 42.00
Griddle, octagonal, 13" w 51.00
Ice bucket, glass lid 36.00
Omelet pan, plastic handles, 16" x 6"
    .... 35.00
Pan, triangular, domed metal lid
    .... 56.00
Pans, triangular shape, domed glass lids, made to fit together in a circle, set of 3 .... 93.00
Platter, 10" x 13" 21.00
Roaster, domed metal lid, 15" x 10"
    .... 105.00
Salt and pepper shakers, teapot form, glass bases, aluminum tops, 3" h, pr 71.00
Skillet, glass lid, 2 handle covers, clip-on handle 91.00
Tray, round, 15-1/2" d 40.00
Turkey roaster with lid, 19" x 10"
    .... 155.00
Water pitcher, tilted ball shape, plastic handle 430.00

❖ Guitars

Guitars do occasionally show up at flea markets. And, if you're the strumming type, ask to try it out before agreeing on a purchase price. Interest in vintage guitars has increased during the last few years, spirited on by record setting prices at auction.

Periodicals: *Twentieth Century Guitar,* 135 Oser Ave, Hauppauge, NY 11788; *Vintage Guitar Classics,* P.O. Box 7301, Bismarck, ND 58507.

Gibson, J45, 1980 .... 1,300.00
Singing Cowboy, wooden, 1941, red and yellow stenciled campfire scene 155.00
Stanford, imitation rosewood finish
    .... 95.00
University, rosewood back and sides, vine and leaf pattern, spruce top, ebony guard plate, mahogany neck, MOP trim, c. 1905-10 .... 250.00

❖ Gunderson

In the late 1930s, Robert Gunderson took over the old Pairpoint Glass operations. Using the name Gundersen Glass Works, the new company manufactured tableware until 1952. One of the most distinctive glass colors made by Gunderson is Peach Blow. Their interpretation of this antique glass shades from a faint opaque pink to white to deep rose.

Bottle, peachblow, pink shading to white, 2-1/2" w, 6" h 110.00
Cornucopia, white shading to light pink to dark pink base, ruffled, etched mark, 6-1/4" h 395.00
Cup and saucer, peachblow, glossy finish, c1953 .... 325.00
Goblet, glossy finish, deep peachblow color, applied Burmese glass base 295.00
Jug, burgundy, applied handle, c1910, 5-1/2" w, 7-3/4" h
    .... 125.00
Luncheon plate, deep raspberry to pale pink, matte finish 375.00
Paperweight, white rose, green leaves 425.00
Vase, crystal, controlled bubble paperweight base, c1950, 10" h
    .... 185.00

H

For exciting collecting trends and newly expanded areas look for the following symbols:

⚙ Hot Topic

★ New Warman's Listing

(May have been in another Warman's title.)

❖ Haeger Potteries

Haeger Pottery has an interesting history. Established as a brickyard in Dundee, Illinois, in 1871, the company began producing an art pottery line in 1914. Their high quality luster glazes and soft pastels met with success. A line named "Royal Haeger" was introduced in 1938. Members of the Haeger family are still involved with the pottery.

Collectors' Club: Haeger Pottery Collectors of America, 5021 Toyon Way, Antioch, CA 94509.

Basket, stork, pink, base chip, 8-1/2" h, 10-1/2" w 35.00
Bowl, shell form, 18" l 18.00
Candy dish, cov, textured white, sgd "Royal Haeger" 12.00
Figurine
    Cocker spaniel puppy, reclining, 2-3/4" h 25.00
    Hound, brown, 4" h 40.00
    Swan with uplifted wings, light gray and brown, 9" l 46.00
    Warlord, pink, 12" h, 12" w 125.00
Flower pot, 4-1/4" h, 5-1/2" dia 20.00
Pitcher, pink, RG-28, 6" h 55.00
Planter
    Bassinet, blue, 5" h, 7" l 12.00
    It's A Boy, light blue, 3-3/4" h, 4-1/4" sq 16.00
    Madonna with Cherub, blue, 11" h 35.00
    Wheelbarrow, 7" l 15.00

Haeger gazelle, pink high-gloss glaze, paper tag, 1968, 21-1/2" high, $125.

Vase
    Cylinder, white, R670, 9" h. 12.00
    Gazelle, green with navy blue feathering, R-706 and R-707, 15" h, pr 100.00
    Lily, blue, green and pink, R-446, 1930s-1940s, 14" h 100.00
Wash bowl and pitcher, yellow, embossed leaves and flowers in gold, pitcher 6" h, bowl 7-1/2" dia 25.00

❖ Hagen Renaker

The Hagen Renaker name is recognized for producing quality miniature figurines and other accessories.
Figure
    Appaloosa and Colt, 3" h ... 18.00
    Buckskin Mare, 2-1/2" h 12.50
    Duck, female lying down, male standing, Studio Line, male 6-3/4" h, pr 175.00
    Hippos, mother 2" h, baby 1" h, 1995 .... 8.50
    Michael, Walt Disney's Peter Pan, 1" h 225.00
    Pedro the Chihuahua, Walt Disney's Lady and the Tramp 125.00
    Pegasus, standing figure 2" h, reclining figure 1" h, 1995 .... 15.00

Saddlebred Horse, Honora, 8" h 600.00
Snow White, orig Walt Disney label 250.00
Tramp, Walt Disney's Lady and the Tramp, 2-1/4" h 195.00
Trusty, Walt Disney's Lady and the Tramp, 1-7/8" h 75.00
Wall plaque, irregular shape, caveman style, high glaze
    Butterfly, 14" x 9" 250.00
    Fawn, 10-1/2" x 5" 175.00
    Fish, 7" x 12" 250.00
    Fish, 19" x 8" 350.00
    Reindeer, 10-1/2" x 15" ... 250.00

❖ Hair Related

Today we've got a commodity the Victorians couldn't get enough of—hair. And to think that we pay barbers and beauticians to cut it off! During the Victorian era, people saved every loose strand of hair in dresser jars called hair receivers. When enough hair had been accumulated, it was used to make jewelry and ornate flower wreaths. Of course, all of the voluminous hair that was so popular during that time had to be brushed and tucked in place with hair combs, barrettes, etc.

References: Mary Bachman, *Collector's Guide to Hair Combs*, Collector Books, 1998; Christie Romero, *Warman's Jewelry*, 2nd ed, Krause Publications, 1998.

Ornamental hair comb, mottled tortoiseshell, hand-carved fretwork, $85.

Collectors' Clubs: Antique Comb Collectors Club International, 8712 Pleasant View Rd, Bangor, PA 18013; Antique Fancy Comb Collectors Club, 3291 N River Rd, Libertyville, IL 60048; National Antique Comb Collectors Club, 3748 Sunray Dr, Holiday, FL 34691.

Hair brush, sterling silver, Art Nouveau style, wear to bristles
....125.00
Hair comb
   Celluloid, engraved grapes, tortoise shell look 12.00
   Celluloid, rhinestone trim ...45.00
   Gutta percha, French jet, Victorian..............................95.00
   Mexican silver, mkd "Made en Mexico, 925" 15.00
   Sterling silver, 3 turquoise stones, wave shape 45.00
Hair pick, single-prong hair ornament, imitation ivory, gracefully twisted top, diecut filigree, 7" l
....35.00
Hair pin, silver twisted work, two-pronged comb, Victorian, c1890, 5" l 75.00
Hair receiver, top with center hole, porcelain, roses dec 85.00
Jewelry
   Brooch, central oval glazed compartment with braided light brown hair, scrolled frame, convex back, 10k yg, c1840
....195.00
   Locket, oval, beveled-edge glass front and back, braided knot of gray hair, plain gold filled frame, c1850 ....200.00
Wreath, ornate flowers made from hair, paper leaves, other period decorations, 19" x 23" shadow box 145.00

❖ Hall China

Hall China Company was located in East Liverpool, Ohio, and produced semi-porcelain dinnerware. By 1911, Robert T. Hall had perfected a non-crazing vitrified china, allowing the body and the glaze to be fired at one time. Initially, Hall's basic product was dinnerware for hotels and restaurants. Eventually, the line was extended to include premiums and retail wares, such as Autumn Leaf for the Jewel Tea. An extensive line of teapots was introduced around 1920, and kitchenware was introduced in 1931. The company is still in business today.

Collectors' Club: Hall China Collector's Club, P.O. Box 360488, Cleveland, OH 44136.

For additional listings, see *Warman's Antiques & Collectible, Warman's Americana & Collectibles, Warman's American Pottery & Porcelain*, and Autumn Leaf in this edition.

Bean pot, Orange Poppy 95.00
Bowl, Orange Poppy, silver rim, 9" dia...35.00
Casserole, cov, Rose White 30.00
Cereal bowl, Pastel Morning Glory
....17.50
Coffeepot, Orange Poppy, Great American 85.00
Cookie jar, Tootsie, inside chips
....128.00
Creamer, Lazy Daisies, Kraft...15.00
Cup and saucer
   Blue Bouquet 25.00
   Lazy Daisies, Kraft..............15.00
   Red Poppy 10.00
   Taverne 20.00
Custard cup, Orange Poppy 6.50
Drip jar, Red Poppy 30.00
Gravy boat, Serenade 40.00
Jug
   Radiance..............................48.00
   Rose White, 7-3/4" h..........48.00
Mixing bowl, Crocus, 7-1/2" dia
....55.00
Onion soup, cov, Red Dot........48.00
Pie plate, Pastel Morning Glory
....32.00
Platter, Cameo Rose, medium
....40.00
Pretzel jar, cov, Taverne 195.00

Hall mixing bowl, 7-1/2" diameter, $14.

Sugar bowl, cov, Mount Vernon
....20.00
Sugar shaker, handle, Crocus
....150.00
Stack set, Red Poppy 75.00
Teapot
   Aladdin, cobalt blue, gold trim
....50.00
   Baltimore, yellow 50.00
   Doughnut, cobalt 165.00
   Globe, emerald green, gold trim
....115.00
   Individual size, dark green, chip on lid, 4" h....................10.00
   Los Angeles, cobalt.........160.00
   Red Poppy, New York shape
....80.00
Tom and Jerry set, bowl, 12 mugs, black, gold lettering...........65.00
Vegetable bowl
   Cameo Rose 30.00
   Red Poppy 25.00

❖ Hallmark

Hallmark is an American success story. In 1913, brothers Joyce and Rollie Hall established their company to sell Christmas cards. Through purchases of printing and engraving plants, they developed into a nationwide company. After World War II, they expanded and attracted famous artists to the company. One of Hallmark's most popular lines, the Keepsake Ornament series, was started in 1973.

References: Rosie Wells, ed, *The Ornament Collector's Official Price Guide for Past Years' Hallmark Ornaments and Kiddie Car Classics*, 12th ed, Rosie Wells Enterprises, 1998.

Periodicals: *Hallmarkers*, P.O. Box 97172, Pittsburgh, PA 15229; *The Ornament Collector*, 22341 E Wells Rd, Canton, IL 61520.

Collectors' Club: Hallmark Keepsake Ornament Collectors Club, P.O. Box 412734, Kansas City, MO 64141.

Cookie cutter, Peanuts, Lucy holding package, Snoopy in a Santa hat, Linus holding lights and Charlie Brown holding ornament, set of 4 ....100.00
Greeting card, birthday, black characters, copyright Hall Brothers, Inc., c1940s, 4" x 5" 25.00

1993 Holiday Barbie ornament, Hallmark, 1st in a series, MIB, $55.

Jewelry, Valentine pin 10.00
Magazine advertisement, Thanksgiving cards adv, 1959......... 5.00
Ornament,
    Barbie, 1993, 1st in series, orig box 55.00
    Bummy, Nature's Angels, 1st in series, 1-1/4" h, orig box 22.50
    Calico Mouse, Merry Miniatures, 1977, 2-1/4" h 100.00
    Enterprise, 1991, MIB......225.00
    From Our House To Yours, 1992 .... 10.00
    Frosty Friends, Eskimo and Husky in igloo, 2nd in series, 1981, no box, 2" h.......350.00
    Heavenly Angel, 1992, MIB, 3" h 32.00
    Mustang, Classic Car series, 1992, MIB......................48.00
    Noel Railroad, Coal Car, miniature, 1990, 2nd in series 24.50
    Puppy's Best Friend, 1986, worn orig box 28.00
    Snowman, Merry Miniatures, 1976, 2-1/4" h 70.00
    Superman lunch box, 1998, tin, 3-1/4" x 2-1/2" 13.50
    Twelve Days of Christmas, 8 Maids A Milking............. 25.00
    World-Class Teacher, 1992, 3-1/4" h, MIB 9.00

1957 Corvette ornament, Hallmark, 1st in Classic American Cars series, 1991, MIB, $100.

✪ Halloween

Among holiday collectibles, Halloween is second only to Christmas. Early Halloween items have a distinctive look that appeals to many collectors.

References: Pamela Apkarian-Russell, *Collectible Halloween,* Schiffer Publishing, 1997; —, *Halloween: Collectible Decorations and Games*, Schiffer Publishing, 2000;—, *More Halloween Collectibles: Anthropomorphic Vegetables and Fruits of Halloween*, Schiffer Publishing, 1998.

Periodicals: *BooNews*, P.O. Box 143, Brookfield, IL 60513; *Trick or Treat Trader*, P.O. Box 499, Winchester, NH 03470.

Reproduction Alert.

Candle, jack-o-lantern, 4" h 15.00
Cookie cutter
    Aluminum, startled cat, 3-1/4" w 7.00
    Halloween Trick Or Treat Cookie Cutters set, MIB 50.00
Costume, child's
    Dr. Kildare 45.00
    Flipper, cloth, black velvet trim 50.00
    Fred Flintstone 25.00
    Howard the Duck, Collegeville, 1986, orig box 60.00
    I Dream of Jeannie, 1960s 125.00
    Indiana Jones.....................80.00
    Pac Man............................40.00
    The Fonz, Happy Days, Ben Cooper, 1976, orig box 35.00

Cup, paper with handle, orange with black cats, bats, trees and full moon, C.A. Reed & Co., Williamsport, Pa., 3-3/4" h.............. 5.00
Hat, cardboard and crepe paper, black and orange, Germany, 4" h 17.50
Horn, litho tin with plastic end, witch on broom, spider webs and stars, Kirchhof, 6-1/2" l...... 20.00
Jack-o'-lantern
    Black cat, cardboard, mouth insert with small tear, Western Germany..................... 475.00
    Devil, compressed paper, face restored, 6-3/4" h........ 500.00
    Pumpkin, cardboard, face with lipstick design, Germany, 1915-1920, 4-3/4" h.... 550.00
    Pumpkin, cardboard, worn paper inserts in eyes and mouth, Germany, 3-1/2" h 225.00
    Pumpkin, tin, nose doubles as a horn, U.S. Metal Toy Co., wear, 5" h, 6" dia......... 148.00
Mask
    Deputy Dawg, 1960s......... 32.00
    Dr. Doolittle, 1960s............ 10.00
    Esso Tiger, 1960s.............. 16.00
    I Dream of Jeannie, 1970s .. 3.00
    Mork from Ork 3.00
    Rabbit, 1960s.................... 10.00
    Sabertooth Tiger, 1950s...... 3.00
    Yogi Bear, 1950s 15.00
    Zorro, large brim, 1960s.... 35.00
Napkin, shows black cat, jack-o'-lantern man & woman, bats and moon................................. 5.00

Halloween postcard, $30.

Nodder, skeleton, papier-mache, gray with black, green and white accents, 1930s-1940s, Japan, 5-3/4" h..............................90.00

Noisemaker

Skillet-shape, litho tin with wooden clappers, shows witches, cats, skeletons, etc., U.S. Metal Toys, 8" l, 4" w 45.00

Twirl-type, litho tin with wooden handle, shows witch, black cat and owl, scratches, 5" l 45.00

Party favor, cardboard paper face, plastic disc, eyes move, Japan 45.00

Table decoration, black cat, tissue-paper construction, H.E. Luhr, 9-1/4" h, 6" w 32.00

Tambourine, litho tin

Black cat motif, 7-1/4" dia 195.00

Jack-o'-lantern motif, 6-1/4" dia 175.00

Toothpick

Black cat head, papier-mache, 1940s, Japan, 1" x 1-1/2" 18.00

Jack-o'-lantern, papier-mache, 1940s, Japan, 1" x 1-1/2" 18.00

Skull, papier-mache, 1940s, Japan, 1" x 1-1/2"..........18.00

Witch, papier-mache, 1940s, Japan, 1" x 1-1/2"..........18.00

Trick-or-Treat bag, cloth, orange with black ghost chasing man and woman, black vinyl handles, stains 16.00

❖ Handkerchiefs

Aaacchhooo! Today we grab for a box of disposable tissues, but that's not what our grandmothers did. Vintage etiquette called for well-dressed folks to carry a well-pressed handkerchief, just in case a sneeze was waiting. Remember those gallant gestures in the movies where the gent would whip out his handkerchief for the damsel in distress? And, of course, grandma had to have the proper place to store her hankies.

Reference: Rosanna Mihalick, *Collecting Handkerchiefs*, Schiffer Publishing, 2000.

Embroidered handkerchief, $2.

Apron, made of 4 matching handkerchiefs with pink rose motif, pink rickrack trim 25.00

Embroidered, "E" monogram and floral spray, hand-rolled hem, linen, 13-1/2" sq 16.00

Florals

Gladiolas, scalloped hem, cotton, 15-1/2" sq 15.00

Orange poppies and wheat motif, hand-rolled hem, linen, 14-1/4" sq 15.00

Handkerchief box, pink silk lining, lace and floral trim, sq 45.00

Humorous, Pekingese, hand-rolled hem, cotton, by Burmel, small stains, 14-1/2" sq 15.00

Souvenir type

London, rayon, 13-1/2" sq 17.50

Montana, scalloped edge, cotton, 14" sq 22.00

Texas, hand-rolled hem, cotton, some fading, 13" sq.......15.00

❖ Hanna-Barbera

The partnership of William Denby Hanna and Joseph Roland Barbera developed slowly. They both worked for MGM, and when a new cartoon division was started in 1937, they were teamed together. For twenty years they worked under this arrangement, creating such classics as Tom and Jerry. After striking out on their own, they began producing cartoons for television and created such great characters as Huckleberry Hound, the Jetsons, and the Flintstones. In 1966, Taft Communications purchased the company.

Flintstones jelly glass, Fred and Barney Play Ball, 4-1/4" high, $12.50.

Animation cel, Yogi Bear, late 1970s/early 1980s, single 5-1/2" image of Yogi on laser background, 13" x11" 85.00

Ashtray, Barney bowling, pottery, Arrow Houseware Products, Chicago, 5-1/4" x 8" 90.00

Book, *Jetsons' Word Search Puzzles*, 1978, 64 pgs, unused 10.00

Camera, Fred Flintstone, 1976, 3-1/4" x 3-3/4" 20.00

Comic book

The Flintstones at the New York World's Fair, official fair souvenir.............................25.00

Space Ghost, Comico, 1987, 48 pgs...................................7.00

Cookie jar, Yogi Bear, American Bisque...........................450.00

Doll, plush, Barney Rubble, Nanco, 1989, 14" h 22.00

Figure, Scooby, metal, orig foil label, 2-3/4" h 60.00

Flashlight, interchangeable faces, Fred Flintstone, Huckleberry Hound and Yogi Bear, 1975, MOC 15.00

Lamp, Quick Draw McGraw, plastic, 22" h 20.00

Lunch box, miniature, Quick Draw McGraw, litho tin, 1999, 5-1/2" x 5"...8.00
Mug, Fred Flintstone, Flintstone Multiple brand Vitamins, 1968, 3-1/4" h...............................8.00
Pinback button, Tom and Jerry Go For Stoehmann's Bread, 1950s, 1-1/8" dia...........................27.50

❖ Hardware

Decorative and ornate hardware has graced our homes for decades. Vintage hardware items are popular with those who are restoring antique homes, those who want to add a unique touch to a newer home, or collectors who simply appreciate the beauty of the object.

Reference: H. Weber Wilson, *Antique Hardware Price Guide*, Krause Publications, 1999.
For additional listings, also see Doorknobs in this edition.
Door knocker, figural fox head, cast iron 85.00
Door push plate, bronze, Windsor pattern, Sargent, c1885, 16" h 150.00
Knob, 6-sided, 1" h, 1" dia
    Black glass..........................12.50
    Clear glass...........................7.50
Mail slot and receiver, "Letters"
    Cast iron, Gothic pattern, 2-1/2" h, 8" w..............195.00
    Nickel-plated cast brass, 2-1/2" h, 7" w..............195.00
    Cast brass, 2-1/2" h, 7-1/2" w 165.00
Outlet plate, copper, ivy design, 4-3/4" h, 3-1/4" w...............31.00
Shelf bracket, wrought iron, ornate scrolling pattern, pr............20.00
Switch plate, copper
    Gingko design, 5" h, 3" w...30.00
    Gingko design, for double push-buttons, 5" h, 4-7/8" w...45.00

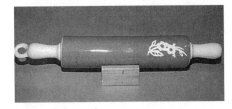

Blue Cameo rolling pin, Harker Pottery, 14-3/4" long, $100.

❖ Harker Pottery

The Harker Company was one of several East Liverpool, Ohio, firms. Founded by Benjamin Harker around 1840, the company produced yellow ware items using the natural clay deposits from the surrounding area. White ware was first made about 1879. Dinnerware and table accessories were the order of the day until the plant was destroyed by fire in 1975.
For additional listings, see *Warman's Americana & Collectibles* and *Warman's American Pottery & Porcelain.*
Batter bowl, Petit Point Rose...65.00
Cake server, Petit Point Rose..20.00
Casserole, cov, Petit Point Rose 65.00
Cheese plate, Cactus Blooms, 11" dia...60.00
Cookie jar, cov, Modern Tulip ..85.00
Creamer, Kriebel's Dairy, Hereford, Pa. 50.00
Cup and saucer, Cameo, Shell Ware, blue 17.50
Dinner plate, Petit Point Rose 15.00
Fork, Apple 40.00
Pie plate, Cameo, Dainty Flower, blue.......................................75.00
Platter, Ivy, large 75.00
Rolling pin, Cameo, blue 75.00
Salad bowl, Red Apple 27.50
Spoon, Amy 60.00
Teapot, cov
    Hallow, some flakes 75.00
    Ivy 200.00
Vegetable bowl, Red Apple 32.00

❖ Harlequin China

This bright and cheery pattern was made by Homer Laughlin and originally sold by F.W. Woolworth Co. When it was introduced in the 1930s it was available in bright yellow, spruce green, maroon, and mauve blue. Eventually, the line was produced in all of the Fiesta colors except ivory and cobalt blue. The line was discontinued in 1964 and then reissued in 1979. The reissued pieces were made in turquoise, yellow, medium green, and coral. Look for the Homer Laughlin back stamp on most pieces.

Harlequin blue eggcup, 3-7/8" high, $28.

Dinnerware

After-dinner cup, chartreuse ... 95.00
After-dinner cup and saucer
    Maroon............................ 100.00
    Red.................................. 130.00
    Spruce............................. 195.00
Ashtray, saucer, red 90.00
Casserole, cov
    Chartreuse 240.00
    Maroon............................ 200.00
    Spruce............................. 195.00
    Yellow.............................. 165.00
Creamer, individual, green.... 125.00
Deep plate, medium green ... 125.00
Eggcup, double
    Gray 40.00
    Mauve 30.00
    Red................................... 40.00
    Rose.................................. 38.00
    Spruce............................... 42.00
    Turquoise 25.00
Marmalade, maroon.............. 325.00
Nappy, medium green........... 195.00
Nut dish, rose........................ 95.00
Pitcher, ball, spruce 95.00
Plate
    7" dia, medium green 45.00
    10" dia, medium green 135.00
    10" dia, red 25.00
Spoon rest, yellow 295.00
Sugar, cov, gray or maroon..... 45.00
Teapot, cov
    Gray 185.00
    Red................................... 95.00
    Rose............................... 100.00

Tumbler, red or yellow 65.00
Figure
Cat
    Mauve 175.00
    Spruce 275.00
    Yellow 175.00
    White and gold.................160.00
Donkey
    Gold trim 80.00
    Mauve 225.00
    Spruce 325.00
    Yellow and gold...............250.00
Duck
    Maroon...........................275.00
    Spruce 175.00
    Yellow 245.00
Fish
    Gold trim 80.00
    Maroon...........................350.00
    Yellow 250.00
Lamb
    Gold 125.00
    Mauve 325.00
    White and gold.................125.00
Penguin
    Maroon...........................285.00
    Yellow 250.00
    White and gold.................125.00

❖ Harmonica and Related

Harmonicas used to be the musical choice of those who couldn't afford fancy instruments. Their rich sounds are still enjoyed today. Flea markets are a wonderful place to look for vintage harmonicas, many of which will still be in their original boxes.

Figurine, Precious Moments, "Lord Give Me A Song," girl with harmonica, 5" h 35.00
Harmonica
    The American Ace Harmonica, Hohner-Panarmonic, orig box 28.00
    Bell Bird, orig box..............18.00
    Hohner Blues Harmonica, orig box 10.00
    Hohner Little Lady #39, orig box, 1-1/2" l..........................49.00
    Hohner Marine Band, #1896, orig box 10.00
    Hoosier Boy, Germany, 4" l 35.00

Horner Super Chromonica Chromatic, with case.............48.00
Woody Woodpecker Harmonica, nodding head, red plastic, 5-1/2" h..........................25.00
Key chain, Harmonica for the Musically Hopeless, small plastic harmonica, orig blister pack......3.50

❖ Hartland Plastics

Hartland Plastics, a small midwestern company based in Hartland, Wisconsin, produced a wide variety of plastic models. Their detailed, finely molded figures included horses, dogs, gunfighters and baseball players, as well as religious statuettes and cake-top decorations. The company was founded in 1939, but it wasn't until the late 1940s that the first of their famous horses was released.

References: Gail Fitch, *Hartland Horses and Dogs*, Schiffer Publishing, 2000.
Baseball
    Yogi Berra, 1960s, mask missing 250.00
    Roberto Clemente, limited edition, orig box, 7" h 150.00
    Whitey Ford, orig box, 6-1/2" h 125.00
    Babe Ruth, 1960s 275.00
    Warren Spahn, 1959-63, freestanding version 159.00
    Ted Williams, 1960s.........350.00
Dale Evans 75.00
Horse
    3-Gaited Saddlebred Mare, light color woodcut, 7" scale series 40.00
    Western, 5" series..............15.00
    Bay Draft, Tinymite, 2" h 12.00
    Bay Foal, mahogany..........12.00
    Mustang, rearing, woodgrain 30.00
Pony Express, rider and horse 138.00
Religious figure, 6" h 9.50
Wells Lamont Thunderchief...155.00
Wyatt Earp and horse.............80.00

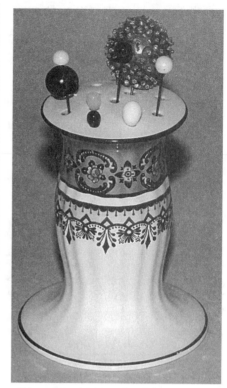

Porcelain hatpin holder, 5" high, $60.

❖ Hatpin Holders and Hatpins

Hatpins are coming back into vogue with collectors. Perhaps it's the renaissance of large hats, or maybe it's the romance that hatpins evoke. Whatever the reason, more and more hatpins are entering the flea market scene, and prices are rising. Of course, if you're going to collect hatpins, you've got to have a few hatpin holders to display your treasures.

Collector's Clubs: American Hatpin Soc, 20 Monticello Dr, Palos Veres Peninsula, CA 90274; International Club for Collectors of Hatpins and Hatpin Holders, 15237 Chanera Ave, Gardena, CA 90249.
For additional listings, see *Warman's Antiques & Collectibles* and *Warman's Jewelry*.
Doll, porcelain half doll, arms folded, satin dress as cushion for hatpins, 9" h 125.00

Hatpin
Ball, rhinestones, 8-1/4" l ... 48.00
Beaded and sequined head, black, 2-3/8" x 1-1/4" dia, 6-1/4" l 75.00
Embossed copper top, bezel set coral colored stone, 8" l 95.00
Faceted glass, black, 2-1/4" x 1-1/4" dia, 5-5/8" l 150.00
Filigree, blank place for monogram, tip broken off, 1" dia, 4-5/8" l 75.00
Filigree, teardrop, 3/4" l head, 7-5/8" l 65.00
Gold lustered metal, screw-type, 1920, 6-1/2" l 20.00
Iridized metal head, faceted dome, 1-3/4" dia, 11-1/4" l 125.00
Military insignia, 2" dia, 9-1/2" l 125.00
Wood, black ebonized head, metal separator, 11-1/2" l 100.00
Hatpin holder, porcelain
Austrian, hp blue flowers, 5" h 45.00
Bavarian, hexagonal, pastel florals, mkd "Z. S. & Co.," 4-3/4" h 45.00
Germany, yellow roses, 6-1/2" h 90.00
Nippon, pink roses, green leaves, gold trim, 4" h 100.00
Souvenir, Capitol Building, Washington, D.C., 4-1/2" h 125.00

❖ Hats, Lady's (Vintage)

A well-groomed lady used her hat to complete her ensemble. Some vintage hats are large and colorful, while others are a little more demure. There has been a resurgence of hat collecting, perhaps due to popular movies featuring stars in large bonnets. Whatever the reason, our hats are off to those who enjoy this field of collecting.

Reference: Susan Langley, *Vintage Hats and Bonnets*, 1770-1970, Collector Books, 1997.

Felt
Black, small bowl crown, short back brim, trimmed in black ostrich feathers, black ribbon with bow in back, orig label "Yowell Drew Ivey Co., Daytona Beach" 125.00
Brown, wide brim, beige feathers, green netting, 1930s 125.00
Rose, net and chiffon layers, flowers and pearls, wire frame on each side for secure fit, label "Mary Louis Shaker-Shaker Heights" 45.00
Sapphire blue, Art Deco style, small matching bow and netting 40.00
Straw
Black, large brim, fabric crown, orig label "Schiparallei Jr. Paris" 70.00
Black, flowers in pink, rose and white, green leaves, orig label "Neiman Marcus" 40.00
Navy, feathers and veil, small turned up brim, orig label "Gage Brothers & Co., Chicago, New York, Since 1856" 70.00
Velvet, black, red poppies, fully lined, wire in brim, narrow back brim 60.00

❖ Haviland China

Haviland China has an interesting history in that it was founded in America by importer David Haviland, who then moved to Limoges, France, to begin manufacturing and he was quite successful. His sons, Charles and Theodore, split the company in 1892. Theodore went on to open an American division in 1936 and continued to produce dinnerware. The Haviland family sold the firm in 1981.

Reference: Nora Travis, *Evolution of Haviland China Design*, Schiffer Publishing, 2000.

Collectors' Club: Haviland Collectors International Foundation, P.O. Box 802462, Santa Clarita, CA 91380.

For additional listings, see *Warman's Antiques & Collectibles* and *Warman's American Pottery & Porcelain.*

Haviland Limoges bowl with flowers, 8-1/8" x 9-9/16", $45.

Bone dish, turtle dec 65.00
Bowl, hp yellow roses, 8" dia .. 37.50
Butter dish, cov, Gold Band, mkd "Theo Haviland" 48.00
Cake plate, Baltimore Rose, #1151, #1 blank, gold trim 145.00
Chop plate, Chrysanthemum, #88, 11" dia 80.00
Coffee cup, Marseille 25.00
Compote, ftd, reticulated, gold trim 175.00
Creamer and sugar, small pink flowers, scalloped, gold trim.... 65.00
Cup and saucer, Montmery..... 30.00
Dinner service, Gold Band, service for 12........................... 1,000.00
Plate
Blue flowers, green leaves, 7-1/2" dia 15.00
Princess, 9-1/2" dia 24.00
Rajah, mkd "Theo Haviland," 6" dia 8.00
Platter, Baltimore Rose, large, #1151, smooth blank, gold trim 170.00
Relish dish, Marseilles, #48, 8-1/2" dia 30.00
Tea cup and saucer, small blue flowers, green leaves 28.00
Teapot, Baltimore Rose, #1151, #1 blank, missing lid 165.00
Vegetable dish, Marseilles, #9 45.00

❖ Hawaiiana

Aloha! Some collectors are just naturally drawn to colorful Hawaiian objects. Perhaps it's the smiles of the hula girls or their alluring dance. Prices are beginning to escalate for items in this category. Be aware that objects actually made in Hawaii tend to cost more than items imported from Japan.

Bell, Hula Girl, ceramic, "Hawaii" written across skirt, "Made in Japan" sticker, 4-1/2" h......36.00

Charm bracelet, surfer and hula girl, 7 charms, silvertone.........29.00

Dress, lounging, 1960s, Honolulu designer Pomare Tahiti.....60.00

Figurine, hula girl, Josef Originals, International Series, orig Hawaii Poem string tag, 4" h.........80.00

Handkerchief, "Aloha Hawaii," embroidered hula girl, MIB, set of 4....................................30.00

Magazine ad, "Take A Trip," Hawaii Tourist Bureau, 1934, from *Fortune Magazine*....................8.00

Menu, S.S. Lurline, Matson Lines, "Hawaii's Decisive Hour" print by Savage, 1956, 21" x 13-1/2"..59.00

Pillow cover, Honolulu, tropic themes and poem to mother, 17-1/4" sq plus fringe........50.00

Plate
Aloha from Hawaii, Hula maids and other colorful scenes, gold trim, 8" dia.............25.00

Hawaii National Park brochure, $3.

Red Anthurium, from Flowers of Hawaii series, Santa Anita Pottery, 1949, 10-1/4" dia 40.00

Postcard, real-photo
Mauna Kea, unused..........12.00
Pineapples at Harvest Time - Hawaiian Islands, unused 12.00

Record, "Hawaii, Melodies from Paradise," Longines Symphonette Recording Society, presentation set, cover scuffed 13.00

Salt and pepper shakers, figural suitcases, pr...........................24.00

Sheet music
"Aloha Oe: Farewell to Thee," H.M. Queen Liliuokalani, torn 3.00
"Hawaii Will Be Paradise Once More," 1947....................5.00

Scarf, Hawaiian Hula, silk, faded, 35" sq 19.00

Shirt, man's
1960s, Islander 45.00
1970s, Royal Hawaiian 40.00

Stereoview
"Papaya Trees in the Mauna Loa Valley Hawaii," Keystone View Co., #10154.............6.00
"Royal School, Honolulu, Hawaii," Keystone View Co., #10161 ....12.00

Swizzle stick
Hale Koa Hotel on the Beach, Waikiki, 6" l.....................1.00
Kahala Hilton, Honolulu, 6" l 1.00
Spencecliff Restaurant's, 5-1/2" l 1.00

Tin, Hawaiian Coconut Snow, Lihue Kauai, Hawaii, 10-oz..........35.00

Travel brochure, Hawaii Tourist Bureau, Honolulu, 1942, wear, 11" x 8-1/2" 15.50

View-Master reel, Hawaii Five-O, 1973, pack of 3 reels, booklet 22.00

❖ Hazel Atlas

Hazel Glass Company merged with the Atlas Glass & Metal Company in 1902 to form Hazel Atlas. The company, based in Washington, Pennsylvania, aggressively developed ways to automate the glassware industry. Their primary output consisted of tableware, kitchen items, and tumblers.

Red Dots mixing bowl set, Hazel Atlas, 4 bowls, 6-5/8" to 9-1/2" diameter, $100.

References: Gene Florence, *Collectible Glassware from the 40s, 50s, 60s*, 4th ed, Collector Books, 1998; —, *Kitchen Glassware of the Depression Years*, 5th ed, Collector Books, 1995 (1997 value update).

Bowl, cobalt, metal holder....... 60.00

Cereal bowl, Cowboy, white opaque glass, black cowboy scenes 25.00

Custard cup, green 5.00

Berry bowl, mkd "Hazel Atlas," 4-1/4" dia 4.50

Child's mug, animal characters, bottom mkd "H/A," some wear to dec, 3" h.......................... 22.00

Creamer, Aurora, blue, 4-1/4" h 25.00

Dinner plate, Moderntone, pink, 1940s, 9" dia...................... 7.50

Drinking glass, frosted, Florida souvenir, yellow state image, sailfish, alligator, palm tree and flamingo, 5" h.................. 12.00

Gravy boat, Florentine #2, yellow 65.00

Lemon reamer, green 20.00

Mixing bowl, Ivy, nested set of 4 .... 80.00

Salad plate, Moderntone, mint green, 1940s, 6-3/4" dia...... 5.50

Salt and pepper shakers, grapes, Hazel Atlas symbol on bottom, some wear to tops, pr 10.00

Seltzer bottle, clear, ruby flashed, white painted flowers, chrome fittings, red painted wooden knob, 14" h 100.00

Sherbet, Moderntone, pink, early
   1950s 5.00
Snack set, cup and oblong plate with
   cup ring
   Capri Seashell, light blue...18.00
   Seashell, crystal.................22.50
Sugar bowl, cov, Ovide, black, 2
   handles................................5.00
Syrup pitcher, green, tin lid, 6" h
   ....70.00
Tom and Jerry set, 2-qt punchbowl,
   six 6-oz mugs 75.00

❖ Heisey Glass

Heisey Glass is a name most collectors recognize. That H in a diamond logo is easy to spot. But, did you know that Heisey didn't mark any glass until 1901 and then used paper labels for years before starting to use the diamond mark. The Heisey Glass Company was known for its brilliant colors and excellent quality crystal.

References: Neila Bredehoft, *Collector's Encyclopedia of Heisey Glass, 1925–1938*, Collector Books, 1986 (1997 value update); Shirley Dunbar, *Heisey Glass, The Early Years: 1896-1924*, Krause Publications, 2000; Gene Florence, *Elegant Glassware of the Depression Era*, 7th ed, Collector Books, 1997.

Periodicals: *Heisey Herald*, P.O. Box 23, Clinton, MD 20735; *The Heisey News,* 169 W Church St., Newark, OH, 43055; *The Newscaster*, P.O. Box 102, Plymouth, OH 44865.

Collectors' Clubs: Bay State Heisey Collectors Club, 354 Washington St, East Walpole, MA 02032; Heisey Collectors of America, 169 W Church St, Newark, OH 43055; National Capital Heisey Collectors, P.O. Box 23, Clinton, MD 20735; Southern Illinois Diamond H Seekers, 1203 N Yale, O'Fallon, IL 62269.
Reproduction Alert.
For additional listings, see *Warman's Antiques & Collectibles* and *Warman's Glass.*
Animal
   Goose, wings half up 90.00
   Plug horse, Oscar............115.00
   Sparrow 140.00

Heisey pitcher, 7" high, $95.

Ashtray, Old Sandwich, #1404, moongleam, individual size70.00
Basket, #480.........................225.00
Bowl, Rose, 13" dia, shallow ...40.00
Cake plate, Rose, pedestal ...325.00
Candelabra, Ridgleigh, bobeches and prisms, 7" h, pr 140.00
Candlesticks, pr
   #18, 9" h.........................100.00
   Lariat, 2-lite 60.00
Candy dish, cov, recessed panels, crystal and black enamel, gold dec....................................45.00
Champagne
   Minuet 35.00
   Tudor..................................20.00
Cheese comport, ftd, Crystolite 25.00
Cheese plate, Crystolite, 2 handles, 8" dia 45.00
Cocktail
   Lariat, moonglo cutting.......15.00
   Rosalie...............................12.00
Creamer and sugar, Twist, Sahara 170.00
Cruet
   Old Sandwich.....................60.00
   Pleat and Panel, flamingo..65.00
Coaster, Colonial, 4-1/2" dia......5.00
Cocktail
   Colonial.............................14.00
   Steeplechase, Sahara........90.00
Cup and saucer, Empress, yellow 42.00
Goblet
   Narrow Flute 30.00
   Provincial 19.50
   Tudor..................................17.50
Iced tea tumbler, ftd, Plantation 75.00

Jug, Queen Anne, dolphin ftd, silver overlay 125.00
Nappy, Colonial, 6-1/4" dia 4.00
Plate
   Colonial, 4-3/4" dia..............6.50
   Empress, yellow, 8" dia 24.00
   Orchid Etch, 7-1/4" dia 24.00
Punch cup, Crystolite.............10.00
Sandwich plate, center handle, Rose 225.00
Sherbet, Orchid Etch 24.00
Spring salad bowl, Crystolite .. 90.00
Tankard, Greek Key 265.00
Toothpick holder, Waldorf Astoria 115.00
Tumbler, ftd, Rose Etch 50.00
Vase, Prison Stripe, cupped, 5" h 65.00
Wine, Orchid Etch...................75.00

⭐ Hess Trucks and Oil Company Promos

We've got Hess Gas to thank for starting a wonderful line of collectible gas-related vehicles. Remember to save the original boxes and packaging for these collectible toys.
1971, Hess............................ 800.00
1980, Hess............................ 300.00
1984, 1986, and 1987, Hess each.................................. 150.00
1990, Hess.............................. 55.00
1992, BP Oil, tanker............... 30.00
1992, Exxon, tanker............... 95.00
1993, BP Oil, car carrier 30.00
1993, Exxon, Mack truck 25.00
1993, Phillips 66, Marx tanker bank 30.00
1993, Sunoco, Marx tanker bank 40.00
1994, Citgo, tanker, orig card 150.00
1994, Mobil, Marx tanker bank 45.00
1994, Texaco, tanker 50.00
1995, BP Oil, transporter and cars 35.00
1995, Exxon, transporter and cars 45.00
1995, Sinclair Refining, tanker 80.00
1995, Texaco, tanker 30.00
1996, Crown Petroleum, fire truck 25.00
1996, Texaco, tanker, Olympics 30.00

1997, Exxon, tanker, chrome...25.00
1997, Gate, wrecker................25.00
1997, Sunoco, racing team trans-
    porter...................................25.00
1997, Texaco, 95th anniversary train
    set 300.00
1998, Crown Petroleum, tanker
    ....30.00
1998, Marathon, tractor trailer
    ....45.00
1998, Texaco, Fire Chief tank
    ....55.00
1999, Exxon, wrecker, gold 35.00
1999, Hess 40.00
1999, Texaco, Millennium tanker
    ....40.00
2000, Hess 35.00
2000, Mobil, car carrier............40.00
2000, Texaco, center tanker....40.00

❖ Higgins Glass

Working in a Chicago studio, Frances Stewart Higgins and Michael Higgins designed some exciting glassware in the early 1950s. Dearborn Glass provided space for them between 1958 and 1964 when their works were mass-produced. Their unique double layered glass was usually signed with a gold screened signature. By 1966, they returned to their own studio and changed their focus a bit. Pieces made after 1970s have an engraved signature on the back. The company is still in business today.

Ashtray
    Green and gold, 7-1/2" sq
        ....260.00
    Jeweled, implosion plate, gold
        highlights, 8-1/2" dia ...185.00
Bowl
    12" dia, green and yellow stripes,
        gold signature 275.00
    14-1/2" dia, Dottie, six layers of
        glass, tree formation,
        engraved signature 950.00
Charger, summer season dec,
    etched signature, 15" dia
        ....550.00
Dish, ftd, daisies dec, 8-1/2" dia
        ....100.00
Plate
    7-1/2" dia, pink, blue and yellow
        stripes, etched signature with
        stick man logo 100.00
    9-1/2" dia, Arabesque pattern,
        ruffled edge, central flower,
        engraved signature 325.00

Platter, purple ground, green and
    light purple stripes, gold signa-
    ture, orig paper label, 12-1/2" l
    ....115.00
Tray
    Dinner Dwarf, black and cara-
        mel, raised stickman signa-
        ture, 5" sq....................175.00
    Pocket watches, gold signature,
        10" x 14".....................285.00
Vase, turquoise blue, wide flat rim
    with ruffled edge, sgd under rim,
    3-1/2" h 325.00

★ Historic Recreations

Most of us were introduced to historic recreations such as Colonial Williamsburg during field trips and family vacations. The products made at these sites, along with the souvenirs these attractions spawned, are finding new life in the collections of historic-minded individuals.

Booklet
    Edison Institute Museum &
        Greenfield Village, 1940s, 68
        pgs 2.50
    Historic Williamsburg, Virginia,
        1951, 6 pgs, 8" x 9".........1.00
    Official Guidebook & Map to
        Colonial Williamsburg, 1953,
        104 pgs 4.50

Williamsburg Pottery vase, 5" high, $10.

Brochure, *Jamestown, Virginia*, 2-
    fold, published by National Park
    Service & Association for the
    Preservation of Virginia Antiqui-
    ties, 1957, 8-1/2" x 24"........ 1.00
Candlestick, chamberstick-type, Wil-
    liamsburg Pottery, gray with blue
    decor, 4-1/4" h, 2-3/4" dia ... 7.00
Pipe, red clay, Jamestown Colony,
    mkd "1607 Jamestown 1907"
    and "Patented July 31, 1906,"
    2" h 75.00
Sampler, cross-stitch, Colonial Will-
    iamsburg replica, dated 1699-
    1779, stain, 12" x 10"...... 200.00
Tankard, pewter, Williamsburg Res-
    toration, Stieff Pewter, 4-3/4" h
    .... 50.00
Ticket, student-military, Colonial Will-
    iamsburg, 1956, 3-1/2" x 6-1/4"
    .... 2.50

❖ Hobby Horses

Children love hobby horses. From primitive homemade wooden creations to exquisite professionally made examples, these stick-and-head toys were loved and ridden for hours.

Also see Rocking Horses in this edition.

Cisco Kid, played-with cond.... 30.00
Colt 45, vinyl head, wood stick,
    played-with cond................ 5.00
Mobo, c1920 .... 475.00
Rich Toys, played-with cond ... 15.00
Snoopy, vinyl head, 36" l wood stick,
    played-with cond................ 5.00

❖ Hockey Cards

As with baseball, basketball, and football trading cards, hockey cards are plentiful. A good price guide is essential to understanding the sporting card market.

Reference: *Standard Catalog of Football, Basketball and Hockey Cards*, 2nd ed, Krause Publications, 1996.

Periodicals: *Sports Cards Magazine & Price Guide*, 700 E State St, Iola, WI 54990; *Sports Collectors Digest*, 700 E State St, Iola, WI 54990.

Donruss, 1997, complete set .. 20.00

Fleer Ultra Series I, 1992-93, set of 250 cards 11.00
McDonald's, 1991, set of 31 cards 11.50
Score, 1990-91, set of 440 cards 8.00
Topps
    1987, complete set 115.00
    1990-91, set of 396 cards.... 7.00
    1992-93, set of 396 cards.... 7.00
Upper Deck, 1995, complete... 55.00

❖ Hockey Memorabilia

Whether you're into field hockey or ice hockey, flea markets are a great place to score a goal with this collectible.

Book, *Hockey's Great Rivalries*, Stan Fischler, Random House, 1974, hardcover, 151 pgs.... 6.00
Comic book, *Wayne Gretzky*, 1990s 7.00
Doll, Kermit the Frog NHL doll, McDonald's, 12" h 10.00
Figurine, Rod Gilbert, by Sports Impressions, 1994, limited edition of 3,950 pcs, NRFB, 6" h 35.00
Mask, PCI, autographed by Patrick Roy 70.00
Plaque, wooden, "Wayne Gretzky, Mr. Offense, The Great One," with Premier card of Gretzky playing for the Los Angeles Kings, 6" x 4-1/4" 10.00
Puck, autographed Mario Lemieux 60.00

National Hockey League puck, Art Ross Tyer, $15.

Eric Lindros 28.00
Sign, New England Whalers, stenciled, shows sperm whale and boat, 1976, made by Hitchcock Furniture Co., 18" x 24" ...125.00
Starting Linuep figure
    Ed Belfour, 1998 ....12.50
    Dominik Hasek, 1998.........16.50
    Gordie Howe, 1995, Timeless Legends 10.00
    Brian Leetch, 1994.............15.00
    Mark Messier, 1996............12.50
    Felix Potvin, 1998 ....12.50
    Joe Sakic, 1996 ....17.50
    Brendan Shanahan, 1996..10.00
Toy, Hockey Smurf, 1979.........28.00

❖ Holiday Collectibles

Holidays have long been commemorated through a variety of collectibles, from postcards to cookie cutters. Here's a sampling of what's available.

Reference: Lissa Bryan Smith and Richard Smith, *Holiday Collectibles*, Krause Publications, 1998.

Periodicals: *Pyrofax Magazine,* P.O. Box 2010, Saratoga, CA 95070; *St. Patrick Notes,* 10802, Greenscreek Dr, Suite 703, Houston, TX 77070.

For additional listings, see Christmas, Easter, and Halloween in this edition.

Bookend, cast metal, Thanksgiving motif, 4-1/2" h, pr 40.00
Candy box, shamrock shape, cardboard, green, litho shamrocks on top, 8-1/2" h 17.50
Candy container, turkey, composition, metal legs, removable head, 5" h 65.00
Cookie cutter, aluminum, turkey, 3" x 4" 5.00
Nodder, Irish boy, bisque, Germany, 3" h 48.00
Pinback button
    "Carter/Mondale Campaign Kickoff, Labor Day 1976" green on white with red donkey caricature, red stars, 1-3/4" dia 12.00
    "Labor Day March for Human and Labor Rights, Sept 6, 1976, Raleigh, North Carolina," black and white sketch of people with signs, 3" dia 14.00

Thanksgiving postcard, two turkeys in dirigible, embossed, $7.50.

    "Labor Day, Sept. 4, 1989," Mickey Mouse 10.00
Plate
    Ceramic, "The Fourth of July," Americana Holidays Collection, 1st in series, 1978, Edwin M. Knowles China Co., Bradford Exchange, 8-1/2" dia 30.00
    Sterling silver, Thanksgiving, artist Stevan Dohanad, 1st annual, 1972, Franklin Mint, orig box, 8" dia.............. 45.00
Postcard
    Independence Day, 2 Victorian children with firecrackers, 1910 postmark................ 8.00
    New Year, elves and clock, 1910 .... 3.50
    New Year, calendar design, angels, 1911 .... 18.00
    Thanksgiving, Pilgrim child, by Whitney, 1919 postmark 6.00
    Thanksgiving, Clapsaddle, Pilgrim child with gun and turkey, 1918 .... 30.00
Puzzle, "First Thanksgiving," Big Star Picture Puzzle, orig box, 10" x 13-1/2" 15.00
Tip tray, litho tin, Thanksgiving motif of boy with turkey, C.D. Kenny, Baltimore.......................... 90.00

❖ Holly Hobbie

This cute country gal first appeared on the scene in the late 1970s, spreading her special brand of sunshine for several years thereafter. Holly Hobbie and her friends often had inspirational messages.

Bell, annual, bisque 40.00
Brunch bag, vinyl, zipper closure, Aladdin Industries, 1978, orig thermos 65.00
Children's play dishes, plastic, large plate, 7 smaller plates, 2 mugs, mkd "Aluminum Specialty, Chilton Toys, Manitowoc, Wis.," 10 pcs 25.00
Coffeepot, 1973, 8" h 35.00
Doll
    Amy, 15" h 30.00
    Fancy, MIB 25.00
Figure
    Holly's Little Friend, 1971, MIB 50.00
    Robbie, seated with toy train 25.00
Halloween Costume, Ben Cooper, American Greetings, small child size, worn 15.00
Limited edition plate, Mother's Day, 10-1/2" dia 35.00

Holly Hobbie Coca-Cola glass, "Friendship makes the rough road smooth," 6" high, $3.

Lunch box, metal, several different scenes, 1979 .... 35.00
Plaque, "Love is a Way of Smiling with Your Heart," ceramic, 1973 .... 18.00
Teapot, white porcelain, green trim, green and brown Holly, "Tea for two is twice as nice," 5-3/4" h 32.00
Tidbit tray, 3 tiers, white porcelain, yellow, gold, orange and black Holly with cat and flowers, "Happiness is having someone to care for," gold trim, gold metal handle, base mkd "Holly Hobbie Porcelain, World Wide Arts, Inc., Cleveland, Ohio," 1972, 13" h 45.00
Toy sewing machine, plastic, mkd "Durham Industries," 1975 .... 20.00

✪ Holt-Howard

The partnership of brothers John and Robert J. Howard with A. Grant Holt created an import company in 1948 in Stamford, Connecticut. Robert designed some novelty ceramic containers that proved to be very successful.

Reference: Walter Dworkin, *Price Guide to Holt-Howard Collectibles and Related Ceramic Wares of the '50s and '60s*, Krause Publications, 1998.

Candle climbers, pr
    Angels, Noel 60.00
    Mice 25.00
    Santa, orig box 35.00
Candleholders, pr
    Angel 28.00
    Santa 28.00
Christmas angels 40.00
Cocktail cherries 90.00
Cocktail olives 90.00
Ketchup, Pixieware 70.00
Salt and pepper shakers, pr, Pixie 400.00
Sewing box, Kitty, tongue tape measure 200.00
String holder, cat head 80.00
Baby feeding dish, warmer, horse, orig tail stopper, paper label and black stamp mark, 1958, 8-3/4" l, 5" h 195.00
Christmas ornament, Santa, paper, boxed set of 6 .... 24.00

My Fair Lady head vase, Christmas theme, 1959, 4-1/8" h, missing earrings, $55.

Drinking glass, Santa, mkd "1959 Holt Howard," 3" h, 2" dia, some paint missing, set of 4 .... 25.00
Jam 'n Jelly condiment jar, Rooster, mkd, c1962, 4-1/2" dia, small chips to paint 45.00
Lady's head vase, orig Christmas ball dangle earrings, holly, necklace, paper label, 1959, 4" h, 4" w, small nick on hair 80.00
Snack plate, pie crust edge, indent for cup, matte finish, stamped "1962 Holt Howard," foil Japan sticker, 8-1/2" dia 7.50
String holder, cat, orig sticker, 4-3/4" h 110.00

❖ Home Front Collectibles

While the "boys" were off to World War II, there was a real effort here at home to influence those left behind to contribute to the war effort. Today, these items and their powerful messages are becoming choice collectibles.

Reference: Martin Jacobs, *World War II Homefront Collectibles*, Krause Publications, 2000.

Bookmark, "Prevent Forest Fires," stiff orange paper, Hitler and Hirohito at top with blazing forest fire in background, US Dept of Agriculture, black and white reverse with text, 2-1/2" x 7" 45.00
Game, "V for Victory" 40.00

"Welcome Home Our Heroes" pinback button, 1-1/4" diameter, $5.

Jewelry
    V-shaped victory pin, sterling sil-
        ver with 30 rhinestones,
        1-1/2" h, 1-1/4" w 60.00
    "Sweetheart" in script, sterling
        silver, gold-plated and
        red/white/blue Bakelite, orig
        box, 1-1/2" sq 102.50
Matchbook, V for Victory, War Bond
    promotion, Diamond Match Co.,
    unused, 1-1/2" x 3-3/4" 12.00
Membership card, Slap-A-Jap, Char-
    ter Member, black-and-white
    cartoon of Uncle Sam slapping
    Japanese soldier to ground,
    unused, 2-1/2" x 4" 50.00
Puzzle, "Keep 'Em Flying," fighter
    planes, Perfect Picture Puzzle,
    "For Victory Buy United States
    Savings Bonds and Stamps"
    logo, 19-1/2" x 15-1/2" 50.00
Sticker, "Salvage Will Win The War,"
    cartoon image of Japanese sol-
    dier choking on "v" of word "sal-
    vage," 1-1/2" x 2" 25.00
Window banner, fabric panel, printed
    in red, white, blue and bright
    gold, loop for hanging, 8-1/2" x
    12" 35.00

❖ Homer Laughlin

The Homer Laughlin Company is another dinnerware manufacturer that helped make East Liverpool, Ohio, a busy place. This company was producing white ware by the late 1880s. When the firm was sold to a group of investors from Pitts-burgh, expansion soon followed. New plants were built in Ohio and West Virginia, and the dinnerware lines increased. Besides giving us such interesting patterns as Fiesta, and Harlequin, the firm also designed Kitchen Kraft and Riviera, plus thousands of others designs.

Periodical: *The Laughlin Eagle*, 1270 63rd Terrace S, St. Petersburg, FL 33705.

For additional listings, see *Warman's Americana & Collectibles* and *Warman's American Pottery & Porcelain.*

Baker, Mexicana, oval 25.00
Bowl, Cavalier, egg shell, numbered,
    set of 4 .... 20.00
Butter, cov, Virginia Rose, jade
    .... 80.00
Casserole, cov, individual, Conchita
    .... 225.00
Casserole, cov, large
    Conchita 125.00
    Mexicana 145.00
Cereal bowl, ftd, Rhythm, char-
    treuse, 5-1/2" dia 5.00
Cup, Rhythm, forest green or gray
    .... 7.00
Deep plate, Mexicana 45.00
Dessert bowl, Rhythm, yellow, 5-1/4"
    dia 3.00
Fruit bowl, Mexicana 15.00
Nappy, Rhythm, yellow, 8-3/4" dia
    .... 18.00
Pie baker, Mexicana 37.50
Plate, Virginia Rose, 9" dia 7.50
Platter, Rhythm, yellow, 11-1/2" l
    .... 12.00
Soup bowl, Rhythm, yellow 9.00
Tray, Virginia Rose 30.00

Rhythm pattern gravy boat, Homer Laughlin, 9" long, $15.

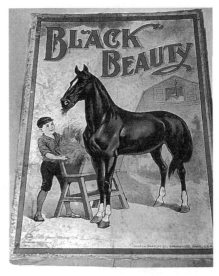

Black Beauty game, Milton Bradley Co., $65.

❖ Horse Collectibles

Some collectors specialize in items related to the care of horses, others search for items used for riding, and some prefer items with images of horses.

Bank, Beauty, cast iron, 4-1/2" h
    .... 300.00
Bells, worn leather strap with over
    40 nickel bells, tug hook . 225.00
Bit, eagle, mkd "G. S. Garcia"
    .... 775.00
Book, *Quarter Horses: Story of Two
    Centuries*, Robert M. Denhardt,
    Univ. of Oklahoma Press, 1967,
    192 pgs 12.00
Brooch, horseshoe shape, flat-cut
    Bohemian garnets, gold filled
    .... 310.00
Clock, brass horse standing next to
    western saddle, wood base,
    United 170.00
Contest flyer, Dan Patch, illus
    .... 28.00
Cookie jar, rocking horse, Regal
    .... 285.00
Curry comb, tin back, leather han-
    dle, early 1900s 45.00
Game, Pony Express, cast-metal
    horses, 1940s 85.00
Lasso, horsehair 135.00
Magazine, *Western Horseman*, vol
    1, #1, 1935 .... 30.00

Men's brush, horse head figural handle 10.00
Mug, Clydesdales, Budweiser, Christmas, Ceramarte, 1985 ....50.00
Postcard, bucking bronco, cowboy flying off, rodeo in Prescott, Ariz., 1920s 15.00
Rosette, brass, Civil War.........25.00
Saddle, McClellan type, large fenders for leg protection, early 1900s 900.00
Saddle blanket, Navajo, early 1900s 950.00
Spurs, Crockett, arrow shank 700.00
Tray, Genessee Twelve Horse Ale, horse team illus, 12" dia .. 115.00

❖ Horse Racing

Man's love for competition has long been reflected in horse racing. Here's a sample of some collectibles on today's market.

Collectors' Club: Sport of Kings Soc, 1406 Annen Ln, Madison, WI 53711.
Also see Kentucky Derby Glasses in this edition.
Ashtray
    Count Fleet, sgd by Lynn Bogue Hunt, ceramic, 5-1/4" sq 30.00
    Kentucky Derby, 1976, Galt House, Louisville, smoke glass, 7" dia 30.00
    Kentucky Derby, 1977, Galt House, Louisville, ceramic, 6-3/4" dia........................30.00

Tile, "Favonius, Derby Winner 1871," ATCO, 6-1/8" sq. $30.

Pinback button
    "Geo. Taylor, Jockey, M. McLoughlin Colors," blue and gold, High Admiral Cigarettes back paper, early 1900s 35.00
    "Loates, Celebrated English Jockey," red, white and pale blue racing clothes, American Pepsin Gum back paper, early 1900s 25.00
    "Silky Sullivan Winner", multicolor, white ground, blue letters, c1950 ....20.00
    Topeka Derby Day, Sept 13, 1904, sepia...................20.00
Print, Currier & Ives, "The Grand Racer Kington, by Spendthrift," 1891, unmatted, unframed 475.00
Sheet music, Dan Patch March 40.00
Soup cup, china, "Beautiful Wheeling Downs," mkd "Shenango Restaurant China Soup Cup," 3-1/2" h, 3-1/4" dia 30.00
Souvenir plate, Jorge Velasquez, Meadowlands jockey, Belcrest Fine China, copyright 1983 by Daily Racing Form, Inc, 8-1/2" dia......................................25.00
Trophy, silver, typical 50.00

⚙ Hot Wheels

Harry Bradley, an automotive designer; Howard Newman, a Mattel designer; Elliot Handler, chairman of Mattel; and Jack Ryan, also of Mattel, joined forces to produce the first diecast Hot Wheels cars in 1968.

References: Bob Parker, *The Complete Book of Hot Wheels*, 4th ed, Schiffer Publishing, 2000; Michael Thomas Strauss, *Tomart's Price Guide to Hot Wheels*, 3rd ed, Tomart Publications, 1998.

Periodicals: *Hot Wheels Newsletter*, 26 Madera Ave, San Carlos, CA 94070; *Toy Cars & Vehicles*, 700 E State St, Iola, WI 54900; *Toy Shop*, 700 E State St, Iola, WI 54900.

Accessories
Case, Sizzlers Race 75.00
Full Curve Accessory Pak 12.00
Gas Pumper, Mattel.................12.00
Snake Mountain Challenge 20.00

Cars and Trucks
Beach Bomb, green 75.00
Bulldozer, #34 .... 28.00
Camaro Z28, #33, red, chrome base 46.00
Chevy, '57, Ultra Hots, #47 ....110.00
Corvette, billionth 10.00
Custom Firebird, blue 40.00
Delivery Truck, #52 .... 32.00
Designer Dreams.................... 17.50
Dump Truck, #38, steel bed...... 7.00
Earthmover, #16 .... 85.00
Ferrari, #312, red enamel 50.00
Fire Truck, 1980...................... 2.00
Fireworks 20.00
Fleetside, purple 35.00
Ford Bronco, #56, turquoise ... 18.00
Golden Knights VW Bug 20.00
GT Racer, #598, 1995, NRFP... 3.00
Hard Rock Café I 25.00
Jiffy Lube, milk truck, red 10.00
John Glenn 8.00
Marrow Foundation 30.00
McDonald's, Tattoo Machine, 1993, NRFP 3.00
Mercedes 500 SL, 1997, NRFP 26.00
Penske 70 Mustang Mach 1 ... 15.00
Penske S'Cool bus, silver 13.00
Porsche, 50th anniversary 39.00
Tail Gunner, #29..................... 75.00
Tractor Trailer, 1979................. 1.00
Van de Kamps, mail in premium, NRFP, Hiway Hauler Truck, 1996 .... 24.00

Set
25th anniversary, 1993, NRFP, 5 cars 38.00
30th anniversary, 30 cars...... 150.00
Christmas, 1999..................... 55.00
Christmas, 2000..................... 55.00
Drive-In, 3 cars 30.00
Holiday, 1995 .... 80.00
Lowrider................................. 25.00
Muscle Cars, Set #1, 2 cars.... 15.00
Night at the Races 18.00

❖ Howdy Doody

"What time is it kids? Howdy Doody Time!" Every Howdy Doody Show started with Buffalo Bob Smith asking the Peanut Gallery that question. It was a great kids show, and today's collectors are happily searching for items relating to Howdy, Mr. Bluster, Clarabelle, and the other characters.

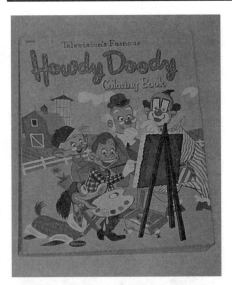

Howdy Doody Coloring Book,
Whitman, 1953, unused, $35.

Collectors Club: Doodyville Historical Society, 8 Hunt Ct, Flemington, NJ 08822.
Bath mitt, terry cloth, 8-1/4".....35.00
Book
  Howdy Doody's Circus Book, Little Golden Book, 1950 ..35.00
  Howdy Doody & Santa Claus, Little Golden Book, 1955, 1st ed 32.00
Comic book, *Howdy Doody,* #3 1950, cover damage 8.00
Cookie jar, Purinton Pottery, 9-3/4" h 900.00
Cup, yellow plastic, Howdy Doody's face at top, Gotham Ware 30.00
Game, Howdy Doody Card Game, Russell Mfg. Co., orig box 71.00
Jelly glass, "Here Comes Music for Doodyville Circus," Welch's, variation with no animals in circus wagon, early 1950s 35.00
Key chain, 3-dimensional, NRFP 4.50
Marionette
  Howdy Doody, composition, 14" h...........................475.00
  Clarabelle, new strings, 14" h 300.00
  Princess Winter, Spring, Summer, Fall, composition, cracked, 14" 500.00
Night light, head moves, wear, 6" h 275.00

Pinback button,
  "It's Howdy Doody Time!," orange and white...........15.00
  "Official Howdy Doody Button," orig card, 3-1/2" 25.00
Toy, Howdy Doody Flub-A-Dub push-up toy, #177, Kohner, tail missing, 5-1/4" h..............245.00

❖ Hubley Toys

Hubley Manufacturing was founded in Lancaster, Pennsylvania, in 1894. The company's first toys were made of cast iron. By 1940, cast iron had been phased out and replaced with other metals and plastic.

Periodicals: *Toy Cars & Models,* 700 E State St, Iola, WI 54990; *Toy Shop,* 700 E State St, Iola, WI 54990.
Bookends, Hunting Dog, bronze, orig paint, c1925, 4-1/2" h, pr 195.00
Cap gun
  Army .45-caliber pistol, nickel-plated, brown checkered grips, finish, 1945, 6-1/2" l 75.00
  Hawk .45-caliber automatic, plastic pearlized grip, 5-1/4" l 45.00
  Pet.......................................15.00
Doorstop, Lilies of the Valley, cast iron, mkd 146, 10-1/2" h, 7-1/2" w 250.00
Toy, airplane
  Single prop, die-cast, orange and yellow, folding wings, 11" wingspan 145.00

Bell Telephone truck, white metal, painted olive green, Hubley, $50.

U.S. Army, retractable wheels, paint chips, tires cracked, 7-1/2" wingspan, 6" l..... 75.00
P-38, paint chips, 7-1/2" x 8 1/2" 50.00
Toy, automobile
  Car of the Future, late 1930s, tires need replaced, 5-1/4" l 65.00
  Milk Cream Truck, 1930s, 1 tire missing, paint chips, 3-3/4" l 365.00
  Racer, cast iron, c1934-36, orig paint, new tires, 5-3/4" l 250.00
  Railway Express truck, 1930s, paint chips, tires cracked 300.00

❖ Hull Pottery

In 1905, Addis E. Hull purchased the Acme Pottery Company in Crooksville, Ohio. In 1917, the A.E. Hull Pottery Company commenced producing art pottery, novelties, stoneware and kitchenware, including the Little Red Riding Hood line that would become one of their best sellers. Most items had a matte finish with shades of pink and blue or brown as the dominant colors.

Following a disastrous flood and fire in 1950, J. Brandon Hull reopened the factory in 1952 as the Hull Pottery Company. These newer pieces usually have a glossy finish and tend to have a more modern look. The company currently produces items for florists, e.g. the Regal and Floraline lines.

References: Susan *and* Al Bagdade, *Warman's American Pottery and Porcelain,* Wallace-Homestead, 1994; Barbara Loveless Gick-Burke, *Collector's Guide to Hull Pottery,* Collector Books, 1993; Joan Hull, *Hull, The Heavenly Pottery,* 6th ed, self-published, 1999; Brenda Roberts, *The Ultimate Encyclopedia of Hull Pottery,* Collector Books, 1995; Mark and Ellen Supnick, *Collecting Hull Pottery's Little Red Riding Hood,* rev ed, L-W Books, 1998.

Periodical: *Hull Pottery Newsletter,* 7768 Meadow Dr, Hillsboro, MO 60350.

Bow Knot wall pocket, Hull Pottery, $135.

Collectors' Club: Hull Pottery Assoc, 11023 Tunnel Hill NE, New Lexington, OH 43764

For additional listings, also see *Warman's Americana & Collectibles.*

Coaster/ashtray, gingerbread man 20.00

Cornucopia
    Blossom Flite, pink and black, 12" l 105.00
    Ebbtide, Mermaid on Shell, rose and turquoise glaze, 7-1/2" h, 9" w 200.00

Head vase, Newborn, #92, 5-3/4" h 65.00

Pitcher, Magnolia, yellow matte glaze, #5, 7" h 185.00

Planter, Parrot 60.00

Salt and pepper shakers, pr
    Apple 25.00
    Mushroom, 3-3/4" h 20.00

Tea set, Blossom Flite, teapot with lid, creamer, sugar with lid 200.00

Teapot, House and Garden, 5-1/4" h 30.00

Tray, gingerbread man, brown 65.00

Vase
    Art Stoneware, 40-H-7, cracks, 6-5/8" h 90.00
    Bow-Knot, B10, 10-1/2" h 495.00
    Magnolia, blue and rose matte glaze, #1, 8-1/2" h 225.00
    Magnolia, blue and rose matte glaze, #12, 6-1/2" h 95.00
    Serenade, pastels, 8-1/2" h 100.00
    Wildflower, rose shading to yellow, W5, 6-1/2" h 95.00

Woodland Gloss, W15 double bud vase, 2-tone green, 8-1/2" h 150.00

Wall pocket, Sunglow, whisk broom shape, #82, 8-1/2" h 125.00

Window box, Woodland Gloss, rose shading to lime-green, W14, 4" h, 10" l 80.00

❖ Hummels

Based on original drawings by Berta Hummel, these charming children have delighted collectors for generations. Production of her figurines started in 1935.

References: Carl F. Luckey, *Luckey's Hummel Figurines and Plates*, 11th ed, Krause Publications, 1997; Robert L. Miller, *Hummels 1978-1998: 20 Years of Miller on Hummel Columns*, Collector News, 1998.

Collectors' Clubs: Hummel Collector's Club, 1261 University Dr, Yardley, PA 19067; M.I. Hummel Club, Goebel Plaza, Rte 31, P.O. Box 11, Pennington, NJ 08534.

Annual plate, Singing Lesson, 1979 .... 50.00

Annual Bell, bas relief, 3rd ed, 1980, MIB 70.00

Candleholder, Silent Night, #54, incised crown mark, orig candle 800.00

Postman, 110, 5-1/4" high, $125.

Telling Her Secret, full bee mark, 196, 6-3/4" high, $170.

Christmas plate, 1st ed, 1971, orig box, 7-1/2" dia 720.00

Figure
    Apple Tree Girl, #141/I, 6" h 290.00
    Book Worm, #3/I 490.00
    Chicken Licken 240.00
    Crossroads, #331, 6-3/4" h 360.00
    Doll Mother, stylized bee mark 135.00
    Farewell 325.00
    Friend or Foe, #434 .... 285.00
    Good Shepherd, #42/0, incised crown mark, full bee, 6-1/4" h 600.00
    Happy Birthday, #176/0, 6" h 245.00
    Holy Child, #70, incised crown mark, full bee 600.00
    Just Resting 175.00
    Letter To Santa Claus, #340 .... 350.00
    Mischief Maker 290.00
    Playmates, #580/0 .... 200.00
    Sensitive Hunter 240.00
    She Loves Me, She Loves Me Not 225.00
    Strolling Along, #5, full bee mark, 5-3/4" h 550.00

Hummel look-alike figurines, 3-1/2" high, pair, $12.

❖ Hummel Look-Alikes

A number of companies have produced figures that resemble the more-expensive, popular Hummels. Always check for the familiar Hummel mark, but don't be surprised to find another maker's identification mark or label.

Boy, standing
    Hands behind back 15.00
    Next to fence 20.00
Girl, standing
    Holding basket 17.50
    Reading book 15.00
    With cat, 1973, Avon 10.00

❖ Hunting

Flea markets make great hunting, whether you're looking for big game or small treasures. Substitute a camera for the usual rifle or trap, and bring along a bag to tote your catch in.

Periodical: *Sporting Collector's Monthly*, P.O. Box 305, Camden Wyoming, DE 19934.

Collectors' Clubs: Call & Whistle Collectors Assoc, 2839 E 26th Place, Tulsa, OK 74114; Callmakers & Collectors Assoc of America, 137 Kingswood Dr, Clarksville, TN 37043.

Book
    Handling Your Hunting Dog, 3rd ed, by J. Earl Bufkin, Purina Mills, 1942, 64 pgs 15.00
    The Story of American Hunting and Firearms by the editors of Outdoor Life, McGraw-Hill, 1959, 172 pgs 10.00
Call
    Duck, Herter's orig box 40.00
    Turkey, orig box 35.00
Charger, hunt scene, Royal Stafford, 13" dia 60.00
Figurine, hunting dogs, Royal Dux, 8" h, 10-1/2" w 325.00
License
    Deer, New York State, 1936, pin-back style 35.00

Game, New York State, 1918, red and white, serial number in blue, brass lapel stud fastener, 1-1/2" dia 75.00
Magazine, *Hunting and Fishing*, April 1935 .... 24.00
Photograph
    Hunter with ducks, hand-tinted, dated 1930, framed, 12-1/8" x 19-1/4" 20.00
    Hunting club members posing with shotguns, 6" x 8" 145.00
Postcard, exaggeration, "Salted," real-photo postcard of hunter salting tail of huge rabbit, W. H. Martin, 1909 postmark 15.00
Poster, "Remington Game Load Game," shows various wildlife, 26" x 18-1/2" 200.00
Watch fob, Dead Shot, brass rim, multicolor celluloid insert, reverse inscribed "Dead Shot Smokeless Powder Manufactured by American Powder Mills, Boston, Mass.," 1920s 175.00

1909 postcard, woman with gun, $5.

For exciting collecting trends and newly expanded areas look for the following symbols:

✪ Hot Topic
★ New Warman's Listing

(May have been in another Warman's title.)

❖ Ice Cream Collectibles

Cold and creamy, ice cream can be the perfect accompaniment to a few hours at the flea market. But, if your tastes run to ice cream collectibles instead, some great examples may be waiting for you, too.

Collectors' Clubs: National Association of Soda Jerks, P.O. Box 115, Omaha, NE 68101; The Ice Screamers, P.O. Box 465, Warrington, PA 18976.

Ashtray, glass, "Carnation Ice Cream," stains 10.00
Booklet, Eckels Ice Cream Co., Baltimore, 23 pgs 11.00
Box, Sclater's Superior Ice Cream, Marion Drug Co., Marion, Va. 12.00
Cone holder, Sealtest Ice Cream, "Get the best - Get Sealtest," red with white lettering, paper with a metal rim, 5" h 12.00
Mold
    Flag on a shield, E.&Co., NY, 3-1/2" x 4" 195.00
    George Washington on shield, mkd 456, 4-1/2" x 4".... 195.00
    George Washington on hatchet, E.&Co., NY, 1092, 3-1/2" x 3-3/4" 195.00
    Liberty Bell, mkd 605, 3-1/2" X 4" 52.00
    Wishbone, mkd 322, 5-1/2" x 4" 145.00
Pinback button, celluloid, Arctic Rainbow Ice Cream Cones, 1912 .... 30.00

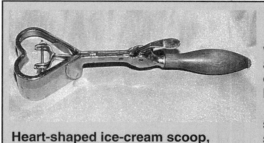

Heart-shaped ice-cream scoop, $12,500.

Salt and pepper shakers, Safe-T Cup ice cream cone, 3-1/2" h, pr 35.00
Scoop
    Gilchrist #12, 11" l 55.00
    Gilchrist #31, wooden handle, 10-1/2" l 58.00
    Kingerly #12, dated Sept. 4, 1894 ....325.00
Top, litho tin with wooden shaft, "Ask for Jersey Maid Milk and Ice Cream" and "Can You Spin It-80 Seconds," red on cream ground, 1915 patent date.................20.00
Towel, linen, embroidered ice cream sundae, 15" x 26" 12.00
Toy, ice cream truck, tin, friction, Japan, 1960 on license plate, wear, 3-1/2" h, 8" l 85.00
Trade card, The Crown Ice Cream Freezer, shows cherubs, American Machine Co., Philadelphia, 2-7/8" x 4-3/8"....................15.00
Tray, "Southern Dairies, Sealtest Ice Cream," paint loss, scratches, rust..................................115.00
Whistle, plastic, Dairy Queen, ice cream cone shape, 3-1/4" h 10.00

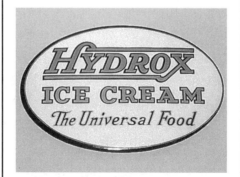

Hydrox Ice Cream sign, celluloid over cardboard, 4-5/8" x 6-5/8", $90.

A real treat

I scream. You scream. But we would all really scream if we ran across one of these gems priced only a few dollars at a flea market.

For collectors, this heart-shaped ice cream scoop is something akin to the Holy Grail, as noted by its value.

❖ Ice Picks

An ice pick was once a necessary household utensil. Today collectors search for examples with interesting shapes and advertising slogans. Most ice picks consist of a wooden handle with a metal pick. Expect to find examples with wear and minor rusting.

1939 World's Fair, San Francisco 23.00
Clarkson Peoples Coal & Ice .. 12.50
"Drink Coca-Cola, Delicious and Refreshing," wooden handle, 8" l 25.00
Dr. Pepper.............................. 5.00
Keystone Ice Co., "Markley & Oak Sts. Phone 2684," all metal 18.00
Maretta Ice Co., "Phone 7," worn wooden handle, 8-1/4" l 7.00
Seaboard Ice Co., "Coolerator," all metal, 8-1/2" l................... 18.00
Standard Ice Co.," Use Kris Kleer Ice, Ice for All Purposes," wooden handle, 8-1/2" l.... 10.00
Union Ice Company 10.00
"Use The Year Round, Dependable Ice Service, Those Who Really Know Prefer ICE, Save With Ice," wooden handle 4.00

❖ Ice Skating

Ice skating is actually an old pastime, going back to a time when skates were handmade and much cruder than today's finely shaped skates. Collecting ephemera related to skating is also quite popular with today's generation.

Animation cel, Mickey and Minnie Mouse on ice pond, from 1930s short, laser background, 10" x 12" 60.00

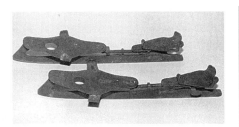

Adjustable cast-iron ice skates, Peck & Snyder's American Club, $20.

Costume, Terri Lee, MIB........435.00
Doll
    Bradley, porcelain, limited ed of
        5,000, 12" h....................37.00
    Ideal, Dorothy Hamill, 1970s,
        with rink, orig box..........31.00
Figurine, Precious Moments, "Drop-
    ping In For Christmas," boy skat-
    ing, 5-1/2" h.......................55.00
Ice skates
    Child's, aluminum, leather
        straps, beginner's type, dou-
        ble runners, c1950........20.00
    Figure, white leather uppers,
        metal blades, worn, c1960
        ....10.00
    Hockey, brown leather uppers,
        wide blades, c1960.......25.00
Magazine cover, *The Associated*,
    Jan. 18, 1914, cover art of cou-
    ple walking with ice skaters in
    background.......................89.00
Program
    Holiday On Ice, 30th anniversary,
        1975..............................20.00
    Ice Follies, Philadelphia, 1960
        ....5.00
Tray, Coca-Cola, 1941, woman with
    skates.............................185.00

❖ Illustrators

Many flea market adventurers are starting to specialize in one or more specific illustrators. You'll see them scouring through magazines for illustrations and advertisements by their favorites. Other collectors of illustrated items devote their search to prints, calendars, books, and other types of ephemera.

Periodicals: *Calendar Art Collectors' Newsletter*, 45 Brown's Ln, Old Lyme, CT 06371; *The Illustrator Collector's News*, P.O. Box 1958, Sequim, WA 98232; *The Philip Boileau Collectors' Society Newsletter*, 1025 Redwood Blvd, Redding, CA 96003.
Books
    Chandler, Howard, *An Old
        Sweetheart of Mine* by James
        Whitcomb Riley, 1903 ...65.00
    Fisher, Harrison, *Love Finds the
        Way* by Paul Leicester Ford,
        Dodd Mead & Co., 1904
        ....75.00
    Peat, Fern Bisel, *The Sugar-
        Plum Tree and Other Verses*
        by Eugene Field............45.00
Magazine cover
    Fisher, Harrison, *Saturday
        Evening Post*, May 18, 1907,
        "The Man Hunt".............80.00
    Fisher, Harrison, *Saturday
        Evening Post*, June 19, 1915,
        "Horse Woman".............75.00
    Fisher, Harrison, *Ladies Home
        Journal*, September 1909
        ....50.00
Postcard
    Atwell, Mabel Lucie..............9.00
    Clapsaddle, Ellen Hattie.....25.00
    Outcault, R. 17.50
Print
    Smith, Jessee Wilcox, "Gold-
        ilocks and the Three Bears,"
        1907 copyright, 16" x 10-3/4"
        ....90.00

Birds, **softcover, Fern Bisel Peat, The Saalfeld Publishing Co., 1943, $15.**

Leyendecker, J.C., "Pay Day,"
    1906 copyright, P.F. Collier
    and Son, 16" x 10-3/4".. 80.00
Remington, Frederic, "Shadows
    at the Water Hole," 1907
    copyright, P.F. Collier and
    Son, 16" x 10-3/4"......... 70.00

❖ Imari

Imari is a Japanese porcelain that dates back to the late 1770s. Early Imari has a simple decoration, unlike later renditions that are also known as Imari. As the Chinese and, later, the English copied and interpreted this pattern, it developed into a rich brocade design.
Bowl, blue and white, scalloped rim,
    early 20th C, 15" dia 225.00
Charger, 19th C 550.00
Dish, shaped rim, all-over flowering
    vine dec, gilt highlights, 9-1/2"
    dia 150.00
Jardiniere, hexagonal, bulbous,
    short flared foot, alternating fig-
    ures and symbols, stylized
    ground, 10" h 265.00
Sauce tureen, Boston retailer's
    mark, imp "Ashworth Real Iron-
    stone," 6-1/8" h, 5-1/4" w, 9-1/4" l
    .... 325.00
Teabowl and saucer, floral spray dec
    .... 215.00

❖ Imperial Glass

Bellaire, Ohio, was the home of Imperial Glass Company, founded in 1901. Through the years they have produced pressed glass in patterns that imitate cut glass, art glass, animals figures, as well as elegant tableware.

Collectors' Club: National Imperial Glass Collectors Soc, P.O. Box 534, Bellaire, OH 43906.
Berry bowl, Katy Blue, opalescent,
    flat, rim............................. 30.00
Bowl, Diamond Quilted, black,
    crimped, 7" dia.................. 20.00
Cake stand, ftd, Cape Cod, 4" h, 10"
    dia.................................... 55.00
Candy box, cov, ftd, Grape, milk
    glass, satin finish.............. 40.00
Cereal bowl, Katy Blue, opalescent
    .... 65.00
Cocktail, Cape Cod................. 12.00

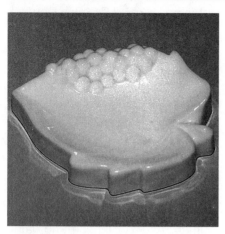

Milk glass leaf-shaped dish with grapes, Imperial, 4-3/4" long, $6.

Cracker jar, cov, Americana, milk glass 60.00
Creamer and sugar, Cape Cod 15.00
Cup and saucer, Cape Cod 7.50
Figure, pony stallion, caramel, c1970 .... 65.00
Jug, Doeskin, milk glass, 36-oz, 8" h 50.00
Juice, ftd, Cape Cod 8.00
Nappy, Quilted Diamond, marigold, stress fracture in ring handle 35.00
Parfait, Cape Cod 11.00
Plate
    Cape Cod, Verdi, 8" dia 15.00
    Diamond Quilted, black, 8" dia 15.00
Punch bowl set
    Crocheted, crystal, bowl, 12 cups 300.00
    Mount Vernon, 15 pcs 90.00
Salt and pepper shakers, Cape Cod, Verdi, pr 45.00
Toothpick holder, blue/purple carnival glass, scalloped top, mkd "IG," nick on base 30.00
Tray, Cape Cod, 12" l, 7" w 75.00
Tumbler, Katy Blue, opalescent, 10-oz 65.00
Vase, bottle shape, cased, orange ext, white int, 6-1/2" h, 4-1/2" dia 275.00

❖ Indiana Glass

The good news is that Indiana Glass Company has a colorful history, dating back to 1907, when it was founded in Dunkirk, Indiana. The bad news is that some of the company's more popular patterns have been reproduced over the years. Flea market shoppers can distinguish vintage Indiana Glass from newer pieces by examining color and the detail of the pattern.
Bowl, Daisy, amber, 9-1/4" dia 35.00
Candlestick, Constellation with Grape, pattern #0753, silver overlay, c1972, pr 92.00
Fairy lamp, Sandwich pattern, amber, 7" h 20.00
Pitcher, Pear pattern, amber, Tiara, c1970, 9-1/4" h 75.00
Plate, Preztel pattern, clear, tab handle, minor scratching 3.00
Sherbet, clear, 3-1/2" h 9.00
Tumbler
    Horseshoe pattern, green, c1930, 5" h 45.00
    Lorain pattern, yellow, c1929, 5" h 38.00

✦ Indian Jewelry

Indian jewelry is abundant at most flea markets. Bargains can be found in collectible Indian jewelry, but vintage Indian jewelry is getting quite pricey. Buy pieces because they appeal to you. Make sure the craftsmanship is good, and the stones are secure in the settings. Watch for signs of heat-stabilized turquoise when considering collectible Indian jewelry.
Barrette, silver 45.00
Beads, turquoise, from Sleeping Beauty mine, graduated disks, leaf design pendant 2-1/2" l, overall 20" l 225.00
Bolo tie, Navajo, hand-made, woven leather tie, tipped in sterling silver, sgd "Sterling," mkd by artist 112.00
Bracelet
    Navajo, silver leaf design on matte black ground, ten Kingman turquoise stones, engraved "D" on back, by J. Delgarito 200.00
    Squash blossom design, Morenci turquoise nugget and coral accent, silver, drop style, stamped "MLS," attributed to Loren Begay 55.00
    Zuni, silver, hummingbird and flower, turquoise, coral, mother-of-pearl and tortoise shell, engraved on back "Made by Bobby & Corraine, Zuni, N.M." 220.00
Fetish necklace
    Santo Domingo, shell, turquoise and coral triangle pieces, bird pendant with upraised wings, c1940, shortened 55.00
    Zuni, silver beads, inlaid pendant with silver leaves and inlaid basket center figure in turquoise, coral and jet, mother-of-pearl background, stamped artist's mark on back, beads have some dents, by Wylie Hill, 14-1/4" l 275.00
    Zuni, 1 strand, silver, birds, bears, frogs and turtles, tubular silver rain spacers, 28" l 250.00
    Zuni, 3 strands, tortoise shell, silver cones at clasp, 26" l 315.00
Necklace
    24" l, spiderweb 2-1/4" l, turquoise center, Navajo 465.00
    24" l, beaded medallion with bird motif 3-1/2", white, yellow, green, black, blue and red 15.00
    26-1/2" l, Heishi, 38 turquoise nuggets, silver beads and cones 90.00
Ring, man's, Navajo
    Silver and turquoise, feathers around cabochon 120.00
    Silver, coral, and turquoise 110.00
Squash blossom necklace
    Hopi, shadowbox style, silver, 15 blue diamond turquoise stones, 13" l 275.00
    Navajo, 2 strands of silver beads, 20 turquoise nuggets, 13" l 275.00
Suite, squash blossom necklace, bracelet and ring, Navajo, Royston turquoise settings, silver beads, rope twist details, 20 stones in necklace, 16-1/2" l 715.00

❖ Ink Bottles

Before the invention of the ball-point pen, ink was sold in bottles. Because most examples date to the 1800s, they can be quite expensive if found in good condition.

Periodical: *Antique Bottle and Glass Collector*, P.O. Box 187, East Greenville, PA 18041.

Barrel shape, blue-green, rim chips, 4" h, 2-1/2" dia 95.00
Bourne Benby, stoneware, English, c1860, 4-7/8" h, 2-3/8" dia 15.00
Carter's, cobalt, cathedral shape, 6-sided, master ink 225.00
Carter's Washable Ink, orig box missing flap, 10-1/2" h 85.00
Empire Ink, "Williams Black Empire Ink, New York," lime green, tooled mouth, smooth base, some damage to label 200.00
Harrison's Columbia Ink, octagonal, light green 75.00
Sawyers Crystal, clear glass, 6-1/4" h 12.00
Senate Ink Co., house shape, "Bank of Writing Fluid, Manuf by Senate Ink Co., Philadelphia," aquamarine, tooled sq collared mouth, some fading to label, 2-5/8" h 325.00

Aqua ink bottle, applied lip and collar, circa 1880, 3" high, $12.

Porcelain inkwell, white ground, pink edge, gold floral decoration, German, $60.

❖ Inkwells

Small receptacles designed to hold ink were a necessity in the days of quill pens and steel dip pens. Inkwells were most commonly made of glass and pottery, because the ink would not adversely affect those substances. Inkwells have become quite popular with collectors, who search for examples made of glass, bronze, pewter, pottery, and even wood. Particularly fascinating are the miniature wells designed for children's desks.

References: Veldon Badders, *Collector's Guide to Inkwells, Book I* (1995), *Book II* (1997), Collector Books; Jean and Franklin Hunting, *The Collector's World of Inkwells*, Schiffer Publishing, 2000; Ray and Bevy Jaegers, *The Write Stuff: Collector's Guide to Inkwells, Fountain Pens, and Desk Accessories*, Krause Publications, 2000.

Collectors' Clubs: St. Louis Inkwell Collectors Soc, Box 29396, St. Louis, MO 63126; The Society of Inkwell Collectors, 5136 Thomas Ave S, Minneapolis, MN 55410, www.soic.com.

Bronze, figural, Robert Burns, 19th C, 5-1/2" h 775.00
Delft, square with round lid, c1910 .... 295.00
Glass
  Clear, 2" h, 1-7/8" dia 25.00
  Olive-amber, blown, some wear, 1-1/2" h, 2-3/8" dia 165.00
Hoof, animal hoof, English, Birmingham hallmarks on silver fitting 295.00
Metal, pocket inkwell, glass bottle 56.00

Porcelain, rose/leaves decor, hinged lid, 2-1/2" h 22.50
Snail, clear glass, ground mouth, 1830-70, flat chip 150.00
Teakettle shape, glass, brick red and burgundy slag, ground mouth, brass cap, 1830-60, two small chips 115.00
Treen, sponge-decor, brown and yellow, gilt stenciling, glass insert, "Manufactured by S. Silliman & Co...Conn.," wear to top, 2-1/2" h, 4-1/4" dia 192.50

❖ Insulators

Insulators date to 1837, when the telegraph was developed. Styles have been modified over the years, and collectors have a wide variety of shapes and colors to choose from.

Reference: Mike Bruner, *The Definitive Guide to Colorful Insulators*, Schiffer Publishing, 2000.

Periodicals: *Canadian Insulator Magazine*, Mayne Island, British Columbia V0N 2J0 Canada; *Crown Jewels of the Wire*, P.O. Box 1003, St Charles, IL 60174.

Collectors' Clubs: National Insulator Assoc, 1315 Old Mill Path, Broadview Heights, OH 44147. In addition, there are many local clubs devoted to this hobby.
Armstrong, clear 2.00

Brookfield No. 20 insulator, green glass, 4" high, $4.

Brookfield
Olive green, chip................ 15.00
No. 20, emerald green....... 20.00
W. Brookfield B., aqua 2.00
B.T.C., aqua.............................. 5.00
Harlow Trade Mark, aqua.......... 4.00
Hemingray
E1 B, light lemon................ 90.00
No. 4, 1893 patent, aqua 8.00
No. 14, aqua, crack.............. 5.00
No. 15, aqua, chip................ 5.00
No. 53B, clear..................... 2.00
Gayner, No. 90, aqua 7.00
Lynchburg, No. 31, aqua 7.00
McLaughlin, No. 9, aqua 2.00
Star, aqua............................... 15.00
Whitall Tatum, No. 3, clear, minor
chip..................................... 1.00

❖ Irons

Folks have been trying to keep their clothes pressed neatly since the 12th century. Of course, irons from those days are vastly different than the streamlined appliances we use today.

References: Dave Irons, *Irons by Irons*, self-published, 1994; —, *More Irons by Irons*, self-published, 1997; —, *Pressing Iron Patents*, self-published, 1994.

Periodical: *Iron Talk*, P.O. Box 68, Waelder, TX 78959.

Collectors' Clubs: Club of the Friends of Ancient Smoothing Irons, P.O. Box 215, Carlsbad, CA 92008; The Midwest Sad Iron Collectors Club, 24 Nob Hill Dr., St. Louis, MO 63138-4171.

Cast-iron child's sad iron, 3-5/8" long, $38.

Electric
American Beauty No. 66A, American Electrical Heater Co., Detroit 10.00
Singer model 820476, Singer Sewing Machine Co. 40.00
Gasoline, ball-shaped tank, Diamond Iron, Akron Lamp Co., Akron, Ohio, ... 35.00
Sad iron
Arched scrollwork iron and wood handle with chicken catch, gold repaint, underside of lid mkd "AFG 3," worn old black paint on base, 8-1/4" l ...88.00
Blacklock, cast iron, name cast on handle 15.00
Griswold #2, wooden handle 120.00
Unmarked, cast iron, twisted handle, mkd "18" (lbs) ...45.00
Travel, Universal, electric, cloth cord, wooden handle, made by Landers, Frary & Clark, New Britain, 7-3/4" l 35.00

❖ Ironstone

Charles Mason first patented ironstone in England in 1813. The dense, durable, white stoneware was named "Mason's Patent Ironstone China," even though the reference to china was misleading since the items were actually earthenware. Ironstone derives its name from the fact that iron slag was mixed with the clay used to produce dinnerware and the like. Manufactured throughout the 19th century, ironstone was available in plain white as well as decorated versions.

Collectors' Club: Mason's Ironstone Collectors' Club, 2011 E Main St, Medford, OR 97504.
Bowl, Tamerlane pattern, Oriental design, J.&M.P. Bell, 9-3/4" dia 165.00
Coffee set, white ironstone, yellow and orange daffodils, mkd "Nikko Ironstone, Dishwasher - Oven Safe, Made in Japan," coffee pot 11-1/4" h, creamer and sugar 3-1/4" h, set 40.00
Decanter, hand-painted guardsman, mkd "Mason's, No. 2574," 9-1/4" h 45.00

Tea Leaf ironstone coffeepot, $200.

Dessert set, white ground, 8 decals representing different countries, mkd "Kaysons Fine Ironstone China, Japan, 1966," cake plate 12" dia, 8 plates 7-3/4" dia, set 30.00
Dinner plate, Stratford Stage, mkd "Royal Staffordshire Ironstone" 6.00
Jug, white, Strathmore, #30, mkd "Mason's," wear, 5-1/4" h 100.00
Ladle, white
Flower and fern dec, gray transfer, worn gold edging, 6" l 45.00
Lavender daisies, gold trim, c1895........................... 50.00
Plain, crazed, 10-1/2" l 48.00
Pitcher, Wheat, Furnival, 12" h 165.00
Place setting, Royal Mail, brown and white, mkd "Fine Staffordshire Ironstone...Made in England," 4 pcs 25.00
Plate
Corn & Oats, mkd "J. Wedgwood," c1841, 8-3/4" dia 45.00
Forget-Me-Not, mkd "E&C Challinor," c1862, 8-3/4" dia 45.00
Platter, plain white
14" x 10", mkd "Royal Ironstone China, Alfred Meakin, England" 65.00
15" x 20", illegible maker's mark 220.00

Whites Utica stoneware mug, green and cobalt highlighting, $85.

Blue Ridge teapot, 7" high, 10" long, $125.

1901 Pan-American Exposition clock, gilt brass, charging buffalo, repaired crack, 7" high, not running, $825.

THE HANDIEST THING ON THE KITCHEN SHELF!

Campbell's TOMATO SOUP
USE IT 3 WAYS
AS A SOUP – SAUCE – INGREDIENT

Campbell's tomato soup cardboard store display, $95.

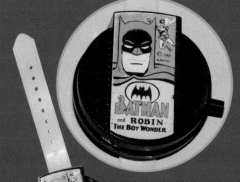

Batman light, wrist-watch form, plastic face with paper label, marked "1966 N.P.P. Inc."and "Bantamlite," face 2-1/4" diameter, strap 7-3/4" long, $110.

Welch's Cat in the Hat jelly glass, $4.

"A Christmas Dinner" game, Parker Brothers, 1897, $1,000.

Mickey Mouse Sunshine Straws, $25.

Uncle Sam printer's block, military background, 1-1/4" high, 4" long, $30.

Roy Rogers plastic figural cup, Quaker Oats, $20.

Butler figural bottle opener, composition, $55.

Staffordshire plate, blue transfer design, "Public Library, Boston," 10-1/4" diameter, $65.

Britains Zoo set, original box, $300.

Coleco Thidwick the Moose, original box, $110.

Roseville Magnolia tea set, blue glaze, $325.

Jade-ite type glassware rolling pin, aluminum screw-on cap, 16-1/2" long, $625.

Fire-King Jade-ite ball jug, $550.

Lunch boxes: Gunsmoke, metal, $180;
Bullwinkle, vinyl, $450.

Gene Autry guitar,
Emenee, original box,
guitar 31" long, $100.

Souvenir china mug, "Totem Pole,
Seattle, Wash." 2-1/8" high, $40.

Haviland cup and saucer, $29.

Woven silk calendar
bookmark, Louisiana
Purchase Exposition,
"St. Louis 1904," 10"
x 3", $150.

Hull piggy bank, 12-1/2" long, $225.

McCoy zebra planter, $575.

Roseville Gardenia vase, 8" high, $125.

Purinton casserole, Apple pattern, $35.

Iris vase, iridescent, 9"
high, $35.

White Castle bridge score pad, unused, $3.

1950s plastic light-up jack-o-lantern, battery-operated, Union Products, 3-1/2" high (excluding wire handle), $65.

Santa Claus rubber squeak toy, Sanitoy, 9" high, $15.

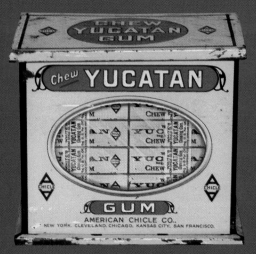

Yucatan Gum display box, lithographed tin, 6" high, 6-3/4" wide, $275.

Occupied Japan bisque figurine, 5-1/8" high, $17.50.

Frankoma Indian figure, brown matte glaze, 8" high, $65.

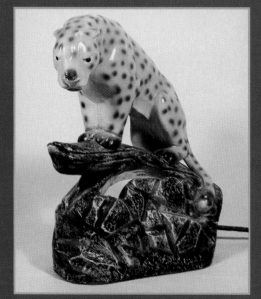

Chalkware leopard television light, $65.

Hallmark 1981 Rocking Horse ornament, MIB, $400.

1975 Kentucky Derby glass, $10.

"J. Palleys Hambone Sweets" cigar advertising plate, hand-painted, 10-1/4" diameter, $90.

Anthropomorphic ceramic figurine, man with onion head, made in Japan, 3-1/2" high, $35.

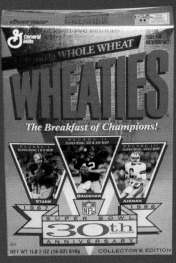

Wheaties box, 30th Super Bowl, 1967-1996, empty, $2.

1910 calendar plate, dog motif, "Compliments of The Summitville Bank," $45.

Everlast aluminum ice bucket, bamboo design, K-shaped finial on lid, $45.

Blue-and-gray stoneware pitcher, man with stein, $85.

A. Kenrick & Sons No. 0 coffee mill, cast-iron case with brass hopper, brass tag with lion, royal crest and unicorn, 6-1/2" high, $120.

Napcoware lady head vase, 5-3/4" high, $95.

Hummel, Chick Girl, full bee mark, 57/l, $155.

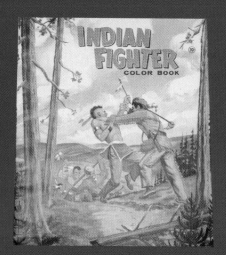

Indian Fighter Color Book, Stephens Publishing Co., 13" x 10-3/4", unused, $15.

Bible Stories Picture Book, Whitman Publishing Co., 1953, $5.

Flower basket doorstop, cast iron, 10" high, $75.

Mammy toaster cover, cloth, 8" plus skirt, $35.

1896 Murat badge, man on running camel, metal, 2-1/2" high, $15.

McDonald's Happy Meal Dalmatian premiums, $1 each.

Holt Howard produced this type of Pixieware in 1959. The base reads "Jam 'n Jelly" and was originally released with a head having green hair. This example is a "marriage" that uses a head from the Cocktail Olives Pixieware Jar of the same period. The value for this type of ware is in the head, so it should be priced at $30, not the $75+ that a completely original Jam 'n Jelly would command.

Green River blotter, $25.

Indian cookie jar, McCoy, 10-3/8" high, $400.

Walt Disney World tin tray, 10-3/4"
diameter, $7.50.

"Gateway, Garden of the
Gods" souvenir tumbler,
frosted finish, $37.50.

Lone Ranger radio with its original box,
$2,800.

Romanesque candlesticks, L.E. Smith Glass,
2-1/2" high, pair, $22.

Red Wing wing ashtray, $45.

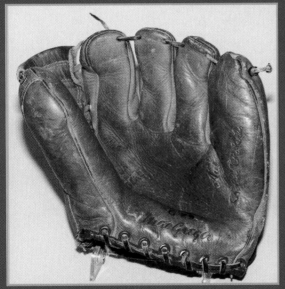

MacGregor baseball glove, Robin Roberts
autograph model, $35.

Art Deco bronze nude bookends, marked
"WB" in shield, 8" high, $300.

Indianapolis 500 ticket stub, May 29, 1971, pictures 1970
winner Al Unser, $10.

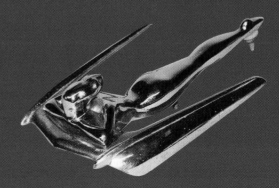

Chromed hood ornament, 10-1/2" long, $65.

Flow Blue soup bowl, Watteau pattern, Doulton, 9-1/2" diameter, $50.

The Calumet Baking Book, 1929, 31 pages, $10.

Starting Lineup Timeless Legends, Tony Esposito, 1997, $10.

Ski tin sign, 12" high, 32" wide, $60.

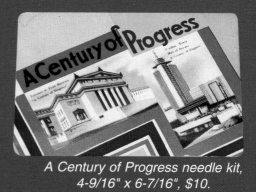

A Century of Progress needle kit, 4-9/16" x 6-7/16", $10.

1991 Hallmark ornament, U.S.S. Enterprise, MIB, $250.

Tiddledy Winks Game, stork motif, $15.

Amberina boot toothpick, L.E. Smith Glass, 4" high, $10.

Kodak Brownie Hawkeye camera, $5.

Carnival chalkware zebra, $45.

Salad plate, Stratford Stage, mkd "Royal Staffordshire Ironstone" 4.00
Soup tureen, cov, underplate, mkd "Bridgewood Porcelaine Opaque" 300.00
Tea set, child's, painted pansies, faded gold trim, worn paint, 15 pcs 75.00
Toothbrush holder, mulberry variant, c1890, 5-1/2" h 75.00
Vegetable bowl, American Hurrah, mkd "J&G Meakin," 8-1/2" l 45.00

❖ Italian Glass

Italian glassblowers have been crafting functional items and whimsical glass novelties for generations. There is strong interest in modern Italian glass. Look for bright colors and flowing forms.

Basket, Hobnail, blue, applied handle 32.00
Bottle, clear, silver overlay, orig sticker, 6" h 32.00
Center bowl, shallow, clear irid, bright blue rim wrap, molded dished pattern at center, Venetian Revival style, 18" dia 300.00
Cordials, etched vining leaves, blue, pink, yellow and green, set of 4 .... 50.00
Decanter set, green, gold floral dec, decanter 10" h, 4 glasses 3" h, set 40.00
Earrings, millefiori, pr 28.00

Italian glass vase, blue, green and clear, 4" high, $48.

Figure, Donald Duck, made by Cristallerie Antonio Imperatore, copyright Walt Disney Productions, MIB, 4-3/4" h 50.00
Vase
  3-3/4" h, oyster white, deep pink and green threading, one side of ruffled rim turned up 100.00
  5-1/2" h, irid, green waves 125.00

❖ Ivory

Ivory is derived from the teeth or tusks of animals. Yellow-white in color, the substance is quite durable and lends itself to carving. Some ivory objects have been highlighted with ink, metal, or stones.

Periodical: *Netsuke & Ivory Carving Newsletter*, 3203 Adams Way, Amber, PA 19002.

Collectors' Club: International Ivory Society, 11109 Nicholas Dr, Wheaton, MD 20902.

Earrings, pierced, hand carved, pr
  Drops suspended from gold filled leaves, c1910, 1-1/4" l 180.00
  Two elephants on a ball, c1910, new gold filled wires, 1" l 75.00
Figure
  Eagle attacking monkey, Japan, 3" h 475.00
  Medicine woman, China, 5-1/4" l 400.00
Measure, whalebone, ivory and exotic wood, American shield inlay, inscribed "WH," 19th C, minor imperfections, 14-7/8" l 200.00
Necklace, hand-carved beads, c1910, pendant 1-1/2" x 1-1/4", overall 15" l, ... 165.00
Rolling pin, exotic wood, baleen spacers, 19th C, cracks, 13-5/8" l 245.00
Seal, intaglio, handle, 19th C, cracks, 3-7/8" l 400.00
Snuff bottle, elephant ivory, carved bird on one side, carved rose on other, gold-tone neck chain, sgd "LRS," orig wand 125.00
Top, carved, sealing wax inlaid scribed lines, 19th C, minor cracks and chips, 2-7/8" l 365.00

For exciting collecting trends and newly expanded areas look for the following symbols:

✪ Hot Topic

✪ New Warman's Listing

(May have been in another Warman's title.)

✪ Jade-ite Glassware

Jade-ite is currently one of the hottest colors in glassware. The name is derived from the jade-like hue of the glass, with the color varying from manufacturer to manufacturer. Anchor-Hocking and McKee are perhaps the best known makers of Jade-ite. First produced around 1920, Jade-ite items are still being made today.

Bowl, 4-1/2" dia 20.00
Bud vase, Jeannette................20.00
Butter dish, cov, 1-lb size 140.00
Canister, dark, Jeannette 90.00
Measuring cup, Jeannette, 2-oz
....50.00
Pitcher, sunflower in base 60.00
Range shaker, sq, mkd "Flour,"
        Jeannette 45.00
Reamer.....................................60.00
Refrigerator dish base, Philbe
....32.00
Salt and pepper shakers, Ribbed,
        Jeannette, 4-1/2" h, pr.....180.00

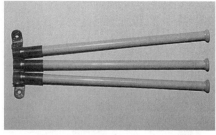

Jade-ite triple-bar towel holder, 10" long, $240.

Skillet, 2 spouts 35.00
Tea canister, sq, light Jade-ite, 48-oz
....165.00
Water dispenser, metal spigot
....160.00

❖ Japanese Ceramics

The term Japanese ceramics covers the entire spectrum of porcelain and ceramic items made in Japan throughout the centuries. As the western world became interested in Oriental things, Japanese ceramics were imported in greater numbers, and they remain treasured objects.

Charger, 2 large iron oxide carp, underglaze blue ground, peonies, stylized waves, flowering branches, Meiji period, 13-1/4" dia...................................350.00
Ewer, red and gilt motif, riverscape and figure dec, loop handle, dragon finial, Kaga, late 19th C 570.00
Plate, Nabeschima style, relief and underglaze blue hibiscus dec, c1900, 8-1/2" dia 225.00
Tea bowl, Raku, hand modeled, irreg straight sides, small recessed ring foot, central well of flower heads, peach glaze, double crackle pattern.................190.00
Teapot, Seven Gods of Wisdom, glazed and unglazed clay, polychrome dec, Banko, 5" h 450.00
Vase, flowing blue dec, fan shape, 20th C 20.00

❖ Japanese Toys

Some of our favorite childhood toys were inexpensive imports from Japan. We loved the colors, the action, and the fact that we could afford them on our pitiful allowances. Now that we're all grown up, many collectors are busy buying back their happy childhood memories. Before making a purchase, check for the original box and make sure all the accessories are present. Top dollar is often paid for toys in excellent working order.

Reference: William C. Gallagher, *Japanese Toys: Amusing Playthings from the Past*, Schiffer Publishing, 2000.

Air Defense Pom-Pom Gun Truck, tin, friction, Linemar, 1950s, 16" l 155.00
Ali and His Flying Carpet, crank wind-up, KO, 1950s 160.00
Boy Playing with Hoops, celluloid wind-up figure, tin hoops, 5" h 55.00
Car, tin friction, 6" l.................. 45.00
Crazy Clown in Crazy Car, litho tin wind-up, MIB................... 175.00
Douglas Sky Rocket, 20" l 140.00
Emergency Utility Truck, tin, TN, 1950s, 8" l....................... 160.00
Fire Chief Car, tin friction, MIB, 9" l 70.00
Guided Missile, Niki, MIB...... 475.00
Happy the Violinist, TPS, MIB 375.00
Harley-Davidson, TN, 1950s, 9" l 170.00
Jet Racer, friction
        Red................................... 95.00
        Silver 90.00
Lotus Racer, battery op, 1960s, 12" l 140.00
Mercedes Convertible 300, friction 75.00
Mr. Dan, man drinking coffee, raises coffee pot, pours and drinks, MIB 95.00
Planet Explorer, battery op, Modern Toys, 1960s, 9-1/2" l 160.00
Reading Bear, turns page of tin book, MIB....................... 145.00
Speed Race Car #20, lavender, Modern Toys, 1950s, 6-1/2" l 155.00
Telephone Bear, tin and cloth, phone rings, picks up phone and places it back on stand, MIB 145.00

❖ Jeannette Glass

Jeannette Glass Company was located in Jeannette, Pennsylvania, and produced mainly depression era glassware. Many of the items they produced from 1900 to 1983 are marked with a "J" inside a square.

References: Gene Florence, *Collectible Glassware From the 40s, 50s, 60s*, 4th ed, Collector Books, 1998; —, *Collector's Encyclopedia of Depression Glass*, 13th ed, Collector Books, 1998.

For additional listings, see *Warman's Depression Glass*.

Ashtray
    Butterfly, clear 7.00
    Cowboy hat, Delphite.........22.75
Banana split dish, oval, clear.....5.00
Beverage set, Willow pattern, c1950, five 5-oz tumblers, 5 plastic coasters, 5 plastic stirring spoons, 6 juice glasses 3-3/4" h, pitcher 9-1/2" h, 22 pcs ...195.00
Candy dish, cov, Stippled Acorn, light marigold 65.00
Canister, cov
    3" h, Jade-ite, Allspice, Ginger, Nutmeg or Pepper, each 72.00
    5-1/2" h, sq, Delphite, Coffee 85.00
Cigarette set, cigarette box 5-1/2" x 3-5/8", 4 ashtrays 3-1/8" sq, orig box 50.00
Compote, pink milk glass 18.00
Creamer, Cubist, pink...............7.00
Drippings jar, cov, Jade-ite 35.00
Mixing bowl, clear, 6" dia.........16.00
Reamer, Delphite.....................90.00
Refrigerator dish, cov
    4-1/2" h, sq, Jade-ite..........20.00
    8-1/2" x 4-1/2", clear 20.00
Salt and pepper shakers, ribbed, Jade-ite, pr 30.00
Tray, sq, handle, pink 18.00
Tumbler, Cubist, green, 9-oz ...75.00

❖ Jelly Glasses

The concept of putting jelly into a glass container with colorful or whimsical decorations no doubt helped boost sales. Collectors today eagerly look for vintage and contemporary jelly glasses.

Archie, Betty and Veronica, 1971 ....10.00
BAMA Racing Collection
    Bobby Allison, 4" h...............1.00
    Bobby Hamilton, 4" h 1.00
Flintstones, Fred And His Pals At Work, Welch's, 4-1/2" h 10.00
Howdy Doody, "Dilly Dally is Circus Big Shot," Welch's, 4-1/4" h 18.00

Welch's Looney Tunes Collector Series jelly glass, 4" high, $3.50.

Jack & Jill, nursery rhyme, 4-3/4" h 8.00
Pooh's Grand Adventure: The Search for Christopher Robin, 4" h 3.00
Spacemen, 2 yellow spacemen, planets, rockets, 1960s, 5" h 18.00
Speedy Gonzales, "Speedy Snaps Up the Cheese," 1974 ....3.00
Tom and Jerry, Tom roller skating toward open manhole........10.00
"World's Fair Seattle 1962, America's Space Age World's Fair, Century 21 Exposition, Seattle, USA 1962," 4-3/8" h 12.00

❖ Jensen, Georg

This designer hailed from Denmark, but he is known worldwide for his jewelry, flatware, and decorative accessories. Most of his creations were produced in sterling silver. Expect to find pieces that are well marked.

Bar pin, sterling silver, mkd "GI #136 Sterling, Denmark," 3-3/4" x 1-1/4" 775.00
Berry spoon, Acanthus, 8-7/8" l 350.00

Brooch, sterling silver, tulips, post-1945 mark, 1-7/8" x 1-1/4" 400.00
Carving knife and fork, Acanthus, stainless blades, 11-1/4" l and 12-1/2" l 325.00
Cuff links, oval, design #75A, post-1945 mark, mkd "Sterling, Made in Denmark," pr 300.00
Key ring, design #208, pineapple decorative ends, sgd "Sterling, Denmark, Georg Jensen" in dotted circle, 1-7/16" dia 225.00
Meat fork, Acanthus, two tines, 8-1/8" l 250.00
Ring, sterling silver, mkd #130 925 Denmark," c1915-27, size 6 ....775.00
Soup spoon, Acanthus, 6-7/8" l 95.00
Tie bar, design #64, post-1945 mark 125.00
Youth knife and fork, Acanthus, 6-3/4" l and 5-5/8" l 180.00

❖ Jewel Tea Company

Most flea market browsers picture the Autumn Leaf pattern when they hear the name Jewel Tea, but the company was actually responsible for a diverse selection of products. The Jewel Tea Company, headquartered in Barrington, Illinois, has been supplying household necessities for years.

Reference: C.L. Miller, *Jewel Tea Grocery Products*, Schiffer Publishing, 1996.

Bank, 1905 truck, Ertl, orig box 65.00
Beverage coaster set, Autumn Leaf pattern, orig box, 9 pcs ...235.00
Christmas ornament, pewter, Oh Come All Ye Faithful, 1980s, orig box 12.00
Cookbook, *476 Tested Recipes*, cover missing corners.........2.00
Flour canister, tin body, white plastic lid, Autumn Leaf dec, 5-3/4" h, 5" dia................................10.00
Laundry soap, Jewel T Jetco Bead Bluing, 8-3/4" x 5-3/4" 85.00
Jar, peanut butter, 3-3/4" h......45.00
Playing cards, Pinochle deck, orig box 225.00

Soap, Shure, 3 bars in box, unused
....85.00
Spice tin, nutmeg, some minor
dents, 3-7/8" sq 145.00
Tin
Fruitcake, 1981 ....20.00
Ginger, 2-oz, 3" x 2-1/4".....95.00
Truck
1926 delivery truck, 100th anni-
versary, Tootsietoy, MIB
....16.00
Banner truck, replica of 1950s
delivery truck...............325.00
Urn, Jewel Best Coffee, made by
West Bend, orig box........525.00

❖ Jewelry, Costume

Jewelry with faux stones became fashionable in the 1920s, thanks to Coco Chanel. Initially, designers were copying real gemstone jewelry, but soon they began creating their own exciting pieces.

References: Maryanne Dolan, *Collecting Rhinestone & Colored Jewelry*, 4th ed, Krause Publications, 1998; Christie Romero, *Warman's Jewelry*, 2nd ed, Krause Publications, 1998.

Collectors' Clubs: Leaping Frog Antique Jewelry and Collectable Club, 4841 Martin Luther Blvd, Sacramento, CA 95820; National Cuff Link Soc, P.O. Box 346, Prospect Heights, IL 60070; Vintage Fashion & Costume Jewelry Club, P.O. Box 265, Glen Oaks, NY 11004.

Reproduction Alert
Bracelet
Bangle, sterling silver, scrolling
abstract design, Lobel, 1960s,
sgd 340.00
Charm, 8 charms, gold-tone
links, Coro, sgd 40.00
Cuff, silver, center band of 6 oval
amethysts, imp marks,
unknown Mexican maker, mid
20th C, wear, 6-1/4" l 90.00
Heart padlock, sterling, 1897
....90.00
Link, sterling silver, lily pad
design, Danecraft, sgd ..65.00
Rhinestones, panther, black
enamel trim, Ciner, sgd
....215.00

Weiss butterfly, 2-1/8" high, 2-5/8" wide, $45.

Brooch
Cameo, faux carnelian surrounded by clear rhine-
stones, scrolled mounting,
Coro 32.00
Circular, green enameled leaves
combined with prong-set
stones of varying shapes and
sizes, bright silvertone setting,
small rhinestone accents,
mkd "Bond Boyd," 2-1/8" dia
....45.00
Daisy, white enamel flower, yel-
low center, red ladybug, green
stem and leaf, Weiss.....30.00
Fan, Oriental design, gold-tone,
bamboo handle, sgd "Haskell"
....50.00
Feather, sterling silver, Nye,
3-3/8" l..........................48.00
Starfish, gold-tone, green, brown
and gold rhinestones, Flo-
renza 65.00
Choker, pavé faux turquoise links,
center aurora borealis rhinestones, gold-tone casting,
Kramer, late 1950s, sgd.....45.00
Cross, filigree, 18k yg, 3 large pearls
....120.00
Cuff links and tie clip set
LaMode Originals, black stone
and goldtone, orig box...25.00
Mask shape, unmkd...........12.00
Square, gold-plated, inset MOP
disk................................18.00
Swank, gold- and silver-plated,
orig box 25.00
Earrings, clip, pr
Aurora borealis, blue rhine-
stones, Weiss................27.50

Dangling, chandelier type, crystal and rhinestone, Carnegie
.....................................60.00
Silver-tone filigree, chocolate
pearl and rhinestone trim
....4.00
Turquoise egg-shaped glass
dangles, gold tops, mkd
"Kramer" 30.00
Earrings, screw-back, egg shaped
cherry red drops, white background, blue edge, copper,
1950s, mkd "Hogan-Bolas," pr
....45.00
Necklace
Faux pearls, double strand, knot-
ted, aurora borealis stone
clasp, Vendome, 16" l... 48.00
"X" design with rhinestones,
Crown Trifari, 14" l........65.00
Wheat style links, small spacers,
gold tone, Francois, Coro,
15" l, 1937 ....27.50
Pendant
Lion, gold-colored metal, carved
amber tortoise shell type
Bakelite, ivory Bakelite ring,
c1960............................70.00
Teardrop, polished faux coral,
plastic, gold trimmed open
center, Sarah Coventry, gold-
tone chain 28" l.............20.00
Tie bar, gold-plated, abstract design
....2.00
Tie tack
Car, gold-plated, Sarah Coventry
....4.00
Initial, "G", silver-plated 2.00

❖ Johnson Brothers

Three English brothers founded Johnson Brothers in 1883. Their dinnerware business flourished, and a fourth brother joined the firm in 1896. He was charged with establishing a stronghold in the American market. Ultimately, this venture was so successful that additional factories were established in England, Canada, and Australia. By 1968, Johnson Brothers had become part of the Wedgwood Group.
Bread and butter plate, Old Britain
Castles, blue dec on white 12.00
Breakfast set, Lily of the Valley,
5 pcs 155.00

Chippendale platter, Johnson Bros., 10" x 12", $50.

Butter dish, cov, Eternal Beau . 72.00
Cereal bowl, Old Britain Castles,
    blue dec on white 18.00
Coffeepot, Eternal Beau 105.00
Creamer and sugar, Friendly Village
    .... 35.00
Cup and saucer
    Brooklyn pattern, flow blue, mkd
       "Royal Semi Porcelain,
       Johnson Brothers, England,"
       c1900 .... 100.00
    Countryside, cup 3" h, saucer
       7" dia 55.00
    Harvest Time, cup 3" h, saucer
       7" dia 55.00
    Old Britain Castles, blue dec on
       white 20.00
Dinner plate
    Brooklyn pattern, flow blue, mkd
       "Royal Semi Porcelain,
       Johnson Brothers, England,"
       c1900, 8-3/4" dia 100.00
    Old Britain Castles, blue dec on
       white 22.00
Dinner service, Coaching Days, ser-
    vice for 10 .... 275.00
Fruit bowl, Old Britain Castles, blue
    dec on white 10.00
Gravy boat, Provincial, blue border
    .... 75.00
Plate, Mt Rushmore, imported for
    Sunset Supply, Keystone,
    10-3/4" dia 15.00
Platter, Heritage Hall, brown.... 95.00
Relish, Friendly Village, 3-part
    .... 38.50
Salad plate, Old Britain Castles, blue
    dec on white 15.00
Saucer, Cherry Thieves, mkd
    "Staffordshire Old Granite Made
    in England by Johnson Brothers"
    .... 5.00

Soup bowl, Old Britain Castles, blue
    dec on white 22.00
Teapot, Athena 75.00
Vegetable bowl, coupe shape
    Athena.............................. 75.00
    Game Birds 68.00
    Hearts & Flowers 135.00

❖ Jordan, Michael

Can you believe it? This basket-ball legend retired on January 13, 1999. As a result, values for collectibles relating to this sports legend will most certainly increase.

Reference: Oscar Gracia, *Collecting Michael Jordan Memorabilia*, Krause Publications, 2000.

Book, *For the Love of the Game*,
    Michael Jordan, 1st ed, paper-
    back 10.00
Comic book, *Sports Superstars*, #1,
    Michael Jordan, 1992, Revolu-
    tionary Comics 8.00
Cup, McDonald's NBA Looney
    Tunes All Star Showdown, 1995,
    Michael Jordan and Bugs Bunny,
    scratched 1.00
Fast-food premium, miniature foot-
    ball, McDonald's, Fitness Fun
    Challenge, 1992, orig package
    .... 3.50
Magazine, *Sports Illustrated*, March
    13, 1989, "Chicago's Indomitable
    Michael Jordan" 5.00
Photograph, wire service, 1989, Chi-
    cago Bulls Michael Jordan and
    Cleveland Cavaliers Horace
    Grant.................................... 3.50
Pinback button, "Me and Michael are
    Madly for Bradley 2000," red and
    blue lettering, 2-1/4" dia 7.50
Trading card, baseball, Upper Deck,
    1994, #661 .... 50.00
Trading card, basketball
    Collector's Choice, 1994, #238
    .... 25.00
    Collegiate Collection, 1990, #3
    .... 18.00
    Fleer, 1996-97, #13 .... 3.00
    NBA Hoops, 1991, #30 .... 3.00
    SkyBox, 1992, #41 .... 2.00
    Topps Stadium Club, 1993, #1
    .... 8.00
    Upper Deck Hologram, 1992,
       AW4 .... 12.00

❖ Josef Originals

Even though a printer originally misspelled the name of this company, Tom and Muriel Joseph George had success on their hands shortly after they started in 1946. Eventually, production was moved to a Japanese factory, with Muriel continuing to create the designs. The company was sold to Applause, Inc. in 1985.

Reference: Jim and Kaye Whitaker, *Josef Originals*, Schiffer Publishing, 2000.

Periodical: *Josef Original Newsletter*, P.O. Box 475, Lynnwood, WA 98046.

Bottle, kangaroo and baby, 6" h
    .... 95.00
Cat, white Persian, paper label
    .... 115.00
Doll, California January........... 80.00
Figure
    Angel Praying 25.00
    At Home, 6-1/2" h 115.00
    Black Native Girl, orig spear
    .... 85.00
    Birthday Girl, 10th birthday
    .... 40.00
    Down to Sleep 45.00
    Dress Up Like Dad 45.00

Josef Originals musical figurine, 5-3/4" high, $55.

Elf Mending Pants.............25.00
Hawaiian Hula Girl.............80.00
Mistletoe Boy 20.00
Puff 40.00
Teddy 35.00
Wee Folks.........................25.00
Music box, boy and girl feeding bird,
    5" h...................................80.00
Night light, mouse...................45.00
Pie bird, yellow chick, 3-1/4" h
    ....90.00

❖ Jugtown Pottery

Although serious about their craft of pottery making, Jugtown founders Jacques and Juliana Busbee were noted for their offbeat operation. The pottery was established in 1920 and was in business until 1958. Ben Owens was one of their most talented potters, Jacques did most of the designing, and Julie took care of promotion.

Bowl, domed lid, orange glaze,
    minor glaze flakes, 4-1/4" h,
    5-1/2" dia..........................85.00
Candlestick, experimental green-
    blue lead glaze, c1963, small
    flake, 17-1/2" h 412.50
Cup and saucer, brown glaze, minor
    flakes................................75.00
Figurine, pedestal chicken, salt-
    glazed, "Jugtown Pottery A.P.,"
    made by Al Powers, 1960-62,
    7" h.................................302.50

Jugtown rolled-edge plate, orange glaze, chips, 8-7/8" x 10-3/4", $45.

Jug
    Frogskin green glaze, incised
        bands, 5" h 35.00
    Salt-glazed, incised wheat on
        shoulder, 1977, 10" h ..110.00
Pitcher, orange-yellow swirlware,
    1940s-50s, small chip......935.00
Vase
    Vernon Owens sig, 1988, 6-1/4"
        h, 5" dia 75.00
    Oriental style, Chinese blue,
        early 1930s, 5" h 770.00
    Oriental style, frogskin glaze, late
        1920s, 2 handles, 5-1/2" h
        ....935.00
    Oriental style, frogskin glaze, late
        1920s/early 1930s, 8-1/4" h,
        ....825.00

❖ Jukeboxes

Let's spin those tunes! Jukeboxes provided many hours of musical entertainment, and, with the proper care and maintenance, these early entertainment centers can still delight.

Periodicals: *Always Jukin',* 221 Yesler Way, Seattle, WA 98104; *Antique Amusements, Slot Machines & Jukebox Gazette,* 909 26th St NW, Washington, DC 20037; *Coin-Op Classics,* 17844 Toiyable St, Fountain Valley, CA 92708; *Gameroom Magazine,* P.O. Box 41, Keyport, NJ 07735; *Jukebox Collector,* 2545 WE 60th Court, Des Moines, IA 50317.

Note: All prices are for fully restored machines.

AMI
    Continental II, 1962...... 6,500.00
Rock-ola
    Model 1422 .... 6,000.00
    Tempo 4,500.00
    Tempo II 3,300.00
Seeburg
    Entertainer................... 2,000.00
    Mardi Gras, 1977 .... 2,000.00
    Matador, 1973 .... 1,800.00
    Model 201 .... 5,700.00
    Model 202 .... 5,700.00
    Model B........................ 6,000.00
    Model C........................ 7,000.00
    Model G........................ 6,600.00
    Model LPC, 1963 .... 1,700.00
    Model Q-160, 1959 ...... 1,800.00
    Sunstar........................ 2,000.00
Wurlitzer
    Model 2610, 1962 .... 2,400.00
    Zodiac, 1971 .... 1,800.00

For exciting collecting trends and newly expanded areas look for the following symbols:

⚙ Hot Topic

☆ New Warman's Listing

(May have been in another Warman's title.)

❖ Kaleidoscopes

Changing colors and patterns as they turn, kaleidoscopes date to a time when entertainment didn't involve a remote or a computer screen. Look for examples with interesting designs and colorful elements.

Brass case, multicolor crystals, leather carrying case, English, c1910 ....400.00
Brass-colored metal, 5" l 100.00
Paper case, child's, multicolor bits of paper, c1950 ....5.00

Woody Woodpecker kaleidoscope, 8-1/4" high, 1971, $13.

Paper case, child's, Hallmark, decorated with Peanuts characters, rainbow colors on turning cylinder, 9" l 10.00
Paper case, multicolor bits of glass, Corning Glass Museum, c1980 ....15.00
Tin case, tin screw caps for ends, multicolor crystals 200.00

❖ Kanawha

West Virginia was home to this glass company that produced colored glass and crackle glass. Kanawha Glass marked its wares with paper labels.

Basket, amberina crackle, 5-1/4" h 55.00
Creamer and sugar, yellow crackle, applied handles 48.00
Pitcher
   Amberina crackle, long neck, applied amber handle, 8-1/4" h...........................70.00
   Cased, red ext, milk white int, grape leaf design, applied handle, 6-1/2" h.............50.00
   Orange crackle, elongated spout, applied handle, 14-1/2" h.......................75.00
Syrup pitcher, ruby crackle, applied amber handle, cork stopper, stainless steel top, 6-3/4" h 65.00
Vase, crackle
   Amberina, 8" h 70.00
   Yellow, 3-1/2" h 25.00
Vinegar cruet, red crackle, applied yellow handle, 6" h 48.00

❖ Keeler, Brad

Brad Keeler got his start making flamingo figurines that he sold to various California department stores. Once his business expanded, Keeler continued to design the pieces himself, but other individuals created the molds and glazes. Keeler died in 1952, ending a promising career at an early age.

Figure, bird
   Canary, unmkd, 4-1/2" h 35.00
   Cockatoo, #35, shades of pink, mkd 80.00
   Flamingo, #1, head up, male, light crazing, 12" h.......215.00
   Flamingo, #3, head down, female, 7-1/2" h 145.00
   Flamingo, #3, head up, male, 9-3/4" h.....................185.00
   Oriole, #39, apricot and black, 7-1/2" h 75.00
   Rose colored, #17, 6" h..... 70.00
Lobster dish
   3 compartments, gray tone, 12-1/2" l, 12-1/2" w 125.00
   5 compartments, deep red, mkd "Brad Keeler Made in USA 872," 7" l, 12" w 125.00
Planter, Pride & Joy, dog 50.00
Serving dish, crab, 11" 80.00
Tray, figural lettuce leaf, figural tomato relish container 85.00

Keen Kutter No. 12 knife and fork set, oak dovetailed box, $100.

❖ Keen Kutter

Keen Kutter was the brand sold by the E.C. Simmons Hardware Company. Their fine tools were welcome in the workshop and the garden as well as in the kitchen.

Reference: Jerry and Elaine Heuring, *Collector's Guide to Keen Kutter*, Collector Books, 2000.

Collectors' Club: Hardware Companies Kollectors' Club, 715 W 20th Ave, Hutchinson, KS 67502.

Can opener, patent Sept 20, 93 .... 25.00
Food chopper, orig booklet 15.00
Hatchet 30.00
Letterhead, 1911 .... 12.00
Pencil clip, 1950s, ... 17.50
Pinback button, celluloid, red logo, 3/4" dia............................ 58.00

Pocketknife, pearl...................28.00
Scissors, 6-3/4" l 20.00
Razor, red Bakelite, 4" l..........19.00
Waffle iron 90.00

❖ Kennedy, John F.

Many people were fascinated with JFK and his family during his life. Since his tragic death, collectors have continued to keep his memory alive.

Collectors' Club: Kennedy Political Items Collectors, P.O. Box 922, Clark, NJ 07066-0922.
Autograph, signed letter, as Senator in 1957 .... 1,200.00
Bank, "John F. Kennedy 1917-1963," plaster bust painted bronze, 7" h 25.00
Book
   John F. Kennedy: War Hero by Richard Tregaskis, paperback 15.00
   John F. Kennedy President by Hugh Sidey, Crest, 1964, rev ed, water stain............... 10.00
Bottle, Wheaton, "Ask not what your country can do for you..." ..25.00
Cigar band, set of 4 different JFK bands 250.00
Comic book, *John F. Kennedy, Champion of Freedom*, 1964 ....8.00

Framed photograph, the Kennedys, Karsh of Ottowa, 10" x 8", $10.

Magazine, *Life*
   Nov. 29, 1963, devoted to assassination..........................25.00
   Dec. 6, 1963, devoted to funeral 25.00
Paperweight, sulphide, cameo set against translucent green ground, Baccarat, 1963, 2-3/4" dia..................................165.00
Plate, pewter, Hamilton Mint, 9" dia 110.00
Salt and pepper shakers, pr Figural, JFK seated in rocking chair, "Copyright Arrow 1962" 75.00
Porcelain, JFK decal on 1, Jackie on other, gold trim 40.00
Spoon, silver-plated, bust of JFK, "35th President 1961-1963," bowl emb "Friendship 7," Wm. Rogers Mfg. Co. 25.00

❖ Kentucky Derby Glasses

The Run for the Roses is perhaps the best-known horse race in the world. Collectors are equally excited about the fact that this event signals the arrival of a new commemorative drinking glass each year. Examples from the 1940s through the 1960s are comparatively scarce at flea markets, but Derby glasses from later decades are available and affordable.
1960...............................60.00
1973...............................35.00
1974...............................25.00
1979...............................15.00
1986...............................10.00
1993.................................8.00

❖ Kewpies

Rose O'Neill's Kewpies made their first appearance in art form in a 1909 issue of *Ladies Home Journal*. These charming characters caught the attention of Joseph Kallus, whose Cameo Doll Company produced the first Kewpie dolls in 1913. In the intervening years, several different companies have produced O'Neill's designs, including Lefton and Enesco.

1979 Kentucky Derby glass, $15.

Periodical: *Traveler*, P.O. Box 4032, Portland, OR 92708.

Collectors' Club: International Rose O' Neill Club, P.O. Box 668, Branson, MO 65616.
Bank, chalkware, back incised "Cast/Craft, Toledo, O," orig paint and glitter, 12" h 155.00
Blanket, felt fabric, fleshtone images, blue sky, tan buildings, red stitched border, 1914 Rose O'Neill copyright.................. 8.00
Candy container, glass, patent date on base 100.00
Doll
   2-1/2" h, celluloid, some paint missing 20.00
   8" h, chalk, black skin tone 65.00
   9" h, vinyl, jointed at neck, shoulders and hips, mkd "Cameo, orig pantaloons," two small discoloration marks 45.00
   10" h, vinyl, head turns, mkd "Cameo" 75.00

13" h, vinyl, orig tag, mkd
"Cameo" 95.00
Figure, Lefton
Bewildered.........................12.00
Content, 5" h.......................27.50
Holding foot, 3" h 12.00
On belly, 3-3/4" l.................12.00
Puzzled, 5" h......................27.50
Winking, 5" h......................30.00
Night light, figural, orig foil sticker
"Lefton Trade Mark Exclusives
Japan," 6-1/2" h.................75.00
Pendant, small.........................10.00
Postcard, "Can't think of an earthly
thing to say, 'Cept I hope you are
happy Valentine's Day," Kewpie
writing valentines, © Rosie
O'Neill, postmarked Feb 12,
1925, published by Gibson Art
Co......................................20.00

❖ Key Chains

Everybody has a couple of key chains saved, whether in a desk drawer, a pocket, or even a collection. Key chains are wonderful collectibles for children—relatively easy to find and usually inexpensive.

Collectors' Club: License Plate Key Chain & Mini License Plate Collectors, 888 Eighth Ave, New York, NY 10019-5704.
Amoco, flicker, "As You Travel Ask Us," back with place for name and address......................12.00
Ballantine Light Lager Beer, 3-ring motif, plastic, red and white, 3" h 10.00
Batman, PVC head, Funatics, MOC 2.00
Coca-Cola, Spanish version, 1960s, 1-1/2" dia 8.00
Copple Motor Co., Chrysler-Plymouth, Mound City, Kan., flicker, Hula dancer 12.00
Curious George, pewter, Danforth 16.00
Esso Happy Motoring Key Club, black plastic disk with silver accent lettering, company name on front, serial number on back, on 3" x 5" white card, red accent text, stapled 4" l gold accent key chain, c1950, unused 24.00
Ford, metal, mkd "Karriers USA" 4.00
Good Luck Penny, circular, "Keep me and never go broke," penny dated 1957........................12.00

Horse, key chain in mouth, 5" h 30.00
Johnson Feed Service, Feeding Grinding & Mixing On Your Farm, Griffin, Ga., flicker... 12.00
License plate, Missouri, 1968 ....10.00
Minnie Mouse, plastic, 4" l 5.00
Silly Putty, small egg-shaped container, MOC......................... 3.75
Super Bowl XXX, 1996, NRFP 6.00
Three Stooges, MOC............. 20.00
Vincent System, Exterminators - Fumigators, Tampa, Florida, flicker 12.00
Western Auto, Over 50 Years of Service, metal......................... 15.00
Winnie the Pooh, brass colored 4.00

❖ Keys

We've all got some keys saved—keys from our first car or first house, the key to a diary or a bicycle lock. Flea markets almost always have a selection you can choose from when seeking to add to a collection.

Collectors' Club: Key Collectors International, 1427 Lincoln Blvd, Santa Monica, CA 90401.
Cabinet
Brass, decorative bow....... 12.00
Nickel-plated, lyre design bow 6.50
Car
Ford, Model T, diamond mark 3.50
MGB, 1973, orig leather fob 7.50
Packard, logo key................ 8.00
Door
Bronze, Keen Kutter bow, 4" l 8.00
Steel, standard bow and bit 4.50
Folding, bronze and steel, jack knife............................. 17.50
Hotel
Bit type, steel, bronze tag.... 4.50
Pin tumbler, plastic tag........ 2.50
Jewelers, brass, 6-point.......... 22.00
Padlock, Yale, 2-1/4" h.............. 5.00
Railroad
C & O 18.50
IC RR 15.00
TT RR.............................. 22.00
Watch, brass and steel, loop bow, folds 7.50

GE Plastics key chain, back mkd "25 Years, 1960 1985, Reaching for the horizon...and beyond!," pewter, 1-1/2" diameter, $13.50.

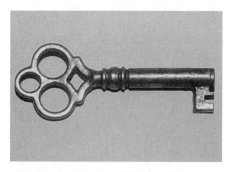

Metal desk key, 2" long, $2.

❖ Kitchen Collectibles

The kitchen is probably the one room in the house that generates more collectibles than any other room. When one considers all the equipment needed to prepare food and the dishes required to serve and store food, it isn't surprising. Somehow, many gadgets make their way to the back of the cupboard when the latest and greatest contraption arrives on the scene. Often, it's those old timers that become the basis for a collection of kitchen items.

References: Linda Fields, *Four & Twenty Blackbirds: A Pictorial Identification and Value Guide for Pie Birds*, self-published; Linda Campbell Franklin, *300 Years of Housekeeping Collectibles,* Books Americana, 1992; —, *300 Years of Kitchen Collectibles*, 4th ed, Krause Publications, 1997; Don Thornton, *Apple Parers,* Off Beat Books, 1997; —, *Beat This: The Eggbeater Chronicles*, Off Beat Books, 1994. Don Thornton.

Periodicals: *Cast Iron Cookware News*, 28 Angela Ave, San Anselmo, CA 94960; *Cookies*, 9610 Greenview Ln, Manassas, VA 20109; *Griswold Cast Iron Collectors' News & Marketplace*, P.O. Box 521, North East, PA 16428; *Kettles 'n Cookware*, P.O. Box B, Perrysville, NY 14129; *Kitchen Antiques & Collectibles News*, 4645 Laurel Ridge Dr, Harrisburg, PA 17110; *Piebirds Unlimited*, 14 Harmony School Rd, Flemington, NJ 08822.

Collectors' Clubs: Assoc of Coffee Mill Enthusiasts, 5941 Wilkerson Rd, Rex, GA 30273; Cookie Cutter Collectors Club, 1167 Teal Rd, SW, Dellroy, OH 44620; Corn Items Collectors Assoc, 613 N Long St, Shelbyville, IL 62565; Eggcup Collectors' Corner, 67 Stevens Ave, Old Bridge, NJ 08857; Griswold & Cast Iron Cookware Assoc, 54 Macon Ave, Asheville, NC 28801; International Soc for Apple Parer Enthusiasts, 735 Cedarwood Terr, Apt 735B, Rochester, NY 14609; Jelly Jammers Club, 110 White Oak Dr, Butler, PA 16001; Kollectors of Old Kitchen Stuff, 501 Market St, Mifflinburg, PA 17844; National Reamer Collectors Assoc, 47 Midline Ct, Gaithersburg, MD 20878-1996; Pie Bird Collectors Club, 158 Bagsby Hill Lane, Dover, TN 37058.

For additional listings, see *Warman's Antiques & Collectibles* and *Warman's Americana & Collectibles.*

Angel food pan, 10" dia 28.00
Canister, house shape, roof as lid, Avon, set of 4.....................55.00
Dipper, gourd, 17" l.................35.00
Egg poacher, red enamel, gray enamel insert, 3-3/4" x 8" ..24.00
Egg separator, aluminum, 9" l....7.00
Hot pad holder, black boy, chalkware, 1940s, chips, 8" h 55.00
Iced tea dispenser, black base and cov, Lord Calvert Hotel, Baltimore, Md., 1940s.............375.00

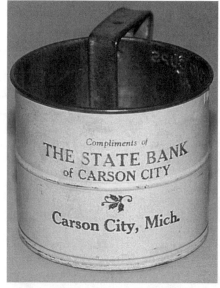

Flour sifter, "The State Bank of Carson City, Mich.," $45.

Mouli-Julienne, rotary cutter, 3 interchangeable cutting and shredding discs, c1950, orig box 30.00
Set, cookie cutter, biscuit cutter, donut cutter and pastry cutter, mkd "Calumet," Wear-Ever Aluminum, made in USA, set of 4 .... 14.00
Spoon rest, pear shape, red plastic, mkd "Fuller Brush Co.".........5.00
Strawberry huller, Nip-It, 1906 .. 4.00
Teapot and salt and pepper shakers, aluminum, 4-cup teapot, cov with red finial, orig strainer with red handle, mkd "Highly Polished Aluminum, Made in Japan," orig box 25.00
Vegetable grater, tin, iron back, wood handle, old blue paint, Schroeter 40.00
Wall plaque
    Fruit, 1950s, paint scuffed... 8.00
    Parrot, chalkware, chips, 10" x 6" 12.00

❖ Kitchen Glassware

One area of kitchen collection that is brightly colored and durable is kitchen glassware. What started as a few manufacturers who were determined to create glass ware that could go from the stove to the table to the refrigerator has given us products few of us could live without, such as Pyrex and Corningware.

Reference: Gene Florence, *Kitchen Glassware of the Depression Years*, 5th ed, Collector Books, 1995 (1997 value update).

Collectors' Club: National Reamer Collectors Assoc, 47 Midline Ct, Gaithersburg, MD 20878-1996.

For additional listings, see *Warman's Americana & Collectibles* and *Warman's Glass.*

Batter bowl, black ships dec ... 25.00
Bowl
    Kellogg's, green 75.00
    Orange Dot, custard, 8" dia 32.00
Butter dish, cov
    Criss-Cross, blue, 1/4-lb size 125.00
    Federal, amber, 1-lb size... 35.00

2-cup measure, light green, $20.

Canister, cov, round, Seville Yellow,
    coffee, sugar or tea, 48-oz
    .... 135.00
Cheese dish, cov, slicer, opaque
    white 90.00
Flour shaker
    Deco, ivory, black lettering
    .... 45.00
    Roman Arch, ivory 45.00
Fruit bowl, Sunkist, pink 335.00
Grease jar
    Red Dots, white 30.00
    Seville Yellow, black trim.... 35.00
Measuring cup
    Crystal, Kellogg's 8.00
    Green, Kellogg's 22.00
    Seville Yellow, 4-cup 125.00
Mixing bowl, Criss-Cross, blue
    7-1/2" dia 85.00
    8-1/2" dia 100.00
Refrigerator bowl, cov, round, Jen-
    nyware, pink, 16-oz 48.00
Refrigerator dish, cov
    4" x 4", Criss-Cross, blue... 35.00
    4" x 8", Criss-Cross, blue
    .... 100.00
Salt and pepper shakers, pr
    Jennyware, ftd, pink........... 55.00
    Ships, red trim, red lids 55.00
Salt box, crystal, 4-1/2" x 3-3/4"
    .... 25.00
Spice set, green lids, Scotty Dog
    dec, green tiered holder, cinna-
    mon, ginger, red pepper,
    paprika, mustard, cloves, all-
    spice, set of 7 .... 325.00
Sugar bowl, Roman Arch, custard,
    red dot 60.00
Tom & Jerry set, custard, bowl and
    12 mugs 135.00

Kitchen Kraft salad fork, green, slight nick to one tine, 10" long, $85.

❖ Kitchen Kraft

Kitchen Kraft is a line of kitchen-ware that was produced by Homer Laughlin during the early 1930s. The pieces feature floral decals, and most of the items are marked "Kitchen Kraft" and/or "Oven-Serve."
Casserole, cov
    Cobalt blue, 8-1/2" dia 110.00
    Yellow, individual size 90.00
Cream soup bowl, double handles,
    pink...................................... 7.50
Jar, cov
    Cobalt blue, small 500.00
    Green, large 390.00
Mixing bowl, cobalt blue, adv for
    Sherwood Rye, 6" dia 250.00
Pie plate, yellow, 9" dia............ 20.00
Platter, oval, yellow................. 50.00
Salad fork
    Green 115.00
    Yellow.............................. 245.00
Salad spoon, red 200.00
Salt and pepper shakers, red, pr
    .... 95.00

❖ Kitchen Prayer Ladies

These pretty ladies entered the kitchen scene in the 1970s and gently reminded us of the power of prayer as we bustled about.
Bank, pink.............................. 275.00
Bell, pink, stress line on back ..60.00
Bud vase................................ 160.00
Canister, Instant Coffee
    Blue................................. 175.00
    Pink................................. 130.00
Coffee mug, blue 325.00
Cookie jar
    Blue................................. 350.00

Kitchen Prayer Lady napkin holder, Enesco, 6-1/4" high, $30.

Pink 350.00
Crumb pan 60.00

❖ Kliban

Who is that black and white cool cat? Kliban! He's available in many shapes and sizes, on almost any type of object imaginable. The one constant, however, is his trademark sly smile.
Candlestick 50.00
Candle tin, 2-1/2" h 28.00
Checkbook cover, rollerskating
    .... 15.00
Mug, "Eat Them Mousies," English
    origin 27.50
Pin, pewter, flying, 2" l............ 27.50
Placemat, woven, rect, red and
    white, unused, pr 20.00
Plate, wearing sneakers, Kiln Craft,
    9" dia................................ 22.00
Poster, Top Cat 6.00
Pot holder 5.00
Sleeping bag, light use 22.00
Teapot, Sigma Trend Setter 47.50
Tumbler, plastic, 4-1/4" h 30.00
Wastebasket, 12" h................. 65.00

❖ Knowles, Edwin M. China Company

Some collectors associate the name Edwin M. Knowles China Co. with fine dinnerware. Others correlate it with limited edition collector plates. The firm was founded in West Virginia in 1900 and continued producing quality wares until 1963. The company used several different marks, and should not be confused with Knowles, Taylor, & Knowles, another manufacturer of fine dinnerware.

Berry bowl, Yorktown, wheat dec
.... 8.00
Bread and butter plate, Beverly
.... 4.00
Bowl, Mexican motif 35.00
Cake plate, Yorktown, white ground, blue daisies 7.50
Cup and saucer, Yorktown, floral dec
.... 15.00
Doll, Little Red Riding Hood, MIB
.... 30.00
Gravy boat, attached underplate, Williamsburg 40.00
Mother's Day plate, Norman Rockwell, 1984 .... 35.00
Plate, Moss Rose, 10-1/4" dia ... 9.00
Platter, Mexican motif 47.50
Sauceboat, stand, Mayflower
.... 35.00
Soup bowl, Yorktown, floral dec
.... 8.50
Souvenir plate, San Francisco Bay, Alcatraz, Treasure Island, 10" dia 75.00

Bluebird oval dish, Knowles, Taylor & Knowles, 5-1/8" x 9-3/8", $40.

❖ Knowles, Taylor & Knowles

Knowles, Taylor & Knowles was located in East Liverpool, Ohio. In business from 1854 to 1931, their production included ironstone, yellowware, and fine dinnerware, as well as translucent china known as Lotus Ware. Knowles, Taylor & Knowles used as many as nine different marks.

Baker, Victory, rose medallion, c1925, 9-1/2" l 20.00
Butter dish, cov, round, gold band, orig drainer insert 45.00
Casserole, cov, Victory, 10" l ... 35.00
Chamber pot, white ground, gold medallions and dec 45.00
Chamber set, blue floral transfer print, gold trim, 5 pcs 130.00

Dinner plate, Grapevine, 10-1/4" dia
.... 10.00
Platter
    Bittersweet, 15" l 25.00
    Coronado, 14-3/4" l 20.00
    Plymouth, 13" l 20.00
Tier, Ebonnette, 3 snack plates, black and white 12.00
Vegetable bowl, roosters in center, hens around edge 15.00

❖ Korean War

This sad time in the world's history is remembered by veterans and collectors. Flea markets are starting to see more items relating to the Korean War as well as later conflicts.

Cigarette lighter, engraved 25.00
Decanter, "Korean War Statue Dedicated 1984," base mkd "Mount Hope, American Legion, Limited Edition, 1984," 12-1/4" h . 130.00
Helmet, aviator, gold dome helmet with goggles and electronics, with liner and earphones
.... 255.00
Medal, Bronze Star, 1953, with documentation 47.50
Newspaper, *Record Herald*, Korean War news 5.00
Pass, Safe Conduct, UN 35.00
Patch
    Foxy Few, 12th Fighter Squadron 355.00
    Utron Five, Navy 85.00
Pin, veteran 9.50
Postcard
    Battleship, 1952 postmark... 3.00
    Sailor's prayer, 1951 postmark
    .... 4.00
Tour jacket 155.00

L

For exciting collecting trends and newly expanded areas look for the following symbols:

⊙ Hot Topic
☆ New Warman's Listing

(May have been in another Warman's title.)

❖ Labels

Labels are colorful, plentiful, and usually inexpensive. Used to identify an almost endless variety of products, they make wonderful collectibles.

References: Joe Davidson, *Fruit Crate Art*, Wellfleet Press, 1990; Lynn Johnson and Michael O'Leary, *En Route: Label Art from the Golden Age of Air Travel*, Chronicle Books, 1993; Ralph and Terry Kovel, *The Label Made Me Buy It*, Crown Publishers, 1998; Gordon T. McClelland and Jay T. Last, *Fruit Box Labels: An Illustrated Guide to Citrus Labels*, Hillcrest Press, 1995; Gerard S. Petrone, *Cigar Box Labels: Portraits of Life, Mirrors of History*, Schiffer Publishing, 1998.

Periodical: *Banana Label Times*, P.O. Box 159, Old Town, FL 32860.

Collectors' Clubs: The Citrus Label Soc, 131 Miramonte Dr., Fullerton, CA 92365; Fruit Crate Label Soc, Rte 2, Box 695, Chelan, WA 98816; International Seal, Label and Cigar Band Soc, 8915 E Bellevue St., Tucson, AZ 85715; Soc of Antique Label Collectors, P.O. Box 24811, Tampa, FL 33623.

Cigar box
    Club House, 6-1/2" x 8" 12.00
    Edmund Halley, inner box label, shows astronomer with telescope and globe............ 12.00
    Mark Twain, inner box label, image of Twain, vignettes of Tom Sawyer and Huck Finn 15.00

Clover Farm brand green beans, unused, water damage, 50 cents.

    Quaker Cigar......................7.00
    White Cat, cigar box label, 7" x 8-3/4"............................15.00
Fruit and vegetable
    Buffalo Apples, Watsonville, Calif., shows buffalo........7.00
    Homer, oranges, Orange Heights, Calif., shows pigeon 7.00
    Independent, apples, 1931 copyright, Liberty Bell design, 8-3/4" x 10"......................3.00
    Lake Wenatchee Pears, lake scene, framed, 12-1/8" x 14-3/4"..........................35.00
    Merry Christmas, 5" x 8" 4.00
    Og-Na Tomatoes, Ogna Indian, framed, 9-1/2" x 18-1/2" 32.00
    "Oh Yes! We grow the Best California Pears"....................4.00
    Red Head, 9" x 10-1/2" 8.00
    Red Lion, Exeter, Calif., shows roaring lion 5.00
    Redman, blue ground, 8-1/2" x 10"..................................10.00
    Safe Hit Texas Vegetables, Welasco, Tex., baseball player in stadium, 1940s, small size 10.00
    Shamrock Navels, Placentia, Calif., shows shamrock, mountains and orange grove 7.00
    Up North, apples, 9" x 10"....5.00
    Yakima Chief, 8-1/2" sq........9.00
Hotel luggage
    Hotel California, Paris, swan and Champs-Elysees, 1920s-30s, 4" sq 14.00
    Hotel Quirinal, Rome, Italy, green, white and red, 2-1/2" x 4", varnished 8.00
    Oriental Hotel, Kobe, Japan, "Operated by Toyo Kisen Kaisha - Kent W. Clark, Manager," pre-World War II, varnished.......................14.00

❖ Labino

Keep your eyes open for studio glass by Dominick Labino. Prices are rising quickly for marked items.
Creamer, light green, mkd "Labino 6-1975," 4-3/8" h............. 220.00
Vase
    4-1/2" h, bulbous, opaque white, brownish red flames, cased in clear, mkd "Labino 11-1974" 275.00
    4-3/4" h, sculpture type, clear, amber veiling pink, mkd "Labino 12-1982" 500.00
    4-3/4" h, sculpture type, 4-bubble design in pink veiling, gold flecks, cased in clear, mkd "Labino 11-1978" 470.00
    4-3/4" h, unsymmetrical, irid light green, mkd "Labino 1968" 250.00
    4-7/8" h, opaque black, subtle ruby swags, mkd "Labino 1969" 350.00
    5-1/4" h, sculpture type, clear, amber center, hour glass opening, red and black flames, mkd "Labino 9-1974" 485.00
    6" h, bulbous, opaque metallic irid green, purple highlights, mkd "Labino 1964" 385.00
    8-1/2" h, amethyst, second gather of glass in 6 root-like prunts, mkd "Labino 1960" 440.00

❖ Lace

Collecting lace became a hobby for the wealthy around 1940. Collectors were dedicated to their hobby and devoted a great deal of time and effort to acquiring and studying various examples. As time passed, some of these collections were sent to museums, and others were dispersed. Now, once again, collectors are eagerly searching for antique lace.

References: Elizabeth Kurella, *Guide To Lace and Linens*, Antique Trader Books, 1998; ——, *Secrets of Real Lace,* The Lace Merchant, 1994; ——, *Pocket Guide to Valuable Old Lace and Lacy Linens*, The Lace Merchant, 1996; ——, *The Complete Guide To Vintage Textiles*, Krause Publications, 1999.

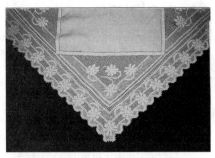

Lace tea cloth, white linen center, circa 1900, 54" square, $150.

Periodical: *The Lace Collector*, P.O. Box 222, Plainview, MI 49080.

Collectors' Club: International Old Lacers, P.O. Box 554, Flanders, NJ 07836.

Bridal veil, cathedral length, white lace trim, 1950s 90.00

Collar, Duchesse bobbin lace, roses, daisies and scrollwork design, c1870, 5" at center back, 32" l 125.00

Curtain, machine-made lace, ecru, 36" x 72" 75.00

Doily, round, needle lace, rose design, 6" dia 20.00

Yardage, machine-made Valenciennes lace, cotton, floral and scrollwork design, 4", 1-yard 10.00

✶ Ladders

Flea markets are good places to find used ladders, often at bargain prices. Those examples that are aged and weathered are being snatched up for their decorative appeal. If you're more concerned with functionality, be sure to check for sturdiness. It will save you from any nasty surprises if called upon to rescue a neighbor's kitten in distress.

Aluminum, extension type, working cond 20.00

Wood, painting type, paint spatters 15.00

Wood, primitive, some wear
   3-foot, narrow 18.00
   6-foot 12.00
   10-foot 5.00

❖ Lady's Head Vases

Planters and vases in the shape of a lady's head are common sights at any flea market. But, did you ever notice how many variations and styles there are? These holders were popular with florists from the 1940s through the early 1960s.

Collectors' Club: Head Vase Society, P.O. Box 83H, Scarsdale, NY 10583.

Baby, blond hair, open mouth, pink ruffled bonnet tied under chin, pink dress, unmkd, 5-3/4" h 20.00

Carmen Miranda 125.00

Cowboy, brown hair, blue eyes, yellow hat and neckerchief, yellow star-shaped badge, unmkd, 6" h 35.00

German Shepherd, mkd Japan, 6" h 125.00

Howdy Doody 45.00

Jackie Kennedy, orig foil label, mkd "#E-1852, INARCO," 6" h 650.00

Napcoware
   7-1/2" h, #C7495 .... 295.00
   8-1/2" h, #C7496 .... 445.00
   9-1/2" h, #C7497 .... 525.00

Nurse, short blond hair, raised right hand, painted fingernails, white cap with Red Cross insignia, white uniform with gold accents, unmkd, 5-3/4" h 70.00

Polynesian, Shawnee 60.00

Lady's head vase, $75.

❖ Lalique

Many collectors associate the name Lalique with French glass, but did you know that Rene Lalique started his artistic career as a jewelry designer? His early molded glass brooches and pendants were highlighted with semiprecious stones and are eagerly sought by Lalique collectors today. By 1905, he had devoted himself to making glass tableware, and by 1908 he had begun designing packaging for cosmetics and perfumes. Most of his glass was marked.

Collectors' Club: Lalique Collectors Society, 400 Veterans Blvd, Carlstadt, NJ 07072.

Reproduction Alert.

For additional listings, see *Warman's Antiques & Collectibles* and *Warman's Glass*.

Ashtray, inscribed "Lalique France" 75.00

Bowl, Bagatelle-style, ftd, bird dec, base inscribed "Lalique France" 100.00

Cigarette lighter, butane, lion, base inscribed "Lalique France" 175.00

Perfume bottle, sq colorless bottle, Richard Hudnut Master Violet, orig contents, labels intact, some wear 145.00

Tumbler, molded with 8 recessed full-length figures, engraved "Lalique France" on base, modern, 4" h 175.00

Urn, Marc Lalique design, Dampierre, 5-1/4" h 195.00

Vase

   Eglantines, frosted oval, polished thorny branches and rose blossoms, center base inscribed "R. Lalique," 4-1/2" h 400.00

   Elongated bulbous form, 8 notched lobes, designed by Marie-Claude Lalique, engraved "Lalique France" on base, 13-1/2" h 200.00

Ceramic pony lamp, 8" high (excluding fixture), $15.

✲ Lamps

Flea markets are great places to find all kind of lamps and replacement parts. When considering a purchase, check to see that all necessary parts are included. As a precautionary measure, any vintage lamp should be rewired before placed into service.

Periodical: *Light Revival*, 35 W Elm Ave, Quincy, MA 02170.

For additional listings, see *Warman's Antiques & Collectibles, Warman's Americana & Collectibles,* and *Warman's Glass.*

TIAS Top 10

The following list ranks the most highly sought collectibles on the Internet during 2000.

1. Avon	6. Noritake
2. China	**7. Lamps**
3. Cookie jars	8. McCoy
4. Roseville	9. Clocks
5. Furniture	10. Books

Source: www.tias.com

Children's
ABC blocks, wood and plastic, linen-over-cardboard shade 25.00
Hobby horse, wood, tail missing, no shade 2.00
Sesame Street characters, plastic and wood 15.00
Lava, red flakes move when heated 70.00
Motion
Antique cars, Econolite, 1957, 11" h 125.00
Fountain of Youth.............120.00
Snow scene, bridge, Econolite 175.00
Radio, Michael Lumitone.......200.00
Stenographer's, clamps onto desk, Emeralite 395.00
Table
Milk can, metal base, repainted, decals added, no shade 10.00
Small stoneware crock, brown-and-white linen shade ...35.00
Television
Dragon motif, Mirmar, Calif. 85.00
Leopard, ceramic 65.00
Wall, tole, peach ground, white floral trim...................................10.00

✦ Lap Desks

Because they were portable, lap desks (or folding desks as they were sometimes called) were the laptop computers of the 18th and 19th centuries. They also provided a firm writing surface as well as a place to store papers and writing instruments. Some examples are quite ornate, having locks, drawers, and even secret compartments.

Black lacquer, mother-of-pearl inlay of flowers, leaves and grape clusters, 4" h, 14" w, 10" d 600.00
Mahogany, brass bands, green leather writing surface, 6-1/2" h, 17" w, 9-3/8" d................. 650.00
Mahogany, satinwood inlay, Victorian, replaced leather writing surface, repairs to underlying wood 395.00
Rosewood, mother-of-pearl inlay, velvet writing surface, 4-1/2" h, 13" w, 10-1/4" d.............. 760.00
Walnut, velvet writing surface, 8-1/2" d x 12" x 5-1/2" 295.00

✦ Laundry

It's Monday; must be wash day. Somewhere between pounding clothes against a rock along the creek and tossing them into a Maytag washer came the washboard. Most washboards had a galvanized metal scrubbing surface in a wooden frame; however, glass and pottery inserts were also made, with the latter being especially valuable. A number of other items were also used to assist in early laundry duties, including sprinklers, dryers, and a whole host of cleaning agents. Also see Clothes Sprinklers, Irons, and Soap in this edition.

Bag, cloth
2 black laundresses, 29" x 20" 35.00
Embroidered "Laundry" and with flowers, stains............... 10.00
Booklet, *Washee Washee Laundry List,* The Really & Britton Co., Chicago, 1905, 11" x 5" 26.00
Box, Cook's Washing and Blueing, 5" h 30.00
Crate, Gold Dust Soap, embossed with images of Gold Dust Twins, paper label on ends, no lid, 8-1/4" h, 29-3/4" w, 16-1/2" d 295.00
Figurine
Precious Moments, "Be Not Weary In Well Doing," laundry girl, 6" h 70.00
Napco, "Washday," girl doing laundry, 5-1/4" h 39.00
Ruler, folding, 3-section, celluloid, "Quaker City Laundry, Souvenir of the National Export Exposition, Fall 1899" 25.00

Vel detergent box, Colgate-Pal-molive-Peet Co., unopened, 12-ounce, $20.

Sprinkler, metal, Jack and Jill decal 20.00
Trade card, "Higgins' German Laundry Soap," shows sailors and young lady, removed from scrapbook 5.00
Washboard
　Glass insert, wooden frame, National Washboard Co., No. 860 ....30.00
　Graniteware, blue scrubbing surface, wooden frame, National Washboard Co., Soap Saver, 24" h, 12-1/2" w........... 115.00
　Mother Hubbard, wooden rollers, 1 dowel cracked, 22-1/4" h, 12-1/4" w.....................105.00

❖ Law Enforcement Collectibles

Collectors actively investigate flea markets for items to add to their collections of law enforcement memorabilia. Some have a desire to honor those who risk their lives to keep the peace, while others enjoy the sense of history that's attached to these items.

References: Matthew G. Forte, *American Police Equipment*, Turn of the Century Publishers, 2000; Monty McCord, *Law Enforcement Memorabilia*, Krause Publications, 1999.

Periodical: *Police Collectors News*, RR1, Box 14, Baldwin, WI 54002.
Button, uniform, brass-tone, 3/4" dia
　Toledo Police.......................8.00
　Cincinnati Police, scales of justice....................................8.00
　Philadelphia Police...............8.00
Comic book
　Police Comics, #1 ....975.00
　Police Comics, #20 ....325.00
Envelope, D.A. Farrell, Sheriff of Mills County, Glenwood, Iowa, late 1800s..........................12.00
Magazine, *National Police Gazette*, December 1947 ....15.00
Patch, uniform, Correction Department, City of New York, shield shape, 4-1/4" x 3-1/2" 6.00
Photograph, Police & Shore Patrol, 1940s, small tears, 11" x 14" 13.00
Plate, Royal Canadian Mounted Police, shows 3 Mounties on horseback, Wood & Son, Burslem, England, 10" dia 12.00
Postcard, Mounted Police Squad on Parade in Manhattan, hand-tinted, unused......................9.00
Toy
　Patrol, battery-op, remote control, twin propellers, litho tin and plastic, late 1960s/early 1970s, Japan, 6-1/2" l ...36.50

Railway Police badge, D.L.&W. Railroad, nickel-plated brass, 1920s, $85.

Motorcycle, Marx, litho tin with siren............................. 400.00
Volkswagen police car, tin, Taiwan, 1970s, MIB, 9" l.... 67.00

❖ Lefton China

Founded by George Zoltan Lefton, this company has created china, porcelain, and ceramic tableware, animals, and figurines. Lefton wares are well marked, and some also include a Japanese factory mark.

Reference: Loretta DeLozier, *Collector's Encyclopedia of Lefton China*, vol. 1 (1995), vol. 2 (1997), v. 3 (1999), Collector Books; Ruth McCarthy, *More Lefton China*, Schiffer Publishing, 2000.
For additional listings, see *Warman's Antiques & Collectibles*.
Bookends, tigers, #6663 .... 35.00
Candy box, cov, heart-shaped, red and white, doves, #5597... 22.00
Egg
　Chick with rose on lid, paper label, chips 15.00
　Roosters and chick on lid, paper label, #3429.................. 25.00
Figure
　Birthday Boys 30.00

Lefton bisque figurine, girl with cat, 6" high, $8.

Chiropractor, 10" h 15.00
Madonna and Child, #543.. 75.00
January Angel, #3332........ 22.00
Three Pigs 35.00
Mug
Elf handle, green, #4284.... 15.00
Grant................................. 35.00
Jackson............................. 35.00
Salt and pepper shakers, Mammy
and Chef, pr 40.00
Snack set, Fleur de Lis........... 50.00
Teapot, To A Wild Rose, #2561
.... 165.00
Wall plaque, roosters, #397, pr
.... 30.00

❖ Lenox

Walter Scott Lenox opened his porcelain factory in 1906, employing potters and decorators, whom he lured from Belleek. Fine Lenox is almost translucent in appearance. The firm is still in business and many factory outlet stores sell their products.

For additional listings, see *Warman's Antiques & Collectible* and *Warman's American Pottery & Porcelain.*

Bowl
Acanthus leaf shape, ivory
ground, gold trim, 9" l.... 48.00
Christmas, 4" sq 15.00
Coffee pot, Cretan #0316 ...... 165.00
Cream soup, Tuxedo, green mark
.... 42.00

Lenox Serenade vase, 6" high, $30.

Cup and saucer
Alden................................. 25.00
Golden Wheat.................... 35.00
Figure
Snow Queen 70.00
Stardust............................. 70.00
Night light, Leda and Swan, white
bisque, sgd, dated, 10" 600.00
Platter, Oak Leaf, platinum trim,
13-1/2" l 75.00
Salt, molded seashells and coral,
green wreath mark, 3" dia .35.00
Tea strainer, hp small pink flowers
.... 72.00
Vase, ivory ground, gold trim, gold
mark................................. 65.00

❖ Letter Openers

These knife-like collectibles are also handy little desk accessories. Constructed of almost any type of material, early manufacturers found them to be wonderful tools for advertising.

Reference: Everett Grist, *Collector's Guide to Letter Openers*, Collector Books, 1998.

Advertising
The Empire Varnish Co., Cleveland, OH, metal, 8" l 7.00
Fuller Brush Man, plastic 8.00
Martin Mfg. Co., Pick Up Beaner, Keck-Gonnerman's Bean Thresher, Phone 325, Bad Axe, MI, celluloid handle, 8-1/2" l 20.00
Pennsylvania Independent Telephone Association, 50th Anniversary, 1902-1952, plastic handle, 8-1/8" l 10.00
Black memorabilia, alligator eating black boy, celluloid, boy is a wooden pencil, Japan, 1930s-40s, 5-1/2" l 97.50
Celluloid, metal blade, 6-1/2" l
....28.00
Political, "Republican Convention 1976 Kansas City, Missouri," black plastic.......................22.00
Souvenir
Chicago's World's Fair, Federal Building, marble handle, metal blade....................95.00
Florida, alligator shape, celluloid
....10.00

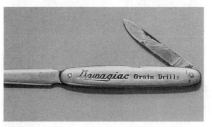

Dowagiac Grain Drills advertising letter opener and knife, $160.

Palo Duro Canyon State Park, wooden, 1935, damage to tip 25.00
Toledo, brass-colored cross, 6-5/8" l 10.00

❖ Libbey Glass

Libbey Glass is a true American success story. Established in Toledo, Ohio, in 1888, Libbey Glass Company produced quality cut glass. Eventually, the company added art glass and pressed wares. Libbey Glass was a frequent exhibitor at World's Fairs, allowing them to advertise their products and promote future lines. Some of their glassware, but not all, is marked.

Bowl, cut glass, Somerset, sgd, 9" dia.............................. 165.00
Candy dish, cov, cut glass, divided, clover shape, hobstar and prism dec, sgd, 7" dia 90.00
Cordial, cut glass, American Prestige, c1930 .... 50.00
Goblet, clear, Liberty Bell pattern, 7" h 25.00
Plate, cut glass, Gloria, 7" dia
.... 165.00
Spooner, Maize pattern, creamy opaque kernels of corn, blue husks, gold trim............... 190.00
Tumbler, light green, lightly swirled ribs, mkd, set of 6 .... 60.00
Wine, Silhouette, clear bowl, black cat silhouette in stem, sgd, 7" h
.... 200.00

Maize pattern condiment set, opaque and green, 6-1/4" high, $770. (Photo courtesy of Jackson's Auctioneers & Appraisers.)

❖ License Plates

As a driver, you won't get far without one of these and few of us can throw them out when new plates are issued. Many of these humble identifiers find their way to flea markets, much to the delight of collectors. Since many states and organizations now issue specialty license plates, watch for those to increase in value too. Beginning license plate collectors should seek out a flea market devoted to automobiles, where common examples range from $2 to $5. Look for examples in good condition, but expect to find some wear.

Attachments
    48-star U.S. flag, 6" x 5-1/2"
    ....35.00
    Shell Motor Oil, metal, 1930s,
      wear, rust, 5-1/4" x 3"....39.00
Political
    "Al Smith," metal, green and
      white.............................60.00
    "All the Way with LBJ," red letters
      on white ground, 1964
      ....22.50
    "Hoover," white on black ground,
      rust, 60% paint..............25.00

States
    California, 1935.................40.00
    Colorado, 1972, rust...........4.00
    Illinois, 1916, rust..............30.00
    Illinois, 1933.....................25.00
    Illinois, 1961.....................18.00
    Kansas, 1971......................5.00
    Maine, 1914, porcelain.......95.00
    Massachusetts, 1915, porcelain
    ....95.00
    North Dakota, 1970.............5.00
    South Dakota, 1934.............5.00
Walt Disney
    Disneyland Paris, Mickey Mouse
    ....30.00
    Disney Surprise 20th Birthday,
      AAA...............................50.00
    Disney Wilderness Lodge Resort
    ....17.00

❖ Liddle Kiddles

Introduced by Mattel in 1965, these half-pint dolls drew a big response from little girls. But that was nothing when compared to the reaction of adult collectors today that eagerly search for these reminders of their childhood. While the dolls themselves constitute the main attraction, accessories and go-withs are also on many want lists.

Beauty Parlor Purse Playset, 1996,
    MIB.....................................5.00
Collector's case, vinyl, holds 8 dolls,
    minor wear, 14-1/2" x 10"..15.00
Colorforms, Dress-Up Kit, trays
    missing, incomplete, box damaged.................................24.00
Coloring book, unused, 1966...43.00
Doll
    Liddle Kiddle Kologne containing Lily Of The Valley doll,
      1960s...........................38.00
    Lola with boat, boat repaired,
      3-3/4" h........................34.00
Play outfit, "Cook 'N," Totsy Corp.,
    orig box..............................45.00
Pop-Up Playhouse, 1967.........45.00

❖ Light Bulbs and Sockets

Because light bulbs were usually thrown away when no longer needed, finding vintage examples—especially those in working condition—can be a real challenge.

Light bulb, $5.

Christmas
    Grape cluster, minor paint loss,
      2-3/4" h...........................9.00
    Pear, paint loss, 2-1/8" h...36.50
    Santa Claus, 2-faced, 3-1/4" h
    ....40.00
    Snowman carrying umbrella,
      milk glass, paint loss, 3-3/4" h
    ....32.50
    Snowman with shawl, milk glass,
      paint loss, 3-3/4" h........32.50
    Rose bud, paint loss, 2-1/4" h
    ....26.50
Edison, early 1900s, mkd "SAC JAC" and "Property of NY Edison Company - Not to be sold," double curl, classic filament
    ....31.00
Edison, Mazda flood light, paper lights, works, 5-1/2" h........28.00
Westinghouse, Edison base, sharp tip, double anchored filament with 3 loops, red patent label with yellow cotton insulation
    ....31.00

❖ Lighters

Cigarette lighters have attracted collectors for years. Watch for examples with figural forms or with interesting advertising. Look for examples in good condition, but exercise caution when trying to determine if a lighter is in working order.

Regens lighter AAA Club insignia, silver-plated, 2-1/8" high, $18.

Collectors' Clubs: International Lighter Collectors, P.O. Box 3536, Quitman, TX 75783; Pocket Lighter Preservation Guild & Historical Society, 380 Brooks Dr, Suite 209A, Hazelwood, MO 63042.

Alligator, ceramic, made in Japan, 1-3/4" h, 5" l 28.00

Boat, Occupied Japan, Bakelite and chrome 148.00

Bottle, Marlboro, wear 8.00

Dodge, 1940s 60.00

Donkey, ceramic, "Japan" on side, Amico, 2" h, 2-1/2" l 35.00

Lays Potato Chips, chrome, Zippo style 20.00

Space Needle, chrome 180.00

Spaniel, ceramic, 3-1/2" h, 4-3/4" l 25.00

Stein, nautical motif, pewter, made in Japan, 5" h 20.00

Winston Cigarettes, penguin design, Japan 10.00

Zippo, ship and a lighthouse design, white on chrome 15.00

❖ Lightning Rod Balls

If you're reading this and wondering just what on earth we're talking about, take a gander at the roof of an old barn the next time you're out in the country. We'll bet you'll spot a colored glass ball up on top of that lightning rod. Lightning rods used on homes and other structures in rural America were often embellished with decorative glass ornaments. Although some were odd shapes, most were round with embossed star or swirl designs. Dark blue and amber were fairly common, but other rare colors such as red can also be found.

References: Russell Barnes, *Lightning Rod Collectibles Price Guide*, self-published; Michael Bruner and Rod Krupka, *The Complete Book of Lightning Rod Balls*.

Periodical: *The Crown Point*, 2615 Echo Ln, Ortonville, MI 48862.

Collectors' Club: Weather or Knot Antiques, 15832S CR 900W, Wanatah, IN 46390.

Classic round shape, amethyst, copper caps, 3-1/2" dia 60.00

D&S

Blue milk glass, 10-sided, with short rod and stand 100.00

White milk glass, 10-sided, copper caps, 4" dia 85.00

Electra round, white milk glass, copper caps, 5-1/8" h, 4-1/8" dia 75.00

Hawkeye, blue milk glass, rounded top with starbursts, tapering bottom, copper caps, 5-1/8" h, 4-3/8" dia 175.00

Moon & Stars, white milk glass, copper caps, 5-1/8" h, 4-3/8" dia 75.00

Ribbed grape

Blue milk glass, copper caps, 5-1/8" h, 4-3/8" dia 100.00

White milk glass, copper caps, 5-1/8" h, 4-3/8" dia 90.00

Round pleat (Barnett Ball), cobalt, copper caps, 5" h, 4-3/8" dia 175.00

Sharp pleated, sun-colored amethyst (orig white milk glass), copper caps, 5" h, 4-1/2" dia ... 75.00

Shinn System, white milk glass, copper caps, 4-1/2" dia 32.00

Smooth round, sun-colored lavender (orig white milk glass), copper caps, 4-1/2" dia 50.00

"Adopt A Puppy," Franklin Mint plate, 8-1/4" diameter, $10.

❖ Limited Edition Collectibles

You're guaranteed to find limited edition collectibles at any flea market you visit. This multi-million dollar market includes many types of objects, with some very dedicated artists and companies offering their wares. Please remember that much of the value of a limited edition object lies with the original box, packaging, etc.

References: Jay Brown, *The Complete Guide to Limited Edition Art Prints*, Krause Publications, 1999; Collector's Information Bureau, *Collectibles Price Guide & Directory to Secondary Market Retailers*, 9th ed, Krause Publications, 1999.

Periodicals: *Collector Editions*, 170 Fifth Ave, 12th Floor, New York, NY 10010; *Collector's Bulletin*, 22341 East Wells Rd, Canton, IL 61520; *Collectors Mart Magazine*, 700 E State St, Iola, WI 54990; *The Treasure Trunk*, P.O. Box 13554, Arlington, TX 76094.

Collectors' Clubs: International Plate Collectors Guide, P.O. Box 487, Artesia, CA 90702. There are also many company-sponsored clubs, as well as local groups.

For additional listings, see *Warman's Antiques & Collectibles* and *Warman's Americana & Collectibles.* Also see specific makers, such as Bing & Grondahl in this edition.

Christmas ornament
    Angel, Danbury Mint, 4" h..48.00
    Candy cane, Wallace Silver-
        smiths, 1986.................35.00
    Christmas Castle, Reed & Bar-
        ton, 1980......................80.00
    Heavenly Strings, Anri, 1989
        ....150.00
    Hummel, Schmid, 1978 .....12.00
    Sleigh bell, silver-plated, Wallace
        Silversmiths, 1992........30.00
    Snowflake, sterling silver,
        Gorham, 1973...............95.00
Figure
    Kay's Doll, River Shore, 1982
        ....45.00
    Marilyn Monroe, Royal Orleans
        Porcelain......................40.00
    Norman Rockwell, Back to
        School, Dave Grossman,
        1973..............................45.00
    Our Puppy, Anri, 1985 ....70.00
    Out of Step, Schmid, 1985
        ....25.00
Plate
    Annie and Grace, Edwin M.
        Knowles, MIB.................40.00
    Ashley, Gone with the Wind
        Series, Edwin M. Knowles,
        MIB.............................100.00
    Cardinal, Audubon Society, 1973
        ....50.00
    Caroling, Disney, Schmid, 1975
        ....15.00
    Christmas in Mexico, Royal
        Doulton, 1973................10.00
    Down the Alps, Schmid, 1987
        ....60.00
    Easter, 1980, Edwin M. Knowles,
        MIB................................30.00
    Flowers for Mother, Schmid,
        1974..............................85.00
    Follow the Yellow Brick Road,
        Wizard of Oz.................20.00
    Hummingbird, Edwin M.
        Knowles, 1986, MIB......24.50
    Laurie & Creche, Zolan......45.00
    Robin, Edwin M. Knowles, 1986,
        MIB................................24.50
    Sunday Best, Reco, 1983..50.00
    Valentine's Day, Edwin M.
        Knowles, 1981, MIB......20.00
    Wood Duck, Franklin Mint, 1972
        ....115.00

❖ Lincoln, Abraham

This famous American president is a favorite among collectors. Lincoln memorabilia is also a favorite with many museums, and genuine vintage articles can be prohibitively expensive. Contemporary items bearing Lincoln's likeness are more reasonably priced, however.

Avon bottle, Lincoln bust, cologne,
    orig box, 7" h 22.50
Bank, cast metal, bronze finish,
    5-1/2" h.............................75.00
Bust, bronze, c1900, 15" h 98.00
Calendar plate, 1911, Lincoln por-
    trait, "Compliments of Chas.
    Seepe & Sons, Peru, Ill.," 9" dia
    ....95.00
Newspaper, *Harper's Weekly*, March
    2, 1861, "Abraham Lincoln, the
    President-Elect, addressing the
    people from the Astor House
    balcony"............................40.00
Plate, commemorative
    150th anniversary of Lincoln's
        birth, Lincoln image, floral
        border, Enoch & Ralph
        Woods, 1959, 10" dia 40.00
    Centennial of christening of Lin-
        coln, Ill., 1953, Stetson China
        Co., 10-1/4" dia 18.00

"Abraham Lincoln's Old Home, Springfield, Illinois" souvenir china tumbler, made in Germany, 3-3/4" high, $40.

Stereoptican card, The Birthplace of
    Abraham Lincoln, Keystone
    View Co., back stained 4.00
Tobacco silk, image of Lincoln with
    facsimile signature, black on
    white, 3" h 100.00

❖ Lindbergh, Charles

Collectors are fascinated with this early aviator and his adventures. Look for printed items, commemorative pieces, and even textiles that pertain to his many flights.

Bank, G&T, 1928.................. 300.00
Book
    The Lone Eagle: Lindbergh,
        Blakely Printing Co., Chi-
        cago, 1929, color portrait
        photo, 20 pgs, stiff paper 8" x
        9" 35.00
    War Within and Without, diaries
        and letters of Anne Morrow
        Lindbergh, Harcourt Brace
        Jovanovich, 1980, dj....... 8.50
Children's book, *Boy's Story of
    Charles Lindbergh,* hardcover
    .... 5.00
Cigarette card, 1927 .... 26.00
First day cover 2.25
Magazine, *Time,* June 13, 1938,
    color cover of Lindbergh and sci-
    entist working on Fountain of
    Age, 76 black-and-white pages,
    8-1/2" x 11" 15.00
Pin, Lucky Lindbergh 22.00
Plate, yellow glazed china, color
    graphics of smiling Lindy, plane
    over ocean between Statue of
    Liberty and Eiffel Tower, "First To
    Navigate The Air In Continuous
    Flight From New York To Paris-
    1927," Limoges China Co.,
    8-1/2" dia 24.00
Postcard, 3-1/2" x 5-1/2"
    Red-tinted, Lindbergh in cockpit
        of Spirit of St. Louis 15.00
    Sepia-tone photo of Lindbergh
        with unidentified gentleman
        on ornate balcony, Under-
        wood copyright, unused
        .... 25.00
Sheet music, *Lindbergh: The Eagle
    of the U.S.A.,* Howard Johnson
    and Al Sherman, 1927 ...... 55.00
Tapestry, New York to Paris ...115.00

Embroidered table scarf, 10" x 15", $2.50.

❖ Linens

No dining room or bedroom is properly dressed without an assortment of linens. Today's collectors treasure these textiles. Some pieces were hand-made and exhibit exquisite craftsmanship, although machine-made examples have a beauty all their own. Enjoy them, but use them with care.

Reference: Elizabeth Kurella, *Guide to Lace and Linens*, Antique Trader Books, 1998.

Periodical: *The Lace Collector*, P.O. Box 222, Plainview, MI 49080.

Collectors' Club: International Old Lacers, P.O. Box 554, Flanders, NJ 07836.

Boudoir pillow, peach linen, embroidered, lace trim, satin bows in each corner, 10" x 14" 120.00
Doily
   Crocheted, pink and cream, 7" sq 5.00
   Embroidered, oval, shaped scalloped edge, scrolled design, 10" x 7" 6.50
Dresser scarf, Damask, embroidered, 31-1/4" x 17" 25.00
Handkerchief
   Oriental motif, orig silver tag "Hermann Irish Linen," 15" sq 17.50
   Place de la Concorne Paris, 7" sq 12.00
   Place des Eetre Paris, 7" sq 10.00
   Purple petunias and green crocuses, orig label "Pure Linen, Hand Rolled," 12" sq 17.50

Napkin, linen, 25" sq, set of 6 ..20.00
Pillow cover, linen, embroidered, 19" x 13-1/2" 25.00
Tablecloth and napkins
   Damask, light blue, some minor stains, 79-1/2" x 60", 4 napkins 15-1/2" sq...............50.00
   Irish linen, 4 matching napkins, orig box, never used, 54" sq 30.00
Tea towel, Irish linen, hand embroidered
   Comical Couple, 19-1/2" x 13-1/4"..........................15.00
   Dogwoods, slight use, 18-1/2" x 12" 15.00
   Purple pansies, white ground, fringed edge, 18" x 20"..18.00

❖ Little Golden Books

Read me a story! From the time Simon & Schuster published the first Little Golden Book in 1942 until today, millions of stories have been read. Collectors have many fun titles to choose from, and everyone is sure to have a childhood favorite.

Reference: Steve Santi, *Collecting Little Golden Books*, 4th ed, Krause Publications, 2000. The following pricing information is from this title.

Collectors' Club: Golden Book Club, 19626 Ricardo Ave, Hayward, CA 94541.

***The Little Red Caboose**, Little Golden Book, 1953, $10.*

Note: All listings are first editions.
Bedtime Stories, 1942 .... 40.00
Brave Eagle, 1957 .... 16.00
Brownie Scouts, 1961............ 15.00
Bugs Bunny's Birthday, 1950 .. 14.00
A Day at the Zoo, 1950............. 8.00
Dinosaurs, 1959..................... 6.00
Farmyard Friends, 1956 .... 7.00
Exploring Space, 1958............. 7.00
Five Little Firemen, 1948 ....11.00
The Gingerbread Man, 1965..... 6.00
Gunsmoke, 1958 .... 20.00
Heidi, 1954............................. 8.00
The Jetsons, 1971 .... 25.00
The Jungle Book, 1967............ 8.00
Let's Fly a Kite, Charlie Brown, 1987 .... 5.00
Little Black Sambo, 1948, 42-pg edition.................................. 150.00
The Monster at the End of this Book, 1971..................................... 5.00
My Kitten, 1964...................... 16.00
The New Baby, 1948 .... 15.00
The Night Before Christmas, 1955 .... 25.00
Noel, 1991 .... 2.00
The Pokey Little Puppy, 1942 .... 40.00
The Rescuers, 1977 .... 7.00
Rudolph the Red-Nosed Reindeer, 1958..................................... 7.00
The Sailor Dog, 1953.............. 20.00
Stories of Jesus, 1974 .... 6.00
Tarzan, 1964 .... 20.00
Tootle, 1945 .... 45.00
The Saggy Baggy Elephant, 1947, ... 20.00
Wild Kingdom, 1976.................. 6.00
The Wizard of Oz, 1975............ 8.00

❖ Little Orphan Annie

Little Orphan Annie has been the subject of comic strips, books, radio shows, and even a modern musical.
Book
   Little Orphan Annie and Chezzler, Big Little Book, 1933, cover taped on.............. 25.00
   Little Orphan Annie in Cosmic City, 1933, spine missing, wear............................. 15.00
Doll, plastic, Knickerbocker, 1982 .... 15.00
Glass, Sunday Funnies, 1976, 5-1/2" h 15.00

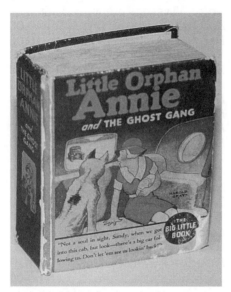

***Little Orphan Annie and The Ghost Gang*, Big Little Book, worn, $25.**

Mug, ceramic, Annie holding an Ovaltine mug, The Wonder Co., Chicago, 3" h 100.00
Plate, "Daddy Warbucks," Knowles, 1982, 8-1/2" dia 37.50
Shaker with lid, plastic, Ovaltine 80.00
Toothbrush holder, bisque, "Orphan Annie and Sandy," mkd Japan, 4" h 145.00
Toy stove, orig green paint, 1930s, 4-1/2" x 5" 125.00

❖ Little Red Riding Hood

This storybook character has been portrayed on all manner of items, the most popular of which are the pottery pieces sold by Hull. Some people feel that Hull manufactured the blanks and sent them to Royal China and Novelty Company in Chicago for decorating. Others think that Hull contracted with Royal China for both production and decoration. In any event, prices have escalated for these charming figures.

Reproduction Alert.
Allspice jar 375.00
Bank, standing 575.00
Canister
    Cereal 950.00

Little Red Riding Hood salt and pepper shakers, 1 with damage, 3" high, pair, $75.

Coffee 750.00
Sugar 600.00
Tea 750.00
Cookie jar
    Gold stars, red shoes 300.00
    Poinsettia trim 300.00
Creamer, tab handle 275.00
Flour canister 375.00
Match holder, Little Red Riding Hood and Wolf, striker, Staffordshire 75.00
Milk pitcher 400.00
Mustard, orig spoon 250.00
Salt and pepper shakers, pr
    3-1/4" h, incised "135889," gold trim 140.00
    5-1/2" h 150.00
Sugar bowl, cov, crawling 275.00
Teapot, cov 325.00

❖ Little Tikes

When it comes to toys, many surges in collectability begin as adults start buying back the items they remember from childhood. With that being the case, expect Little Tikes items to continue to grow in popularity. Flea markets are excellent sources for these plastic playthings. Because the items were mass-produced, look for examples in prime condition.
Doll house, with family, furniture, horse and car, blue roof, 21" h, 28" w, 17" d 95.00
Fishing set, pole, hook, 10 fish 12.50

Grandma's House, with grandma, girl and accessories 34.00
Mansion dollhouse, 3-story, 32" h, 44" w, 18"d 65.00
Noah's Ark, with Noah, lion, giraffe and sheep 8.00
Pirate, 4" h 4.00
Roadway set, 68 pcs, with train, people, station, bridge and accessories 26.50
School bus, 9 figures 9.00
Stable set, with swinging doors, fence, horses and accessories 73.00

Nesting Little Tikes farm animals, plastic, discontinued set of 5, 5-1/8" to 1-5/8", $10.

❖ Lladró Porcelain

Brothers José, Juan, and Vincente Lladró established this Spanish ceramics business in 1951. The company produces ceramic figurines and flowers. This segment of the collectibles market underwent a period of speculation several years ago. It remains to be seen whether the high prices realized at that time will remain in place when those items return to the marketplace.

Collectors' Club: Lladró Collectors Society, 1 Lladró Dr, Moonachie, NJ 07074.

Girl wearing nightgown, pigtails, puppy on lap, 7" h 125.00
Girl with lamb, 10-3/4" h 65.00
Pepita, sombrero 175.00
Puppy, butterfly on tail, 4" h .. 250.00
Spanish policeman 100.00
Wedding couple 45.00

❖ Locks and Padlocks

Locks and padlocks have been around since the 1600s, so collectors have much to choose from. Many will specialize in a particular type of lock or will focus on products produced by a particular manufacturer.

Collectors' Club: American Lock Collectors Assoc, 36076 Grenada, Livonia, MI 48154.

Reproduction Alert.

Ames Sword Co., Chicopee, Mass., bronze, no key 150.00
Champion 6 Lever, brass, no key 28.00
Commemorative, Pan-American Exhibition, man riding buffalo, emb, brass, 1901 .... 95.00
Douglas Air Inc., Yale and Town, no key, 1-1/2" w 19.00
Leader, no key, some rust, 2-7/8" h 5.00
Miller, brass, no key, 3-1/2" h, 2-1/2" w 19.00
Railroad
    L&N, Yale, pink tumbler 25.00
    NC&StL, switch type, Yale, figure-8 back 30.00
    Union Pacific, switch type, brass lever 45.00
Yale Junior, 2-3/4" h 32.00

Keen Kutter advertising lock, $125.

❖ Loetz Glass

This pretty Austrian glass often features bright iridescent colors, and some examples can be found with metal ornamentation. Produced at the same time Tiffany was inspiring the art glass world, Loetz glass was similar in color and in shape to pieces produced by Tiffany. Some pieces are signed, but not all.

For additional listings, see *Warman's Antiques & Collectibles* and *Warman's Glass.*

Basket, brilliant green mottled on clear ground, irid blue and purple finish, 6-1/2" h, 5" w 100.00
Bowl, rolled rim, applied green tadpoles, irid white ground, 4" h, 7" dia 110.00
Bowl and stand, irid deep ruby shading to irid pale green, 5 crimps, 3 chased metal studs, reticulated 4-ftd stand, 8" x 4" 400.00
Candlesticks, slender baluster form, raised circular foot, gold irid, 9-1/2" h, pr 300.00
Dish, 3 applied pulled-out handles, gold base, sgd in pontil with monogram "M" and "L," 2-3/4" h, 8-1/2" dia 200.00
Rose bowl, ruffled purple, irid raindrop dec, 6-1/2" dia 265.00
Vase
    6-1/2" h, tadpole neck, white irid ground, green rigaree..200.00
    6-3/4" h, 4-3/4" dia, cranberry, irid fan and swirl optic, bulbous bottom, 3 dimples 190.00
    8" h, 4-5/8" dia, amethyst, eggshell irid, bulbous bottom 235.00
    8-1/2" h, irid green, pimpled texture, polished pontil, mkd "Loetz, Austria" 450.00

❖ Lone Ranger

The Lone Ranger and his Indian pal Tonto rode into our lives on the silver screen, over the radio waves, and through the television. For those wishing to collect, there is a plethora of items from which to choose.

Periodical: *The Silver Bullet*, P.O. Box 553, Forks, WA 98331-0553.

Lone Ranger gun and holster set, holster only, original box, $500.

Collectors' Club: Lone Ranger Fan Club, 19205 Seneca Ridge Ct, Gaithersburg, MD 20879-3135.
Book
    The Lone Ranger and the Menace of Murder Valley, Big Little Book, 1938, spine detached 20.00
    The Lone Ranger and the Warhorse, 1951 .... 30.00
Cap gun, "The Lone Ranger, Hi-Yo Silver," trigger missing, 9-1/4" l 65.00
Coloring book, 1959................ 50.00
Comic book, *Lone Ranger and Silver*, #369, Dell, 1951 .... 22.00
Game, Lone Ranger Game, Parker Brothers, 1938, faded cover, wear 75.00
Hair brush, wooden................. 25.00
Halloween mask, 1960s.......... 30.00
Holster, 2-gun set, no guns, 1976, Gabriel 45.00
Squirt gun, plastic, figural, hat broken 50.00
Target game and gun, target 27" x 16" 300.00
Toy, Lone Ranger Hi-Yo Silver, tin windup, Marx, 8" h 295.00

Christmas Collection, 1987 Edition Mistletoe Basket, 7-1/2" high, $75.

❖ Longaberger Baskets

Made in Dresden, Ohio, these baskets attract a lot of attention and have a huge following. Sold mostly through home shows, baskets have begun entering the secondary market. To achieve high prices, baskets must be in mint condition. Liners and protectors add to the value, as does a maker's signature.

Bayberry basket, fabric liner, protector, "K. S. Lanam" wooden lid 60.00
Booking basket
   Ambrosia, 1994..................25.00
   Chives, fabric liner, protector, 1995............................40.00
Baking basket, Crisco American, napkin liner, protector, non-Longaberger wooden lid, 1993 ....95.00
Bee basket, protector, 1996, 8-1/2" x 8-1/2" x 5" 105.00
Cake basket, swing handles, fabric liner, protector, 1993..........50.00
Dresden Tour, fabric liner, protector, 1993 ....45.00
Easter basket, fabric liner, protector
   1993, large..........................45.00
   1993, orig J.W., sgd...........70.00
   1996.....................................35.00

Flowerpot basket, fabric liner, protector, 1994...................40.00
Gingerbread basket, orig product cards, 1990, 10" x 6" x 4" ..95.00
Heartland, small purse, Longaberger signatures, 1993................50.00
Hostess basket
   Appreciation, 1996.............35.00
   Christmas Evergreen, fabric liner, protector, 1995......90.00
   Easter, 1991.......................45.00
   Sleigh bell, fabric liner, protector, wooden lid, 1994 ....85.00
   Wildflower, protector, 1994 ....75.00
Key basket
   Medium, fabric liner, 1989..25.00
   Medium, green accent weaving, protector, 1994 ....30.00
   Small, green accent weaving, protector, 1994 ....25.00
   Small, red accent weaving, protector, 1995 ....20.00
   Tall, 1993............................20.00
Lilac basket, fabric liner, protector, tie-on, 1994.........................40.00
Measuring, Holiday, protector, 1990, 13" 80.00
Mother's Day, 1989, 7" x 5" x 3-1/2" 85.00
Pantry basket, protector, 1989 ....45.00
Patriot basket, All-American, fabric liner, divided protector, 1997 ....30.00
Petunia basket, fabric liner, protector, 1997..............................35.00
Pumpkin basket, swing handle, orange and black trim........50.00
Season's Greetings, fabric liner, 1992...................................55.00
Sentiments Basket, red trim, artist sgd and dated, 3" d, 4" sq 85.00

❖ Lotton, Charles

A contemporary studio glass maker, Charles Lotton started out in a small studio at his home in Sauk Village, Illinois. His exquisite glass creations are sold to select retailers and at some antique shows. Several of the Lotton children are now part of the business. Expect to find pieces signed by Charles or by his son David.

Atomizer, selenium red............85.00

Bottle, long neck, flared lip, mandarin red..............................250.00
Bowl, Leaf & Vine, red ground, sgd "David Lotton" 145.00
Chalice, ftd, mandarin red.....160.00
Paperweight, Dana Flora, pink flower, green leaves, sgd, 1982 ....150.00
Rose bowl, cobalt ground, gold zipper-style pattern.............150.00
Vase, irid selenium red, blue luster draped web pattern, sgd, 8" h, 7" dia..............................795.00

❖ Luggage

Interior decorators have been known to frequent flea markets looking for interesting old suitcases and other travel bags. What they have discovered is that luggage can serve as a wonderful storage container at the same time that it is decorative.

Reference: Helenka Gulshan, *Vintage Luggage*, Phillip Wilson Publishers, 1998.

Child's, round, pink vinyl, black and white poodle dec, zipper closure, pink carrying loop, wear.... 20.00
Hatbox, Louis Vuitton, wood, leather, cloth and brass, painted with stripes and initials, minor damage, 18" x 18" x 9" 995.00
Suitcase
   Belber, gray, shows black porter, 6" h, 20-3/4" w, 16" d.... 35.00
   Samsonite #4635, scorch marks, 6-1/2" h, 24" w, 17-1/4" d 40.00

1930s leather suitcase, Indian profile on both sides, $150.

Train case, brown, light beige stripes, fitted int with mirror, molded plastic handle, 1940s 35.00

Valise, dark brown leather, padded leather handles, some wear 150.00

❖ Lunch Boxes

As a kid, it was always easier to remember your lunch if it was packed in a brightly colored lunch box. And, although the term conjures up images of a plastic container with cartoon characters on the sides, lunch boxes or kits have been around since the mid 1930s.

Periodical: *Paileontologist's Report*, P.O. Box 3255, Burbank, CA 91508.

Note: Prices include lunch box and thermos. All prices from Sharon Korbeck & Elizabeth Stephan, *Toys & Prices*, 8th ed, Krause Publications, 2001.

Plastic
101 Dalmatians, 1990 Aladdin 26.00
Beetlejuice, 1980, Thermos 14.00
Ewoks, 1983, Thermos 25.00
Hot Wheels, 1984, Thermos 70.00
Los Angeles Olympics, 1984, Thermos 25.00
Mr. T, 1984, Aladdin 30.00
Rocketeer, 1990, Aladdin... 15.00
Scooby Doo, 1984, Aladdin 60.00
Smurfs Fishing, 1984, Thermos 20.00

Mork & Mindy tin lunch box and thermos, Thermos brand, $30.

Wayne Gretzky, 1980, Aladdin 130.00
Wizard of Oz, 50th Anniversary, 1989, Aladdin 80.00
Steel
Addams Family, 1974, King Seely Thermos 130.00
Astronaut, dome-top, 1960, King Seeley Thermos 310.00
Batman, 1966, Aladdin..... 230.00
Beverly Hillbillies, 1963, Aladdin 260.00
Bionic Woman, with car, 1977 .... 55.00
Dr. Seuss, 1970, Aladdin .200.00
Flipper, 1966, Thermos 235.00
Happy Days, 1977, Thermos 60.00
Hogan's Heroes dome-top, 1966, Aladdin 390.00
Indiana Jones, 1984, King Seeley Thermos 35.00
Jonathan Livingston Seagull, 1973, Aladdin 75.00
Little House on the Prairie, 1978, King Seeley Thermos .. 115.00
Muppet Babies, 1985, King Seeley Thermos 17.00
Péle, 1975, King Seeley Thermos 120.00
Secret of NIMH, 1982, Aladdin 40.00
Star Trek, dome-top, Aladdin 1,075.00
U.S. Mail, dome-top, 1969, Aladdin 85.00
Vinyl
Alvin and the Chipmunks, 1963, King Seeley Thermos ..540.00
Barbie Softy, 1988, King Seeley Thermos 60.00
Donnie & Marie, 1977, Aladdin, long-hair version.......... 130.00
Kodak Gold, 1970s, Aladdin 105.00
Monkees, 1967, King Seeley Thermos 505.00
Sesame Street, 1977, Aladdin, orange 45.00
Tinker Bell, Disney, 1969, Aladdin 350.00

❖ Lu-Ray Dinnerware

Taylor, Smith & Taylor introduced this pretty pattern in the late 1930s and production continued until the early 1950s. The pastel shades were made in Chatham Gray, Persian Cream, Sharon Pink, Surf Green, and Windsor Blue.

Bowl
Fruit, green, 5-1/2" dia....... 10.00
Vegetable, pink, 9" dia....... 22.50
Casserole, cov, pink.............. 155.00
Cream soup, underplate, pink 135.00
Cup, green, 2-1/2" h.................. 8.00
Eggcup, blue........................... 20.00
Plate, yellow, 9" dia................. 10.00
Platter, pink, 9-1/2" x 13-1/2" .. 22.50
Salt shaker, yellow 12.00
Teapot, pink 65.00
Tumbler, juice, cream.............. 70.00

Lu-Ray blue cup, $5.

For exciting collecting trends and newly expanded areas look for the following symbols:

✪ Hot Topic

★ New Warman's Listing

(May have been in another Warman's title.)

Paperback book, *A MAD Look At Old Movies*, 1973, $1.

❖ MAD Collectibles

Look for Alfred E. Neuman's smug mug on any number of items, from games to timepieces.

Book, paperback
   A MAD Look at Old Movies by Dick De Bartolo, 1966, 1st printing 1.00
   The Bedside MAD by William M. Gaines, 1959, 21st printing 1.00
Bookend, Alfred E. Neuman, gold plastic, black relief, pr........ 35.00

Card game, Parker Brothers, 1980, boxed.............................3.50
Game, Screwball, The MAD MAD MAD Game, 1960, Transogram 75.00
Magazine
   MAD Magazine, December 1973 ....3.00
   MAD Magazine, March 1976 ....3.00
   MAD Star Wars Spectacular, 1996 ....2.00
Model, Alfred E. Neuman, Aurora, 1965, unassembled, orig box, complete 142.50
Skateboard, Alfred E. Neuman 117.50

❖ Maddux of California

Maddux of California was founded in 1938 in Los Angeles. The company produced and distributed novelties, figurines, planters, lamps, and other decorative accessories until 1974.

Ashtray, triangular, gunmetal gray, #731, each side 10-1/2" l...20.00
Bowl, white, flared sides, 2" h, 5-1/2" dia......................................16.00
Console bowl, oblong shell motif, white, 14-1/2" l...................20.00
Figurine
   Bull, blue and white, ...140.00
   Flamingo, 6-1/2" h..............40.00
Planter
   Flamingo, 6" h..................165.00
   Pheasant, white, #527, 11-1/4" h, 7-1/4" w 38.00

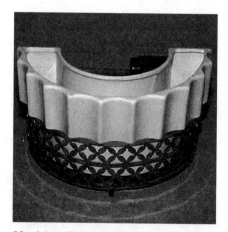

Maddux TV lamp and planter, 6" high, 10" wide, $25.

Television lamp/planter, flamingo, 9-3/4" h 185.00
Vase, double flamingo, unmkd, 5" h 65.00
Vegetable bowl, cov, white with green lid, #3066B, 4-1/2" h, 7-3/4" dia 25.00

❖ Magazines

Magazine collecting offers a unique perspective on American life. By reading the old issues, you can get a clearer idea of what life was like, what products were being advertised, who was making news, etc. Some collectors buy magazines that they can take apart and sell as individual advertisements or articles.

Car Toons, December 1969...... 3.00
Cycle Illustrated, June 1973 ..... 7.00
Fortune, March 1974 .... 3.00
Hit Parader, February 1960, Paul Anka cover.......................... 5.00
Iron Man, December 1962 .... 7.50
Life
   September 1, 1941, Ted Williams 75.00
   December 8, 1941, Douglas MacArthur 8.00
   July 12, 1943, Roy Rogers 55.00
   June 14, 1945, George Patton 35.00
   July 16, 1945, Audie Murphy 46.00

Hot Rod magazine, October 1959, $4.

November 17, 1961, Minnesota Vikings 22.00
September 3, 1968, Beatles 32.50
October 15, 1971, Disney World Opens 265.00
November 1982, test-tube baby 7.00

National Geographic
1901, September 200.00
1906, February 6.50
1923, 12 issues.................52.00
1939, 12 issues.................26.00
1943, 12 issues.................30.00
1948, 12 issues.................18.00
1958, 12 issues...................7.00

Quick Magazine, April 13, 1953, Lucille Ball cover 32.50
The Space Gamer, #6, June/July 1976 ....22.50
True Danger, July 1967 ....17.00

❖ Magic Collectibles

Abracadabra! Magic collectibles can be found at flea markets, but you have to be careful that they don't disappear before your eyes!

Book
Al Baker's Pet Secrets, Al Baker, illus, 1951, sgd by author 125.00
Blitz's Book of Magic: Tricks for Sale, Francois Blitz, New York, 1880 ....600.00
Elusive Magical Secrets, Will Goldston, illus, London, 1912, lock and key, cover badly worn 250.00
Fifty TV Magic Tricks, Marshall Brodien, 1960s..............10.00

Catalog, *Magical Place of Conjuring Wonders, Price List of Mr. J. Bland's Best and Cheapest Conjuring Tricks*, London, 1895 ....450.00

Lobby card
Carter Beats the Devil, Carter the Great, color litho, turbaned Carter playing cards with the devil, Cleveland, c1930 ....400.00
World's Super Magician, Harry Blackstone, RKO Orpheum Theatre, Davenport, 1950s 125.00

Photograph, Harry Blackstone, bust portrait, inscribed by Blackstone, 1939, 8" x 10" 75.00

Poster
El Saba, 3-color, photo of acts, 1937, 24" x 36"............175.00
The Great Virgil, full color, 1940s, 40" x 80" 375.00
Virgil, 3-color, Cheating the Gallows, 1940s, 28" x 41" 250.00

Program, B.F. Keith's Theatre Program, Boston, Dec 19, 1921, including a performance by Houdini, 10-1/2" x 4" 95.00

Set, Master Magic Set, "A Sherms Creation," 1937, MIB 160.00

Toy, Mickey Magician Magic Show, Durham, 1976, NRFB......150.00

Window card, Mind Reading Abilities of Joseph Dunninger, 1926 ....75.00

❖ Magic Lanterns

Here's one of the first types of home entertainment equipment. With a magic lantern, images could be projected and shared for all to see. These do occasionally surface at flea markets. Check to see if the original slides are included with the lantern.

Lantern
Brass, attached alcohol burner 295.00
Delineascope, Spencer Lens Co., Buffalo, 350 slides, orig box 600.00
Germany, orig kerosene burner, 17 glass slides, orig instructions and box............1,890.00
Laterna Magica, orig box and slides 190.00
Optimus, converted to electric 90.00

Slide
Auction scene, Civil War era 15.00
Bearded man 6.00
Berkeley Univ, 1920 ....4.00
Hunt scene, horses, Victorian 2.00
Marching troops 6.00
Mickey Mouse 35.00

❖ Magnifying Glasses

Did you ever play detective and scour the house with a magnifying glass in your hand? Most of us did at one time or another. And, as baby boomers age, perhaps a few of us will be looking for them to help read that fine print in the local newspaper.

Brass and rosewood, matching letter opener, 10" l...................... 50.00
Cracker Jack prize 10.00
Ivory handle, large round glass lens 125.00
Jade handle, large oval glass lens 35.00
Porcelain handle, floral dec, large round glass lens............... 75.00
Wood handle, large round glass lens 27.50

❖ Majolica

Majolica is defined as an opaque tin glazed pottery. Made for centuries, most majolica pieces consist of designs with naturalistic elements such as flowers, leaves, insects, and shells. Few majolica pieces are marked.

Periodical: *Majolica Market*, 2720 N 45 Rd, Manton, MI 49663.

Collectors' Club: Majolica International Society, 1275 First Ave, Suite 103, New York, NY 10021.

Majolica plate with parrots, $85.

Reproduction Alert.

For additional listings, see *Warman's Antiques & Collectibles, Warman's American Pottery & Porcelain,* and *Warman's English & Continental Pottery & Porcelain.*

Butter dish, cov, insert, Shell and Seaweed, Etruscan, minor rim nicks to lid 660.00

Butter pat

    Butterfly, Fielding, stains..220.00

    Grape, Clifton, rim nick 145.00

    Horseshoe, Wedgwood ...300.00

Calling card tray, fox with duck, Continental, rim chips 100.00

Compote, Argenta Ware, molded dish, assorted fruit on basketweave body, Wedgwood, England, imp mark, c1880, 4-5/8" h 460.00

Deep dish, oval, Argenta Ware, molded floral designs, imp Wedgwood mark, star-form frame with imp mark, c1882, 11-7/8" l 420.00

Dish, figural, boy pulling rect cart, 4 wheels, English, c1885, slight foot rim hairline, 9-3/8" l ..750.00

Fruit bowl, oval, Argenta Ware, St. Louis, molded body of flowering branches with butterfly and dragonfly, Wedgwood, England, imp mark, c1882, hairlines on foot rim, 12" l 200.00

Jardinière

    10-3/4" h, cobalt ground, oval portraits in relief, floral festoon, Wedgwood, England, imp mark, c1871, glaze loss, hairlines, repair 375.00

    12-1/4" h, magnolia pattern, pink and yellow glazes, Wedgwood, England, imp mark, c1887 ....230.00

Plaque, Villerory & Boch, lilies of the valley dec, large leaves with finely molded white flowers, mustard ground, reticulated, 12" 175.00

Plate, Pond Lily, minor glaze loss, 9" dia 150.00

Smoking set, monk, tobacco and cigarette holder, orig cover, match holder, and striker, 8" x 6" x 6" 225.00

Teapot, monkey handle, ostrich spout, clutched by two hands, behind spout is face of bearded man, scene of people and village on side, chipped finial, 8" h 150.00

Tea trivet, round, multicolor ...155.00

Tile, red rose center, shaded blue ground, mkd "Made in England, H & R Johnson, Ltd.," 6" sq 45.00

Umbrella stand, relief iris, streaked brown, green and ochre, 18-1/2" h, 9-3/4" dia 350.00

Vase

    11" h, 5-1/2" dia, applied duck, full-relief bamboo and water plants, cream glossy cylinder, gold trim 270.00

    11-1/2" h, figural, black boy and girl, tulip form leaf base, pink flower and bud, boy with basket of food, girl with tray of food, pr 700.00

❖ Marbles

Playing the game of marbles may not be as popular as it once was, but collectors are still able to find great examples at flea markets. Many collectors specialize in a particular type of marble, such as agates, clambroths, clay, or end-of-day examples. Contemporary studio glass blowers are creating some interesting specimens also.

Reference: Paul Baumann, *Collecting Antique Marbles,* 3rd ed, Krause Publications, 1999.

Collectors' Clubs: Marble Collectors Unlimited, P.O. Box 206, Northboro, MA 01532; Marble Collectors Soc of America, P.O. Box 222, Trumbull, CT 06611; National Marble Club of America, 440 Eaton Rd, Drexel Hill, PA 19026.

Akro Agate Co., machine-made

    Blue oxblood 65.00

    Helmet patch.......................2.50

    Lemonade corkscrew........15.00

    Set, "60 Game Marbles No. 00, Vitro Agate Co., Parkersburg, W.Va.," unused..............85.00

    Slag.....................................1.00

Benningtons.............................1.00

Clays......................................10.00

End-of-day onionskin, 3/4" dia 35.00

Glazed painted china..............10.00

Lutz

    Banded, 1" dia 250.00

    Clear, 7/8" dia 200.00

Onion marble, 1-1/4" diameter, $190.

    End-of-day onionskin, 3/4" dia 300.00

    Ribbon, 1" dia.................. 800.00

Marble King Co., machine-made

    Bumblebee 1.75

    Cub scout 5.00

    Wasp 5.00

Mica, 1-1/2" dia 200.00

Oxblood

    5/8" dia, limeade.............. 140.00

    3/4" dia 105.00

Peltier Glass Co.

    Peerless patch 5.00

    Slag 20.00

    Two-color, Rainbow, old type 1.50

Sulphide

    Bear, 1-1/2" dia.................. 95.00

    Sheep, 1-3/4" dia............. 125.00

Swirl

    Banded, 1" dia.................. 65.00

    Divided core, 3/4" dia 18.00

    Latticino core, 1-1/2" dia.... 75.00

    Ribbon core, 3/4" dia......... 75.00

    Solid core, 3/4" dia 25.00

Unglazed painted china 5.00

❖ Marx Toys

Louis Marx founded the Marx Toy Co. in 1921. He stressed high quality at the lowest possible price. Marx toys tend to be very colorful, and many can be found with their original box, which greatly enhances the price.

Donald the Demon plastic Nutty Mads figure, Marx, 1963, 5" high, $15.

Reference: Tom Heaton, *The Encyclopedia of Marx Action Figures*, Krause Publications, 1998.

Periodical: *Toy Shop*, 700 E State St, Iola, WI 54990.

Astronaut figure, white plastic, 5-1/2" h 10.00
Bagatelle
    Combat, 1950s, NMIB 50.00
    Pop A Puppet, 1950s, orig box
    .... 25.00
Dora Dipsy car, tin windup 350.00
Fireman ramp walker with hose
    .... 110.00
Jumpin Jeep, tin windup 215.00
Honeymoon Express, tin windup,
    orig box 350.00
Midget Racer #5, tin windup, 5-1/4" l
    .... 175.00
Rollover Plane, tin windup, 1940s,
    5" l 165.00
Scottie Dog, tin windup, orig box
    .... 215.00
Shady Glen Stock Ranch semi tractor and trailer, "Arrow Truck Lines" and "Shady Glen Stock Ranch" decals, 16-1/2" l 85.00
Toytown dairy wagon, tin, yellow and red wagon, black horse ... 450.00
Train set, #532, 4 cars, 10 pcs of track, box torn 200.00
Tricky Taxi, tin windup, 4-1/2" l
    .... 85.00
Zippo The Climbing Monkey, 9-1/2" l
    .... 200.00

Tin #12 Marx windup race car, metal wheels, 16" long, $225.

❖ Matchbox Toys

Matchbox toys were developed by Lesney in 1953. The name reflected the idea that there was a miniature toy packed in a box that resembled a matchbox. The toys were first exported to America from England in 1958 and were an instant success.

Collectors' Clubs: Matchbox Collectors Club, P.O. Box 977, Newfield, NJ 08344; Matchbox U.S.A., 62 Saw Mill Rd, Durham, CT 06422; The Matchbox International Collectors Assoc, P.O. Box 28072, Waterloo, Ontario, Canada N2L 6J8.

Ambulance, Mercedes, MIB 24.00
Big Tipper, MIB 24.00
Canteen Truck, 2-1/2" l 22.00
Dodge Daytona Turbo, 1994 ..... 1.00
Ferrari F40, 1988 .... 1.00
Ford Cortina 10.00
Ford Escort 1.00
Ford Transit, 1978 .... 2.00

Matchbox Caterpillar bulldozer, No. 64, 1979, $3.

International Ltd. Trailer, 1979 .. 2.00
Jaguar 50.00
Jennings Cattle Truck, no back gate, 4-1/2" l 30.00
Korean Airlines Airbus, Sky Busters, 1988, MOC, 4-1/4" l 35.00
Merry Weather Fire Truck 40.00
Minnie Mouse Car, Walt Disney Productions, 1970s, MOC 50.00
Nissan 300 ZX Turbo, 1986 ...... 1.00
Pontiac Firebird SE, 1982 .... 1.00
Rig, 1993, NRFP 6.00
Toll Truck 10.00
Train Car, green, 1978 .... 28.00
Wells Fargo Truck, #69, 1978
    .... 24.00

❖ Matchcovers

Matchcovers have been on the scene since the early 1900s, but any examples from before the 1930s are considered scarce.

Collectors' Clubs: Rathkamp Matchcover Society, 1359 Surrey Rd, Vandalia, OH 45377; American Matchcover Collecting Club, P.O. Box 18481, Asheville, NC 28814, www.matchcovers.com.

The Aloha Room at the Heartman Hotel- Hawaiian Foods, British Royalty commemorative, Their Most Gracious Majesties to Canada, May 15-June 15th, 1939, cover only 18.00

Hunt's Tomato Sauce matchcover, 1963, $3.

Champion Spark Plugs, 1930s
....2.00
Lion Match Co., N.Y................32.00
Dr. Pepper, 1930s....................25.00
Dutch Boy Paint, Ulrich Paint &
    Glass....................................3.00
Howard Johnson 7.00
Military design, shows barracks and
    flagpole, World War II vintage,
    Universal Match Corp., San
    Francisco.............................6.00
Nu-Grape....................................9.00
Patriotic, World War II, "Buy More
    War Bonds, We Must Win, Our
    First Duty," cover only..........3.00
Reddy Kilowatt 4.00

❖ Match Holders and Match Safes

Matches were precious commodities many years ago. Care had to be taken to keep matches dry, but still handy. Match holders can be found in almost every medium, ranging from table or mantle top containers to wall containers. Match safes, on the other hand, are small containers used to safely carry matches in a pocket. Many are figural and can be found in many metals. Some match safes will also have a striking surface.

Chick figural match holder, painted pot metal, hinged head, striker on base, repainted, 3" high, $50.

TIAS Top 10

The following list ranks the most highly sought collectibles on the Internet during 2000.

1. Avon
2. China
3. Cookie jars
4. Roseville
5. Furniture

6. Noritake
7. Lamps
8. **McCoy**
9. Clocks
10. Books

Source: www.tias.com

Collectors' Club: International Match Safe Assoc, P.O. Box 791, Malaga, NJ 08328.

Amish farmer, figural, cast iron, hanging, 6" h, 4" w...........210.00

Art Nouveau, sterling silver, 2-1/2" x 1-1/8" 135.00

Ceresota Flour, emb die-cut tin, hanging, boy slicing bread, 5-1/2" h 440.00

Graniteware, gray, double pockets, 5-1/8" h, 4-3/8" w.............225.00

Little Red Riding Hood, Regal China 800.00

Stoneware, Whites Utica, salt-glazed

    Plain, tooled pattern, minor surface roughness, mold mark #1, 3" h..........................44.00

    "American Brew Co., Rochester, N.Y.," eagle inside badge, small impact fracture on rim, 2-3/4" h......................220.00

    "Westcott & Parker, Dealers in Coal & Wood, Utica, N.Y.," 3" h...............................275.00

Veuve Cliquot, figural champagne bottle..............................450.00

Walnut, Eastlake style, double pockets, wall-hung, 10" x 6" 105.00

Wooden, barrel-form, brown and tan sponge-painted, 2-1/8" h 115.00

World's Fair, 1904 Exposition, Palace of Manufacturing & Palace of Mines & Metallurgy, metal 65.00

⊛ McCoy Pottery

The J.W. McCoy Pottery was established in Roseville, Ohio, in 1899. Initially, the company produced stoneware and some art pottery. In 1911, three area potteries (Brush Pottery Company, J.W. McCoy Pottery Company, and Nelson McCoy Sanitary Stoneware Company) merged to create the Brush-McCoy Pottery Co. The new company produced all kinds of utilitarian ware, including cookie jars, garden items, and kitchenware.

References: Sharon and Bob Huxford, *Collector's Encyclopedia of Brush-McCoy Pottery*, Collector Books, 1996; —, *Collectors Encyclopedia of McCoy Pottery*, Collector Books, 1980 (1997 value update); Martha and Steve Sanford, *Sanfords' Guide to Brush-McCoy Pottery, Book 2*, Adelmore Press, 1996; —, *Sanfords' Guide to McCoy Pottery*, Adelmore Press, 1997.

Lotus Leaf flowerpot, McCoy, 5" high, $60.

Reproduction Alert.

For additional listings see, *Warman's Antique & Collectibles, Warman's Americana & Collectibles,* and *Warman's American Pottery & Porcelain.*

Brush-McCoy

Bowl and flower frog, Onyx pattern in greens, blues, black and rust, bowl 7" dia 127.50

Flower frog
    Duck form, 2" h, 4" l 175.00
    Turtle form, 5" l, 3" w 100.00

Frog, sitting
    5-1/4" l 35.00

Frog, reclining
    10" l.................................. 150.00

Jardiniére
    Pastel Ware, embossed flowers and leaves, ivory with green accents, 6" h 130.00
    Swallows, brown and green matte glaze, 7" dia 85.00

Jug, Onyx, brown, with stopper, 10" h 150.00

Lantern, Cat patio lantern, 12-1/2" h 125.00

Mug
    Davy Crockett, cream and brown glaze 65.00
    Old Sleepy Eye style, 4-1/2" h 260.00

Musical decanter, blue Onyx, with stopper, 11" h 375.00

Pitcher
    Keg shape, brown glaze 70.00
    Kolor Kraft, #331, dark-green glaze, 6-1/2" h 85.00
    Relief Grape, rose glaze, 4-1/2" h, 4" w 45.00

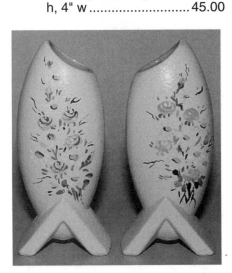

Capri bud vases, McCoy, 7-1/4" high, pair, $25.

Woodland pattern, brown glaze, 7" h..............................120.00

Planter
    Boat on Waves, white, glaze nick, 12-1/2" l.................60.00
    Frog, green, 5-1/2" l 40.00
    House and Garden, green glaze, 5" h, 11" l 50.00
    Madonna, white, 9" h 40.00
    Majolica Ware, 5-1/4" h, 6-1/2" dia 70.00
    Peanut, matte glaze 50.00
    Duck, yellow, 3" h...............15.00

Vase
    Art Vellum Fawn, red glaze, 5" h, 6" dia 100.00
    Gladiola, pink, 12" h...........70.00
    Onyx, green 70.00
    Ringed, #508, green, 8" h 55.00
    Ringed, #508, white, 8" h...40.00

Wall pocket, dog and doghouse, chip, 8" h, 7" w...................80.00

McCoy

Cookie jar
    Mammy, 11" h 295.00
    Rooster 225.00
    Squirrel............................225.00

Jardiniére, green....................185.00

Lamp, Cowboy Boots, replaced shade, 14" h 150.00

Planter
    Bird, double cache pot 45.00
    Duck, 1940s 57.50
    Gondola, black, 11-1/2" l....45.00

Sprinkler, turtle, 11" l................55.00

Tankard, Buccaneer, green, 8-1/2" h 110.00

Teapot, Daisy, pale-green and brown, 1940s, 6" h, 9-3/4" l 65.00

Vase
    Bird of Paradise, green, 8" h 45.00
    Brown Onyx, 7" h 45.00
    Green Onyx, 7" h 45.00
    Triple flowers, yellow, 7" h, 8-1/4" w 90.00
    Sailboat, pedestal, blue......50.00

❖ McDonald's

It might be the sight of those golden arches, or it might be the growling of your tummy that convinces you to head to McDonald's. In any event, if you've got children with you when you go, you'll most certainly go home with a fast-food collectible.

Ronald McDonald plastic tumbler, $3.

Periodical: *Collecting Tips Newsletter*, P.O. Box 633, Joplin, MO 64802.

Collectors' Club: McDonald's Collectors Club, 255 New Lenox Rd, Lenox, MA 01240.

Bank, 1953 Ford delivery van, Ertl, 1/25 diecast, copyright 1996, orig box and key 25.00

Doll, Hamburglar, played-with cond 15.00

Employee cap, flattened service cap, blue cardboard headband with yellow arch symbol on each side, white mesh open crown, mid-1960s, unused, 12-1/2" x 11-1/2"............................. 15.00

Lunch box, Sheriff of Cactus Canyon, Aladdin, 1982, orig thermos, orig hang tag 175.00

Map, Ronald McDonald Map of the Moon, 1969........................ 7.50

Mug, Garfield, c1987, set of 4 .... 12.00

Patch, cloth, Ronald McDonald, red, white, blue and yellow stitching 2.00

Puppet, hand, plastic, Ronald McDonald, c1977................ 2.00

Salt and pepper shakers, pr Original building shape...... 16.00

Speedy Fries and Shake,
4-1/2" h 16.00
Snow globe, 101 Dalmatians, MIB
....25.00
Teeny Beanie Babies, from 1998
series, Pinchers, Happy, Bongo,
Mel, Inch and Twigs, set of 6
....50.00
Valentines, strip of 6 different valentines, 1978.........................3.00

❖ McKee Glass

Founded by the McKee Brothers in 1853, this glassware company remained in production until 1961. Their output included pattern glass, depression-era glass, kitchenware, and household wares.

Batter bowl, Jade-ite................45.00
Bottoms up tumbler, light emerald,
patent #77725, orig coaster
.... 175.00
Butter dish, cov, Seville Yellow, sgd
on lid and base, flake on bottom,
1-lb size 80.00
Candleholder, double, Rock Crystal,
5-1/4" h.............................35.00
Creamer, custard.....................24.00
Dresser tray, milk glass 35.00
Egg cup, custard 8.50
Pitcher, Wild Rose and Bowknot,
frosted, gilt dec...................75.00
Range shaker sets
Lady, salt, pepper, flour and
sugar...........................135.00
Roman Arch, custard, blue dots,
salt, pepper, flour and sugar
....................................135.00
Refrigerator box, cov, white, 8" x 5" x
2-1/2"................................95.00

McKee covered "Butter" dish, green, 3-1/4" x 6-5/8", $65.

Salt and pepper shakers, pr
Roman Arch, black, 4-1/4" h
....65.00
Laurel pattern, custard.......42.00
Sandwich server, center handle,
Rock Crystal, red.............165.00
Tom and Jerry set, punch bowl and
10 cups, red and green dec
....150.00
Tumbler, Seville Yellow...........17.50

❖ Medals

One way to honor a hero was to present him with a medal. Many of these awards were passed down through families as treasured mementos. Other medals include those that are commemorative in nature.

Commemorative
Dwight D. Eisenhower Inaugura-
tion, 1953, bronze, Medallic
Art Co., 2-3/4" dia..........80.00
Mercedes-Benz, South American
dealerships, shows airplane,
auto and boat, mkd 1885-
1913 ....17.50
Pan-American Games, Sao
Paulo, Brazil, 1963, bronze, in
Portuguese, 2" dia.........14.50
Military
American Legion, 1-1/4" dia
....8.00
Bronze Star, engraved name,
with ribbon bar and lapel pin,
1960s, in presentation case
....40.00
Connecticut Foot Guard, 1st
Company of Foot Guards, 5
years of service 25.00
USS Puget Sound, orig box
....35.00
Religious
St. Anne's Shrine Fiskdale near
Sturbridge, Mass., pewter,
gold-colored trim, 1-1/2" h
....5.00
St. Dominic Pray for Us, shows
Virgin Mary with infant Jesus,
mkd Italy, 1" x 5/8"...........2.00
St. Jude Thaddeus Intercede for
Us, Infant of Prague Shrine
New Haven, Conn., brass-col-
ored, 5/8" dia 2.00
Sports
Rowing, 1-1/8" dia................9.00
Tennis, 1-1/8" dia 8.50

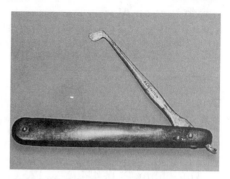

Folding scalpel, A.L. Hernstein, plastic tortoiseshell case, 5-7/8" long (open), $60.

❖ Medical Items

Ouch! Collectors of medical items certainly aren't squeamish as they search flea markets for new items to add to their collections. Some folks concentrate on medical apparatus and instruments, while others focus on other aspects of the profession.

Bleeder, 3 folding blades, copper
and brass, 18th C, 3-3/4" l
.... 225.00
Box, Red Cross Sterilized Gauze,
Johnson & Johnson 8.00
Doctor's bag, leather.............. 33.00
Letterhead, Reinle-Salmon Co.,
maker of druggist fixtures, 1912
.... 3.50
License, Registered Pharmacist,
The Board of Pharmacy of the
State of New Jersey, 1944
.... 30.00
Manual, *John's First Aid Manual,*
1919, 8th ed...................... 24.00
Mortar and pestle
Brass 70.00
Wooden........................... 247.50
Order form, mentions opium, Craw-
ford's Drug Store, Atlantic City,
N.J. 8-1/2" x 10-1/2".......... 20.00
Tooth extractor, bronze, 4-1/2" l
.... 130.00

❖ Meissen

Meissen is a fine porcelain with a long and interesting history. Briefly, the original factory dates to 1710 in Saxony, Germany. Over the years, decorating techniques were developed that led to the creation of beautiful pieces that are eagerly sought by collectors today. Each period of the Meissen story features different styles, colors, and influences. The factory is still in business today.

Many marks have been used by Meissen over the years. Learning to read those marks and ascertain the time period they represent will enhance a collector's knowledge of this lovely porcelain.

Reproduction Alert.

For additional listings and background information, see *Warman's English & Continental Pottery & Porcelain* and *Warman's Antiques & Collectibles.*

Ashtray, Onion pattern, blue crossed swords mark, 5" dia........... 80.00

Bread and butter plate, Onion pattern, 6-1/2" dia................... 75.00

Dessert dish, painted red rose and foliage center, bouquets at corners, c1770 .... 225.00

Dessert plate, floral dec, 20th C, 7" dia, set of 4........................ 50.00

Figure, young man and woman gathering eggs from under tree, white glaze, blue crossed swords mark, late 19th C 275.00

Hot plate, Onion pattern, handles 125.00

Teabowl and saucer, 3 purple flowers, green leaves, early 19th C, chip................................. 325.00

Urn, white, gilt trim, 2 delicate snake-form handles, pr ... 500.00

Vase, floral dec, 20th C, 3" h... 80.00

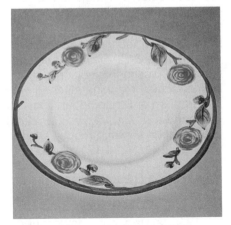

Metlox Camellia plate, 9" diameter, $5.

Vegetable dish, cov, Onion pattern, 10" sq 150.00

❖ Melmac

Melmac is a trade name associated with thermoset plastic dinnerware made by American Cyanamid. Although first introduced for commercial use, Melmac became popular with housewives in the 1950s. Collectors today search for pieces in very good condition with interesting colors and shapes.

Collectors' Club: Melmac Collectors Club, 6802 Glenkirk Rd, Baltimore, MD 21239.

Child's set, bunny dec, Oneida, used, plate 8-1/4" dia, cereal bowl 6-1/2" dia, dessert bowl 4-3/4" dia 8.00

Creamer and sugar, blue, mkd "Made in Canada," 3" h 17.50

Magazine advertisement, Boonton Ware, Melmac Dishes Guaranteed Against Breakage, 8-1/2" x 11"...................................... 2.00

Platter, pink, N416, 13-3/4" x 9-3/4" 8.00

Set

    Avocado fruit bowls, bread plates and cups, white saucers, service for 8........................ 20.00

    Normandy Rose, MIB, 4-pc place setting............................. 27.00

    Shasta Daisy, dinner plates, salad plates, cereal bowls, cups and saucers, Texas Ware, service for 6 .... 60.00

Wall pocket, sq gray saucer as backplate, green cup as pocket, mkd "Maherware, 2, Made in USA" 10.00

❖ Metlox Pottery

After its formation in 1927, Metlox manufactured outdoor ceramic signs. During the Depression, the company reorganized and began producing dinnerware. During World War II, the factory was again retooled so that workers could make machine parts and parts for B-25 bombers. After the war, dinnerware production resumed along with the creation of some art ware. The factory finally closed in 1989.

For additional listings and history, see *Warman's Americana & Collectibles* and *Warman's American Pottery & Porcelain.*

Bowl

    Ivy, 5-1/2" dia..................... 20.00

    Sculptured Grape, 8-1/2" dia 16.00

Bread server, California Provincial 60.00

Casserole, cov, Sculptured Grape, 1-qt............................... 50.00

Cereal bowl, Sculptured Daisy 12.00

Chop plate

    Palm..................................... 10.00

    Rose-A-Day......................... 8.00

Cookie jar, Clown................. 200.00

Creamer

    Rose-A-Day...................... 10.00

    Sculptured Grape 15.00

Cup and saucer

    California Provincial 17.50

    Sculptured Grape 10.00

Dinner plate, Della Robbia........ 8.00

Dinner service, California Ivy, 47-pc set................................... 330.00

Figure, Dobbin horse and buggy, repaired leg..................... 120.00

Gravy, attached underplate, Sculptured Grape...................... 27.50

Miniature, White House, orig sticker 175.00

Mustard jar, Red Rooster........ 48.00

Place setting, Liberty Blue, 5 pcs 35.00

Platter, Provincial Rose........... 70.00

Salad bowl, California Strawberry 55.00

Salad plate, Sculptured Grape, 7-1/2" dia 8.00

Salt and pepper shakers, Sammy Seal, pr 75.00

Soup bowl, Camellia California 17.50

Sugar, cov, Sculptured Grape 22.00

Vegetable bowl, cov, Poppytrail 100.00

Vegetable bowl, divided, Rose-A-Day 10.00

❖ Mettlach

Most collectors think of steins when they hear the name "Mettlach," but this German company also produced very fine pottery, including plates, plaques, bowls, and teapots. One of their hallmarks is underglaze printing on earthenware, achieved by using transfers from copper plates. Relief decorations, etched decorations, and cameos were also used. Individual pieces of Mettlach are well marked.

Periodical: *Beer Stein Journal*, P.O. Box 8807, Coral Springs, FL 33075.

Collectors' Clubs: Stein Collectors International, 281 Shore Dr, Burr Ridge, IL 60521; Sun Steiners, P.O. Box 11782, Fort Lauderdale, FL 33339.

Coaster, #1264, girl on swing and boy on bicycle, print under glaze, one chipped, 5" dia, pr 260.00
Plaque
    #1044-542, portrait of man, blue delft dec, 12" dia 125.00
    #1108, incised castle, gilt rim, c1902, 17" dia 230.00
Stein
    #1027, relief, face and floral dec, beige, rust and green, inlaid lid, 1/2-liter 215.00
    #2057, etched, festive dancing scene, inlaid lid, 1/2-liter
    .... 325.00
    #2755, cameo and etched, 3 scenes of people, Art Nouveau design between scenes, inlaid lid, 1/4-liter 560.00
    #2833B, 1/2-liter 350.00
Vase, #1808, stoneware, incised foliage dec, 10" h, pr 230.00

Mettlach stein showing fiddler and rabbit, 8" high, $500.

❖ Microscopes

Microscopes are included in the field of scientific instrument collecting, a category that has really taken off recently. If considering a purchase of a microscope, check to see that all the necessary parts are included. And remember, value is enhanced by original documentation, boxes, slides, etc.

Collectors' Club: Maryland Microscopical Society, 8261 Polk St, McLean VA 22102.

Booklet, Gilbert microscope, 1960, 75 pgs 5.00
Catalog, *Biological and Chemical Supplies and Apparatus*, 1930s, microscope cover, 24 pgs .. 24.00
Microscope
    Gilbert, toy, 1956, orig box
    .... 59.00
    New Gem Microscope, Bausch & Lomb Optical Co, Rochester, 75-300x. 7-1/4" h 80.00
    Regency, 100-400x, dovetailed wooden box, 7-7/8" h 75.00
    Spencer, mkd "CENCO/Spencer/USA," double optical turret, orig case, 11" 175.00
    World's Fair, 20th Century Microscope, Pan-American Exposition, Buffalo, orig box 75.00

Sears microscope, 3 lenses, 8" high, $6.50.

❖ Militaria

Throughout history, men have marched off to war. Those who return often bring mementos of their travels. Years later these treasures end up at flea markets where eager collectors find them.

References: Many good reference books are available that cover all periods of military history.

Periodicals: *Men at Arms*, 222 W Exchange St, Providence, RI 02903; *Militaria Magazine*, P.O. Box 995, Southbury, CT 06488; *Military Collector Magazine*, P.O. Box 245, Lyon Station, PA 19536; *Military Collector News*, P.O. Box 702073, Tulsa, OK 74170; *Military Images*, RD1 Box 99A, Henryville, PA 18332; *Military Trader*, P.O. Box 1050, Dubuque, IA 52004; *North South Trader's Civil War*, PO Drawer 631, Orange, VA 22960; *Wildcat Collectors Journal*, 15158 NE 6th Ave, Miami, FL 33162; *WWII Military Journal*, P.O. Box 28906, San Diego, CA 92198.

Collectors' Clubs: American Society of Military Insignia Collectors, 526 Lafayette Ave, Palmerton, PA 18071; Assoc of American Military Uniform Collectors, P.O. Box 1876, Elyria, OH 44036; Company of Military Historians, North Main St, Westbrook, CT, 06498; Imperial German Military Collectors Assoc, 82 Atlantic St, Keyport, NJ 07735; Militaria Collectors Society, 137 S Almar Dr, Ft Lauderdale, FL 33334; Orders and Medals Society of America, P.O. Box 484, Glassboro, NJ 08028.

Reproduction Alert.

For additional listings, see *Warman's Antiques & Collectibles* and specific topics in this edition.

Handkerchief, machine-stitched emblem of Strategic Air Command 22.00
Identification airplane model, World War II, 11-1/2" l, 17" wingspan
    .... 80.00
Map, Pacific Theater, Esso premium
    .... 18.00
Newspaper, *The Wardial*, April 14, 1945, military base newspaper for Ward Island, Corpus Christie, Texas, 16 pgs 15.00

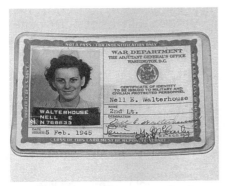

U.S. War Department identification, issued 1945, 2-3/4" x 4", $10.

Paperweight, West Point, sulphide, marching cadets holding 2 flags, 3" dia 35.00
Pennant, felt
  Admiral Farragut Academy, eagle, buoy with anchor and cadet, 28" l 25.00
  Camp Pickett, Va., red background with eagle, 25" l 25.00
  West Point, logo of eagle on shield, 26" l 25.00
Photograph, black and white, 5" x 7", slightly faded
  U.S.S. Arizona 15.00
  U.S.S. Los Angeles............ 12.50
Pin, Naval officer insignia, eagle over shield and pair of anchors, sterling silver with gold wash, 1" dia 32.00
Poster, World War I, "Join the Red Cross," Howard Chandler Christy, creases, edge wear 25-1/2" x 19-1/2"............. 250.00
Tie tack, R.C.A.F. Reserves, 3/4" sq 26.00
Token, U.S. Marine Corp, Third Battalion, brass....................... 10.00
Wings, Army Air Force, AWS, 1-1/8" l.............................. 28.00

❖ Milk Bottles

Before the advent of paper and plastic containers, milk was sold in glass bottles. Today's flea markets often contain great examples of different sizes and designs. Keep your eyes open for interesting slogans.

Reference: John Tutton, *Udderly Beautiful*, self-published, no date.

Periodical: *The Udder Collectibles*, HC73 Box 1, Smithville Flats, NY 13841.

Collectors' Club: National Assoc of Milk Bottle Collectors, 4 Ox Bow Rd, Westport, CT 06880.
Bonfoey's Dairy, Three Rivers, Mich., pyro label, 1/2-gal ...15.00
Country Delights, 2-tone green pyro label, 1-gal 32.00
Delview, Fresh, Milk, Tuscaloosa, Ala., pyro label shows a woods, 1-qt 8.00
Farm Fresh, Grade A Dairy Products, Chester, Ill., orange pyro label, 1/2-pt....................5.00
Foremost Dairy, embossed, 1-qt 28.00
Handy's Putnam Gold Dairy Products, Greencastle, Ind., red pyro label, 1-qt...........................15.00
Heber Valley Milk Depots, "It's the Modern Way," orange pyro label shows boy and girl, 1/2-pt 13.00
Pennsupreme, 1-pt..................16.00
Sanitary Dairy, Chisholm, Maine, 1/2-pt 5.00
Wallis Dairy, New Castle, Pa., orange pyro label of cows and dairy, 1-gal 65.00
W.B. Baker, Birmingham, Ala., emb, 1/2-pt 18.00

Light-blue turkey figurine, repro milkglass, 2-3/4" high, $5.

❖ Milk Glass

Milk glass is an opaque white-bodied glass that was produced by many manufacturers. Early in the 20th century it was a popular choice for tableware and accessories. By the early 1960s, preferences had cycled again, and milk glass was fashionable once more.

References: Several older reference books are wonderful tools for determining makers and pattern names.

Collectors' Club: National Milk Glass Collectors Society, 46 Almond Dr, Hershey, PA 17033.
Animal covered dish
  Hen, basketweave base.. 175.00
  Lion, English...................... 95.00
  Setter, sgd "Flaccus," repair to lid 150.00
Bowl, Daisy, all-over leaves and flower dec, open scalloped edge, 8-1/4" dia 85.00
Celery vase, Blackberry, scalloped rim, 6-5/8" h 115.00
Creamer and sugar, Trumpet Vine, fire-painted dec, sgd "SV" 135.00
Easter egg, emb chick 60.00
Jar, cov, owl, figural 45.00
Mug, Ivy in Snow 45.00
Soap dish, cov, orig drainer, Wheat 125.00
Spooner, Monkey, scalloped rim 140.00
Tumbler, Royal Oak, fire-painted dec, green band................ 50.00

❖ Miniature Bottles

Flea markets are great places to find these clever bottles. Often they are samples, or they were designed to provide single servings for restaurant or commercial use.
Acme Beer, stubby, decal 6.50
Budweiser, stubby, paper label 17.50
Carstairs, lipstick shaped, 1950s 8.00
Fort Pitt Beer, stubby 3.00
Gold Bond Beer 20.00
Hamms Preferred 5.00
Maple Farms, Vt., maple syrup. 1.00
Old Dutch, stubby 24.00
Tavern Pale............................ 12.00

**Pabst miniature bottle, 4-1/4"
high, $17.50.**

❖ Miniatures

The world of tiny objects is truly a fascinating one. Some collectors are attracted to the craftsmanship shown by these tiny treasures, while others are more interested in finding examples to display. Keep scale in mind when purchasing miniatures for use in a doll house.

Periodicals: *Doll Castle News*, P.O. Box 247, Washington, NJ 07882; *Miniature Collector*, Scott Publications, 30595 Eight Mile Rd, Livonia, MI 48152; *Nutshell News*, 21027 Crossroads Circle, P.O. Box 1612, Waukesha, WI 53187.

Miniature Occupied Japan tea set, 6 pieces plus lids, some damage, tray 3-1/2" diameter, $30.

Collectors' Clubs: International Guild Miniature Artisans, P.O. Box 71, Bridgeport, NY 18080; National Association of Miniature Enthusiasts, 2621 Anaheim, CA 92804-3883.

Amoire, tin litho, purple and black 35.00
Bed, 4-poster, mahogany stain, hand-made 40.00
Blanket chest, 6-board construction, old worn paint dec 200.00
Christmas tree, decorated 50.00
Clock, metal.............................40.00
Desk, Chippendale style, slant front, working drawers 65.00
Fireplace, Britannia metal fretwork, draped mantel, carved grate 65.00
Living room set, Empire style, sofa, fainting couch, two chairs, 4pcs 350.00
Sofa, porcelain and metal........35.00
Stove, Royal, complete..........120.00
Table, tin, painted brown, white top, floral design 35.00
Umbrella stand, brass, ormolu, emb palm fronds, sq.................65.00
Wash bowl and pitcher, cobalt glass, minor chips 275.00

❖ Mirrors

"Mirror, mirror on the wall..." Mirrors are something we all depend on, and many of us use them as decorative accents in our homes and offices. Flea markets are great sources for interesting examples in almost every decorating style.

Hand mirror
    Bakelite with rhinestones, butterfly design 40.00
    Celluloid, Art Deco design 37.00
    Celluloid, plain, beveled glass 23.00
Hanging
    Chippendale style, mahogany, molded frame, worn silvering on glass, 20th C., 20" h, 12" w 82.50
    Curly maple, frame and liner, 20th C, 17-1/2" h, 27-1/2" w 220.00
    Tramp art frame, dark finish over varnish, stepped sawtooth border, stacked geometric designs, 15" h, 17-1/2" w 275.00
Pocket mirror, advertising
    "I Wear Skeezix Shoes, Outgrown before Outworn," shows birthstones with comic image, 2-1/4" dia 85.00
    Garland Stoves & Ranges, minor flaking, 1-3/4" dia.......... 75.00
    V.T. and L.S. Schosser, Hagerstown, Md., dentists, pictures teeth, celluloid, 2" dia 285.00
    Womelsdorf Vol. Fire Dept., shows fire truck, 2-1/4" dia 55.00
Shaving mirror, mahogany veneer on pine, line inlay, bowfront case, turned feet, 2 drawers, adjustable mirror with turned posts, repairs, 23-1/2" h, 18-1/2" w, 7-1/2" d..................... 137.50

Ludlow Ambulance Service pocket mirror, $45.

❖ Model Kits

Plastic scale models were introduced in England in the mid 1930s. The popularity of these kits reached a high in the 1960s, but the oil crisis of the 1970s caused a setback in the industry. Understand that the character the model is based on has more to do with determining value than does the kit itself.

Reference: Bill Coulter, *Stock Car Model Kit Encyclopedia and Price Guide*, Krause Publications, 1999.

Collectors' Clubs: International Figure Kit Club, P.O. Box 201, Sharon Center, OH, 44274; Kit Collectors International, P.O. Box 38, Stanton, CA 90680.

Periodicals: *Toy Cars & Models*, Krause Publications; *Scale Auto Enthusiast Magazine*, Kalmbach Publishing.

Apollo spacecraft, Revell, unbuilt
....58.00
Comet jet, unbuilt 14.50
Corvette, 1989, AMT Ertl, MIB
....10.00
Jet fighter, Guillows, unbuilt..... 10.00
Klingon Battle Cruiser, Star Trek: The Next Generation, AMT Ertl, MIB 23.00
Mercedes-Benz 500K roadster, 1935, paperboard, Wrebbit, MIB
....30.00
Metaluna Mutant, Jumbo Series Model #20, built, 15" h..... 125.00
Model T, 1909, Gabriel, unbuilt
....45.00
Robin, The Boy Wonder, Revell, 1999 re-release, MIB......... 15.00

Chopped Mini model kit, Model Products Corp., $15.

Suzuki RV90, Heller, MIB 19.00
Visible Man, Revell, dated 1977, unbuilt..................................15.00
Vostol, first Russian spacecraft, Revell, unbuilt....................70.00

❖ Monroe, Marilyn

Marilyn Monroe was a model turned actress who captured the hearts of moviegoers in the 1950s. Her tragic life has been the subject of numerous books, magazine articles, television shows, etc.

Reference: Clark Kidder, *Marilyn Monroe Cover to Cover*, Krause Publications, 1999.

Collectors' Club: All About Marilyn, P.O. Box 291176, Los Angeles, CA 90029.

Book, *Strange Death of Marilyn Monroe*, 1964 ....95.00
Calendar, 1974, orig envelope
....30.00
Commemorative coin, Marilyn on one side, Joe DiMaggio on other, 1-1/2" dia 10.00
Doll, emerald evening gown, Collector's Series, MIB 25.00
Magazine
    Eye, August 1955...............13.00
    Look, July 5, 1960..............25.00
    Tempo, July 1953...............10.00
    Stare Magazine, June 1953
    ....20.00
Plate, Lady in Red, Up Close and Personal series, 3rd issue, Bradford Exchange, 8-1/8" dia
....35.00
Ornament
    Carlton, 1998, MIB.............13.00
    Hallmark, 1999, 3rd in series, orig box 25.00
Trading card, Series L, 20th, Fox 26, biography in Dutch.............25.00

❖ Monsters

Perhaps it was those Saturday afternoon matinees, or those science-fiction books we read as kids that caused so many collectors to seek out monster related memorabilia. And, those lucky folks are finding plenty of their favorite demons at flea markets.

Chalkware King Kong, $60.

References: Dana Cain, *Collecting Monsters of Film and TV*, Krause Publications, 1997; John Marshall, *Collecting Monster Toys*, Schiffer Publishing, 1999.

Periodical: *Toy Shop,* 700 E State St, Iola, WI 54990.

Book, *It's Alive: The Classic Cinema of Frankenstein*, 1981 .... 7.00
Figure, Dracula, hard rubber, 1986, 8" h 30.00
Film, 8mm, black-and-white
    "Doom of Dracula" with Boris Karloff, orig box 22.00
    "Monster from a Prehistoric Planet," American International Pictures, Super 8, 1967
    .... 51.00
Flashlight/key chain, Wolfman, Universal, MOC...................... 15.00
Magazine
    Fangoria, #1, August 1979 50.00
    Horror Monsters, #9, Fall 1964
    .... 22.00
    Monster World, #1, 1964... 10.00
    Monster World, #6, 1965... 10.00
    World Famous Creatures, #1, one corner missing 45.00

Model kit, Frankenstein, Horizon, unbuilt................76.00
Poster, Frankenstein and the Monster from Hell, 1-sheet, 27" x 41"................10.00
Window card, Robot Monster, reprint................20.00
Toy,
Dracula, made by Telco, battery-op, 1992, MIB................75.00
The Wolfman, Marx, 4-1/2" h................20.00

❖ Moon & Star Pattern

This popular glassware pattern has its origins in America's pattern glass industry. Adams & Co. of Pittsburgh, Pennsylvania manufactured an extensive line called Palace. The L.G. Wright Co. began reproducing that pattern in a broad spectrum of colors and called the design Moon & Star. The molds have changed hands several times since then, but the pattern is still being made.

For additional Adams listings, see *Warman's Pattern Glass Price and Identification Guide.*

Ashtray, amberina................20.00
Banana boat, ruby, 12-1/2" l, 5-1/2" h................80.00
Basket, green, LE Smith................55.00
Canister, green, LE Smith, 9-1/2" h................35.00
Compote, green, LE Smith................42.50

Compote, golden amber, 6-1/2" high, 6-1/8" diameter, $40.

Creamer and sugar, amber................40.00
Cruet, blue................45.00
Dinner plate, clear, Weishar................15.00
Goblet, blue................18.50
Sherbet, clear, Weishar................15.00
Toothpick holder, green, LE Smith................9.00
Tumbler, blue, Weishar................17.50
Vase, amber................20.00
Water set, LE Smith, pitcher, four 13-oz tumblers................185.00
Wine, Adams................35.00

❖ Morgantown Glass

Founded in Morgantown, West Virginia, this manufacturer of handmade glass created lovely household items and tableware. The colors produced by Morgantown are bright and clear, and the company introduced several innovative techniques and forms to the industry.

Collectors' Club: Old Morgantown Glass Collectors' Guild, P.O. Box 894, Morgantown, WV 26507.

For additional listings, see *Warman's Antiques & Collectibles* and *Warman's Glass.*

Champagne
Jockey, crystal................50.00
Monroe, red and crystal................35.00
Claret, Golf Ball, red................75.00
Cocktail
Chanticleer, Copen blue................35.00
Golf Ball, Stiegel Green................35.00
Majestic, red and crystal................32.50
Compote, Palmer, green stem, 7-1/2" h, 5-1/4" dia................80.00
Cordial
Mayfair, crystal................35.00
Plantation, cobalt................145.00
Goblet, Golf Ball, cobalt................55.00
High ball, Mexicana, 5" h................115.00
Ivy ball, Golf Ball, red, 4" w................95.00
Oyster cocktail, Sunrise Medallion, blue, slight wear................190.00
Parfait, Golf Ball, cobalt................125.00
Plate, Mexicana, Ice, 6" dia................18.00
Tumbler, Carlton, etch #778, crystal................35.00
Wine, Old English, Spanish red................35.00

❖ Mortens Studio

Collectors identify the name Mortens Studios with finely crafted porcelain dog figurines.

Airedale, #742, 4-1/4" h................85.00
Boxer, sitting, 2-1/2" h................52.00
Borzoi, #749................145.00
Cocker spaniel, nose chip, 2-3/4" h................47.50
Dachshund................65.00
English setter................150.00
Fox terrier................185.00
Mustang, 7-1/2" h................45.00
Palomino, ear damaged, 8" h................85.00
Pomeranian, #739, 4" h................55.00
Pug, #738................145.00
Spaniel................80.00

❖ Morton Potteries

Morton Pottery Works was established in Morton, Illinois, in 1922. Production of dinnerware, earthenware, and table accessories continued until 1976. The company also specialized in kitchenware and novelties for chain stores and gift shops.

Cookie jar
Basket of fruit................55.00
Panda................85.00
Figurine
Deer, chip, 2-3/8" h................8.00
Lamb, green, 2-3/8" h................12.00
Kangaroo, white, 2-5/8" h................11.00
Squirrel, 2" h................8.00
Nightlight
Old woman in a shoe, yellow and red................45.00

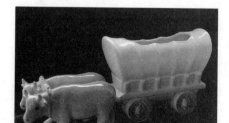

Morton Pottery Co. planter, covered wagon with attached oxen team, $55.

Teddy bear, brown, hand-painted 50.00
Pie bird, 5" h............................75.00
Planter, rabbit, umbrella, blue egg 20.00

❖ Moss Rose Pattern

Several English and American pottery companies made this pretty pattern. The pink rose bud with leaves makes it easy to identify this pattern. Some pieces also have gold trim.

Butter pat, mkd "Meakin," sq ...25.00
Cake plate, 2 emb handles......40.00
Coaster, mkd "Nasco".............12.95
Creamer and sugar, mkd "Haviland, Limoges" 150.00
Cup and saucer, mkd "Haviland, Limoges" 30.00
Dinner plate, mkd "Haviland," 9-1/2" dia 25.00
Egg, hairline crack at top, 6-1/4" h 22.00
Gravy boat, matching underplate, mkd "Green Co., England" 35.00
Juicer......................................38.00
Nappy, mkd "Edwards," 4-1/2" dia 18.50
Sauce dish, mkd "Haviland," 4-1/2" dia 20.00
Sugar bowl, cov, mkd "Rosenthal" 35.00
Teapot, bulbous, gooseneck spout, basketweave trim, mkd "T&V" 95.00

Moss Rose platter, W.H. Grindley & Co., England, 8-1/2" x 9-3/4", $35.

❖ Mother's Day Collectibles

The first Mother's Day celebration was held in Philadelphia, Pennsylvania, in 1907, but it wasn't until 1914 that it became a national observance. Most of us think of cards, flowers, and candy as the traditional Mother's Day gifts, but there is also a wide selection of items to commemorate the day, including ornaments and limited edition collector plates.

Limited edition plate
Bing and Grondahl, Hare and Young, H. Thelander, 1971, 6" dia 40.00
Precious Moments, "Mother's Day 1990," Samuel J. Butcher, 4" dia 7.00
Schmid, "Devotion for Mother," Sister Berta Hummel, 1976 ....32.50
Magazine, *MAD*, #79, June, 1963, Special Mother's Day Issue 15.00
Magazine ad, Western Union, "Remember Your Mother," 1955 ....6.00
Ornament for mother-to-be, hen nesting on bowed wrapped egg, mkd "Hallmark Handcrafted," 1992, orig box...................20.00
Planter, ceramic, white, swans, FTD 3.50
Table decoration, tissue paper type, image of Victorian Mother, "Remember your mother on Mother's Day. Second Sunday in May," 11" x 14"...................15.00

❖ Motorcycle Collectibles

Most people who are interested in motorcycle collectibles either ride this unique form of transportation or did so in the past. Whatever their motivation, it's a field that is growing, and these collectibles are sure to increase in value.

Collectors' Clubs: American Motorcycle Assoc, P.O. Box 6114, Westerville, OH 43081; Antique Motorcycle Club of America, P.O. Box 300, Sweetser, IN 46987-0300; Women on Wheels, P.O. Box 546, Sparta, WI 54656-9546.

Friction-powered Harley-Davidson Auto Cycle motorcycles, original boxes, $875 each.

Catalog, Harley-Davidson Motorcycles, accessories catalog, blue and yellow accents, 1954, 36 pgs, 8-1/2" h, 11" w..........25.00
Flyer, Harley-Davidson Motorcycles, Christmas, accessories, Baltimore, Md. dealer imprint, some inked notations, 6" x 9" 10.00
Magazine tear sheet
Harley-Davidson, Farm Life, 1919 ....2.00
Honda Mini Trail, 1969, large sheet..............................2.50
Member card and patch, card 2-1/4" x 4", buff paper with orange accents, American Motorcycle Association, typewritten member identification, 1952 expiration date, fabric patch 2" x 2-1/4", green, red and yellow on blue ground......................35.00
Patch, Harley-Davidson Motorcycles, embroidered, gold trademark in center, flanked by silver wings on black felt ground, early 1950s, 7-1/2" 75.00
Stationery, white sheet, 2" red, pink and gray logo, Indian Motorcycles Dealer, profile of Indian head at left, text "Motorcycles for Sport, Business, and Police," wheel and wing design across top, Alabama dealer imprint, 3-digit phone number, c1920, 8-1/2" x 11" 20.00

❖ Movie Memorabilia

Going to the movies has always been a fun event. Today's collectors actively seek memorabilia from their favorite flicks or items that are related to a particular star or studio.

Black-and-white movie still, "The Texan," Gary Cooper and Fay Wray, 8" x 10", $5.

Periodicals: *Big Reel*, P.O. Box 1050, Dubuque, IA 52004; *Collecting Hollywood Magazine*, P.O. Box 2512, Chattanooga, TN 37409; *Goldmine*, 700 E State St, Iola, WI 54990; *Movie Advertising Collector*, P.O. Box 28587, Philadelphia, PA, 19149.

Book

 Crime Movies: An Illustrated History, 1980, softcover........ 9.00

 Encyclopedia of Western Movies, 1984 .... 25.00

 Fabulous Fantasy Films, 1977 .... 7.00

 David O. Selznick's Hollywood, 1980, 1st ed 35.00

Sheet music, *As Time Goes By*, Casablanca, 1942, cover shows Humphrey Bogart, Ingrid Bergman and Paul Henreid 65.00

Trading cards

 Alien 3, 1992, Star Pics, with wrapper 8.00

 Alien, 1979, Topps 2.00

 Batman, 1966, Topps....... 125.00

 Batman, Series 2, 1989, with sticker set, Topps 12.00

 Batman Returns, Super Premium, 1992, with wrapper, Topps 15.00

 Terminator 2, 1991, with offer cards, Impel 5.00

 Terminator 2, 1991, sticker set, Topps 8.00

Pinback buttons

 Casper 4.00

 Flubber................................. 5.00

 Quest for Camelot............... 2.00

 Time Cop 4.00

 Titanic 11.00

 What Dreams May Come 3.00

❖ Movie Posters

Posters are a specialized area of movie collectibles. Created by the studios to promote their movies, posters are usually brightly colored and make wonderful display pieces. One of the most common types of poster measures 27" x 41" and is called a "one sheet."

Periodicals: *Collecting Hollywood*, American Collectors Exchange, 2401 Broad St., Chattanooga, TN 37408; *Hollywood Collectibles*, 4099 McEwen Drive, Suite 350, Dallas, TX 75244; *Movie Poster Update*, American Collectors Exchange, 2401 Broad St., Chattanooga, TN 37408.

Note: The following listings are all full-color one sheets, unless otherwise noted.

Blazing Saddles.....................250.00

Cannes Film Festival, 50th Anniversary...................................150.00

Clockwork Orange, Italian 200.00

The Comedians, MGM, 1967, minor margin damage, 60" x 40" 95.00

Every Which Way But Loose 150.00

Guys and Dolls 600.00

Love Story 500.00

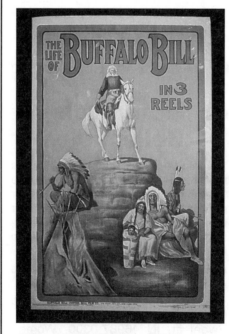

"The Life of Buffalo Bill," $1,950.

Melody Time, Walt Disney, 1948, margin deterioration from dampness, 60" x 40"............... 150.00

New York, New York 200.00

Saturday Night Fever, soundtrack promotion version 75.00

The Searchers, oversized.... 350.00

Straw Dogs 200.00

Taxi Driver, Italian 150.00

Utah Wagon Train, Republic Picture, 1951, margin damage, tear, 58" x 40"................................ 150.00

❖ Moxie

Originally called Moxie Nerve Food and intended to be taken with a spoon, Moxie was first sold in Salem, Massachusetts, in 1876. Created by Augustin Thompson, the mixture was one of a number of patent medicines he sold to supplement the income from his medical practice. Several years later, wanting to capitalize on the popularity of soft drinks, Thompson modified his medicine. By 1884, Moxie was being sold in carbonated form, and it is still sold today.

Collectors' Clubs: Moxie Enthusiasts Collectors Club of America, Route 375, Box 164, Woodstock, NY 12498; New England Moxie Congress, 445 Wyoming Ave., Millburn, NJ 07041.

Bag, paper, 1932 copyright, stain, tear, 11" x 9-1/4" 45.00

Bottle

 Moxie embossed on shoulders, pale green, 7-oz, 7-3/4" h 10.00

 Moxie Nerve Food, Lowell, Mass., pre-1900, some clouding, small chips, hairline in neck, 10" h.................... 95.00

Fan

 Eileen Pery, all paper, 5-1/4" x 8-3/8" 95.00

 Muriel Ostriche, edge damage, 8-1/4" x 9".................... 95.00

Pinback button, litho tin, diecut

 Moxie man, face shot...... 125.00

 Moxie woman, orig card, 2" h, 1-3/4" w 550.00

Sign

 Tin over cardboard, "Drink Moxie," 2-1/2" x 10" 325.00

 Cardboard, easel-back, diecut, Fred Archer, 8" h, 10-3/8" w 185.00

Tip tray, litho tin, woman with glass of Moxie, 6" dia 140.00

Sheet music, "Just Make It Moxie for Mine," 1904, $18.50.

❖ Mugs

While no one is sure when the first mug was produced, many early pottery manufacturers did include mugs in their patterns. Collectors tend to focus on advertising mugs or those related to a particular character.

British commemorative
    Royal Silver Jubilee, 1952-1977,
      mkd Royal Grafton 25.00
    Wedding of Prince Andrew and
      Sarah Ferguson, July 23,
      1986, Creemore China and
      Glass, Creemore, Ontario
       ....25.00
Carnival glass, Orange Tree pattern,
    red, Fenton 600.00
Ceramic, "Mother," mkd Germany
     ....26.00
Glass, clear, Dad's, barrel shape,
    5-1/4" h 4.00
Lusterware, emb "Present," violets
    deco, base mkd "J.C.S. Co.,
    Germany" 55.00
Milk glass, Dunkin Donuts 6.00
Pattern glass
    Fighting Cats, clear, 2-1/4" h
       ....32.00
    Cut Log, 3-1/4" h 32.00
Plastic, advertising
    Hires, scratches 1.50

Mr. Peanut, yellow, 1970s .. 12.00
Nestlés' Quik bunny, 4" h
     ....12.00
Toby, made by Lego, Japan, 4-1/2" h
    Pirate 60.00
    Pirate and parrot 60.00

❖ Mulberry China

Mulberry china is similar to flow blue, but the design is a dark purple that appears almost black in some cases. The name derives from the resemblance of the color to crushed mulberries. Many of the same factories that produced flow blue also manufactured mulberry items.

Creamer
    Corean 120.00
    Marble, Wedgwood 90.00
Cup and saucer, handleless .. 125.00
Gravy boat, Calcutta.............. 110.00
Plate
    Avon, 9-3/4" dia..................40.00
    Calcutta, Edward Challinor,
      8-1/2" dia ....95.00.
    Corean, PW & Co, 7-3/4" dia
       ....50.00
    Corean, PW & Co, 9-3/4" dia
       ....65.00
    Foliage 70.00
    Horticultural, 9" dia...........125.00
    Neopolitan, 9-1/4" dia 85.00
    Ning-Po, R. Hall & Co., 9" dia
       ....95.00

A&W Root Beer mug, 4-1/2" high, $7.

Pelew, E. Challinor, 8-1/2" dia
     ....115.00
Vincennes, by John Alcock, 7"
    dia................................. 40.00
Washington Vase, Podmore
    Walker & Co., 8-3/4" dia
     ....100.00
Platter
    Foliage, A. Walley, 15-1/4" l
       ....275.00
    Foliage, 11" l.................... 175.00
Teapot, 7" h........................... 395.00

❖ Music Boxes, Novelty Types

Music boxes were invented by the Swiss around 1825. They can now be found in many shapes, sizes, and materials. When buying a music box at a flea market, ask the dealer if it works properly and perhaps you'll hear the pretty tune.

Collectors' Club: Musical Box Society International, 12140 Anchor Ln SW, Moore Haven, FL 33471.

Ballerina, pink, metal base, some
    wear 50.00
Birdcage, singing bird, German
     .... 250.00
Children on merry-go-round, wood,
    figures move, plays "Around the
    World in 80 Days," 7-3/4" h
     .... 30.00
Christmas tree, revolving, German
     .... 65.00
Dancing dude......................... 90.00
Eastere Egg, tin, hand crank .. 25.00
Evening in Paris, illus of different
    cosmetics, velvet and silver box
     .... 125.00
Piano, silver-plated, red velvet lining
     .... 45.00
Snowball, glass, Frosty the Snow-
    man, red wooden base, 5" h
     .... 12.00
South of the Border................. 35.00

❖ Music Related

Perhaps you're the type who likes to whistle while browsing at a flea market. Bet you'll find some music-related collectibles while you regale your fellow shoppers with a happy tune.

**Costume jewelry pin, 2-1/2"
high, $5.**

Periodical: *Goldmine*, 700 E State
St, Iola, WI 54990.
Also see Sheet Music and related
  categories in this edition.
Book
  History of English Music, Lon-
    don, 1895 .... 20.00
  Songs for the Family, yellow
    hardcover, c1960 .... 10.00
Bookmark, figural grand piano, cellu-
  loid, printed adv 25.00
Calendar print, dogs playing piano
  .... 5.00
Catalog, McKinley Music Co., Chi-
  cago, Ill., 1903, 50 pgs 20.00
Guitar pick, used 1.00
Hat, marching band, blue and white,
  white plume, worn 10.00
Music stand, chrome, folding type
  .... 2.00
Piano instruction book, beginner,
  green cover, worn 2.00
Piano roll cabinet, Adam style,
  mahogany veneer, painted panels on doors, incomplete applied
  ornament, English, 38-1/4" h,
  40" w, 16" d 330.00
Sign, emb tin, Mason & Hamlin
  Grands & Upright Pianos, Boston, New York, Chicago, shows
  grand piano, framed, 19-1/2" x
  27" 300.00

❖ Musical Instruments

The musical instruments generally found at flea markets have been
used as practice instruments, or
have been under the ownership of
children. Expect to find wear, and
understand that your purchase will
probably need some repairs before it
can make music again.

Periodicals: *Concertina &
Squeezebox*, P.O. Box 6706, Ithaca,
NY 14851; *Jerry's Musical Newsletter*, 4624 W Woodland Rd, Minneapolis, MN 55424.

Collectors' Clubs: American Musi-
cal Instrument Society, RD 3, Box
205-B, Franklin, PA 16323; Auto-
matic Musical Instrument Collectors
Assoc, 919 Lantern Glow Trail, Dayton, OH 45431; Fretted Instrument
Guild of America, 2344 S Oakley
Ave, Chicago, IL 60608; Musical Box
Society International, 887 Orange
Ave. E, St. Paul, MN 55106; Reed
Organ Society, Inc., P.O. Box 901,
Deansboro, NY 13328.
Accordion, black lacquer, brass, silver and abalone inlay, keys and
  decorative valve covers with
  carved mother-of-pearl, needs
  repair, some damage 95.00
Bassoon, 15-keyed, maple, brass
  mounts and keys, c1900,
  50-1/4" l 460.00
Bugle, nickel-plated, minor dents,
  wooden case with black paint
  .... 100.00
Clarinet, 10-keyed boxwood, key of
  C, brass mountings, brass keys
  with round covers, c1860, orig
  mouthpiece, 21-1/2" l 400.00
Cornet, silver-plated brass tubing,
  engraved at the bell, three piston
  valves with pearl buttons, Lyric,
  The Rudolph Wurlitzer Co. USA,
  stamped "P21766," fitted case, 2
  period mouthpieces, turning
  crook and mute 150.00
Flute, Firth Hall and Pond, 8 keys,
  crocuswood and nickel silver
  mounts, inlaid lip plate, nickel-sil-
  ver keys with salt spoon cup
  cover, adjustable stopper c1855,
  stamped "Firth, Hall & Pond,
  Franklin Sq, New York, 1242," fitted mahogany case, 26-1/4" l
  .... 230.00
Melodeon, rosewood veneer, lyre
  shaped ends, ivory and ebony
  keyboard, 4-1/2 octaves, mkd
  "Carhart & Needham, New
  York," wear and veneer damage,
  lyre and bench mismatched, one
  bellows rod is missing, 28" h,
  32-1/2" w, 16-1/4" dia 175.00
Orguinette, "Mechanical Orguinette
  Co., New York," small roller
  organ, walnut case, silver stenciled label and dec, working
  cond, paper rolls, 10" h, 12" w,
  9-1/4" dia 500.00

**Hand-painted "Mexico" maraca
with wooden handle, $12.**

Pianola, Aeolian, quartersawn oak,
  foot pedals, repairs required to
  bellows, 60 orig rolls, 36" h,
  45" w 400.00
Pitch pipe, walnut, book form, paper
  label on int, "WN," crack, 6" l
  .... 200.00
Ukulele, The Serenader, B.&G.,
  N.Y., double binding, celluloid
  fingerboard and head 250.00
Zither, Columbia, 47 strings, c1900
  .... 275.00

❖ My Little Pony

It is said that the idea for My Little
Pony came about when research by
Hasbro discovered that young girls
see horses when they close their
eyes at night. The result: ponies that
even city kids can keep. My Little
Pony memorabilia has been putting
smiles on the faces of girls, young
and old, since 1982.

Reference: Debra L. Birge, *The
World of My Little Pony*, Schiffer
Publishing, 2000.
Alarm clock, Bubbles 47.00
Figurine, bisque, First Born by Extra
  Special, 4" l 19.50
Key chain, Morning Glory, detach-
  able with rainbow-colored comb
  .... 4.00
Pony
  Applejack, 1983 .... 7.50
  Firefly, with brush and ribbon,
    orig card 9.00
  Merry Treat, 2nd of 3 Christmas
    ponies, 1984 .... 13.50
  Morning Glory, Birthflower
    Ponies, September 1982
    .... 26.00
  Nightglider, 1984 .... 35.00

N

❖ Napkin Rings

Figural napkin rings are useful collectibles. Victorian silver and silver plate napkin rings, including examples having a whimsical nature, often are available at flea markets.

Aluminum, engraved "World's Fair, St. Louis, 1904," and flag ..50.00
Bakelite
    Angelfish, marbled blue, c1940
        ....70.00
    Elephant, navy blue, c194065.00
    Popeye, decal face, caramel
        color 145.00
    Rabbit, green, shows wear
        ....65.00
    Rocking Horse, red..........225.00
Pewter, turtle, 2-1/2" h.............28.00
Porcelain, sunbonnet girl, mkd
    "Erphila Czechoslovakian," 2" x
    4" 72.00

Silver napkin ring with hallmarks, 1-3/4" diameter, $12.50.

Silver
    Eagle, Meriden, 2" h 125.00
    Leaf and barrel, tarnished..45.00
Silvered metal, cuff style, double
    band..................................20.00
Silver-plated, flowers on lily pad, top
    emb with fan and flowers, sgd
    "Middletown Quad Plate #97"
    ....100.00

✩ ⊙ NASCAR

It's a pretty cool sport when you think about it—guys racing cars that, except for the abundance of colorful advertisements, look like they could have come out of your driveway. When it comes to racing collectibles, nothing's hotter. Are you racing off to a flea market? You should find plenty of good NASCAR collectibles to choose from.

Also see: Racing Collectibles, Auto Bank
    1991, Jeff Gordon, Carolina Ford
        Dealers, NASCAR Club Bank
        ....68.00
    1998, Terry Labonte, Monte
        Carlo, Kellogg's Corny Bank,
        1:24, MIB......................65.00
Barbie, 50th Anniversary NASCAR
    Barbie, MIB......................30.00
Comic book, NASCAR Christmas
    100, 1991, unused..............5.00
Die-cast
    1992, Pit Stop Showcase, Ford
        #98 and 6 pit crew figures,
        1:43 scale, Racing Champi-
        ons 15.00
    1994, Rusty Wallace #2, Premier
        Edition, 1:64 scale, Racing
        Champions, MIB............45.00

Dale Earnhardt playing cards in collector tin, $10.

    1997, Transporter Truck, 1:64
        scale, Racing Champions,
        MIB.............................. 25.00
    1998, 1978 Trans Am, #00,
        3-1/4" l 12.00

❖ Nautical

Anchors Aweigh! Nautical items can encompass things with a nautical theme or items that were actually used on a ship.

Periodicals: *Nautical Brass*, P.O. Box 3966, North Ft. Myers, FL 33918; *Nautical Collector,* P.O. Box 949, New London, CT 06320.

Collectors' Club: Nautical Research Guild, 62 Marlboro St., Newburyport, MA 01950.

For additional listings, see *Warman's Antiques and Collectibles Price Guide.*

Bookends, pr
    Anchors, brass, mounted on faux
        stone base, 8" h........... 47.50
    Whale's heads, bronze verdigris
        finish, 5-1/2" h.............. 50.00
Diorama, ship, old paint dec, c1920
    .... 585.00
Diving helmet, Russian, 3-bolt
    .... 1,295.00
Folk art, carved fish, wood plaque,
    c1940, life size
    Pickerel 265.00
    Rainbow trout.................. 295.00
    Salmon........................... 345.00
Key chain, ship's wheel, leather
    attached to medallion, "VN Bal-
    boa," 1" dia 25.00
Model, English motor launch, steam
    powered, c1950, 44" l, 7-1/2" w
    .... 850.00
Plaque, White Star Line, thick brass
    plate, engraved words, mounted
    on varnished mahogany board,
    18" x 7" 375.00
Porthole, hinged brass, rect, WWII
    era................................... 975.00
Print
    Clippers *Ariel & Taiping*, M. Dawson, 26" x 31" 65.00
    Cutty Sark, *Racing Home*, M. Dawson, 20" x 28" 65.00
    Ship *Triumphant,* Frank Vining Smith, 22" x 32" 38.50

Ship compass, 10" dia magnetic compass, teakwood box, polished brass gimball ring, U.S. Navy, World War II era, made by John E. Hand & Co. 750.00

Table lamp, brass boat cleat, ship's wheel, sea navigation chart lamp shade, 15" h 235.00

❖ Nazi

The National Socialist German Workers Party was created on February 24, 1920, as a program to revive the depressed German economy and spark government revitalization. Today the influence of this political party is referred to as Nazi.

Armband, Hitler Youth 100.00

Belt buckle

    Hitler Youth 45.00

    Nazi Railway, Deutche Reichsbahn 135.00

Cigarette card, Adolf Hitler

    Hiking in woods....................2.50

    On navy ship.........................5.00

Envelope, Hitler birthday stamp, 1940 ....20.00

Identification card, Hitler Youth membership 98.00

Medal, Mother's Honor Cross, gold version, 1938.....................82.00

Pin, Hitler Youth membership, diamond shape, red, white and black enamel 48.00

Pincushion, figural, Hitler 5" h 325.00

Plaque, tin, Adolf Hitler, from building in Prague, 8-1/4" h x 7" 175.00

Hitler pincushion, painted plaster, original tag, 4-3/4" high, $75.

❖ New Martinsville Glass

Founded in 1901, the New Martinsville Glass Manufacturing Company was located in West Virginia. Its glassware products ranged from pressed utilitarian wares to some innovative designs and colors.

Animal

    Baby bear, head straight....60.00

    Seal, holding ball, light lavender, candle holder.................75.00

    Rooster, crooked tail 95.00

Ashtray, Moondrops, red 35.00

Basket, 9-1/2" h, 12" w, Janice, black 190.00

Bitters bottle, Hostmaster, cobalt blue.....................................75.00

Bookends, pr, clipper ships......95.00

Bowl, Teardrop, crystal, 3 ftd, 11" dia, 4" h 45.00

Cake plate

    Janice, 40th Anniversary silver overlay.........................45.00

    Prelude, pedestal foot........10.00

Candlesticks, pr

    Janice, red 200.00

    Moondrops, #37/2, 4" h, brocade etching.........................130.00

    Prelude, #4554, 5" h 130.00

    Radiance, 2-lite 230.00

Candy box, Radiance, 3 part, amber, etch #26..........................160.00

Champagne, Moondrops, red..40.00

Console bowl, Janice, ftd, crystal 38.00

Console set, Radiance, crystal, 12" bowl pr 2-lite candlesticks 125.00

Cordial, Janice, red, silver trim 40.00

Creamer and sugar, Janice, red 48.00

Cup and saucer

    Janice, red 30.00

    Radiance, amber................30.00

Decanter, Moondrops, amber ..80.00

Figure, crystal

    Baby bear, 3-1/2" h 65.00

    Polar bear, 4" h 95.00

    Squirrel, 5" h 55.00

Guest set, 9-1/4" w x 5-3/4" l tray, 6-1/4" h pitcher, 3-1/8" h tumbler, pink, slight flea bites 190.00

Ivy ball, Janice, light blue.........95.00

Lamp, 10" h, Art Deco style, pink satin, black enamel accents 45.00

Pitcher, Oscar, red 100.00

Punch cup, Radiance............15.00

Punch ladle, Radiance, red... 125.00

Relish, Radiance, amber, 3 part 15.00

Swan, Janice, crystal 38.00

Tumbler

    Amy, #34, ftd 22.50

    Janice, red, 10 oz, ftd........35.00

    Moondrops, cobalt blue, 5 oz 24.00

    Oscar, red.........................20.00

Vanity set, 3 pc, Judy, green and crystal or pink and crystal 100.00

Vase, Radiance, #4232, 10" h, crimped, etch #26 ....140.00

❖ Newspapers

Saving a newspaper about a historic event or memorable occasion seems like such an easy thing to do. Happily for newspaper collectors, folks have been doing that for centuries. Flea markets are a great place to find these interesting publications.

Collectors' Club: Newspaper Collectors Society of America, 6031 Winterset, Lansing, MI 48911.

Man Walks On Moon, New York Times, July 21, 1969, $25.

Cincinnati Weekly Herald and Philanthropist, Nov. 22, 1843, feature on "Mr. Adams and the Colored People" 45.00
Hagerstown Daily Mail, Hagerstown, Md., April 6, 1964, "Hero's Homage Paid MacArthur" 25.00
The Hartford Daily Times, Oct. 11, 1876, predicts election of Tilden 45.00
Metropolis Planet, Metropolis, Ill., June 28, 1973, Superman souvenir edition 35.00
New York Times, July 21, 1969, Man Walks on the Moon 25.00
The Washington Daily News, July 12, 1972, "FAREWELL" headline, final edition of publication 30.00
The Youths Medallion, Boston, Mass., April 17, 1841 .... 40.00

❖ Nicodemus Pottery

Made in Ohio by Chester Nicodemus, this pottery is especially noted for a variety of charming animal figurines.
Cabinet jug, yellow & brown on ferrostone, 4-1/4" h 75.00
Figurine
    Fox terrier, 4-1/2" h, 9" l ... 425.00
    Robin, 4-1/2" h 100.00
Flower frog, Madonna, 10-1/2" h 210.00
Salt and pepper shakers, green and brown, 3-1/2" h, pr 72.50
Vase
    Turquoise, 5-1/2" h 180.00
    Yellow, 5" h 52.50

❖ Niloak Pottery

Niloak Pottery was located near Benton, Arkansas. The founder of the company, Charles Dean Hyten, experimented with native clays and tried to preserve their natural colors. By 1911, he had perfected a method that gave this effect, a product he named Mission Ware. The pottery burned but was rebuilt. It reopened under the name Eagle Pottery and by 1929 was producing novelties. Several different marks were used, helping to determine the dates of pieces. By 1946 the company went out of business.

Niloak Mission Ware vase, 5-1/4" high, $100.

Collectors' Club: Arkansas Pottery Collectors Society, 12 Normandy Road, Little Rock, AR 72007.
For additional listings, see *Warman's Antiques and Collectibles Price Guide, Warman's Americana & Collectibles,* and *Warman's American Pottery and Porcelain.*
Candlestick, Mission Ware, 10" h 245.00
Canoe, 2-1/2" h, 8" l 61.00
Creamer, Ozark Dawn 35.00
Planter
    Deer, blue, 4-1/2" h 35.00
    Dutch shoe, tan 40.00
    Elephant, pink 30.00
    Frog, brown, 4-1/2" h 55.00
    Squirrel, white 65.00
    Swan, blue, 7-1/2" h...........65.00
Vase
    Mission Ware, flared lip, 4" h 110.00
    Mission Ware, 4-3/4" h.....280.00
    Mission Ware, hourglass form, 5-1/2" h.........................175.00
    Mission Ware, corseted waist, 6-1/2" h.........................215.00
    Mission Ware, 10-1/2" h...495.00
    Ozark Dawn, twisted handle, 6" h 155.00
    Ozark Dawn, 8-3/4" h.......200.00
    Pink, twisted design, 6-1/2" h 30.00

❖ Nippon China

From 1891 until 1921, *Nippon* was the mark Japan used on hand-painted porcelain made for export. However, in 1921, the United States required all imported Japanese wares to be marked *Japan.*

There are more than 200 documented marks or backstamps for Nippon. For some makers, the color of the mark helps determine the quality of the piece. Green was used for first-grade porcelain, blue for second-grade, and magenta for third-grade. Other types of marks were also used.

Sadly, today there are marked reproductions that can be very deceiving. Carefully examine any piece, study the workmanship, and thoroughly investigate any marks.

References: There are several older reference books that provide information about marks and various makers.

Collectors' Club: Contact the International Nippon Collectors Club, 112 Oak Lane, N., Owatonna, MN 55060 to find a chapter in your local area.
Reproduction Alert.
For additional listings, see *Warman's Antiques and Collectibles Price Guide.*
Ashtray, black cat on roof 125.00
Biscuit jar, ftd, hp roses, gold beading, deep teal background, 7" h, 6" dia............................... 395.00
Bowl
    Eagle and shield design, blue and gold, green "M" in wreath mark, 9-3/4" dia 45.00
    Scalloped edge, floral and gold border, green "M" in wreath mark, 7-1/2" dia 20.00
Cake plate, 2 handles, 10" dia..20.00
Candy dish, divided, scenic design, blue rising sun mark.......... 50.00
Celery tray, pink flowers.......... 60.00
Child's cup and bowl, pulled out face, googlie eyes, red bow tie 175.00
Chocolate set, chocolate pot, five cups and saucers, hp pink roses, light green leaves, gold trim and beading, blue rising sun mark, 10" h 425.00

Reproduction Nippon hat-pin holder.

Buyer beware!

Don't believe everything you see.

That's good advice when it comes to buying antiques and collectibles. It's not that a person should be a cynic. However, the existence of reproductions, fakes, forgeries, and fantasy items have led collectors to approach the marketplace knowledgeably and with caution.

The phrase "caveat emptor"—let the buyer beware—is especially true for anyone interested in Nippon porcelain. Few areas of the antiques market have been plagued by reproductions bearing more fake marks than Nippon.

This hatpin holder is a prime example. An unsuspecting buyer might assume it's an authentic piece of Nippon, since it's marked. However, the mark is a fake—one of many. Therefore, this hatpin holder has no value as an antique.

One of the best resources providing information about such bogus items is *Antique & Collectors Reproduction News*, a monthly newsletter. For information, phone (515) 274-5886 or write to ACRN, P.O. Box 12130, Des Moines, IA 50312.

Cider set, pitcher and 4 mugs, hp grapes and leaves pattern, gilding 375.00
Cup and saucer, Orange Blossom pattern, gold trim, blue mark 30.00
Mayonnaise set, underplate, spoon, floral border, magenta "M" in wreath mark 50.00

Mustard pot, scenic design, green "M" in wreath mark, 3-1/2" h 40.00
Plate, two handles, floral and gold border, red and green mark, 10-1/2" dia 35.00
Relish, cov, scenic design, gold trim, matching spoon, green "M" in wreath mark, 4" h 50.00

Serving tray, center handle, floral dec, magenta "M" in wreath mark 20.00
Spoon holder, gold and white 60.00
Vase
    Florals, gold trim, 11" h.... 450.00
    House and trees scene, ivory ground, gold painted grape leaves, green Morimura mark, 8" h 375.00
    Trees, lake, and floral scene, elephant handles, "M" in wreath mark, 9-1/2" h, pr........ 375.00

❖ Nodders and Bobbin' Heads

Here's a collecting category that folks never seem to tire of. Perhaps it's the whimsical nature of these pieces or the idea that there is constant motion. Whatever, there are plenty of examples to be found at flea markets.

Reference: Tim Hunter, *Bobbing Head Dolls 1960-2000*, Krause Publications, 1999.

Collectors' Club: Bobbin' Head National Club, P.O. Box 9297, Daytona Beach, FL 32120.

Football player, made in Japan, 6-1/2" high, $32.

TIAS Top 10

The following list ranks the most highly sought collectibles on the Internet during 2000.

1. Avon
2. China
3. Cookie jars
4. Roseville
5. Furniture
6. **Noritake**
7. Lamps
8. McCoy
9. Clocks
10. Books

Source: www.tias.com

Nodder
- American League umpire, 8-1/2" h 45.00
- Cat, porcelain, hairline 85.00
- Cowboy, Japan, 5" h 65.00
- Cowgirl, "Let's Kiss," Japan, 5-1/2" h 65.00
- Chinaman, Japan, 6-1/2" h 65.00
- Elephant, celluloid, S.A. Reider & Co., Germany................ 65.00
- Elephant, in green overalls, Hong Kong, 4" h 35.00
- Goose, S.A. Reider & Co., U.S. Zone, Germany, 1-1/2" h, 3-1/2" l........................... 65.00
- Hawaiian boy, "Let's Kiss," Japan, 5-1/2" h.............. 85.00
- Hawaiian girl, "Let's Kiss," Japan, 5-1/4" h.............. 85.00
- Lion, fleece, plastic teeth ... 22.00
- Mickey Mantle, 1962........ 700.00
- Oakland Athletics, 1988, 8-1/2" h 45.00
- Pluto, plastic, 1 ear missing 40.00
- Robin Hood, Japan, 6" h.... 85.00
- Scottie, celluloid, windup, Occupied Japan 125.00
- St. Louis Cardinals football player, plaster, 6-1/2" h 130.00

Nodder/bank
- Black policeman, Nassau, black pants, white hat and jacket, doubles as bank.......... 145.00
- Colonel Sanders, plaster, 7-1/2" h 165.00
- Golfer, club missing 75.00
- Oriental girl 57.50

❖ Norcrest

Not a lot of information has been printed about this porcelain maker, but many folks are finding their products to be charming and worth collecting.

- Anniversary plate, 45th, 10-1/2" d 10.00
- Bank, wishing well, blue bird and bucket at edge, 7" h........... 14.50
- Cup and saucer
  - Golden Wheat pattern, red mark 5.00
  - Pine Cone pattern 7.50
- Figure
  - Boy with cart 7.00
  - Dalmatian, 1960s, 6-1/4" l.. 15.00
  - Giraffe 35.00
  - Poppy, #F447, August........ 12.00
- Salt and pepper shakers, pr
  - Hula Girl and Ukelele Boy, paper label, 3-1/2" h 45.00
  - Sad Sack, George Baker, black ink stamp, 4-1/2" h 350.00
- Wall pocket, clock, orig label, 6" h 25.00

✪ Noritake China

Noritake China was founded by the Morimura Brothers in Nagoya, Japan, about 1904. The company produced high-quality dinnerware for export and also some blanks for hand painting. Although the factory was heavily damaged during World War II, production resumed and continues today. There are more than 100 different marks to help determine the pattern and date of production.

Collectors' Club: Noritake Collectors' Society, 145 Andover Place, West Hempstead, NY 11552.

- Bowl, Lusterware, blue ext, white and orange luster int, 5-1/4" dia, 3-1/4" h 85.00
- Candlesticks, pr, gold flowers and bird, blue luster ground, wreath with "M" mark, 8-1/4" h.... 125.00
- Celery set, celery holder, six matching salts, gold trim, green wreath marks.............................. 85.00
- Creamer, Chandon, #7306 ..... 42.00
- Cup and saucer
  - Floroia, #83374 pattern 24.00
  - Margarita pattern.............. 12.00
  - Roanne, #6794................. 18.00
- Dinner plate, Margarita pattern, 9-7/8" dia 18.00
- Dish, handle, red and gold flower border, gold trim, red wreath mark, 5-1/2" w.................. 28.00
- Easter egg, yellow hat with blue trim, blue and pink flowers, dated 1976, satin lined box, 3" h 26.00
- Gravy boat, Carolyn.............. 105.00
- Hair receiver, Art Deco geometric designs, gold luster, wreath with "M" mark, 3-1/4" h 50.00
- Jam jar, cov, basket style, figural applied cherries on notched lid 55.00
- Platter
  - Asian Song, medium 85.00
  - Candice, large 85.00
  - Carolyn, small 82.00
- Salt, swan, white, orange luster 12.00
- Soup bowl, Margarita pattern.. 18.00
- Sugar bowl, cov, Margarita pattern 18.00

Castella plate, Noritake, 9-7/8" diameter, $10.

Vase, medallion with landscape scene on one side, florals on reverse, gold moriage, black background covered with tiny gold roses, gold edge at bottom, some wear to gold, green "M" in wreath mark, c1920, 6" h ..90.00

Vegetable bowl, cov
Bamboo 105.00
Candice..............................95.00

❖ Noritake China, Azalea Pattern

In the 1920s, the Larkin Company of Buffalo, N.Y., became a prime distributor of Noritake China. Two of the most popular patterns they promoted were Azalea and Tree in the Meadow, causing them to be the most popular with collectors today. The design of Azalea pattern includes delicate pink flowers, green leaves on a white background. Many pieces have gold trim, especially on handles and finials.

Bon bon 48.00
Cake plate 40.00
Casserole, cov.........................75.00
Creamer 25.00
Dinner plate............................24.00

Noritake Azalea gravy boat and attached underplate, $50.

Egg cup 55.00
Lemon tray 30.00
Luncheon plate........................15.00
Salad bowl, 10" dia..................37.50
Teapot...................................100.00
Vase, fan 150.00

❖ Noritake China, Tree in the Meadow Pattern

This popular pattern was also sold by the Larkin Company. The pattern shows a scene with a meadow, sky, buildings, and, of course, trees. It's a more colorful pattern than Azalea.

Ashtray, green backstamp, 5-1/4" dia.....................................35.00
Berry set, master bowl with pierced handles, six smaller bowls 75.00
Bowl, green backstamp, 6-3/4" l, 6" dia.....................................30.00
Cake plate, 7-1/2" sq 38.00
Creamer and sugar, red wreath mark 45.00
Demitasse cup and saucer 48.00
Plate, red-brown backstamp, 7-3/4" dia.....................................30.00
Platter, two handles 45.00
Relish tray, 8-1/2" l, red mark ..40.00
Vase, fan shape, green backstamp, 5" w......................................35.00

❖ Northwood Glass

Northwood Glass is a term used to describe the glassware made by both the Northwood Glass Company and Northwood & Company, two distinct glass makers. The histories of these companies are quite interesting and involved. Between them, fine pressed pattern glass, opalescent glass, and Carnival glass were made. The name Northwood has again surfaced as a glass manufacturer as Northwood family descendants are beginning to issue new pieces. Contemporary wares have a different mark than the familiar N or script signature found on vintage pieces. Like many glass manufacturers, not every piece was marked.

Basket, white carnival, basket-weave, open handles, ftd, sgd, 4" h 125.00

Bon bon, Stippled Rays pattern, blue Carnival............................60.00
Bowl, 8-3/4" dia, Blossoms and Shell, marigold Carnival, molded mark............................... 135.00
Butter dish, cov, Cherry and Lattice, ruby and gold flashing, wear, roughness 90.00
Candlestick, 3" h, 5-1/4" dia, Chinese Coral 85.00
Candy dish, cov
Ruffles and Bows, blue opalescent.............................. 45.00
Stretch, blue iridescent, #636 .... 70.00
Compote, Chrysanthemum Sprig, custard, 5" h, 3" dia.......... 80.00
Creamer
Lustre Flute, green carnival 50.00
Pods and Posies, green pattern glass, gold trim 70.00
Regal, blue opalescent...... 60.00
Cruet, Leaf Umbrella, mauve, heat check, no stopper 500.00
Goblet
Grape and Gothic Arches, custard, nutmeg stain......... 75.00
Nearcut, colorless 40.00
Jelly compote, Poppy pattern, green 35.00
Nut bowl, Leaf and Beads pattern, purple carnival 65.00
Pitcher, Ribbed Opal, blue 1,450.00

Peacock Tumbler, Northwood, orange, 4" high, $60.

Salt and pepper shakers, pr, orig
tops
Bow and Tassel pattern, milk
glass..............................65.00
Leaf Umbrella, mauve, cased
.....................................165.00
Sugar, cov
Cherry and Plum pattern, clear,
ruby and green trim.......85.00
Paneled Spring, milk glass,
green and gold dec 125.00
Tumbler, Acorn Burrs, green ...75.00
Water set, Regent, amethyst, pitcher
and six tumblers 800.00

❖ Nutcrackers

Clever devices to release the tasty part of a nut were invented as far back as the 19th century. Collectors today seek out interesting examples in various metals and wood.

Collectors' Club: Nutcracker Collectors' Club, 12204 Fox Run Drive, Chesterland, OH 44026.

Bear, wooden, Black Forest, glass
eyes, curved tail with lever that
operates the mouth, 4-1/2" h, 8" l
.....................................165.00
Crocodile, wooden, full-figure, Swiss
or German, screw press in belly,
8" l 585.00
Dog, graniteware over cast iron,
white on black base, black tail
and lower jaw, 5-3/4" h, 10-1/2" l
.....................................115.00
Dog's head, wooden, Black Forest
style, glass eyes, levered jaw,
mkd "Chalet Minerve & Chalet
Suisse Egger & Bruger…," oval
base, 3-1/2" h, 7" l 520.00
Eagle's head, wooden, Swiss, glass
eyes, levered beak, 6-1/2" l
.....................................310.00
Elephant's head, wooden, glass
eyes, levered mouth, 10-1/2" l
.....................................650.00
Man with umbrella, bearded, smoking a pipe, wooden, German, 1
foot reattached, 8-1/2" h
.....................................570.00
Squirrel, cast iron, 4-1/2" h, 5-1/2" l
.....................................100.00
St. Bernard, metal, advertises L.A.
Althoff Makers of Headlight
Stoves and Ranges Chicago, Ill.,
5-3/4" h, 11" l...................275.00

❖ Nutting, Wallace

The story of Wallace Nutting is a fascinating tale of enterprising an American. Born in 1861, he attended Harvard University and several theological seminaries. In 1904 he opened a photography studio in New York, later other branch studios. By the time he moved to Framingham, Massachusetts, in 1913, he was employing more than 200 colorists, framers, and support staff. Nutting photographed the images that were to be hand colored under his specific directions. Nutting died in 1941, but his wife continued the business. After her death, the business continued until 1971, when the last owner ordered the glass negatives destroyed.

Although the listing below is devoted to his pictures, remember that he also published several books and sold silhouettes and furniture.

References: Michael Ivankovich, *Alphabetical & Numerical Index to Wallace Nutting Pictures*, Diamond Press, 1988; ——, *Collector's Guide to Wallace Nutting Pictures*, Collector Books, 1997.

Collectors' Club: Wallace Nutting Collectors Club, P.O. Box 2458, Doylestown, PA 18901.

A Birch Grove, 11" x 14" 175.00

By the Stone Fence, The Swimming
Pool, 10" x 12" 160.00

Dell Dale Road, 16" x 20" 235.00

The Goose Chase Quilt, 10" x 18"
....375.00

Harmony, 14" x 17" 375.00

The Home Hearth, 10" x 16"..325.00

Honeymoon Blossoms, 12" x 16"
....185.00

June Beautiful, 13" x 16" 195.00

Lingering Waters, 9" x 11" 185.00

The Orchard Brook, 9" x 11"..165.00

A Roadside Pine, 12" x 14" ...165.00

A Stitch in Time, 11" x 13" 295.00

❖ Nutting-Like Pictures

Because Wallace Nutting's pictures were so successful, copycats soon appeared on the scene. Some artists had worked for Nutting and learned the techniques. These pictures are starting to catch the eye of collectors.

Davidson, David
Over the Hills, 7" x 9" 75.00
The Pool, 5" x 7" 60.00
Rivers of Peace, 7" x 9" ... 65.00
The Road Home, 6" x 8" ... 75.00
Haynes, F. Jay
Old Faithful, 8" x 10" 95.00
Great Falls, Yellowstone Park,
13" x 18" 150.00
Harris
Florida Wilds, 4" x 8" 65.00
Tower, Ft. Marion, St. Augustine,
Fla., 12" x 15" 175.00
Sawyer
The Pool, 4" x 6" 60.00
Echo Lake, 7" x 9"............. 65.00
Upper-Flame Falls, 14" x 16"
.... 150.00
Willoughby Lake, 5" x 6" ..110.00
Thompson, Fred
Deep Hole Brook, 5" x 13"
.... 75.00
Fireside Fancy Work, 7" x 9"
.... 110.00
Paring Apples, 7" x 9" 125.00

Standley, "Ute Pass, Manitou, Colorado," hand-tinted photograph, image size 7-3/4" x 3-1/4", $70.

❖ Occupied Japan

To help repair their devastated economy after World War II, the Japanese produced items to export, including porcelain, toys, and all kinds of knickknacks. Today savvy collectors know that items made during the occupation time period might be marked "Japan," "Made in Japan," or "Occupied Japan" as well as "Made in Occupied Japan."

Reference: Florence Archambault, *Occupied Japan For the Home*, Schiffer Publishing, 2000.

Collectors' Club: The Occupied Japan Club, 29 Freeborn St., Newport, RI 02840.

Porcelain figurine with vase, Occupied Japan, 3-1/8" high, $8.50.

Opera glasses, Occupied Japan, 3-3/8" high, 4-1/8" long, $45.

Ashtray, china, souvenir from Florida, shaped like state, black letters, gold trim 15.00

Basket, china, small figural roses and leaves 7.50

Bell, chef holding wine bottle and glass 27.50

Clock, bisque, dancing couple in colonial garb, floral encrusted case, 10-1/2" h 250.00

Figurine

    Couple, 7" x 4-1/2" 35.00

    Cowboy on rearing horse, metal 18.00

    Farm girl with scarf, egg basket beside her, red mark "Made in Occupied Japan," 1-1/4" x 5" 15.00

    Man, 6" h, 2" w base 25.00

    Santa, 7-1/2" h 60.00

Flower frog, bisque, girl with bird on shoulder, pastel highlights, gold trim 48.00

Harmonica, butterfly, orig box 20.00

Mug, boy-shaped handle 15.00

Planter, black cat, red ribbon ... 15.00

Platter, Courley pattern, heavy gold trim 30.00

Tape measure, pig, stamped "Occupied Japan" 45.00

Toy, boy on sled, litho tin wind-up, MIB 150.00

Wall pocket, lady with hat, 5" h 45.00

❖ Ocean Liner Memorabilia

The thought of a leisurely ocean cruise has enticed many to try this mode of travel. Of course they brought back souvenirs. Today collectors are glad they did as they discover these mementos at flea markets.

Collectors' Club: Steamship Historical Society of America, Inc., 300 Ray Drive, Suite 4, Providence, RI 02906.

Ashtray, *Nord Lloyd Europa*, Bakelite, Art Deco, 5-1/2" dia 85.00

Baggage tag, French Line, first class, unused 7.50

Brochure

    Cunard Line, Getting There is Half the Fun, 16 pgs, 1952 .... 7.50

    Italian Line, Six Cruises the Mediterranean and Egypt, 1934 .... 15.00

Cruet set, salt, pepper, glass lined mustard compartment with serving spoon, chromium, English, 1930s, 8" l, 3" h 125.00

Deck plan, *R.M.S.P. Avon*, The Royal Mail Steam Packet, Dec 1909 .... 32.00

Dish, Cunard *R.M.S. Queen Mary*, ceramic, oval, color portrait, gold edge, Staffordshire, 5" l 37.50

Magazine illus, framed, *S.S. Normandie* being escorted by the E. J. Moran tug into slip in N.Y. Harbor, 12" x 15" 125.00

Flag-shaped ashtray, red "M" for Mason Lines, green plastic, 4-3/4" wide, $25.

Map, Norwegian Cruise Lines, *M/S Southward*, map of West Indies and Caribbean Sea, routes, antiquities images, 1970s, framed, 18" x 24"............... 40.00

Menu

S.S. *Leonardo Da Vinci*, January, 1973............................... 6.00

S.S. *Lurline*, Matson Lines, Commodore's Dinner, March 3, 1959, 12" x 9"................20.50

Newspaper Supplement, *Queen Mary, the World's Wonder Ship*, 20" x 24", acid free mat ...125.00

Note paper, Cunard *White Star*, blue 5.00

Passport cover, Red Star Line, fabric, ship illus.......................27.50

Pencil, S.S. *Oceanic*, Caran D'ache lead pencil, plastic case 25.00

Pennant, *R.M.S. Queen Elizabeth*, gray felt, blue, red, white, and black, some fading, 26-1/2" l 25.00

Playing cards, Eastern Steamship Corp., 3/4" x 2-1/4" x 3-1/2" gold foil box, red, and black accents, full color deck, showing ship at sea, yellow and white border, revenue stamp attached to edge flap, c1950......................... 15.00

Poster, *Nord-Lloyd Bremen and Europa*, marketed for American transatlantic travel, conservation framed, 6-1/2" x 9-1/2" 150.00

Souvenir Spoon, Cunard *White Star*, demitasse, silver plated.....20.00

Table knives, Matson lines, "M" scribed on each handle, silverplate, set of 890.00

Tie clasp, Cunard Line *R.M.S. Queen Mary*, gold tone, red, white, and blue enameled ship 18.00

❖ Old Sleepy Eye

Old Sleepy Eye, Minnesota, was the home of the Old Sleepy Eye Flour Mill. The company used an Indian as its symbol. Collectors can also find his image on stoneware premiums that were issued by the mill.

Collectors' Club: Old Sleepy Eye Collectors Club, P.O. Box 12, Monmouth, IL 61462.

Old Sleepy Eye commemorative, 1982 collector's convention, 7" high, $65.

Reproduction Alert.

Bowl, Flemish, rounded bottom, 4" h, 6-1/2" dia 355.00

Butter crock, Flemish, straight-sided, 5" h, 6-1/2" dia 375.00

Cookbook, shaped like a loaf of bread, 4-7/8" x 4-1/4".......175.00

Mug, 4-1/4" h 110.00

Pillow top, Chief Sleepy Eye before the Great Father, known as the Monroe top, 1901 ....500.00

Pitcher, blue and white

No. 1, blue rim, 4-1/8" h ...275.00

No. 1, plain rim, 4-1/8" h ..180.00

No. 2, 5-1/4" h.................275.00

No. 4, blue rim..................410.00

Salt crock, hanging, blue and white, 5-1/2" h, 5-1/4" dia........1,650.00

Vase

Flemish, cylindrical, 8-1/2" h 350.00

❖ Olympic Collectibles

Most of us are familiar with the Olympic rings logo. Watching for those is a great way to spot Olympic collectibles. It's usually easier to find fresh examples at flea markets during years the Olympics are held.

Periodical: *Sports Collectors Digest*, 700 E State St., Iola, WI 54990.

Collectors' Club: Olympic Pin Collector's Club, 1386 Fifth St., Schenectady, NY 12303.

Barbie, Olympic gymnast Barbie, 1995, NRFB......................20.00

Pen and pencil set, Los Angeles 1984, Pentel, $15.

Booklet, viewers guide, 1992 Olympic Winter Games, Albertville 10.00

Bottle opener, 1996, Atlanta, American flag design on one side, 4-1/2" l 12.00

Coca-Cola bottle, 1984, 23rd Olympiad, Los Angeles, 10" h... 12.00

Figurine, 1980, Sam the Eagle, 5" h 8.50

Key chain, 1984, Olympic rings 4.00

License plate, 1996, Atlanta 4.00

Mr. Peanut coin, 1980............. 14.00

Pennant, 1996, Atlanta, Olympic baseball 6.00

Pin, 1996, torch relay, Coca-Cola, 1-1/4" x 1/2" 7.00

Plate

1972 Olympics, Royal Copenhagen, 8" dia 15.00

1992, Winter Olympics Skating, Albertville, France, Budweiser, orig box, 8-1/2" dia 28.00

Platter, 1984, features Olympians, McDonald's, tin, 8" x 11" 9.00

Program, 1996, "The Games of the XXVI Olympiad Centennial Olympic Games," 196 pgs 32.00

Smurf, Olympic Smurf............. 40.00

❖ Orrefors, Kosta Boda

Here's interesting glassware to start collecting. Made in Sweden since 1898, current pieces often reflect their historical antecedents. The crystal used is high quality and the designers certainly develop some interesting shapes and color combinations.

Bowl, crystal, oval indents with wheel cut edges, sgd and numbered, 6-1/2" dia 50.00
Bucket, heavy walled cylinder, transparent teal blue, base inscribed "Orrefors Esp. PA 245-62 Sven Palmqvist" 200.00
Candlesticks, pr, 3" h, 5" dia, crystal, sgd 115.00
Centerpiece bowl, crystal petals, orig sticker, 9-3/4" w, 4" h 265.00
Decanter, 12-1/2" h, squared crystal bottle, Romeo serenading Juliet on balcony, base engraved "Orrefors No. 880" 350.00
Jar, cov, 1000 Windows, sgd and numbered 450.00
Perfume bottle, crystal, orig label, 4-1/4" h 32.00
Rose bowl, round, layered, sgd "Orrefors H 7 48" 200.00
Scent bottle, octagonal, engraved fish and bubbles, 9-1/4" h 180.00
Vase
   Etching of little girl on front, stars etched on back, sgd, 4-3/4" h 340.00

Smokey gray, signed by Sven Palmqvist, 8-1/2" h 100.00
Triangular, crystal, sgd, 7-1/4" h 110.00

❖ Owl Collectibles

Whoo, whoo, who collects owl items—lots of folks! Some are enchanted with the wisdom of this regal bird, while others find owls fun and whimsical. Lucky for them, artists and designers have been incorporating the owl's image into items for years.

Book rack, expandable, owl on each end 55.00
Brooch, Mandle, Japanned mounting, clear rhinestones for the body and head, dark green eyes and ears, 2-1/4" h, 1" w 50.00
Figurine, glass, alpine blue, Boyd, 3-1/2" h 10.00
Letter opener, brass 25.00
Notepad holder, chalkware, figural, 1970, 7" sq 29.00
Pin, Avon, solid perfume sachet, goldtone, 2" h 10.00

Print, Mottled Owl, hand-colored, Beverly Robinson Morris, from Birds of Great Britain, 1895, slight stain, foxing, 10" x 6-3/4" 20.00
Salt and pepper shakers, Shawnee Pottery, 3-3/8" h, pr 35.00
Spoon rest, ceramic, souvenir of San Francisco, shows cable car, has kitchen prayer, 7" x 4-1/2" 20.00
Tin, Red Owl allspice, Red Owl Stores 17.00

Porcelain owl match holder, $20.

For exciting collecting trends and newly expanded areas look for the following symbols:

⊛ Hot Topic

☆ New Warman's Listing

(May have been in another Warman's title.)

❖ Paden City Glass

Founded in Paden City, West Virginia, in 1916, this company made glassware until 1951. Paden City's wares were all hand made until 1948. The glass was not marked, nor was it heavily advertised. Much of their success laid with blanks supplied to others to decorate. Many of their wares were sold to institutional facilities, restaurants, etc. Paden City is known for rich colors in many shades.

Reference: O.O. Brown, *Paden City Glass Mfg. Co., Catalogue Reprints From the 1920s*, Glass Press, 2000.

Bowl, Orchid, ruby, 2 handles, 12" w, 9-3/4" deep 230.00

Cake plate, ftd
    Black Forest, green 125.00
    Crow's Foot, cobalt blue, 11" d 50.00
    Leia Bird, green, 10" dia .. 125.00

Candy box, cov, flat, Crow's Foot Square, crystal, flower cut, 3 ftd, chipped edge of lid 18.00

Compote, cov, #555 line, ruby stained, 9" h, int. rim of cover chipped 80.00

Cup and saucer, Largo, red 32.50

Figure
    Chinese pheasant, light blue, slight nick 260.00
    Pony, light blue, two base chips 200.00

Goblet, Penny line, amethyst .. 18.50

Iced tea tumbler, Penny line, red 22.50

Napkin rings, Party line, set of 6 .... 60.00

Old Fashioned tumbler, Georgian, ruby 15.00

Plate
    Crow's Foot, orchid etch, 10" sq 48.00
    Party line, amber, 6" dia 3.00

Reamer, 4 cup measure base, floral design, pink, 7-1/2" dia 170.00

Sherbet, Penny line, amethyst 12.50

Tumbler, Party line, ftd, amber, 3-1/2" h 9.50

Underplate, crystal, etched leaves, flowers, balls, center depression, 12" dia 28.00

Vase
    Black Forest etch, black, squatty, 6-1/2" h 175.00
    Black Forest etch, black, Regina, 10" h 250.00
    Orchid etch, red, 10" h 395.00
    Utopia etch, black, 10" h .. 195.00

❖ Paden City Pottery

Located near Sisterville, West Virginia, Paden City Pottery was founded in 1914 and ceased operation in 1963. They produced semiporcelain dinnerware with high-quality decal decoration.

Cup and saucer
    Rose 9.50
    Yellow Rose 10.50

Gravy boat, Rose 17.00

Plate
    Far East, 10-1/2" dia 19.00
    Modern Orchid, 9-3/8" dia .. 11.75
    Pink Roses, 9-3/4" dia 10.00
    Rose, 10" dia 12.00
    Shell Crest, tab handled, 10-1/2" dia 20.00
    Yellow Rose, 9-1/4" dia 9.25

Platter
    Forest Green, 12" l 25.00
    Modern Orchid, 9-1/4" l 13.00
    Patio, 12" l 30.00
    Petit Point Bouquet, 12" l ... 25.00
    Rose, oval, 13-3/4" l 35.00
    Shell Crest, 16" l 30.00
    Touch of Black, 14" l 25.00
    Yellow Roses, 14" l 25.00
    Wild Grasses, 12" l 12.00

Salt and pepper shakers, Modern Orchid 16.50

Teapot, Bak-Serv, stains, spot chip 95.00

Vegetable bowl, Yellow Rose, 9" 24.00

Goldilocks and the Three Bears paint-by-number, 11-1/2" x 5-1/2" each, pair, $5.

❖ Paint-by-Number Sets

For those of us who aren't artistically inclined, paint-by-number sets open a world that turns anyone into a first-class artist. Popular-culture figures are favorite subjects. Collectors look for sets that are mint in box. However, buyers are also snapping up many finished products, especially those with unusual subjects.

Blue jays, framed, 13" x 10-1/2" 20.00

French street scene, edge damage, 20" x 16" 37.00

Hunting dogs, 1950s/60s, 16-1/2" x 20-1/2" 17.50

Impalas drinking at African water hole, framed, 12" x 16" 32.00

Jesus and children, framed, 21-1/2" x 27-1/2" 7.50

The Last Supper, 1950s, framed, 18" x 24" 10.00

Lighthouse, framed, 10" x 14" 16.50

Nude, woman sitting on rocks on beach, 12" x 16" 55.00

Roses, still life, 1958, PP Corp, 2 paintings, MIB 7.50

Sunflower Mosaic, artist Brian Shellabear, 18" x 16", MIB 17.00

Pairpoint hat, deep red and white, original label, 4-1/4" high, $75.

❖ Pairpoint

Here's a name that can confuse flea market dealers. Some associate Pairpoint with the Pairpoint Manufacturing Company or Pairpoint Corporation, a leader in silver-plated wares. Others associate it with National Pairpoint Company, a company that made glassware and aluminum products such as windows, and other commercial glassware. Today lead crystal glassware is still made by Pairpoint.

Basket, silver plated, 12-5/8" l, 9-1/4" w, 9-1/4" h, mkd "Pat applied for 12/1904," some wear to plating...........................295.00
Bowl, amethyst glass silver label, unused 75.00
Bride's basket holder, silver plated, figural berries dec, mkd...325.00
Centerpiece bowl, emerald green glass, engraved vintage pattern, 12" dia 425.00
Epergne, center glass vase etched with roses, silver plate holder with matching roses, mkd "Pairpoint Mfg Co., New Bedford, Mass," 11" h 675.00
Fruit tray, silver plated, birds, cherries, and leaves, 11" x 14" 195.00
Mustache cup, silver plated, elaborate floral design, mkd "Pairpoint Mfg Co., New Bedford,

Mass, Quadruple Plate, 2060," 3-1/4" h 45.00
Tea set, silver plated..............300.00
Trophy, copper, 2 fancy handles with feather design, plaque "New Bedford Yacht Club, Ocean Race, won by Nutmeg for fastest time, Aug 5th, 1909," base mkd and numbered, 8-1/2" h, 7" dia 400.00
Tray, silver plated, designer Albert Steffin, 14" l, patented June 28, 1904................................195.00

❖ Paper Dolls

Paper dolls date to the 1880s. Several early magazines, including McCall's, used to include paper dolls in every issue. The book form of paper dolls came into favor in the 1950s. Look for interesting characters and vintage clothing styles.

Periodicals: *Celebrity Doll Journal,* 5 Court Pl, Puyallup, WA 98372; *Cornerstones,* 2216 S. Autumn Lane, Diamond Bar, CA 91789; *Golden Paper Doll & Toy Opportunities,* P.O. Box 252, Golden CO, 80402-0252; *Loretta's Place Paper Doll Newsletter,* 808 Lee Ave., Tifton, GA 3194-4134; *Midwest Paper Dolls & Toys Quarterly,* P.O. Box 131, Galesburg, KS 66740; *Northern Lights Paperdoll News,* P.O. Box 871189, Wasilla, AK 99687; *Now & Then,* 67-40 Yellowstone Blvd., Flushing, NY 11375-2614; *Paper Doll & Doll Diary,* P.O. Box 12146, Lake Park, FL 33403; *Paper Doll Circle,* 5 Jackson Mews, Immingham, NR, Grimsby, S Hubs DN40 2HQ, UK; *Paper Doll Gazette,* Route #2, Box 52, Princeton, IN 47670; *Paper Doll News,* P.O. Box 807, Vivian, LA 71082; *Paperdoll Review,* P.O. Box 584, Princeton, IN 47670; *PD Pal,* 5341 Gawain #883, San Antonio, TX 78218.

Collectors' Clubs: Original Paper Doll Artist Guild, P.O. Box 14, Kingsfield, ME 04947; Paper Doll Queens & Kings of Metro Detroit, 685 Canyon Road, Rochester, MI 48306; United Federation of Doll Clubs, 10920 N Ambassador, Kansas City, MO 64153.

Alice Faye, uncut.....................95.00

Hour of Charm Paper Dolls, The Saalfield Publishing Co., 1943, uncut, $25.

Annie Oakley, 1956, uncut...... 65.00
Barbie's Boutique, Whitman, 1973, uncut 12.00
Betsy McCall Cut-Out/Punch-Out Paper Dolls, Saalfield #1370, 8-1/4" x 11-1/2", copyright 1965, 1966 McCall Corp., USA, 16 full color pages 24.00
Cinderella, Saalfield Publishing Co., 4 dolls, 4 pgs, uncut.......... 20.00
Dotty and Danny on Parade, Burton Playthings, #875, 1935, uncut 35.00
Lucille Ball & Desi Arnaz, Whitman, 1953, uncut....................... 80.00
Mary Poppins, 1973, partially cut 35.00
Miss America Magic Doll, Parker Bros, 1953, uncut............. 24.00
Nanny and the Professor, Artcraft, 1971................................. 24.00
Our Gang, Whitman, 1931, clothes uncut 65.00
Pony Tail, Samuel Gabriel & Sons, uncut................................. 24.00
Sparkle Plenty, uncut 60.00
The Wedding Party, Samuel Gabriel & Sons, uncut 35.00

❖ Paperback Books

Mass-marketed paperback books date to the late 1930s. Collectors tend to focus on one type of book or a favorite author.

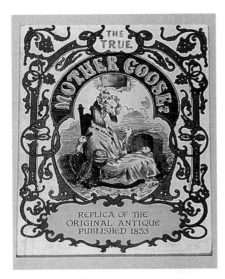

The True Mother Goose: Replica of the Original Antique Published 1833, $8.

Periodicals: *Books Are Everything,* 302 Martin Drive, Richmond, KY 40475; *Dime Novel Round-Up,* P.O. Box 226, Dundas, MN 55019; *Echoes,* 504 E. Morris Street, Seymour, TX 76380; *Golden Perils,* 5 Milliken Mills Road, Scarboro, ME 04074; *Paperback Parade,* P.O. Box 209, Brooklyn, NY 11228.

The Democratic Book 1936.....55.00
Elvis Presley: The King is Dead, Martin A. Grove, 1977 ....6.00
Favorite Christmas Carols, Firestone Tire and Rubber Co., 1955 ....5.00
First Lady, Charlotte Curtis, Pyramid Book, 1962, 1st printing 12.00
The Flood, Prof. Alfred M. Rehwinkel, Good News Publishers 5.00
Flying Saucers in Fact and Fiction, Hans Stefan Santesson, 1968 ....6.00
For Your Eyes Only, Ian Fleming, 1st ed., 1981 ....5.00
John F. Kennedy: War Hero, Richard Tregaskis.........................15.00
The Kennedy Wit, Bill Adler, Bantam Edition, 1965 ....15.00
The Mystery of the Laughing Shadow, Alfred Hitchcock and The Three Investigators, Random House, 1985................3.50
Number 1, Billy Martin (autographed) and Peter Goldenbock, Dell, 1st printing, 1981 ......20.00

The Quotable Mr. Kennedy, Gerald Gardner, 1963....................15.00
Saddle Man, Matt Stuart, Bantam, Sept. 1951, 1st printing........8.00
Spacehive, Jeff Sutton, Ace, 1960 ....8.00
U-Boats In Action, Robert C. Stern, 1977.................................10.00
They Were Expendable, W.L. White, 1941.................................15.00

❖ Paper Ephemera

Paper memorabilia is another one of the fastest-growing collecting areas. Some folks search for bits of nostalgia to decorate with, while others look for interesting pieces of local history or items related to a specific topic. Ephemera takes many forms, from advertisements to books to posters. The listings below are but a sampling of the types of paper items commonly found at flea markets.

Periodicals: *Biblio,* 845 Willamette St., Eugene, OR 87401; *Paper & Advertising Collector,* P.O. Box 500, Mount Joy, PA 17552; *Paper Collectors' Marketplace,* P.O. Box 128, Scandinavia, WI 54977.

Zenith Color TV Operating Instructions, rotating wheel, 10-1/2" x 8-1/8", $3.

Collectors' Clubs: Ephemera Society, 12 Fitzroy Square, London, W1P 5HQ England; National Association of Paper & Advertising Collectors, P.O. Box 500, Mount Joy, PA 17552; The Ephemera Society of America, Inc., P.O. Box 95, Cazenovia, NY 13035; The Ephemera Society of Canada, 36 MacCauley Drive, Thornhill, Ontario L3T 5S5 Canada, plus specialized collector clubs.

For additional listings, see *Warman's Antiques and Collectibles Price Guide.*

Almanac, *Hostetters Illustrated United States Almanac 1876 for Merchants, Mechanics, Miners, Farmers, Planters & General Family Use,* Pittsburgh, loose cover 20.00
Birthday card, Golliwog, 1950s 24.00
Blotter, tiger, None Such Novelty Masks, ink stains, bent corners, 3-1/4" x 6" 10.00
Book
    Children's Guide to Boston, 1946, spiralbound, 10" x 6-1/2" 25.00
    The Little Tin Soldier, Thomson & Taylor Spice Co., Chicago, c1890, 7-1/2" x 5-1/2" ... 25.00
Brochure, John Deere Spring Tooth Harrows, 1949, 16 pgs, 9" x 4" 12.00
Insert card, for Goodrich sport shoes display, 1930s, "Washable in soap and water" shows boxes of Super Suds, Fels-Napha Soap Chips, Ivory Flakes, Kirkman, Rinso, and Ivory Soap, 11-5/8" x 15-1/2" 30.00
Menu, Club Plantation Souvenir Menu, 1950s.................... 20.00
Placemat, Aunt Jemima Restaurant, 1982, Quaker Oats Co., plastic-coated 18.00

❖ Paper Money

Here's another one of those topics where thousands of examples exist, and collectors should be critical of condition. There are many good reference books to help with both issues.

It's a record

As noted in the *Bank Note Reporter*, an auction record was set when an 1890 $1,000 treasury note sold for $792,000. The note is commonly known as the Levitan Grand Watermelon. Only three Grand Watermelons are known to be in private hands.

Jim Davis paperweight, 1995, 3-1/2" high, $7.

References, all from Krause Publications: Colin R. Bruce, II and Neil Shafer, eds., *Standard Catalog of World Paper Money, Specialized Issues*, Volume I, 8th ed.; Chester Krause, *Wisconsin Obsolete Bank Notes and Scrip*; Eric P. Newman, *Early Paper Money of America*, 4th ed., Dean Oates & John Schwartz, *Standard Guide to Small Size U. S. Paper Money*, 2nd ed.; Albert Pick, *Standard Catalog of World Paper Money, General Issues*, Volume II, 9th ed., Arlie Slabaugh, *Confederate States Paper Money*, 9th ed.; Robert E. Wilhite, ed., *Standard Catalog of U. S. Paper Money*, 19th ed.

Periodical: *Bank Note Reporter*, 700 E State St., Iola, WI 54990.

Bank of State of Georgia, 1857 .... 20.00
Bank of Tennessee, 1861, 5 cents 10.00
Consecutive numbers, set of five, $1, CU FRNS, 1995 Star, District B 20.00
Continental Note, Philadelphia, Feb 17, 1776, $2, decorative border, woodcuts 85.00
Djibouti, 20 francs.................... 65.00
Egypt, 10 pounds, 1958 .... 48.00
First Reserve Bank Note, 1929, $5 .... 150.00
Iran, 10000 Rials 45.00
State of Florida, $1 .... 26.00
State of North Carolina, $2 note, 1861 .... 21.00
Tecumseh, Michigan, $1.......... 30.00

❖ Paperweights

About the same time folks invented paper, they needed something to hold it down, so along came the paperweight. They can be highly decorative or purely practical. Look for ones of interesting advertising, perhaps a unique shape, or showing an interesting location.

References: For high end priced antique and modern glass paperweights, consult one of the many standard paperweight reference books.

Collectors' Clubs: Caithness Collectors Club, 141 Lanza Ave., Building 12, Garfield, NJ 07026; International Paperweight Society, 761 Chestnut St., Santa Cruz, CA 95060; Paperweight Collectors Association, Inc., P.O. Box 1263, Beltsville, MD 20704.
For additional listings of traditional glass paperweights, see *Warman's Antiques* and *Collectibles Price Guide and Warman's Glass*.

Cast iron, 7-1/2" l, skeleton hand, realistic 125.00
Glass, rect, advertising
   Coutes Clipper Mfg., Worcester, Mass., illus of pair of clippers, 2-1/2" w, 4" l 75.00
   Donnelly Machine Co., Brockton, Mass., scalloped edge, illus of vintage factory, 3" w, 4-1/2" l 50.00
   Heywood Shoes, shoe illus, titled "Heywood is in it," 2-1/2" w, 4" l 40.00
   J. R. Leeson & Co., Boston, Linen Thread importers, spinning wheel image 80.00
   Oscar R. Boehne & Co., gold scale, 2-1/2" w, 4" l........ 60.00

Glass, modern
   Ayotte, Rick, yellow finch, perched on branch, faceted, sgd, and dated, 1979.. 750.00
   Baccarat, Peace on Earth, sgd 130.00
   Banford, Bob, white flower, yellow flower, brown dots, green leaves, sgd 225.00
   Caithness, Chai, gold symbol, translucent blue background, faceted front window, 3-1/4" dia.............................. 210.00
   Gunderson, rose, white petals, green leaves............... 425.00
   Kaziun, Charles, Millefiori spider lily, green ground, pedestal 365.00
   Lundberg Studios, green spider, light and dark blue web, sgd and dated 1979, 2-3/4" d 250.00
   Murano, cluster of green and white daisies, pink and white cushion, signature cane "Fili Tosi," 2-3/4" dia........... 300.00

Slimy critter

Believe it or not, salamander paperweights—so called because they contain a glass replica of the amphibian—are among the most desirable of all 19th-century French paperweights. The proof is in the price.

In 1998, Sotheby's sold one for $156,500. In 2000, Lawrence Selman of Santa Cruz, Calif., set the bar up another notch when he sold a salamander paperweight for $169,400.

Think you might have one? Start digging through the desk drawers quickly. Only 12 examples are known.

Perthshire, center flower, five silhouette canes, white lace ground, 2-1/4" dia, MIB 135.00
Sturgeon, Sam, fish, controlled bubbles, sgd, dated Aug 1989 ....395.00
Wallace, Matt, anemones and coral, 3-3/4" dia 225.00

Souvenir
Acrylic, torch inside made from materials from Statue of Liberty, 1886-1996, round, 4-1/2" dia 20.00
Glass, Gillinder, Memorial Hall, Philadelphia Exposition, 1876, 5-1/4" l, scratches 350.00

❖ Parrish, Maxfield

Like many illustrators, Maxfield Parrish did commercial work. Today, some of those commercial illustrations are highly sought after by collectors.

Bookplate print, 8" x 10"
The Fisherman and the Genie 65.00
The Sugar Plum Tree 65.00
The Little Peach.................65.00
The City of Brass 65.00
Wynken, Blyken & Nod......65.00
With Trumpet and Drum 65.00
Calendar top, Edison Mazda Reveries, 1927, framed, 6-3/4" x 10-1/4"..............................175.00

Magazine cover
American Heritage, December 1970 ....25.00
Scribner Magazine, 1902...55.00
Matchbook, Old King Cole, St. Regis Hotel, New York, wooden matches............................25.00
Playing cards, The Waterfall, advertise Edison Mazda Lamps, boxed single deck 127.50

❖ Patriotic Collectibles

Three cheers for the red, white, and blue! And three cheers for the collectors who thrive on this type of material. There are lots of great examples just waiting to be found at America's flea markets.

Flag plate, "Compliments of Holstein Mercantile Co., Holstein, Nebr.," 9-1/2" diameter, $35.

Collectors' Club: Statue of Liberty Collectors' Club, 26601 Bernwood Rd., Cleveland, OH 44122.
Bank, Uncle Sam, Puriton 32.00
Costume jewelry
Flag pin, Coro, sterling silver, enamel and rhinestones, 1-1/2" h..........................88.00
"USA" pin, red, clear and blue rhinestones, 1-3/8" h 15.00
Envelope
Civil War, 2-3/4" x 5-1/8" 22.00
"Our Country" across globe, Civil War, unused 6.00
Fan, "America First," die-cut shield, red, white and blue cardboard, sailor raising deck flag, warships in background, biplanes overhead, 7" x 9" 45.00
Magic lantern slide, American flag, 3-1/4" x 4" 48.00
Medal, Victory Liberty Loan, U.S. Treasury Dept....................15.00
Needle book, World's Best, Statue of Liberty, airplane, ship, world, 6 needle packets 20.00
Postcard
Betsy Ross sewing flag........5.00
Santa Claus toasting the holidays with Uncle Sam, "Christmas Greetings," early 1900s 40.00
Sash, Mexican War era, patriotic seal, 39" l..........................625.00
Sheet music, War Songs, 1898, John Church Co., flag cover 48.00
Statue of Liberty, Avon, 7-1/2" h 10.00

Tumbler, red, white and blue bands, gold eagle, 1970s, 4" h 2.00

❖ Pattern Glass

Pattern glass can best be defined as tableware made in a wide range of patterns and colors. Early manufacturers developed machinery to create glassware and as the years went by, the patterns became more intricate. Most pattern glass is clear, but some pieces came in translucent colors. The mass-produced glassware came in hundreds of patterns and a variety of shapes and sizes.

References: There are many older reference books which are good sources for identifing a pattern name, maker, and pieces available. There are also several good resources giving solid information about the reproductions found in today's marketplace.

Collectors' Clubs: Early American Pattern Glass Society, P.O. Box 266, Colesburg, IA 52035; Moon and Star Collectors Club, 4207 Fox Creek, Mount Vernon, IL 62864; The National American Glass Club, Ltd., P.O. Box 9489, Silver Spring, MD 20907.

Reproduction Alert.
For additional listings, see *Warman's Antiques and Collectibles Price Guide, Warman's Pattern Glass,* and *Warman's Glass.*
Items listed are clear unless otherwise noted.
Banana boat, Heart with Thumbprint, ruby stained 155.00
Basket, Dakota, clear, etched dec 205.00
Berry bowl, Inverted Strawberry, 9-1/2" d, scalloped 65.00
Biscuit jar, cov, Minnesota 55.00
Bowl
Delaware, green, oval 65.00
Holly, 9" l, oval, under rim flake 65.00
Bread plate, Horseshoe, double horseshoe handles 70.00
Butter, cov
Crystal Wedding................65.00
Finecut & Panel, vaseline 115.00
Loop and Dart 45.00

Record prices

Early American pattern glass seems to be on the rise and gaining favor with new collectors. It's available in thousands of patterns and affordable enough for collectors to use. However, record-setting prices for pattern glass are always achieved during the annual fall auction conducted by Green Valley Auctions, Inc., Mount Crawford, Va.

Beaver Band goblet $850
Bellflower small cake stand..$5,600
Bellflower rare cobalt blue spoon holder $7,000
Dragon goblet...$1,600
Early Thumbprint covered compote, ball form, 8" dia, 14-1/2" h ..$4,200
Heart with Thumbprint goblet with ruby stained hearts $2,500
Swan Mid Rushes goblet $650
Ostrich, Stork, and Heron goblet (previously unlisted in reference books)..$1,500
Frosted Lion milk pitcher, non-flint, applied handle $5,100
Three Face hollow-stem champagne $4,600
Westward Ho, cov compote, 16" h, 9" dia $1,350

Cake stand
    Heart with Thumbprint 165.00
    Holly................................... 175.00
    Loop and Dart..................... 40.00
    Thousand Eye, apple green
        ....60.00
Castor set, King's Crown, 4 bottles,
    glass stand 175.00
Celery tray, Illinois 40.00
Celery vase, Honeycomb 45.00
Champagne, Lily of the Valley
    .... 165.00
Cheese dish, cov, Illinois 75.00
Compote, cov, high standard,
    Dakota, 5" dia.................... 50.00
Compote, cov, low standard, Loop
    and Dart, 8" dia 65.00
Compote, open, Thousand Eye,
    amber, 6" dia 45.00
Creamer
    Flowerpot........................... 32.00
    King's Crown...................... 50.00
    Paneled Diamond Point, applied
        handle 35.00
    Thousand Eye, blue........... 45.00
Cruet
    Dakota, clear, etched dec
        .... 125.00
    Paneled Thistle 25.00
Eggcup
    Loop and Dart.................... 25.00
    Thousand Eye, vaseline .. 100.00
    Viking 40.00
Finger Bowl, Heart with Thumbprint
    ....45.00
Goblet
    Chain and Shield 28.00
    Curtain Tie Back 20.00

Frazier.................................20.00
Greek Key 20.00
Heart with Thumbprint........65.00
King's Crown.......................35.00
Late Paneled Grape...........20.00
Loop and Dart 25.00
Minnesota 35.00
New Hampshire 20.00
Thousand Eye, amber........50.00
Wheat & Barley, amber......38.00
Hair receiver, Heart with Thumbprint,
    emerald green 100.00
Honey dish, Bleeding Heart.....25.00
Marmalade jar, cov, Illinois 145.00
Nappy, handle
    Crystal Wedding.................25.00
    Thousand Eye, blue...........45.00
Pitcher
    Crystal Wedding, square..120.00
    Feathered Points.................85.00
    Flowerpot 65.00
    Peacock Feather...............85.00
Plate
    Loop and Dart, 6" dia 35.00
    Wheat & Barley, 7" dia 35.00
Punch cup, King's Crown, ruby
    stained 30.00
Relish
    Horseshoe..........................30.00
    Loop and Dart 20.00
    Minnesota 20.00
    Wisconsin............................25.00
Salt, master, Loop and Dart.....20.00
Salt shaker
    Minnesota 25.00
    Three Face..........................75.00
    Willow Oak, blue 40.00
Sauce, Holly, 4" dia.................25.00

Sugar, cov
    Flowerpot 48.00
    Hidalgo.............................. 65.00
Syrup Pitcher, Crystal Wedding
    .... 150.00
Toothpick holder, US Sheraton
    .... 35.00
Tumbler
    Broken Column, ruby stained
        .... 55.00
    Eyewinker........................... 45.00
    Maine 30.00
    Red Block.......................... 40.00
    US Coin........................... 135.00
    Wisconsin.......................... 45.00
Water set, pitcher and 6 tumblers
    Anthemion, green............ 345.00
    Beaumont's Floral, emerald
        green, gold trim 285.00
    Peerless, flint.................. 355.00
    Red Block, ruby stained .. 330.00
Wine
    Bridal Rosette................... 15.00
    Finecut 24.00
    Iowa.................................. 30.00
    Maine 50.00
    Manhattan 15.00

❖ Peachblow Glass

Taking its name from its peach color and shading, this glassware has differences in color and texture from one major glassmaker to another.

Reference: Sean and Johanna Billings, *Peachblow, Collector's Identification & Price Guide*, Krause Publications, 2000.

Reproduction Alert.

For additional listings, see *Warman's Antiques and Collectibles Price Guide* and *Warman's Glass*.

Bowl, peachblow ext., ivory int., applied crystal feet, flower prunt over pontil mark, English, 8-1/2" dia 425.00

Bride's bowl, wavy ruffled rim, cased int., New Martinsville, 11" dia 125.00

Candlesticks, pr, Gundersen 275.00

Celery vase, 5" sq, glossy, Wheeling 300.00

Creamer and sugar, satin finish, ribbed, applied white handles, New England 500.00

Dish, wavy ruffled rim, New Martinsville, 5" dia 100.00
Finger bowl, cased, Webb, 4-1/2" dia 195.00
Lamp shade, light pink shading to dark pink, gold trim, fluted, undulating rim, small chips 295.00
Rose bowl, Wheeling, 4" dia 225.00
Toothpick holder, bulbous, deep color, glossy finish, Wheeling, two cracks in outer casing 70.00
Tumbler, Hobbs, Brockunier, 3-1/2" h, 2-3/4" dia 450.00
Vase, lily form, shading near white to dark pink, New England, 7-3/4" h 975.00
Whimsey, figural pear, attributed to New England, roughness at stem, 5" l 125.00

❖ Peanuts

The comic strip Peanuts has been bringing smiles to faces since 1950. Snoopy, Charlie Brown, Lucy and the rest of the gang are all creations of the late Charles M. Schulz. Peanuts collectibles are licensed by Charles M. Schulz Creative Associates and United Features Syndicate.

Collectors' Club: Peanuts Collector Club, 539 Sudden Valley, Bellingham, WA 98226.
Book, *Here's To You, Charlie Brown*, Fawcett Crest Books, 1962, 21st printing 4.50
Cookie cutters, Hallmark, set of 4, Lucy holding package, Snoopy in a Santa hat, Linus holding lights and Charlie Brown holding ornament 100.00

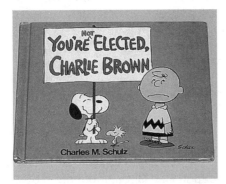

You're Not Elected, Charlie Brown, **World Publishing, 1973, 1st printing, $15.**

Commemorative coin, The Great Pumpkin, 30th anniversary, silver 79.00
Dishes, tin, tray, 3 plates, 3 saucers 105.00
Figurine, porcelain, Life with Peanuts collection
   Schroeder, 4-3/4" h 20.00
   Snoopy, 4-1/2" h 20.00
Lunch box, Have Lunch with Snoopy, domed, 1968, King Seeley Thermos 50.00
Musical figurine, ceramic, Charlie Brown, Lucy, Linus, Sally, Snoopy and Woodstock at Christmas Tree, Schmid, 1984, plays Joy to the World, 8" h 200.00
Pinback button, Charlie Brown, celluloid, 1-1/4" dia 20.00
Soap dish, Avon, Snoopy, 7" l 10.00
Telephone, Snoopy And Woodstock, 13-1/2" h 82.50
Thermos, Charlie Brown, 1969, 3-1/2" h 5.00
View-Master reel, It's a Bird, Charlie Brown, GAF, 1973, 3 reels, top flap detached 25.00

❖ Pedal Cars

Pedal cars date to about 1915, when they were made to closely resemble automobiles of the day. War-time material supplies curbed growth for a few years, but these popular toys gained popularity again, just in time for special cars issued to tie into television programs of the 1950s and 1960s.

Periodical: *The Wheel Goods Trader*, P.O. Box 435, Fraser, MI 48026.

Collectors' Club: National Pedal Vehicle Association, 1720 Rupert NE, Grand Rapids, MI 49505.
Blue Streak, blue and white, BMC 450.00
Coca-Cola Truck, red and white, AMF 500.00
Comet, Murray 775.00
Earthmover, Murray 1,100.00
Fire truck, orig ladders 325.00
Junior Trac, AMF 250.00
Mustang, AMF 800.00

1998 Hallmark ornament, '55 Murray Pedal Tractor & Trailer, original box, $25.

Safari wagon, AMF 50.00
Studebaker, Midwest Industries, restored 950.00
Tin Lizzy, green, Garton 500.00

❖ Pencil Clips and Paper Clips

Companies developed a clever way to help folks remember their names, advertising on both paper clips and pencil clips. Most advertising was on a metal or celluloid disk.
Diamond Crystal Salt, celluloid 18.00
Morton's Salt, It Pours 10.00
The Page Milk Co., celluloid ... 48.00
Red Goose Shoes 12.00
Reddy Kilowatt Power, V, patriotic, 1942 .... 10.00
7-Up 10.00

❖ Pencil Sharpeners

Figural pencil sharpeners are starting to catch on with collectors. Look for examples in good condition.
Cannon on wheels, bronzed metal, 3" l 6.50
Coffee grinder, double-wheel, metal, painted red, Hong Kong, 3" h 7.50
Covered wagon, metal and plastic, Hong Kong, 3-1/4" l 4.50

Space Shuttle figural pencil sharpener, metal and plastic, 4-7/8" high, $5.

Dallas Cowboy helmet, plastic, 1-1/2" h.............. 10.00
Farm lantern, metal, blue paint, clear plastic globe, Hong Kong, 2-3/4" h.............. 6.00
Franklin Roosevelt, 32nd President, 1882-1945, bronzed metal bust, 3" h.............. 10.00
Hep Cats, decal, Bakelite, Walt Disney, crack, 1-1/4" dia......... 45.00
John Kennedy, 35th President, 1917-1963, bronzed metal bust, 3" h.............. 12.50
Popeye, figural, Bakelite, 1929, 1-3/4" h.............. 75.00
Porky Pig, waving, orig box....... 3.25
Ronald McDonald, August 1984 Happy Meals, 2" h.............. 4.00
Sewing machine, figural, plastic, Germany, 1970s, 2" sq...... 19.00
Stagecoach, bronzed metal, 2-1/2" l 6.50
Submarine, bronzed metal, 5" l 7.50
Tweety Bird, orig bag................. 3.25
Volkswagen Beetle, bronzed metal, 3-1/2" l 7.50

❖ Pennants

Rah Rah! Pennants used to be the flag of choice for sporting events and parades. Today they have become colorful collectibles.
1933 Chicago World's Fair, 25" l 42.00
1957 Eisenhower-Nixon Inauguration, Washington, D.C., 25-1/2" l 60.00
1996 Olympic baseball, Atlanta 1996 .... 6.00
Atlantic City, scenes Steel Pier, Convention Hall and bathing, 27" l 45.00
Cincinnati Redlegs, 1 tassel missing, 29" l 55.00
Cleveland Indians American League Champions 140.00
Democratic National Convention, Atlantic City, 1964, black and white picture of Lyndon Johnson in shield, 29" l 30.00
Empire State Building, "The tallest man-made structure in the world, 102 floors, 1,472 ft. high, Souvenir of Empire State Building, New York City," 26-1/4" l....15.00
Gettysburg, Pa., dated 1938, shows Virginia State Monument, 17-1/2" l 18.00
Howe Caverns, dated 1958, shows pagoda, 17-1/4" l 18.00
Lumbermen's Memorial, image of lumberjacks, 1940s, 26" l ..27.00
Meramec Caverns, Jesse James' hideout, Stanton, Mo., 26"l 29.00
Mt. Washington, White Mountains, N.H., dated 1957, shows World's First Cog Railway, 17-1/4" l 18.00
Navy, yellow and blue, 5-1/2" l 15.00
New Jersey Turnpike, 25" l......22.00
Newark Airport, airplane in clouds, 25" l 25.00

Felt pennant, French Lick, Ind., red and white, $12.50.

N.R.I. (National Radio Institute), Pioneer Home Study Radio School, Washington, D.C., 1920s/30s, 28" l.............. 29.00
Pennsylvania Turnpike, 25" l .. 25.00
Philadelphia Eagles, 1940s/50s, 28" l.............. 35.00
South Carolina, black boy sitting on bales of cotton, 27" l 45.00
Souvenir of Gettysburg Battlefield, panorama of the Gettysburg Battlefield and monuments, 1930s/40s, 28" l 26.00
Swarthmore College, c1960, moth holes 3.75

❖ Pennsbury Pottery

Taking its name from the close proximity of William Penn's estate, Pennsbury, in Bucks County, Pennsylvania, this small pottery lasted from 1950 until 1970. Several of the owners had formerly worked for Stangl, which helps explain some of the similarities of design and forms between Pennsbury and Stangl.
Ashtray
    Doylestown Trust.............. 30.00
    What Giffs, Amish pattern . 20.00
Bird
    Bird on Nest 300.00
    Goldfinch, #102 .... 200.00
Creamer, Rooster, 4-1/2" h 45.00
Cup and saucer, Black Rooster pattern.............. 20.00
Dinner plate, Hex pattern........ 17.50
Eggcup, Red Rooster pattern . 25.00
Milk pitcher
    Amish Family, 6-1/2" h 175.00
    Yellow Rooster, 7-1/2" h.. 150.00
Mug, Schiaraflia Filadelfia, owl and seal 30.00
Pie plate, Rooster, 8" dia 65.00
Plaque
    Amish Family, 8" dia.......... 55.00
    B & O Railroad, 5-3/4" x 7-3/4" 65.00
Teapot, Red Rooster pattern... 65.00
Tea tile, 6" dia, skunk "Why Be Disagreeable".............. 60.00
Tray, Yellow Rooster, 8" l 50.00

Advertising pencil, "Colonial is good Bread," unused, 7-1/2" long, $1.

❖ Pens and Pencils

Before computers, folks actually wrote letters with pens and pencils! Today some collectors find interesting examples at flea markets.

References: Paul Evans, *Fountain Pens Past & Present*, Collector Books, 1999; Stuart Schneider and George Fischler, *The Illustrated Guide to Antique Writing Instruments*, 3rd ed, Schiffer Publishing, 2000.

Periodical: *Pen World Magazine*, P.O. Box 6007, Kingwood, TX 77325.

Collectors' Clubs: American Pencil Collectors Society, RR North, Wilmore, KS 67155; Pen Collectors of America, P.O. Box 821449, Houston, TX 77282.

Pen

    Cartier, 14k, large, 2 dents 260.00

    Conklin, Endura Model, desk set, 2 pens, side-lever fill, black marble base 135.00

    Dunn, black, red barrel, gold filled trim, c1920............45.00

    Moore, lady's, black, 3 narrow gold bands on cap, lever fill 75.00

    Sheaffer Lifetime Stylist, gold filled metal, professionally engraved clip, 1960s.....35.00

    Wahl, lady's, ribbon pen, double narrow band on cap, 14k #2 nib, lever fill, 1928.........80.00

    Waterman's, black, gold trim, clip, unused...................50.00

Pencil

    Brown-McLaren MFG. Co., Hamburg, Mich., Detroit Office-7340 Puritan Ave., Phone UNiversity 3-3520, Redipoint, USA, celluloid................10.00

    Conklin, rolled gold, initials engraved on clip............85.00

    Electric Café, Detroit, Michigan, clip mkd "Wearever," some paint missing 9.00

    Mr. Peanut, engraved on both sides of clip, some paint missing from top hat 12.00

⬡ Pepsi-Cola

"Pepsi-Cola Hits the Spot!" That line was part of a popular 1950s jingle. Pepsi collectibles today are hot, just as the beverage itself has remained popular since it was first introduced in the late 1890s.

Reference: Phil Dillman and Larry Woestman, *Pepsi Memorabilia...Then and Now*, Schiffer Publishing, 2000.

Collectors' Club: Pepsi-Cola Collectors Club, P.O. Box 1275, Covina, CA 91722.

Limited-edition Pepsi-Cola reproduction bottle, 12-ounce, $4.

"Bigger Better" Pepsi thermometer, tin, 16" high, $250.

Blotter, "Pepsi and Pete, The Pepsi-Cola Cops," Pepsi bottle with 2 cartoon characters, 1930s, cond. 8.75-9............................... 60.50

Bottle cap, green, c1910......... 50.00

Bottle opener, metal, bottle shape, "America's Biggest Nickel's Worth," rust, 2 3/4" l.......... 44.00

Carrier, 6-pack, wooden, "Buy Pepsi-Cola," red/blue, 1930s-1940s, cond. 8-8.5............ 93.50

Clock, bottlecap shape, plastic, "Drink Pepsi-Cola, Ice Cold," white background, 11" dia 165.00

Clock, lightup, glass face, metal case, "Say Pepsi Please" 16" sq 209.00

Cooler, metal, "Drink Pepsi-Cola" in white, blue background, 18-1/2" h, 18" w, 13" d.................. 88.00

Glass, clear with syrup line, 1930s-40s, two-color decor, 10 oz 13.00

Menu sign, "Have a Pepsi" beside bottlecap, "Pepsi-Cola, the Light Refreshment" at bottom, black chalkboard area, yellow/white striped background, 1950s, 30" h, 20" w 71.50

Salt and pepper shakers, plastic, 1-pc, "The Light Refreshment" under bottlecap logo, 1950s, orig box 66.00

Sign

Celluloid, button-type, "Ice Cold Pepsi-Cola Sold Here," red name, white text, blue/white/blue background, 1940s, 9" dia 330.00

Tin, "Say 'Pepsi, Please,'" on bottle with white oval label beside angled bottlecap, yellow background, 1960s, 48" h, 18" w 176.00

Tin, die-cut, bottlecap shape, "Pepsi-Cola," crazing, 14" dia 140.00

Thermometer, tin

"Have a Pepsi" at top, bottle cap/"The Light Refreshment" at bottom, yellow with V-shaped white area, 1950s, 27" h............................ 231.00

"Pepsi-Cola" bottlecap logo at top, "More Bounce To The Ounce" at bottle with red/white/blue ribbon, white background, rounded top and bottom, 27" h, 8" w 275.00

❖ Perfume Bottles

Decorative and figural perfume bottles have remained a popular area of collecting for generations. Perfume bottles can be found in a variety of sizes, shapes, and colors, as well as price ranges. Look for examples with matching stoppers and original labels.

Collectors' Clubs: International Perfume Bottle Association, P.O. Box 529, Vienna, VA 22180; Miniature Perfume Bottle Collectors, 28227 Paseo El Siena, Laguna Niguel, CA 92677.

Atomizer

Cambridge, stippled gold, opaque jade, orig silk lined box, 6-1/4" h................ 150.00

White opalescent swirl glass perfume bottle, plastic lid, 3-3/4" high, $8.

Devilbiss, clear, threaded dec, 4" h, #127 .... 45.00

Boxed set

Evening In Paris............... 135.00

Hudnut, Sweet Orchid, 3" h, 1920s 45.00

L'Heure Bleue, fluted and scrolled design, Guerlain fitted box 90.00

Cut glass, Button and Star pattern, rayed base, faceted stopper, 6-1/2" h 125.00

Figural

Decanter shape, glass, opaque blue ground, enameled white leaves and grape garlands, dragonfly in center, three gold applied ball feet, clear ground stopper 125.00

Genie slippers, glass, cork stoppers, paper labels, "Rose Oil and Cologne by H. P. & C. R. Taylor, Phila," some damage to orig labels, pr........... 125.00

Purse shape, sterling silver, gilded int., mkd "John Turner, Birmingham," 1792 ...... 250.00

German, green glass body, colored enamel coat of arms dec, matching green stopper, 2" h 65.00

Lay-down type, satin glass, Diamond Quilted pattern, shading yellow to white, 6" l 415.00

Mary Gregory, cranberry ground, white enameled girl dec, colorless ball stopper.............. 175.00

❖ PEZ

PEZ was invented in Austria as a cigarette substitute. Eduard Haas hoped his mints would catch on when he named it PEZ, an abbreviation for pfefferminz (the German word for peppermint). By 1952, a tabletop model arrived in America, but it was not until the container was redesigned for children that the candy caught on. Many popular characters get periodic design updates, giving collectors variations to search for.

Reference: Shawn Peterson, *Collector's Guide To PEZ, Identification & Price Guide*, Krause Publications, 2000.

Periodicals: *PEZ Collector's News*, P.O. Box 124, Sea Cliff, NY 11579; *Toy Shop*, 700 E State St, Iola, WI 54990.

Aardvark, orange stem, loose. 10.00

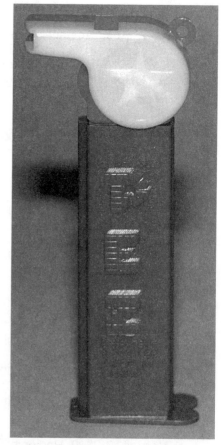

Red, white and blue PEZ whistle-shaped dispenser, with feet, $3.

Alpine Boy, purple hat and shoes, loose 6.50
Ant, green stem, loose 8.00
Aral, Gas, blue hat and shoes, loose 6.00
Barney Bear, 1970s 12.00
Boy with hat, PEZ Pal, 1960.... 12.00
Charlie Brown, frown, MIP 8.00
Clown, Merry Melody Maker, MOC 5.00
Donald Duck, no feet, MIP 27.50
Fozzie Bear, 1991 .... 3.00
Icee 5.50
Inspector Clouseu, yellow stem, loose 6.00
Kermit, mkd "Made in Hungry" .. 7.50
Lamb, mkd "Made in Yuglosavia" 6.00
Mariner, blue hat, black shoes, loose 7.50
Muselix, orange stem, loose.... 12.00
Parrot, Merry Melody Maker, MOC 8.50
Penguin, Melody Maker, MOC 12.00
Pilot, white hat, black shoes, loose 6.00
Pink Panther, pink stem, loose 12.00
Rabbit 7.50
Santa, mkd "Made in Yuglosavia" 8.00
Shell Gas, yellow hat, red shoes, loose 7.00
Smurf
    Boy, blue stem 3.00
    Papa, red stem 3.00
    Smurfette, yellow stem 14.00
Tom 6.00
Tuffy 7.50
Whistle, 1960s 2.50

❖ Pfaltzgraff

Here's a name most flea marketers associate with dinnerware. However, Pfaltzgraff originally started as a stoneware company. By the early 1950s, company officials realized their future was in dinnerware production, and production successfully shifted toward that goal.

Butter dish, Village 10.50
Canister, coffee, Yorktowne 12.00
Casserole, Aura, 12" x 8" 14.00
Cookie jar, Kroger 50.00
Child's mug, bear faces 10.00
Cup and saucer
    Christmas Heirloom 7.50
    Yorktowne 5.00

Custard, Village, set of 4 .... 12.00
Dinner plate
    Gazebo 10.00
    Gourmet 12.00
    Windsong 12.00
    Yorktowne 10.00
Goblet, Village, set of 4 .... 14.00
Honey pot, cov, Village, 5-1/4" h 21.00
Platter, Folk Art, oval, 14" l 10.00
Salad bowl, Village, set of 8 .... 10.50

❖ Phoenix Bird China

Phoenix Bird China ia a blue-and-white dinnerware made from the late 19th century through the 1940s. The china was imported to America, where it was retailed by several firms, including Woolworth's, and wholesalers such as Butler Brothers.

Collectors' Club: Phoenix Bird Collectors of America, 685 S. Washington, Constantine, MI 49042.

For additional listings and a detailed history, see Warman's Americana & Collectibles.

Cup and saucer 10.00
Eggcup, double cup 15.00
Plate
    Dinner, 9-3/4" dia 48.00
    Luncheon, 8-1/2" dia 17.50
Platter, oval, 14" l 95.00
Soup dish, 7-1/4" dia 35.00
Teapot, squatty 42.00

❖ Phoenix Glass

Phoenix Glass Company, founded in Beaver, Pennsylvania, in 1880 initially made commercial products but later shifted to art glass. The company's molded and sculptured wares are what most dealers think of as "Phoenix" glass.

Collectors' Club: Phoenix & Consolidated Glass Collectors Club, P.O. Box 3847, Edmond, OK 73083.

Ashtray, Phlox, large, white, frosted 90.00
Basket, pink ground, relief molded dogwood dec, 4-1/2" h 65.00
Bowl, Swallows, purple wash 150.00
Candlesticks, pr, blue ground, bubbles and swirls, 3-1/4" h 65.00

Phoenix Glass lamp, white ground, red berries with green leaves, bronze-plated base, 22" high, $145.

Charger, blue ground, relief molded white daffodils 100.00
Ginger jar, cov, frosted ground, bird finial 80.00
Planter, white ground, relief molded green lion, 8-1/2" l 95.00
Vase
    Bellflower, burgundy pearlized ground 95.00
    Philodendron, Wedgwood blue, white ground 160.00
    Wild Geese, pearlized white birds, light green ground 195.00

Eagle cabinet card, Jones Studio, Madison, Wis., 6-1/2" x 4-1/4", $90.

❖ Photographs

Photograph collecting certainly is one way to add "instant ancestors" to those picture frames you'd like to hang. Many photographs are found at flea markets. The market for vintage photos has received increased attention, in part because they are easy to sell over the Internet. Look for photographs that have interesting composition or those that give some perspective to the way an area once looked.

Reference: O. Henry Mace, *Collector's Guide to Early Photographs*, Krause Publications, 1999.

Collectors' Clubs: American Photographic Historical Society, 1150 Avenue of the Americas, New York, NY 10036; National Stereoscopic Association, P.O. Box 14801, Columbus, OH 43214; The Photographic Historical Society, P.O. Box 39563, Rochester, NY 14604.

Albumen print
Baseball game, mounted, 5-1/4" sq 125.00
Cowboy on horse with dog doing a trick on back of the horse, 1920-1930s, mounted, 5" x 7" 48.00

Man with horse-drawn moving van in front of building with sign for "Pacific Transfer Company," dated 1913, identified in pencil as Portland, Ore., mounted, 5" x 7" ...60.00
Navy sailors, one in a Red Cross cart in front of tents, cart mkd "USN Medical Dept. N.C.," removed from photo album, 4-1/4" x 2-3/4" 3.00
Cabinet card, 6-1/4" x 4-1/2"
3 young brothers, smallest sitting in Express wagon, Savannah, Ill., imprint 37.50
Identical twins, Willow City, N.D., imprint 30.00
Memorial floral arrangements, Massillon, Ohio, imprint, mounted on cream stock 6.00
Main Street, Dorchester, Wisc., 1890s, mounted on cream stock 15.00
Carte de viste (CDV)
Boy on toy rocking horse, Louisiana, Mo., imprint .. 45.00
Girl with bisque doll 14.00

❖ Pickard China

Wilder Pickard founded this company in 1897 in Chicago. China blanks imported from Europe were hand-painted by company artists. Signed pieces are especially sought.

Collectors' Club: Pickard Collectors Club, 300 E Grove St., Bloomington, IL 67101.
For additional listings, see *Warman's Antiques and Collectibles Price Guide* and *Warman's American Pottery & Porcelain*.
Bon bon, basket style, four sided, gold 45.00
Cake plate, open gold handles, Desert Garden pattern 185.00
Hatpin holder, all over gold design of etched flowers, c1925 .... 50.00
Mug, poinsettia flowers, gold banding and trim, sgd "N. R. Clifford" 265.00
Perfume bottle, yellow primroses, shaded ground, artist sgd and dated 1905, gold stopper 200.00
Plate
Currants, 7-1/2" dia 75.00
Peaches, gilded and molded border, sgd "S. Heap," 9-1/8" dia 110.00

Pickard China mug, poinsettias, by N.R. Clifford, gold banding and rim, 6-7/8" high, $275.

Platter, roses, gilded border, sgd "Seidel," 12" dia 275.00
Tea set, teapot, creamer, sugar, and cake plate, pink apple blossoms and green leaves, gilded trim, artist sgd 550.00
Vase, three large dark poppies, gold, rust, and brown dec, sgd "Gasper," 9-1/2" h 365.00

❖ Picture Frames

Here's a category few people admit to collecting, but most of us have many of these in our homes. Flea markets are a good place to find interesting frames. Make sure you take measurements if you're looking for a certain size frame and bring that tape measure along to the flea market.
Celluloid, 8" x 6-1/4" 70.00
Curly maple, good curl, 16-1/4" x 16" 385.00
Grain-decor, pine, 17" x 14" .. 385.00
Horseshoe-form, white paint, gilt liner, 17-1/4" x 13-1/2" 95.00
Oak
Cross-corner, leaves in corners, 17" x 15" 45.00

Gesso border in gold, 30" x
25-1/2" 132.50
Shells, 8-1/2" x 6-1/2" 65.00
Tramp art
Cross-corner, 7" x 6" 115.00
Divided for 2 photos, gold paint,
minor damage, 13-1/2" h,
26-1/2" w 250.00
Walnut
Cross-corner, gilt liner, 8" x 7"
.... 125.00
Oval, deep, 13-1/2" x 11-1/2"
.... 40.00
Shadowbox type, gilt liner,
14-1/2" h, 12" w 75.00

❖ Pie Birds

These little birds with their beaks wide open are a bit unusual looking when found out of their natural habitat. Designed to act as a vent for a pie with a top crust, they work well, but many collectors won't think of using them for baking. New examples abound.

Reproducton Alert.
Baby Chick, English 85.00
Bird, Shawnee, 5-1/2" h 85.00
Bluebird 75.00
Eagle, Boyd 45.00
Elephant, mkd "Nutbrown Pie Funnel, Made in England," trunk
raised 185.00
First Day of Spring, baby chick in
egg 40.00
Lady, blue dress, pink apron, holding
cherry pie, flowers at base, 4" h
.... 25.00
Mama bear, blue dress, English
.... 95.00
Mammy, black 245.00
Pirate, English 85.00
Rooster
Art Deco, 5-1/4" h 175.00
Cleminson, 4-1/2" h 95.00

❖ Pierce, Howard

Howard Pierce was a California potter who designed and created interesting figurines, dinnerware, and some accessories.
Dealer sign 75.00
Dish, brown and white, 1950s, 13" l
.... 24.00

Figure
Bulldog, Marine Corps, U.S.M.C.
on base, 5" h 200.00
Cat trio, cream and brown matte
finish, unmarked.........200.00
Giraffe trio, brown matte finish,
largest stamped...........200.00
Mouse 27.50
Owls, pr...........................48.00
Penguin, 7" h 85.00
Raccoon...........................75.00
Robin................................46.00
Sparrows, trio....................55.00
St. Francis of Assisi, holding
bird, 12" h 195.00
Vase, Wedgwood jasper style, light
green ground, white cameo of
Oriental boy on one, girl on
other, 5-3/4" h, pr..............48.00

❖ Pig Collectibles

"This little piggie went to market..." Actually lots of piggies are heading to flea markets so that collectors can give them a new home. Some collectors specialize in famous characters, like Babe or Porky Pig, while others prefer figurines.

Collectors' Club: The Happy Pig Collectors Club, P.O. Box 17, Oneida, IL 61467.
Advertising trade card, "Try Wright's
Little Liver Pills," shows 5 pigs
....12.00
Ashtray, green ceramic base, figural
pink pig 5.00

"My System" bisque pig figurine, Germany, 2-3/4" high, 3-3/4" wide, $40.

Bank, pig shape, ceramic, pink and
white, multicolored flowers, curly
tail, 1950s 30.00
Cutting board, pig shape, homemade, well used.................. 2.00
Figure
Lobster pulling leg of red pig
......................................115.00
Pig riding in canoe, c1930
.... 65.00
Playing cards, "Hearts are
Trumps," 3-1/2" h.........115.00
Purse, black bisque pig sitting on
top of green purse, 2-1/4" h
.... 80.00
Well, gold pig, orange roof, mkd
"Souvenir of Chicago, Made
in Germany," 1930s 65.00
Match holder, pair of pink bisque
pigs, "Scratch My Back" and "Me
Too".................................. 120.00
Pinback button, Swift's, multicolored
carton of smiling pig wearing
rope noose while seated in frying
pan, c1901 .... 45.00
Toothpick holder, pink pig holding
camera............................... 95.00

❖ Pigeon Forge Pottery

Among the array of regional pottery commonly found at flea markets is Pigeon Forge Pottery, made in the Tennessee town of the same name. Capitalizing on the popularity of the tourist trade, many pieces were sold as souvenirs. The market is still being established for Pigeon Forge Pottery. Look for artist-signed pieces and unusual glazes.
Bear, figurine, 4-1/4" h 17.50
Bowl, tan exterior, blue interior,
5-1/4" dia 20.00
Butter molds, mustard color, set of 4,
snowflake, flower, 2 swans,
impressed designs, 4"....... 15.50
Cream pitcher, Dogwood pattern,
4" h 9.00
Jug, miniature, 5" h 12.50
Mug, tan, brown owl, blue interior
.... 10.00
Racoon, D. Ferguson, 5-1/4" h
.... 44.00
Teapot, brown, squatty form,
3-1/2" h 6.00
Tile, aqua, 3 yellow flowers, D. Ferguson, 5-3/4" sq............... 114.50
Vase, blue, Dogwood pattern,
3-1/2" h 6.00

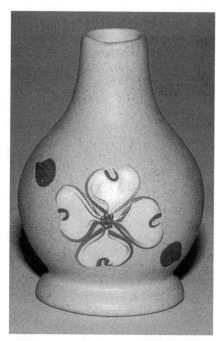

Dogwood vase, Pigeon Forge, 3-1/4" high, $4.

❖ Pinback Buttons

Here's a form of advertising that was an instant hit and is still popular. Look for interesting pinback buttons with advertising and political slogans of all types. Many early manufacturers included a paper insert that further exclaimed the virtues of the product. An insert adds value to a pin. Bright colors and good condition are also important.

Amoco, Join The American Party, American Gas, litho tin 18.00
Batman and Robin Fan Club, 1960s 10.00
Diamond C Hams, celluloid, 1-1/2" dia 95.00
Gore '88 .... 7.50
I'm a Beech-Nut, Wearer Qualified to Win 15.00
Kennedy '80, 1-3/8" dia 10.00
Lucky Strikes Again, 2-1/2" dia 25.00
Meet Me At The Bon-Ton, shows Santa Claus, 1-1/4" dia 28.00
Mickey Mouse Club, black and white, 7/8" dia 50.00

Green Hornet "Hornet Sting" pinback button, $10.

Official Mickey Mouse Store, 1-1/4" dia 18.00
Ritz Crackers 14.00
Super Hero Hornet Society, Green Hornet membership, 3-1/2" dia 25.00
White Rose Bread 10.00

❖ Pin-Up Art

Charles Dana Gibson is credited with creating the first pin-up girl with his famous Gibson Girls in the early 1900s. Other famous artists followed, creating pretty girls for calendars, magazines, advertisements, etc. It wasn't until the 1920s, when the film industry got involved, that their clothes seemed to be less important. Later pin-up artists, including Vargas, Elvgren, and Moran, helped create the modern image of pin-up art.

Periodicals: *Glamour Girls: Then and Now*, P.O. Box 34501, Washington, DC 20043; *The Illustrator Collector's News*, P.O. Box 1958, Sequim, WA 98382.

Calendar
Devorss, 1944 .... 45.00
MacPherson, 1953, Models Sketchbook, 9-1/2" x 12-1/2", spiral bound paper, wall type, 12 monthly pages, sgd full color art 75.00

Petty, Esquire, 1955, desk, 5-3/4" x 6-1/4", white cardboard eagle frame, dark red diecut opening around 12 monthly cardboard sheets 45.00
Petty, Fawcett, 1947 .... 70.00
Greeting Card
Bettie Page, artist Olivia 7.00
Bride, Varga 9.00
Cowboy, artist Olivia 6.00
Gum card, 2-1/2" x 3", Gum Inc., American Beauties, Elvgren art, full color, unsigned artwork, titled captions, 1940s 15.00
Magazine, *Esquire*, Christmas, 1943, Varga fold-out, 10" x 13", 320 pgs 45.00
Pocket knife, 3-3/4" l, silvered steel, two blade, black and white cello insert, one side with standing nude, hands held discreetly over mid-torso, wearing high heels, similar dec on other side, c1940 .... 30.00
Print
Elvgren, Two Cushion, sultry girl in red dress playing billiards, 5" x 7", matted 55.00
Rubens, Fox and Wolf Hunt, 1937, published by US Government Art Committee, headed by Eleanor Roosevelt, heavy paper, 9" x 13" 25.00
Vargas Girl, 1960s Playboy, captioned "Mr. Farnsworth,...," 8-1/4" x 11" 12.00
Stand-up card, 4-3/4" x 10" diecut cardboard, perforations for folding to form model figure standing on triangular display, full color Moran art, titled "Aiming To Please," pretty redhead archer, mini skirt, red high heels, c1950, unused 15.00

❖ Pisgah Forest

This American potter made interesting wares. They used a layered or cameo technique, giving an interesting texture to their work. Most of their wares are clearly marked and dated.

Dish, cov, blue-green, 1935, 4" h, 4-1/2" dia 135.00
Jar, cov, aqua, 4" h, 2-1/2" dia 110.00
Mug, cameo, clog dancers, Walter Stephen 115.00

Teapot, white cameo relief of pioneering scene, light blue ground, 1951, Stephen.................225.00

Vase

    Cameo, covered wagon and riders on horseback, blue ground, 1953, Walter Stephen, 5-1/2" h........302.50

    Crystalline, 1943, 6-1/2" h

    ....395.00

    Green, 11" h.....................325.00

    Green, 5" h 90.00

❖ Planters

Flea markets are great places to find planters of every type. Unfortunately, many of us have brown thumbs and are soon left with a pretty container and little foliage. However, with careful inspection, you just might find out that your favorite planter is a piece of Westmoreland glass or McCoy pottery. Additional listings for planters can be found throughout this book; look under specific companies and also Lady's Head Vases.

Bambi, mkd "Walt Disney Productions" 65.00

Butterfly on log, brown and white, glossy glaze, mkd "Shawnee USA 524"...........................12.00

Cactus and cowboy, natural colors, Morton 17.50

Cat, coral glaze, green box, McCoy, 1950 ....12.00

Shawnee chicken planter, 6-1/2" high, $30.

Fawns, standing pair, McCoy, 1957 ....35.00

Flamingos, facing pair, 10" l...150.00

Gondola, yellow, McCoy 20.00

Mallard, head down, Royal Copley 22.00

Parrot, white, orange accents..15.00

Pheasant, mkd "Napcoware," small chip 10.00

Straw hat, yellow, blue ribbon 17.50

Turkey, brown, Morton 15.00

❖ Planters Peanuts

The Planters Nut and Chocolate Co. was founded in Wilkes-Barre, Pennsylvania, in 1906. In 1916 the company held a contest to find a mascot, and Mr. Peanut came to life by 1916. He has remained a popular advertising icon.

Reference: Jan Lindenberger, *Planters Peanut Collectibles Since 1961*, Schiffer Publishing, 1995.

Collector's Club: Peanut Pals, P.O. Box 652, St. Clairsville, OH 43950.

Reproduction Alert.

For additional listings, see *Warman's Americana & Collectibles*.

Bank, plastic, set of 4, solid colors, red, cobalt, green, tan......176.00

Beach ball, 13" dia...................22.00

Box, cardboard

    "Planters Roasted Peanuts," oval red medallion shows peanut lettered "The Peanut Store," 10" h, 6-1/4" sq............143.00

    "Planters Salted Nuts, fresh, Roasted To You," shows bowl of peanuts, 1940s-1950s 11.00

Can, litho tin, Planters Pennant Brand Salted Peanuts, red pennant with Mr. Peanut, 5 lb, 8" h, 6-1/4" dia 55.00

Coloring book

    50 States, 1970s 15.00

    American Ecology, 1970s ..15.00

    Presidents of the United States, unused 20.00

Costume, Halloween, Mr. Peanut, plastic mask, plastic/cloth peanut-body, orig shipping box, 1960s, mint.......................99.00

Planter's Cocktail Peanuts tin, 1938 copyright, 3" high, 3-1/4" diameter, $10.

Fan, cardboard, "Planters Peanuts, Always Speeding Ahead," Mr. Peanut in peanut-shaped car, c1940, 5-1/4" h, 8" w.......467.50

Jar, glass, countertop

    4 Corners Peanut jar, bottom mkd "Made in U.S.A." 209.00

    6-sided jar, yellow printing on all sides, bottom mkd "Made in U.S.A." 264.00

    8-sided jar, 1 side plain for label, 7 sides embossed, chips, bottom mkd "Made in U.S.A." 60.50

    8-sided jar, embossed on all sides 121.00

    Fired-on enamel label, "Planters Peanuts 5¢," and Mr. Peanut, red and blue, embossed back, orig red tin lid, c1940, 9" h, 5" w, 7-5/8" d..................198.00

Lighter

    Bic, 1970s 15.00

    Peanut shape, "Planters" in black, unused orig box, 2-5/8" l 203.50

Mask, cardboard, unused, smiling peanut face with monocle, 7-3/4" x 8-1/4" 232.00

Mechanical pencil, 1970s 15.00

Radio, transistor, plastic, yellow Mr. Peanut design, unused, orig box/mailing carton, mint, 10" h, 5" w................................110.00

Tennis balls, Dunlop, can of 3 ....24.00

Toy, plastic, windup, Mr. Peanut figure walker, 1950s, 8-1/2" h
Tan body, black arms/legs/hat, works............................ 412.50
Green, works 440.00
Red, works....................... 550.00
Yellow, works 605.00
Whistle, figural, 1970s............... 5.00

❖ Plastic

It's hard to imagine life without plastics. Today collectors actively search for early plastics, including acrylics, Bakelite, and celluloid.

For a more detailed history and additional listings of plastics, see *Warman's Americana & Collectibles* and Bakelite and Celluloid in this edition.

Alarm clock, key wind, Black Forest, works, octagonal translucent green case 30.00
Business card holder, sea shells suspended in rect acrylic base 6.50
Dress clip, green opaque Lucite, triangular, chevron design, rhinestone trim 20.00
Mirror, hand, beveled acrylic handle and frame, U-shaped mirror, sterling silver floral ornament, c1946 .... 55.00
Napkin ring, translucent Lucite, sq shape, rounded edges, circular center, c1960, 4 pc set 12.00
Paperweight, translucent Lucite cube, suspended JFK half dollar, c1965 .... 10.00
Push puppet, Santa, holding bell, mkd "Made in Hong Kong for Kohner" 60.00
Wall shelf, translucent neon pink, 30" l, 6" d, 1970s 25.00

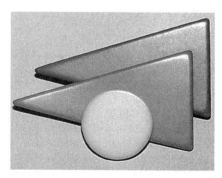

Costume jewelry plastic pin, 2-5/8" long, $5.

Picturesque Canada souvenir playing cards, published by Canadian Pacific Railroad News Service, $35.

❖ Playing Cards

What we know today as playing cards were developed in 1885 by the U.S. Playing Card Company of Cincinnati. However, Americans had been using cards for games and entertainment since the 1700s. Look for interesting designs, complete sets, and original boxes.

Collectors' Clubs: Chicago Playing Card Collectors, 1826 Mallard Lake Drive, Mariette, GA 30068; 52 Plus Joker, 204 Gorham Ave., Hamden, CT 06514; International Playing Card Society, 3570 Delaware Common, Indianapolis, IN 46220.

1965 New York World's Fair, "52 Outstanding World's Fair Exhibits, Memorable Illustrations In Color," Stancraft, 2-part plastic box, promotional sleeve, sealed 55.00
American Airlines..................... 10.00
Boys Town Souvenir Paying Cards, double deck, shows the famous "He ain't heavy, Father, he's my brother" scene, Brown & Bigelow, mint.......................... 60.00
Chessie System, double deck, sealed............................... 40.00
Frisco Railroad, sealed............ 22.00
Jeff Gordon, double deck, in collector's tin, 1999, NRFB 12.00
Quilt design, "Patchwork," double deck, Hallmark, 1 joker missing, plastic box....................... 8.00
Raggedy Ann, Hallmark, orig box 25.00

Texas souvenir deck, "Historical facts about Texas," features "Home of the President of the United States" mid-1960s, sealed 24.00
Texas souvenir deck, Lone Star design on back, c1915, used, box in poor cond. 32.00
U.S. Military Vertical Vehicles, double deck, Vertol Aircraft Corp., Morton, Pa., plastic holder 40.00
Woman with dogs, double set, Congress 28.00

❖ Playsets

Marx dominated the market for playsets in the 1950s and 1960s, producing a wide variety of the multipiece toys. Other makers and newer sets have followed, including some contemporary reproductions of popular vintage playsets. However, collectors remain most keenly interested in early examples.

Values are from *Toys & Prices*, 8th ed. 2001, Krause Publications, for playsets in excellent condition.

Adventures of Robin Hood, Marx, 1956................................. 750.00
Battleground, Montgomery Ward, 1971................................. 275.00
Cape Canaveral, Sears, 1959 .... 325.00
Daniel Boone Frontier, Marx 230.00
Fort Apache, Sears, 1972....... 90.00
Galaxy Command, Marx, 1976 .... 30.00
Johnny Apollo Moon Launch Center, Marx, 1970..................... 135.00
Lone Ranger Ranch, Marx.... 250.00
Modern Service Center, Marx, 1962 .... 210.00
Rin Tin Tin at Fort Apache, Series 500, Sears, 1956 .... 475.00
Roy Rogers Double R Bar Ranch, March, 1962.................... 300.00
Strategic Air Command, Marx 520.00
Untouchables, Marx, 1961.... 975.00
Walt Disney's Zorro, Series 1000 Marx, 1958 .... 775.00
Sears, 1972.................. 500.00

❖ Playskool

Remember wooden Lincoln Logs and Tinkertoys? Does anyone recall Weebles, which wobble but don't fall down? Those are some of the most popular toys made by Playskool, which was founded in 1928. Playskool products are still largely designed for children 6 years old and under. Flea markets are a prime hunting ground for all manner of Playskool toys, both vintage and contemporary.

Colored blocks, cardboard canister, 1972 ....22.00
Dressy Bessy, 1970, stuffed cloth, 1 button missing, 18" h.........48.50
Play set
   Sleep Dolly Sleep, Pullman A-756, tin, 1920s 405.00
   Holiday Inn, orig box, missing 2 pcs 205.00
Puzzle
   Airplane, #330-16, 15 pcs..12.00
   Balloon Man, #360-18, 21 pcs 10.00
   Cookie's Seasame Street Number, Sesame Street, train motif, #105, 5 pc 15.00
   Steam Shovel, #360-29, 18 pcs 12.00
Skaneateles Train, Track and Blocks set, 1960s, orig box, #S950, 55 pcs..............................102.50
Zoo, late 1960s/early 1970s, complete with animals..............95.00

✪ ★ Pokémon

This big collecting phase at the end of the millennium attracted much interest with youngsters. As with most flash-type collectible phenomenon, reproductions arrived on the scene early and have caused confusion and frustration. Unless you're buying for the sheer pleasure of collecting, know your dealer's reputation well.

Reference: *The Ultimate Unofficial Pokémon Price and Players Guide,* 2000, Krause Publications, 700 E. State St., Iola, WI 54990

Action Flipz cards, ten packs of four unopened cards, premier edition 13.00

Toys
   Mew, #151, comes with Pokeball, light-up, Burger King premium, battery needs to be replaced 40.00
   Togepi, bean bag, Burger King premium 9.50
Trading cards
   Dark Blastoise, non-holo, 1st edition 30.00
   Dark Dragonite, non-holo...15.00
   Flareon, holo foil, #3 ....16.00
   Hitmonchan, holographic 9.00
   Kangaskhan, holo foil, #5...18.00
   Meowth Common, #62.......62.00
   Misty's Poliwrath, non-holo 15.00
   Pokémon Chansey, holographic 13.00
   Pokémon Clefairy, holographic 13.00
   Vaporeon, holo foil, #12 .....15.00

❖ Pocketknives

Pocketknives have been made in various forms and with different types of handles and blade materials. Some collectors search out pocketknives from specific makers, while others specialize in certain handles or advertising knives.

References: Bernard Levine, *Levine's Guide to Knives and Their Values,* Krause Publications, 1997; Jack Lewis and Roger Combs, *The Gun Digest Book of Knives,* 5th ed., Krause Publications, 1997; Jim Sargent, *Sargent's American Premium Guide to Pocket Knives & Razors,* 4th ed., Books Americana, 1995; Ron Stewart and Roy Ritchie, *Big Book of Pocket Knives,* Collector Books, 2000; J. Bruce Voyles, *IBCA Price Guide To Antique Knives,* 2nd ed., Krause Publications; —, *IBCA Price Guide to Commemorative Knives, 1960-1990,* 2nd ed. Krause Publications; Joe Kertzman, *Knives 2001,* 21st ed., Krause Publications, 2001.

Periodicals: *The Blade,* 700 E. State St., Iola, WI 54990; *Knife World,* P.O. Box 3395, Knoxville, TN 37927.

Ka-Bar pocketknife, dog's head, $550.

Collectors' Clubs: American Blade Collectors, P.O. Box 22007, Chattanooga, TN 37422; Canadian Knife Collectors Club, Route 1, Milton, Ontario L9T 2X5 Canada; National Knife Collectors Association, P.O. Box 21070, Chattanooga, TN 37421.

Advertising, "Canadian Club, Best in the House," mkd "Stainless Steel, Japan," normal wear 20.00
Barlow, blade mkd "Colonial Prov. USA," 2 blades, 3-1/2" l folded 95.00
Camillus
   Babe Ruth, facsimile signature on side, 2-1/2" 125.00
   #702, stainless 17.50
   4 line stamp, black composition handle, mkd "Camillus Cutlery, Camillus, NY, USA," 3 blades, pre 1942...........18.00
   4 line stamp, bow tie shield, black composition handle, 3 blades, pre 1942...........20.00
Case
   XX #799, single blade 15.00
   XX USA, 3 dots, #31048, single blade..............................18.00
Forestmaster, blade mkd "Colonial," 4 blades, used, some rust, 3-3/4" l folded 25.00
Hammer Brand, loop missing, 2-1/4" l 10.00
Hoffritz, Switzerland, stainless, 2 blades and scissors, adv "American Greetings," 2-1/4" d....25.00
Remington, 2 blade, one blade missing, rusted, bone handle, 3-1/4" l 15.00
Schrade Cutlery, Captain DL-2, Dura Lens diamond nail file, precision scissors, pen blade, mkd "Snap On".....................................12.00

Texas Centennial, cream colored handle with bull, bale of hay, state flag, state emblem, and "1836-1936," 2 different sized blades 72.00

Thornton, red handle, 2 blades, well used, 3-1/2" l 55.00

Zippo, 2 blades, adv "Trio Mfg Co., Inc.," 2" l 18.00

❖ Pocket Watches

Pocket watches never go out of style and currently are quite fashionable. When shopping for a pocket watch at a flea market, ask a lot of questions as you carefully examine the watch—who made it, when, where, has it been repaired or cleaned recently, does it keep the proper time, etc.

Periodical: *Watch & Clock Review,* 2403 Champa St., Denver, CO 80205.

Collectors' Clubs: American Watchmakers Institute, Chapter 102, 3 Washington St., Apt 3C, Larchmont, NY 10538; Early American Watch Club Chapter 149, P.O. Box 5499, Beverly Hills, CA 90210; National Association of Watch & Clock Collectors, 514 Poplar St., Columbia, PA 17512.

American Waltham Watch Co.

14K yellow gold, model 1890 movement, size 6, fancy hunting case, scalloped edges, engraved and dated 1897 on front cover 700.00

Gold filled case, size 16, Roman numeral dial, elk on back, c1891, open face 250.00

Silver, Deuber coin silver, model 1883 movement, size 18, open face, c1891, small chip and ding to case 295.00

Elgin National Watch Co.

Gold tone, open face 325.00

White metal, 16 size, fancy edges and back, c1906, open face, replaced crystal 250.00

Yellow gold filled, model 2 movement, 12 size, three-quarter plate, hunter case, pendant set, c1916 .... 395.00

Eterna, pendant, 18K yg, rect form, black line indicators, hallmark 230.00

Hampden, nickel, large, open face 475.00

Howard, 14K white gold, 17 jewels, matching chain, open face 450.00

U.S. Watch Co., 14K yg, hunter, size 6, white dial, black Roman numerals, subsidiary seconds dial, engraved floral and scroll motifs on case 245.00

❖ Political and Campaign Items

As the cost of getting elected to political office continues to spiral upward, we can thank our forefathers for establishing the practice of creating items with their image or slogan. Intended to passively generate votes, these political items are now eagerly sought by collectors.

Periodicals: *The Political Bandwagon,* P.O. Box 348, Leola, PA 17540; *Political Collector,* P.O. Box 5171, York, PA 17405.

Jugate postcard, Taft and Sherman, "Our Choice," $14.

Collectors' Clubs: American Political Items Collectors, P.O. Box 340339, San Antonio, TX 78234; Third Party & Hopefuls, 503 Kings Canyon Blvd., Galesburg, IL 61401.

Reproduction Alert.

For additional listings, see *Warman's Antiques and Collectibles Price Guide* and *Warman's Americana & Collectibles,* as well as specific topics in this edition, including John F. Kennedy, Abraham Lincoln, and Presidential.

Book

Balance, Senator Al Gore, Houghton, Mifflin Co., 1992, first edition, ... 15.00

Blind Ambition, The White House Years, John Dean, Simon and Schuster, orig shrinkwrap 5.00

Clinton, Portrait of Victory, Warner Books, photographs by P. F. Bentley, 1993, dj 20.00

Kennedy and Roosevelt, The Uneasy Alliance, Michael R. Meschloss, W. W. Norton and Co., 1980, first edition .. 10.00

Life of James G. Blaine, The Plumed Knight, 1893, printing error 30.00

Lyndon's Legacy, A Candid Look at The President's Policymakers, Frank L. Kluckhorn, Davin-Adair Co., 1964, first edition, dj 5.00

Pictures I've Kept, A Concise Pictorial Autobiography, Dwight D. Eisenhower, Doubleday and Co., 1969, first edition 20.00

Putting People First, How We Can All Change America, Governor Bill Clinton and Senator Al Gore, Times Books, 1992, paperback, first edition 7.50

The Buzzards, Janet Burroway, Little, Brown & Co., 1969, first edition, novel about American politician, his family, etc. 6.00

Dress, Hubert Humphrey, red, white, and blue, 8-1/2" h black and white facial photo of Humphrey on front and back, 32" l 85.00

Earrings, clip back, red, white, and blue oval shaped stones, gold tone metal backings 25.00

Mechanical bank, Boss Tweed Tammany, 1873......................750.00

Pinback button
Bush/Quayle, 1992, 1-1/2" dia 75.00
Nixon's The One, orig wrapper, 1" dia...........................125.00

Poster
Humphrey/Muskie, name in big letters, birds, fish, trees, stars, and rising sun, numbered 30 of 115, sgd and dated by artist D.I. Stovall 1/9/71, stiff poster board stock 125.00
Reagan/Bush, Vote Republican, Palm Beach, framed, 22" x 27"................................75.00

Record, "The Voice of President John F. Kennedy, highlights from Nomination Acceptance Speech and Inaugural Address," Golden Memorial Record, photos labeled "Wide World Photos," printed in USA, yellow label 125.00

Toy, truck set, Winross, trailer and cab, Clinton/Gore and Bush/Quayle, 1992, NRFB 110.00

❖ Poodles

In the 1950s, poodles were supreme! From poodle skirts to television lamps, they were the favorites of many kids. Collectors enjoy reliving some of that nostalgia at flea markets by finding those friendly pink, white, or black poodles they loved as a kid.

Ashtray, black, some wear to ear and face, 4-1/2" 5.00
Autograph dog, white vinyl, signatures, 1950s, 4-1/2" x 7".... 18.00
Beanie Baby, Gigi, MWBT and protector 18.00
Jewelry Box, wood, white, poodle dec, sgd "Kellerman Jewel Case, Japan," 1960s, 10" x 6" 25.00
Figure, Paulette.......................30.00
Lamp, television type, poodle and puppy, mkd "Kron," 1950s, 13" h 160.00

Pin
AJC, brass color, clear rhinestone eyes, 2" x 2" 25.00
Beau, sterling, 1-1/2" x 1-3/4" 35.00

Spaghetti poodles figurine, 5-1/4" high, 4-1/2" long, $130.

Stein, Parisian Poodle, orange body, ivory pom-poms, purple hair bow, mkd "Lea Stein, Paris" on clasp, 1-1/2" x 1-1/2".............................95.00
Tortolani, gold-tone, faux pearls and red rhinestone eye, 1-1/2" x 2-1/4" 85.00
Pillow, poodle design, tiny rhinestone accents, tassels on each corner, 16" sq 165.00
Pincushion, metal and fabric, nodding head and tail 35.00
Pincushion and tape measure, ceramic, brown, tongue pulls out as tape measure, mkd "Wales, Made in Japan," 6" h 48.00
Planter, ceramic, pink, c1940, 6-1/2" h, 8-1/2" w, 3-1/2" d 45.00
Playing cards, yellow and blue backgrounds, Congress Playing Cards, Cell-U-Tone Finish, used 35.00
Purse, wool, gold embellishment, large..................................56.00
Salt and pepper shakers, pr, egg shape, one with yellow poodle, other with blue poodle, flowers, butterfly, raised relief, orig plastic stoppers and Enesco stickers 25.00
Wall plaque, chalk, white head, illegible imp mark, 4-1/2" l, 4-1/4" w 30.00

❖ Porcelier

Porcelain light fixtures, small appliances and a variety of tableware were some of the items produced by Porcelier Manufacturing Company, which was in business between 1926 and 1954. Collectors look for flawless items, wanting any gold trim to be unworn and items such as light fixtures to have their original pulls.

Reference: Susan E. Grindberg, *Collector's Guide to Porcelier China*, Collector Books, 1996.

Collectors' Club: Porcelier Collectors Club, 21 Tamarac Swamp Rd., Wallingford, CT 06492-5529.

Coffee set, percolator, sugar and creamer, lavender-blue bell platinum design 130.00
Coffeepot, Dutch couple, 4 pcs, 12-3/4" h 85.00
Cream and sugar, Field Flowers, platinum 22.50

Light fixture
Ceiling-mount, 2 sockets, white with pink lilacs, needs rewired, no mounting hardware, 11" x 6-1/4" 30.00
Wall-mount, circular back, socket arm, white with red roses, gold accents, rewired, replaced socket $129.00

Teapot
Nautical, shows sailboats, 8" h 48.00
Floral pattern, hairline, 5-1/4" h 15.00

Porcelain teapot, Nautical, 8" h, $48.

Hearthside, rim chip, 6-3/4" h
....25.00

Waffle iron, Barock-Colonia, gold
dots variation...................187.50

❖ Portrait Plates

Portrait plates and other types of wares with portraits of prominent people were made as decorations. Displays of American leaders could subtly express a political affiliation. Other portrait plates were made with busts of lovely women and were intended only for decorative display.

Gibson Girl, brown hair, blue-green
ground, shaded purple to pink
ground, shaped gold rim, artist
sgd, mkd "Austria".............50.00

Mrs. Lincoln, 6" dia, Imperial China
....85.00

Napoleon, Louisiana Purchase souvenir, fair buildings on rim, blue
and white earthenware, high
glaze, Victoria Art Company,
N.Y. 10" dia......................300.00

Queen Louise, white dress, pink
sash, gold rim, sgd "Mme A-K,
France," 8-1/2" dia...........180.00

Woman, brown curly hair, star band
on forehead, cream gown, brown
border with gold overlay, mkd "C.
T. Germany" and eagle mark
....45.00

Woman, brown hair, pale purple
fringed lavender shawl on shoulder, gold stenciled inner rim,
green border, blue "Victoria Austria" mark.........................125.00

Martha Washington portrait plate, "Souvenir of Washington, D.C.," Capsco, 7-1/4" diameter, $3.50.

New National Museum, Washington, D.C., 1913 postmark, $3.

❖ Postcards

Ever wonder what happened to all those postcards tourists have sent over the decades? Postcard collectors are searching flea markets for them. Some buyers specialize in local history cards, while others seek a specific maker or artist. Most are reasonably priced, but recently some rare postcards have sold for record prices.

References: Ron Menchine, *Tuff Stuff's Baseball Postcard Collection*, Tuff Stuff Books, 1999; Robert Reed, *Advertising Postcards*, Schiffer Publishing, 2001.

Collectors' Clubs: There are many regional collectors clubs. Contact one of these national organizations to find out about a chapter near you. Deltiologists of America, P.O. Box 8, Norwood, PA 19074; Postcard History Society, P.O. Box 1765, Manassas, VA 22110.

Advertising, Griffin's Waffle Syrup,
unused...............................15.40

Bank, Buffalo, NY, Buffalo Savings
Bank, Buffalo Square, 1900s
....6.50

Cats, four kittens, "Greetings from
the Kills," early 1900s..........6.00

Christmas, little girl and doll, silk
insert, Wolf and Co., NY, writing
on back.............................10.00

Dogs
Happy Birthday, "We're sending
these puppies to say, Have a
Happy Birthday," photo of
beagles by Roberts.........6.00

Pekingese, "Just a Few Lines,"
B B London, Series No. G 53,
printed in Germany.........9.00

Pug, "Grace and Remembrance
to You," Oval Panel Series, G.
D. & D. L., printed in Germany
....8.50

Scottish Terrier and Westie, titled
"A Double Scotch from Pitlo-
chry," also includes illus of
Loch Faskall, The Dam, Festival Theatre, and Athoil Road
....10.00

Yorkshire Terrier, photo by Virginia Kay, Columbia Wholesale Supply, Hollywood, CA
....6.00

Easter, Easter angel, early 1900,
never used............................9.00

Flowers
Violets, celluloid, textured, emb
flowers, dated 1913, used
....12.00

Interior, Will Roger's house in Pacific
Palisades, CA, real photo type
....5.00

Pretty Lady
Cowgirl on horseback, The Belle
of the Plain, traces of glue
....8.00

Dear Heart, pretty lady wearing
large hat, copyright 1908, previously glued into album
....10.00

Railroad, chrome
Erie Railroad.......................3.50
Milwaukee Railroad.............3.00
Southern Pacific Limited.....3.00
Southern Pacific Railroad....3.00
Steam Town USA................2.00
Vista-Dome Zephyr.............3.50

Restaurant, Hollywood Cabaret Restaurant, Broadway, 48th, NYC
....10.00

River scene, Ohio river boat in canal
locks at Louisville, Kentucky,
linen.....................................6.00

Street scene
Santa Fe, chrome................3.00

Real-photo postcard, swimmers, unused, $5.

Valentine

Cupid with arrows, "You stole a heart! Love's law is plain, that bids you part, with one again" 6.00

Tuck, poster girl, series #231, unused 30.00

Two cupids tending love fire, 1900 .... 8.75

❖ Posters

Posters have long been an effective communication tool. Their size, bright colors, and great illustrations caught the attention of many passersby. Today they are treasured and becoming more available at flea markets.

Periodicals: *Biblio*, 845 Willamette St. Eugene, OR 87401; *Collecting Hollywood*, American Collectors Exchange, 2401 Broad St., Chattanooga, TN 37408; *Movie Poster Update*, American Collectors Exchange, 2401 Broad St., Chattanooga, TN 37408.

For additional listings, see *Warman's Antiques and Collectibles Price Guide* and *Warman's Americana & Collectibles*, as well as Movie Posters in this edition.

1940 Golden Gate International Exposition poster, 18" x 13-1/2", $575.

Central Hudson Line, Newburgh/Poughkeepsie/Kingston, shows man and woman with binoculars at railing, "B.B. Odell" on life preserver, with trip dates, 45-1/2" x 29-1/2" 715.00

Chevrolet, "We Airline-Check When We Chevy Tune for Top-Flight Performance," mechanic working on car, 44" x 17" 170.50

Clyde, Beatty-Cole Bros Combined Circus, the World's Largest Circus, "Clyde Beatty in Person," Roland Butler, Lion tamer, 19" x 26" 90.00

Crossman Bros. Seeds, Rochester, N.Y., woman holding basket of "New Crop, New Black-Eyed Wax Bean," 24" x 18" 1,072.50

Family Fun Night, Disneyland, May 16, 1971, 12" x 9" 45.00

Give It Your Best, 48-star U.S. flag, World War II, 28-1/2" x 20" 60.00

"I Summon You to Comradeship in the Red Cross," Harrison Fisher illustration, World War I, heavy wear at edges, tears, creases, 40" x 28" 335.00

I Want You, Uncle Sam Army recruiting poster, 1975, 14" x 11" 80.00

Nixon/Agnew, 44" x 30" 450.00

NRA Code (National Recovery Administration), blue eagle, 1934, cardboard 14" x 11" 39.00

Post Toasties, "Sweet Memories," 1909, framed, 21-3/4" x 16-1/2" 575.00

Tin Cans Going to War, World War II, orig wooden frame, 36" x 30" 150.00

Wings Cigarette, Piper Cub giveaway, 1940s, cardboard, 30" x 20" 145.00

❖ Powder Jars

Containers to hold powder were a staple of a lady's dressing table. The boxes were often decorative or whimsical. Today collectors are charmed by them.

Celluloid lid, frosted green glass jar base, wear to emb black design on top, 3-1/2" h, 4-1/4" w ... 28.00

Covered jar, O.&E.G., Royal Austria, 3-1/2" diameter, $35.

Glass

Clear, elephant on top, raised trunk 28.00

Clear, lady sitting in front of beveled mirror 55.00

Clear, lady's portrait under lid, reverse painted highlights, box shape, wear to paint, 3" x 4" 85.00

Clear, My Pet 40.00

Clear, woman with child, 9" h, inside nick 145.00

Frosted, green, Art Deco lady 250.00

Frosted, green, Cameo lady 225.00

Frosted, green, Crinoline Girl 145.00

Frosted, green, hand painted flowers 26.00

Frosted, pink, elephant, trunk down 65.00

Frosted, pink, scottie, small rough spot 25.00

Hobnail, clear, opalescent white hobnails, 4-3/8" dia 25.00

Iridescent, marigold, figural poodle on top 32.00

Pink, Annette 75.00

Limoges, Remy Delinieres & Company, matte black, gilding, mkd "AG," 1895 .... 295.00

Musical, dresser jar, 8-1/2" h 60.00

❖ Precious Moments Figurines

Created by Samuel J. Butcher in 1978 and produced by Enesco, Precious Moments are now in their third decade of production. This popular line of collectibles features cute kids with inspiring messages. The collectibles include figurines, mugs, ornaments, and plates. Collectors should enjoy their Precious Moments, but not hope to reap great rewards on the resale of these objects.

References: Rosie Wells, *Rosie's Secondary Market Price Guide for Enesco's Precious Moments Collection*, 16th ed, Rosie Wells Enterprises, 1998; *Precious Collectibles*, 22341 E. Wells Rd., Canton, IL 61520.

Collectors' Club: Enesco Precious Moments Collectors' Club, P.O. Box 99, Itasca, IL 60143.

Birthday Club, Clown Drummer, B-0001, Charter Member figure, 3-3/4" h 80.00

God's Speed, little boy jogging with dog, base dated and mkd "Jonathon & David" 85.00

God Understands, triangle mark, string tag, no box 125.00

Healer of Broken Hearts, 6" h . 55.00

Lord Bless You and Keep You, bride and groom, 6" h 65.00

Love Lifted Me, older boy helping younger friend tumbling from wagon, 5-1/2" h 80.00

Loving is Sharing, little boy sitting on bench, sharing ice cream with dog, 4-3/4" h, 4" w 95.00

Make a Joyful Noise, string tag, no box 85.00

Peacemaker, 1979, 5" h 55.00

Praise the Lord Anyhow, #82, orig string tag, orig box 80.00

This Is Your Day To Shine, little girl being helped by kitten and puppy, 6" h 80.00

Thou Art Mine, little boy and girl with turtle, writing in sand, 5-1/4" h 70.00

❖ Premiums

Saving box tops and barcodes has been a way to get a promotional item from a favorite company. Many early premiums promoted radio and cowboy heroes. Some of these vintage treasures have become quite valuable.

Periodicals: *Box Top Bonanza*, 3403 46th Ave., Moline, IL 61265; *Premium Collectors Magazine*, 1125 Redman Ave., St. Louis, MO 63138; *The Premium Watch Watch*, 24 San Rafael Drive, Rochester, NY 14618; *The Toy Ring Journal*, P.O. Box 544, Birmingham, MI 48012.

Catalog
  Kellogg's Funny Jungleland Moving Pictures, 1932 .... 48.00
  Octagon Soap Premium List, 1930 edition 38.00
  Wrigley's Gum Mother Goose premium booklet, 1915 .. 55.00

Decoder, Lil Orphan Annie Secret Society Decoder, 1935, brass with silver outer rim 65.00

Mask, Cisco Kid, paper, Schulze Butternut White Bread. 1949, 12-1/2" w 30.00

Postcard, Tony the Tiger, 3-5/8" x 5-5/8", Tony with camper's gear, "Hi, It's Gr-r-eat Here At" as he points to sign post, black and white art on reverse, various messages to be checked off by sender, including plug for Kellogg's cereals, mid-1960s 12.00

Ring, Cap'n Crunch, plastic, blue figure on red base 295.00

Sign, Squirt doll, paper banner offering 18" h vinyl doll with fabric outfit through participating store of direct mail, 1962, Squirt Co. 40.00

❖ Presidential

Collectors who follow the candidates to the White House have additional collectibles to gather. Tried-and-true presidential collectors will add to their campaign paraphernalia by gathering inaugural and other collectibles generated by the office holder. Other presidential memorabilia might deal with family members.

Periodicals: *The Political Bandwagon*, P.O. Box 348, Leola, PA 17540; *Political Collector*, P.O. Box 5171, York, PA 17405.

Collectors' Club: American Political Items Collectors, P.O. Box 340339, San Antonio, TX 78234.

First-day cover, autographed by Gerald Ford 60.00

Inaugural program
  Bill Clinton, glossy content, full color photos, 24 pgs 15.00
  Lyndon Johnson, gold presidential seal, Jan 20, 1965, full color and black and white photos and text 20.00

Inaugural ticket, 1941, pr 40.00

Magazine cover, *Time*
  Johnson and Goldwater collage, Sept. 25, 1964 .... 5.00
  Johnson and Humphrey, Sept. 4, 1964 .... 8.00
  President Clinton, December 1998 .... .50
  President Johnson, Man of the Year, Jan. 1, 1965 .... 8.00

Newspaper, *Mobile Register*, April 13, 1945, "President Roosevelt Dies at Warm Springs" 6.00

Nodder, Dwight Eisenhower, composition, brown hat, blue coat, c1956, 6" h 100.00

Paperweight
  Dwight D. Eisenhower, sulphide, Baccarat, cameo, grid-cut base, 1963, 2-3/4" dia 325.00
  Franklin D. Roosevelt dime motif, made for Imperial Glass by Lenox, 1977 .... 15.00

Pencil, Hoover for President, 1928, yellow, unsharpened 20.00

Plate, ceramic
  President and Mrs. Dwight D. Eisenhower, America's First Family, 9" dia 8.00
  U.S. presidents, ending with John F. Kennedy 15.00

Postcard
  President and Mrs. Taft, 1909 inauguration 25.00
  President Roosevelt and Family 10.00

Sheet music, *The New Frontier*, black and white portrait of Kennedy on cover, facsimile signature, red, white, and blue flag, capitol dome on cover 27.50

Stereoview
  The President and Mrs. McKinley, floral border 15.00
  Tomb of Late President McKinley, Canton, Ohio, tinted 6.00

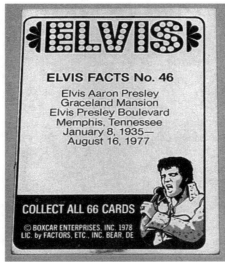

Elvis Facts Card No. 46 of 66, Boxcar Enterprises, 1978, $10.

❖ Presley, Elvis

"You ain't nothin' but a hound dog…" Elvis was quite a hit in his day. Even after his death in 1977, memorabilia sales remain strong. Fans still flock to his home and swoon when they hear his songs.

Collectors' Clubs: Elvis Forever TCB Fan Club, P.O. Box 1066, Pinellas Park, FL 33281; Graceland News Fan Club, P.O. Box 452, Rutherford, NJ 07070.

Album, LP
   "Our Memories of Elvis", black label, DNT 75.00
   "Personally Elvis", blue label, double pocket, silhouette 50.00
   "Spinout", black label, DOT, RCA, white top 35.00
   "Welcome to My World," black label, DNT 30.00
Bubble gum cards, complete set, unopened card packs, issued by Boxcar Enterprises, Inc., 1978 .... 135.00
Calendar, 1977, Tribute to Elvis, Boxcar Enterprises, 12" x 13" 50.00
Cassette tapes, boxed set of 3 tapes, limited edition, poster, book 15.00
Cookie jar, riding in car 100.00
Decanter, McCormick Distillery, porcelain
   Music box base plays "Blue Hawaii," Aloha Elvis, shows Arizona Memorial, 16" h 295.00

Music box base plays "Don't Be Cruel," Taking Care of Business in a Flash emblem, 15" h, MIB 275.00
Music box base plays "Loving You," mkd "Young Elvis '55," 16" h, MIB.................... 275.00
Portrait bust, orig booklet titled "1935-1977, The End of an Era," 15" h, MIB........... 275.00
   Singing pose, 14" h, MIB .275.00
Doll, Barbie Gift Set, "Barbie Loves Elvis," 1996, MIB 130.00
Magazine, *Saturday Evening Post*, July/August, 1985, "Legends that Won't Die"................... 10.00
Portrait, sgd by artist Ivan Jesse Curtin, mounted on wooden frame, c1960.................... 125.00
Puzzle, The King, Springbok, 1992, 1000 pieces 50.00
Sheet music, 1954, "Love Me Tender" 35.00

❖ Princess Diana

Her tragic death in 1997 stopped the world for a brief time. Collectibles ranging from things made during her lifetime, such as wedding commemoratives, and later memorial pieces are readily available at flea markets.

Ale glass, Royal Wedding........ 32.00

Beer can, Felinfoel Brewery, Wales, 1981, official Royal Wedding commemorative, bottom opened 15.00
Brooch, memorial heart pin, orig card................................... 50.00
Calendar, 1998, still sealed..... 10.00
Coach replica, Matchbox, replica of coach used in wedding, made for Her Majesty's 40th Anniversary, limited edition, MIB .. 65.00
Doll, porcelain, flower girl, pastel yellow dress, white roses, Danbury Mint, 11" h 195.00
First-day cover, Marshall Islands 3.00
Postcard, birthday card type, photo of Diana and Charles, unused 10.00
Slippers, figural head of sleeping Diana and Charles, c1980, unused, orig tags 48.00
Tea towel, Irish linen, portraits of Diana and Charles, Prince of Wales plumes, 28-1/2" x 18-1/2" 20.00
Thimble, HRH Prince William of Wales, to commemorate his 1st birthday, portrait of Prince and Mother, June, 1983 .... 27.00
Tin, engagement photo, banner on top "Royal Wedding, July 1981," mkd "Regent Ware, Made in England," minor dent 22.00
Trade card set, full unopened package, Press Pass................ 95.00

❖ Prints

Prints are a great way for the common folk to have copies of fine artwork for their homes or offices. Currier & Ives was one of numerous publishers that reproduced a variety of artwork. Today's limited-edition prints compete for the same collector dollars.

References: Jay Brown, *The Complete Guide to Limited Edition Art Prints*, Krause Publications, 1999; Michael Ivankovich, *Collector's Value Guide to Early 20th Century American Prints*, Collector Books, 1998. Plus there are many other excellent reference books available about prints, fine arts, and artists.

"The Christian Martyrs," photogravure, Gebbie & Husson Co., 10-3/4" x 16-1/4", $25.

Periodicals: *Journal of the Print World*, 1008 Winona Road, Meredith, NH 03253; *On Paper*, 39 E. 78th St., #601, New York, NY 10021.
For additional listings, see *Warman's Antiques and Collectibles Price Guide.*

Reproduction Alert.

Currier & Ives

    The Deacon's Mare, framed, light water staining on bottom margin, 13-1/2" x 7-1/2" 247.50

    Fruit Piece, framed, 13" x 16" 137.50

    James Polk, Eleventh President of the United States, period decor frame, light water stains, top margin worn, 14" x 9-7/8" 220.00

    Jay Eye See, Record 2:10, cherry frame, stains, minor damage, edge repair, 13-3/8" x 17-5/8" 165.00

    Lady Washington, period veneer frame with chips, slight stains, 1 small pc missing from margin 275.00

Fox, R. Adkinson, The Westwinds, ...75.00

Kellogg & Comstock

    The Angler, girl reading letter to man fishing, grain-decor frame, margin tear, stains, fold line, 9-3/4" x 14" ... 137.50

    The Fruit, light stains, walnut cross-corner frame, short margin tear, 10" x 14"....88.00

    Napoleon, hand-colored, 1870, 17" x 13".......................225.00

Thompson, William

    Memory Lane, 12" x 16-1/2" 100.00

    Winter Moonlight, 1939, snow scene, 8" x 10" 55.00

★ Pull Toys

Simple toys made to delight young children have been collected for decades. Many are homemade and those often contain a certain charm that appeals to collectors. Look for examples that are in good condition and have all their parts. Don't be surprised if the favorite little one in your life wants to play with these colorful toys.

Bouncing Buggy, Fisher-Price, c1973.................................10.00

Bunny, pink plastic bunny, wooden wheels, 7" h, 5" l 15.00

Chiming Turtle, Fisher-Price....22.00

Dog, Fisher-Price, c1993, 5" l..10.00

Elephant, wooden, mkd "Montgomery Schoolhouse, Inc., Vermont," orig tail and pull cord, some wear to edges, 7-1/4" l 20.00

Mary Had A Little Lamb, hand painted plaster, wooden wheels 85.00

Mickey Mouse Locomotive, Mickey as conductor, Pluto and Donald Duck on stickers on one side, Minnie and Goofy on other, red, green, orange, and yellow balls in globe pop up and down as toy moves, Mickey also moves, makes clanging noise, worn paint.................................12.00

Pixie Face, green hat and mouth, red, green, and blue face, Bakelite and wood, mkd "Cinderella Mfg. Co., Jackson, Mich.," 1940s..............................120.00

Slinky Dog, from Toy Story, fair condition, 8" l...........................10.00

Wooden rooster pull toy, 6" high, 7" long, $35.

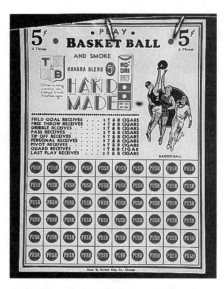

Play Basket Ball punchboard, Havana Blend Cigars, 1930s, 10" x 7-1/4", $17.50.

❖ Punch Boards

Feel like taking a chance? For those lucky collectors who enjoy finding punch boards, flea markets often offer several choices.

Beat the Seven 25.00

Charley Board, 25 cents each, 9" x 10" 20.00

Elvgren's Flashy, 11-7/8" x 9-5/8" 50.00

Fancy Fives, 11-7/8" x 9-5/8" .. 50.00

Five Tens 24.00

Lulu Bell 18.00

Nickel Special, shows Lucky Strike pack, pre-World War II, 500 punches at 5 cents each... 45.00

Pick A Cherry, fruit seal........... 24.00

Sunshine, risque 45.00

Take Me Home....................... 15.00

❖ Puppets

Puppets come in all shapes and sizes, from hand operated to elaborate marionettes to ventriloquist dummies and little push puppets, giving collectors a real variety. The fun part about collecting puppets is that all probably have made people laugh and smile, and probably still have lots of smiles left to share with their new owners.

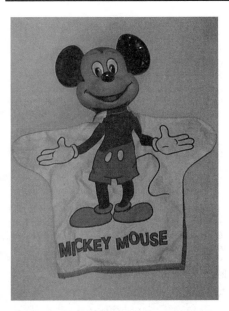

Mickey Mouse hand puppet, 10" high, $15.

Hand, all used condition
  Boglin, purple, yellow eyes,
    1980s, 8" h 16.00
  Donkey, Kamar 10.00
  Goofy, Gabriel, 1977 .... 10.00
  Pinocchio, Gund, soft plastic
    head, printed cotton body
    .... 50.00
  Snuggle Bear 8.75
  Tweety Bird, 10" h 13.50
  Witchiepoo, Remco, 1971, orig
    paper sticker on back
    .... 140.00
Marionette, all used condition
  Clown 42.00
  Mr. Bluster 635.00
  Howdy Doody, cloth body, vinyl
    head and hands, body mkd
    "Goldberger Doll Co., Made in
    Hong Kong," head mkd
    "Eegee," one arm and hand
    damaged, 12" l 30.00
  McCarthy, Charlie, composition,
    12" h 125.00
  Pinocchio, Walt Disney Enter-
    prises, composition, 12" h
    .... 125.00
  Princess Winter, Spring, Sum-
    mer, Fall, cracks to composi-
    tion head, 14" l 500.00
  Siamese Temple Dancer
    .... 130.00
Push puppet, used condition
  Atom Ant 25.00
  Cowboy on White Horse, by
    Kohner, Socko label 45.00

Donald Duck 30.00
Fred Flintstone 80.00
Mickey Mouse 30.00
Olive Oyl 35.00
Pluto 25.00
Popeye 35.00
Santa Mouse 35.00
Terry the Tiger 30.00
Ventriloquist dummy, all used condi-
  tion
  Bart Simpson, custom made
    .... 200.00
  Bozo 42.00
  Jerry Mahoney 60.00
  Three Stooges 100.00
  Willie Talk, Horsman 42.00

❖ Purinton Pottery

Purinton Pottery is another Ohio pottery company that made dinnerware and some table wares. Founded in Wellsville, the company was in business from 1936 to 1959.
Periodical: Puritan Pastimes, P.O. Box 9394, Arlington, VA 22219.
Cookie jar, rooster, 11" h 525.00
Creamer, miniature, apple, 2" h
  .... 15.00
Cruet set, intaglio 36.00
Dutch jug, apple, 6" h, 8" w 35.00
Pitcher, fruit, qt, 5-1/2" h 55.00
Plate, intaglio, 9 3/4" 18.00
Platter, intaglio, 12-1/2" 22.00

Purinton flour canister, 9-1/2" high, $50.

Salt and pepper shakers, apple, jug-
  style, 2-1/2" h, pr 25.00
Serving dish, intaglio, 11-1/4" . 22.00
Snack set, apple 32.50
Sugar, cov, apple, 5" h 38.50
Teapot, red ivy, crack, 5" h 25.00
Tumbler, apple 20.00
Wall pocket, apple, 4" h 127.50

❖ Purses

Here's an item most ladies wouldn't be without. Collectors are intrigued with the styles, colors, and different textures of purses from bygone eras.
Alligator, brown, designer type
  .... 50.00
Bamboo, boxy style, 13" x 14", one
  small red knob missing 65.00
Beaded
  Enameled pink, blue, and yellow,
    frame stamped "Whiting and
    Davis" 200.00
  White with pastel colored beaded
    flowers, mkd "Made in Hong
    Kong," 9" x 5" 40.00
Evening
  Brocade, Art Deco, engraved
    gold filled frame 75.00
  Faille, black, marcasite set
    mounting, gold onyx mono-
    gram, c1930 .... 70.00
  Satin, pink, silver bugle beads,
    ivory colored seed pearls, sil-
    ver frame and clasp, trimmed
    in white rhinestones, silver
    chain handle, Jolle Original,
    9" x 7-1/2" x 1" 110.00

Coin purse, imitation alligator skin, $5.

Lucite, trapezoid, cream colored, gold-tone frame, rigid handle, snap clasp, navy lining and side gussets, c1950, 8" w 185.00
Mesh, sterling silver, short silver chain, hallmarked London 1916, 4-1/4" h, 5-1/5" w............. 105.00
Straw, two handles, gold-tone ball type clasp, c1950 .... 20.00

❖ Puzzles

What's got lots of pieces and hours of fun? Puzzles. Puzzles have been around about as long as the Americas, starting as ways to keep children occupied. By the 1890s, adults wanted to have some fun too, leading the creation of more intricate examples. Ask the dealer if the puzzle is complete and if any pieces are damaged. Missing pieces can drastically reduce the price.

Collectors' Club: American Game Collectors Association, P.O. Box 44, Dresher, PA 19025.
For additional listings, see *Warman's Antiques and Collectibles Price Guide.*
Alpine Beauty, Picture Perfect Puzzle, 1940s, 15-1/2" x 10-1/8" 15.00
Dumbo, Jaymar Specialty 11" x 14" 15.00
E.T., Craft Master, 5 pcs, 11" x 8-3/8" 5.00
First In The Heart Of His Countrymen, Corker Picture Puzzle, Whitman Publishing Co. 15.00
The Fonz, Happy Days, HG Toys, 1976, 14" x 10".................. 15.00
The Future Champion, English setter with pup, Guild 12.00

"Never Too Late to Learn," Perfect Picture Puzzle, $6.50.

Jesus Learned Many Things in the Carpenter's Shop, Little Folks Bible Picture, Warner Press, 14 pcs, 7-3/4" x 6-3/4" 5.00
Mother Goose, 1954, Sifco Co., 10" x 8" 16.00
Mr.T., 1982, sealed, 14" sq 13.50
Rolling to Victory, Tuco 32.00

❖ Pyrex

Pyrex was developed by the researchers at Corning Glass in the early 1910s. By 1915, Corning launched its Pyrex line with a 12-piece set. Fry Glass Company was granted permission to produce Pyrex under its Fry Oven Glass label in 1920. Cooks today still use many Pyrex products. This kitchenware collectible is just starting to become popular with many people. Don't overlook advertising and paper ephemera dealing with Pyrex.

Reference: Barbara Mauzy, *Pyrex*, Schiffer Publishing, 2000.
Baker, cov, delphite blue, 6-3/4" x 4-1/4" 22.00
Bean pot, cov, clear, 2 qt 12.00
Casserole, cov, 2 qt, round, robin's egg blue base, clear cover, light use 15.00
Double boiler, mkd "Flameware" 17.50
Freezer server, Butterprint 12.00
Mixing bowl set, four nested bowls, solid colored exterior, white int., one yellow, green, orange/red, and blue............................. 40.00
Percolator, Flameware, Deluxe, 4 cup size 45.00
Pie plate, clear, 10".................. 10.00
Refrigerator set, Butterprint pattern, 8 pc set............................. 45.00
Serving dish, Bluebelle 20.00

Pyrex serving dish, wheat pattern, 7-1/2" diameter, $8.

❖ Pyrography

It's an interesting concept—give someone a hot tool and tell him to go burn a design on a piece of wood. That is essentially what pyrography was all about. Skilled artisans introduced the form to America in the mid-1800s, but it became a hobby for the masses around the turn of the century, when several companies began offering items with designs stamped on them for burning. The Flemish Art Company of New York was the largest producer of pyrography products, and the term Flemish Art has become synonymous with burnt wood pieces of that era. The hobby was most popular from 1890 to 1915.

Reference: Frank L. Hahn, *Collector's Guide to Burnt Wood Antiques*, Golden Era Publications, 1994.
Book rack, folding, 18" l 80.00
Box
    Book-shaped, woman wearing crown, 2 pcs, 1905, 4" x 3-1/2" x 1-1/2" 45.00
    Hand-painted, cherries design 42.00
Chair-table, floral and other decor, sides with 2 large oval cutouts, 47" h 495.00
Utensil box, 3" h, 12" w, 9" l.... 35.00
Gameboard, triangle-design surface, owl on reverse, 11" x 14" 104.50
Handkerchief box, hand-painted, 9" sq................................. 65.00
Plaque
    Dutch girl with cookie jar, painted floral border, 12" x 9" 65.00
    Indian maiden in headdress, oval 85.00
Plate rack, fruit motif, 12" h, 42" l 220.00
Spoon holder, 3 dancing Dutch girls, slots for 8 spoons.............. 55.00
Wastebasket, woman's bust and grapes decor, square, scalloped top, 14" h 71.50

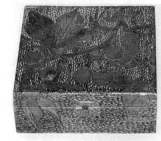

Pyrography box with hand-painted cherries and leaves, broken clasp, 2-1/2" high, 6" square, $10.

❖ Quilts

Colorful bits and pieces of material sewn together make up quilts. Wonderful examples can be found at flea markets, from vintage, hand-made, one-of-a-kind quilts to newer designer quilts.

References: There are many excellent quilt identification books available to collectors. Many collectors are also quilt makers and may find the quilt books by Krause Publications of interest, including Patricia J. Morris and Jeannette T. Muir's *Worth Doing Twice, New Quilts from Old Tops.*

Periodical: *Quilters Newsletter,* P.O. Box 4101, Golden, CO 80401.

Collectors' Clubs: American Quilter's Society, P.O. Box 3290, Paducah, KY 42001; The National Quilting Association, P.O. Box 393, Ellicott City, MD 21043.

Broken Star, orange, yellow, green, red, brown, blue, and white painted calico patches, red and white calico Flying Geese border, Penn., 19th C 475.00

Crazy, pieced velvet, multicolored, arranged in 16 squares, colorful velvet border, late 19th C, 72" x 74" 900.00

Cross and Crown, yellow, red, and olive patches, yellow borders, red backing, 84" x 83" 450.00

Fan, multicolored pieces, red accents, trimmed in red, 74" x 85" 485.00

Floral Medallions, pastel pink, green and yellow appliques, swag border, minor stains, 82" x 90" 420.00

Four Patch, green, brown, red, and blue printed calico horizontal panels, diamond and zigzag quilting, Mennonite, Penn., 19th C 230.00

Grandmother's Flower Garden, blue, pink, yellow, and green, 20th C 500.00

Log Cabin, yellow, brown, red, green, brown, pink, and white bars, broad red and black borders, rope quilting, red, yellow, and green calico backing, 81" x 81" 250.00

Nine Patch variation, blue, gray, and tan, white background and backing, 73" x 72" 365.00

Pineapple Medallion, pink calico and white, 76-1/2" x 94"..........395.00

Serrated Square, pink and green calico, shell and diamond quilted, 82" x 84"..............325.00

Star of Bethlehem, yellow, pink, purple, green, gray, and blue, white ground, pink and green borders, c1940, 85" x 85" 725.00

Sunbonnet Sue, some wear, 1930s 125.00

Tulip, ivory sq cotton squares, vivid red and gold appliqué tulips, green stems, banded green border, 76" sq 900.00

❖ Quimper

Known for its colorful peasant design, Quimper is a French faience that dates to the 17th century. As times and styles changed, patterns were also influenced but still continued to have a certain charm that is special to Quimper.

Reference: Sue and Al Bagdade, *Warman's English & Continental Pottery & Porcelain,* 3rd ed, Krause Publications, 1998.

For additional listings, see *Warman's Antiques and Collectibles Price Guide.*

Box, horn shape, male peasant with bagpipe, décor riche border, "Henroit Quimper" mark .. 565.00

Butter dish, cov, 2 small chips 350.00

Cake plate, pedestal base, black haired male peasant playing bagpipes, surrounded by floral sprays and floral garland border, pattern repeated on underside and base, mkd "HR Quimper" on front................................. 385.00

Cigarette holder, brown bust of camel on sides, dark red and blue arrowheads on border, blue shaped base, mkd "Henriot Quimper 82F" mark......... 575.00

Cookie plate, female peasant, blue, orange, red, and green florals, dark red inner chain border, orange and blue outlined rim, blue handles, yellow ground, mkd "Henriot Quimper France 110"................................. 200.00

Cup and saucer, orange, yellow, green and blue bird, orange borders, mkd "Henriot Quimper France" 125.00

Plate, male peasant in blue pantaloons, green jacket, black hat, green, yellow, blue and rust florals, green and rust border with blue dots, yellow, green, and blue lined rim, "HB" mark, 9" dia 300.00

Tray, Breton Broderie pattern, male and female portraits facing each other in center, wide cobalt blue border with raised orange dashes and dots, scalloped rim, "HB Quimper" mark......... 325.00

For exciting collecting trends and newly expanded areas look for the following symbols:

⊙ Hot Topic

☆ New Warman's Listing

(May have been in another Warman's title.)

❖ Racing Collectibles, Auto

"Start your engines" is music to the ears of racing collectors. Auto racing has become one of the hottest spectator sports of the 1990s. This category looks at some of the collectibles spawned by motor sports.

Collectors' Club: National Indy 500 Collectors Club, 10505 N. Delaware St., Indianapolis, IN 46280.

Also see NASCAR

Bottle, Jim Beam, Indianapolis 500, 1970 ....50.00
Hot Wheels, Hydropane, 1997, NRFP 5.00
Indianapolis 500 program, 1964 ....36.00

Floyd Clymer's Indianapolis Race History, 1947, $40; *Floyd Clymer's 1961 Indianapolis 500 Mile Race Yearbook*, 1961, $70.

Lighter, Zippo, Indianapolis 500
1994 ....50.00
1997 ....30.00
Photograph, wire service photo, 1989 Indianapolis 500
Rick Mears with wife Chris and father Bill 3.50
Rich Vogler..........................3.50
Tom Bigelow........................3.50
Trading cards
1992 Grid Formula 1, Premier Edition, factory sealed, 200 cards 5.00
1996, Indy 500 Racing League inaugural season card set and Racing Champions die-cast pace car, box opened, cards sealed...........................16.00

❖ Racing Collectibles, Other

If you're not into auto racing, there are other racing collectibles that can be found at flea markets. Keep your eyes open for air racing, dog racing, and other fast-paced collectibles.

Collectors' Club: Sport of Kings Society, 1406 Annen Lane, Madison, WI 53711.

Ashtray, Kentucky Derby, 1976, glass 29.00
Book, *Tactics Strategy Yacht Racing*, Joachim Schult, 1970, Dodd Mead.................................10.00
Cigarette card, World's Marathon Record Set by W. Kolehmainen of Finland, 1925...................8.00
Cup, restaurant china, Beautiful Wheeling Downs, Shenango, 3-1/4" h 29.00
Pinback button
American Air Races, mechanic, red and cream, 1923 .....50.00
Dan Patch Days, brown horse, white ground, 1967, Savage, Minn. commemorative celebration 25.00
Jockey portrait, American Pepsin Gum 30.00
Los Angeles National Air Races, red and white, 1928.......75.00

Postcard
Dog racing, Hialeah, Miami, Fla. 7.00
Greyhound track, Derby Lane, St. Petersburg, Fla. 4.00
Toy, Racing Motorcycle, litho tin, friction, Japan, 1960s, 3-3/4" l 18.00

❖ Radio Characters and Personalities

The golden age of radio created a whole cadre of heroes and characters for the listeners. Like the stars of today, these folks had fan clubs and created premiums and memorabilia to meet the demands of the earliest collectors.

Periodicals: *Friends of Old Time Radio*, P.O. Box 4321, Hamden, CT 06514; *Hello Again*, P.O. Box 4321, Hamden, CT 06514; *Nostalgia Digest and Radio Guide*, P.O. Box 421, Morton Grove, IL 60053; *Old Time Radio Digest*, 10280 Gunpowder Rd, Florence, KY 41042.

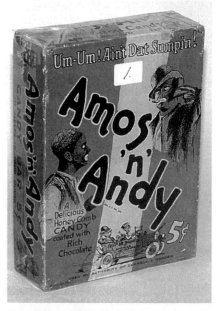

Amos 'n' Andy candy box, cardboard, Williamson Candy Co., 12" high, 8-1/2" wide, $280.

Collectors' Clubs: National Lum & Abner Society, #81 Sharon Blvd, Dora, AL 35062; North American Radio Archives, 134 Vincewood Dr, Nicholasville, KY 40356; Radio Collectors of America, 8 Ardsley Circle, Brockton, MA 02402.

Blotter, The Shadow, orange, blue, and white, red silhouette, 1940s 28.00

Book

All About Amos 'n' Andy and Their Creators Correl & Gosden, 1929, 128 pgs, illus 55.00

'R You Listening? Tony Wons, radio scrapbook, CBS, Reilly & Lee, 1931, 1st ed., dj ...9.00

Flashlight, Jack Armstrong, cardboard, red metal ends, c1939 ....25.00

Game, Amos 'n' Andy Shooting Game, Transogram Co., early 1930s, wear.......................75.00

Magazine, *Post*
Arthur Godfrey, 1955 ....10.00
Jack Benny article, 1963....15.00

Map, Jimmy Allen, full color, printed letter on back, 1934.........125.00

Membership badge, Pilot Patrol, Phantom...........................32.00

Newsletter, Jimmy Allen, red, white, and green holiday design and signatures on front cover, black and white photos on back, 4 pgs 65.00

Photo, Fiber McGee and Molly, black and white glossy, cast members, late 1930s, 8-1/4" x 12" 40.00

Pinback Button
Adventurers Club, Frank Buck, 1936 ....20.00
Magic Club, Mandrake the Magician 60.00
Uncle Don, Taystee Bread 55.00

Puzzle, Amos 'n' Andy, Pepsodent premium, 1931 ....42.00

Ring, Jack Armstrong, Dragon's Eye, crocodile design, green stone, 1940 ....150.00

Stamp album, Jimmie Allen Flying Club Stamp Album, stamps mounted inside, 1936........85.00

Valentine, Joe Penner, mechanical diecut, Joe holding duck on shoulder, inscribed "I'll Gladly Buy A Duck," c1935 ....30.00

Whistle, Jimmie Allen, brass, c1936 ....30.00

Whistle ring, Jack Armstrong, Egyptian symbols, orig mailing envelope, c1938......................135.00

❖ Radios

Today a radio brings us news, weather, and some tunes. But to generations past, it brought all those things plus laughter, companionship, and entertainment. The mechanical device that allowed connection to this new exciting world was developed and refined at the beginning of the 20th century. New technology caused changes in the shapes and materials of early radio receivers.

References: There are many older reference books to help identify radios.

Periodicals: *Antique Radio Classified*, P.O. Box 2, Carlisle, MA, 01741; *Antique Radio Topics*, P.O. Box 28572, Dallas, TX 75228; *Horn Speaker*, P.O. Box 1193, Mabank, TX 75147; *Radio Age*, 636 Cambridge Rd, Augusta, GA 30909; *Transistor Network*, RR1, Box 36, Bradford, NH 03221.

Collectors' Clubs: Antique Radio Club of America, 300 Washington Trails, Washington, PA 15301; Antique Wireless Assoc., 59 Main St., Bloomfield, NY 14469; New England Antique Radio Club, RR1, Box 36, Bradford, NH 03221; Vintage Radio & Phonograph Society, Inc., P.O. Box 165345, Irving, TX 75016.

Also see: Transistor Radios

Arvin, #522A, ivory metal case, 1941 ....65.00

Crosley, Liftella, 1-N, cathedral 185.00

Novelty
Green Giant Niblets corn box 30.00
Hi-C Berry Berry juice box 39.00
Jaguar XKE, plastic, Japan, 1960s, no antenna 75.00
Pet evaporated milk can 49.00
Radio Shack D-cell battery 38.00

RCA Victor radio, Art Deco styling, $200.

Twix candy bar, orig box.... 60.00
Philco Deco, Model 39-7, restored 185.00
RCA Victor, marbleized Catalin, rusty red, tuner not working 695.00
Stromberg-Carlson, "The Dynatomic," Model 1500-H, Bakelite 65.00
Zenith
Model H511W long-distance radio 110.00
Table radio, Bakelite, mkd 7G01Z, 8" h, 14" w, 8" d 79.00
Model 808, tombstone radio, 1934, no sound........... 175.00
Model 500D, plastic, 1959 .... 55.00

❖ Raggedy Ann

Who's always got a smile? Of course, it's Raggedy Ann. This happy creation of Johnny Gruelle has lived on for decades. You can find her, Andy, their dog and friends in children's literature and all kinds of decorative accessories.

Reference: Susan Ann Garrison, *The Raggedy Ann & Andy Family Album*, 3rd ed. Schiffer Publishing, 2000.

Children's book
Raggedy Ann & Hoppy Toad, McLoughlin, 1940 .... 95.00
Raggedy Ann & Laughing Brook, Perks, 1946 .... 30.00
Raggedy Ann & Marcella's First Day At School, Wonder Book, #588 .... 22.00

**Raggedy Ann and Andy, 15"
high, pair, $25.**

Raggedy Ann Stories, Volland,
1918, 1st ed., Johnny Gruelle,
color pictures, light use
....65.00
*Sweet and Dandy Sugar Candy
Scratch and Sniff Book*,
Golden Press, 1976, well read
.... 15.00
Cookie jar
California Originals, incised mark
on lid and "859 USA,"
13-3/4" h 175.00
Certified International, 11" h
.... 125.00
Creamer, figural, foil label, Royal
Sealy, 4-1/2" h 35.00
Doll
Georgene Novelties, 1947, 19" h
......................................265.00
Hasbro Commemorative Edi-
tion, 1996, 12" h............40.00
Knickerbocker, Raggedy Ann
and Andy, 1960s, 30" h
......................................250.00
Game, Raggedy Ann's Magic Peb-
ble Game, Milton Bradley, copyright 1941 Johnny Gruelle Co.,
orig box 95.00
Lunch box, plastic, Raggedy Ann
and Andy on front, orig thermos
....75.00
Music box, ceramic, Raggedy Ann
and Andy, plays "This Old Man"
....45.00
Nodder, 5" dia head, 5-1/2" h
.... 175.00
Print, copy of orig Johnny Gruelle
drawing, 6" x 9" 35.00
Pop-up book
Raggedy Ann and Andy, 45 rpm
record, 1974, played with
....5.00

*Raggedy Ann & the Daffy Taffy
Pull*, 1972 ....15.00

❖ Railroad Collectibles

All Aboard! Transportation of
goods and passengers across this
great country was a dream of the
early railroad men. Today, we take it
for granted that these giants will
keep moving along tracks laid so
many years ago. Collectors can tell
you about their favorite rail lines or
types of collectibles.

Periodicals: *Key, Lock and Lantern*,
3 Berkeley Heights Park, Bloomfield,
NJ 07003; *Main Line Journal*, P.O.
Box 121, Streamwood, IL 60107;
Railfan & Railroad, P.O. Box 700,
Newton, NJ 07860-0700; *Trains*,
P.O. Box 1612, Waukesha, WI
53187; *US Rail News,* P.O. Box
7007, Huntingdon Woods, MI 48070.

Collectors' Clubs: Canadian Rail-
road Historical Association, 120 Rue
St. Pierre, St. Constant, Quebec J5A
2G9 Canada; Chesapeake & Ohio
Historical Society Inc., P.O. Box 79,
Clifton Forge, VA 24422; Illinois
Central Railroad Historical Society,
14818 Clifton Park, Midlothian, IL
60445; New York Central System
Historical Society, Inc., P.O. Box
58994, Philadelphia, PA 19102-
8994; Railroad Enthusiasts, 102
Dean Rd. Brookline, MA 02146;
Railroad Club of America, Inc., P.O.
Box 8292, Chicago, IL 60680; Rail-
roadiana Collectors Association, 795
Aspen Drive, Buffalo Grove, IL
60089; Railway and Locomotive His-
torical Society, P.O. Box 1418, West-
ford, MA 01886; Twentieth Century
Railroad Club, 329 West 18th St.,
Suite 902, Chicago, IL 60616.
Book, *Oliphant's Earning Power of
Railroads 1946*, James H. Oliphant & Co., 1946, 556 pgs...10.00
Brochure, Florida East Coast Rail-
way & Steamship Co., January,
1900, 39 pgs...................150.00
Button, uniform, "Baggage Master,"
silvertone, 3/4" dia 8.00

Caboose marker, Atlantic Coast Line
RR Co., 1900, 4-way lamp
.... 385.00
Calendar, Burlington Zephyr, 1943
.... 90.00
Catalog, Erie Railroad, Co., New
York, NY, 32 pgs, 1918 ..... 42.00
China, dish, Santa Fe Super Chief
.... 65.00
Coaster, Central RR, New Jersey,
Statue of Liberty logo, set of 6
.... 15.00
Coloring book, Union Pacific RR
giveaway, 29 pgs, 1954 .... 20.00
Commemorative plate, 10-1/2" dia,
B & O Railroad, blue transfer
scene of Harper's Ferry, Lam-
berton China, 13-1/4" dia turned
wood frame 165.00
Creamer, Baltimore & Ohio RR,
Centenary pattern, Lamberton
China, 3-3/4" h 210.00
Funnel, Pennsylvania RR, metal,
9" h 40.00
Hat rack, overhead type, coach,
wood and brass, 6 brass double-
sided hooks..................... 200.00
Head rest cover, PRR, tan ground,
brown logo, 15" x 18"........ 15.00
Lantern, Penn Central RR, red globe
with logo, Adlake, 10" h 95.00
Magazine, *Railway Age* 5.00
Membership card, American Associ-
ation Railroad Ticket Agents,
1931................................. 10.00
Menu, Amtrak, Good Morning, single
card, 7" x 11"....................... 3.50

**Brotherhood Railroad Trainmen
button, $5.**

Padlock, Rock Island, orig key
....35.00
Pass
    Ft Wayne, Cincinnati & Louis-
       ville and White Water, 2-1/2" x
       3-3/4" white card, green
       accents, purple ink stamp fac-
       simile signature of president,
       1889 ....12.00
    Ohio, Indiana, and Western,
       2-1/4" x 3-3/4", black and
       white, ornately printed, signed
       in ink by general manager,
       1889 ....12.00
Patch, South Shore Line, embroi-
    dered, 3-3/8" x 1-1/2" 9.00
Plate, Baltimore & Ohio RR,
    Shenango, 10-1/2" dia.....120.00
Ribbon, Brotherhood of Railroad
    Men, Grand Union Picnic, Har-
    risburg, PA, June 27, 1901,
    1-7/8" x 3-3/4", beige, gold
    accent lettering..................10.00
Sign, Seaboard RR, "Explosives,"
    1948 ....19.00
Spike, chromed, Chesapeake &
    Ohio RR, engraved 1944-1970,
    retirement presentation, 6" l
    ....25.00
Step, Pullman RR Station, wood,
    hand cut out on top, 21" w, 10" h
    ....25.00
Sugar tongs, Canadian Pacific, SP,
    mkd "England"...................20.00
Timetable
    Atchison, Topeka & Santa Fe,
       1954 ....12.50
    Erie Railroad, 1907............32.00
    L&N Kansas City Southern, 1955
    ....8.50
    Southern Pacific RR, 1915
    ....22.00

✪ Ramp Walkers

Here's a collectible where the prices might be a surprise to you. Remember those little plastic toys we all played with as a kid, no batteries required, just a sturdy surface that we could tilt so the little critter could walk away. Well, today collectors are walking all over flea markets to find them.

Cow, plastic, 2-1/4" h...............45.00
Cowgirl, plastic, c1945, 6-1/2" h
....95.00

California Raisin ramp walker, 4-3/4" high, $3.

Donald Duck, pushing wheelbarrow,
    Marx, plastic, 1950s.........120.00
Elephant, plastic, Hong Kong,
    2-1/4" h 65.00
Farmer, plastic, 2-5/8" h...........60.00
Hop and Hop, marching soldiers,
    Marx, 2-3/4" h 20.00
Little Girl, plastic, orig weight ball,
    6-1/2" h 115.00
Mickey Mouse, 3-1/4" h...........24.00
Nanny pushing carriage...........22.00
Penguin Ramp, plastic, Hong Kong,
    2-5/8" h 60.00
Popeye and Wimpy, plastic, Marx,
    c1964, orig box, never played
    with 80.00
Soldier, wood and cloth, c1920,
    4-3/4" h 65.00

✪ Razor Blade Banks

Razor blade banks were designed as a safe place to deposit used razor blades, hence the name. Just because they were useful, they didn't have to be ordinary. Many ceramic manufacturers created whimsical figural banks, which nicely complement the tin and advertising razor blade banks also found at flea markets. The listings below are all for ceramic or pottery banks.

Barber head, Ceramic Arts Studio
....82.00
Barber pole 80.00

Frog 15.50
Happy shaver, Cleminson.......18.00
Hobo 20.00
Mule, adv for Listerine on bottom
....25.00

✪ Reamers

Feel like putting the squeeze on something? How about an orange, lemon, or grapefruit? Reamer collectors know just how to make their favorite juice and end up sweetly smiling when making a new purchase to add to their collection. They will tell you that reamers can be found in all types of materials, shapes, and sizes.

Collectors' Club: National Reamer Collectors Association, 47 Midline Court, Gaithersburg, MD 20878.

China
    Bavaria, white, red, yellow, and
       green flowers dec, gold trim, 2
       pc type..........................60.00
    England, white, orange, and yel-
       low flowers, 3-1/2" h 68.00
    Germany, Goebel, yellow, 5" dia
    ....60.00
Figural, china
    Elephant, nick on trunk.... 300.00
    Pear, yellow and orange glaze,
       green leaves, 2 pc type
    ....55.00
Glass
    Pink, Criss-Cross, Hazel Atlas,
       orange size.................295.00
    Transparent green, pointed
       cone, tab handle, Federal
    ....30.00
    Vaseline green, emb "Sunkist,"
       McKee 48.00

Criss Cross reamer, green, 6" diameter, $15.

Metal

Dunlap's Improved, iron hinge, 9-1/2" l 35.00

Kwicky Juicer, aluminum, pan style, Quam Nicholas Co. 10.00

Nasco-Royal, scissors type, 6" l 10.00

Wagner Ware, cast aluminum, skillet shape, long red seed dams beneath cone, 2 spouts 20.00

❖ Records

Spin me a tune! Records have evolved from early cylinders for Thomas Edison's first phonographs to the vinyl disks of today. This music can cross into other collecting areas devoted to specific artists such as Elvis or because of the subject matter on the record's album sleeve or protective box. Quickly gaining in popularity are children's records having an image imprinted on the vinyl.

Periodical: *Goldmine*, 700 E State St, Iola, WI 54990.

Reference: Tim Neely, *Goldmine Price Guide to 45 RPM Records*, 3rd ed., Krause Publications, 2001. Plus there are many other good reference books available.

ABC Wide World of Sports, 33 rpm, 1970, narrated by Jim McKay 25.00

The 500 Hats of Bartholomew Cubbins, RCA Victor, $40.

Allen Brothers, *Glorious Night Blues,* Victor 50.00

Belafonte, Harry, LP, *Streets I Have Walked,* 1963....................35.00

Blue Ridge Mountain Girls, *She Came Rolling Down The Mountain,* Champion 12.00

Bye Bye Birdy, Columbia, orig cast, 1980.................................17.50

Chubby Checker, *Limbo Party,* Parkway, LP, 1962 ....20.00

Chuck Berry, *Johnny Bgoode,* 78 RPM, Chess 10.00

Crosby, Bing, *The Songs I Love,* six long play records, mint in orig case 75.00

Disneyland Davy Crockett, record storybook, copyright 1971, 24 pgs......................................35.00

Duke Ellington, *Jubilee Stomp,* Okeh, 41013, 1938............15.00

Glenn Miller, *Glenn Miller Story,* Unbreakable, LP, Decca, 1954 ....22.00

Oklahoma, Decca, orig cast, 1953 ....42.00

Presley, E., *Touch of Gold,* Volume 2, EPA-5101, maroon label 85.00

Roy Rogers, Dale Evans, *Jesus Loves Me,* Camden, 1960, LP 30.00

Shari Lewis Party Record, 6" sq black and white thin cardboard vinyl-coated sheet, 5-3/4" dia vinyl record with black and white photo of Shari, 2 puppets, Allied Creative Services, Inc., c1950 ....25.00

Superman the Movie, 1978, 2 record set, LP 24.00

Teardrops, *The Stars Are Out Tonight,* Josie 30.00

To Kill A Mocking Bird, Ava, 1963 ....15.00

Welling & McGhee, *Ring the Bells of Heaven,* Champion, 1966 ....17.50

❖ Red Wing Pottery

Red Wing is a generic term that covers several manufacturers that produced utilitarian stoneware and ceramic dinnerware in Red Wing, Minnesota. The trademark red wing is the most recognizable symbol used in Red Wing, but other marks also identify the pottery.

Paneled bowl with red and blue sponging, Red Wing, 10-1/4" diameter, $150.

Collectors' Clubs: Red Wing Collectors Society, P.O. Box 50, Red Wing, MN 55066; The RumRill Society, P.O. Box 2161, Hudson, OH 44326.

For additional listings, see *Warman's Americana & Collectibles* and *Warman's American Pottery & Porcelain.*

Celery dish, Lotus pattern, Concord shape, 11-1/4" l 35.00

Cookie jar, Chef Pierre, rim chip, discoloration 40.00

Crock, 2 gallon, large wing ... 100.00

Floor vase, embossed designs, bronze-like glaze, Red Wing Union Stoneware Co., hairline, 22" h 330.00

Jug, 5 gallon, beehive shape, Red Wing Union Stoneware Co. 635.00

Pitcher, Bobwhite, 12" h.......... 65.00

Platter, Random Harvest, 13" l 30.00

Soup bowl, Lotus pattern, Concord shape, 6-3/8" dia, set of 6 .... 70.00

Bob White handled gravy, Red Wing, 9-1/2" long, $25.

Teapot, Town & Country, rust color, chip 175.00

Vase

Cornucopia, light gray with burgundy ivy, 8-3/8" h 65.00

Pedestal, Classic line, blue, 8-1/4" h 27.50

Water cooler, 3 gallon, no lid 400.00

❖ Redware

American colonists began making redware in the late 17th century, using the same clay as for bricks and roof tiles. Ready availability of the clay meant that items could be produced in large quantities. The lead-glazed items retained their reddish color, hence the name redware, although various colors could be obtained by adding different metals to the glaze. Modern craftsmen have kept the redware tradition alive and can be found working in several parts of the country today.

References: Susan and Al Bagdade, *Warman's American Pottery and Porcelain*, 2nd ed., Krause Publications, 2000; William C. Ketchum Jr., *American Redware*, Henry Holt and Company, 1991; Kevin McConnell, *Redware: America's Folk Art Pottery*, Schiffer Publishing, 1988.

Bank, acorn form, painted brown, gold textured cap, 4-1/2" h 264.00

Bowl, Foltz Pottery, tulip sgraffito decor in cobalt, dated 1980, 14-1/2" dia 137.50

Canning jar, John Bell, orange glaze, cylindrical shape, impressed "J. Bell" on bottom, side repairs, chips, 5-5/8" h, 4-5/8" dia 425.00

Charger, Breininger Pottery, flowers in green and brown, yellow slip ground, green flourish decor around edges, 14" dia 93.50

Crock, John Bell, light greenish-brown glaze, slightly rounded sides, impressed "John Bell" below collar, cracks, 4-3/8" dia 270.00

Fish mold

Stahl Pottery (Powder Valley, Pa.), mottled brown glaze, dated 1939, glaze imperfections, 3" h, 11" l 165.00

Unmkd, vintage, spiraled flutes, scalloped rim, brown sponging on pinkish-amber ground, wear, slight hairline, 8" dia 137.50

Jar

Stahl Pottery, dark reddish-brown glaze, ovoid, shoulder handles, mkd "Made in Stahl Pottery by Thomas Stahl, April 16, 1936," chips, hairline, 3-3/4" h 82.50

Unmkd, vintage, mottled brown glaze, tooled lines, flared rim, handle, 5-1/8" h, 4-5/8" dia 330.00

Jug, ovoid, dark-brown glaze, black running spots around shoulder and strap handle, tooled foot and neck, old edge chips, 8" h 550.00

Pie plate

2-line swag decor, yellow slip, imperfections, 11-1/2" dia 247.50

3-line, yellow slip, wavy decor, wear, hairlines, 8-1/2" dia 440.00

4-line, yellow slip, wear, hairline, 8" dia 412.50

❖ Regal China Corporation

Here's a chinaware maker that was owned by Jim Beam Distilleries. Their wares include those wonderful decanters you think of as Beam bottles, plus several types of advertising wares and items made for clients including Quaker Oats and Kraft Foods.

Canister, Old McDonald's Farm, gold trim

Coffee, horse lid 235.00

Flour, Grandpa lid 225.00

Pretzels, Grandma lid 300.00

Sugar, Grandma lid 225.00

Cookie jar, cov

Barn 300.00

Kraft Teddy Bear 90.00

Quaker Oats 85.00

Creamer, Old McDonald's, rooster 135.00

Decanter, Jim Beam, empty

Antique Trader, 1968 .... 10.00

Cat, 1967 .... 10.00

Cherubs, 1974 .... 12.00

Ford, 1978 .... 25.00

Hawaii, 50th State 15.00

Ohio 10.00

Sailfish, 1957, 14" h 10.00

Telephone, 1979 .... 13.00

Lamp base, 12-3/4" h, Davy Crockett 125.00

Salt and pepper shakers, pr, Old McDonald's Farm, barrels, gold trim, 4" h 125.00

Teapot, Old McDonald's Farm, duck, 7-1/2" h 300.00

Tobacco jar, Fox, Jim Beam 60.00

❖ Religious Collectibles

Hunting for religious collectibles at flea markets is a great idea, but not in lieu of going to church services. (Well, perhaps before or after Sunday services.) However, no matter when you shop, you're likely to find something of interest.

"My Kitchen Prayer" plaque, $15.

Collectors' Clubs: Foundation International for Restorers of Religious Medals, P.O. Box 2652, Worcester, MA 01608; Judaica Collectors Society, P.O. Box 854, Van Nuys, CA 91408.

Book, *Jesus Lover of My Soul* by C. Wesley, 1907, 20 pgs, spine damage, mildew 10.00

Figurine
    Plastic, Madonna, blue rhinestone halo, paint peeling, 3-3/4" h 4.00
    Precious Moments, "Jesus Loves Me", 1976, 1 of orig 21 .... 55.00
    Precious Moments, "Jesus Is The Answer," cross mark, 4-1/2" h 105.00

Menorah, porcelain, Lenox, 6" h, 12" l 100.00

Paperweight, Star of David design, white stardust canes, Millefiori garland, cobalt ground, Perthshire, limited to production of 300, 2-1/2" dia 110.00

Pinback button, Vacation Bible School, tin, 3/4" dia 3.00

Print, *Head of Christ* by Warner Sallman, framed, 16-1/4" x 13-1/2" 35.00

❖ Riviera

This popular Homer Laughlin pattern was introduced in 1938 and sold by the Murphy Company. Not all pieces were marked, but some have a gold backstamp. Riviera was produced in Laughlin's Century shape in dark blue (considered rare), light green, ivory, mauve blue, red, and yellow.

Periodical: *Laughlin Eagle,* 1270 63rd Terrace, South, St. Petersburg, FL 33705.

Butter dish, 1/2 lb, red 150.00
Casserole, cov
    Light green 95.00
    Mauve blue 110.00
Creamer, light green or red 18.00
Cup and saucer, ivory 125.00
Deep plate, ivory 45.00
Juice pitcher, mauve blue 350.00
Juice tumbler, light green 85.00

Nappy, yellow 50.00
Oatmeal bowl
    Ivory 95.00
    Light green 85.00
    Mauve blue 85.00
    Red 95.00
    Yellow 85.00
Sugar bowl, cov
    Light green 30.00
    Mauve blue 45.00
    Red 45.00
Teapot, light green 185.00
Tumbler, handle
    Light green 55.00
    Mauve 75.00
    Red 95.00

❖ Road Maps

Today's road maps are a far cry from the early guide books that provided written descriptions of how to get from Point A to Point B. While most maps are readily affordable, earlier examples, especially those with colorful covers, have taken the hobby to a new price level.

1928 Texaco road map, $350.

Central & Western United States, Deep Rock Gasoline, 1960s 10.00
Hawaii, Shell Oil Co., 1961, 1/4" tear 8.00
Illinois, Sinclair, 1962 .... 3.00
Indiana, Rand McNally, 1924 .. 95.00
Indiana Official Highway Map, 1970-71 .... 3.00
Mid-Atlantic Region, Delaware, Maryland, Virginia and West Virginia Road Map with Pictorial Guide, Esso, 1952 .... 7.50
Nevada, Chevron/Standard Oil, 1960 .... 5.00
Pennsylvania Official Highway Map, 1972-73 .... 3.00
Portland, Flying A, 1963 .... 8.00

❖ Robots

These mechanical marvels have delighted moviegoers and science fiction buffs for years. The first documented robot is Atomic Robot Man, created in 1948. The Japanese dominated the robot market. By the 1970s, production had moved to Hong Kong and other foreign countries. Some older Japanese robots are commanding big prices (see boxed story).

Reference: Jim Bunte, Dave Hallman and Heinz Mueller, *Vintage Toys: Robots and Space Toys*, Antique Trader Books, 1999.

Periodicals: *Robot World & Price Guide*, P.O. Box 184, Lenox Hill Station, New York, NY 10021; *Toy Shop,* 700 E State St, Iola, WI 54990.

For additional listings, see *Warman's Americana & Collectibles*.

Action figure, Robot Zone, five 2-1/2" h figures, 1985, mkd "Made in British Colony of Hong Kong," MOC 25.00
Bank, wind-up, plastic, dumps coin in slots when revolving, mkd "Made in Hong Kong," orig box 25.00
Figure
    Lost in Space, chrome version, Trendmasters Classic ... 60.00
    Rosie, Jetson's, plastic, Applause, orig sticker, 1990 .... 25.00

Top, Shogun Rocket, plastic, Mattel, 1978, MIP 15.00

Toy

Cosmos Robot, battery-operated, plastic, Kamco, China, 1980s, MIB, 12-1/2" h ... 38.00

Fighting Robot, tin litho, battery-operated, Japan, 1960s, C-8.5 .... 245.00

Lost in Space, battery-operated, Remco, C-9 .... 685.00

Moon Stroller, wind-up, arms swing, moving radar, mkd "Made in Hong Kong," 3-1/4" h, orig box with slight wear 35.00

Morgan TR2 Talking Robot, Hong Kong, orig box 65.00

Mystery Action, battery-operated, bump-and-go-action, plastic, mkd "Made in Hong Kong," orig box, 8-1/2" h 25.00

Rascal, wind-up, mkd "1978, Tomy Corp., Made in Taiwan," MIP, 2" h 20.00

Robot Sentinel, battery-operated, walks, arms move, lights, 4 shooting missiles, plastic, mkd "Made in China by Kamco," 1980s, 13" h, MIB 55.00

Saturn, battery operated, walks, lights up eyes, mkd "Made in Hong Kong by Kamco," missiles missing, 13" h 38.00

Sentinel Robot, plastic, made by Kamco, China, 1980s, MIB, 13" h 31.00

Silver-colored, wind-up, mkd "Made in Hong Kong," 4" h, orig box 35.00

Robot driving a Mercedes, tin friction toy, gun sparks, $350.

SP-1, friction, blue and red space ship, Japan, 1950s, 6-1/2" l 330.00

Space Tank, ME 091, China, orig box, 1980s 275.00

Sparky Robot, wind-up, silver and red, flashes, 1950s, Japan, 8" h, C-9 .... 355.00

Tang, General Foods, 7-1/4" h 30.00

TR2 Talking, mkd "Made in Hong Kong," orig box 65.00

Ultra 7, wind-up, made by Biliken, Japan, orig box, 8-1/2" h 300.00

❖ Rock 'n Roll

"Rock, Rock, Rock Around the Clock!" Remember the good ol' days with *American Bandstand* and the great singers Dick Clark introduced us to? No matter what kind of music you associate with rock 'n roll, chances are good that some neat collectibles will be rocking at your favorite flea market.

Reference: Joe Hilton and Greg Moore, *Rock-n-Roll Treasures*, Collector Books, 1999.

Belt, Michael Jackson, metal buckle, Lee, 1984, 29" l 30.00

Book

KISStory, autographed by band members, coffee table size 175.00

Mick Jagger: Primitive Cool, Christopher Sanford, St. Martin's, 1994 .... 12.00

Rock Elvis, 1994, 240 pgs 24.00

The Honeymoon Is Over, Shirley and Pat Boone, autographed, 1977, 185 pgs 22.50

Woodstock 69, Scholastic Book Services, 1970 .... 25.00

Book cover, orange and red title paper, 3 black and white book covers, one with Pat Boone, one with Sal Mineo, third generic singer, 1958 Cooga Mooga Products, Inc., N.Y., unused in clear plastic bag 18.00

Colorforms, KISS, MIB 27.50

Comic book

AC/DC, early 1990s 15.00

Frank Zappa, #32, 1991 .... 20.00

Jane's Addiction, early 1990s 15.00

Janis Joplin, #63 .... 15.00

Music Comic #4, The Cure, complete with two trading cards 20.00

Queensryche, early 1990s 20.00

Doll outfit, Michael Jackson, c1984, LIN, MOC 28.00

Figure, Dave Clark Five, Remco, Rick, Mike, Dennis 95.00

Game, Duran Duran into the Arena, Milton Bradley, 1985 .... 18.00

Halloween costume, child's, Donny, Marie, or Jimmy Osmond, orig costume, mask, box, each 35.00

Lunch box, The Osmonds, metal, orig thermos, unused, 1973 .... 95.00

Magazine, *Frank Zappa Record Review*, Feb, 1980 ....25.00
Pinback button, black and white photo
    Bob-a-Loo, WABC, disc jockey 70.00
    Dick Clark, dark green ground 15.00
    Frankie Avalon-Venus, bright pink ground 25.00
Record case, cardboard, full color photo and signature of Dick Clark, blue, white plastic handle, brass closure, holds 45 rpm records 45.00
Salt and pepper shakers, pr, ceramic feet, mkd "Rock-N-Roll Indiana," mkd "Japan," 2-3/4" l 6.00
Tie clip, Dick Clark *American Bandstand*, gold-tone metal.......15.00
View-Master reel, Last Wheelbarrow to Pokeyville, Monkees, orig booklet...............................12.00

❖ Rockwell, Norman

One of America's most beloved artists, Norman Rockwell, was born in 1894. By the time he died in 1978, he had created more than 2,000 paintings. Many of these paintings were reproduced as magazine covers, illustrations, calendars, etc. Rockwell's ability to capture the essence of everyday life has attracted people to his work for generations. Besides the artwork, many of Rockwell's illustrations have been used in designs of limited-edition collectibles.

Collectors' Club: Rockwell Society of America, P.O. Box 705, Ardsley, NY 10502.
For additional listings, see *Warman's Antiques and Collectibles Price Guide* and *Warman's Americana & Collectibles.*
Bell, Love's Harmony, 1976, wooden handle, 9" h 45.00
Dealer sign, porcelain figure standing next to plaque, c1980, 5-1/4" h...........................125.00
Doll, Mary Moline, made in Germany
    Anne 70.00
    Mimi 70.00
    Tina....................................70.00

***Saturday Evening Post* magazine, September 1958, Norman Rockwell cover, 14" x 11", $40.**

Figure
    Dave Grossman Designs, Inc., The Graduate, 1983 ......35.00
    Gorham, Jolly Coachman, 1982 ....50.00
    Lynell Studios, Cradle of Love, 1980 ....85.00
    Rockwell Museum, Bride and Groom, 1979 ....95.00
Ignot, Franklin Mint, Spirit of Scouting, 1972, 12 pc set 295.00
Magazine cover
    Boys' Life, June, 1947........45.00
    Family Circle, Dec, 1967....15.00
    Red Cross, April, 1918.......25.00
    Saturday Evening Post, Jan. 26, 1918 ....95.00
    Saturday Evening Post, Feb. 18, 1922 ....90.00
    Saturday Evening Post, April 19, 1950 ....85.00
    Saturday Evening Post, Sept. 7, 1957 ....35.00
    Saturday Evening Post, Jan. 13, 1962 ....20.00
    Scouting, Dec., 1944..........15.00
Plate
    Dave Grossman Designs, Huckleberry Finn, 1980 ....45.00
    Four Seasons, 1975, set of four 85.00
    Franklin Mint, The Carolers, 1972 ....175.00

Gorham, Boy Scout, 1975 ....65.00
Lynell Studios, Mother's Day, 1980 .... 45.00
River Shore, Jennie & Tina, 1982 ....45.00
Rockwell Museum, First Prom, 1979 .... 35.00
Rockwell Society, A Mother's Love, first edition, 1976 ....38.00
Royal Devon, One Present Too Many, 1979 ....30.00

❖ Rogers, Roy

This popular cowboy hero made a positive impression on many young minds. Today collectors are drawn to Roy Rogers memorabilia to remember and commemorate the morals and honesty he stressed.

Reference: Ron Lenius, *The Ultimate Roy Rogers Collectibles Identification and Price Guide*, Krause Publications, 2001. P. Allan Coyle, *Roy Rogers and Dale Evans Toys & Memorabilia*, Collector Books, 2000.

Collectors' Club: Roy Rogers-Dale Evans Collectors Association, P.O. Box 1166, Portsmouth, OH 45662-1166.
Camera 110.00
Comic book
    Roy Rogers #5, May 1948, Dell, wear........................... 100.00
    Roy Rogers #20, 1949, wear 20.00

***Roy Rogers and the Sure 'Nough Cowpoke*, Tell-A-Tale Books, Whitman, 1952, $40.**

Roy Rogers #72, 1953, wear 25.00
Guitar, orig box, 1950s 140.00
Horseshoe game, hard rubber horseshoes......................190.00
Lantern, cracked, incomplete, 8" h 75.00
Old Japan china plate from the Roy Rogers Museum, shows cactus varieties in the Western Desert, 7" dia 32.00
Pocketknife............................60.00
Ring, branding iron, brass, 1948, Quaker 195.00
Watch, Roy and Dale 120.00

❖ Rookwood

Founded in 1880, Rookwood Pottery underwent a metamorphosis as it produced a varying line of wares that ranged from highly detailed artist-decorated vases to production-line figural paperweights. The distinctive mark used indicates the clay or body mark, the size, the decorator mark, a date mark, and the factory mark. Learning to accurately read these marks will enhance your understanding and appreciation for Rookwood Pottery.

Ashtray, owl, green high glaze, 1950, 4-1/4" h.................. 125.00
Bookend, elephant, white, 1936, 5-1/2" h............................225.00
Bowl, blue matte glaze, 1925, mkd as a second, 3-3/4" h, 9" dia 450.00
Candlestick, mauve, 1916, 7-3/4" h, base 5-1/8" dia 250.00
Cocktail shaker, green glaze, 1951, 12" h, 8" w 700.00

Rookwood 1929 fox ashtray, blue glaze, 6-3/4" diameter, chipped ear, $90.

Paperweight
Canary, white, 1946, 3-5/8" h 145.00
Cocker spaniel, 24k gold, 1985, 4" h..............................95.00
Gazelle, white, 1934, 4-1/2" h 250.00
Rooster, 1946, 5" h 350.00
Vase
High glaze, hand-painted floral decor by E.T. Hurley, 7-1/4" h 895.00
Matte glaze, Arts & Crafts style, blue, 1912, 8-3/8" h 440.00
Matte glaze, purple, 3 angular handles, 1929, 4-7/8" h 300.00
Vellum glaze, narcissus decor, E.T. Hurley, 1929, 6-7/8" h 1,320.00
Vellum glaze, grape decor, Margaret McDonald, 1912, 6-7/8" h 660.00

❖ Rose Bowls

A rose bowl is defined as a round or ovoid bowl with a small opening. Crimped, pinched, scalloped, petaled, and pleated designs are common. They held potpourri or rose petals.

Amethyst, irid finish, etched "Thos. Webb & Son, England," minor rim flakes, 4-1/2" h...........175.00
Bohemian, amber stained cut to clear, grape and vine dec, 3-1/2" h 20.00
Carnival glass, Northwood Drapery, marigold...........................325.00
Custard glass, ovoid, rose and swag dec, nutmeg stain highlights, ftd, chips on one foot 20.00
Fenton cranberry, orig stand....42.00
Milk glass, Katy pattern, Imperial 10.00
Pattern glass, Puritan pattern, 2-1/4" h 50.00
Porcelain, blue glaze over white base, white int., oval scene captioned "Water St., Shullsburg, Vt.," gold outline.................40.00
Satin
Blue shaded to white, DQ, 3-3/4" h..........................65.00
Raspberry pink shading to white, 4-1/2" h..........................25.00

Yellow, herringbone, 6" h... 65.00
Venetian, gold and pink, 4-1/2" dia 35.00

❖ Roselane Pottery

This California pottery was founded in 1938 in Pasadena. Production included dinnerware and accessories. Roselane Pottery is perhaps best known for its figures, many of which have jeweled eyes and are known as "Sparklers" to collectors.

Bust, Oriental, pearl luster glaze, 9" h, pr 30.00
Console bowl, black matte ext., turquoise glaze int., 1950s, 13-3/4" l 25.00
Figure, Sparklers
Basset Hound.................... 15.00
Cat..................................... 40.00
Chihuahua......................... 57.00
Deer, pair.......................... 15.00
Dog family 42.00
Elephant............................ 50.00
Giraffe 22.00
Quail, 6" h......................... 45.00
Siamese Cat and Kittens, 4-1/4" h 40.00
Swimming Duck 50.00

❖ Rosemeade Pottery

Located in Whapeton, North Dakota, from 1940 to 1961, this pottery created many figures and novelties. They are known for their accurate wildlife designs.

Ashtray
Bear, emb "Breckenridge, Minnesota" 315.00
Duck................................. 50.00
Bell, elephant 300.00
Boot, orig label "Rosemeade No. Dak.," 3-7/8" h.................. 30.00
Figure, Chinese Ringneck Pheasant, 11-1/2" l.................... 195.00
Flower frog, rust colored, script mark, 3" h......................... 25.00
Flower pot, tulip design, light green, 3" h 45.00
Pansy ring, white, 8-1/2" d, 2" h 35.00

Range shaker, Paul Bunyan.... 60.00
Salt and pepper shakers, pr
    Bears, 3" h 80.00
    Gopher, large 145.00
    Leaping deer.................... 145.00
    Mice 35.00
    Pheasants......................... 35.00
    Running Rabbits 145.00
    White duck, orig paper label
    .... 50.00
Vase, creamy green with pink high-
    lights, Arts and Crafts style, orig
    sticker, 1940, 5" h............ 125.00

❖ Rosenthal China

Rosenthal China has been made in Selb, Bavaria, since 1880. Major production centers around dinnerware and some accessories.

Cake plate, grape dec, scalloped
    ruffled edge, ruffled handles,
    12" w 75.00
Creamer and sugar, pate-sur-pate
    type blue cherries dec 125.00
Cup and saucer, San Souci pattern,
    white................................. 20.00

Rosenthal China hatpin holder, poppies decoration, gold accents, 4-7/8" high, $90.

Demitasse cup and saucer, Marie
    pattern 25.00
Figure, clown, 6" h 225.00
Lemon plate, handles, hp, peacock,
    early 1920s, sgd "Knapp"
    ....300.00
Plate, comic lion dec, 4" d 20.00
Vase
    Modeled owls on branch, 7" h
    ....165.00
    Multicolored roses, 11" h
    ....125.00

✪ Roseville Pottery

In 1892 the J.B. Owens Pottery was renamed Roseville Pottery Co., taking its name from the Ohio town where the manufacturer was based. From the late 19th century until the business was sold to Mosiac Tile Co. in 1954, Roseville produce a vast quantity of art pottery and dinnerware.

In the 1930s and 1940s the company hit full stride with numerous lines of mass-produced pottery that remain highly popular with collectors today. Unfortunately, reproductions of many of those designs were released in the 1990s. Although those imported reproductions can be easily detected by knowledgeable collectors, the fakes continue to fool many people who see the name Roseville and think they're buying a vintage piece of pottery.

Roseville Iris basket, pink to green glaze, 10" high, $180.

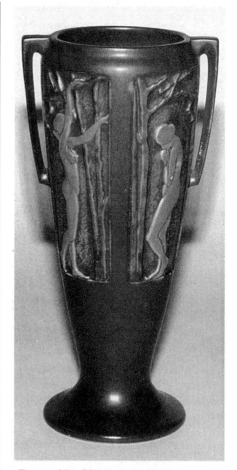

Roseville Silhouette vase, browns, 11-1/2" high, $600.

Reference: Mark Bassett, *Introducing Roseville Pottery*, Schiffer Publishing, 1999.

Collectors' Club: Roseville's of the Past, P.O. Box 656, Clarcona, FL 32710.

Reproduction Alert.

For additional listings, see *Warman's Antiques and Collectibles Price Guide, Warman's Americana & Collectibles,* and *Warman's American Pottery & Porcelain.*

Baby plate, Juvenile line, chicks
    motif, hairline 275.00
Basket
    Bleeding Heart, #360, 9-1/2" h
    .... 395.00
    Clematis, #389, 10" h 275.00
Bookend
    Bleeding Heart, green with pink,
    1 repaired, pr 335.00
    Peony, pink, #11, pr........ 315.00

TIAS Top 10

The following list ranks the most highly sought collectibles on the Internet during 2000.

1. Avon
2. China
3. Cookie jars
4. **Roseville**
5. Furniture
6. Noritake
7. Lamps
8. McCoy
9. Clocks
10. Books

Source: www.tias.com

Bowl, Persian, 3 handles, restoration, 3-1/8" h, 8" dia 295.00
Candlesticks, pr
    Columbine, blue, #1145 ..... 90.00
    Ixia, #1125, green 75.00
    Snowberry, mauve, #1CS1 .... 75.00
Conch shell, green, #453, 6" h 215.00
Cookie jar, Clemantis, brown 300.00
Cornucopia, #190, 6" h 220.00
Flowerpot and saucer, Zephyr Lily, green, #672, 5" h 255.00
Hanging basket, Zephyr Lily, green, small chip 245.00
Jardiniére
    Florentine, cream and green, 8" h, 12" dia 325.00
    Fuschia, #347, 6" h 395.00
Vase
    Blackberry, #572, 6" h 635.00
    Fuschia, brown, #898, 8" h 325.00
    Futura, gray/green, #380, 6" h 625.00
    Ming Tree, green, #581, 6" h 175.00
    Pine Cone, gold and brown, #838, 6" h 265.00
Wall pocket
    Apple Blossom, green 550.00
    Gardenia, brown, 8" h 150.00
    Maple Leaf, 8-1/2" h 75.00
    Snowberry, blue, 8" h 180.00
Window box, Zephyr Lily, green, #1393, 3" h, 10" l 210.00

❖ Royal Bayreuth

Another Bavarian firm, Royal Bayreuth traces its history to the late 1790s. The company is still in business, producing dinnerware. Royal Bayreuth is well known to collectors for its figural lines that were popular in the late 1880s. One interesting type of porcelain Royal Bayreuth introduced is Tapestry Ware. Placing a piece in fabric, then decorating and glazing and firing the item caused the texture of this ware.

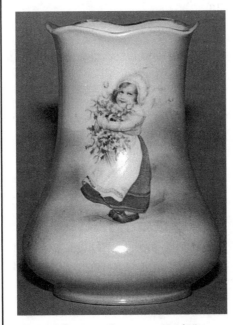

Royal Bayreuth vase, 5-1/4" high, $285.

Reference: Mary J. McCaslin, *Royal Bayreuth: A Collector's Guide, Book II*, Glass Press, 2000.

Collectors' Clubs: Royal Bayreuth Collectors Club, 926 Essex Circle, Kalamazoo, MI 49008; Royal Bayreuth International Collectors' Society, P.O. Box 325, Orrville, OH 44667.

For additional listings, see *Warman's Antiques and Collectibles Price Guide* and *Warman's English & Continental Pottery* and *Porcelain*.

Ashtray
    Devil and Cards 500.00
    Elk 225.00
Bowl, Snow Babies, 6" dia 325.00
Candy dish, lobster 140.00
Celery tray, tomato pattern 95.00
Cracker jar, grapes, green dec, no lid 95.00
Creamer, figural
    Bird of Paradise 225.00
    Clown, red 275.00
    Eagle 200.00
    Elk 55.00
    Frog, green 250.00
    Pear 290.00
Creamer, tapestry
    Brittany women, double handle, 4" h 125.00
    Mountain sheep, hunt scene, 4" h 110.00
Cup and saucer
    Boy with turkey 125.00
    Man in boat fishing 125.00
Hatpin holder, courting couple, cut-out base, gold dec, blue mark 400.00
Match holder, tapestry, Arab scene 100.00
Milk pitcher, 3-1/2" h, pinched spout, mountain sheep 125.00
Mustard, cov
    Sunbonnet Babies 395.00
    Tomato, figural leaf underplate 125.00
Pitcher, turkey and cock fighting, 7" h 375.00
Plate, 7-1/2" dia
    Man and dogs 95.00
    Man in boat fishing 95.00
Plate, boy and donkeys, 8-1/2" dia 95.00
Salt and pepper shakers, rose tapestry, pink roses, pr 375.00

Vase, peasant women and sheep, silver rim, 3 handles, blue mark 60.00

Wall pocket, strawberry 265.00

✿ Royal China

Manufactured in Sebring, Ohio, from 1924 to 1986, Royal China made a large variety of dinnerware patterns. Collectors today are particularly fond of several patterns, including Currier & Ives, Bucks County, Colonial Homestead, Fair Oaks, Memory Lane, Old Curiosity Shop, and Willow Ware.

Collectors' Club: Currier & Ives Dinnerware Collectors Club, RD 2, Box 394, Hollidaysburg, PA 16648.

For additional listings and more detailed history, see *Warman's Americana & Collectibles.*

Bread and butter plate
    Bucks County.......................2.50
    Old Curiosity Shop...............3.50
Butter dish, cov
    Colonial Homestead 30.00
    Willow Ware........................27.50
Casserole, cov
    Bucks County......................72.00
    Old Curiosity Shop, tab handles 100.00
Coffee mug
    Colonial Homestead 20.00
    Old Curiosity Shop..............30.00
    Willow Ware........................22.00
Creamer
    Currier and Ives 7.50
    Willow Ware..........................5.00

Old Curiosity Shop plate, Royal, 10-1/8" diameter, $5.

Cup and saucer
    Bucks County.......................3.75
    Colonial Homestead.............3.00
    Currier and Ives 4.50
    Memory Lane 5.00
    Willow Ware.........................4.50
Dinner plate
    Bucks County.......................5.00
    Colonial Homestead.............5.00
    Currier and Ives 6.00
    Old Curiosity Shop...............4.50
    Willow Ware.........................4.00
Fruit bowl
    Bucks County.......................2.75
    Currier and Ives 3.50
    Old Curiosity Shop...............3.00
Gravy boat, underplate, Old Curiosity Shop...................................28.00
Pie plate, Willow Ware, 10" dia 25.00
Platter
    Colonial Homestead, meat, 11-1/2" l 20.00
    Willow Ware, oval, 11" l......25.00
Salad plate
    Bucks County.......................8.25
    Willow Ware........................10.00
Salt and pepper shakers, pr
    Bucks County......................20.00
    Old Curiosity Shop.............20.00
Soup bowl
    Colonial Homestead.............8.50
    Willow Ware........................10.00
Sugar bowl
    Bucks County, tab handles 20.00
    Currier and Ives, angled handles 17.50
    Memory Lane, angled handles 12.00
Teapot, Old Curiosity Shop....100.00
Vegetable dish, divided, Fair Oaks 28.00

❖ Royal Copenhagen

Many collectors think of Royal Copenhagen as making blue and white Christmas plates. However, this Danish firm has also made dinnerware, figurines, and other tablewares.

Bowl, reticulated blue and white, round 125.00

Royal Copenhagen vase, dogwood spray and butterflies, 4-1/2" high, $170.

Christmas plate
    1981 .... 35.00
    1982 .... 50.00
Cup and saucer, #1870........... 75.00
Figure
    Fawn with Parrot 570.00
    Lady with deer, 9-3/4" h... 350.00
    Nude with dog, glaze blemish, 11-1/2" h 900.00
Inkwell, Blue Fluted pattern, matching tray........................... 165.00
Plate, #1624, 8" dia................. 50.00
Tray, Blue Fluted pattern, 10" l 65.00
Vase, sage green and gray crackled glaze, 7" h,..................... 150.00

❖ Royal Copley

Royal Copley was a trade name used by the Spaulding China Company of Sebring, Ohio. Concentrating on the tableware and the novelty market, Royal Copley was sold through retail stores to consumers who wanted a knick knack or perhaps something pretty to use on their table.

Royal Copley bluebird planter, 5-1/4" diameter, $20.

Reference: Joe Devine and Leslie C. & Marjorie A. Wolfe, *Collector's Guide to Royal Copley, Book II*, Collector Books, 1999.
Periodical: *The Copley Courier*, 1639 N Catalina St, Burbank, CA 91505.

Baby mug, fish handle, as is ...	60.00
Bank, rooster	
Green, gold trim	70.00
Multicolored	50.00
Dish, bluebird	15.00
Figure	
Blackamoor Woman	45.00
Mallard Duck, 7" h	20.00
Rooster, deep pink, yellow, dark green, brown, and black, 8" h	50.00
Lamp, Flower Tree	70.00
Planter	
Blackamoor princess, 1950s	50.00
Blossom, large	8.00
Cow	20.00
Deer head, 9-1/4" h	50.00
Kitten with yarn, c1942-57	42.00
Mallard Duck	30.00
Puppy and mailbox	15.00
Wall pocket	
Blackamoor prince	70.00
Pirate, raised lettering mark	50.00

For exciting collecting trends and newly expanded areas look for the following symbols:

✪ Hot Topic
★ New Warman's Listing

(May have been in another Warman's title.)

❖ Royal Doulton

This English firm has had a long and interesting history. The company produced a variety of figurines, character jugs, toby jugs, dinnerware, Beswick, Bunnykins, and stoneware. One popular dinnerware line is known as Dickens Ware, named for the Dickens characters included in the design. The listings below are a sampling of Royal Doulton found at flea markets.

References: Susan and Al Bagdade, *Warman's English & Continental Pottery & Porcelain*, 3rd Edition, Krause Publications, 1998; Jean Dale, *Charlton Standard Catalogue of Royal Doulton Animals*, 2nd ed., Charlton Press, 1998; ——, *Charlton Standard Catalogue of Royal Doulton Beswick Figurines*, 6th ed., Charlton Press, 1998.

Periodicals: *Collecting Doulton*, BBR Publishing, 2 Strattford Ave, Elsecar, Nr Barnsley, S. Yorkshire, S74 8AA, England; *Doulton Divvy*, P.O. Box 2434, Joliet, IL 60434.

Collectors' Clubs: Heartland Doulton Collectors, P.O. Box 2434, Joliet, IL 60434; Mid-America Doulton Collectors, P.O. Box 483, McHenry, IL 60050; Royal Doulton International Collectors Club, P.O. Box 6705, Somerset, NJ 08873; Royal Doulton International Collectors Club, 850 Progress Ave, Scarborough, Ontario M1H 3C4, Canada.

Royal Doulton Mine Host toby mug, 3-3/4" high, $120.

Animal	
Brown Bear, HN2659	175.00
Bunnykins, Aerobic	150.00
Cat with Bandaged Paw, 3-1/4" h	45.00
Dalmatian, HN1113	250.00
Elephant, Flambe, HN489A	200.00
Fox Terrier, HN1068	1,750.00
Pine Martin, HN2656	275.00
Stalking Tiger, Flambe, HN809	700.00
Winnie the Pooh, boxed set of Pooh, Kanga, Piglet, Eeyore, Owl, Rabbit, and Tigger, Beswick	650.00
Character jug	
Cardinal, large	150.00
Pickwick, miniature	85.00
Christmas Carol plate	
#1, 1982	35.00
#2, 1983	35.00
Figure	
Best Friends, HN3935, designed by Alan Maslankowski, 1995	100.00
Biddy Pennfarthing, HN1834	175.00
Bridget, HN2070, 1951-1973, gold, brown, and lavender, designer L. Harradine, green backstamp and registration marks, 7-3/4" h	465.00
Cherie, HN2341, designed by M.Davies, 1966-92, green backstamp	135.00
Christmas Morn, HN3212	145.00
Danielle, HN3001, designed by P. Gee, c1990-96, white, green backstamp	150.00
Family, HN2720, designed by E. J. Griffiths, 1981, 12" h	190.00
Happy Anniversary, HN3254, designed by D. V. Tootle, 1989, 12" h	175.00
Jane Eyre, HN3842, designed by Pauline Parsons, 8-1/4" h	375.00
Rose, HN1368	85.00
Sit, HN3123, designed by Alan Maslankowski, c1991, 4-1/2" h	120.00
Sweet and Twenty, HN1298, designed by L. Harradine, 1928-69, green backstamp, 5-3/4" h	425.00

Wigmaker of Williamsburg,
  HN2239......................300.00
Plate
  Alfred Jingle.....................145.00
  Bottom from Mid Summer's Night
    Dream.......................185.00
  Gullivers...........................95.00
  Henry VIII........................135.00
  Orchids.............................85.00
  Sir Andrew.......................180.00
  Toxophilite........................95.00

❖ Royal Dux

Here's lovely porcelain, made in Bohemia starting about 1860. Some of the most popular designs are the Art Nouveau inspired wares. Look for a distinctive raised triangle mark or acorn mark to help identify genuine Royal Dux.
Figure
  Boy with accordion.............65.00
  Bulldog, pink triangle mark, blue
    stamped circle "Czech
    Republic".....................110.00
  Elephant, pastel blue, white, and
    beige, triangular gold mark,
    stick, oval "Made in Czech
    Republic" sticker, 4-1/4" h
    ....50.00
  Poodle, 7-1/2" l.................75.00
  Sheep Herder, #2261, and Peas-
    ant Girl, #2262, 9" h, price for
    pr...............................250.00
Jardiniére, rect, large molded flower
  handles, center Art Nouveau
  maiden in flowing robes, 7-5/8" h
  ....850.00

Dog figurine, Royal Dux, pink triangle mark, 11-3/4" long, $90.

Vase, 6-1/2" h, 3-3/4" l, Art Deco,
  gold sticker, back stamp "Royal
  Dux Bohemia, Hand Painted,
  Made in Czech Republic," raised
  pink triangle, 6 incised numbers
  ....60.00

❖ Royal Winton

Known best for its chintz patterns, Royal Winton also made other dinnerware and tablewares. The firm was started by the Grimwade brothers and some marks bear their name in additional to Royal Winton and other information.
For additional listings, see *Warman's English & Continental Pottery & Porcelain* as well as Chintz in this edition.
Candlesticks, pr, Delphinium, hand
  painted, octagonal.............80.00
Cup and saucer, Spring #2506
  ....125.00
Figure, Dickens character, Sam
  Weller, red jacket.............155.00
Jug, 8-1/2" h, Fish, gurgles when
  pours..................................45.00
Place setting, Ivory, mkd "Wye,"
  black Art Deco design with multi-
  colored flowers..................12.00
Snack set, plate and cup, Tiger Lily
  pattern...............................85.00
Soup plate, Rosebud pattern,
  8-1/4" d.............................15.00
Tea cup
  Eversham pattern, 2-3/4" h
    ....95.00
  Hibiscus, gold trim, 2-3/4" h
    ....28.50
Teapot, Old Canada, scenes and
  gold trim, 1953...................21.75

❖ Royal Worcester

Here's another venerable English pottery that's a favorite with collectors. Some of the porcelains are hand decorated while others take advantage of a transfer print decoration technique, which Royal Worcester perfected. Look for a mark, which will help date the piece, give clues as to the decorator, etc.

Royal Worcester basket, cane-weave base, twisted reed handle, purple mark, circa 1891, 5-3/4" high, $500.

For additional listings, see *Warman's Antiques and Collectibles Price Guide* and *Warman's English & Continental Pottery & Porcelain.*
Bud vase, bulbous, triangular han-
  dle, reticulated leaf design, ivory
  ground, hp floral trim, gold
  accents, purple crown mark, reg-
  istration mark....................75.00
Cup and saucer, Imari pattern,
  c1910.................................48.00
Egg coddler, silver lid with ring on
  top
  3" h, peach on front, leaf with
    berries on back.............20.00
  3 1/4" h, two different bird scenes
    on each coddler, mkd "Royal
    Worcester Porcelain, Made in
    England," pr..................30.00
Figure
  Politician, white glaze, hat rim
    restored, minor staining
    ....300.00
  Saturday's Child, boy......130.00
  The Thief.........................225.00
Mustard pot, cylindrical, blue and
  white transfer, floral clusters, floral finial, first period, mid 18th C,
  4" h.................................325.00
Plate, bird center, blue enamel and
  gilt floral rim, c1886, set of 10
  ....300.00

Sauce boat, geometric band above foliate molded body, painted floral sprays, oval foot, c1765, pr 275.00

Urn, cov, pierced dome top, painted floral sprays, basketweave molded base, early 20th C, 11-1/2" h 200.00

Vase, floral dec, gilt trim, reticulated, 3-1/4" h............................ 115.00

Waste bowl, floral molded ext., floral spray int., lambrequin border, c1765, 5" dia 200.00

❖ Roycroft

Roycroft is a familiar name to Arts and Crafts collectors. The Roycrofters were founded by Elbert Hubbard in East Aurora, New York. He was a talented author, lecturer, and manufacturer. Perhaps his greatest contribution was the campus he created with shops to teach and create furniture, metals, leather working, and printing.

Collectors' Clubs: Foundation for the Study of Arts & Crafts Movement, Roycroft Campus, 31 S Grove St, East Aurora, NY 14052; Roycrofters-At-Large Association, P.O. Box 417, East Aurora, NY 14052.

Book, *Little Journey*, memorial edition, set of 14...................240.00

Bracelet, hammered sterling silver 225.00

Chair, armchair from Grove Park Inn, mkd GPI, orig leather seat, 41" h 3,750.00

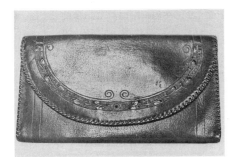

Roycroft tooled-leather purse, 5-3/4" x 10-1/8", $175.

Etching, Elbert Hubbard 65.00

Humidor, brass, 5" h, acid-etched finish, discoloration 200.00

Jug, stoneware, brown glaze, 5" h 15.00

Stand, Little Journey's stand, oak, orig finish, 26" h, 26" w, 14" d 1,150.00

Vase, hammered copper, orig patina, minor wear to base, 4-1/2" dia 425.00

Wastebasket, mahogany, copper corners, orig finish, 13" h, 10" sq 1,150.00

❖ R.S. Germany

R. S. Germany wares are also known as Schlegelmilch porcelain, in reference to the brothers whose potteries in the Thuringia and Upper Silesia region of Poland/Germany produced wares from the 1860s until the 1950s. Generally R. S. Germany porcelain is decorated with florals and detailed backgrounds. Handles and finials tend to be fancy.

Biscuit jar, cov, roses dec, satin finish, loop handles, gold knob, 6" h 95.00

Bon bon dish, pink carnations, gold dec, silver-gray ground, inside looped handle, 7-3/4" l.......45.00

Bread plate, Iris variant edge mold, blue and white, gold outlines, steeple mark.....................115.00

Bride's bowl, floral center, ornate ftd stand.................................95.00

R.S. Germany covered sugar, floral design, 5" high, $45.

Chocolate pot, white rose florals, blue mark 95.00

Demitasse cup and saucer, pink roses, gold stenciled dec, satin finish, blue mark................95.00

Nut bowl, cream and yellow roses, green scalloped edge, 5-1/4" dia 65.00

Plate, white flowers, gold leaves, green ground, gilded edge, dark green mark, gold script signature, 9-3/4" dia 45.00

Tea tile, peach and tan, green-white snowballs, RM over faint blue mark............................... 165.00

R.S. Prussia pitcher, poppies, red mark, 10-1/4" high, $820.

❖ R.S. Prussia

Like R. S. Germany, R.S. Prussia was porcelain made by Reinhold Schlegelmilch in the same region. Designed to be used for export, the wares are mostly table accessories or dinnerware. Pieces of R. S. Prussia tend to be more expensive than R.S. Germany, primarily because of better molds and decoration.

Collectors' Club: International Association of R. S. Prussia Collectors, Inc, 212 Wooded Falls Rd, Louisville, KY 40243.

Reproduction Alert.

Bowl, Hidden Images, portrait of woman, additional molded florals, pastel green ground, 10" d 250.00

Butter dish, cov, porcelain insert, cream and gold shading, pink roses, raised enamel trim 715.00

Cake plate, floral with 3 medallions of cherubs 500.00

Cake plate, turkey and evergreens 500.00

Celery dish, green florals....... 175.00

Chocolate set, cov chocolate pot, 6 cups and saucers, pink and red roses, gold luster, angular handles, red mark 995.00

Ferner, mold 876, florals on purple and green ground, unsigned 175.00

Hair receiver, green lilies of the valley flowers, white ground, red mark 95.00

Plate, poppies dec, raised molded edge and gilt trim, 8-3/4" dia 75.00

Spoon holder, pink and white roses, 14" l 200.00

Toothpick holder, pink and white roses, green shadows, jeweled, six small feet, red mark ...250.00

❖ Ruby-Stained Glass

Pattern glass with ruby-stained highlights can be a great find at flea markets. Look for examples that are in good condition with little wear to the ruby staining and gold trim. Many pieces of ruby stained glass were used as souvenirs and are engraved with names, places, and dates.

Berry set, Tacoma pattern 7 pc 310.00

Compote, Tacoma pattern..... 110.00

Dish, canoe shape, Tacoma pattern 75.00

Mug
    Button Arches pattern, engraved "Mother" 35.00
    Heart Band pattern 30.00

Rose bowl, Tacoma pattern.....85.00

Ashtray, "Doris 1947," 2-1/4" x 4", $10.

Spooner, Royal Crystal pattern 75.00

Syrup
    Late Block Pattern, orig top 300.00
    Pioneer's Victoria pattern, orig top 350.00
    Prize pattern, orig top.......325.00
    Truncated Cube pattern ...250.00

Toothpick holder
    Double Arch pattern.........195.00
    Harvard pattern..................80.00
    Pleating pattern.................85.00
    Prize pattern....................135.00

Tumbler, Riverside's Victoria pattern 85.00

Water set, water pitcher and six tumblers
    Art Novo pattern...............425.00
    Hexagon Block pattern.....325.00
    Loop and Block pattern....465.00
    Pioneer's Victoria pattern 350.00

❖ Rugs

Rug styles and the techniques for making them have changed greatly over the years. Embroidered rugs date to the early 19th century. Braided rugs, made from strips of fabric that were braided and then sewn together to form a circular or oval shape, were first popular in the second quarter of the 19th century. Hooked rugs, which were introduced about 1830 and came into vogue in the 1850s, were crafted from homemade designs as well as from commercial patterns.

Most rugs found at flea markets are later examples of those styles, with many being machine-made. Especially popular today are hooked rugs with bold graphic designs or pictorials with a folkish flair. Never buy a rug without carefully examining the piece beforehand, checking for damage and repairs.

References: Joel and Kate Kopp, *American Hooked and Sewn Rugs: Folk Art Underfoot*, E.P. Dutton, 1975; Mildred Cole Peladeau, *Art Underfoot: The Story of Waldoboro Hooked Rugs*, American Textile History Museum, 1999; Jessie A. Turbayne, *Hooked Rug Treasury*, Schiffer Publishing, 1997.

Collectors' Club: RugNotes, 12700 Ardennes Ave., Rockville, MD 20851.

Bambi and Thumper, Belgium, 22" x 36" 60.00

Hooked
    Collie, landscape ground, birds in air, border in stripes of red, blue and white, 30" x 48" 495.00
    Lighthouse 34-1/2" x 22" 200.00
    Horse, running, impressionistic multicolor ground, 24" x 34" 192.50
    Cabin scene, 29" x 50".... 275.00
    Tulips, daffodils, lilies and iris, white central oval ground, gray border, 54" x 35" 357.50

Indian, Navajo, Stunning Storm pattern, woven by Alice Yazzie, 41" x 26" 875.00

Mickey and Minnie Mouse on flying broom, 21" x 41" 200.00

Penny, 6-sided, tan, orange, blue, dark- and light-green circles on tan ground, staining, minor damage, 19-1/4" x 33" 220.00

Rag
    Oval, gray, green, tan, blue and red, 23" x 30"...............148.00
    Runner, stripes of red, green, white and black, 33" w, 120" l 220.00

Uncle Scrooge McDuck, 21" x 34" 175.00

❖ RumRill Pottery

This American art pottery has been around, literally. At different times, RumRill Pottery has been made by the Red Wing potteries (and sold by a sales force located in Little Rock, Ark), Florence Pottery in Ohio, and Shawnee Pottery, also in Ohio. Knowledgeable collectors can identify when and where a piece of RumRill was made.

Bulb bowl, Class pattern, chartreuse exterior, olive-green interior, 9" dia 40.00

Planter
    Log 60.00
    Scalloped, pink, E12, 7" dia
    .... 15.00

Seal, black, glass bowl on nose, 8" h
.... 250.00

Vase
    Grecian, 2-handle, blue, 9-1/2" h
    .... 85.00
    Octagonal, orange and yellow drip glaze, Arts & Crafts design, 287, 5-1/4" h 95.00
    Urn-shape, off-white with pink speckled overlay, H-4, 9" h
    .... 148.00

❖ Russian Items

Flea markets are great places to find Russian collectibles. From beautiful amber from the Baltic region to pieces commemorating events, there is a lot of variety. Russian craftsmen were known for their exquisite work in silver, enamels, and lacquer.

Beads, amber, graduated, screw closure, 28" l 375.00

Box, lacquer, Fedoskino, Tzar surveying wonders of Dvidon's Country 575.00

Commemorative coin, Russian scientist A.C. Popov, 1984, 1 Ruble
.... 25.00

Compact, sterling, Catherine the Great on front, puff missing
.... 175.00

Paper dolls, man, woman, 3 men on donkey, angel with wreath, single sheet, 20" x 14" 12.00

Plate
    Double-headed eagle crest, hand-painted, 12" dia ... 95.00
    St. Petersburg Palace, 1991, 7-3/4" sq 22.00
    Tianex, Bradford Exchange, 1988, 7-3/4" dia 15.00

Wine cup, silver, Slavic flowers decor, 19th C., 2-1/2" h ... 125.00

S

For exciting collecting trends and newly expanded areas look for the following symbols:

⚙ Hot Topic

★ New Warman's Listing

(May have been in another Warman's title.)

❖ Salt and Pepper Shakers

What table would be complete without a pair of salt and pepper shakers? Flea markets are great places to spot novelty and decorative sets. Most can add a smile to even a sleepy head! Generally the salt shaker has larger or more holes than the pepper.

Reference: Irene Thornburg, *The Big Book of Salt & Pepper Shaker Series*, Schiffer Publishing, 1999.

Collectors' Club: Novelty Salt & Pepper Shakers Club, P.O. Box 3617, Lantana, FL 33465.

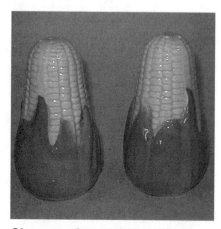

Shawnee Corn King salt and pepper shakers, 5-1/4" high, pair, $35.

For additional listings, see *Warman's Antiques and Collectibles Price Guide* and *Warman's Antiques & Collectibles*.

Bugs Bunny and Taz with football 15.00
Chicks emerging from egg-shaped cups, script mark "Japan," 4-1/2" h 60.00
Donald Duck and BBQ 15.00
Duck and egg, 3-1/4" h............27.50
Fishermen, Black men, mkd "Ucago China, Hand Painted Japan," blue ink stamp mark, 5-1/2" h 275.00
Golliwoggs, orange and white outfits, 3-1/2" h 225.00
Kissing Dutch Boy and Girl, mkd "Made in Japan"...............225.00
Mickey and Piano 15.00
Milk cans, copper....................20.00
Minnie Mouse and Vanity 15.00
Pluto and doghouse.................15.00
Poodles...................................40.00
Rabbits, yellow, snuggle type, Van Telligen 42.00
Refrigerators, GE, 1930 style refrigerator, milk glass................30.00
Tombstones, wood, black lettering 10.00

❖ Salts, Open

Before the advent of salt shakers, open salt containers were used on tables. Frequently there was a master salt to hold this precious condiment. Another way of dispensing salt was individual salts, often called salt cellars, one per place setting, along with a tiny spoon. The individual salts were usually sold as sets and can be found in silver, silver plate, and various types of glassware.

Periodical: *Salty Comments*, 401 Nottingham Road, Newark, DE 19711.

Collectors' Clubs: Central Mid-West Open Salt Society, 10386 Fox River Drive, Walnut Springs, Newark, IL 60541; Mid-West Open Salt Society, 9123 S Linden Rd, Swartz Creek, MI 48473-9125; New England Society of Open Salt Collectors, 62 Clear Pond Drive, Walpole, MA 02081; Open Salt Collectors of the Atlantic Region, 71 Clearview Lane, Biglerville, PA 17307-9407; Open Salt Seekers of the West (Northern Chapter), 84 Margaret Drive, Walnut Creek, CA 94596; Open Salt Seekers of the West (Southern Chapter), 2525 East Vassar Drive, Visalia, CA 93292; Salt Collectors' South East, 1405 N Amanda Circle, Atlanta, GA 30329-3317.

Bavaria, lavender ext., gold int., mkd "Bavaria," 1-1/2" dia 18.00
Cut glass, master, green cut to clear, silver-plated holder, 2" h . 120.00
Intaglio, individual, bronze basket frame with "jewels," burnished gold scene on body, 8-sided 80.00
Limoges, peach flowers, white ground, gold trim, three small feet..................................... 30.00
Lusterware, swan, mkd "Made in Japan by Noritake," 2" h ... 27.50
Mercury glass, silvered, 2-1/4" dia 115.00
Pattern glass, individual
    Fine Rib, flint 35.00
    Hawaiian Lei...................... 35.00
    Three Face........................ 42.00
Pattern glass, master
    Barberry, pedestal 45.00
    Jacob's Ladder, pedestal base 40.00
    Snail, ruby stained............. 75.00
Pewter, master, cobalt blue liner, pedestal 70.00

Jacob's Ladder master salt, pressed glass, $35.

Royal Bayreuth, individual, lobster
claw 85.00
Silver plated, cobalt blue glass liner,
2-1/2" dia 22.00
Sterling silver, whale, crystal salt,
mkd "Sterling, Germany,"
3-1/2" h 60.00

❖ Sand Pails

Bright lithographed metal sand pails have gained popularity in recent years. Made by several of the major toy manufacturers, they were designed with all types of characters and childhood scenes. Look for ones with bright colors. Most collectors prefer very good examples, but will tolerate some dents and signs of use.

Cowboy chased by Indian, Ohio Art,
with shovel 100.00
Easter scene, bunnies and chicks,
6" h 85.00
Flowers, metallic blue, Ohio Art,
1960s, 9-1/2" h 37.00
Man selling flower from cart, 6" h
....32.00
Red Riding Hood, Ohio Art, 7-7/8" h
....75.00
Safeguard soap, children, lion, elephant and kangaroo, 5" h ..19.00
Under the Sea design, Ohio Art,
9-1/2" h 37.00

Mickey Mouse sand pail, J. Chein & Co., 4-3/8" high (excluding handle), 5" diameter, $75.

Sarreguemines character jug, Lawyer, majolica, $120.

❖ Sarreguemines

This porcelain is another example of tin-glazed earthware, like Majolica. It was made in France and can be found in all types of designs, some quite whimsical. Some have the name impressed on the back.

Basket, quilted green body, heavy
leopard skin crystallization, 9" h
....250.00
Character jug, lawyer.............125.00
Cup and saucer, Orange, Majolica
....50.00
Demitasse cup and saucer, cup dec
inside and out 40.00
Dish, cov, Majolica, 6-1/2" l....300.00
Ewer, tall, cylindrical, 13" h 150.00
Humidor, man with top hat.....175.00
Pitcher, ugly man's head, blue int.,
Majolica 275.00
Stein, high relief dec, mkd "Sarreguemines/1237/215/Y,"
8-1/4" h 195.00

❖ Scales

Whether it's the scales of justice or a candy scale, collectors like to find interesting examples to add weight to their collections.

Reference: Bill and Jan Berning, *Scales,* Schiffer Publishing, 1999.

Collectors' Club: International Society of Antique Scale Collectors, 300 W. Adams, Suite 821, Chicago, IL 60606.

Balance, V.W. Brinckerhoff, New
York, cast iron, scroll designs,
brass pans, 7-1/4" h, 14-3/4" w
....85.00
Candy scale, white enamel, 2-lb
capacity, Eureka Automatic
Scales, No. 35864, with pan, 20"
h, 13" w 195.00
Kitchen scale
Montgomery Wards Family
Scale, 25-lb capacity 35.00
Universal Family Scale, 24-lb
capacity, 1865 patent date
...................................40.00
Spring
Fray's Improved Spring Balance, brass and iron, 48-lb,
14-3/8" l 30.00
Penn Scale Mfg. Co., brass and
iron, 100-lb, 17-1/2" l, wear
...................................35.00
Morton & Bremner, iron, brass
face, 24-lb, 9-1/4" dia round
tin pan, 11" l 35.00

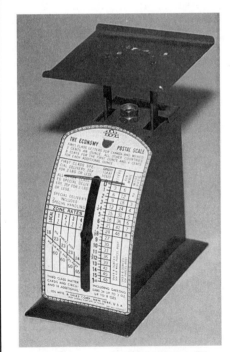

The Economy Postal Scale, No. 500, 1st-class postage was 3 cents per ounce, original box in rough condition, $12.

❖ Schafer & Vater

The first factory of Schafer and Vater was located in Rudolstadt, Thuringia, from about 1890 to 1962. They made porcelain dolls, figurines, and novelty wares of all types.

For additional listings, see *Warman's English & Continental Pottery & Porcelain.*

Bottle, figural, One of the Boys
.... 150.00
Box, cov, olive green bisque, gold and bronze accents, white glazed emb cameo of lady and cupid on lid, chip on lid, 5" x 3"
.... 225.00
Cup and saucer, pale blue rose as cup, petal form saucer, minor wear to gilt 75.00
Mug, figural, elk 50.00
Pin tray, figural, lady golfer 235.00
Pitcher, figural
    Lady with cape, blue 130.00
    Man, hat and cane, blue and white 125.00
Pitcher, jasperware, dark green, white cameo woman's portrait, 3" h 50.00
Plaque, jasperware, dark green, white dec, mkd #2870, artist #18, 12" h 275.00
Rose bowl, cherubs, two rams head handles, mkd "5660," 3-1/4" h
.... 230.00
Shaving mug, raised relief elk, tan, shades of brown, light tan, rusty-orange, glossy white int... 115.00
Urn, jasperware, blue and white, man and woman planting tree, 2-1/2" h 50.00
Vase
    Bisque, handles, bluish-gray, white bird on handle, tree trunk design, emb berries, nick on bird, 2" h 45.00
    Jasperware, lilac, raised Art Nouveau dec, large cobalt blue jewels, iridized and crystallized glaze, c1900-20, 6-1/4" h 225.00

❖ Schoop, Hedi

Hedi Schoop Art Creations represents another California pottery. This one was located in North Hollywood from 1942 to 1958. The company is well known for its detailed figures and other tablewares.

Bowl, 8" w, 4-1/4" h, handcrafted, mkd 75.00
Figure
    Dutch Boy and Girl, 11" h, missing one pail 95.00
    Lady, seated, holding bowl, tinted bisque, high glaze turquoise, 12" h 300.00
    Oriental Couple, carrying pottery buckets with rope handles, white, blue, and black, 12" h and 13" h 300.00
Planter
    Butterfly, green and gold, pr
    .... 175.00
    Lady, full skirt, 7" w, 9" h, minor chips, cracks, water damage to back.......................... 30.00
Vase
    8" h, feather design 110.00
    8-1/2" h, 8-1/4" dia, c1940 .90.00

❖ Schuco

Founded by Heinrich Muller and Herr Schreyer in 1912, Schreyer and Co. adopted the name Schuco for its line of toys. Often having ingenious mechanisms, Schuco toys were made from the 1930s to 1950. Originals are marked "Germany" or "U.S. Zone Germany."

Other markings indicate a reissued toy.

Beach Buggy, worn orig box
.... 195.00
Curvo 1000 Motorcycle, red shirt, brown pants, green cycle, orig box, missing end flap....... 680.00
Car
    Akustico 2002, 5-5/8" l 185.00
    Examico 4001, 5-3/4" l.....300.00
Clown Fiddler, made in U.S. Zone Germany, 1950s, box with restored flaps, 4-1/2" h 275.00
Dancing Tippo, one shoe torn, 5-3/4" h 165.00
Motorcycle, Motodrill 1006, windup, 1960s, 5-1/2" l 485.00
Pig musicians, fife, violin and drums, set of 3............................. 990.00

Scotties cast-iron doorstop, 6" high, 9" wide, $115.

❖ Scotties

Scotties are one of the most recognizable dog breeds. Some attribute this to President Franklin Roosevelt and his dog, Fala. Others identify Scotties with Jock from Lady and the Tramp. Many Scottie collectibles are found with black dogs and red and white accents. Scottie images can be found on every type of item, and they bring a smile with their cheerful attitude.

Reference: Candace Sten Davis and Patricia Baugh, *A Treasury of Scottie Dog Collectibles, Vol. II*, Collector Books, 2000.

Collectors' Club: Wee Scots, P.O. Box 1597, Winchester, VA 22604.

Bookends, wooden, 5" h, pr.... 32.00
Bowl, running Scotties design, red on white ground, faded 18.00
Christmas card, 2 black Scotties on front, single-sided, 1930s.... 6.00
Cocktail shaker, glass, black Scottie, red checkered border........ 15.00
Doorstop, cast iron, 2 dogs, orig paint, 6" h, 8-3/4" l 225.00
Glass, red and black design, 1940s, 6-1/4" h, set of 4 .... 42.00
Ice tub, glass, 8 black Scotties around outside, red checker border, 1940s, 4-1/4" h 55.00
Salt and pepper shakers, figural, pr
    Black and white 32.00
    Orange Scotties playing instruments........................... 75.00
Toothbrush holder, porcelain, 3 dogs, Japan, 4" h............ 125.00

❖ Sebastian Miniatures

Marblehead, Massachusetts, was the home for Prescott Baston's Sebastian figurines. He started production in 1938 and created detailed historical figurines or characters from literature. Finding a figure with the original label adds to the value of these little charmers.

Collectors' Clubs: The Sebastian Exchange Collector Association, P.O. Box 10905, Lancaster, PA 17605; Sebastian Miniature Collectors Society, 321 Central St, Hudson, MA 01749.

Aunt Betsy Trotwood, wear 20.00
Building Days Boy, blue label
.... 35.00
Colonial Carriage 80.00
Ezra, yellow label 30.00
Gibson Girl 90.00
House of Seven Gables 100.00
In the Candy Store, green and silver
    Marblehead label 135.00
Mrs. Cratchit, light blue label, 2-1/2"
    h, wear to paint, chip 20.00
New England Town Crier, figure
    standing next to dealer's plaque,
    base nick 20.00
Pecksniff, light blue label, 3" h
.... 20.00
Pioneer Couple, blue label, top of
    rifle broken, chip on back .. 25.00
Sailing Days Girl, red label 35.00
Sea Captain, #132 .... 30.00
Snow Days Girl, #6253, orig box
.... 35.00
Mark Twain 120.00
William and Hannah Penn 200.00

❖ Sesame Street

"Sunny day, everything's A-Ok!" That's the song Sesame Street collectors sing as they gleefully search through flea markets for the growing number of items related to Big Bird, Elmo, and the rest of the Sesame Street gang. Wise collectors know to watch for knockoffs—cheap, unlicensed imitations of Sesame Street products. Most of the copycats aren't worth adding to a collection.
Bank, Cookie Monster, MIB 24.00

Big Bird figurine, Gorham, with original box, 7-1/2" high, $22.50.

Book, *Sesame Street L & M Book*,
    Funk & Wagnalls, copyright
    1978, hardcover 4.00
Cookie jar, Big Bird, pale yellow,
    11-1/2" h 55.00
Cup, plastic, Cookie Monster on
    one, Big Bird on other, 1977,
    each 5.00
Game, Walk Along Sesame Street,
    Milton Bradley, orig box, c1975
.... 20.00
Halloween costume, child's, Big
    Bird, orig costume, mask, box
.... 10.00
Record, *Hits from Sesame Street,
    Vol. III,* Peter Pan Records, 45
    rpm 4.00
Plush toy
    Baby Piggy, 1987 .... 8.00
    Christmas Elmo, Tyco, 1997
    .... 18.00
    Cookie Monster, laughs, says
        "Oh Boy Oh Boy," 1996
    .... 18.00
    Kermit the Frog, Fisher-Price,
        1976, some wear 15.00
    Kermit the Frog, NHL,
        McDonald's, 1995 .... 10.00
    The Count, Tyco, 1997 .... 6.00
Pop-up book, *Grover's Superprise,*
    1978 .... 12.00
TV Guide, Cookie Monster on cover,
    July, 1971 .... 15.00

❖ Sevres and Sevres-Type China

Sevres porcelain at a flea market—sure, not every dealer carries it, but some pieces of this fine French porcelain show up at flea markets. Just like today, when Sevres porcelain became so popular, imitations were made. Those are often considered "Sevres type" and are also found at flea markets. Carefully check the mark and decoration of an item before buying it. Many reproduction Sevres pieces exist, including some older fakes.

For additional listings, see *Warman's Antiques and Collectibles Price Guide* and *Warman's English & Continental Pottery & Porcelain.*

Compote, polychrome transfer
    printed figural landscapes,
    bronze mounts, 20th C, 5-1/4" h,
    price for matched pair 175.00
Luncheon plate, central gilt six-
    pointed star, border with hunt
    scenes, 9-3/4" d, price for 6 pc
    set 325.00
Pin box, cov, cartouche of romantic
    couple on cover, blue ground,
    oval, 6-1/2" l 275.00
Salt, 1-3/4", hp roses, paneled blue
    and white ground 58.00
Vase, gilt ground, enamel Art Nou-
    veau stylized leaf and flower
    design, printed mark, 6" h
.... 645.00

Sevres cup and saucer, bird in landscape, 18th century, $250.

Sewer tile spaniel, 10" high, $250.

❖ Sewer Tile

Also called sewer pipe, sewer tile was produced from about 1880 through the early 20th century. Draining tiles and sewer tiles were produced at the factories, but the workers often spent their spare time creating other items of utilitarian or whimsical nature. Although some molded pieces were made, much of the production was one-of-a-kind items. Pieces that are signed and/or dated are especially prized.

Ohio is recognized as the leading producer of sewer tile, but other states, including New York, Pennsylvania, and Indiana, all had a strong presence in the sewer tile market.

For additional listings, see *Warman's Country Price Guide.*

Alligator, Ohio, 15" l 440.00
Bank, dog, seated Spaniel, slot in back of head, round opening on bottom, minor glaze flakes, probably Tuscarawas County, Ohio, 10-1/2" h 220.00
Cat, seated, glaze with copper speckles, small chips, 1 front foot missing, 7" h 330.00

Dog, seated, Spaniel
    5-1/2" h, minor edge chips
        .... 192.50
    8-1/4" h, incised detail up the back, over the head and down the front leg, incised collar and chain, deep-brownish red glaze, oval base, minor base chips 275.00
    10-1/2" h, light-brown glaze
        .... 330.00
Owl, perched on log, 20th C., 8-1/2" h 165.00
Planter, stump
    17" h, 10" dia, 4 branches
        .... 330.00
    26" h, 9" dia, hand-tooled bark, 3 branches 220.00
Umbrella stand, tree trunk design, applied roses, chips on flowers, 25-1/2" h 330.00

❖ Sewing Collectibles

"A stitch in time saves nine," or so thought Ben Franklin. Today collectors find lots of sewing memorabilia at flea markets. From tiny needle holders to interesting sewing machines, it just takes a little hunting, like finding a needle in a haystack.

Collectors Clubs: International Sewing Machine Collectors Society, 1000 E Charleston Blvd, Las Vegas, NV 89104; National Button Society, 2730 Juno Place, Apt 4, Akron, OH 44313; Toy Stitchers, 623 Santa Florita Ave, Milbrae, CA 94030.

For additional listings, see *Warman's Antiques and Collectibles Price Guide* and *Warman's Americana & Collectibles.*

Advertising trade card, Clark's Thread 7.50
Darning egg
    Ebony, sterling handle 100.00
    Porcelain, marbleized finish, one piece, 5-1/2" l 12.50
    Wood, 5-1/2" l, age crack ... 10.00
Dress form, wire and cloth 50.00
Embroidery hoop, clamp for table, wood 85.00
Hook rug machine, c1920 .... 25.00

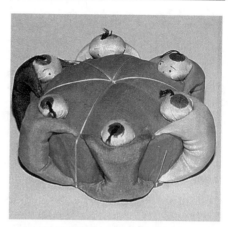

Chinamen pincushion, 3-1/2" diameter, $5.

Instruction manual
    Domestic Sewing Machine, model 725 .... 10.00
    Singer Sewing Machine 400w, 106, 107, 108, 109 and 110, dated 1948 .... 10.00
Machine, Singer Featherweight, Model 221, black case, attachments, c1941 .... 400.00
Needle book, Liberty National Life Insurance Co., Birmingham, Alabama, Statue of Liberty on front, one needle pack 8.00
Needle case, egg shape, wood, mkd "The Columbian Egg," Germany, orig needles 155.00
Pincushion
    Chinese figures surrounding cushion 5.00
    Sewing drawer, thread spindle on case, orig red paint .. 90.00
    Victorian, velvet, fruits and flowers 35.00
Quilt frame, large, fancy scroll work ends 150.00
Sewing basket, wood, silhouette designs on side, c1930, 10" x 9" 45.00
Sewing bird, gilt finish, pincushion 180.00
Sewing machine, Betsy Ross, Gilbrater Mfg. 295.00
Sign, Coats & Clark's Quality Threads, porcelain 900.00
Spool, woolen, mill type, 8-1/2" h, old blue paint 10.00
Thimble holder, carved acorn 70.00
Toy machine, "Singer Sewhandy No. 20," unused condition, orig box, 7" l 325.00

Butcher occupational shaving mug, $100.

❖ Shaving Mugs

"Shave and a hair cut, 2 bits!" Oh how we'd love to pay those prices again. And probably finding a barber who still uses old-fashioned shaving mugs might just be harder than finding vintage shaving mugs at a flea market. There are several different types of shaving mugs; fraternal, generic; and scuttles. By far the most popular are the occupational style mugs, made exclusively for use in barbershops in the United States. Introduced shortly after the Civil War, they were still being made into the 1930s. Unlike shaving mugs used at home, these mugs typically had the owner's name in gilt. The mug was kept in a rack at the barbershop, and it was used only when the owner came in for a shave. Occupational shaving mugs, which have a hand-painted scene depicting the owner's line of work, are especially prized.

References: Ronald S. Barlow, *Vanishing American Barber Shop*, Windmill Publishing, 1993; Keith E. Estep, *The Best of Shaving Mugs*, Schiffer Publishing, 2001; —, *Shaving Mug and Barber Bottle Book*, Schiffer Publishing, 1995.

Collectors' Club: National Shaving Mug Collectors Assoc, 1608 Mineral Spring Rd, Reading, PA 19602-2229.

Museums: Atwater Kent History Museum, Philadelphia, PA; Barber Museum, Canal Winchester, OH; Lightner Museum, Saint Augustine, FL.

For additional listings, see *Warman's Antiques and Collectibles Price Guide* and *Warman's English & Continental Pottery & Porcelain*.

Elk flanked by gold floral swags, transfer design, Germany ..60.00
Floral and scrolls, transfer design, late 19th C, 3-3/4" h 45.00
Forget Me Not, transfer design, Germany, 3" h 45.00
Levi Strauss & Co., from the Antique Miniature Shaving Mug Collection, Franklin Porcelain, 1982, 2-1/2" h 12.50
Milk glass, 1927 Mercedes, mkd "Surrey," with shaving brush, 3-1/4" h 8.00
Occupational, hand-painted
Finish carpenter, man planing a board, name above, floral sprigs on sides, handle crack, 3-3/4" h 357.50
Pretzel maker, baker with over-sized pretzel, lettering and trim possibly redone, cond. exc, 3-5/8" h 880.00
Patriotic, flying bald eagle with U.S. flag and leaves/berries in claws, gilt ribbon across flag with name, wear, 3-1/2" h 220.00

❖ Shawnee Pottery

From 1937 until 1961, Shawnee Pottery operated in Zanesville, Ohio. The company made kitchenwares, dinnerware, and some art pottery. Two of their most recognized patterns are Corn Queen and Corn King.

References: Susan and Al Bagdade, *Warman's American Pottery & Porcelain*, Wallace-Homestead, 1994; Jim and Bev Mangus, *Shawnee Pottery*, Collector Books, 1994, 1998 value update; Mark Supnick, *Collecting Shawnee Pottery*, L-W Book Sales, 2000.

Collectors' Club: Shawnee Pottery Collectors Club, P.O. Box 713, New Smyrna Beach, FL 32170.

Shawnee Sunflower ice-lip pitcher, 7-1/4" high, $55.

Cookie jar
    Happy, Dutch boy 385.00
    Mugsey, blue scarf, 11-3/4" h 600.00
    Smiley Pig, tulip decor, 11-1/4" h 400.00
Creamer, Puss-n-Boots 85.00
Figurine
    Goldfish, 3-1/4" h............... 16.00
    Elephant, yellow, 3-1/4" h.. 18.00
    Frog, chip, 2-1/4" h............ 13.00
Pie bird, Pillsbury, 5-1/2" h...... 85.00
Pitcher
    Chanticleer, figural chicken 150.00
    Ball, embossed fruit, 7" h 135.00
Planter
    Deer and Fawn, 6" h, 6-1/2" w 27.50
    Old Mill 25.00
Salt and pepper shakers, pr
    Milk Can, 3-1/4" h.............. 22.50
    Mugsey............................ 245.00
    Puss-n-Boots..................... 67.50
    Smiley Pig, 3-1/4" h........... 67.50
Teapot, Granny Ann.............. 175.00
Wall pocket, Wheat................. 35.00

❖ Sheet Music

Here's a topic that might get you humming along. Sheet music is especially popular today, perhaps because of the nostalgic appeal of the old tunes or the interesting cover art. You might want to check that old piano bench to see what titles are stored there.

"There's A Gold Mine In The Sky," Bing Crosby cover, $10.

Periodical: *The Rag Times*, 15522 Ricky Court, Grass Valley, CA 95949.

Collectors' Clubs: City of Roses Sheet Music Collectors Club, 13447 Bush St SE, Portland, OR 97236; National Sheet Music Society, 1597 Fair Park Ave, Los Angeles, CA 90041; New York Sheet Music Society, P.O. Box 354, Hewlett, NY 11557; Remember That Song, 5623 N 64th St, Glendale, AZ 85301; Sonneck Society for American Music & Music in America, P.O. Box 476, Canton, MA 02021.

Any Bonds Today, Irving Berlin 16.00
A Woman In Love, Guys & Dolls, photo of Brandy & Sinatra . 25.00
Coast Guard Forever............... 15.00
Couldn't Sleep A Wink Last Night 12.50
Down Yonder, Spade Copley .. 10.00
Father of the Land We Love, 1931 .... 8.00
Five Minutes More................... 12.50
If Washington Could Come To Life, 1906 .... 15.00
It's Always You 12.50
Keep 'Em Flying..................... 15.00
Little Red Hen, UB Iwerks, cartoon graphics............................. 28.00

Love & Marriage 12.50
My Arms, Donna Reed and Robert Walker 10.00
No Orchids For My Lady.......... 15.00
Now Is The Hour, Bing Crosby 12.00
One Zy, Two-Zy, 1964.............. 12.00
Paper Doll, Sinatra 15.00
The Ballad of Davy Crockett, 1954, from Disneyland television production 25.00
The Blond Sailor, 1945 .... 15.00
The Marines' Hymn, 1942 .... 15.00
When The Robin Calls Its Mate, Then I'll Call You, 1912......20.00

❖ Shelley China

The Shelley China Company has been in business in Longton, England, since the mid-18th century, producing figurines and dinnerware. Many of the dinnerware patterns are known for interesting shapes. Expect to find a variety of decoration and marks since this firm has been around for so long.

Collectors' Club: National Shelley China Club, 5585 NW 164th Ave, Portland, OR 97229.

Child's plate, "Little Blue Bird, How He Sings, So Happy on My Plates and Things," Mabel Lucie Attwell illus, 7" dia............150.00
Cup and saucer
    Country Garden, pattern #2500, Ludlow shape 85.00
    Maytime, pattern #13452, Henley shape, beige trim ...155.00
    Morning Glory, Dainty shape 85.00
    Orange pattern.................170.00
    Scilla, pattern #2511 ....85.00
    Shamrock pattern...............85.00
    Syringa pattern..................85.00
Demitasse cup and saucer
    Begonia, pattern #13427....85.00
    Red Rose & Daisy, pattern #12425 ....85.00
    Rosebud, pattern #13291 ..85.00
Eggcup, Rose..........................18.00
Gravy boat and underplate, Dainty Blue 525.00
Pin dish, Regency, Dainty shape, sq, tab handle, gold trim 65.00

Place setting, Block pattern, #11787, yellow, black, and silver, 3 pcs 380.00
Platter, medium, Dainty, blue 350.00
Teapot, cov, Rosebud pattern, Dainty shape................... 395.00
Tea Set, Woodlands pattern, teapot, plate, two cups and saucers, milk jug, sugar................. 750.00
Vase, hand painted over transfer dec, matte finish, green mark and "799/8590," 8-1/2" h. 395.00

❖ Shoe-Related Collectibles

Perhaps you know the old woman who lives in a shoe, or just like to buy shoes! Whatever the reason, flea markets can be a great place to find nifty additions to a shoe collection.

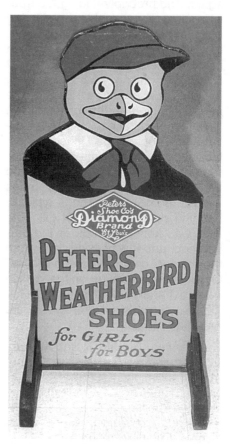

Peters Weatherbird Shoes sidewalk sign, painted wood, decorated on both sides, 44" high, 20" wide, $650.

Ladies' brown high-top shoes, scuffed toes, $85.

Charm, baby shoe, silvertone, 1/2" l 3.50
Cookie jar, Old Woman in a Shoe, Fitz & Floyd, 1986 ....165.00
Dutch shoe, wooden, Heineken Beer, 9" l.............................23.00
Miniature, man's cordovan wingtip, French Shriner & Urner Men's Shoes, 5-1/4" l....................65.00
Pinback button, Dottie Dimple, D.P. Ramsdell Sweet & Co., celluloid, wear, 1-1/8" dia 50.00
Shoe
    Fenton, milk glass, 4-1/4" h 33.00
    Occupied Japan, porcelain, 2-1/2" l..............................4.00
    Porcelain, red roses decor, 8" l 28.00
Souvenir of Windsor, Canada, porcelain, 4-1/2" l....................65.00
Trade card, Tappan's Shoes, motif of 2 bare feet 15.00

❖ Shot Glasses

Here's a flea market collectible that's almost always available. Watch for interesting sets of shot glasses with their original decanter or those boxed in an unusual way. Souvenir shot glasses have always been a popular memento to take home. They are usually plentiful and reasonably priced.
Adam's Rodeo, blue lettering, 2-1/2" h..............................15.00

Crackle glass, 3-1/8" h.............15.00
Frosted, flamenco dancers and drink recipes, Federal, 2 oz..........5.00
Harvard, red lettering.................5.00
Say When!, frosted, 4 humorous illustrations, Anchor Hocking 7.50
Souvenir of Detroit, shows Model T, frosted, Anchor Hocking, 2 oz 5.00
Sterling sliver, 1930s 78.00

❖ Signs

Advertising signs have been a staple of flea markets for many years. With the many signs available, great examples can be found in all price ranges and made from different types of materials. Bright colors and appealing graphics are important, but condition is always critical.
For additional listings, see *Warman's Advertising Price Guide.*
Atlantic, pump sign, porcelain, white letters on red ground, 9" x 13" 90.00
Barber Shop, porcelain flange, 12" x 24" 260.00
Barq's Root Beer, "Drink Barq's, It's Good," embossed tin, NOS, 12" x 30" 100.00
Bell System, Public Telephone, bell logo in center, porcelain flange, 18" sq 275.00
Dr. Pepper, tin, bottle-cap shape, 10-2-4 logo, 24" dia 410.00
Entrance, reverse-painted glass, 3-3/4" x 18".........................22.00
Ex-Lax, "Dependable Home Remedies, Ex-Lax, The Chocolate Laxative," hardboard, NOS, 10" x 15" 15.00

Kurfees Paints flange porcelain sign, 14" x 20-1/4", $30.

Bridge Out sign, painted wood, 8" x 36", $65.

Hires R-J Root Beer With Real Root Juices, embossed tin, red and black bulls-eye, 12" dia 82.50
Mail Pouch, "Chew Smoke Mail Pouch," porcelain, 3-3/4" x 18" 230.00
"Men" and "Women," porcelain, 2-sided, red on white ground, each 7" x 20"....................110.00
Orange-Crush, "Ask For Orange-Crush Carbonated Beverage," embossed tin, 1940s, 12" x 20" 165.00
Street sign, Albany, N.Y., porcelain over metal
    North Pearl Street 55.00
    Clinton Avenue.................. 55.00

❖ Silhouette Pictures

Silhouette pictures are decorative plaques with rounded or convex frames over a black image. Having foil or colored backgrounds, they were a later generation's answer to the old hand-cut silhouettes, thus the name.
Dresser box, wood, red metal trim, large heart shaped cutout on top with dancing silhouettes, lined int. with mirror, 8-1/2" x 6-1/2," wear 50.00
Picture, convex glass type
    Equestrian jumping fence.. 40.00
    Fairies, painted background, 1929 .... 35.00
    Hearts, shows suitor, mkd "Deltex" 24.00
    Lady, seated at vanity, hairbrush in hand.......................... 40.00
    Lady with bird in cage, pale pink background, silver stars, 8-3/4" x 10-1/2"............ 60.00

Lovebirds, boy courting girl, 2 lovebirds watching, foil accents on dress and boy's suit 30.00
Victorian couple 40.00

❖ Silver, Plated and Sterling

Every flea market has great examples of silver in sterling and also silver plate. Look for hallmarks and maker's mark to determine the age of a piece, its silver content, and perhaps the country of origin. Also check for signs of silver polish hidden in crevices, often an indication that a piece has been polished for years. When examining plated silver, some wear is acceptable if it doesn't detract from the overall appearance. For additional listings, see *Warman's Antiques and Collectibles Price Guide.*

Silver Plate
Bank, clown with umbrella 35.00
Champagne bucket, cylindrical, bracket handles, applied scroll border band, monogram, Simpson, Hall, Miller & Co., 9" h 275.00

Silver-plated sugar bowl/ spooner, bird finial, R&R Mfg. Co., 10" high, $140.

Child's mug, two handles, engraved 30.00
Meat dome, Victorian, bright cut with panel of foliage swags and roses, beaded base edge, twisted branch handle, monogram, maker's mark, 18" x 10-1/2" 250.00
Punch bowl, cylindrical, reeded circular foot, applied flowers at rim, International Silver, 12" dia 200.00
Toast rack 45.00
Tray, rectangular, center chased with scrolls, trellis, and foliage, gadrooned and foliate handles, English, 27" l 150.00
Wine cooler stand, Art Deco, Reed & Barton 200.00

Silver, Sterling
Baby spoon, ornate curled handle
    Cupid 65.00
    Mother Goose 60.00
Child's mug, single handle, engraved bands, monogram 45.00
Cigarette/compact case, chain, all-over scrolling 110.00
Curling iron, ornate handle 50.00
Glove hook, ornate handle 30.00
Glove stretcher, ornate 60.00
Grape shears, grape motif dec 90.00
Nail file, 6-1/2" l, head of woman as handle 30.00
Teapot, Kingston pattern, Wallace 250.00
Whistle, chain, Reed and Barton, sterling, MIB 45.00

❖ Skateboards

Whooosh, skateboarding around a flea market would be too fast to spot all the great buys. However, if you're in the market for a vintage skateboard, you'll want to slow down, so you don't miss a good buy. Look for early wooden boards with bold graphics.

Reference: Ryhn Noll, *Skateboard Retrospective, A Collector's Guide,* Schiffer Publishing, 2000.
Black Night, wood, graphic of Black Night, clay wheels, 1960s, 22" l, 5-3/4" w 55.00

Butcher block style, wood, Power Paw red plastic wheels, 23-1/2" l, 6-1/2" w 32.00
Charlie's Angels, Jill, 1977 ...... 45.00
Hawaii Super Surfer, wood, graphics of Hawaii Islands and "Hawaii" painted on top, clay wheels 50.00
Pro-Line 66-99, see-thru gold plastic, Jacksonville, Fla. 65.00
Roller Derby, Mustang 15, blue, gold trim, horse graphic, ball bearing wheels, 21" l, 5" w 55.00
Valterra Dragon, wood, 27" l, 8" w 20.00

❖ Sleds

You won't find the infamous "Rose Bud" sled at a flea market, but you might be able to find some other interesting examples. There are many variations of sleds, some made for boys, girls, singles, doubles, and even some with wheels for those who lived in "snowless" climates. Don't overlook sled-related collectibles.

Inkstand, brass, sled figural, glass well 195.00
Pencil box, sled shape, wooden, 8-1/2" l 200.00
Plate, Hummel, shows boy on sled, 1975, orig box, 7-5/8" dia.. 65.00
Postcard, Christmas Greetings, 2 children on sled, 1915 postmark 15.00
Sled, wooden
    Dog oval decal and "Wagner Make," 30-1/2" l 300.00
    Flexible Flyer, No. 60J, 1960s, 60" l 40.00
    Rocket Plane, Flexible Flyer type, 51" l 55.00
    "Hustler" painted on red ground 360.00
    Running horse design, 19th C., 26" l 150.00

❖ Slot Machines

The first slot machine, the Liberty Bell, was developed by Charles Fey in San Francisco in 1905. Advancements were made through the years by several of the manufacturers. Some were enhancements to the playing action, others to prevent players from cheating.

Periodicals: *Antique Amusements, Slot Machines & Jukebox,* 909 26th St NW, Washington, DC 20037; *Chicagoland Program,* 414 N Prospect Manor Ave, Mt Prospect, IL 60056; *Chicago Land Slot Machine & Jukebox Gazette,* 909 26th St, NW, Washington, DC 20037; *Coin Drop International,* 5815 W 52nd Ave, Denver, CO 80212; *Coin-Op Classics,* 17844 Toiyabe St, Fountain Valley, CA 92708; *Coin-Op Newsletter,* 909 26th St, NW, Washington, DC 20037; *Coin Slot,* 4401 Zephyr St, Wheatridge, CO 80033; *Loose Change,* 1515 South Commerce Street, Las Vegas, NV 89102.

Jennings
    Little Duke, 1933, orig cond.
    .... 3,500.00
    Standard Chief, 10-cent
    .... 1,2100.00
Mills
    Lion Head, 1932, 25-cent,
        restored 3,000.00
    War Eagle, 1931, 25-cent,
        restored 3,200.00
Wattling, Rol-A-Top, twin jackpot,
    back doesn't open 2,420.00

Bar 7 slot machine, $350.

It's a record

The record price for a slot machine sold at auction is $143,000 for this Fey Liberty Bell. It was sold in 1995 by James D. Julia, Inc.

Fey Liberty Bell, $143,000. (Photo courtesy of James D. Julia, Inc., Fairfield, Maine.)

❖ Smokey Bear Collectibles

Since 1947, Smokey Bear has been telling us, "Remember, only you can prevent forest fires." The character was created by the U.S. Forest Service in 1944, when he appeared on a poster warning of the dangers of forest fires, which threatened the country's lumber supply during World War II. The lovable character, always seen with his campaign hat, starred in an animated television show from 1969 to 1971.

Ashtray set, aluminum, 4 pc,
    embossed image of Smokey,
    4" dia 20.00
Bank, ceramic, Norcrest, Japan
    .... 195.00
Coloring and activity book
    Smokey Bear Color & Activity Book, 1971, 126 pgs, used
    .... 8.00
    Smokey Bear's Story of the Forest, Florida Forest Service, 1959, 15 pgs, unused 25.00
Comic book, *The True Story of Smokey Bear,* 1969 .... 25.00
Hand puppet, plush, Ideal, 1965
    .... 195.00
Pinback button, I'm Smokey's Helper, 2-3/4" dia 4.50
Plush figure, hard plastic hat, Dakin tag, 1985 .... 65.00

Salt and pepper shakers, figural, Norcrest, Japan, 3-3/4" h, pr
    .... 55.00
Sign, "Prevent Forest Fires," 1960s, 18" x 24" 195.00

❖ Smurfs

Smurfs made their debut in 1958, as secondary characters for a story illustrated by Pierre Culliford, better known as Peyo. It wasn't long before these little blue guys and gals were taking center stage. Collectors know to watch for figurines, toys, records and other Smurf memorabilia at flea markets.

Collectors' Club: Smurf Collectors Club International, 24 Cabot Road W Massapequa, NY 11758. Website: www.smurf.com

Animation cel, matted, mkd "#240 21 65," 11" x 14" 95.00
Card game, 1982, MIB 12.00
Figure
    Smurf-O-Gram, Doctor's Orders, Get Well Soon 10.00
    Smurf with Go-Cart, MIB ... 15.00
    Super Smurf, with hobby horse, MIB 5.00
Key chain, figural, 2-1/4" h 5.00
Lunch box, plastic, Thermos Co.1987, no thermos 32.00
Mushroom cottage, Peyo Schleich, orig box, description in English, French and German, 1970s, MIB
    .... 55.00

The Hundredth Smurf, Random House, 1982, $2.50.

Ornament, wearing red hat, 1978
.... 1.25
PEZ 12.00
Puppet, hand, Pecor, 1981 ...... 12.00
Stuffed toy
    Amour Smurf 12.00
    Baby Smurf, pink, 16" l 25.00
    Baseball Smurf, baseball shirt,
        baseball in hand, orig side
        tag, 1982 .... 2.00
    Blue, 1979, 16" h 20.00
    Papa, sitting, 10" h, soiled ... 6.00
    Smurfette 12.00
    St. Patrick's Day 14.00
    Sweetheart Valentine 12.00
Telephone, mkd "H. G. Toys," 1982,
    numbers faded, slight wear
    .... 20.00
Wind-up toy, blue and white, mkd
    "Wallace Berry Co., Hong Kong,"
    1980 .... 12.00

❖ Snack Sets

A snack set is the combination of a plate or tray with an indent to hold a cup. Perfect for a snack in front of that new invention, television, or perhaps just the item to serve refreshments on the patio. Many glass and dinnerware services included these items in the 1950s. Whole sets can be found in original boxes, perhaps attesting to the fact that although they were a great wedding present, the idea never really caught on.

Periodical: *Snack Set Searchers*, P.O. Box 158, Hallock, MN 56728.

Anchor Hocking
    Fleurette, 8 pcs in orig box, some
        damage to box 18.00
    Grape, clear, grape and leaf
        design, orig box 26.50
    Primrose, Anchorglass, milk
        glass, 11" l plate, 8 pc set
        .... 25.00
Bavaria, bone china, purple roses
    dec, 7-1/2" dia plate 15.00
California Pottery, bright orange,
    1960s, 4 pcs, orig sticker "Cal-
    Style Ceramics Torrance Calif
    #2433" 40.00
Federal, Yorktown, orig boxed set
    .... 16.00
Fire-King, Soreno, green, 9-3/4" dia
    plate, 2-1/2" h cup 5.00
Hand painted, pink flowers with yel-
    low centers, green leaves, gold
    edge, artist sgd "G. H. T. 1940,"
    8-1/2" x 7-1/4" plate, 3-1/2" d x
    1-7/8" h cup 27.50
Hazel Atlas
    Capri Sea Shell pattern, light
        blue 18.00
    Sea Shell, crystal, 10" x 6-1/2"
        tray, 3-1/2" d x 2-1/2" h cup
        .... 22.50
Lefton, Golden Wheat, 8" snack
    plate with tab handle, low scal-
    loped ftd cub, gold trim 12.50
Noritake, kidney shaped plate,
    white, blue luster trim, black
    lines, black floral dec, green
    mark, 8-1/2" x 7" plate, 3-1/4" h
    cup 35.00
Porcelain, Oriental design, purple,
    red, gold, light blue, yellow, and
    olive green, 8" dia plate 15.00
Shelley, Flowers of Gold, pattern
    #141287, Dainty shape 130.00

Milk glass snack set, 10-1/4" x 7-1/4" tray, set of 6, $27.50.

Steubenville, Woodfield pattern, 2
    Tropic Green, 2 Salmon Pink, 4
    Dove Gray, 9" plate, 4-1/4" w x
    2-1/2" h cup, 16 pc set, one
    chipped plate 60.00

Snow Baby, $145.

❖ Snow Babies

Here's a debate that's never really been settled—some folks feel that the original snow babies were designed to commemorate Admiral Peary's trip and his little daughter. Others believe they were just cute German figurines. Expect to find their little snowsuits encrusted with bits of shiny sparkles, adding to their whimsical characteristic.

Reproduction Alert.

Bear, walking on four paws ... 100.00
Elf, 1-1/2" h 75.00
Snow baby riding bear, red, white,
    and maroon, 2-7/8" h 165.00
Snow baby on sled 82.75
Snow baby playing banjo, stamped
    "Germany" 145.00
Snow baby waving 160.00
Snow man, standing 70.00

❖ Snow Globes

Some folks refer to these as snow globes, others prefer the name snowdomes. Whatever you call them, the fun is to shake the paperweight-type ball and see the snow fly through the water and swirl around the featured character. Many companies created snow globes over the years. The objects remain a popular souvenir for tourists.

Periodical: *Roadside Attractions,* 7553 Norton Ave, Apt 4, Los Angeles, CA 90046.

Collectors' Club: Snowdome Collectors Club, P.O. Box 53262, Washington, DC 20009.

For additional listings, see *Warman's Americana & Collectibles.*

Berta Hummel, Tree Trimming Time 68.00
Betty Boop, musical, plays "Red Roses for a Blue Lady," 1995 ....55.00
Chevrolet 1958 Corvette, musical, plays "Little Red Corvette," white base with Chevy logo, Westland, MIB 45.00
Cherub kneels in prayer, licensed by Kristen Haynes, Westland 15.00
Cherub on cloud, holding star, iridescent silvery moon, licensed by Kristen Haynes, Westland 15.00
Coca-Cola, Heritage Collection, polar bear scene, authorized seal, plays Coke theme, retired 1996 ....60.00
Disney 75th anniversary, fiber optics 75.00
Easter Bunny train, Glama, retired, 4" l 10.00
Happy bunny with chick, Glama, 3" h 10.00
Little girl gazing at rose, resin pedestal base, Westland, MIB 20.00
Little Mermaid, Ursula 52.00
101 Dalmatians, McDonald's giveaway 2.25
Souvenir, Florida, coral, tethered fish, rect, 2" x 1-1/2" x 2-1/2" 6.00
Teletubbies 36.00
Winnie the Pooh......................30.00
Yogi Bear..................................3.00

❖ Soakies

Remember those great figural plastic bottles we got bubble bath in when we were kids? Collectors happily relive those days as they search flea markets for those bottles, now called "soakies."

Alvin Chipmunk, red 20.00
Atom Ant..................................40.00
Augie Doggie............................55.00
Beauty and the Beast 5.00
Bozo Clown 35.00
Bugs Bunny, some paint loss ..25.00
Casper Ghost 35.00
Chewbacca..............................10.00
Cinderella, movable arms........25.00
Deputy Dawg, small..................20.00
Dick Tracy, crack at neck.........25.00
Dopey Dwarf............................25.00
Dum Dum 65.00
Elmer Fudd..............................35.00
Frankenstein............................95.00
Mickey Mouse, lots of wear to paint 5.00
Mighty Mouse, small................25.00
Mummy, green head and hands, white body 175.00
Pinocchio................................25.00
Pluto, with hat..........................25.00
Punkin Puss, repainted............65.00
Santa Claus 10.00
Squiddly Diddly........................75.00
Sylvester Cat, some paint loss 35.00
Tennessee Tuxedo 45.00
Topcat, red or blue vest 45.00
Wendy Witch 45.00
Woody Woodpecker 25.00

❖ Soap Collectibles

If you're not into cleaning up with soakies, how about some soap collectibles. Again, flea markets are a great place to find all kinds of ephemera relating to soap, as well as some great examples of vintage soap. Don't overlook vintage illustrations used in advertising.

Miniature hotel soap, Hartness House, Palmolive, Wheeler-Williams, 1-1/2" x 2-1/4", $1.

Box
    Aristocat Kitten Soap, 1970s, Avon 65.00
    Peets Washing Machine Soap, goat image, 6" x 5 3/8" 125.00
    White King, lg, 1933 ....25.00
Brochure, Larkin Soap, 1885 .. 17.50
Soap saver, wire with basket-like head, 9-1/2" l 12.50
Pocket mirror, Dingman Soap, 1-7/8" dia......................................40.00
Ruler, Glory Soap Chips, folding, celluloid, Swift & Co., trademark, 1919 calendar, 5-1/2" l......35.00
Sign, Ivory, porcelain, blue and white, 3-1/4" x 21"..........330.00
Tin, Pax Soap, rooster, Packwood Mfg. Co., St Louis, 1940, 5-1/2" x 3-1/4" 28.00
Trade card, Babbitts Soap, "A Thing of Worth is a Joy Forever," Uncle Sam among men comparing Babbitts Soap to gold..........9.00

❖ Social Cause Collectibles

Here's a topic where collectors find memorabilia related to their favorite cause. Feel free to interpret this area as you see fit, for isn't that what social causes are all about?

Reference: William A. Sievert, *All For the Cause: Campaign Buttons For Social Change, 1960s-1990s*, Decoy Magazine, 1997.

Badge, "Old Newsboys Day Globe-Democrat Fund For Children," attached purple ribbon, gold lettered text "Old Newsboy," c1960 ....7.50
Flicker card, "The Tin Woodman," Heart Assn premium, colorful image pointing to his heart "Take Care Of Your Heart," Heart Assn inscription on back, c1960, 2-1/4" x 3-1/4," 35.00
Loom, miniature, old stringing, shuttles, some weaving intact, black stamp "N.R.A. We Do Our Part," green label "Oslind Miniature Loom," 9-1/2" x 12-1/2" ... 250.00
Pinback button
    Eat Grapes, purple grapes, white ground, c1970 ....8.00

Flowers for Peace, orange psychedelic lettering, yellow background, 1-3/4" d.....40.00
Keep the Faith Baby, Adam Clayton Powell, c1960..........12.00
I Support Lesbian and Gay Rights, black and white, dark pink heart, Texas, c1960 ....10.00
Linda Lovelace for President, 1-3/4" d, cello, red, dark blue, and white lettering, early 1970s 25.00
Support the Equal Rights amendment, dark blue and white...............................10.00
Take a Hippie to Lunch, black lettering, bright yellow ground, 1-1/2" d 15.00

❖ Soda

Getting thirsty? Collectors from around the country tend to call carbonated beverages by different names – it's "soda" to some, "soda pop" to others, and "pop" in other regions. Whatever your passion, flea markets are a great place to find collectibles that will "wet your whistle."

Periodical: *Club Soda,* P.O. Box 489, Troy, IN 83871.

Collectors Clubs: Dr. Pepper 10-2-4 Collectors Club, 3508 Mockingbird, Dallas, TX 75205; Grapette Collectors Club, 2240 Highway 27N, Nashville, AR 71852; National Pop Can Collectors, P.O. Box 7862, Rockford, IL 61126; Painted Soda Bottle Collectors Association, 9418 Hilmer Drive, La Mesa, CA 91942; Root Beer Float, P.O. Box 571, Lake Geneva, WI 53167.

For additional listings, see *Warman's Advertising Price Guide.*

Can, Dad's Root Beer, tin, conetop, 1940s-50s, qt 154.00
Cooler, Drink Dr. Pepper, airline style, 16" h, 18" w, 9" d....187.00
Coupon, Hires Root Beer, druggist stamp on front, 1-3/4" x 3".95.00
Door pull, Enjoy Kist Beverages, Here's Refreshment, litho tin 66.00
Fan, 75 Years Good, Dr. Pepper, Good For Life, cardboard 143.00

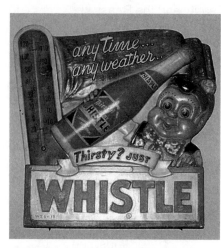

Whistle chalkware thermometer, 12-1/2" square, $170.

Mug, Buckeye Root Beer, ceramic, figural handle, cracks, chips, 6-1/4" h 22.00
Playing cards, Dr. Pepper, 1946, woman in red dress, 10-2-4 logo in corner, orig box 385.00
Postcard, Cherry Smash, Our Nation's Beverage, portrait of George Washington, glass of product inset on axe, embossed 302.50
Sidewalk marker, Enjoy Grapette, Walk Safely, brass, round, 1940s-50s..........................50.00
Sign
    Drink Canada Dry, metal flange, white shield with crown, chips, scratches, 14-1/2" x 17-1/2" 100.00
    Drink Dr. Pepper, Distinctively Different, embossed tin, shows pop-tab can, 1960s, 54" x 18"......................121.00
    Drink Orange-Crush, Naturally - It Tastes Better, orange ground, 1940s-50s, 40" sq 250.00
    Drink Sun Spot, tin, 9-3/4" x 12" 185.00
    Enjoy Orange Crush, celluloid, 9" dia 71.50
Thermometer
    Cheer Up by bottle, round with dial, 12" dia.................495.00
    Drink NuGrape Soda, A Flavor You Can't Forget, tin, rounded top and bottom, shows 6 bottles, 16" x 6-3/4" 100.00

❖ Soda Fountain

Soda fountains are another icon of a bygone era. However, a variety of soda fountain collectibles draw keen interest on today's collectibles market.

Collectors' Club: National Association of Soda Jerks, P.O. Box 115, Omaha, NE 68101; The Ice Screamers, P.O. Box 465, Warrington, PA 18976.

Barbie, Soda Fountain Sweetheart Barbie, Coca-Cola, 1st in series, MIB 250.00
Dispenser, Buckeye Root Beer, tree trunk shape, minor chips. 375.00
Fountain jerk heads, Liquid Mechanical Co., 15", pr 125.00
Glass, Hershey's, clear, 5-3/4" h, pr 22.00
Jar, Borden's Malted Milk, glass 175.00
Milkshake machine, Hamilton Beach, triple head, green.. 75.00
Seltzer bottle, cobalt, Babad's Miami Seltzer Co. 100.00
Straw holder, pressed glass, clear Cradle shape, 1910s....... 250.00
    Cylindrical, red metal lid, 1950s 175.00
Syrup jar, white porcelain, metal lid/pump, set of 4 .... 125.00

❖ Souvenirs

Vacations are always too short. Maybe that's what compels us to bring home mementos of those days. Flea markets are a good place to look for souvenirs.
Ashtray
    Souvenir of New York City, metal, Statue of Liberty in the center, other landmarks around the edge, oval, 4-3/4" x 3-3/4" 15.00
    Souvenir of Queen Elizabeth, metal, shows ship......... 15.00
Bank, Souvenir of Florida, ceramic, black boy on pig, 1940s-50s 155.00
Basket, Souvenir of Crosby, Minn., frosted, gold accents, 4-3/4" h 28.00
Bathtub, Souvenir of Craig, Iowa, milk glass, molded legs, 5-1/4" l 27.50

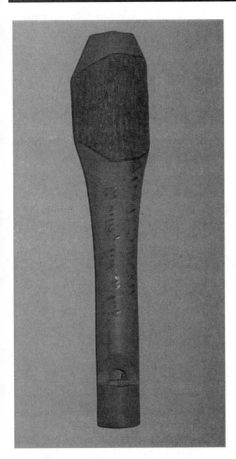

Great Smoky Mountain Park wooden whistle, 5" long, $5.

Cream and sugar, San Francisco, shows Golden Gate Bridge, dragonware, 2-3/4" h......... 35.00
Pillow cover
    Souvenir of Cheyenne, cowboy motif 20.00
    Washington, D.C., verse, fringe, 12" sq............................. 8.50
Sheet music, *A March to Eisenhower*, Souvenir of Inauguration 1953, red, white and blue cover shows American flag, sketch of White House and bluetone image of Eisenhower, 1953 .... 10.00
Tablecloth, Alaska 30.00
Teabag holder, Souvenir of Florida, ceramic, teapot shape, chips, 4-1/4" x 3-1/4"...................... 4.00
Trade card, Souvenir of the Virginia Exposition, With Compliments of Walter A. Wood, shows log cabin with black banjo player, farm machinery.......................... 45.00

❖ Souvenir China

These porcelain souvenirs have images of the places or events. Early examples were hand-painted in England and Germany, specially made for merchants in the United States. Souvenir china can be found in a variety of forms, from ashtrays to plates to pitchers to vases.

Periodical: *Antique Souvenir Collectors News*, P.O. Box 562, Great Barrington, MA 01230.
For additional listings, see *Warman's Americana & Collectibles* and *Warman's Antiques and Collectibles Price Guide*.
Bank, Marion, VA, Smith County Courthouse, barrel shape, 3" h 80.00
Box, cov, Rushville, IL, Wester School, black transfer, made by Wheelock...........................76.00
Chamberstick, Brant Rock, MA, National Electric Signaling Co., From Bluefish Rock, Aladdin style, 2-1/4" h, 6-3/4" l 160.00
Cup, Waukesha, WI, Bethesda Spring, shows pavilion and bandstand, 3" h 90.00
Plate
    Beaumont, TX, A Gushing Gusher, made by Wheelock, 7-3/4" dia.......................90.00

"Regent Spring, Excelsior Springs, Mo." souvenir china plate, Wheelock China, 3-7/8" diameter, $45.

"Clifton Suspension Bridge" souvenir china teapot, 5" high, $60.

Boston, Bunker Hill, blue transfer design, 9" dia................ 25.00
Northport, ME, Northport Hotel, mkd Germany, 6-5/8" dia 76.00
Olathe, KS, State Deaf and Dumb Institution, made by Wheelock, 8" dia......... 152.50
St. Louis, Souvenir of St. Louis, St. Louis World's Fair, 8-1/2" dia............................. 180.00
Williamsport, Pa., The River and Market Street Bridge, made by Wheelock, 7-1/2" dia 60.00
Match holder, Grand Falls, Nebr., cobalt, Germany 51.00
Teapot, Little Falls, N.Y., High School, 5-1/2" h 105.00
Toothpick holder, Alexandria, Va., Christ Church, 2-1/2" h 51.00
Tumbler, Bridgton, Maine, views of Public Library, Sunrise Rock and Scene From Ingalls Grove, 3-5/8" h 110.00
Vase
    Cripple Creek District, Colo., The Independence Mine, cobalt, 2 handles, Germany, 3" h 130.00
    Lapeer, MI, Nepessing Street, 4-7/8" h 68.00

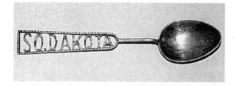

"So. Dakota" souvenir spoon, $30.

❖ Souvenir Spoons

Collecting souvenir spoons has become more popular in the past few years. Collectors are starting to admire the tiny treasures often for their colorful decoration as well as the place they honor. The following is a sampling of sterling silver souvenir spoons.

Periodical: *Spooners Forum*, c/o Bill Boyd, 7408 Englewood Lane, Raytown, MO 64133

Collectors' Clubs: American Spoon Collectors, 7408 Englewood Lane, Kansas City, MO 64133; Northeastern Spoon Collectors Guild, 52 Hillcrest Ave., Morristown, NJ 07960.
For additional listings, see *Warman's Americana & Collectibles*.
Atlantic City, oar shape, shows sailing ship and lighthouse, Codding Bros. & Heilborn, 4" l 18.00
Grant's Tomb, Tiffany, goldenrod handle, 4-1/4" l 24.00
Lookout Mountain, Chattanooga, TN, Incline Railroad in bowl, floral pattern handle, 4" l 20.00
Miami, The Old Cape Florida Light in bowl, Miami Biscayne Bay Florida on handle, reverse has Indian Chief Osceola on bowl, Seminole Soffkee Spoon on handle, by Gorham for Greenleaf & Crosby Co., 4-1/4" l 30.00
New York City, Statue of Liberty, city seal in bowl, Shiebler, 4-1/4" l 75.00
San Diego Skyline, mission, fruit, Paye & Baker, Old Palms, 5-5/8" 59.00
Tacoma, Wash., Old Church, gold-washed bowl, state handle, Mayer Bros., 5-3/8" l 29.00

Vermillion, S.D., gold-washed bowl, view of the university building, Whiting, 5" l 24.00

❖ Space Adventurers, Fictional

Space adventurers have always fascinated folks, from Buck Rogers in 1929 to the early awaited sequels to Star Trek. We're spellbound by their adventures—taken to new places and returned safely at the journey's end.

References: Dana Cain, *UFO & Alien Collectibles Price Guide*, Krause Publications, 1999; Rex Miller, *The Investor's Guide to Vintage Character Collectibles*, Krause Publications, 1999; Stuart W. Wells, III, *Science Fiction Collectibles Identification & Price Guide*, Krause Publications, 1998.

Collectors' Club: Galaxy Patrol, 22 Colton St, Worcester, MA 01610.
For additional listings, see *Warman's Americana & Collectibles*.
Activity Book, *Battlestar Galactica*, Wonder Books, Universal City Studios, Inc., unused 10.00
Book
    Buck Rogers, 25th Century A. D., Big Little Book, Whitman, 1938, Cocomalt premium 48.00

Jetsons mug, back side advertises Carnation Hot Cocoa Mix, $3.

Buck Rogers in the 25th Century, Kellogg's, 1932, 32 pgs 300.00
Buck Rogers in the 25th Century, Big Little Book, 1933 .... 35.00
Major Matt Mason-Moon Mission, George S. Elrick, Little Big Book, 1968, worn cover 26.00
Tom Corbett's Wonder Book of Space, Marcia Martin, Wonder Books, 1953 .... 12.00
Booklet, *Meet Major Matt Mason-Mattel's Man in Space,* 1965 .... 18.00
Code wheel, Captain Midnight 20.00
Comic book
    Space Family Robinson/Lost In Space, 1965, World Distributors 20.00
    Space Ghost, 1987, Hanna-Barbera 7.00
    Lost in Space, #13, Voyage to the Bottom of the Soul, 1993, Innovation, sealed in orig plastic with poster 8.00
Crayon box, Buck Rogers Crayon Ship, cardboard, 6 colored pencils, c1930 .... 175.00
Die-cast, Lost in Space Jupiter 2, with bonus film clip, MOC ... 5.00
Figure, Buck Rogers, Buck, Dr. Huer, Dale, Friend, Monster, painted lead, each 42.00
Flashlight, Captain Astro, wrist type, Bantamalite, c1967, MOC 45.00
Gun, Captain Video Secret Ray Gun, red plastic flashlight, secret message instructions, Power House Candy premium 90.00
Helmet, Steve Canyon, 1959, orig box 125.00
Lunch box
    Buck Rogers in the 25th Century, metal, with plastic thermos, 1979, Aladdin 55.00
    Space: 1999, metal, with thermos 58.00
Match cover, Buck Rogers, Popsicle adv 17.50
Wallet, Battlestar Galactica, vinyl, 1971, Larami, MOC 18.00

Apollo, Man on the Moon Coloring Book, Artcraft, 1969, 11" x 8-1/2", unused, $20.

❖ Space Exploration

In a day when space shuttle flights are commonplace, we've lost the excitement associated with early space flights. Nonetheless, space-related memorabilia, from the days of Sputnik to today's missions to Mars, is available to collectors. Flea markets are a great place to find such items.

Periodical: *Space Autograph News,* 862 Thomas Ave, San Diego, CA 92109.

For additional listings, see *Warman's Americana & Collectibles.*

Book, *Neal Armstrong: Space Pioneer,* Paul Westman, 1980, hardcover, 64 pgs.............. 15.00
Clock, Apollo 11, animated windup, ivory case, Lux Clock Co. 145.00
Drinking glass, Apollo 13, 4-1/8" h 2.00
Jewelry, pin, Apollo 11, 1969, dated 7-20-69, 1-1/2" h 29.00
Magazine, *Life,* July, 4, 1969, Apollo, "Off to the Moon" 15.00
Newspaper
    Madison Capital Times, Madison, Wis., May 5, 1961, "U.S. Man Blasted Into Space; Shepard's Back Safe" ... 25.00

The Washington Evening Star, Washington, D.C., July 21, 1969, Apollo Edition 45.00
Plate, "John H. Glenn Jr., Feb 20, 1962, First American to Orbit the World," 9-1/4" dia...............25.00
Paperweight, glass, Apollo 11, 1969, "One small step for man, one giant leap for mankind" around border, Fenton, 4" dia 160.00
Photograph, Space Shuttle Orbiter 101 crew, Official NASA photo 4.00
Record, *The First Man On The Moon,* Apollo 11 flight, 45 rpm 20.00
Stamp, Mercury Space Exhibit cover, 1962, 14th National Postage Stamp Show labels.....10.00
Token, Apollo 13, Shell Oil, 1970, 1-1/8" dia 12.00

❖ Space Toys

Now that we've done some imagining about space adventurers and real space heroes, how about some toys to round out our experience? Flea markets are sure to yield some out-of-this-world treasures.

References: Jim Bunte, Dave Hallman and Heinz Mueller, *Vintage Toys: Robots and Space Toys,* Antique Trader Books, 1999; Dana Cain, *UFO & Alien Collectibles Price Guide,* Krause Publications, 1999; Stuart W. Wells, III, *Science Fiction Collectibles Identification & Price Guide,* Krause Publications, 1998.

Periodical: *Toy Shop,* 700 E. State St., Iola, WI 54990.

Flash Gordon Rocket Fighter - Marx 1930's, MIB, $450.

Also see Robots.
Action figure, Commander Sisko, Deep Space Nine, 1994, MIB, 5" h 8.00
Bagatelle game, space theme, rockets and moon graphics, 14" x 8" 25.00
Board game, Space Pilot board game, Cadaco Ellie, 1951, ... 62.50
Flying saucer, litho tin, space pilot, revolving antenna, swivel lighted engine 395.00
Helmet, Space Patrol, cardboard, 1950s............................ 235.00
Model kit, Vostok, Russian space ship, Revell, 1969 .... 70.00
Play set, Space Shuttle Space Set, plastic, 11 pcs, 1984, Hong Kong, unsealed................. 25.00
Ray gun, Atomic Space Pistol, tin, 1960s, Japan, 6-1/2" l....... 24.00
Space ships
    Apollo, battery-op, Japan, MIB 275.00
    Eagle Lunar Module, battery-op, Daishin, Japan, 1969, MIB 320.00
    Gemini, litho tin, plastic windshield broken, 6" h...... 100.00
Top, Space Top, litho tin, 1950s 45.00

❖ Spark Plugs

Spark plug collectors are quite at home at flea markets devoted to automobiles. They look for interesting spark plugs, boxes, and other ephemera.

Champion
    J-9 14 MM, 13/16" hex, MIB 10.00
    Maytag, 14 MM, red lettering, used............................ 30.00
    V-3, airplane 15.50
    W-18, oversized 6.00
Red Head, 1-1/2" pipe thread, unused............................ 40.00
Western Auto
    Endurance Red Seal, box only, 1950s............................ 2.00
    Wizard, orig box, MIB.......... 3.00

Spatter glass miniature lamp, Beaded Swirl pattern, brown and green, 8-7/8" high, $275.

❖ Spatter Glass

This colorful glassware is so named because of the spatters found in the clear glass body. The misnomer "end of day glass" has been associated with spatter glass for years. These colorful combinations weren't unplanned; instead, many are terrific examples of a glass blower showing off his craft.

Basket, multicolored spatter, white int., cased, applied crystal thorn handle, polished pontil, Stourbridge, England, c1880 7" h, 6" w triangular body 285.00

8" h, 6-1/4" w, sides pinched to form ruffled top 295.00

Creamer, 4" h, multicolored spatter, white int., cased, applied crystal handle, English 125.00

Vase
4-1/4" h, multicolored spatter, cased, Stourbridge, c1880 .... 75.00

5" h, silver and multicolored spatter, mica flecks, white int., cased, attributed to Stevens & Williams 195.00

7-1/4" h, white, yellow, and pink spatter, cased, applied crystal handles, English, c1880 .... 325.00

Water set, Leaf Mold, cased cranberry spatter, 6 pcs 850.00

❖ Spongeware

Ever see pottery that looked like someone had taken paint and just sponged all over the piece—well that's spongeware. Extensively produced in England and America, spongeware items were most commonly blue and white, but yellowware with mottled tans, browns, and greens was also popular. The design was achieved by sponging, spattering, or daubing on the color, and it was generally applied in an overall pattern. Care should be taken when examining a piece of spongeware, as modern craftsmen are making some examples that rival their antique ancestors.

References: William C. Ketchum Jr., *American Country Pottery: Yellowware and Spongeware*, Alfred A. Knopf, 1987; Kevin McConnell, *Spongeware and Spatterware*, 2nd ed., Schiffer Publishing, 1999.

Reproduction Alert. Reproductions and contemporary examples are quite common.

Note: All listings are blue-and-white unless otherwise noted.

For additional listings, see *Warman's Antiques and Collectibles Price Guide* and *Warman's Country Price Guide*.

Bank, pig, brown and green sponging, pierced eyes and coin slot, 6" l 209.00

Bowl
11-1/2" dia, green and brown sponging, glaze flakes 330.00

12" dia, blue sponging above and below blue stripe ..275.00

12" dia, blue sponging overall 412.50

Spongeware cuspidor, 4-3/4" high, 7" diameter, $80.

Bowl, mixing
4" h, scalloped panels on sides, glaze wear in bottom, rim hairline 165.00

10" dia, 4-3/4" h, blue, heart panels, large glaze imperfection on interior 137.50

12" dia, 5-1/2" h, molded arched panels 275.00

Butter crock
"Butter" in oblong border, sponged band above and below, sponged lid, bail handle, lid cracked, 3-3/4" h, 5-3/4" dia 192.50

"Butter" framed with dark chicken-wire sponging, orig lid, 2 rim chips filled, 3-3/4" h 247.50

Good Luck pattern, 5" h, 7-1/2" dia 225.00

Chamber pot with handle, overall sponging, 5-1/2" h, 10" dia 121.00

Custard, minor surface wear, hairline crack, 2-3/4" h 44.00

Nappy, 3-1/4" h, 10" dia 247.50

Pitcher
Bulbous form, double bands around top and base, sponged body, 9-3/4" h 632.50

Lattice design, brown and green sponging, yellow body, rim chips, 9-1/4" h 88.00

Miniature, brown and green chicken-wire sponging, 3" h 220.00

Plain form, dark chain-link sponging, large interior rim chip, 9" h 302.50

Wild Rose, roses highlighted in cobalt, upper and lower part of pitcher sponged, small surface chip, 9" h 412.50

Spittoon, blue bands, imperfections, 5" h, 7-1/2" dia 100.00

Teapot, chips on lid and spout 700.00

Wash pitcher, bulbous base, 3 blue lines around body 302.50

❖ Sporting Collectibles

Whatever sport is your passion, you're bound to find some interesting examples of ephemera and other collectibles while browsing a flea market.

Reference: Sports Collectors Digest Editors, *Sports Collectors Almanac*, Krause Publications, 1998; Tom Mortenson, *2000 Standard Catalog of Sports Memorabilia*, Krause Publications, 1999.

For additional listings, see *Warman's Antiques and Collectibles Price Guide*, *Warman's Americana & Collectibles*, and specific categories in this edition.

Charm, male archer, sterling silver 28.00

Magazine, *The Sporting News*, Oct. 24,1970, Johnny Bench cover 10.00

Pendant, metal, crossed arrows, attached to ribbon safety pin, "Class A, 1942" on back, 3/4" sq 22.00

Postcard, Soldier Field and Field Museum, Grant Park, Chicago, 1937 postmark, $5.

Pinback button
American Bowling Congress 1932, 32nd Annual Tournament, Detroit 82.00
Devil's Lake Regatta, blue and white, 1934 .... 15.00
U.S. Open Tennis Championship, 1975 .... 18.50

Plate, hunter walking in brook with 5 dogs, Royal Bayreuth, chip, 7-1/2" dia 65.00

Tie tack, male archer, sterling silver 22.00

Tobacco card
Jackie Brown, boxer, 1935, Sporting Events & Stars series, J.A. Pattreioux, yellowing 5.00
E.W. Higgins, cycler, 1935, Sporting Events & Stars series, J.A. Pattreioux 5.00
Fred Welsh, boxer, Series of Champion Athletes & Prize Fighters series, Mecca Cigarettes 35.00

❖ Sporting Goods

So, you'd rather participate in sports than watch? Needing some kitschy decor items for your family room? Well, head for the flea market and look for some of these neat collectibles.

See specific listings for fishing, skateboards, etc.

Baseball glove, professional model
Del Ennis, Wilson 60.00
Draper Maynard, D&M 110.00
Grover Alexander 130.00
Joe DiMaggio, Spalding 50.00
Pee Wee Reese, pre-World War II 75.00

Catalog
Kirtland Bros. Sporting Goods, 1924, 16 pgs 12.50
Timberwolf Cutlery and Sporting Goods, Winter 1983, Clanton, Ala., 48 pgs 4.00

Football, Dowdle Sporting Goods 68.00

Minnow bucket, green canvas, collapsible, No. 08, Mfd. by the Planet Co., West Field, Mass., 7-1/2" h 155.00

Roller skates, Glove Roller Skates No. 197, Marvel Beginners Ages 2-5, orig box, 1 leather strap missing 35.00

Snowshoes, pr 125.00

Keds basketball shoes, $35.

❖ Staffordshire Items

The Staffordshire district of England is well known for the quality porcelain produced there through the centuries. This region was home to many potteries that supplied dinnerware, table items, and novelties such as mantel figures and toby jugs.

For additional listings, see *Warman's Antiques and Collectibles Price Guide* and *Warman's English & Continental Pottery & Porcelain*.

Bank, cottage shape, 5-1/4" h, repairs 195.00

Box, cov, oval, raised panels, finial, green, black, and gold traces 60.00

Chamber pot, cov, 9" h, Columbia, mkd "W. Adams," short hairline in bottom 80.00

Cup and saucer, handleless, dark blue transfer of vase with flowers, imp "Clews," small chips, wear 95.00

Figure
Gentleman, seated, book and spectacles, polychrome enamel, damaged, old repairs 275.00
Rabbit, black and white, green and brown base, 3-1/4" h, wear and enamel flaking 315.00
Squirrel, sitting upright, holding nut, naturalistic stump base, ear repaired 125.00

Mantel ornament, cottage, Potash Farm, hairlines, 9" h 175.00

Plate, blue feathered edge, emb rim design, 10" dia 55.00

Red-transfer Staffordshire plate, $15.

Waste bowl, Forget-Me-Not, red transfer, edge roughness, 5-5/8" dia 60.00

❖ Stamps

Stamp collecting has long been one of the most popular hobbies. Like many other hobbies, it is crucial that participants spend time reading and researching stamps and their values.

References: George Cuhaj, ed., *Krause-Minkus Standard Catalog of Canadian & United Nations Stamps*, Krause Publications, 1998; Arlene Dunn, ed., *Brookman Price Guide for Disney Stamps,* 2nd edition, Krause Publications, 1998; Robert Furman, *The 1999 Comprehensive Catalogue of United States Stamp Booklets, Postage and Airmail,* Krause Publications, 1998, plus many others.

Periodical: *Stamp Collector,* 700 E State St, Iola, WI 54990, plus others.

Collectors' Clubs: American Philatelic Society, P.O. Box 8000, State College, PA 16803; International Stamp Collectors Society, P.O. Box 854, Van Nuys, CA 91408. Contact either one of these to inquire about local chapters.

❖ Stangl

Stangl Pottery was an active pottery in the Flemington, New Jersey, area. They produced colorful dinnerware, table wares and are well known for their interesting bird figurines.

References: Robert C. Runge Jr., *Collector's Guide to Stangl Dinnerware*, Collector Books, 2000.

Collectors' Club: Stangl/Fulper Collectors Club, P.O. Box 538, Flemington, NJ 08822.

For additional listings, see *Warman's Antiques and Collectibles Price Guide* (Stangl Birds) and *Warman's Americana & Collectibles* (dinnerware).

Basket, #3414.........................20.00
Butter dish, cov, Country Garden 42.00
Child's dish and cup, ABC's, chip on rear of plate 85.00
Chop plate, Harvest.................42.00
Cigarette box, cov, goldfinch ...55.00
Coffeepot, Blue Rooster 90.00
Creamer, Blue Rooster 27.50
Cup and saucer
    Country Garden 20.00
    Harvest............................22.00
    Terra Rose 24.00
    Town and Country, brown 20.00
Decorative plate, quail, small chip on back..................................25.00
Dinner plate
    Country Garden 40.00
    Terra Rose 15.00
    Thistle 19.50
Eggcup, Country Garden.........15.00
Gravy boat, Thistle 24.00

Town and Country sugar and creamer, brown and white, Stangl, pair, $30.

Mug, Town and Country, blue . 22.00
Teapot, Harvest......................80.00
Vase, orange, #3102, 7" h 75.00
Wig stand, lady's head, brown 500.00

❖ Stanhope

Remember those Easter Eggs that you peeked in one end to see an Easter scene at the other end? That's a large form of a Stanhope. Stanhopes are little scenes tucked in miniature holders. Sometimes the cases are shaped like cameras and the viewer sees different images when holding the camera up to the light. Other Stanhopes are shaped like tiny binoculars.

Disney 40th anniversary, a scene from "Aladdin's Oasis" at Disneyland 4.00
Easter egg, composition and plastic, blue egg, multicolored scene, c1950 .... 5.00
Eiffel Tower, binoculars shape, bone, brass ring, c1900, 1-1/2" l. 55.00
Garfield, General James A., scenes and incidents from his life, 1831-1881 .... 100.00
Lord's Prayer, cross shape, silvertone, baguettes dec, 1950s, 1-1/2" l, 1" w..................... 35.00
Napoleon, figure, 2" h, bronzed 80.00
Rock City, plastic camera with 15 views, mkd "Brownie Mfg Co., West Germany," 2-1/4" x 1-1/4" 10.00
Rome, Coliseum, St. Peters, binoculars shape, 1-1/8" l............ 35.00
Rosary 21.50
The Apparition of Knock County, Mayo, Ireland, bone, 1-5/8" l 22.00

❖ Stanley Tools

Some of the finest tools were created by the Stanley Tool Co. Today they are increasingly collectible. Look for examples free of rust and damage, but expect to find some wear from usage.

Periodical: *Stanley Tool Collectors News*, 208 Front St, P.O. Box 227, Marietta, OH 45750.

Brace and eclipse bit, No. 945-10 ....22.00
Doweling jig, No. 59, nickel-plated, orig box 30.00
Folding measure
    No. 27, 24".......................10.00
    No. 38, 24" 20.00
Level, No. 27, 9" l....................10.00
Plane
    No. 4 ....50.00
    No. 45 ....150.00
    No. 48, tongue and grove 120.00
    No. 78 rabbet plane, orig box
    ....110.00
Router, No. 71-1/2..................60.00
Vise No. 700..........................45.00

❖ Star Trek

"Beam Me Up Scotty" certainly is a phrase many collectors associate with Star Trek. The adventures of this space team started on television in September 1966 and lasted until June 1969. By 1978 syndicated broadcasts were reaching 51 countries, while the number of Star Trek fan clubs kept growing. *Star Trek, the Motion Picture* was released in 1979, followed by additional movies.

Collectors' Clubs: International Federation of Trekkers, P.O. Box 84, Groveport, OH, 43125; Starfleet, 200 Hiawatha Blvd., Oakland, NJ 07436; Star Trek: The Official Fan Club, P.O. Box 111000, Aurora, CO 80042.

Action figure
    Gowron, ritual Klingon attire, *Star Trek: The Next Generation,* 1994 series, second set, MIB, 5" h..............................45.00
    Montgomery Scott, 1994, MIB, 5" h..............................30.00
    Mordock the Benzite, *Star Trek: The Next Generation,* 1994 reissue, MIB..................26.00
Children's dishes, *Star Trek: The Motion Picture,* bowl, cup and tumbler, hard plastic 35.00
Dress, mid-1980s, mint 160.00
Game, Star Trek Game, 1983 copyright 30.00
Matchbook, Star Trek, *The Motion Picture,* 1977, cover only.....9.00
Micro Machine, U.S.S. Enterprise, fold-out ship with 4 figures, 10" l 25.00

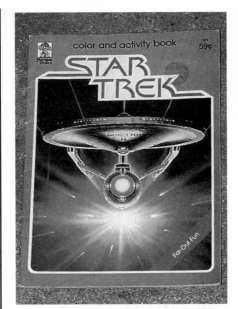

Star Trek Color & Activity Book, 1982, Merrigold Press, $5.

Pin, Star Trek: Deep Space Nine, 1993, Paramount Pictures, 1-1/2" h................................4.00
Plate, All Good Things, 1994, *Star Trek: The Next Generation,* no box....................................17.50
Trading card
    Star Trek, 1993, SkyBox, factory-sealed box of 36 packs 35.00
    Star Trek - The Original Series, 1996, 30th anniversary set, meal cards, set of 6, factory-sealed box.....................11.00

❖ Star Wars

"May The Force Be With You" as you search for collectibles from this series of science-fiction movies. George Lucas brought such special effects to the screen that fans of all ages were mesmerized. 20th Century-Fox was clever enough to give Kenner a broad license to produce movie-related toys and items, creating a wealth of Star Wars materials for collectors.

References: James T. McCallum, *Irwin Toys: The Canadian Star Wars Connection*, Collector's Guide Publishing, Inc., 2000; Stuart W. Wells, III, *Science Fiction Collectibles Identification & Price Guide*, Krause Publications, 1998.

Periodical: *The Star Wars Collector,* 20982 Homecrest Court, Ashburn, VA 22011.

Collectors' Club: Official Star Wars Fan Club, P.O. Box 111000, Aurora, CO 80042.

Action figure
    Chewbacca, 1978, with weapon, pouch and ammunition belt, mint, 12" 70.00
    Luke Skywalker, 1996, MIB 60.00
Book, *Star Wars: A Pop-up Book*, Random House, 1978, one section missing......................25.00
Costume, C-3PO, Ben Cooper, 1977 ....35.00
Game
    Escape from Death Star Game, 1977 ....35.00
    Ewoks Save the Trees, 1984, sealed..........................25.00
    Wicket the Ewok and Friends in a Food Gathering Adventure Game, Parker Brothers, 1983, NM................................45.00
Helmet, Darth Vader, Don Post, orig box, 1977 ....115.00
Mug
    Luke Skywalker, Sigma 24.00
    Obi-Wan Kenobi, Rumph, 1977 ....135.00
Play set, Rebel Pilot/Hoth, Micro Machines, MIP 15.00

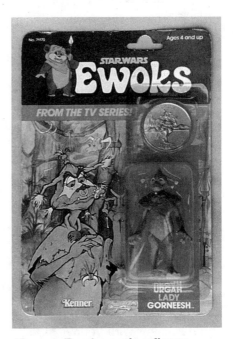

Kenner Ewoks action figure, Urgah Lady Gorneesh, $22.50.

Postcard, Greetings Earthlings,
    Droids .... .25
Poster, Luke Skywalker, Coca-Cola,
    24" x 18" 18.00
Shampoo, Yoda, 6-1/2" h 35.00

❖ St. Clair Glass

Molds from defunct glass companies were used by St. Clair, which produced items in new colors as well as pieces in colors similar to the originals. The glass is usually marked and is eagerly sought by collectors.

Bell, Rosette pattern, chocolate
    glass, 6-1/4" h 55.00
Bicentennial plate, blue carnival,
    5-1/2" dia 40.00
Candleholder, paperweight base,
    red florals, applied glass handle,
    sgd, 11-1/2" dia 55.00
Figure, buffalo, caramel slag ... 40.00
Paperweight
    Apple, red 82.00
    Bell shape, turquoise, sgd
    .... 55.00
    Bird, yellow, sgd 50.00
    Blue flowers 40.00
    Owl, sulfide, yellow base, sgd
        "Maude and Bob" 180.00
    Pear, green 100.00
    Turtle, clear and brown, sgd
        "Maude and Bob," 1982
    .... 155.00
    Yellow flowers, 10" dia 70.00
Salt, open, wheelbarrow, caramel
    slag 15.00
Toothpick holder, Indian, yellow,
    2-3/4" h 30.00
Tumbler, Cactus, cobalt blue ... 28.00

St. Clair teapot-shaped ring holder, clear with yellow, blue, red and white flowers, 4-1/4" high, 6" long, $60.

Steiff cat with blue ribbon, glass eyes, 7" long, $65.

❖ Steiff

Steiff bears and toys are recognized by their button ear tag. Steiff's first teddy bear appeared in 1903 and was an instant hit. The company remains in business, and collectors know the name means quality and a well-made toy.

Reference: Dee Hockenberry, *Steiff Bears & Other Playthings*, Schiffer Publishing, 2000.

Collectors' Clubs: Steiff Club USA, 225 Fifth Ave, Suite 1033, New York, NY 10010; Steiff Collectors Club, P.O. Box 798, Holland, OH 43528.

Bunny, Manni, button 85.00
Circus seal, with ball, on stand
    .... 85.00
Hen, gold and black spotted feathers, yellow plush head, felt tail,
    black button eyes, c1949 ... 85.00
Kangaroo, plush, glass eyes, 2 plastic Joeys in pouch 70.00
Leopard 90.00
Llama, standing, white, brown spots
    .... 110.00
Owl, 10" h 75.00
Parrot, Lora, glass eyes 75.00
Rabbit, jointed, mohair, 6-1/2" h
    .... 110.00
Squirrel, Perri, plush 45.00
Teddy bear
    Light brown plush, glass eyes,
        jointed, c1950 .... 350.00
    Tan mohair, ear button, chest
        tag, jointed, c1980 .... 75.00

❖ Steins

Finding steins at flea markets is great fun. Look for advertising or novelty steins, and don't overlook the limited ones made to commemorate a special event, such as a fire truck housing.

Periodical: *Regimental Quarterly*, P.O. Box 793, Frederick, MD 21705.

Collectors' Club: Stein Collectors International, P.O. Box 5005, Laurel, MD 20726; Sun Steiners, P.O. Box 11782, Fort Lauderdale, FL 33339.
For additional listings, see *Warman's Antiques and Collectibles Price Guide.*

Avon, vintage automobiles, 1979, no
    box, 8-1/2" h 19.50
Budweiser
    50th anniversary, 1933-1983, 3rd
        in Holiday series, Clydesdales
        on snow scene with cabin
    .... 100.00
    Basketball, 1991, orig box
    .... 15.00
    Frog, Albert Stahl and Co.,
        9-1/2" h 210.00
Figural
    Ape, dressed in hobo tuxedo
        jacket, top hat, drinking from
        stein, smoking pipe, pewter
        thumb rest, 9-1/2" h 100.00
    Jolly Man, sitting on stump, playing accordion, pewter thumb
        rest and lid rim, 9-1/2" h
    .... 150.00

Cobalt stein, silver-plated lid, 4-1/4" high, $35.

Budweiser stein, 1988 Collectors Series, $22.

Monk, #3, fat monk with book, pewter handle, by Gertiz, West Germany, 7" h 125.00

Greentown Glass, Troubadour, pale yellow, 5" h 29.00

McCoy, Spirit of '76, 8" h 35.00

Mekelbach, half liter, Hassfurt Township, pewter lid and thumb rest, raised lettering and seal on lid, German inscription on front, blue and white border and green wreath, 5-1/2" h 100.00

Mettlach

#171, half liter, figures representing monthly activities, blue background, inlaid top, pewter rim and thumbrest, 9-1/2" h, minor rubbing 90.00

2-1/4-liter, PUG, pewter lid and thumbrest, print of musical cherubs, man and woman performing ceremony, 17" h 250.00

Oakland Raiders, National Football League Collector's Stein, 7-1/2" h 15.00

Oktoberfest, German beer garden scene, Ceramarte, 1996, 5-3/4" h 20.00

Olympics, deep relief, full color, official logo, Atlanta, 1996, mkd "Made in Brazil, Ceramarte," 5-3/4" h 25.00

❖ Stereoptican and Cards

Here's another way to bring antiques into your family entertainment area. Think of a stereoptican as the precursor of the modern View-Master. Stereopticans were made as tabletop and hand-held models. Stereoviews covered many topics, from comedies to disasters, and from everyday scenes to tourist sites.

Collectors' Club: National Stereoscopic Association, P.O. Box 14801, Columbus, OH 43214.

Stereoview

Birthplace of Abraham Lincoln, Keystone 4.00

Bristol, Steamship scene ... 18.50

Cemetery Gatehouse, Gettysburg, Anthony # 2388 .. 350.00

Civil War, Libby Prison, Anthony #3365, yellow mount 45.00

Crystal Palace, yellow mount 27.50

Deer hunting, Keystone #26396 .... 8.50

Eskimo Dog Team on Trail, Hopedale, Labrador, Keystone 10.00

Fishing in the Pool, copyright 1903, T. W. Ingersoll, No. 499 .... 6.00

Fireman, steam pumper, 1870 .... 50.00

Funeral of Abraham Lincoln, Anthony #2948 .... 75.00

Stereoview, "Salute to the Colors, West Point Academy," 1925, worn corners, $3.

Panoramic View of Washington, D.C., Underwood & Underwood 15.00

Picking Cotton on a Mississippi Plantation, Keystone #9506 .... 30.00

Princess Gray Paws, Keystone #34467 .... 10.00

Portland Fire, 1866, Soule #469 .... 12.00

Savannah, Bonaventura Cemetery 10.00

Viewer

Hand-held, aluminum hood, wooden folding handle 125.00

Hand-held, Sears Roebuck, with 56 cards...................... 125.00

Hand-held, walnut, screw on handle, velvet hood 115.00

Table top, Bates-Holmes, paper or wood hood.............. 195.00

Table top, Bowstills Graphoscope 695.00

Table top, Keystone, school and library type, black crinkle metal finish 95.00

❖ Steuben Glass

The Steuben Glass Works was established in Corning, New York, in 1904. The company produced many types of glass, from crystal to art glass. A trip to the Corning Museum is always a treat that includes seeing the glass made. Look for the traditional fleur-de-lis mark on Steuben Glass, although not all pieces are marked. Beware of faked signatures. For additional listings, see *Warman's Antiques* and *Collectibles Price Guide* and *Warman's Glass*.

Bowl, blown into mold, amber, catalog #7696 .... 300.00

Champagne, ruby, crystal stem, catalog #6521, set of 8 .... 500.00

Cologne, 5" h, catalog #6887

Flemish Blue, ... 225.00

Wisteria 300.00

Compote, Cerise, ruby and crystal, twisted stem, catalog #6043 .... 325.00

Perfume, Verre de Soie, green jade stopper, catalog #1455 ... 300.00

Puff box, Green Jade, catalog #2910 .... 325.00

Steuben Aurene bowl, gold iridescent, pedestal foot, 4-3/4" high, 11" diameter, $315.

Salt, gold Aurene on calcite, pedestal foot, 1-1/2" h, 2-1/2" w 375.00
Sherbet set, catalog #2960, gold Aurene stemmed bowl, calcite stem, matching undertray, sgd "F. Carder Aurene" on base 300.00
Vase
  Celeste Blue, catalog #6298, fan shape, optic ribbed version, triple wafer stem, pedestal base stamped with fleur-de-lis mark 320.00
  Rosaline, catalog #345 ....300.00

❖ Stocks and Bonds

Just as today's Wall Street stocks and bonds fluctuate, so do the prices of vintage stocks and bonds, just not as quickly. Many collectors enjoy researching the companies that issued stock; some enjoy the intricate vignettes.

Periodical: *Bank Note Reporter,* 700 E State St, Iola, WI 54990.

Collectors' Clubs: Bond and Share Society, 26 Broadway at Bowling Green, Room 200, New York, NY 10004; Old Certificates Collector's Club, 4761 W Waterbuck Drive, Tucson, AZ 85742.

Atchison, Topeka & Santa Fe Railroad, $1000 bond, two vignettes of railroad station interior, issued 20.00
Ben-Hur Motor Car, globe vignette, issued but not canceled, 1917 ....85.00

Carson City Controller's Office Warrant, March 8, 1888, Carson Gas Co. 40.00
Ford International Capital Corporation, $1000 bond, 1968......15.00
Fruit of the Loom, script certificate for fractional share of common stock, 1938 ....7.50
King Productions, Inc., unissued stock certificate book, 9-3/4" x 16" black textured hardbound book, 26 green bank note design stock certificates, vignette of two workers in factory, wheels and turbines against city skyline, bound, serially numbered, c1940 ....75.00
Milwaukee Street Railway, incorporated under the laws of New Jersey, c1880 ....50.00
New York City Revenue Bond, 1858 ....45.00
Nickel Plated Railway, June 4, 1957 ....40.00
Packard Motor Car Company, August 7, 1951, one share 30.00
Pennsylvania New York Central Transportation Co., 100 shares, blue on white, black vignette, Sept 11, 1968 ....50.00
Pepsi-Cola United Bottlers, vignette of goddess holding world globe and Pepsi bottle, issued 15.00
State of New York, Canal Department, Draper, Toppan & Co., NY, engravers, 1842 ....18.50
United Airlines, $1000 share, 1970s 7.50

❖ Stoneware

Crocks and jugs are forms of stoneware. Early potters boasted of its durability and added cobalt blue lettering to advertise their location, or perhaps a flower or bird as decoration. Pieces which exhibit slightly pitted surfaces are referred to as having an "orange peel" glaze. Stoneware items are impervious to liquid and extremely durable, making them ideal for food preparation and storage. The most desirable pieces are those with unusual cobalt decorations.

"Home Made Preserves" crock, $50.

References: Georgeanna H. Greer, *American Stonewares: The Art and Craft of Utilitarian Potters*, Schiffer Publishing, 1999; Kathryn McNerney, *Blue & White Stoneware*, Collector Books, 1996; Terry Taylor and Terry & Kay Lawrence, *Collector's Encyclopedia of Salt Glaze Stoneware*, Collector Books, 1997.

Collectors' Clubs: American Stoneware Association, 208 Crescent Ct, Mars, PA 16066-3308; American Stoneware Collectors Society, P.O. Box 281, Bay Head, NJ 08742; Blue & White Pottery Club, 224 12th St, NW, Cedar Rapids, IA 52405; Collectors of Illinois Pottery & Stoneware, 308 N Jackson St., Clinton, IL 61727; Red Wing Collectors Society, Inc., P.O. Box 14, Galesburg, IL 61401; Southern Folk Pottery Collectors Society, 1828 N Howard Mill Rd, Robbins, NC 27325-7477; Uhl Collectors' Society, 80 Tidewater Rd, Hagerstown, IN 47346.

Museums: Bennington Museum, VT; Brooklyn Museum, NY; DAR Museum, Washington, DC; Henry Ford Museum, Dearborn, MI; Henry Francis DuPont Winterthur Museum, DE; Museum of Ceramics at East Liverpool, OH; Shelburne Museum, VT.

For additional listings, see *Warman's Country Price Guide.*

Canning jar

Hamilton & Jones, Greensboro, Pa., salt-glazed, cobalt stencil, minor chips, 8-1/2" h 132.00

Mason Fruit Jar, Union Stoneware Co., Red Wing, Minn., 1/2-gal, bristol glaze, blue inkstamp mark 220.00

Unmarked, salt-glazed, 4 brushed stripes on front, minor chips, 1/2-gal, 8" h 209.00

Churn

Uhl Pottery Co., Acorn Wares ink stamp, 2-gal, bristol glaze 150.00

Unmarked, 5-gal, salt glaze, cobalt stencil of two roses beneath round wreath with "5", hairline 192.50

Crock or storage jar

Jas. Benjamin Stoneware Depot, Cincinnati, O., 2-gal, salt-glazed, cobalt stencil, crack 77.00

C.W. Braun, Buffalo, N.Y., 6-gal, salt-glazed, cobalt sunflower decor, crack................. 247.50

Salt-glazed jug with simple cobalt decoration, $80.

Burger & Co., Rochester, N.Y., 3-gal, salt-glazed, wreath variation 412.50

N. Clark & Co., Lyons, 3-gal, saltglazed, ovoid, brushed cobalt flower, chips 275.00

J. Fisher & Co., Lyons, N.Y., 2-gal, salt-glazed, brushed tulip............................ 220.00

James Hamilton & Co., Greensboro, Pa., 3-gal, salt-glazed, cobalt stencil and freehand stripes, double handles, minor stains, chips 385.00

Lyons, 1-gal, salt-glazed, brushed flower, crack ..132.00

New York Stoneware Co., Fort Edwards, N.Y., 3-gal, saltglazed, large bird on plume, orig lid, cinnamon clay 577.50

J.&E. Norton, Bennington, Vt., 2-gal, salt-glazed, dotted floral decor, minor rim chip...605.00

Union Stoneware Co., Red Wing, Minn., 20-gal, bristol glaze, four birch leaves, ink stamp mark 286.00

Jug

John Burger, Rochester,N.Y., 2-gal, salt-glazed, poppy decor 440.00

Cowden & Wilcox, 1-gal, saltglazed, freehand cobalt flower with petals and scrolled leaves, chip 450.00

A.P. Donaghho, Parkersburg, W.Va., 2-gal, salt-glazed, beehive shape, stenciled "2" in circle motif above name, minor spout chips........247.50

Hamilton & Jones, Greensboro, 2-gal, salt-glazed, ovoid, cobalt stencil and freehand decor, minor chips on neck 302.50

T. Harrington, Lyons, 4-gal, saltglazed, ovoid, brushed leaf, stains..........................247.50

C.W. Weaver, Stoneware Depot, Cincinnati, Ohio, 2-gal, saltglazed, cobalt stencil, handle cracked, small chips....110.00

Unmarked, bee-sting decor, 3-gal, salt-glazed, beehive shape, handle cracked 247.50

Strawberry Shortcake metal lunch box with plastic thermos, $20.

❖ Strawberry Shortcake

Who's that freckle-faced kid in the puffy bonnet? It's Strawberry Shortcake, of course. Strawberry Shortcake memorabilia is both available and affordable, meaning it's perfect flea market material as well as a great collectible for children and adults.

Collectors' Clubs: Strawberry Shortcake Collectors' Club, 1409 72nd St, North Bergen, NJ 07047-3827; Strawberry Shortcake Doll Club, 405 E Main Cross, Greenville, KY 42345.

Carrying case, strawberry shape 15.00

Jewelry

Charm Set, Apricot, Lemon, Custard, some wear.......... 100.00

Necklace, Strawberry Shortcake, hand over mouth 25.00

Ring, Strawberry Shortake 20.00

Comforter, Strawberry Shortcake, some wear 15.00

Doll

Angel Cake with Souffle, MIB 45.00

Apricot with Hopsalot, MIB 65.00

Lem & Ada with Sugar Woofer, MIB 90.00

Mint Tulip with Marsh Mallard,
MIB................................80.00
Strawberry Shortcake, 1st ed.,
MIB................................75.00
Game, board, slight play wear
Berries to Market Game, American Greetings Corporation,
c1979 ....35.00
Strawberry Shortcake Berry-Go-Round, Parker Brothers,
c1981 ....25.00
Lunch box, Aladdin, thermos missing, C-8.........................25.00
Pillow panel, Strawberry Shortcake
train, uncut 27.00
Playset
Lime Chiffon, Dance n' Berry-cise, 1991, MIP 35.00
Strawberry Shortcake, Berry
Beach Park, 1991, MIP
....45.00
Sleeping bag, Strawberry Shortcake, some wear 15.00

❖ String Holders

The string holder developed as a useful tool to assist the merchant or manufacturer who needed tangle-free string or twine to tie packages. The early holders were made of cast-iron, with some patents dating to the 1860s. Among the variations to evolve were the hanging lithographed-tin examples with advertising and decorative chalkware examples. In the home, string holders remained a useful kitchen element until the early 1950s.

Look for examples that are bright and colorful, free of chips or damage, and include the original hanger.
Apple, chalkware, 7-3/4" h 95.00
Black man and woman, chalkware,
matched pair 275.00
Boy, top hat and pipe, chalkware,
9" h 125.00
Cast iron, ball shape, designed to be
hung from ceiling...............75.00
Cat, ball of twine, white cat,
red/orange ball, chalkware, 7" h
....75.00
Cat, ball of twine and bow, black cat,
white face, green bow, chalkware, 6-1/2" h 100.00
Chef
Black, chalkware, 8" h 165.00

Chalkware cat string holder, 6-3/4" high, $75.

White, chalkware, 7-1/4" h
....145.00
Dome, clear etched glass, cobalt
band around rim and base,
engraved flowers, mid-19th C,
minor chips 172.50
Dutch girl, chalkware, 7" h 100.00
Kettle shape, cast iron, embossed
"S.S.S. For The Blood," missing
handles, 4-1/2" h, 5" dia ..110.00
Mammy, holding flowers, chalkware, 6-1/2" h 185.00
Pear, chalkware, 7-3/4" h 85.00
Pineapple, face, chalkware, 7" h
....165.00
Senor, chalkware, bright colors,
8-1/4" h 90.00
Strawberry, chalkware, 6-1/2" h
....115.00

❖ Structo

Founded in 1909 in Freeport, Illinois, this company's earliest products were construction toys. Sturdy metal toy vehicles were added to the line about 1919. Ertl bought Structo's toy patents and designs in 1975.
Army Cub Jeep, #200, pressed
steel, orig box 75.00

Cargo truck, steel, #702.......... 75.00
Cattle Farms truck and trailer, metal
.... 220.00
Dump Truck, diecast, painted white,
red sheet metal body, extension
frame, dual rubber tires, side
decals, 12" l, MIB............ 225.00
Fix It Tow Truck, #910, pressed
steel, MIB....................... 200.00
Hook and ladder truck........... 450.00
Overland freight truck, #704 ... 90.00

❖ Stuffed Toys

Steiff was the originator of stuffed toys. By the middle of the 20th century, stuffed toys of every type, color, and animal were made. Some were sold in stores, others used for carnival prizes. Today many of these animals find their way to flea markets, hoping someone will give them a new home.

Periodical: *Soft Dolls & Animals*, 30595 Eight Mile, Livonia, MI 48152.
Bucky Badger, University of Wisconsin mascot, Animal Fair, 1960s,
23" h 36.00

Squirrel stuffed animal, 7-1/2" high, $15.

Cat, tiger-striped, Purrfection, Gund, 1985 Collectors Classic Limited Edition #1174, 15" h 16.00

Dinosaur, Animal Fair, late 1970s, 26" l 15.00

Dumbo, Character Novelty Co., 14" h 88.00

Lion, standing, Animal Fair, 1979, 15" h 24.00

Paddington Bear, Holiden Eden, 16" h 16.00

Parrot, plush, glass eyes, Merrythought, 16" h 325.00

Polar bear, Always Coca-Cola emblem 7" h 10.00

Winnie the Pooh, Japan, 4-1/2" h 1.50

❖ Sugar Packets

Here's a sweet topic. Collectors used to find many of their most interesting examples while traveling and enjoying diners and restaurants. Many sugar packets have interesting scenes or advertising, and some were made in sets. Today some sugar packets are finding their ways to flea markets. Because the collecting interest is relatively small, expect to find sugar packets for as little as 25 cents.

New York World's Fair sugar packet, Domino, $3.

Milk glass sugar shaker, Waffle pattern, 7" high, $45.

❖ Sugar Shakers

Two sweet categories in a row! Sugar shakers, also called muffineers, were designed to sprinkle powdered sugar, so the holes in their tops tend to be large. When looking for sugar shakers, check to see that the top and bottom started life together. Like salt shakers, tops do wear out. Replacement tops detract slightly from the value.

Coin Spot, cranberry, new lid 150.00

Mt. Washington, opaque white ground, flowers dec, orig top 350.00

Nippon, white, gold beading 65.00

R. S. Prussia, pearl finish, shaded roses and green leaves, scalloped base, red mark 250.00

Spanish Lace
Blue opalescent, light blue color 275.00
Vaseline opalescent 300.00

Tomato shape, Mt. Washington 410.00

❖ Sunbonnet Babies

These cute little gals did everything in their large-brimmed sunbonnets. They washed and ironed and played on all types of material, from postcards to Royal Bayreuth china.

Book, *Sunbonnet Babies*, 1902 .... 90.00

Cake plate, babies washing, Royal Bayreuth, 10-1/4" dia 400.00

Cup and saucer, babies fishing, Royal Bayreuth 250.00

Pictures, watercolor, professionally framed, 13-1/2" x 9-3/4", pr 160.00

Plate, babies ironing, Royal Bayreuth 110.00

Postcard, Weekly series, set of 7 .... 85.00

Quilt, Sunbonnet Sue and Sam, summer weight, c1910, some wear 45.00

★ Sunday School

Jesus loves me, this I know. Anyone who's sat through Sunday school has probably sung that song. Sunday school items can be readily found at flea markets. Looking to start a collection on a budget? This is one area where most items remain readily affordable. Anyone who's looking for Sunday school items really does have a prayer of finding them.

Book
International Sunday School Lessons, 1918 .... 15.00
Sunday School is Fun, 1948, with dust jacket 7.50

Cards, lesson cards, 1901-05, set of 47, 3" x 4" 26.00

Magazine, *Sunday School Magazine*, November 1881, Southern Methodist Publishing House 3.50

Pin
Christian, brass and enameled 12.50
Lutheran Sunday School, 8-year pin, 10K gold 1" dia 5.00

Postcard, Rally Day, 1924 .... 3.50

Football-theme Sunday School postcard, $1.

Record, Little Marcy Sings Sunday
   School Songs 22.50
Songbook
   *Bradbury's Golden Shower of
   Sunday School Melodies,*
   1862 .... 18.00
   Sunday School Songbook, 1870
   .... 15.00

❖ Super Heroes

Shazam! Super heroes have been influencing the minds and checkbooks of collectors for decades. Batman, Green Hornet, Captain Midnight, Superman, and all kinds of villains have come to life from comic books, radio, television, and movie tales.

References: Ted Hake, *Hake's Price Guide to Character Toys,* 3rd ed, Gemstone Publishing; Rex Miller, *The Investor's Guide to Vintage Character Collectibles,* Krause Publications, 1999.

Periodical: *The Adventures Continue,* 935 Fruitsville Pike, #105, Lancaster, PA 17601.

Collectors' Clubs: Air Heroes Fan Club, 19205 Seneca Ridge Club, Gaithersburg, MD 20879; Batman TV Series Fan Club, P.O. Box 107, Venice, CA 90291; Rocketeer Fan Club, 10 Halick Court, East Brunswick, NJ 08816.

For additional listings, see *Warman's Americana & Collectibles* and related topics in this edition.

Coloring book
   Flash Gordon, 1958, unused
   .... 30.00
   Six Million Dollar Man, Saalfield,
   unused 20.00
Comic book
   The Amazing World of Superman, 1973, map of Krypton
   .... 8.50
   Aquaman #4, August 1962
   .... 34.50
Costume
   Aquaman, Ben Cooper, 1967
   .... 210.00
   Wonder Woman, 1980s 15.50
Cape, Superman, homemade,
   c1975 .... 20.00
Doll, Wonder Woman, MIB 90.00
Figure
   Captain America, wind-up,
   5-1/2" h, MIB 90.00
   Thor, wind-up, 5-1/2" h, MIB
   .... 110.00
Gun
   Batman Escape Gun, 1966,
   MOC 45.00
   Superman Krypton Ray Gun
   .... 475.00

8mm movie, Captain Marvel in "Curse of the Scorpion," $27.50.

Pinback, Green Hornet Society
   membership pin, 3-1/2" dia
   .... 25.00
Puzzle
   Aquaman, action scene, Whitman, 1967 .... 45.00
   Wonder Woman puzzle, 130 pcs
   .... 9.50
Ring, Incredible Hulk face, 1977
   .... 15.00
Spoon, Green Hornet figure on handle, 1955 .... 20.00
Toy, Spider-Man Helicopter, NRFB
   .... 115.00
Wallet, Superman, leather and plastic, made in Hong Kong, 1976
   .... 27.50

❖ Surveyor's Equipment

Keep your eyes open while out surveying at your favorite flea market. Perhaps you'll spot an interesting piece of used surveying equipment. With today's electronics and computers, many old rods and transits are being sold. Instruments with original cases are worth more. Time will tell whether collectors like their instruments brightly polished or with the original patina.

For additional listings, see *Warman's Antiques and Collectibles Price Guide.*

Alidade, Keuffel & Esser Co., Model No. 5093A, high-post plane table, 10" telescope, one beveled edge, strider level, orig case, c1940 .... 360.00
Compass, W. Davenport, Philadelphia, detachable brass sight vanes, worn fitted dovetailed mahogany case with brass fittings 920.00
Level, Worth, 12', plumb, brass top
   .... 35.00
Sight level, Dieterich, leather case
   .... 80.00
Military level, Berger & Sons, Boston, 9-1/4" l, telescope with high precision vial, c1950 .... 375.00
Tape measure, English land surveyor measuring tape, 30'
   .... 78.00
Transit, Bostrom, orig box 50.00

Swankyswig, Cornflower No. 2, dark blue, $2.

❖ Swankyswigs

Collectors never seem to tire of finding these little glasses. Kraft Cheese Spreads were originally packed in these colorful juice glasses as early as the 1930s. Over the years many variations and new patterns have been introduced.

Collectors' Club: Swankyswigs Unlimited, 201 Alvena, Wichita, KS 67203.

Antique, brown coal bucket and
    clock, 3-3/4" h......................5.00
Bands, red and black.................3.00
Bustlin' Betsy...........................5.00
Checkerboard, green, red, and dark
    blue, 3-1/2" h....................25.00
Deer and squirrels, brown, 3-3/4" h
    ....8.00
Dots and circles, black, blue, green,
    or red..................................4.50
Elephants and birds, red, 3-3/4" h
    ....8.00
KiddieCup, pig and bear, blue ...2.00
Modern flowers, dark and light blue,
    red or yellow
    Cornflower 3.25
    Forget-me-not......................3.25
    Jonquil 3.00
Roosters, red, 3-1/4" h 6.00
Sailboat, red, green, or dark blue,
    racing or sailing 25.00

❖ Swarovski Crystal

The Swarovski family traces its glassmaking tradition to Austria in 1895. Today the company is still identified with high-quality crystal. Look for a swan logo on most pieces. The original box and packaging add to an item's value.

Periodicals: *Swan Seekers News*, 9740 Campo Road, Suite 134, Spring Valley, CA 91977; *The Crystal Report*, 1322 N. Barron St., Eaton, OH 45320.

Collectors' Clubs: Swan Seekers, 9740 Campo Road, Suite 134, Spring Valley, CA 91977; Swarovski Collectors Society, 2 Slater Road, Cranston, RI 02920.

Charm, musical clef note, enamel
    and crystal, 1-3/4" h...........15.00
Christmas ornament, snowflake,
    1990...................................35.00
Figure
    Bear, miniature, 1-1/8" h ..200.00
    Butterfly, miniature, 1" h ...125.00
    Dachshund, large, 3" l......125.00
    Dragon, Society member, "Fabulous Creatures," 1997..595.00
    Elephant, large, frosted tail
    ....115.00
    Lion, Society member, "Inspiration Africa," 1995, stand
    included......................750.00
    Rabbit, large.....................250.00
    Whale, "Care for Me," last of
    "Mother & Child" series, 1992
    ....475.00
Fur clip, gold-tone, crystal stones,
    sterling silver setting, sgd
    "Eisenberg Original, Sterling,"
    2-1/2" h, pr......................695.00
Paperweight, pyramid, helio, small,
    1990, orig box and certificate
    ....595.00
Pendant, red and black enameled
    child's sled, crystal on top, 2" h
    ....35.00

For exciting collecting trends and newly expanded areas look for the following symbols:

⊙ Hot Topic

✶ New Warman's Listing

(May have been in another Warman's title.)

Indianapolis Motor Speedway Motel swizzle stick, 6-1/4" long, $2.

❖ Swizzle Sticks

Here's another example of something people tend to save as a souvenir. Who hasn't tucked one into their pocket? After awhile you've got a collection started, so why not search for some more examples during your next trip to a flea market.

Aluminum, golf club shape, "O'Donnell's Sea Grill" on shaft, "Stolen in Washington, D.C." on other
    side, pr 15.00
Commemorative, plastic
    Aircal, 5" l 1.00
    Beefeater, clear, red lettering, 7" l
    .... .25
    Hard Rock Café, guitar at top,
    9" l 2.00
    Howard Johnson's, 5-1/2" l
    .... 1.00
    Lawrence Welk Welkome Inn,
    6" l 1.00
    Mirage, Las Vegas, 6" l 1.00
    Savarin Restaurant, 6" l 1.00
    Ski Southwest, 4" l 1.00
    S.S. Independence, 5-1/2" l
    .... 1.00
    The Royal Lahaina Hotel..... 1.00
    The Sands, Las Vegas........ 1.00
    TWA, 6" l 1.00
Glass
    Amber, 6" l.......................... 3.00
    Christmas Tree.................... 7.00
    Nude, waist-up, twisted light
    brown hair.................... 55.00
Plastic
    Hawaiian girl....................... 1.00
    Mr. Peanut, Everybody Loves A
    Nut................................. 5.00
    Sword .... .25

❖ Syracuse China

Founded in Syracuse, New York, in the mid 1800s, this china company is still in operation. Along with the many dinnerware patterns produced over the years are pieces for commercial accounts, such as the C&O Railroad. The company's restaurant wares are especially popular with collectors.

Ashtray, Irish setter in center, front mkd "Stuart Bruce," some hairline cracks from use, 4-1/2" dia
.... 10.00

Creamer, Chessie, C&O Railroad
....20.00

Cup and saucer, Adobe Ware, Rodeo Cowboy, stenciled "Adobe Ware, Syracuse China, 5-EE USA," c1950 ....38.00

Place setting, Chicken in the Rough, golfing rooster, 4 pc set 95.00

Plate

AAA, 50th anniversary, Oct. 4, 1950, mkd "Iroquois China, Syracuse, NY"................55.00

Black Waiter, Homestead Hotel, Hot Springs, VA, 10-1/2" dia
.... 110.00

Caprice, 10-1/2" dia 5.00

George Washington Hotel, Jacksonville, FL, 1959, 10" dia
.................................20.00

Platter, Sabella, fish chef logo, green mark, 12" x 9-1/2" 35.00

Soup bowl, Anderdsen Restaurant, Pea Soup Characters, Hap-Pea and Pea-Wee, 9" dia..........45.00

❖ Syrup Pitchers

Here's another specialized type of glassware for your table or sideboard. It was designed to hold syrup. Look for metal tops to be in good condition, but some use-related wear is acceptable.

Coin Spot & Swirl, blue opalescent
.... 185.00

Coreopis, red satin................ 350.00

Daisy & Fern, cranberry opalescent
.... 210.00

Hazel Atlas, clear body, plastic top
.... 90.00

Inverted Thumbprint, blue..... 200.00

Lattice, blue opalescent 335.00

T

For exciting collecting trends and newly expanded areas look for the following symbols:

⚙ Hot Topic

✶ New Warman's Listing

(May have been in another Warman's title.)

❖ Taylor, Smith & Taylor

Taylor, Smith & Taylor was started by W.L. Smith, John N. Taylor, W.L. Taylor, Homer J. Taylor, and Joseph G. Lee in Chester, West Virginia, in 1899. By 1903 the firm reorganized and the Taylors bought out Lee. By 1906 Smith bought out the Taylors. The company continued making dinnerware and table wares until 1981, when the plant closed. The Smith family sold its interest to Anchor Hocking in 1973.

For additional listings, see *Warman's Americana & Collectibles* and the LuRay pattern in this edition.

Bowl
    Autumn Harvest 40.00
    Vistosa, cobalt blue, 8" dia
        .... 65.00
Butter dish, cov, Empire 20.00
Cake plate, Laurel, 10-1/4" dia 12.00
Casserole, cov
    Autumn Harvest 38.00
    Pattern #1377, Empire shape, red, blue, green and yellow, gold trim, c1941 .... 45.00
Chop plate
    Plymouth 20.00
    Vistosa, light green, 11" dia
        .... 85.00
Creamer and sugar, Vistosa, light green 45.00
Cup and saucer
    Marvel 6.00
    Vogue 6.50

Dinner plate
    Empire, 10" dia 12.00
    Fairway, 9-1/2" dia 8.50
    Pebbleford, 10" dia 10.00
Gravy boat, underplate, Indian Summer 45.00
Pan, cov, Chateau Buffet, Pebbleford, blue int. 62.00
Platter, LuRay, pastel green, medium 75.00
Salad bowl, Marvel 17.50
Salt and pepper shakers, pr, Versatile 6.00
Sauce boat, underplate, Pattern #1377 .... 45.00
Soup bowl, Vistosa, deep yellow
        .... 24.00
Teapot, Vistosa, deep yellow ... 85.00
Vegetable dish, cov
    Autumn Harvest 40.00
    Silhouette 95.00

❖ Teapots

To devoted tea drinkers, the only way to properly brew a cup of tea is in a teapot. Thankfully there are many wonderful examples of teapots available to collectors. From decorative porcelain teapots to whimsical figural teapots, the array is endless.

Reference: Tina M. Carter, *Collectible Teapots*, Krause Publications, 2000.

Periodicals: *Tea Talk*, P.O. Box 860, Sausalito, CA 94966; *Tea Time Gazette*, P.O. Box 40276, St. Paul, MN 55104.

"Jas. Van Dyk, Tea Importer" teapot, brown over white, 3-1/2" high, $40.

For additional listings, see specific companies, such as Hall China, in this edition.

Figural
    Betty Boop 35.00
    Dickens character, Beswick, English 85.00
    Doc 35.00
    Lucy 50.00
    McCormick, black 35.00
    Minnie Mouse 35.00
Porcelain
    English, Abrams, cosy pot, pitcher shape, patents .. 50.00
    English, Wade, Majolica style, basket and fruit 40.00
    German, Royal Hanover, hand painted 75.00

⚙ Teddy Bears

Everybody has loved one of these at some time in their lives, and many collectors start by buying one or two that reminds them of a childhood companion. Whatever the motivation, teddy bears are still one of the hottest collectibles. Look for teddy bears that are in good condition, perhaps showing a sign or two of a little loving. Some collectors are more discriminating about condition and know they may pay a premium.

References: Shawn Brecka, *Big Book of Little Bears*, Krause Publications, 2000; Ken Yenke, *Bing Bears and Toys*, Schiffer Publishing, 2000.

Periodicals: *National Doll & Teddy Bear Collector*, P.O. Box 4032, Portland, OR 97208; *Teddy Bear & Friends*, P.O. Box 420235, II Commerce Blvd., Palm Coast, FL 32142; *Teddy Bear Review*, 170 Fifth Ave, 12th Floor, New York, NY 10010.

Collectors' Clubs: Good Bears of the World, PO Box 13097, Toledo, OH 43613; My Favorite Bear: Collectors Club for Classic Winnie the Pooh, 468 W Alpine #10, Upland, CA 91786; Teddy Bear Boosters Club, 19750 SW Peavine Mountain Road, McMinnville, OR 97128.

For additional listings, see *Warman's Antiques and Collectibles Price Guide*, as well as Steiff and other categories in this edition.

A special bear

Black isn't a traditional color for teddy bears. However, 600 black Steiff bears made in May 1912 were of special significance. They were made by Steiff in Germany and exported to England as a symbol of mourning after the sinking of the Titanic.

When one of the bears was offered at Christie's South Kensington in December 2000, it drew considerable attention. The consignor's great uncle was among the more than 1,500 who perished when the Titanic sank in the icy waters of the North Atlantic.

The child who originally owned the bear took a dislike to the toy, and it was put away—for the next 88 years. When it returned to the light of day, it drew great enthusiasm from collectors and sold for $136,000.

Anker, mohair, mkd "Plustchtiere Aus Muchen," 16" h 215.00
Brooklyn Doll and Toy Co., brown plush, plastic eyes and nose, 1982 ....25.00
Campbell's cheerleader bear ..70.00
Campbell's Super Chief bear ..25.00
Hershey's Cocoa 85.00
Jeane Steel, wearing straw hat, felt collar, and big fabric bow, jointed arms and legs, mkd "Kent Collectibles/Jeane Steele Originals/© 1985," 11-1/2" h 48.00
Koala Me, store display, 10" h 75.00
Laveen bear, Shug, long gray fur, blue corduroy vest, large blue marble eyes, leather snout and paw pads, orig hang tag, 18" h 165.00
Musical, Swiss, 16" h, mohair 350.00
Petsey, Steiff, blond, button.....95.00
Teddy Ruxpin, orig box, 2 tapes, orig books 100.00
This Bear, Possum Trot, brown plush, orig tags 75.00
Yes-No Bear, Schuco, mohair, 20" h, 1950s 1,200.00
Westinghouse, adv, 1983 ....15.00

❖ Telephone Cards

The hobby of collecting telephone cards was a rage in Europe for years before Americans started taking notice of the plastic cards the size and shape of traditional credit cards. Sometimes made in a series, the cards often have interesting designs.

Atlanta Olympic Games, 1996, instructions in Russian.......10.00
Bell Cab Taxi Co., Los Angeles, 1996....................................15.00
John F. Kennedy throwing out the first baseball on 1963 opening day, 1994 ....30.00
Kiwi Collectors Fair, New Zealand 7.00
Kurier, Russian newspaper, instructions in Russian, 1997 ....10.00
Lou Gehrig, 1994.....................15.00
Olympic Games, Soccer, photo of 1928 Uruguay winning team 8.50
Telecom Phonecard, New Zealand's 1st commercial phonecard, 1989, $2 value 10.00
Union Bail Bond Co., Los Angeles, 1997....................................10.00
Wizard of Oz
    Ruby Slippers......................7.50
    Scarecrow..........................12.50
    Tin Man 10.00
Whitney Houston 9.00

❖ Telephones & Related

Talk, talk, talk, that's what we've been doing since this wonderful invention caught on with our ancestors. As technology changes, some folks are starting to notice that perhaps telephones are something to collect. Add to that some interesting ephemera, and you have a great collecting area.

Candy container, Miniature Dial Telephone, glass candlestick telephone, 4-1/4" h 55.00
Lighter, desk phone motif, Occupied Japan 248.00
Postcard
    Bell Telephone Co. Building, Kansas City, MO, 1924... 5.00
    Christmas, girl using candlestick telephone, 1913 postmark 3.50
    Christmas, girl using wall telephone, 1911 postmark.... 4.00
Salt and pepper shakers, pink wall telephone, orig box mkd "Party Line," c1950 ....25.00
Sheet music, *Hello Central Give Me Heaven*, cover shows girl with phone 15.00
Sign
    New York Telephone Co., porcelain, trademark bell, 8" dia 150.00
    United Utilities System, Public Telephone, porcelain, 2-sided, L-shape, flange...........200.00

Oak wall phone, $250.

Telephone

Candlestick, Kellogg 300.00
Co-pay, gray, box with key
.... 95.00
Desk, rotary, blue plastic, Bell
System 30.00
Figural, Bozo, no lights when
rings, Telemania, 12-1/2" h
.... 60.00
Figural, '57 Chevy, red, push-
button, modular plugs,
unused 37.50
Figural, Garfield, Tyco Industries,
Model #1207, 1988 .... 40.00
Figural, Mickey Mouse, 1978,
Western Electric 150.00
Figural, Pizza Inn, cartoon figure
of mustache-wearing pizza
maker, touch-tone, Taiwan,
late 1970s, 10" h 25.00
Figural, Snoopy, push button dial
.... 75.00
Wall, Chicago Telephone Supply
Company, receiver missing,
26" h 200.00
Wall, single box, Kellogg, refin-
ished 200.00
Wall single box, Kellogg, oak
case, mouth base mkd
"Kellogg," 25-1/2" h 200.00
Wall, single box, Western Elec-
tric 190.00
Stock certificate, Associated Tele-
phone Co., 1945 .... 10.00
Telephone Almanac
1940, Bell System Telephone
Subscribers, American Tele-
phone & Telegraph 5.00
1959, Michigan Bell Telephone
Co., slight discoloration ... 2.50
Telephone Book
Beloit, Wisc., 1954 .... 5.00
Villisca, Iowa, 1962 .... 17.50
Washington, D.C. March, 1948,
Yellow Pages Directory, slight
use 55.00
Toy
Fisher-Price telephone pull toy,
2251, 1993 .... 6.00
Junior Phone, battery operated,
Modern Toys, Japan, 1950s, 2
large hard plastic phones,
orig. wiring, instructions, and
fold-out display box 60.00
Ranch Phone, litho tin wind-up,
partial box 125.00

❖ Television Characters and Personalities

"Now on with the show" was Ed Sullivan's promise to the audience waiting to be entertained. Today's flea markets are a great place to find vintage items relating to early television and the many characters who became stars.

Reference: Rex Miller, *The Investor's Guide to Vintage Character Collectibles*, Krause Publications, 1999, plus many others on specific stars and character memorabilia.

Periodicals: *Big Reel*, P.O. Box 1050, Dubuque, IA 52004; *Television Chronicles*, 10061 Riverside Dr, #171, North Hollywood, CA 91602; *The TV Collector*, P.O. Box 1088, Easton, MA 02334.

For additional listings, see *Warman's Americana & Collectibles*, plus other categories in this edition.

Activity set, Captain Kangaroo, shoe box size, c1956, unused 75.00
Advertisement, Red Skelton Pledge of Allegiance, 1969 .... 20.00

Welcome Back Kotter, **Golden All-Star Book, 1977, $5.**

Bank, Romper Room, Do-Bee, Has-
bro 55.00
Big Little Book, *Lassie Adventure in Alaska*, Whitman, 1967 ..... 15.00
Card game
Beverly Hillbillies, Milton Bradley,
complete 24.00
Howdy Doody, orig slide-out box
.... 45.00
Cigar band, Hawaii Five-O, full color
.... 2.50
Colorforms, Daniel Boone, Fess
Parker, 1964, unused 85.00
Coloring book, unused
Beverly Hillbillies, Whitman,
1963 .... 24.00
Gilligan's Island, Whitman, 1965
.... 135.00
Comic book, *I Love Lucy*, Dell, #3,
1954 .... 135.00
Cookbook, *Buffy's Cookbook,* Jody
Cameron, Family Affair 15.00
Doll
Cher, Mego, 12" h 50.00
Honey West, Gilbert, 12" h, MIB
.... 375.00
Six Million Dollar Man, 1973, MIB
.... 35.00
Game
Down You Go, Selchow &
Righter Co., copyright 1954
.... 18.00
Lost in Space 180.00
Mister Ed, Parker Brothers,
copyright 1962, missing dice
and markers 45.00
Road Runner, Milton Bradley,
Warner Bros., 1968 ...... 65.00
Gum card wrapper, Beverly Hillbil-
lies, Topps, 1963 .... 65.00
Halloween costume, child's, orig
costume, mask, box
I Love Lucy 325.00
Mr. Ed 115.00
Lunch box
Charlie's Angels, Aladdin, metal,
6-1/2" h thermos 72.00
Munsters, 1965, lunch box and
thermos 375.00
Magazine, *TV Junior*, March 1959
.... 20.00
Medic set, M*A*S*H, Ja-Ru, copy-
right 1981, 20th Century Fox
Film Corp, 6" x 10" blister card,
MOC 18.00
Mirror, Miss Piggy, Sigma, glazed
ceramic, easel back and hook
for hanging, early 1980s ... 80.00

Night light, Flintstones, Fred and
   Barney 25.00
Nodder, Dr. Kildare, Lego 125.00
Paint set, Winky Dink, licensed by
   CBS, 16" x 12", c1950, MIB
   .... 100.00
Photograph, Robert Redford in "Jer-
   emiah Johnson," ABC Sunday
   Night Movie, Dec 19, 1976
   .... 10.00
Pinback button
   Ben Casey, white, blue letters
   .... 15.00
   Bullwinkle for President, red,
   white, and blue flag, c1972,
   2-1/4" d 40.00
Puppet, hand
   Captain Kangaroo 3.00
   Gumby 28.00
Push puppet
   Huckleberry Hound 45.00
   Pebbles 50.00
Toy
   Flying Nun, Ray Plastic Inc.,
   c1970 Screen Gems, Inc.,
   color photo of Sally Field,
   plastic figure, launching unit,
   some wear to orig box ... 50.00
   Starsky & Hutch, diecast car, 3" l,
   metal and plastic, 1970s
   .... 35.00
Wallet, CHiPS, orig display card,
   MGM, MOC 20.00
Waste can, Laugh-In, litho metal
   .... 45.00
Whistle, Dragnet 15.00

❖ Television Sets

Used television sets are something that occasionally show up at
flea markets. Often their size and
bulk finds them still sitting on the
truck or in the back of a booth.
Before plugging in a vintage television set, have someone knowledgeable check over the circuits and old
tubes.

Collectors' Clubs: Antique Wireless Association, 59 Main St, Holcomb, NY 14469-9336; Mid-Atlantic
Radio Club, P.O. Box 67, Upperco,
MD 21155.

GE, portable, cream colored plastic
   case, black and white, working
   condition, one knob chipped
   .... 25.00
Hallicrafters, T-54, c1950 .... 250.00
Philco, reconditioned, floor model
   .... 325.00
Pilot, TV-37, magnifier model 120.00
RCA, CT-100, first RCA color set
   .... 550.00
Zenith, portable, black plastic case,
   black and white, working condition 35.00

❖ Temple, Shirley

Her smile and curly hair were her
trademarks as she stole the hearts
of moviegoers in the 1940s. Her
mother carefully licensed items with
her image, including dolls, glassware, jewelry, and soap. More
recently, several companies have
revived interest in Shirley Temple by
creating new collectibles with vintage images. Beware of reproductions, especially copies of cobalt
glassware.

Reproduction Alert.

Book, *Story of Shirley Temple*, 1934
   .... 28.00
Doll, Ideal 1982, Captain January,
   1982 .... 60.00
Doll dress, 1930s, for 18" or 20" doll,
   orig tags 90.00
Figure, limited edition, Nostalgia
   Collectibles, made in Japan
   Curly Top 60.00
   Standup and Cheer 60.00
Movie book, *The Little Colonel*,
   Saalfield, hardcover, black and
   white movie scenes, full color
   front cover 40.00
Pinback button, Ideal Dolls 75.00
Plate, limited edition, Nostalgia Col-
   lectibles, made in Japan
   Baby Take A Bow 65.00
   Standup and Cheer 65.00
Pocket mirror, 1937 Fox Film Corp.
   .... 35.00
Scrapbook, Saalfield #1722, copy-
   right 1936, full color front and
   back covers, Shirley wearing
   pink dress, white bonnet, spiral
   binding, used 40.00

Sheet music, *Goodnight My Love*,
   name written in pencil on front
   .... 21.00

❖ Tennis Collectibles

Tennis anyone? Here's another
sport where the collectibles are starting to command increased attention.
Look for ephemera and equipment
with endorsements by famous players.

Autograph, Billie Jean King, 8" x 10"
   photo 22.00
Book, *How to Improve Your Tennis*,
   Harry "Cap" Leighton 7.50
Cigarette card, 1931 Lawn Tennis
   series
   Lakeman, Jan Fry 10.00
   Wilmer Allison 10.00
   Jacques Brugnon 7.00
Decanter, Ezra Brooks, tennis
   player, 1973, 14" h 20.00
Figurine, Precious Moments, "Serv-
   ing The Lord"
   Boy tennis player, olive branch
   mark, 1985, 5-1/2" h 35.00
   Girl tennis player, olive branch
   mark, 1985, 5" h 45.00
Pin, tennis racket, green enamel,
   mkd Gerry's, 2-1/2" l 4.00

**MacGregor tennis racket, Frank
Parker autograph model, $25.**

Swizzle stick, tennis racket shape,
blue plastic 1.00
Tennis balls
    Dunlop, Mr. Peanut 9.00
    Dunlop, Vinnie Richards 25.00
    MacGregor, red and white plaid
        can 25.00
    Spaulding, Pancho Gonzales,
        blue label...................... 20.00
    Wilson, Jack Kramer illus, red
        and white...................... 55.00
Tennis racket
    Dayton, 1923 patent 70.00
    Knickerbocker, wood.......... 45.00
    Spaulding, needs restringing
        .... 10.00
    Wilson Sporting Goods, Mau-
        reen Connolly, full color por-
        trait on handle, 1950s ... 25.00
    Wright & Ditson Championship,
        26" l.............................. 50.00
Valentine, German, honeycomb tis-
    sue type, girl with tennis racket
    and bag of balls, 1920s, 5" h
    .... 26.00

❖ Thermometers

We've got Galileo to thank for the first practical thermometer. There have certainly been a few advances since that 1593 start. One of the most collectible types of thermometers are those used as advertising. Look for examples that are free of rust or damage. You might also want to check the accuracy of the reading.

Reference: Curtis Merritt, *Advertising, Thermometers*, Collector Books, 2001.

Collectors' Club: Thermometer Collectors Club of America, 6130 Rampart Dr, Carmichael, CA 96508.
Reproduction Alert.
For additional information, see *Warman's Americana & Collectibles* and *Warman's Advertising.*
Advertising
    The Baltimore Tank and Tower
        Co., celluloid, 6-1/4" x 2"
        .... 95.00
    Chesterfield, They Satisfy, tin,
        13" h........................... 132.00
    Drink Double Cola, You'll Like It
        Better, tin, 1960s, 17" h
        .... 165.00

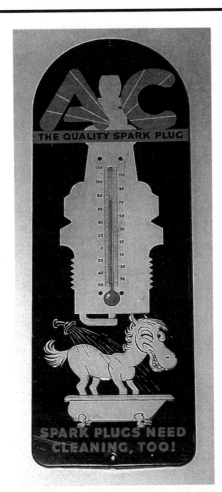

AC Spark Plugs tin thermometer, 21" x 7-1/2", $450.

Dr. A.C. Daniels' Famous Veterinary Medicines, Home Treatment For Horses and Cattle, Dog Remedies, painted wood, 20-3/4" x 5"................. 385.00
For Best Results Feed Your Dog Ken-L-Ration, tin, 26-3/4" x 7-1/4"........................... 175.00
Phillips 66, plastic, 14" l 16.00
Sylvania Radio Tubes, tin, rounded top and bottom, 39" x 8".......................... 75.00
Figural
    Cat, Enesco, 5" h 20.00
    Wishing well, chalkware, 6-3/4" h
    .... 22.00
Souvenir
    Florida, alligator motif, Japan, 1950s, 8-3/4" l 18.00
    Ruby Falls, Lookout Mountain, elephant, doubles as bank, brown ceramic, 4-7/8" h .. 9.00

❖ Thimbles

Thimble, thimble, who's got the thimble? Collectors do! And, they enjoy their tiny treasures. Finding thimbles at flea markets is probably easier than it sounds since there are so many different kinds of thimbles—advertising, commemorative, political, porcelain, and metal.

Periodical: *Thimbletter*, 93 Walnut Hill Rd, Newton Highlands, MA 02161.

Collectors' Clubs: The Thimble Guild, P.O. Box 381807, Duncanville, TX 75138; Thimble Collectors International, 8289 Northgate Dr, Rome, NY 13440.
Aluminum, plain 4.00
Commemorative
    California, gold-tone, white background with bear, 3/4" l. 10.00
    Mackinaw Bridge, copper-tone, showing bridge 10.00
    Virginia Beach, silver-tone, seagull 10.00
Figural, ceramic, 2-1/4" h
    Donald Duck...................... 15.00
    Goofy............................... 15.00
    Minnie Mouse................... 17.50
Miniature, Arcadia, gold thimble, gold thread........................ 30.00

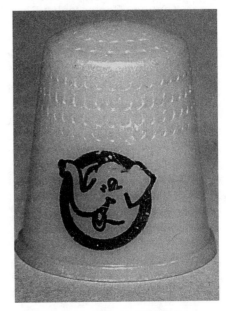

Plastic Republican thimble, local candidate's name on back, 25 cents.

Porcelain
    Anniversary, violet flower, gold
        band, mkd "Fine Bone China,"
        Ashleydale, England 8.00
    Blue and red flowers, mkd "Avon"
        .... 6.00
    Bird 5.50
    Orange flowers 5.00
    Queen Mother.................... 12.00
    Pink and blue flowers........... 6.00
Silver, plain, 5/8" l..................... 5.00

❖ Ticket Stubs

Here's another collectible that
most of us have tucked in a drawer
and probably have almost forgotten.
However, there are dedicated collectors of tickets for all kinds of
events—charities, sporting event,
theatrical shows, expositions, fairs,
etc. Most tickets are small in size
and easy to display in an album.
Children's Day, March 31, 1894, *San
    Francisco Chronicle*, coupons
    attached, unused............. 135.00
Led Zeppelin, Arizona State Univ.,
    ticket dated March 6, 1977, con-
    cert actually held July 20, 1977
    .... 50.00
Political
    Inaugural Ball, 1981,
        Reagan/Bush, John F.
        Kennedy Center for the Per-
        forming Arts, red, white, and
        blue, gold inauguration seal
        .... 10.00
    Republican Convention, 1964,
        San Francisco, elephant, and
        shield logo, "Entertainer" Pass
        .... 6.00

**1969 Indianapolis 500 ticket
stub, pictures Bobby Unser,
$10.**

Stevenson Rally, Memorial Audi-
    torium, Thursday, Nov 1
    (1956), red, white and blue
    .... 17.50
Railroad
    PA RR 50
    Pitt & Lake Erie, passenger,
        1918 ....2.00
Rose Bowl, 1952 ....55.00
Ship, *Italia Societa Di Navigazione
    Marco Polo*, from Valparaiso to
    La Guaira............................6.00
World's Fair
    Panama-Pacific International
        Exposition, tan and brown,
        Nov 2, 1915, used 45.00
    Souvenir of the California Mid-
        winter International Exposi-
        tion, souvenir, San Francisco
        Day, July 4, 1894, four Fair
        buildings on back, 4-3/4" x
        3-1/2"............................85.00

❖ Tiffany Studios

Louis Comfort Tiffany was an
interesting man. While he was a
patron of arts and crafts, he was
also a skilled craftsman. Although he
worked in many mediums, he is
most acclaimed for his glass creations and designs. Flea market
shoppers should be aware that most
"signed" Tiffany glass pieces were
not signed by Louis Tiffany. Never
buy a piece of Tiffany glass based
solely on the signature.

Reproduction Alert.
For additional listings, see *Warman's
    Antiques and Collectibles Price
    Guide* and *Warman's Glass*.
Bowl, squared dimpled form, trans-
    parent aquamarine, foot
    inscribed "L. C. Tiffany Favrile,"
    4-1/4" d, 2-1/2" h, price for pair
    ....490.00
Calling card receiver, bronze, mkd
    "Tiffany Studios"................75.00
Candlestick, heavy walled amber
    glass stick, 10 prominent swirled
    ribs, fine gold luster, inscribed
    "L.C.T.," labeled, 6-3/4" h
    ....400.00
Desk accessories, Zodiac pattern,
    bronze

**L.C. Tiffany Favrile compote, iri-
descent blue, 4-1/2" high, 8"
diameter, $1,200.**

Calendar holder 95.00
Rocker blotter 120.00
Paper rack, bronze, Chinese pat-
    tern, dark patina, some green
    wash in pattern recesses, three-
    tier, imp "Tiffany Studios New
    York 1756," some metal corro-
    sion 260.00
Serving fork, sterling silver, Wave
    Edge pattern 150.00
Tile, pressed molded irid blue glass,
    stylized blossom motif, imp
    "Patent Applied For," small chip,
    4" sq............................... 375.00
Vase
    Elongated bulbous body, 10
        prominent ribs below flattened
        rim, gold irid, inscribed "L.C.
        Tiffany Favrile," and number,
        7-1/4" h 525.00
    Oval body, teal blue, lined in opal
        white glass, smooth matte
        lustrous surface, inscribed
        "L.C. Tiffany Favrile 1753E,"
        5-3/4" h 750.00

❖ Tiffin Glass

Founded around 1888, A.J.
Beatty & Sons made glass in Tiffin,
Ohio. The factory became part of the
United States Glass conglomerate
and continued to provide high-quality glassware. The company closed
in 1980, ending a long tradition that
included many types of glassware
produced in brilliant colors.

Reference: Ed Goshe, Ruth Hem-
minger, Leslie Pina, *'40s, '50s & '60s
Stemware by Tiffin*, Schiffer Publishing, 1999.

Tiffin elephant paperweight, controlled bubbles, Twilight core, 6-1/2" high, $475.

Collectors' Club: Tiffin Glass Collectors' Club, P.O. Box 554, Tiffin, OH 44883.

Bud vase, Cherokee Rose, 6" h 38.00

Champagne
    Charlton 22.00
    Mystic............................26.00
    Rosalind.........................20.00

Cocktail, Cherokee Rose.........16.00

Cordial
    June Night.......................40.00
    Rambling Rose 28.00

Goblet
    Cherokee Rose.................32.00
    Mystic.............................28.00
    Rosalind..........................30.00

Parfait, Mystic........................27.00

Sherbet, Cordelia, crystal, high type 15.00

Tumbler
    Rambling Rose, flat 13.00
    Rosalind, ftd.....................20.00

Vase, black satin, red poppies dec, #16255 ....125.00

Wine
    Rosalind...........................25.00
    Thistle 17.00

❖ Tiles

Tiles have been used as a functional design element for decades. Collectors have also recognized the beauty of tiles and search them out. Examples range from inexpensive souvenirs to more pricey art pottery examples.

American Encaustic Tiling Co., white, black design of horseman riding through brush, 4-1/4" sq 48.00

Batchelder, imp bird design, blue ground, imp mark, 6" sq, price for pair 175.00

Delft, windmill 25.00

California Art, landscape, tan and green, 5-3/4" sq 65.00

Hamilton Tile, knight motif, green and brown, 12" x 6" 290.00

Marblehead, blue and white ships, 4-5/8" sq, price for pair 125.00

Minton Hollins & Co., urn and floral relief, green ground, 6" sq .48.00

Mosaic Tile Co., Delft windmill, blue and white, framed, 8" sq....55.00

Pin, Pewabic Pottery tile, stylized tree on green ground, "Pewabic Detroit 1997," 1-1/2" sq 55.00

Souvenir
    Washington, D.C., Bicentennial, 1776-1976, 200 Years of Progress..........................6.00
    Myrtle Beach, S.C., boating and beach scene, blue on white 6.00
    Old Deerfield, Massachusetts, black on white 5.00

Rebekah tile, National Tile Company, 4-3/8" square, $20.

West Dennis, Mass., The Lighthouse Inn.......................6.00
U.S. Encaustic Tile Works, flowered wreath, light green, 6" sq .. 20.00

❖ Tins

One of the most decorative aspects of collecting vintage advertising is to collect tins. They were designed to catch the consumer's eye with interesting graphics and/or colors. Today collectors seek them out for many of the same reasons.

For additional listings, see *Warman's Advertising.*

American Lady Coffee, slip lid, 3 lb, 9-1/2" h 154.00

Buster Popcorn, 10 lb, 9-1/2" h 75.00

Canco Candy, 5 lb tin, Piggies dec 235.00

Campfire Marshmallows, Campfire Kitchens, 7-1/4" d, 2" h 70.00

Colgate Talc for Men, Invisible, Soothing, Refreshing, blue on white, 3-1/4" h.................. 27.50

Constans Brand Coffee, slid lid, 9-1/2" h 22.00

Cream Dove Blanched and Salted Whole Peanuts, white dove in blue medallion, 10 lb....... 165.00

Donald Duck Coffee, keywind, 1 lb 742.50

Elite Powder, A Perfect Foot Powder, 4-1/8" h 34.00

Evening In Paris, round, 5" h .. 10.00

Festive Popcorn, cardboard, circus performers, unopened, 5-1/4" h 330.00

Honor Peanut Butter, no lid, 25 lb, 9-1/2" h 105.00

Italina Antacid, 1930s 30.00

Jack Sprat, black-eye peas, paper label, unopened, 12 oz, 7" h 50.00

Johnson & Johnson Baby Talc 60.00

Libbey's Miniature Asparagus 95.00

Log Cabin Syrup, blacksmith scene, 5" h 330.00

Mammy Salted Peanuts, pictures Mammy, some wear..... 2,500.00

Monarch Cocoa, 3" h 50.00

Mount Cross Coffee, J. S. Brown Mercantile Co., 3 lb, 7-1/2" h 70.00

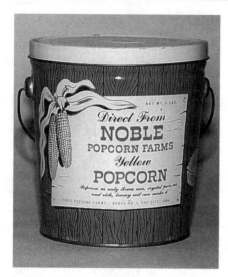

Noble Popcorn Farms pail, tin, 6-1/2" high, 5-7/8" diameter, $20.

National Biscuit......................... 15.00
Old Master Coffee, 9-1/4" h, 5-1/2" d, 3 lb, snap lid, few dents
.... 75.00
Omar Cigarettes 15.00
O-So-Easy Mop, 1920s 50.00
Plee-zing, no graphics.............. 7.00
Rawleigh's Cocoa, sample, 2-1/4" h
.... 60.00
Red Rooster Coffee, keywind, 1 lb
.... 72.00
Red Wolf Coffee, keywind, 1 lb
.... 144.00
Royal Blue Stores Coffee, keywind, tall version, 1 lb 115.00
Rose Kist Popcorn................... 48.00
Runkel's Cocoa, sample, 1-1/4" h
.... 66.00
Shur-Fine, no graphics............. 7.00
Shotwell's Marshmallow, cake design, 3-1/2" h, 5-1/2" dia
.... 82.50
Sudan Spice, graphics 9.00
Twas the Night Before Christmas, candy, Art Deco style....... 245.00
Widlar's Spice, no graphics....... 7.00

❖ Tinware

Edward and William Pattison settled in Berlin, Connecticut, in 1738, becoming America's first tinsmiths. Before that time, the pieces of tinware used in the Colonies were expensive imports. It wasn't until the discovery of tin near Goshen, Connecticut, in 1829 that tinplate was produced in America. The industrial revolution ushered in machine-made, mass-produced tinware, and by the late 19th century, the hand-made era had ended. Tinware with painted decorations is known as toleware.

References: Marilyn E. Dragowick, ed., *Metalwares Price Guide,* Antique Trader Books, 1995; John Player, *Origins and Craft of Antique Tin & Tole,* Norwood Publishing, 1995.

Periodical: *Let's Talk Tin Newsletter,* 1 S Beaver Ln, Greenville, SC 29605.

Museum: Cooper-Hewitt Museum, New York, NY.
Coffeepot
  Gooseneck, flared gallery foot, inverted conical top, stamped banding, arched tapered ribbon handle with handle brace, rounded hinged lid, wooden turned finial, 10" h 250.00
  Punched heart and floral motif, V-shaped spout, 10" h
......................................550.00
Comb holder, hanging, mirrored
....95.00
Cookie cutter, cat, 4" h 145.00

Advertising egg separator, "The South Bend Malleable Range, All-ways Preferable," $20.

Cream pail, stamped banding around sides, arched bail handle, early solder repair, 8-3/4" h, 5-3/8" dia 60.00
Flour bin from Hoosier cabinet, 31" h
.... 125.00
Food mold, 3 fruits, tin and copper
.... 135.00
Lunch kettle, hinged lid, 2 hinged brass handles, mkd "Champion," 1917 patent date, interior with removable tray and insulated container, minor rust, 5-7/8" h, 9-3/4" w, 6-1/4" d 75.00
Tray, painted village scene, "Concord 1839," copper-painted rim with flowers, 15" x 18-1/2"
.... 192.50
Wall pocket, shaped back with large arched top having crimped rim and large round hole for hanging, arched top flanked by 2 small circular elements, full-width rectangular pocket at bottom with tapering front, some rust, 7-5/8" h, 5-1/8" w, 1-3/8" d
.... 200.00

❖ Tip Trays

Tip trays are small colorful trays left on a table so that a patron could leave a tip for the wait staff. Their colorful lithographed decoration makes them an interesting collectible to many collectors. Because these little beauties saw a lot of use, carried coins, etc., expect to find signs of wear, perhaps some denting.

For additional listings, see *Warman's Advertising.*

Reproduction Alert.

C.D. Kenny, Baltimore, boy with turkey, round 90.00
Cleveland and Buffalo Line, shows ship, 4-1/8" dia................ 400.00
Clysmic, King of the Table Waters, woman with bottle, oval 80.00
El Verso Cigar, man smoking in den
.... 60.00
Japan Rose Soap, James S. Kirk & Co., Chicago, back worn, 4-1/4" dia 250.00
Prudential Insurance, The Prudential, 2-1/2" x 3-1/2" 20.00

Tip tray, "New Store, New Goods, Anthony & Cowell Co., At The Old Stand," tin, $15.

Quick Meal Ranges, oval, 4-1/2" x 3-3/8" 255.00
Treasure Line Stoves & Ranges, The D. Moore Co. Limited, Hamilton, Ontario, 7-1/2" x 4-1/8" 290.00

❖ Titanic Collectibles

There are two types of Titanic collectibles. The older are those that were generated when the great ship was built and launched. The public then was eager for news about this disaster just as we would be today. There were newspaper reports, books, and other memorabilia. The second classification of Titanic memorabilia relates to the recent movie and its popularity.

Collectors' Clubs: Titanic Historical Society, 208 Main St, Indian Orchard, MA 01151; Titanic International, Inc, P.O. Box 7007, Freehold, NJ 07728-7007.

Book, *Wreck & Sinking of the Titanic*, Marshall Everett, 1912, worn condition 150.00
Key chain, Titanic, White Star Line, MOC 3.95
Magazine, *National Geographic*, December, 1985 .... 2.25
Model kit, Minicraft 350 scale, Japan, 30" l, MIB 55.00
Movie prop, certificate of authenticity Oar lock, brass 450.00

Passageway lamp, brass 250.00
Newspaper, *Daily Mirror* 35.00
Photograph, movie set, set of 27 4" x 6" photos, showing film crews, actors, 1977 .... 35.00
Print, 6" dia round sealed bubble frame, shells and seaweed dec on frame 250.00

❖ Toasters

You need a good breakfast to help you get through a hard day at the flea market. Better include some toast in that feast. That breakfast staple has been around for generations, and the toaster has been evolving too. Watch for interesting designs and shapes in toasters. However, like other electrical appliances, be careful if you try to use any vintage toaster.

Periodical: *A Toast To You*, 26245 Calle Cresta, Temecula, CA 92590.

Collectors' Club: Electric Breakfast Club, P.O. Box 306, White Mills, PA 18473-0306; Upper Crust, P.O. Box 529, Temecula, CA 92593.

Capitol Products, #50, tin and chrome, 1930s 45.00
Cornet-CGNN Appliance Co., Winsted, CT, Art Deco styling, orig cord................................... 40.00
General Mills, 2 slice pop-up, chrome body, wheat dec, black Bakelite base, early 1940s 38.00

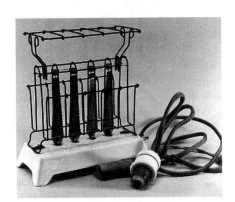

GE Model D-12 electric toaster, removable warming rack, 1908 patent date, $135.

Knapp Monach Reverso, light weight nickel plated body, rounded corners, black painted base, flip-flop doors with tab handles 35.00
Landers, Fray & Clarke, EE-947, 1915, orig cord.................. 75.00
Ohio Art, child's, play toaster, mkd "Pfaltzgraff," 8" 2, 5-1/2" h 18.00
Radiant Roast 65.00
Sunbeam, Model B, flat, chrome body, round reeded legs, hexagonal Bakelite feet, double wire cages flip over horizontally, small drop bail handles for carrying, 1920s, 5" x 9".................. 145.00
Toast-A-Lator, conveyor belt toaster 125.00

Goodrich Silvertowns, green glass insert, 6-1/2" dia, $65.

❖ Tire Ashtrays

Miniature tires and round ashtrays were a marriage just waiting to happen. When the two came together, they created tire ashtrays—a perfect advertising medium. These interesting items are becoming harder to find, especially the earlier examples.

Firestone
Clear glass insert, 6-1/2" dia 50.00
Red and black swirled plastic insert............................. 82.00
Goodrich, clear glass insert with white advertising for Amarillo, Texas, merchant 50.00

U.S. Royal Master, clear glass insert, 5-7/8" dia 30.00
U.S. Tire, blue slag glass insert 88.00
Vogue Tyre, clear glass insert, 2-1/2" dia 28.00
Western Auto, marbleized Bakelite insert, 6" dia 33.00

❖ Tobaccoania

Tobaccoania is a term coined to reflect the joys of smoking, and includes cigar, cigarette, and pipe smoking. As a collectible, tobaccoania seems to be as strong today as it was several years ago.

Collectors' Club: Society of Tobacco Jar Collectors, 3011 Falstaff Rd, #307, Baltimore, MD 21209-2960.
For additional listings, see *Warman's Advertising*.
Humidor, walnut, metal liner, 5-3/4" h, 6-3/8" dia 19.00
Plate, tin, Havana Post, Morning English, La Tarde-Castello, woman holding jug 150.00
Pouch, orig contents
    Arrow 15.00
    Bigger Hair, 5" h 30.00
    Buckeye, Mellow Chewing Tobacco, 5" h 5.00

Porcelain dog's-head tobacco jar, pipe in mouth, multicolor glaze, 5" high, $195.

Harp 15.00
Star, empty 10.00
Sure Shot, 5" h 20.00
Uncle Daniel, 3-1/2" h 15.00
Sign
    Red Coon Tobacco, cardboard 278.00
    Edgeworth Tobacco, metal over cardboard, 9-1/4" x 13-1/4" 475.00
Tobacco cutter
    Enterprise Mfg. Co., Philadelphia, April 13, 1875 patent 195.00
    Drummond's Good Luck Tobacco Cutter, American Machine Co., 16" l 185.00
Tobacco Jar
    Fisherman 275.00
    Old Man 350.00
    Scotsman 275.00
    Tobacco silk, zebra, 2" x 3" 10.00

❖ Tobacco Tags

The colorful tags used to identify bundles of tobacco that were sold at country tobacco auctions have become collectible. Watch for interesting shapes, names or places to help identify the original locale of the tag.

Collectors' Club: Tobacco Tin Tag Collectors Club, Route 2, Box 55, Pittsburg, TX 75686-9516.
Bachman's Fiddle 18.50
Battle Axe 9.00
Bull of the Woods 6.00
Brown & Williamson, Sun Cured 10.00
Close Figures 28.00
Favorite 8.00
Flat Iron 13.50
Golden Slipper 6.00
Gravely's Second 10.00
Harvey's Nat'leaf 8.00
Legal Tender 9.50
Little Henry 11.50
Little Mattie 9.50
New Coon 28.00
New Moon 10.00
Old Bob 28.00
Old Lorillard Climax Plug, 5/8" dia 3.00
Old Navy, Zahm 5.00

Penn's Red J. 6.00
Ram's Horn Sun Cured 10.00
Rich and Ripe 13.00
Scotten's Brown Slag 10.00
Sickle 6.00
Spur 22.50
Sun Cured 10.00
Taylor Made 6.00
Uncle Sam 14.00

Buckingham tobacco tin, 3-3/4" high, 4-1/2" diameter, $75.

❖ Tobacco Tins

Everybody remembers the old joke about letting Prince Albert out of the can. Today's collectors of tobacco tins search for Prince Albert and many other colorful characters who grace the front of tobacco tins.
For additional listings, see *Warman's Advertising*.
Bowl of Roses, vertical pocket tin, short version, man smoking in chair, 3-5/8" h 242.00
Dill's Best, vertical pocket tin, 4-1/2" h 44.00
Edgeworth Junior, Extra High Grade Tobacco, vertical pocket tin 72.00
Fashion Cut Plug Tobacco, lunch box, 4-1/2" h, 7-1/2" w 385.00
Golden Rod Plug Cut, 1-3/8" h, 4-3/8" w, 3-3/8" d 40.00
Golden Sceptre, vertical pocket tin, rounded corners 250.00
Guide, vertical pocket tin, outdoorsman, 4-1/4" h 335.00

Qboid vertical pocket tin, both sides concaved, 4" high, $65.

Hi-Plane Smooth Cut Tobacco, round, 6-1/4" h 220.00
J.G. Dill's Best Cube Cut Plug, 4 oz, 2-3/4" h 55.00
Lucky Strike Roll Cut, vertical pocket tin, 4-1/4" h 92.00
Picoback, The Pick of Tobacco, screw lid, 1/2-lb, round, 4-1/2" h 35.00

❖ Tokens

Tokens are small medallions or coin-like objects. Some tokens were used in lieu of currency for transportation, such as a railroad token. Other tokens were forms of advertising or perhaps were used for admission to an event. Look for tokens where you tend to find coins and medals.

References: Many coin reference books also contain information about tokens.

Collectors' Clubs: Active Token Collectors Organization, P.O. Box 1573, Sioux Falls, SD 57101-1573; American Numismatic Association, 818 N Cascade Ave, Colorado Springs, CO 80903-3279; American Vecturist Association, P.O. Box 1204, Boston, MA 02104-1204; National Token Collector's

"The Cathedral Church of St. John the Divine, Souvenir of Pilgrimage, New York," gold, 1-1/2" diameter, $1.

Association, P.O. Box 5596, Elko, NV 98902; Token & Medal Society, P.O. Box 366, Brayntown, MD 20617-0366.

Chief Of The Sixes, Product Of General Motors 25.00
Chuck E. Cheese Pizza Time Theatre, Ogden, Utah / In Pizza We Trust, 1980, 1" dia 1.00
General Motors Motorama, 1956 .... 20.00

"Good Luck Souvenir, Pan-American Exposition, Buffalo, N.Y.," encased 1901 Indian-head penny, 1-1/2" diameter, $10.

Houston Transit Authority, Houston skyline, 7/8" dia 2.00
Ford, 30th Anniversary, 1933, copper 30.00
Green River Whiskey, goldtone, 1-1/4" dia 45.00
Pierce-Arrow, brass, 1-3/4" dia 60.00
Union Pacific, "A sample of the aluminum in the new Union Pacific Train built by Pullman Car & Mfg. Corp., ALCOA Aluminum Co. of America," 1-1/4" dia 10.00
World's Fair and Expositions
1939 New York World's Fair, brass, Communications Building 9.00
1939 Golden Gate International Exposition, San Francisco Bay, 1-1/4" dia 15.00
Expo '74, Spokane, Wash., U.S. Pavilion, silver, 1-1/2" dia 8.00

★ Tonka

Named after Minnesota's Lake Minnetonka, Tonka Toys was created by the Mound Metalcraft Co. in 1946. The company changed its focus from small farm implements to toy trucks after the success of its Steam Shovel and Crane in 1947. In 1955, Mound Metalcraft Co. changed its name to Tonka Toys, Inc. and in 1991, Hasbro, Inc bought Tonka. When purchasing a Tonka, look for play wear, rust, and make sure that any small pieces (i.e. lights, grill, fire hoses, sirens, gates, etc.) are intact as this will affect the value. Also be aware of items that have been restored—dealers should represent them as restored, not new.

Airlines Tractor Set, 2 baggage carts 150.00
Camper, #1070, purple metal, white plastic camper top, mini, 1970s, MIB 90.00
Cement Mixer, 1970s 150.00
Construction Set, #3109, red and black box art, sealed in orig box 600.00
Crawler, 1970s 150.00
Dump Truck, 1970s 150.00
Dump Truck, red and green, Tonka, 1955 .... 100.00

1964 Tonka Dump Truck, $20.

Dune Buggy, #2445, bumper chain, 1970s, MIB 90.00
Pickup, red body, white roof 225.00
Stables Set, #1104, light blue metal, mini, 1970s, MIB 450.00
Universal Jeep, MIB 125.00

❖ Tools

Considering this great country was built from the ground up, tools have been with us for a long time. Treated properly, good tools last for years, many eventually making their way to flea markets. Tool collectors tend to find flea markets to be like gold mines when they are searching for something new to add to their collections.

Collectors' Clubs: Collectors of Rare & Familiar Tools Society of New Jersey, 38 Colony Ct, New Providence, NJ 07974-2332; Early American Industries Association, 167 Bakersville Rd, South Dartsmouth, MA 02748; New England Tool Collectors Association, 11-1/2 Concord Ave, Saint Johnsbury, VT 05819; Tool Group of Canada, 7 Tottenham Rd, Ontario MC3 2J3 Canada, plus many regional and specialized groups.

Anvil, 4" l, "Compliments of John Fink Metal Works, San Francisco and Seattle Wash".... 30.00
Axe head, single bit, Black Raven 20.00
Broad axe, W. Hunt, 6" h, orig handle 50.00

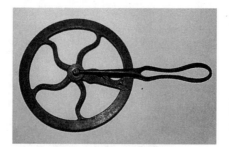

Traveler, used for measuring barrels and other round objects, cast iron, $25.

Carving chisels, S.J. Addis Cast Steel, Masonic hallmark, set of 12 .... 125.00
Draw knife, D.R. Barton 1882, 22" l, orig finish 85.00
Foot measure, Korrecto, directions on back 32.00
Ice saw, 78" l 89.00
Measuring tape, Lufkin. 100' ... 65.00
Plane, Doscher Plane & Tool Co., Saugatuck, Conn., 9-1/2" l 55.00
Router, unmarked, wrought iron, 1/2", wood handles, needs cleaning 25.00
Saddle maker's knife, H.G. Comph & Co., Albany, NY, crescent shape, rosewood handle, orig tooled leather scabbard 45.00
Socket chisel
    9/16" gouge, mkd "Lakeside" 15.00
    1-1/4" gouge, mkd "Butcher Cast Steel," handle split 15.00
    2", heavy, needs handle 17.00
Woodworking plane, "The Cincinnati Tool Co. Hargrove" on blade, spoke shave, 10-1/2" l 45.00
Wrench
    John Deere JD 50, 6" l 19.00
    Morrison #260 multi-wrench, 10-1/4" l 9.00
    Unmkd, twisted handle 45.00

❖ Toothbrush Holders

Getting kids to brush their teeth has been a challenge for decades. One way to help this activity was a character to hold toothbrushes. They certainly make a neat collectible. Because many were made of plaster or bisque, expect to find some damage and loss to the paint.

Collectors' Club: Toothbrush Holder Collectors Club, P.O. Box 371, Barnesville, MD 20838-0371.
Drum major, tube tray 90.00
Girl with dog, tube tray 80.00
Lone Ranger, plaster, painted, 4" h 75.00
Mickey and Minnie Mouse, bisque 350.00
Mickey Mouse, bisque, one arm moveable, other connected to body, string tail missing, paint worn, late 1930s 225.00
Soldier 85.00
Three Pigs 155.00

❖ Toothpick Holders

Here's another accessory that has been present on the table or sideboard since Victorian times. Typically they are high enough for a toothpick to stand on end and large enough to hold many toothpicks. Over the years, toothpick holders have been made in all different types of materials.

Collectors' Club: National Toothpick Holders Collectors Society, P.O. Box 417, Safety Harbor, Fl 34695-0417.
Bisque, Kate Greenaway-style little girl standing beside basket 75.00

Caramel slag glass toothpick holder, swan motif, 2-1/2" high, $25.

China
Meissen, clown 70.00
Royal Bayreuth, elk 120.00
R.S. Prussia, pink and green luster ground, floral trim
.... 45.00
Glass
Cut glass, pedestal, chain of hobstars dec 150.00
Milk glass, parrot and top hat, c1895 .... 45.00
Pattern glass
Daisy and Button, blue 75.00
Kansas 45.00
Texas, gold trim 50.00
Silver plate, chick standing next to egg, engraved "Just Picked Out," Victorian, plate very worn .. 25.00

❖ Torquay Pottery

This English pottery is often called Motto Ware because it usually contains a motto written into the clay. Some of the sayings are quite humorous. The pieces were hand decorated and usually well marked.

Collectors' Clubs: North American Torquay Society, 12 Stanton, Madison, CT 06443; Torquay Pottery Collectors Society, 23 Holland Ave, Cheam, Sutton, Surrey SM2 6HW UK.

Bowl, Allervale, "Du'ee mak yerzel at 'ome," 3-3/4" dia 18.00
Candle holder, "Last in bed put the light out," 5-3/4" dia 120.00

Torquay pot with lid, 4-1/2" high, $40.

Console bowl, Kingfisher, 9-1/2" dia, 3" h 195.00
Creamer, house dec, "Don't make a fool of pleasure" 26.00
Finger bowl, "Time Ripens All Things," 4-1/4" dia 27.00
Shaving mug, scuttle, "The nearer the razor, the closer the shave," Dad on back, 6-1/2" h 215.00
Teapot, small, house dec, 4" h
.... 120.00
Tulip vase, hand painted, cobalt blue ground, hummingbird and floral design, black mark and #32, 7-1/2" h 98.00
Vase, Kingfisher, 3-1/4" dia, 10" h
.... 175.00

❖ Tortoiseshell Items

The mottled brown design known as tortoiseshell was so popular with Victorians that many items were made of actual tortoise shells as well as being imitated in glassware and pottery. With the invention of celluloid and plastics, imitations saw a revival. Today, real tortoiseshell falls under the protection of the Endangered Species Act. But, remember when many vintage tortoiseshell items were made, the entire tortoise was being used for food and other purposes, so the shell was also used.

Box, cov, circular, painted figure by riverscape, French, late 19th C, minor losses, 3" dia 495.00
Calling card case, mother-of-pearl and ivory inlaid dec, c1825, 4" x 3" 225.00
Glove box, domed lid, ornate ivory strapping, sandalwood int., 3-1/2" h 375.00
Snuff box, oval, silver dec, 1-1/2" x 3" 325.00
Travel set, case, comb, nail file, hand mirror, shoe horn, hair brush, soap box, toothpaste box, toothbrush box, powder box, nail buff, monogrammed "B.M.A," case worn 40.00

❖ Toys

Every toy at a flea market is collectible, though some toys have greater value. Factors that influence price include age, condition, the original box, desirability, and maker. Probably the most deciding factor in the purchase of an antique toy is the one that makes the heart of the collector skip a beat, something that says that toy is important. The sampling below is just a mere peek into the giant toy box that many flea markets represent to collectors.

References: Ted Hake, *Hake's Price Guide to Character Toys*, Gemstone Publishing, 2000; Sharon and Bob Huxford, *Schroeder's Collectible Toys*, 7th ed., Collector Books, 2000; Dana Johnson, *Collector's Guide to Diecast Toys & Scale Models*, 2nd ed., Collector Books, 1998; Sharon Korbeck and Elizabeth A. Stephan, *Toys & Prices*, 8th ed, Krause Publications, 2000; Mike and Sue Richardson, *Diecast Toy Aircraft*, New Cavendish, 1998; Elizabeth Stephan, *O'Brien's Collecting Toy Cars & Trucks*, 3rd ed, Krause Publications, 2000; —, *O'Brien's Collecting Toys*, 9th ed, Krause Publications, 1999.

Periodicals: *Antique Toy World*, P.O. Box 34509, Chicago, IL 60634; *Model and Toy Collector Magazine*, P.O. Box 347240, Cleveland, OH 44134; *Toy Farmer*, 7496 106th Ave, SE, Lamoure, ND 58458; *Toy Shop*, 700 E State St, Iola, WI 54990.

Collectors' Clubs: American Game Collectors Association, P.O. Box 44, Dresher, PA, 19025; Antique Toy Collectors of America, 2 Wall St, 13th Floor, New York, NY, 10005; Canadian Toy Collectors Society, 67 Alpine Ave, Hamilton, Ontario L9A 1A7 Canada; Gamers Alliance, P.O. Box 197, East Meadow, NY 11554; plus many regional and specialized clubs.

Auburn Rubber "Auburn" racer, 6" long, $15.

Smith-Miller Mobiloil truck, $450.

For additional listings, see *Warman's Antiques and Collectibles Price Guide* and *Warman's Americana & Collectibles*, as well as specific company listings in this edition.

Airplane, 1940s, 9" wingspan, blue and red, white wooden wheels, metal propeller, wings fold at hinges, Wyandotte........... 145.00

Boxing gloves, child size, Benlee, 2 pairs in box...................... 125.00

Bunny, three-wheeler bike, litho tin wind-up, mkd "MTU, China" 65.00

Camper truck, all tin, litho, friction, 8" l, MIB 175.00

Charleston Trio, litho tin wind-up, 1921, C-8 .... 700.00

Coney Island Roller Coaster, 22" w, 15" deep, two large bus type cars, bright graphics, Techonix, Germany, MIB 395.00

Coupe, rumble seat, A.C. Williams, 4-3/4" l, c1930, small chip on bottom of seat 195.00

Dipper Bug, pull toy, 1950s, MIB 85.00

Double decker London bus, adv for Mobil and Shell, all tin, rubber wheels, friction, 7" l, MIB . 175.00

Duck, blue shirt, red bandanna, big orange star badge, rubber, mkd "The Walt Disney Company Tootsie Toy Made in China," 5-1/4" h.............................. 35.00

Dandy Jim, litho tin wind-up, Unique Art, 1922........................... 700.00

Dump truck, litho tin wind-up, mkd "England," C-8 .... 200.00

Easy Bake Oven, Kenner's, 1960, orig mixes and box 140.00

Easy Show, Kenner's, 1960, six movies, orig box 140.00

Evel Knievel Skycycle, Ideal Toys, diecast, MIB 125.00

Ferris wheel, colorful seats and graphics, Ohio Art 295.00

Fire Chief Car, pull toy, metal, clanging bell, T. Cohen, 1940s, MIB 275.00

Flying Patrol Set, Tootsietoy, MIB 175.00

Ford sedan, Tootsietoy 40.00

Gibbs Teeter Totter, painted tin, c1905, C-9 ....350.00

Give A Show Projector, Kenner, boxed................................35.00

Hansom Limo, 6" l, cast-iron, Kenton 300.00

Horse-drawn cart, cast-iron, Kenton 350.00

Indian Joe, Alps, NMIB 65.00

Katerina, Shako figure, litho tin, Lindstrom, 1930s 175.00

Jack in the box, Beanie & Cecil 160.00

Johnny Toymaker, played with condition, orig box 60.00

Mercury, 1949, Tootsietoy........95.00

Musical clown, Mattel, MIB 210.00

Policeman on motorcycle, tin, friction, MIB 75.00

Pontiac, 1950, Tootsietoy 95.00

Race car
    Auburn Rubber...................65.00
    Buffalo Toys, Red Streak, C-7.5 ....200.00
    Schuco, green, key wind, MIB 190.00

Roadster, red and black, Wyandotte, 7" l 175.00

Suzy Homemaker plastic oven, electric, 1968, Deluxe Topper Corp., 14" high, 9-1/2" wide, $25.

Shooting gallery, litho tin wind-up, tin target, orig darts, Wyandotte 290.00

Shuttling freight train, Cragston, battery operated, MIB 295.00

Sky Ranger, tin zeppelin and prop plane revolving around naval tower lighthouse, Unique Art, 1930s 390.00

Stake truck, cast-iron, Kenton 350.00

Trombone, 10" l, tin, brass-color, works 60.00

UPS package car, brown hard plastic truck, orig brown and white box, copyright UPS 1977, friction, 2" x 5-1/2" x 2-1/2" box 45.00

UPS truck, hard plastic, clicker on front tires, copyright UPS, Made in China, 1977, 5-1/2" l 45.00

Whirlybird, 25 men attack team, Remco, 1960s, orig box.. 275.00

❖ Toy Dimestore Soldiers

Children have been fascinated with three-dimensional lead, iron, rubber, and plastic toy soldiers for many years. About the time of World War II, dimestores started to carry soldiers, which immediately became popular with youngsters. The toys could be purchased one at a time, making each set unique, unlike the English lead soldiers, which were sold in sets.

Periodicals: *Old Toy Soldier*, 209 N Lombard, Oak Park, IL 60302; *Plastic Figure & Playset Collector*, P.O. Box 1355, LaCrosse, WI 54602; *Plastic Warrior*, 905 Harrison St, Allentown, PA 18103; *Toy Shop*, 700 E State St, Iola, WI 54990; *Toy Soldier Review*, 127 74th St, North Bergen, NJ 07047.

Aircraft spotter, Manoil........... 27.50

Army motorcycle with sidecar, Barclay 50.00

Bandit, hands up, Grey Iron.... 42.00

Baseball player, Auburn Rubber 35.00

Bicycle dispatch rider, soldier, Manoil 25.00

Bomb thrower, 2 grenades in pouch, Manoil 20.00

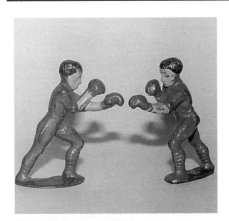

Manoil boxers, $60 each.

Boy in travel suit, Grey Iron 10.00
Bugler, prewar, tin helmet, Barclay
.... 20.00
Cadet officer, Grey Iron 20.00
Charging soldier with tommy gun,
    Auburn Rubber 12.00
Colonial soldier, Grey Iron 17.50
Cowboy, mounted, firing pistol, Bar-
    clay 24.00
Crawling soldier, Barclay 15.00
Deep sea diver, 65 on chest, Manoil
.... 18.00
Farmer, sowing grain, Manoil .. 20.00
Flag bearer, postwar, Manoil ... 24.00
Football player, Auburn Rubber
.... 35.00
Indian chief, Barclay 12.00
Knight with pennant, Barclay ... 15.00
Lineman, football player, Auburn
    Rubber 25.00
Machine gunner, kneeling, Auburn
    Rubber 15.00
Marine officer, prewar, marching,
    sword, blue uniform, tin hat
.... 27.50
Navy doctor, in white, Barclay, flat
    underbase 15.00
Nurse, white uniform, Barclay
.... 24.00
Officer, postwar, pot helmet, Barclay,
    orig sword........................ 175.00
Pirate, Barclay 15.00
Policeman, raised arm, Barclay
.... 12.00
Red Cross nurse, Auburn Rubber
.... 30.00
Sailor, blue uniform, Barclay.... 15.00
Searchlight, Auburn Rubber 30.00
Soldier in gas mask and with flare
    gun, Manoil....................... 20.00
Wounded soldier, Manoil 17.50

❖ Toy Train Accessories

Toy train accessories, like Plasticville houses, tunnels, miniature figures, and fences, are often found at flea markets. Look for these tiny treasures to add to your train set-up.

Airport Hanger, Lionel 36.00
Bachman Hotel, Plasticville, HO 6.00
Billboard, Plasticville 10.00
Diner, Plasticville, orig box, some
    wear 25.00
Fence and gate, Plasticville 3.25
Foot bridge, Plasticville, #1051
.... 7.00
Gas station, Plasticville, MIB ... 66.50
Green house, Plasticville, MIB
.... 65.00
House, Plasticville
    Brick-look 8.00
    Cape Cod 10.00
    Ranch................................. 5.00
Moving and storage van, Plasticville,
    NRFB 35.00
Outhouse, Plasticville, O or S gauge
.... 10.00
Spruce trees, pr, Plasticville 9.00
Trestle set
    American Flyer, #780 .... 42.00
    Lionel, #111 .... 24.00
Union Station, Plasticville 18.00
Waiting room, American Flyer, metal
.... 30.00

Water tower
    American Flyer, red and white
        checkerboard sides, bubbling
        type 100.00
    Lionel............................... 82.00
    Plasticville 6.00

❖ Toy Trains

Toy trains are one of the most popular types of toys that collectors invest in today. Early toy trains were cast iron and quickly progressed to well-crafted examples using different types of metals and materials. American Flyer, Ives, and Lionel are among the most recognized makers. The prices listed below are for sets of trains.

References: Excellent references exist for every kind of toy train.

Periodicals: *Classic Toy Trains,* P.O. Box 1612, Waukesha, WI 53187; *LGB Telegram,* 1573 Landvater, Hummelstown, PA 17036; *Lionel Collector Series Marketmaker,* Trainmaster, 3224 NW 47th Terrace, Gainesville, FL 32606; *O Scale Railroading,* P.O. Box 239, Nazareth, PA 18064; S. *Gaugian,* 7236 Madison Ave, Forest Park, IL 60130.

Collectors' Clubs: American Flyer Collectors Club, P.O. Box 13269,

John Deere HO Scale Train Set, $400.

Tracking the market

Mention "John Deere," and most people think of tractors. However, a variety of collectible items have been made to promote the popular farm equipment manufacturer, including this train set.

Oddly enough, there was little interest when this John Deere HO Scale Train Set was first made available at a John Deere parts meeting in 1985. Accordingly, few sets were ordered. Enter the supply-and-demand factor, and as interest climbed, so did prices on the secondary market. Having originally sold for $69.95, the train jumped to as high as $500 within a year. As the initial frenzy subsided, the value readjusted to its current level of $400.

Made by Athearn, Inc., of Compton, Cal., the electric train consists of an engine, tanker, boxcar, flatbed with two John Deere tractors, caboose, and track. Other John Deere train sets have also been made.

Pittsburgh, PA 15234; LGB Model Railroad Club, 1854 Erin Dr, Altoona, PA 16602; Lionel Collectors Club of America, P.O. Box 479, LaSalle, IL 61301; Lionel Operating Train Society, 18 Eland Ct, Fairfield, OH 45014; Marklin Club-North America, P.O. Box 51559, New Berlin, WI 53151; Marklin Digital Special Interest Group, P.O. Box 51319, New Berlin, WI 53151; The National Model Railroad Association, 4121 Cromwell Rd, Chattanooga, TN 37421; The Toy Train Operating Society, Inc, Suite 308, 25 West Walnut St, Pasadena, CA 91103; Train Collector's Association, P.O. Box 248, Strasburg, PA 17579.

American Flyer
  Burlington Zephyr Streamliner, passenger, O gauge.... 725.00
  Minnie Ha-Ha, locomotive, 3 coaches, orange and gray, minor wear 295.00
  Passenger, #253 locomotive, two #610 cars, #612 dark green, maroon inserts, 1924, O gauge 295.00
Ives, passenger set, locomotive, tender, 3 cars, S gauge 150.00
Lionel
  Freight, #33, #35, #36, olive green, S gauge, 1920 .... 350.00
  Passenger, #352E, #10 locomotive, #332 baggage car, #339, coach, #341 observation car, 1926, S gauge, orig box, minor wear to locomotive 550.00
Marx, Seaboard Air Line RR Co., citrus colors, boxed set 450.00

❖ Tramp Art

Here's a hot part of the flea market scene! Now considered to be folk art by some, these pieces were crafted by someone with limited materials, tools, and sometimes skill. By adding bits and pieces together, layers became objects such as picture frames, boxes of all kinds, etc.

References: Michael Cornish and Clifford Wallach, *They Call It Tramp Art,* Columbia University Press, 1996; Helaine Fendelman and Jonathan Taylor, *Tramp Art: A Folk Art Phenomenon,* Stewart, Tabori & Chang, 1999; Clifford A. Wallach and Michael Cornish, *Tramp Art: One Notch at a Time,* Wallach-Irons Publishing, 1998.

For additional listings, see *Warman's Country.*

Comb box, hanging, arched scalloped back with layered notch-carved rosette in center accented with small round white porcelain knobs, front of open box slopes forward and has scalloped top edge, double dart-shaped ornament on front, dark-red paint, 10-1/8" h, 8-3/4" w 110.00
Doll dresser, 3 drawers, old white repaint, gold trim, worn, age cracks, 21-1/2" h, 15-1/2" w, 8-3/4" d 357.50
Frame
  12-1/2" h, 10-1/8" w, applied notch-carved molding with hearts and X's around sides, stained finish 110.00
  23" h, 21" w, gold and silver repaint on inner liners and outer border, dark orig finish in-between, graduated strips of wood stacked and chip-carved, minor wear, holds 8" x 10" picture 495.00
Jewelry box, hinged lid, 4 square layered notch-carved feet, 1 back foot missing, 6" h, 14" w, 8-1/4" d, ... 140.00
Mirror, frame with dark finish over varnish, stepped sawtooth border, stacked geometric designs, 15" h, 17-1/2" w 275.00
Sewing stand, dark orig finish, 4 molded legs, applied sawtooth trim, shelf in base, well at top with handles on each side, large rectangular pincushions on front and back, lid missing, 27" h, 18-1/4" w, 13-1/4" d 412.50

1986 Transformers Decepticon Breakdown, part of the Stunticons, $5

★ Transformers

The first generation of Transformers were released in 1984 and introduced GenX children to good-guy Autobots fighting bad-guy Decepticons. These toys transform from robot to vehicle and featured cars and trucks before expanding to include planes, motorcycles, cassettes, and even the space shuttle. Transformers mint-on-the-card or mint-in-sealed-box command the highest prices. The Marvel comics series, television series and even *Transformers the Movie* established well-known characters, like Autobot leader Optimus Prime, that hold even higher values.

Air Hammer, MOC, C-9 .... 15.00
Blurr, 1986, missing gun, loose 20.00
Bonecrusher, MOC, C-9 .... 60.00
Buzzsaw, MOC, C-9 .... 50.00
Claw Jaw, MOC, C-9 .... 30.00
Devastator, 1985, loose 85.00
Grimlock, 1985, sword missing, loose 70.00
Inferno, MISB, C-9 .... 15.00
Injector, MOC, C-8 .... 10.00
Omega Supreme, 1985, C-9, loose 85.00
Optimus Prime, 1984, MIB, C-7, decals unopened 225.00
Outback, 1985, C-8, loose 10.00
Overdrive, 1985, C-8, loose.... 25.00
Polar Claw, MISB, C-9 .... 60.00
Powrpinch, MOC, C-6............. 12.00

Scraper, 1984, gun missing, loose
....8.00
Sky Shadow, MOC, C-8 ....10.00
Sunstreaker, 1984, C-9, C-7 box
....150.00
Swoop, 1985, loose, C-9 ....110.00
Tigatron, MOC, C-8 ....40.00
Trailbreaker, 1984, C-9, C-8 box
....140.00
Tripredacus, MISB, C-8 ....30.00
Wheeljack, 1984, C-9, C-6 box
....120.00
Wolfgang, MOC, C-8 ....45.00

❖ Transistor Radios

Remember how cool it was to walk around as a teenager, holding your radio up so only you could hear it! Those transistor radios spelled freedom from electrical cords and sometimes were even in funky shapes and colors. Most of us didn't care that they only got AM stations, it was the "old folks" that listened to FM anyway. Today collectors like to find transistor radios with original cases, instructions, and little wear.

Bulova, transistor, orig case 45.00
Emerson, #888, Vanguard, transistor, portable, 1958 ....65.00

Polaroid novelty transistor radio, 4-1/2" high, $15.

GE, P-910C, aqua 12.50
Guild Radio, telephone shape, crank changes stations, 18" h 95.00
Lionel, MIB..............................35.00
Panasonic, 1950s, blue 55.00
Radio Shack, shaped like D-cell battery....................................38.00
Realtone 6 ....48.00
Silvertone, #9205, transistor, plastic, 1959 ....42.00
Sony, TFM-151, transistor, 1960
....60.00
Toy telephone and cigarette lighter, plastic, 1950s, 5-1/2" h 20.00
Tropicana...............................15.00
Zenith
    RG 47J, Hong Kong.............4.00
    Royal 500 Deluxe...............45.00
    Royal 710 ....30.00

❖ Transportation

Memorabilia relating to the transportation of goods and people has long been a favorite with collectors. Perhaps it's the romance of the open road or the fun of finding out about faraway places. Whatever the mode of transportation, you'll find some ephemera relating to it.

Reference: Barbara J. Conroy, *Restaurant China: Identification & Value Guide For Restaurant, Airline, Ship & Railroad Dinnerware*, Collector Books, 1998.

Periodical: *Airliners*, P.O. Box 52-1238, Miami, FL 33152.

Collectors' Clubs: Bus History Association, 965 McEwan, Windsor Ontario N9B 2G1 Canada; Central Electric Railfans' Association, P.O. Box 503, Chicago, IL 60690; International Bus Collectors Club, 1518 "C" Trailee Dr, Charleston, SC 29407; Steamship Historical Society of America, Inc, Ste #4, 300 Ray Dr, Providence, RI 02906; Transport Ticket Society, 4 Gladridge Close, Earley, Reading Berks RG6 2DL England.

Blotter, Firestone Bicycle Tires, black, white, orange, and blue, 1920s, unused 20.00
Booklet, St. Lawrence route to Europe, Canadian Pacific, 1930, 16 pgs, 8" x 11"...............25.00
Bus calendar, Greyhound, 1940
....80.00

Fan, Air India, adv.....................4.00
Game, Pirates & Travelers, 1911, tri-fold board, boxed pcs 120.00
Map, Greyhound Routes, folded
....10.00
Luggage tag, Canadian Pacific, stringed cardstock, red, white, and blue ship signs, c1930, 5" x 3" 15.00
Stickpin, brass, bug pedaling bicycle, mkd "Compliments of United States Tire Co.," 1920s.....27.50
Ticket holder, blue plastic, TWA logo
....2.00
Traffic light, rewired................85.00

❖ Traps

Snap! Gotcha! Hunters have been trapping since the old days when fur traders trapped and traded goods. Today many traps are considered to be collectible. Be careful if you test one of these!

Collectors' Clubs: National Trappers Assoc, 456 N Main St, P.O. Box 550, New Martinsville, WV 26155; North American Trap Collectors Association, P.O. Box 94, Galloway, OH 43119-0094.

Blake & Lamb Model #21, Hawkins Co. 15.00
Jump #13, beaver 46.00
Newhouse #15, bear.............400.00
Sargent & Co. #1, muskrat 22.50
Triumph #4 ....30.00
Ranger #42 ....130.00
Mousetrap, wire and wood, domed, 4-1/2" h, 4-3/4" sq 55.00
Minnow, green glass, 9-3/4" l
....150.00

Lobster trap with float, $50.

❖ Trays

Trays are another type of advertising collectible. Like tip trays, expect to find interesting lithographed scenes and advertising for all types of products. Also expect to find some signs of usage.

Reproduction Alert.

For additional listings, see *Warman's Advertising*.

Jim Beam, plastic, 17" x 11" 9.00
Bartlett Spring Mineral Water, 13" dia 150.00
Bozo, TV tray, some rust 30.00
Buffalo Brewing Co., scratches and soiling, 13" dia 100.00
C.D. Kenny Co., Christmas motif of girl with doll, holly border, 10" dia 230.00
Dick & Bros' Quincy Beer, factory scene, early wagons and automobilia, some chipping to rim, fading, scratching 200.00
Enterprise Brewing Co., Old Tap Ale, toothless happy old man, minor wear to rim, some staining to background 175.00
Golden West Brewing Co., factory scene, early trolleys and horse drawn carts, American Art Works, some chipping and soiling 300.00
Happy Birthday Mickey Mouse, Cheinco, 1978, 14" dia 45.00
Kaiser Willhelm Bitters Co., oversized bottle with trademark label, "For Appetite and Digestion" 70.00
Knickerbocker beer, metal, 13" dia 15.00

Shurtleff's Ice Cream tray, red and white, tin, 12" x 17", $65.

Maier Brewing, woman in orange outfit, Maier trademark on side, ©1909, Kaufmann & Strauss Co. litho, some overall scratching 100.00
Moerlein Beer, trademark "Crowned Wherever Exhibited" in fancy filigree, rim shows different expositions, Chas. W. Shonk Co., minor inpainting 50.00
National Brewery Co., White Seal Beer, factory scene, horse drawn wagon, early blob top bottle, Griesedieck Bros, proprietors, chipping and scratching ... 185.00
Pacific Brewing & Malting Co., Mt. Tacoma illus, orig 1912 work order from Chas. W. Shonk Co. on back 50.00
Paul "Bear" Bryant, College Football's All-Time Winningest Coach, 315th Victory, Nov. 28, 1981, Krystal 30.00
Portrait, Victorian woman with bouquet, porcelain, 2 handles, gold trim, 10" sq 300.00
Stegmaier Brewing Co., factory scene, early railroad and automobilia, minor scratching and rubbing............................. 70.00
Terre Haute Brewing Co., room full of Colonials raise their empty glasses to flying cherubs who are bringing that "Ever-Welcome Beer" 125.00

❖ Trivets

Trivets are handy for holding hot irons and pots. Over the years, some have become quite decorative.

Note: All trivets are cast iron.

Iron rest
  Double Point, IWANTU, Comfort Iron, Strause Gas Iron Co., Phila. Pa., embossed image of gas iron 40.00
  Humphrey Gas Iron & General Specialty Co. 42.50
Kitchen
  Chagrin Falls, Ohio, square with stylized flowers 27.50
  God Bless Our Home, gold, green, red and black paint 4-1/4" dia 14.00
  Good Luck, horseshoe with star in center, mkd 9-35 and VCM, 7" x 4-1/4" 58.00

6 interlooping circles, footed, mkd "J.L.H. 1945 C2," traces of gold, red and green paint, 5-1/2" sq 16.00
Wilton #2, love birds, hearts, brooms and a star 25.00

❖ Trolls

These funny looking characters marched onto the scene in the 1960s. With their bright colors and bushy hair, they have been bringing collectors good luck.

Periodicals: *Troll Monthly*, 216 Washington St., Canton, MA 02021; *Trollin*, P.O. Box 601292, Sacramento, CA 95860.

49ers Troll, NFL, 1998, 4-1/4" h 10.00
Caveman, Mop-Pets by Sarco, 1960s, 5" h........................ 25.00
Cinderella, 12" h 15.00
Marx, talking troll, 18" h 45.00
Wooden, hand-carved, Henning, Norway, 5" h..................... 32.00
Russ Berrie Troll, baby in pajamas, 7-1/2" h 6.00
Treasure Troll, Ace Novelty Co., baby, 11" h 15.00

❖ Trophies

How many of us have received a trophy for some event and it now resides in the back of a closet? Some trophies find their way to flea markets and then attract new buyers. Look for interesting names or dates on a trophy.

Bowling, Bakelite, 1960s....... 108.00
Boy Scouts, figural metal boy on plastic base, 8-1/2" h 35.00
Dog, Best Hound 1962, cup style, silver-plated 220.00
Garfield, on his knee, Arlene's holding needle, "Get the point," Enesco Corp., 4-1/2" h...... 25.00
Golf
  Crystal Lake Country Club, 1931, silver-plated, runner-up, 5" h 5.00
  Figural golfer on marble base, 1973 .... 68.00

Woman's bowling trophy, 9" high, $9.

High school
Mercury figure on black base, District Champ, SDHS Exclamatory League, 1933 .... 110.00
Triumph figure on black base, District High School Exclamatory, 1930 .... 125.00

❖ Tupperware

Tupperware was one of the first household products introduced to modern housewives at parties. By gathering with friends, housewives could see the latest in plastic wares and have a good time too. Today, Tupperware is especially sought in Japan and many European countries. Related booklets and other paper ephemera are destined to become collectibles of tomorrow, just as Tupperware is beginning to show up at flea markets.

Bowl, cov, bright green, 8" dia, 3-1/2" h 6.00
Coasters, pastel, set of six in orig holder, few scratches, 2-7/8" dia 15.00
Child's cup, solid and sippy lid, name in Spanish on back, 6-1/2" h
Cinderella 6.00
Jasmine, Princess Collection 6.00

Tupperware Toys child's play set, 26 pieces total, orange, green, yellow and brown plastic, $15.

Child's playset
Mini-mix set, 1979, complete, MIB 20.00
Mini-party set, 1980, complete, MIB 20.00
Collector plate, Chrissy's Favorite Toy, little girl with bowl on head, orig certificate, 1993, 7-1/4" dia 8.00
Cookbook, *Stacked Cooked Meals*, Meredith, 1990, microwave system 10.00
Cup, Super Bowl XXIX, January 2, 1995, Joe Robbie Stadium, orig top, 7-1/4" h 5.00
Figure, Tupperware Lady, carrying miniature piece of Tupperware in one hand, bag full on her arm, orange skirt and blouse, cream colored jacket and shoes, mkd "Special Edition, Made exclusively for Tupperware, Series II," 7-3/4" h 70.00
Lettuce keeper, green, 7" dia 5.00
Mustard container, mkd, 7-1/2" h 5.00
Pastry sheet, 18" w, 21-1/2" l 5.00
Pepper shaker, light blue, 2-3/4" h 4.00
Salad tongs, blue-green hard plastic, mkd "Tupperware" on handle, 1958, orig box 15.00

❖ Turtle Collectibles

Turtle collectors will not find a flea market slow-going. There will probably be several interesting examples to add to their growing collections.

References: Alan J. Brainard, *Turtle Collectibles*, Schiffer Publishing, 2000.

Beanie Baby, Speedy the Turtle, retired, protector on orig tag 65.00
Earrings, sterling silver, 1" l 8.50
Hat, child's, green 5.00
Pin, Ciner, yellow enameled shell, green rhinestones, red rhinestone eye, 1-1/2" x 1-1/4" . 50.00
Paperweight, cast-iron 35.00
Pill box, sterling silver, 1-1/2" l, 1-1/8" w 35.00
Planter, McCoy 40.00
Tape measure, brushed gold metal, red rhinestone eyes, 3" x 2-1/2" 130.00

Turtle candle, 3" long, $1.

❖ TV Guides

These little television-oriented magazines have been steadily growing in value. There is usually an article about the star featured on the cover, plus other interesting tidbits for television memorabilia collectors.

1953, Queen Elizabeth 12.00
1963, Lucille Ball's newborn baby 400.00
1967, Ed Sullivan 7.50
1973, Bill Cosby 10.00

TV Guide, **Dinah Shore cover, Dec. 15-21, 1956, $3.**

1975, Tony Orlando and Dawn 6.00
1976, George Kennedy 5.00
1976, Redd Foxx 5.00
1977, Frank Sinatra..................5.00
1981, Archie Bunker.................6.50
1982, Michael Landon...............7.50
1984, Pierce Bronsan..............12.50
1986, Farrah Fawcett 5.00
1986, Nicollette Sheridan 5.00
1986, Lucille Ball 15.00

❖ Twin Winton

Twin Winton had production facilities in Pasedena and San Juan Capistrano, California, in the early 1950s. Their wares are well known to cookie jar collectors, but don't overlook some of their other table wares and accessories.

Bank, Hillbilly, barrel mkd "Mountain Dew 100 Proof".................85.00
Cookie jar
  Cat 60.00
  Elf, crack on back...............55.00
  Monk, banner on bottom of robe "Thou Shalt Not Steal," some crazing on head............50.00
  Pot O' Cookies 115.00
  Sailor Elephant, 11-1/2" h, small chip on hat....................45.00
Dealer's sign.........................300.00
Figure, black football player, 6" h, 1972.................................75.00
Napkin holder
  Dutch Girl..........................20.00
  Mother Goose 55.00
Pitcher, Hillbilly, glaze flake on spout 33.00
Salt and pepper shakers, pr
  Kittens 46.00
  Lions 40.00
  Racoons..............................65.00
  Squirrels.............................20.00

❖ Typewriters & Accessories

Tap, tap, ding. Remember the bell that used to ring as you pecked away on a typewriter? Some collectors still hear that sound. You can find them while searching flea markets for vintage typewriters, accessories and related ephemera. Vintage typewriters are another example of where you should thoroughly inspect the keys, motor, and wiring, before trying to use it.

Reference: Michael Adler, *Antique Typewriters*, Schiffer Publishing, 1997.

Periodicals: *Ribbon Tin News*, 28 The Green, Watertown, CT 06795-2118; *The Typewriter Exchange*, 2125 Mount Vernon St, Philadelphia, PA 19130.

Collectors' Club: Early Typewriter Collectors Association, 2591 Military Ave, Los Angeles, CA 90064.

Advertisement
  Royal, 1962 .... 13.00
  Royal Portable, 1970s......... 3.00
Oil can, Smith Premier Typewriter Oiler, 3-1/2" h 22.00
Postcard, Remington Plant 15.00
Ribbon tin
  Carter's Midnight, space motif 16.00
  Columbia Twins................. 15.00
  Eberhard 10.00
  McGregor, 2-1/2" dia 65.00
  Panama............................ 20.00
  Remington........................ 7.50
  Seagull 23.00
  Vogue Royale..................... 5.00
  Webster Star Brand.......... 18.00
Typewriter
  Adler 7, oak case 335.00
  Bing #2, German, with case 150.00
  L.C. Smith #8, 12" carriage 20.00
  L.C. Smith & Corona, Comet 65.00
  Remington, portable, #5.... 40.00
  Simplex 50.00
  Tom Thumb, orig case....... 15.00
  Underwood #5................. 155.00

❖ Umbrellas

While you might not want to open one in your house, it's great fun to find vintage umbrellas and parasols at flea markets. Look for examples in working order with interesting handles and fabrics in good condition.

Beach, beige cloth, long wooden spiked pole, c1940, some wear and fading 40.00
Black, large size, "J" shaped Bakelite handle 45.00
Brown, light beige stripes, clear lucite handle, some wear .. 10.00
Golf, bright red and white, wood handle 35.00
Holly Hobbie, child size, plastic . 7.50
Mickey & Minnie Mouse, Walt Disney Enterprises, Ltd., 1930s, wood handle 185.00
Newscaster, Comcast, black, white and red 10.00
Parasol, beige, boa trim, shepherd's crook handle, c1900 .... 100.00
Parasol, white linen, crochet work trim, c1890 .... 120.00

❖ Unicorns

This mystical beast has charmed many hearts. Today collectors search them out and enjoy finding the various ways they are interpreted in glass, ceramic, and even on paper.

Collectors' Club: Unicorns Unanimous, 248 N Larchmont Blvd, Los Angeles, CA 90004.

Beanie Baby, Mystic the Unicorn, protector on orig tag 18.00

Bell, bronzed pot metal, figural unicorn handle, 6-1/2" h 20.00
Candleholder, Vandor, MIB 12.00
Clipboard, brass 24.00
Figure, ceramic
    Hamilton/Enesco, Starlight Starbright Series, Believe in Miracles 60.00
    Hamilton/Enesco, Starlight Starbright Series, Discover Your Dreams 60.00
    Hamilton/Enesco, Starlight Starbright Series, Hang on to Your Dreams 60.00
    Lefton, gold horns and hooves, pastel pink ribbons, floral accents, #10912, retired, pr 30.00
    White, ivory, blue, and black, fired-on gold horn, applied silk flowers 75.00
Garden ornament, Unicorn Gargoyle, gypsum, Windstone, 13-3/4" h, orig box 85.00
Mirror, hand, Vandor, MIB 10.00
Pin, vermeil, black enameled horn, red, green, blue, and pink cabochons, rhinestone accents, mkd "Reinad," 3-1/2" x 3" 450.00
Print, black and white, sgd "Lisa Johnson, 1979," matted and framed, 11" x 14" 25.00
Sculpture, glass, hand blown, Scott Hartshorn, 4" h 30.00
Stuffed toy
White plush, satin ribbons, shimmering gold horn, iridescent mane 22.00
White plush, silver horn and hooves, Gund, 10" h 10.00
Vase, galloping unicorn, light green, mkd "Hull USA," 11-1/2" h.. 80.00

❖ Universal Pottery

Organized in 1934 by the Oxford Pottery Company, in Cambridge, Ohio, the firm merged and bought several other small potteries over the years. Universal Pottery made dinnerware and kitchenware until 1960, when the company closed. Because of the mergers, several different brand names were used, including Oxford Ware and Harmony House.

Universal custard, set of 4, 2-1/4" high, $10.

Reference: Timothy J. Smith, *Universal Dinnerware and Its Predecessors*, Schiffer Publishing, 2000.
For additional listings, see *Warman's Americana & Collectibles* and *Warman's American Pottery & Porcelain*.

Batter bowl set, Circus pattern, 4-1/2" d, 5-1/2" d, 6-1/2" d, 3 matching lids, one with nick 25.00
Bread box, Cattails 40.00
Casserole, cov, Cattails 20.00
Cup and saucer, Woodvine 12.00
Custard cup, Calico Fruit 6.50
Dinner plate, Rambler Rose ... 10.00
Drip jar, Bittersweet................. 25.00
Gravy boat
    Highland 35.00
    Rambler Rose 12.00
Milk jug, Calico Fruit 30.00
Mixing bowl set, Ballerina, nested set of three, some wear 30.00
Pie server, Cattails.................. 24.00
Platter
    Bittersweet 35.00
    Cattails 35.00
Refrigerator pitcher, Cattails ... 40.00
Salad bowl, Bittersweet 24.00
Salt and pepper shakers, Calico Fruit, pr 20.00
Soup bowl, Rambler Rose 6.50
Sugar bowl, cov
    Baby's Breath.................... 30.00
    Ballerina 35.00
    Cattails 30.00
Vegetable bowl, cov, Cattails .. 30.00
Vegetable bowl, open
    Ballerina 30.00
    Bittersweet 45.00
Water jug, orig stopper............ 35.00

❖ U.S. Glass

Known to collectors and dealers as U.S. Glass, the United States Glass Company started as a conglomerate of several glass houses in 1891. The first wares under this new company were pressed pattern glass. One innovation was the company's States series, made up of pre-existing patterns that were renamed, while others were new designs. As the years went on, U.S. Glass developed some of the newer, sleeker, more elegant Depression-era patterns. The last of U.S. Glass factories to close was Tiffin Glass.

Prices listed below are for clear pieces, unless otherwise indicated.

Banana stand, Colorado, blue. 65.00
Bowl, Bull's Eye and Daisy, ruby stained.............................. 30.00
Bride's basket, Delaware, silver plated frame...................... 75.00
Butter dish, cov, Almond Thumbprint, non-flint..................... 40.00
Cake stand, Connecticut, non-flint 40.00
Celery tray, Vermont, gold trim 30.00
Compote, cov, New Hampshire, high standard, 5" d 5.00
Creamer
    California, emerald green...50.00
    Texas, gold trim.................. 45.00
    Vermont, gold trim.............. 32.00
Finger bowl, Nevada................ 25.00
Goblet
    California, emerald green...55.00
    Galloway, non-flint.............. 75.00
    Manhattan.......................... 25.00
Juice tumbler, Pennsylvania 10.00
Olive, Iowa............................... 15.00
Pickle castor, Galloway, silver-plated holder and lid.................... 85.00
Punch bowl, Almond Thumbprint, non-flint............................. 75.00
Punch cup, Iowa 15.00
Relish, Maryland...................... 15.00
Rose bowl, Galloway 25.00
Salt and pepper shakers, pr
    California 45.00
    Kentucky 24.00
Sauce dish, Nevada................ 10.00
Spooner, Bull's Eye and Daisy 25.00
Sugar, cov
    Colorado............................ 75.00
    Vermont, gold trim............. 35.00
Toothpick, Delaware, rose, gold trim 45.00
Tumbler, Almond Thumbprint, non-flint 20.00
Whiskey, Pennsylvania, gold trim 24.00
Wine, Connecticut, non-flint.... 35.00

❖ Valentines

Collecting Valentine's Day sentiments is a pleasure for many folks. The earliest cards were handmade. After the greeting card business became more fully developed, valentines were included. Many collectors prefer die-cut cards, which are sometimes found with layers or pull-down decorations. Others like mechanical or animated cards, which have a moving part.

Collectors' Club: National Valentine Collectors Association, P.O. Box 1404, Santa Ana, CA 92702.

For additional listings, see *Warman's Antiques and Collectibles Price Guide* and *Warman's Americana & Collectibles.*

Honeycomb tissue
  Children playing house, 1920s, 8" x 5"............................25.00
  Cupid and flower basket, 1926 ....32.00
Mechanical
  Boxer, "You sure are a Knockout Valentine," 8-3/4" h, 8" w 24.00
  Baseball player swinging bat, "I'd sure go to bat for a Valentine Like You," 6-1/4" h.........22.00
  Girl doing dishes, 8" h, 6" w 25.00
  Saxophone player, "My dear Sweetheart I'm making a big noise about you," 5" h ... 10.00
Stand-up, easel-back
  Automobile, windows open 12.00

Mechanical valentine, Charles Twelvetrees design, 1920s, 7" x 8", $22.50.

Cat with parachute, 4-1/2" x 3-1/2"............................29.00
Flower basket, pasteboard, 1918 ....9.00

❖ Van Briggle Pottery

The Van Briggle Pottery was founded in 1869 by an Ohio artist, Artus Van Briggle. For health reasons, he moved his pottery to Colorado Springs in 1901. After his death in 1904, his wife, Anna, continued the pottery for a few years. Reading the marks can give valuable clues as to the date and maker. The really pricey pieces of Van Briggle are early works; prime examples can command hundreds of dollars. However, there are plenty of more ordinary pieces which are great for a beginning collector. Keep in mind, the company is still in business and many current-production pieces turn up at flea markets.

Candlestick, double-socket, mulberry glaze, floral design, 4-1/2" h, pr.....................140.00
Ewer, black glaze, 7-1/4" h 60.00
Paperweight
  Donkey, black glaze, 3-3/4" h 55.00
  Donkey, mulberry glaze, 3-3/4" h 132.00
  Owl, black glaze, 1960s, 9-1/2" h 125.00
  Shell, mulberry glaze, 9" l ..95.00

Planter, donkey, brown glaze, Anna Van Briggle 70.00
Plaque, Indian head, ming turquoise, 4-1/2" h 80.00
Vase
  Bulbous form, floral design, mulberry glaze, 8-3/8" h ... 440.00
  Lorelei, blue mat glaze, 10-7/8" h 209.00
  Low vase, inerlocking circles and lines, blue mat glaze, 1920 ....302.50
  Three Indian, Mulberry glaze, 10-7/8" h 660.00
Wall pocket, daisy design, Mountain Craig Brown glaze, 7-5/8" h 302.50

❖ Vandor

Vandor is a relative newcomer to the flea market scene. Their specialized wares bring vintage characters back to life and are well received. Because the wares are mainly from the 1990s, the original box and packaging should be readily available.

Bank, Howdy Doody 25.00
Cookie jar
  Betty Boop, holiday 35.00
  Grateful Dead, 1998, MIB 125.00
  Mona Lisa..........................85.00
Egg cup, Sweet Pea 45.00
Mug, Brutus 15.00
Music box, Popeye and Olive Oyl 75.00
Picture frame, Betty Boop, copyright K.F.S., 1985, orig paper label 65.00
Salt and pepper shakers, pr
  Beatles fish phone, fish salt shaker, phone pepper, mkd "2000 Subafilms, Ltd., Yellow Submarine product, Trade Mark of Subafilms, Ltd., ©1968, Authorized Beatles Merchandise," MIB 20.00
  Betty Boop and Pup, on motorcycle, 4-1/2" h 24.00
  Bewitched, stove salt shaker, Samatha pepper shaker, 2-7/8" h, MIB.................20.00
  Cat Pais, nodders, 1996....25.00
  Grateful Dead, yellow bear salt shaker, train pepper shaker, 2-1/4" h, MIB................22.00

Man in top hat 15.00
Poodles, NRFB 20.00
Popeye 95.00
Teapot, cover
Betty Boop, car 12.50
Cherry Woods 5.00

❖ Van Telligen

Designer Ruth Van Telligen created some fun characters for the Royal China and Novelty Company of Chicago. Produced by Regal China, the items were limited to a few cookie jar designs and salt and pepper shakers. The cookie jars were made in limited numbers and tend to be hard to find.

Salt and pepper shakers, pr
Bears, yellow, 3-1/2" h 45.00
Black boy and dog 175.00
Bunnies, hugging 25.00
Ducks 75.00
Dutch boy and girl, 3-3/4" h
.... 80.00
Mary and lamb 85.00
Peek-A-Boos, red and white
.... 120.00
Snuggle Hug Love Bugs
.... 125.00

Van Telligan duck salt and pepper shakers, chips, $30.

❖ Vaseline Glass

Vaseline glass is named for its unusual yellow-green color, which is created by adding uranium salts to the glassware batch. Collectors test their vaseline glass with a black light or even a Geiger counter, as it is somewhat radioactive. Production was restricted in later years because of the lack of uranium. This type of glass was made by early American glassblowers up through the early Depression years. The white swirls of the opalescent highlights create a pleasing contrast to the unusual base color.

Reproduction Alert.

Bread plate, Daisy and Button with Crossbars, pattern glass 35.00
Butter dish, cov, Spanish Lace, opalescent, Northwood 445.00
Celery vase, Daisy and Button with Crossbars, pattern glass 50.00
Cologne bottle, 5-1/2" h, 2" sq
.... 250.00
Console set, 10" d compote, matching 9" h candlesticks 500.00
Creamer, Wreath and Shell, opalescent, dec 135.00
Cruet, Everglades, opalescent
.... 275.00
Ice cream set, Daisy and Button, large bowl, serving bowls, some chips, 7 pc set 475.00
Jelly compote, Iris with Meander, opalescent 95.00
Knife rest, barbell shape, faceted ends, 4-7/8" l 95.00
Perfume bottle, Waterfall Nude, Czechoslovakian, 7-1/2" h
.... 225.00
Pitcher, Fluted Scrolls, opalescent
.... 300.00

Yellow Vaseline glass pitcher, Cane pattern, $45.

Spooner, Palm Beach, opalescent
.... 95.00
Sugar, cov, Diamond Spearhead, opalescent 235.00
Toothpick holder, Daisy and Button
.... 35.00
Tumbler, Fluted Scrolls 50.00
Vase, free blown, 8" h 60.00

"Eat 'em Hot" peanut vending machine, $350.

❖ Vending Machines

Got a penny for a gumball? Vending machines with gumballs, peanuts, and other goodies captured many pennies and loose change. These simple vending machines date to about 1910.

References: Several good older reference books exist on this topic and are recommended to those who want to learn more about vending machines.

It's a record

The record auction price for a vending machine is $104,500, paid to acquire The Merchant. The rarity was sold in 1995 by James D. Julia, Inc.

The Merchant, $104,500. (Photo courtesy of James D. Julia, Inc., Fairfield, Maine)

Periodicals: *Antique Amusements Slot Machines & Jukebox Gazette*, 909 26th St NW, Washington, DC 20037; *Around the Vending Wheel*, 54217 Costana Ave, Lakewood, CA 90712; *Coin Drop International*, 5815 W 52nd Ave, Denver, CO 80212; *Coin Machine Trader*, 569 Kansas SE, P.O. Box 602, Huron, SD 57350; *Coin-Op Classics*, 17844 Toiyabe St, Fountain Valley, CA 92708; *Coin-Op Newsletter*, 909 26th St, NW, Washington, DC 20037; *Coin Slot*, 4401 Zephyr St, Wheat Ridge, CO 80033; *Gameroom*, 1014 Mt Tabor Rd, New Albany, IN 47150; *Loose Change*, 1515 S Commerce St, Las Vegas, NV 89102; *Pin Game Journal*, 31937 Olde Franklin Dr, Farmington, MI, 48334; *Scopitone Newsletter*, 810 Courtland Dr, Ballwin, MO 63021.

Aspirin, Winthrop Metal Products, 10¢, 1940s 45.00
Cigar, Malkin Phillies, steel meal, 10¢, 1930s 95.00
Combs, Advance machine, Model #4, 10¢, 1950s 45.00
Gum
 Ford, round globe with Ford decal, chrome finish 150.00
 Jumbo, depicts circus elephant, 15" h 295.00

Mills Automatic Tab, 5-column tab gum vendor, aluminum front, colorful paper sign, green case 295.00
Northwestern, Model 33, 1930s, porcelain, glass globe 15" h 395.00
Victor, 1940s, aluminum front, cylindrical glass, 17" h, restored 245.00
Victor, 1950s, red and black metal case, glass globe, 11" h 195.00
Nut
 Atlas Bantam tray vendor, 1940s, restored, 11" h 395.00
 Eldridge, aluminum, 1936, 8-1/2" h, 4-1/2" w, 4" d 195.00
 Northwest, 1930s, porcelain base and top, frosted globe, embossed name, 15" h 395.00
 Silver King Hot Nut, c1947, red hobnail glass light on top, 15" h 495.00
Matches, Kelley Mfg., boxes, 1¢, 1920s 225.00
Postcard, Exhibit Supply, 1¢, 1930s 125.00
Stamps, Postage and Stamp Machine Co., metal, 5¢ and 10¢, 1948 .... 45.00

❖ Ventriloquist Dummies

Charlie McCarthy and Jerry Mahoney easily come to mind when thinking about vintage ventriloquist dummies. How fascinated we used to be with this form of entertainment. Because there were many amateur ventriloquists, their dummies occasionally find their way to flea markets. Look for well-constructed handmade examples or those produced by well-known doll companies.

Bart Simpson, custom made. 200.00
Boy, handmade, wearing child's blue suit, white shirt 90.00
Bozo 42.00
Jerry Mahoney 60.00
Lester, Paul Winchell, 1973, 25" h 142.00
Groucho Marx, made by Juro, 1977, 30" h 95.00

❖ Vernon Kilns

Founded in Vernon, California, the firm was formerly called Poxon China. After it sold to Faye Bennison in 1931, it was renamed Vernon Kilns. The company then flourished and made high-quality dinnerware and other items. Souvenir plates were among their more successful products. The company folded in 1958, when it sold its trade name, molds, and remaining stock.

Periodical: *Vernon Views*, P.O. Box 945, Scottsdale, AZ 85252.

Ashtray, Frontier Days, 5-3/4" w 80.00
Cake plate, Organdie, 12" dia. 20.00
Chop plate, Hawaiian Flowers, blue, 14" dia 42.00
Coffeepot, Style 165.00
Creamer and sugar, Brown-Eyed Susan 12.00
Cup and saucer
 Chatelaine, topaz 40.00
 Moby Dick, brown 22.00
Dinner plate, Hawaiian Flowers, blue, 9" dia 32.00
Egg cup, Organdie 27.50
Flower pot, matching saucer, Tam O'Shanter 80.00

Chintz sugar bowl, Vernon Kilns, $12.50.

Mug, Brown-Eyed Susan.........25.00
Pitcher
    Raffia, 2 qt 40.00
    Tweed, half pint, streamline, 5" h
    ....80.00
Platter, Painted Rose, oval, 16" l
    ....105.00
Salad plate, Chatelaine, topaz
    ....25.00
Salt and pepper shakers, pr, Gingham 15.00
Souvenir plate
    Georgia, 10" dia.................15.00
    Honolulu, Hawaii, pineapple border, several scenes, mkd "Made Exclusively for the Liberty House by Vernon Kilns, USA," 10-1/2" dia 50.00
    Nebraska University...........30.00
    Oklahoma State Agricultural and Mechanical College, backstamp "Vernon Kilns, designed especially for Creech's, Stillwater, Oklahoma"..........30.00
    Texas Southwest Methodist University, Dallas, backstamp "Made exclusively for Titche-Goettinger Co." 35.00
Teapot, Linda.......................125.00
Tidbit tray, Tam O'Shanter, 3 tiers, wood handle......................45.00

❖ Victorian

This is one of those topics clearly open to individual interpretation. It takes its name from the reign of Queen Victoria, but clearly lasted for years after her reign ceased. Decorators and dealers use "Victorian" to describe things from that era, especially objects that are ornate, richly colored, and often richly textured.

Boudoir chair, lady's, wicker, ornate curliques, bead garlands
....335.00
Bud vase, sterling silver, unidentified hallmarks, 8" h 90.00
Fan, ostrich feathers, ribbon, white, some losses.....................120.00
Frame, double heart shape openings, wood, brass corners, 12" x 13" 60.00
Mirror, beveled, ornate, 12" sq
....155.00
Print, Gibson Girl type portrait, some hand colored accents, framed
....125.00
Rose bowl, glass, rich cranberry color....................................65.00
Sheet, matching pillow case, cutwork and embroidered cherubs, bows, and flowers, 90" sq
.... 110.00
Valance and mantle cloth, silk, large pink roses, moss green background, fringe, 60" x 29" ..225.00

❖ Vienna Art

The Vienna Art Company was responsible for many interesting lithographed-tin items, including numerous advertising pieces. Look for intricate scenes with rich colors. Because this tinware was designed to be used, expect to find scratches or wear.

Calendar, adv Harvard Brewing Co. Pure Malt Beverages, Lowell, Mass USA, lady with large pink ribbons in her hair, white gown, ornamental gilt border......150.00
Plate, adv, 10" dia
    Anheuser-Busch Malt-Nutrine on back, front with lady in low cut diaphanous top..............95.00
    Compliments of the American Sheet and Tinplate Co., Pittsburgh, maid with flowing brunette brown hair, plunging neckline, gilt border 90.00
    Dr. Pepper, beautiful lady holding stem of lilies, silhouetted against floral background, some rim chips, overall soiling and staining.................650.00
    Dr. Pepper, Gypsy lady, some rim chips, staining on back
    ....650.00

Jamestown Exposition, 1907, Pocahontas and John Smith, copyrighted W.H. Owens & Co., Manchester, Va... 125.00
Joslin Dry Goods Co. adv on back, Gypsy lady 90.00
Tray
    9-1/2" dia, adv Joseph Glennons New Brewery, art plate #207, Lenore, blond lady, rose colored gown, burgundy and gilt lined border 80.00
    9-1/2" dia, adv Stegmaier Brewing Co. Wilkes Barre, Pa., lady with flowing hair dec with flowers, cobalt blue border, sapphire blue and gilt dec
    .... 80.00
    10" dia, adv Anheuser-Busch Malt-Nutrine, St. Louis, Mo., lady with flowing brown hair, low gown, green, gold, white, and pink on mantel border, dated 1905 .... 200.00
    10" dia, adv Heim Breweries Select, East St. Louis, Ill., art plate #104, Poesie, lady with flowing brown hair, sprigs of leaves in her hair, pink low-cut gown, gold, cream, brown, and green border.......... 75.00
    10" dia, adv Hotel Majestic, color litho of maiden in rose colored gown, holding vase of flowers, Mocha-type gilt border
    .... 150.00
    10" dia, adv Independent Special Brew Beer, sultry young maid, plunging neckline, long brown flowing hair, red hat with pearls throughout hair, holds pink rose, Victorian burgundy border, red and white flowers, dated 1905 .... 100.00
    10" dia, beautiful maid with white gown, long brown flowing hair, red hat, Art Nouveau green, gilt, and brown border, back mkd "Royal Saxony Art Plate #105, Irene, Chs. W. Shonk Co.".............................. 60.00
    10" dia, bust of beautiful maiden, pink gown, sprigs of leaves, multicolored border, reverse mkd "Royal Saxony Art Plate #104, Poesie, Chs. W. Shonk Co.".............................. 90.00

❖ Vietnam War

With the passing of time since the Vietnam War, there is growing interest in military and civilian items related to the conflict. Items from "The Nam" and those from back in "The World" are seen with increasing frequency at flea markets, where good pieces can still be found at reasonable prices.

Flight jacket, G-1, US Navy, leather, size 40 .... 260.00

Magazine, *Life*, Oct. 20, 1967, "U.S. Prisoners in North Viet Nam" 5.00

MIA bracelet, red aluminum, "Maj Horace H. Fleming III, FL. USMC 10 May 68 SVN" ... 25.00

Lighter, Zippo
  Vietnam 67-68 Long Binh 300.00
  Vietnam 68-69 Qui Nhon, enamel decor 300.00

Pinback button, "Out Now Nov. 6th, Demonstrate Against the War NPAC," 1-3/4" dia 17.00

Poster, cardboard, "Vietnam Moratorium Oct. 15 No Business As Usual Until The Troops Are Home," 13" x 10" 15.00

Shoulder tab, RV Ranger, white silk, light-red border, "23 Vietnamese Ranger Bn" 75.00

GAF View-Master reel No. J23, Godzilla in "Godzilla's Rampage," 1978, $12.50.

Swizzle stick, Sandbox Club, U.S. Naval Hospital Danang RVN, green plastic 5.50

❖ View-Master

Gimme, gimme, I want to see too! Since View-Masters and their reels were first created in 1939, they have been educating and entertaining us. During World War II, shortages caused a cutback in production, until the Army and Navy recognized that this would be a good way to train troops. After the war, demand soared and was met by several different companies.

Collectors' Club: National Stereoscopic Association, P.O. Box 14801, Columbus, OH 43214.

Reels
  Brussels World Fair, c1958, four reel set 48.00
  Cinderella, GAF, 3 reels 28.00
  Eight Is Enough, GAF, 1980, MIP 15.00
  Expo '67 Montreal, general tour 22.00
  Jack & the Beanstalk, Swayers FT-3, c1951 .... 8.00
  Little Black Sambo, View-Master, c1948 .... 90.00
  New York World's Fair, 1964, International area 28.00
  Our Planet Earth, Geology, View-Master Science Series, 3 reels 19.00
  Sleeping Beauty, Swayers FT-10, c1953 .... 8.00
  Snow White & the Seven Dwarfs, "The Magic Mirror," FT-4A 10.00
  Time Tunnel 75.00
  Walt Disney's Peter Pan, "Flight to Never Land," Reel 1 .. 10.00
  Zorro, View-Master B 469, 3 reels, small tear 45.00
Stereoscope
  Sawyer View-Master Model C, 1946-55, with 2 reels 27.00
  View-Master Model E I.O.B. 75.00

❖ Viking Glass

Located in New Martinsville, West Virginia, this glass company has recently ceased production under the last of the original family owners, Dalzell-Viking. Viking produced various brightly colored glassware items through the years and also made some crackle glass. Look for a silver and pink foil label on some items.

Ashtray
  Amber, crackle glass, 7" l.. 15.00
  Tea blue, triangular, orig foil label, 3-3/4" w 17.50
Bookends, owls, dark green, 7" h, pr 68.00
Bowl, amethyst, 1950s............ 25.00
Bust, Madonna........................ 30.00
Candy dish, olive green, Teardrop pattern, 8" h 15.00
Compote
  Amber, part of orig sticker, 8-1/2" dia, 7" h 35.00
  Amberina, 4-3/4" h, 8-3/4" dia 35.00
Cruet, applied handle, orig stopper, 6-1/2" h, amber or green... 30.00
Fairy lamp, red satin 55.00
Figure
  Duck, dark blue 40.00
  Elephant, frosted 20.00
  Penguin, dark blue 65.00
Goblet, orange and gold, 4-5/8" h 12.00
Juice set, cobalt blue, 5 pcs.... 30.00

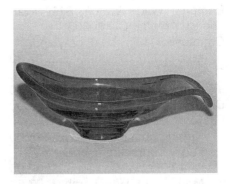

Orange Viking dish, 10" long, $15.

❖ Wade Ceramics

The British firm known as The Wade Group originally made industrial ceramics. By the late 1920s, the company started making figurines, which were well received, and then dinnerware and accessories. Many dealers know the name Wade from the Red Rose Tea premiums.

References: Donna Baker, *Wade Miniatures*, Schiffer Publishing, 2000; Pat Murray, *The Charlton Standard Catalogue of Wade, Vol. Three*, 1998; *The Charlton Standard Catalogue of Wade Whimsical Collectibles*, 4th ed., 1998, Charlton Press.

Collectors' Clubs: The Official International Wade Collectors Club, Royal Works, Westport, Road, Burslem, Stoke-On-Trent, ST6 4AP England; Wade Watch, 8199 Pierson Ct, Arvada, CO 80005.

Candlestick, baby seal, gray and
    black.....................................37.50
Circus figures, set of 15 entertainers
    and animals........................35.00
Dish, ballerina..........................12.00
Figure
    Kissing bunnies................ 115.00
    Lucky Leprechaun, cobbler,
        1950s...........................32.00
    Mary Had A Little Lamb....... 7.50
    Storybook Chimp, wearing skirt
        ....5.00

Ginger jar, red and black flowers,
    white ground.....................32.50
Party crackers, orig box with six
    unopened paper crackers, mkd
    "Wade Whimsies Tom Smith
    Tales For The Nursery Crackers"
    ....55.00
Pitcher, Art Deco Flaxman ware,
    Budgie handle, 10" h....... 115.00
Red Rose Tea figure
    Buffalo.................................3.50
    Camel..................................3.00
    Cockatoo.............................8.00
    Elephant..............................2.50
    Gingerbread Man...............60.00
    Hippo...................................3.00
    Kangaroo 2.50
    Raccoon..............................2.50
    Tiger....................................2.50
Stein, beer barrel shape, sgd "T.J.,"
    7-1/2" h.............................35.00
Teapot
    Character, hp, 8-7/8" l......120.00
    Scottie, 8" l.......................300.00
Tea set, Golden Turquoise, teapot,
    creamer, and sugar..........125.00
Turtle, with lid...........................35.00
Wall plaque, yacht, green, blue, and
    beige.................................45.00

❖ Waffle Irons

An array of interesting waffle irons can be found at most flea markets. Early cast-iron examples were placed over an open fire. Later versions were electrified. Collectors are especially interested in waffle irons with unusual patterns. Watch out for damaged irons and those with missing parts.

Birmingham Stove & Range Co., No.
    8, cast iron 63.00
Crescent, No. 8, Fanner Mfg. Co.,
    Cleveland, Ohio, wire handles
    ....110.00
Freidag, No. #8, cast iron, wire handle, Freidag Mfg. Co. Freeport,
    Ill., LL. #8 .... 10.00
Rainbow, No. 80W, Precision Mfg.,
    Dover, N.J., chrome, wooden
    handles, temperature gauge
    window in top................... 35.00
Stover, No. 28, cast iron, wooden
    handles, Stover Mfg. Co., Freeport, Ill. 110.00
Toastmaster, Model 2D2, electric,
    McGraw Electric Co., Elgin, Ill.
    .... 45.00
Universal China, electric, replaced
    cord.................................. 65.00
Wear-Ever Aluminum, No. 340-1,
    wire handle 25.00
Wright & Bridgeford, Louisville, cast
    iron................................. 120.00

❖ Wagner Ware

Wagner Manufacturing made cast-iron hollow ware, brass castings, and aluminum cookware among other household items. The company prospered from 1891 to the late 1950s under the care of the Wagner family. The firm was bought in 1959 by Textron, which held it until 1969.

Wagner Ware cast-iron ashtray, 1050, 6-1/4" x 4-3/4", $20.

Periodical: *Kettles 'n Cookware,* Drawer B, Perrysville, NY 14129.
Ashtray, skillet shape, red spatter, 3"
.....................................55.00
Child's teakettle, 6" h.............290.00
Corn stick, 13" l 68.00
Muffin pan, 11-hole, 7-1/4" x 10-1/2"
.....................................55.00
Scoop, #912, 9-1/4" l...............24.00
Skillet
    No. 8 ....30.00
    No. 12 ....59.00
Teakettle, wire handle, 6" h ...150.00
Waffle iron, wooden handles ...30.00

❖ Walgreen's Collectibles

Walgreen's is an American institution. Being one of the oldest drug stores in the country contributes to collectors searching for early tins and products with the Walgreen's name. Others concentrate on things relating to other aspects of the store.
Bank, 1913 Ford Model T, Ertl,
    #9531, 1991, mint 18.50
Bottle, vitamins, orig box, 3-1/2" h
....5.00
Box, prescription, 1952 label, Cincinnati 6.50
Restaurant ware, Syracuse China
    Bowl, dessert 4-1/2" dia.....18.00
    Cup and saucer 8.50
    Grill plate, 9-1/2" dia 26.00
    Plate, 7-1/4" dia 35.00
Match cover, 1930s 11.00
Tin, Epsom salt, 1 lb.................9.00

❖ Wallace China

Wallace China was founded in 1931 in Vernon, California, making commercial and residential dinnerware until 1959. The company's western designs are favorites with collectors. The Westward Ho pattern is a good example of the firm's hotel chinaware, while Willow is also popular with Blue Willow collectors. Wallace China is well marked.
Bowl, Chuckwagon, 4" dia.......55.00
Cereal bowl, Magnolia.............20.00
Chili bowl
    Western brands motif.........70.00
    Westward Ho 55.00
Cup and saucer
    Newport 8.00

Yorkshire 8.00
Dinner plate
    Bonanza logo, 9-1/2" dia....20.00
    Daphne 16.00
    Master Pizza, 7" dia 10.00
    Newport.............................15.00
    Rodeo 115.00
    Yorkshire 8.00
Fruit bowl, Yorkshire 4.00
Grill plate, Magnolia.................20.00
Mug, California, green border....8.00
Pitcher, Hibiscus 200.00
Salad plate, Rodeo 70.00
Saucer, El Rancho...................12.00
Serving plate
    Old Hawaii, oval 30.00
    Shadow Leaf.......................20.00
Teapot, individual size, Hibiscus
....55.00

❖ Wall Pockets

Wall pockets are clever pottery holders designed to be hung on walls. Potteries such as Roseville and Weller made wall pockets in the same lines as their vases, bowls, etc. Collectors search for these potteries plus interesting examples from lesser-known makers. Wall pockets were very collectible a few years ago, driven by the decorator market. Today they are becoming easier to find at flea markets, but the prices haven't declined.

Reference: Betty and Bill Newbound, *Collector's Encyclopedia of Wall Pockets, Identification and Values,* Collector Books, 1996, 1998 value update.

Collectors' Club: Wall Pocket Collectors Club, 1356 Tahiti, St. Louis, MO 63128.
Frankoma
Acorn, light brown, mkd "Frankoma
    190" 25.00
Cowboy Boot, blue and white,
    speckled, mkd "Frankoma 133"
....30.00
Japan, Harlequin heads, boy and girl
....65.00
McCoy
    Apple on leaf 50.00

Owl wall pocket, made in Japan, 7-1/2" high, $10.

Bellows............................. 40.00
Cornucopia basket, green and
    white 40.00
Fan, white, pink floral 60.00
Figure of woman in bonnet and
    bow, white, red trim 40.00
Leaf, blue and pink............ 40.00
Morning Glory.................... 50.00
Post Box, green................. 50.00
Sunflower, yellow, with bird
    .... 45.00
Tulip, white 40.00
Yellow, pink floral dec........ 40.00
Roseville
    Foxglove, brown, #1296-8"
    .... 190.00
    Gardenia, brown, #666-8"
    .... 150.00
    Green, matte, 8" l 120.00
    Maple Leaf, 8-1/2" 75.00
    Snowberry, blue, #1WP-8
    .... 180.00
    Three sided, green, 11" l ..110.00
    Tulips, emb flowers, white . 60.00
Shawnee, teapot, pink apple dec
    .... 32.00
Unmarked
    Cornucopia shape, cattail and
    duck dec, blue, 6" h 40.00

Plaster, yellow iris dec, home-
made, 8" l 20.00
Weller
Blue, emb leaf, 7" l 60.00
Glendale, 9-1/2" l 450.00
Iris, blue, 8-1/2" l 50.00
Klyro, 8" h 110.00
Roma, 7" l 130.00
Woodrose 110.00

❖ Watch Fobs

A watch fob is a useful and/or decorative item that is attached to a man's pocket watch by a strap. Its main function is to assist the user in removing the watch from a pocket. The heyday of watch fobs was late in the 19th century, when many manufacturers created them to advertise products, commemorate special events, or serve as decorative and useful objects. Most watch fobs are made of metal and struck from a steel die. Some are trimmed with enamel or may have a celluloid plaque. When found with their original watch strap or original packaging, the value is enhanced.

Collectors' Clubs: Canadian Association of Watch Fob Collectors, P.O. Box 787, Caledonia, Ontario, NDA IAO Canada; International Watch Fob Association, Inc, RR5, P.O. Box 210, Burlington, IA 52601; Midwest Watch Fob Collectors, Inc, 6401 W Girard Ave, Milwaukee, WI 53210.

Reproduction Alert.

For additional listings, see *Warman's Americana & Collectibles.*

Advertising
Brown Gin & Liquors, brass, raised moose head, reverse mkd "Sold by H. Obermauer & Co., Pittsburgh, Pa.," 1-1/2" dia 60.00
Caterpillar, MacAllister Machine Co., Ft. Wayne, Indianapolis, Plymouth, Ind., silvertone, 1-1/2" 45.00
Evening Gazette, baseball shape, scorecard back, 1912 .... 95.00
Foundry & Machine Exhibition Co., 1-3/4" x 1-1/2" 48.00

Roosevelt and Cox brass watch fob, 1920, $100.

Johnston's, the Appreciated Chocolates, woman with platter of confections, plastic, 2-1/8" 40.00
Joliet Corn Shellers 150.00
Kelly Springfield Tires, white metal, raised illus of female motorist, "Kelly Springfield Hand Made Tires" on back, 2" d 80.00
Pontiac, with key chain, 3/4" dia 45.00
Red Goose Shoes, enameled red goose 100.00
Commemorative
American Legion, Cleveland State Convention, 1946, diecut brass 35.00
Princeton University, brass, 1908 .... 48.00
Souvenir Chicago Head Camp, June 19-23, 1917 on one side, Municipal Pier, Chicago, initials MWA and crossed hatchet and mallet on other, metal, 1-7/8" 28.00
World Championship Rodeo Contest, Chicago 45.00

❖ Waterford Crystal

Waterford is easily identified with high-quality crystal. The firm was started in 1729 in Waterford, Ireland. Look for a finely etched mark or a foil type label. Waterford continues to make exquisite glassware today.

For additional listings, see *Warman's Antiques and Collectibles* and *Warman's Glass.*

Christmas ornament, c1995.... 17.50
Claret, Colleen, set of six in orig box, some orig labels.............. 480.00
Clock, ABC block 60.00
Figure
Dolphin 110.00
Eagle 140.00
Lion 150.00
Rocking horse 80.00
Shark 125.00
Frame, ABC block, 4" x 6" 55.00
Goblet, Colleen 65.00
Ornament, Partridge in a Pear Tree, first in series, 1982, orig box and brochure 375.00
Paperweight, Capital 90.00
Sherry, Colleen, set of six in orig box, some orig labels 360.00
Tumbler, Colleen, set of six in orig box, some with orig labels 390.00
Vase
Glendora, 9" h 195.00
#227-974-6200, 9" h 175.00

❖ Watering Cans

Here's a topic that was really hot at last summer's flea markets. It seemed like everywhere you looked there was a watering can. Again, it's the decorator influence that encouraged those with a country-style interior to add a few watering cans. And, while all this flower watering has been going on, more children's vintage lithographed-tin watering cans also appeared on the scene. They too have become an eagerly sought item.

Brass, small dings, 4-3/8" h, 9-3/8" l 8.00
Ceramic, Czechoslovakian, white ground, blue-green shading and trim, 2 swans swimming, 5-1/4" h 60.00
Child's, litho on tin
Ohio Art, turquoise and orange flowers, pink hearts, yellow ground, 8-1/4" h 35.00
Pretty garden, bright colors, c1920, very slight use, 6-1/4" h 150.00
Super Smurf in Shower 10.00

Tin watering can, brass head, $40.

Victorian children in garden, handle loose, scratches, wear, 8" h 60.00
Copper, round, long narrow spout, round closed sprinkler head 66.00
Miniature, doll house size, metal, painted red, flower dec, 1" h 5.00
Sterling silver, narrow spout, small size 45.00
Tin
　　Brass head 35.00
　　Dover, orig label, no sprinkler 25.00
Toleware, some rust and surface abrasion, 16" h, 9-3/4" dia base 115.00

❖ Watt Pottery

Although the name Watt Pottery wasn't used until about 1920, founder W.J. Watt was involved in the pottery business as early as 1886. He worked at several pottery companies before purchasing the Crooksville, Ohio, Globe Stoneware Company. With the help of his sons Harry and Thomas, son-in-law C.L. Dawson, daughter Marion Watt, and numerous other relatives, he began production of this uniquely American pottery. Most Watt dinnerware features underglazed decorations on a sturdy off-white or tan body. Much of Watt dinnerware was sold by Safeway, Woolworth, and grocery chains. A fire destroyed the factory in October 1965, and it was never rebuilt.

Collectors' Club: Watt Pottery Collectors USA, Box 26067, Fairview Park, OH 44126.
Reproduction Alert.
For additional listings, see *Warman's Americana & Collectibles.*
Creamer, Tulip, #62 .... 225.00
Bowl
　　Apple, #04 .... 95.00
　　Apple, #63 .... 100.00
　　Apple, #73, Wisconsin advertising 125.00
　　Raised Pansy, #9 .... 135.00
　　Rooster, #6 .... 105.00
　　Tulip, #65 .... 190.00
　　Tulip, #64 .... 175.00
Casserole, individual, Raised Pansy 145.00
Mug, Starflower, #61 .... 285.00
Pepper shaker, Autumn Foliage, hour-glass shape 90.00
Pitcher
　　Apple, #15 .... 165.00
　　Autumn Foliage, #17 .... 350.00
　　Cherries, #15, with advertising 180.00
　　Rooster, #15 .... 145.00
　　Tear Drop, #15 .... 65.00
Spaghetti bowl, Pansy, 13" dia 100.00

Watt flour canister, Apple pattern, lid damaged, 8-1/2" high, $245.

❖ Weather Vanes

Weather vanes were originally designed to indicate the direction of the wind, showing farmers which way a potential weather system was coming. Look for large weather vanes made of copper, sheet metal, cast or wrought iron, wood, or zinc. Expect to find some signs of weathered wear on vintage weather vanes.

References: Robert Bishop and Patricia Coblentz, *Gallery of American Weather Vanes and Whirligigs,* E.P. Dutton, 1981.

Reproduction Alert. Reproductions of early weather vanes are being expertly aged and then sold as originals.

Collecting Hint: Because they were popular targets for hunters and gun-toting boys, many old weather vanes are riddled with bullet holes. Filled holes generally can be detected with a blacklight.
For additional listings, see *Warman's Country Price Guide* and *Warman's Antiques and Collectibles Price Guide.*
Arrow, copper, ball finial, dents, 13" h, 25" l 345.00
Banner, zinc and wrought iron, banner/arrow finial, 54-1/2" h 690.00
Eagle, hollow copper body, solid zinc head, 15-1/2" h, 18-1/2" wingspan 385.00
Eagle with arrow, sheet iron, black repaint, landing with wings spread, arrow beneath with separate pole and directionals, welded repair, 59" h 605.00
Fish, flat sheet metal, applied fins, green glass eyes cracked, gilt loss, 13-3/4" h, 16" l 1,035.00
Horse
　　Prancing, cast aluminum, over arrow, bullet holes, small size 49.50
　　Running, copper body, zinc head, 16" h, 26" l 2,585.00
　　Running, sheet metal, holes, wear, 16" h, 28" l 220.00

Running, tin, full-bodied, on
arrow, 24" l 825.00
Standing, sheet metal, large tail
to vane, 26" l 110.00
Rooster, sheet iron, reinforced with
riveted iron straps, 36-1/2" h,
27-1/2" l 977.50

❖ Wedgwood

Wedgwood is another name that usually denotes quality. Josiah Wedgwood built a factory at Etruria, England, between 1766 and 1769, after having been in the ceramics business for a few years. Wedgwood's early products included caneware, unglazed earthenware, black basalt, creamware, and jasperware. Bone china was introduced between 1812 and 1822. Over the years these and other wares have been made, marked, and well used. Today, Wedgwood still continues its tradition of fine quality.

Periodical: *ARS Ceramics,* 5 Dogwood Ct, Glen Head, NY 11545.

Collectors' Clubs: Wedgwood International Seminar, 22 DeSavry Crescent, Toronto, Ontario M4S 212 Canada; The Wedgwood Society, The Roman Villa, Rockbourne, Fordingbridge, Hants, SP6 3PG, England; The Wedgwood Society of Boston, 28 Birchwood Dr, Hampstead, NH 03841; The Wedgwood Society of New York, 5 Dogwood Ct, Glen Head, NY 11545; Wedgwood Society of Southern California, Inc, P.O. Box 4385, North Hollywood, CA 91617.

For additional listings, see *Warman's Antiques and Collectibles Price Guide* and *Warman's English & Continental Pottery & Porcelain.*

Basket, Queen's Ware, oval, undertray, basketweave molded bodies, pierced galleries, green and black enamel oak leaves and trim, imp mark, early 19th C, 9" l
....290.00
Bowl, black jasper dip, applied white classical Dancing Hours figures, foliate banding, imp mark, c1962, 10-1/8" 460.00

Wedgwood Jasperware cup and saucer, green and white, 2-1/2" high, $45.

Celery dish, bone china, gilt diamond border, printed mark, foot rim, light gilt wear, c1820
....175.00
Dinner plate, lavender on cream, shell edge 35.00
Egg-shaped box, cov, 1978, incised "Wedgwood, England, V," 2" h, 3" l 65.00
Fruit plate, majolica, turquoise basketweave, 6-1/2" dia 250.00
Game pie, caneware, oval, molded, rabbit finial, imp mark, 1865, 7" l, orig liner cracked 445.00
Match box, jasper, dark blue....90.00
Medallion, jasper, light green dip, oval, portrait of Admiral Richard Howe, imp title and mark, 3-1/2" x 4-1/4" 260.00
Pitcher, black basalt, club, enameled floral dec, imp mark, c1860, 6-1/2" h 345.00
Plaque, jasper, solid black, applied white classical relief of muses, imp mark, 19th C, wood frame, rect..................................490.00
Vase
Creamware, molded grape vines and foliage, painted band of strawberries, mid 19th C, minor damage, 6" h 90.00
Diceware, tricolor, pale blue dip, yellow quatrefoils, white ground, pierced flower frog cover with white applied quatrefoils, #82 of limited edition of 200, mkd "Wedgwood, Made in England, H82HB, 74," c1974, 5-1/4" h, 4-5/8" d
..................................1,275.00

Jasper, black jasper dip, applied white classical relief, Portland, imp "Marshall Field & Co. Wedgwood Exhibition 1918," price for pr, 4" h 690.00
Jasper, solid pale blue, white relief of children playing Blind Man's Bluff, mounted to white marble base, with oval Wedgwood pale blue jasper medallion with white relief of children playing, imp mark, late 18th C, minor damage, modern cover 1,850.00
Wine cooler, redware, fruiting vines on molded body, raised mask handles, imp mark, early 19th C, 10" h......550.00

❖ Weller Pottery

Samuel Weller opened a small pottery factory near Zanesville, Ohio, in 1872, originally producing utilitarian stoneware. By 1882, he moved to larger quarters and expanded his lines. As the years continued, more designers arrived and the lines were expanded to include commercial wares. As art pottery became popular, Weller developed lines to answer that need. Today, some of the art pottery lines are highly sought. The company stayed in business during World War II, but by 1948 it had ceased operations.

For additional listings, see *Warman's Antiques and Collectibles Price Guide, Warman's Americana & Collectibles,* and *Warman's American Pottery & Porcelain.*

Ewer, Louwelsa, peaches on a vine, decor by Lillie Mitchell, crazed, 12-1/2" h 595.00
Lamp base, Louwelsa, 9" h... 350.00
Mug
Dickensware II, stag head decor, 5-3/4" h 375.00
Aurelian, grapes and leaves decor, glaze imperfections, 4-1/2" h 375.00
Vase
Mat glaze, green with bluebells, green mat glaze..........225.00
Turkish, red with yellow and green drip glaze, 5" h . 195.00

Weller Cameo vase, tan glaze, 13" high, $75.

Muskota, double bud vase, small chip 175.00
Marvo, base chip, 9" h 175.00
Atlas, 6-1/2" h 165.00
Dogwood, 9-1/2" h 125.00
Wall pocket, Glendale, 12-1/2" h 550.00

Weller Sicard vase, 7-1/2" high, $775.

❖ Western Collectibles

The American West has always held a fascination. Whether you're a collector interested in history or a decorator striving to achieve a western motif using authentic items, flea markets yield many items worth rustling up.

Periodicals: *American Cowboy*, P.O. Box 6630, Sheridan, WY 82801; *Boots*, Lone Pine Rd, P.O. Box 766, Challis, ID 83226; *Cowboy Collector Newsletter*, P.O. Box 7486, Long Beach, CA 90807; *Cowboy Guide*, P.O. Box 6459, Sante Fe, NM 87502; *Rope Burns*, P.O. Box 35, Gene Autry, OK 73436; *The Westerner*, P.O. Box 5253, Vienna, WV 26105.

Collectors' Clubs: American Cowboy Culture Association, 4124 62nd Dr, Lubbock, TX 79413; National Bit, Spur & Saddle Collectors Association, P.O. Box 3098, Colorado Springs, CO 80934; Western Americana Collectors Society, P.O. Box 620417, Woodside, CA 94062.

Belt Buckle, bucking bronc, MIB 40.00
Book
   My Sixty Years on the Plains: Trapping, Trading, and Indian Fighting, W.T. Hamilton, 1905, portrait frontispiece, plates by Charles Russell, first edition 150.00
   Old Frontiers: The Story of the Cherokee Indians, John P. Brown, 1938 .... 70.00
   The Cowboys Own Brand Book, Duncan Emrich, hardbound, 1954, ex-library 7.50
Bookends, saddle, rope, boots and hat, Syrocco, 7-1/4" h, 5-1/2" w, pr 79.00
Coasters, cowboy, set of four in holder 15.00
Compact, wooden with boots, hat and cactus 36.00
Cowboy hat, Stetson, pencil roll, orig box 150.00
Figure, cowboy, Stetson 35.00
Holster, leather, double, studs, jewels, 1950s 65.00

Mug, steer head, Western Enamel, 4-3/4" h 22.50
Plate, divided, chuckwagon and cattle brands, 11" dia 55.00
Plate, steer head, Western Enamel, 10" dia 20.00
Saddle, western style, tooled decor, 1970s 225.00
Saddle stand, wood 100.00
Scarf, horses motif, rayon, 28" sq 24.00
Spurs, N&J, brass, horse head, pr, ... 225.00
Wall lamp, cast-iron silhouette of bronco buster 30.00

❖ Westmoreland Glass

Founded in 1899 in Grapeville, Pennsylvania, the Westmoreland Company originally made hand-crafted high-quality glassware. During the 1920s, the company started to make reproductions and decorated wares. Production continued until 1982. Pieces were made in crystal, black, and colored milk glass, among other colors. Milk glass pieces bring the most interest from collectors today.

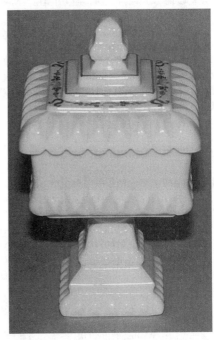

Milk glass wedding bowl, 8" high, $75.

Collectors' Clubs: National Westmoreland Glass Collectors Club, P.O. Box 625, Irwin, PA 15692; Westmoreland Glass Collectors Club, 2712 Glenwood, Independence, MO 64052; Westmoreland Glass Society, P.O. Box 2883, Iowa City, IA 52244.

Animal dish, cov, turkey, goofus coloring, chip on lid, some loss to paint 125.00

Bell Bowl, ruby stained, 11-1/4" d 110.00

Bowl
    Old Quilt, milk glass, 6" dia 18.00
    Paneled Grape, milk glass, 10" dia 50.00

Bud vase, Roses & Bows, milk glass, 10" h, paneled grape dec 45.00

Cake stand, Paneled Grape, milk glass 95.00

Candelabra, 3 light, Paneled Grape, milk glass 285.00

Candlesticks, pr
    Old Quilt, milk glass, 3" h ... 20.00
    Paneled Grape, milk glass, 2-lite 37.50

Candy dish, cov, Old Quilt, milk glass, sq
    High foot 30.00
    Low foot 25.00

Cheese dish, cov, Old Quilt, milk glass 45.00

Cologne bottle, Paneled Grape, milk glass 45.00

Compote, vaseline, 7" h 145.00

Creamer and sugar, Della Robia, milk glass 18.00

Cruet, Old Quilt, milk glass 25.00

Cup, Della Robia 45.00

Cup and saucer
    Paneled Grape, milk glass 22.50
    Plain, beaded edge, milk glass 12.00

Dresser set, Paneled Grape, milk glass, 4 pcs 250.00

Dresser tray
    Daisy, milk glass 20.00
    Paneled Grape, milk glass, decorated 125.00
    Sunflower, milk glass 30.00

Epergne, Paneled Grape, milk glass, 14" h 235.00

Goblet
    Della Robia, milk glass 18.00
    Paneled Grape, milk glass . 18.00
    Thousand Eye, crystal 12.00

Honey dish, cov, Beaded Grape, milk glass, sq 20.00

Iced tea tumbler
    Old Quilt, milk glass, 5-1/4" h, ftd 18.00
    Paneled Grape, milk glass, 12 oz 22.00

Pickle jar, frosted flower pattern, 12" h, 4-1/4" dia 95.00

Pin dish, square, milk glass 7.00

Pitcher, pint, Paneled Grape, milk glass 47.50

Planter, Paneled Grape, milk glass, 5" x 9" 40.00

Plate
    Milk glass, beaded edge, apple dec 12.00
    Old Quilt, milk glass, 8" dia 32.00

Punch set, Della Robia, crystal bell shaped punch bowl, 6 cups 45.00

Salad plate, Della Robia, crystal, dark stained fruit 24.00

Relish, 3 part, Paneled Grape, milk glass 40.00

Tidbit, Beaded Grape, milk glass, 2 tiers.................................... 45.00

Tray
    Grape, milk glass 25.00
    Heavy Scroll, all over gold dec 25.00
    Maple Leaf, 9" dia 12.00

Tumbler, milk glass, ftd
    Apple 20.00
    Old Quilt, 4-1/4" h 10.00
    Peach 20.00

Wedding bowl, Roses & Bows, milk glass, 10" h 75.00

❖ Wheaton Glass

Wheaton Glass is located in central New Jersey and operates a museum and working glass site in Millville. Flea markets are seeing few of their limited-edition bottles and objects. Perhaps this will change as collectors begin to search for Wheaton objects again.

Ashtray, ruby 3.00

Bottle
    George Washington 5.00
    Great American Series, Mark Twain, W72, blue carnival 30.00

Flask, "Skylab I, May 15 - June 22, 1973," light-blue matte finish, Wheaton, 8-1/2" high, $15.

Jenny Lind, set of three, red, green, and cobalt blue .. 12.00

Mother and Daughter, set of two, green 20.00

President Series, 12 bottles 50.00

Bud vase, ruby 10.00

Decanter, Robert F. Kennedy, green 5.00

Paperweight, figural green pepper 20.00

❖ Whirligigs

A variation of the weathervane, whirligigs indicate wind direction and velocity. Often constructed by the unskilled, they were generally made of wood and metal and exhibited a rather primitive appearance. Flat, paddle-like arms are characteristic of single-figure whirligigs, but multi-figure examples are usually driven by a propeller that moves a series of gears or rods. Three-dimensional figures are commonly found on 19th century whirligigs, but silhouette figures are generally indicative of 20th century construction.

Reference: Robert Bishop and Patricia Coblentz, *Gallery of American Weather Vanes and Whirligigs*, E.P. Dutton, 1981.

Indian in canoe, carved and painted wood, paddle arms, 14" h, 18" l 440.00

Man, light-blue outfit, blue hat, rubber arms, composition, looks like weathered wood, contemporary, 24-1/2" h..........................605.00

Man sawing logs, cut tin, wooden base, old worn gold, red, green and black paint, directional in green and black, propeller in green and orange, 32-3/4" l 137.50

Patriotic motif, black man with hat pumping water for woman in polka-dot bandana and with washboard, wooden, propellers in red, white and blue with stars on the ends, white stars along the base, compass stars on the directional, repairs, weathering, 26-1/2" l 1,072.50

Roosters, 2 facing each other, on tower made resembling an oil derrick, painted wood, 62" h 110.00

Woman washing clothes, painted wood, 1930s, 12" h, 15" l 185.00

❖ Whistles

Think referees and police officers are the only ones to use whistles? Think again. During the early 20th century, lithographed-tin whistles made a perfect advertising medium. Fifty years later, plastic examples were advertising pop-culture icons.

Benzo-Gas, Blow Out The Carbon, cylindrical, 1-3/8" h 58.00

Chicken Dinner Delicious Candy, litho tin, 2" l 80.00

Cracker Jack, litho tin, shows trademark boy, 2-5/8" l 110.00

Dragnet, Official Jack Webb Whistle, plastic 12.00

Guitar, litho tin, 2" l 12.00

Pepsi-Cola, 2 miniature bottles 150.00

Robin Hood Shoes, litho tin, flat style, 2-5/8" l.....................95.00

Dragnet / Official Jack Webb Whistle, black plastic, 2" long, $12.

Twinkie Shoes For Girls And Boys, litho tin, balloon shape, 1-1/4" l 125.00

Uncle Sam riding early bicycle, plastic, chips, 3-1/2" h, 4-1/4" l 45.00

Weatherbird Shoes, cylindrical 60.00

❖ White Knob Windups

Just give a twist or two to the little white knob, and these plastic playthings teeter across any hard, flat surface. Because of their small size they are most commonly found in showcases. Only recently have they received much attention, which has started to send prices scurrying. Of course, ask permission to test any white knob windup before buying it. Few nonfunctioning examples are worth owning.

Baby Bert and Ernie, crawling, pr 8.00

Casper Mini Winder, MOC.......26.50

Cat in the Hat, riding scooter pulling carousel, Universal Theme Park exclusive...........................10.00

Cheeseburger wearing sunglasses, exclusive to Restaurant Margaretiville 7.00

Creature from the Black Lagoon 3.00

Donald Duck, Disney Theme Parks 13.00

Dumbo, Disney's Magic Kingdom 11.50

Godzilla.................................3.00

Jets football helmet.................12.00

King Kong 3.00

Pluto..20.00

Strolling Bowling, Tomy............8.50

Winnie the Pooh in safari clothing, exclusive to Disney Animal Kingdom.....................................6.50

Wind-Up Bunny, Easter theme, MOC 2.50

❖ Wicker

Wicker furniture evokes a summertime feeling, even in the cold of winter. Wicker can be found in natural rattan or painted. The Victorians loved it. Today the look is still popular. Look for pieces with original upholstery in good condition and without too many layers of paint. Many pieces of wicker cannot be stripped without damaging the materials.

Chair

Arm, wide flat arm rests continue to back, broad seat, repainted 200.00

Corner, elaborate scrolling, bird cage arms and supports, natural finish 650.00

Photographer's, elaborate scrolled back and arms, painted white 450.00

Ferner, white, metal liner, rectangular, repainted several times 185.00

Footstool, upholstered seat, painted 195.00

Music stand, Wakefield Rattan Co., three shelves, orig paper label, c1883.............................285.00

Rocking chair, Wakefield Rattan Co., serpentine edges, braided trim, wooden rockers, painted white 265.00

Suite, sofa, two matching arm chairs, ottoman, some damage to wicker, worn old upholstery, as found condition 300.00

❖ Winchester

This favorite American firearms manufacturer has a quite a following with collectors. Those with sharp vision can find all kinds of ephemera and advertising.

Winchester roller skates, tattered original box, $85.

Collectors' Club: Winchester Club of America, 3070 S. Wyandot, Englewood, CO 80110.

Ammunition, 50-110-300 for Model 1886 rifles, orig box in good condition, orig labels, 20 cartridges 200.00

Banner, Headquarters for Winchester Rifles & Shotguns, fringed hem, wood rod, 19-1/2" x 29" 150.00

Book, *The Book of Winchester Engraving,* first edition, dust jacket...............................500.00

Calendar, 1915, eagle attacking mountain goats, Forbes Litho Mfg. Co., artist sgd "Lynn Bogue Hunt," paper, framed, 29-1/2" h, 14-1/2" w, calendar pad missing 1,500.00

Catalog
  Winchester Rifles, John Wayne cover, 1982 ....10.00
  Winchester-Western, New Haven, CT, 1976, 5-3/4" x 7-1/2" 40.00

Counter felt, Shoot Where You Aim 175.00

Flashlight, dents, 1923 patent date, 9-1/4" l...............................60.00

Pocket knife, 2-blade, cracked bone handle, 3-3/4" l closed.......65.00

Print, signed, framed, hunter standing tall with his Winchester as ferocious wolves attack, c1906, 29" h, 15-1/4" w 3,300.00

Stickpin, Ask for Winchester Nublack, brass, shotgun shell shape, green enamel shell casing with inscription, early 1900s 125.00

Tin, J. Goldmark's Percussion Caps, made Winchester, some loss to paper labels, 1-1/2" dia 30.00

❖ Winnie The Pooh

A.A. Milne's "tubby little cubby all stuffed with fluff" has become a best friend to countless children. It's no wonder that collectors eagerly seek Pooh, Piglet, Eeyore, and the rest of the gang. Mass marketing of Pooh in recent years has brought a flood of newer collectibles into the market. However, buyers can still find a fair share of vintage Pooh items at flea markets.

Big Golden Book, *Winnie The Pooh and Eeyore's Birthday*, E. Dutton, copyright 1964, 1965 by Walt Disney Productions 35.00

Book
  Winnie The Pooh, Fat Bee, puppet included, produced for Buena Vista home video, 1994, mint 12.00
  Winnie the Pooh and Tigger Too, Disney's Wonderful World of Reading, Grolier, hardcover, 1975, orig cardboard mailer 20.00

Bracelet, Ampaco, Ltd., 1960s, MOC 35.00

Figure, Eeyore, stamped "Walt Disney Productions Japan," 4" l 45.00

Little Golden Book, *Walt Disney Presents Winnie The Pooh, The Honey Tree*, 1977, 19th printing 1.00

Pinback button, Winnie, Disneyland souvenir, c1960 ....12.00

Plush toy, Winnie, tags removed, 12" h 15.00

Puzzle blocks, Disney, sold by Sears, bottom missing from orig box.....................................10.00

Record, *Winnie the Pooh and Christopher Robin Songs*, Disney, 78 rpm, Decca Records..........40.00

Wall decoration
  Train, Disney, particleboard, 35" l 12.00
  Winnie, Tigger, Eeyore, heavy cardboard, c1960 ....40.00

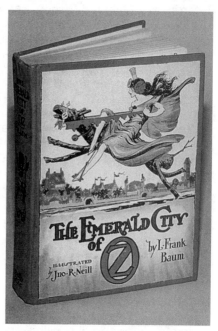

The Emerald City of Oz, Reilley & Lee Co., 1910, $125.

❖ Wizard of Oz

MGM gave birth to an institution when it released "The Wizard of Oz" in 1939, although L. Frank Baum's stories of Oz date to the early part of the 20th century. While vintage Oz items are competitively sought and can be pricey, a variety of contemporary collectibles fit into any person's budget. Among the newer items are numerous pieces commemorating the film's 50th anniversary in 1989.

Periodical: *Beyond the Rainbow Collector's Exchange,* Elaine Willingham, P.O. Box 31672, St. Louis, MO 63131-0672.

Collectors' Clubs: Emerald City Club, 153 E. Main St., New Albany, IN 47150; The International Wizard of Oz Club, P.O. Box 10117, Berkeley, CA 94709-5117.

Book
  The Patchwork of Oz, L. Frank Baum, Reilly & Lee, 1913, no dustjacket 96.00
  The Road to Oz, L. Frank Baum, Reilly & Lee, 1909, loose spine, no dustjacket......71.00

Collector's plate
    Knowles China, 7th in series, man in hot air balloon, art by James Auckland, MIB ... 42.00
    "If I Only Had a Brain," Scarecrow, 1977, orig box, 8-1/2" dia 38.00
Cookbook, *The Wonderful Wizard of Oz Cookbook*, Monica Bayley, hardcover, 1st ed, 1981 ..... 52.00
Cookie jar, Dorothy & Toto, Star Jars, limited production of 1,939, 1994 .... 350.00
Doll, Barbie as Dorothy, Hollywood Legend Series, 1994, MIB 227.50
Drinking glass, Scarecrow, Coca-Cola, 50th anniversary commemorative, 1989, 6" h 10.00
Game, Wizard of Oz Collector's Edition Monopoly Game, Parker Brothers, MIB 85.00
Lunch box and thermos, Aladdin, 50th anniversary, 1989 ...... 73.00
Playset, Wizard of Oz, Mego, complete 250.00
Sheet music, *Over the Rainbow*, 1939, pages separated 43.50

❖ Wolverine Toys

The Wolverine Supply & Manufacturing Company was founded in 1903. The first type of toys produced were lithographed sand toys, followed by girls' housekeeping toys, and then action games, and cars and trucks.

Automatic Coal Loader, litho tin 80.00
Cap't Sandy Andy sand toy, orig box 200.00
Do The Twist, dancer on pedestal, MIB 75.00
Dollhouse with furniture, litho tin, 2-story house with bay window, 5 rooms, 10 pcs plastic furniture, 15" h, 22" w, 12" d 45.00
Drum Major, #27, round base, c1930, 13-1/4" h 225.00
Gee Whiz Racehorse Game, 1930s, 15" l 145.00
Horse-drawn farm wagon, plastic windup, orig box 150.00
Icebox, tin 55.00

Jet Roller Coaster, 12" l 225.00
Kitchen cabinet, #280, 1949, complete with toy groceries, orig box 195.00
Le Mans Pinball, orig box, ...50.00
See and Spell 50.00
Shooting Gallery, orig box 175.00
Streamline Railway pull toy, 1930s, 17-3/4" l 220.00
Sunny Suzy, electric iron, orig box 25.00
Washing machine, metal and heavy glass, hand-crank, 9" h 125.00

❖ Wood Collectibles

Wooden objects of all types are found at flea markets. Look for objects that are interesting, well made, and fit into your decorating scheme. Today's decorators often prefer a weathered look, while others prefer natural finished wood or an aged patina.

Collectors' Club: International Wood Collectors Society, 5900 Chestnut Ridge Rd, Riner, VA 24149.

Apple box, pine, old red paint, conical feet, 10" l 310.00
Artist's model, articulated, minor losses and breaks, late 19th C 1,100.00
Bowl, treen, old worn brown finish, tight are cracks, 6" dia 175.00
Checkerboard, inlaid, mahogany and maple, 20th C, minor veneer damage, 14-3/4" sq 110.00
Churn, stave construction, metal bands, turned lid, dasher, old refinishing, 21-1/2" h 150.00
Cutting board, round top, shaped base, metal blade, 18" l 35.00

Wooden slaw cutting board, $40.

Drying rack, mortised construction, chamfered, shoe feet, old blue repaint over yellow, 24-1/2" w 220.00
Egg timer, candlestick telephone shape, wood, stamped "Cornwall Wood Products, So. Paris, Maine," 5" h 45.00
Niddy noddy, hardwood, old yellow paint, one end with age crack 110.00
Press, orig hardware, patina, dovetailed construction, carved spout, 17" 150.00
Salad bowl, varnished int, bright hand painted flowers, matching serving fork and spoon 25.00
Towel bar, walnut, three horizontal bars on tapering squared posts, scrolled trestle feet, New England, early 19th C, 37-1/2" w 175.00

❖ World's Fairs & Expositions

The first really great world's exposition was the Great Exhibition of 1851 in London. Since that time, there have been many world's fairs, expositions, and celebrations. Today collectors tend to specialize in a particular fair or type of memorabilia.

Periodical: *World's Fair,* P.O. Box 339, Corte Madera, CA 94976.

Collectors' Club: World's Fair Collectors' Society, P.O. Box 20806, Sarasota, FL 34276.

Ashtray
    1933, brass and emb chrome over copper 100.00
    1961, Unisphere, Presented by United States Steel, Made in Japan," 5-3/4" dia 48.00
    1962, Seattle, Space Needle, mkd "Made in Japan," 4" dia 8.00
Foil stickers, New York World's Fair, 1939-40, 4-3/4" x 5-1/2" clear cellophane pack, double-sided sheet with gold, blue, and orange foil stickers on one side, silver, blue, and orange on other side, 12 images on both sides 25.00

1933 Chicago World's Fair felt cap, $45.

Guide book
"Second Edition Official Guide Book," 1939, New York, 5" x 8", softcover, Art Deco style cover of Trylon/Perisphere at night, 256 black and white pgs 25.00
"World's Fair 1934 Official Guide Book," 5-1/2" x 8-1/2", full color Art Deco cover, 192 pages 25.00
Handkerchief, 1939 N.Y., different world costumes 20.00
Hot pad, A Century of Progress, 1933, 6" x 8" cardboard, detailed silver accented relief image of exposition in center, surrounded by transportation theme, dark tan suede covering...........15.00
Key chain, Golden Gate bridge in center, "International Exposition" on bottom, 1-1/4" h....40.00
Magazine, New York World's Fair 1939, *Life* 35.00
Mug, 2-3/4" dia, 5" h, brown glass, designed like mason jar, brass accent metal straps, notched wooden handle, New York Unisphere painted in white on front, Siesta Ware, 1964..............15.00
Pennant, 1939 Golden Gate International Exposition, San Francisco Bay, pastel Portals of the Pacific Building, red ground, 14-3/4" l 45.00
Plate, Knoxville, TN, 1982, 4" dia 20.00
Program, *"Official Daily Program of the Pan American Exposition,"* features for Elmira College Day, Sat, Oct 26, 1901 ....25.00
Salt and pepper shakers, pr, 2" x 3-3/4" h, Eneloid plastic, blue Trylon and Perisphere, orange base, inscribed "New York World's Fair" 35.00

Shot glass, ruby stained, "World's Fair 1933, Leona Hess," 2-1/4" h 55.00
Souvenir Spoon, 1939 N.Y., Theme Building on front, mkd "Pat. Pend., Wm. Rogers Mfg Co." 25.00
Token, Expo '74, Spokane, silvered metal, 1-1/2" dia 8.00
Vinegar bottle, 1939, milk glass 20.00

❖ World War I

Fueled by the assassination of Austrian Archduke Franz Ferdinand by a Serbian national in June of 1914, World War I was set off with Germany invading Belgium and France. Shortly after that, Russia, England, and Turkey joined the war. By 1917 the United States and Italy had become involved. When peace was reached in 1918-19, millions had died and the damage was widespread. Memorabilia relating to World War I was carefully laid aside, hoping it would be the last war. Alas, it was not.

Periodicals: *Men at Arms,* 222 W Exchange St, Providence, RI 02903; *Military Collector Magazine,* P.O. Box 245, Lyon Station, PA, 19536; *Military Collectors' News,* P.O. Box 702073, Tulsa, OK 74170; *Military Trader,* 700 E. State St., Iola, WI, 54990; *Wildcat Collectors Journal,* 15158 NE 6 Ave, Miami FL 33162.

Collectors' Clubs: American Society of Military Insignia Collectors, 526 Lafayette Ave, Palmerton, PA 18701; Association of American Military Uniform Collectors, P.O. Box 1876, Elyria, OH 44036; Company of Military Historians, North Main St, Westbrook, CT 06498; Orders and Medals Society of America, P.O. Box 484, Glassboro, NJ 08028.

Badge, American Red Cross-Military Welfare, cap, enamel.........24.00
Bayonet, orig case...................24.00
Gas mask, carrying can, shoulder strap, canister attached to bottom, German......................50.00
Handkerchief, Remember Me, soldier and girl in center, red, white, and blue edge...................24.00

Real-photo postcard, World War I soldiers on parade, unused, $10.

Helmet, US, 3rd Army insignia 72.00
Magazine, *Red Cross Magazine,* October 1918, battle-scene cover...................................15.00
Medal, British, King George V 65.00
Photograph, Officer Training Camp, Chickamauga Park, Ga., 1917, 7" x 31" 85.00
Postcard, real-photo, soldier in uniform..5.00
Poster, *They Gave Their Lives - Do You Lend Your Savings?*, image of battlefield hilltop cemetery, 30" x 20".................................75.00
Sheet Music
American Patrol March, 1914 ....15.00
What Kind of an American Are You?, Uncle Sam design 20.00
Songbook, *U.S. Army Song Book,* 1918................................40.00
Trench art, pencil holder, shell affixed to base of 3 crossed bullets, 4-3/8" h.....................95.00
Watch fob, flag on pole, USA, beaded, blue....................48.00

❖ World War II

Several world events came together in 1939, leading to World War II. The German Third Reich was engaged in an arms race; the Depression compounded the situation. After Germany invaded Poland, Allied and Axis alliances were formed. From 1942 to 1945, the whole world was involved, and almost all industry was war-related. Peace was not achieved until August 1945. Today collectors are discovering artifacts, equipment, and remembrances of this war.

Reference: Martin Jacobs, *World War II Homefront Collectibles*, Krause Publications, 2000.

Periodicals: *Men at Arms*, 222 W Exchange St, Providence, RI 02903; *Military Collector Magazine*, P.O. Box 245, Lyon Station, PA, 19536; *Military Collectors' News*, P.O. Box 702073, Tulsa, OK 74170; *Military Trader*, P.O. Box 1050, Dubuque, IA 52004; *Wildcat Collectors Journal*, 15158 NE 6 Ave, Miami FL 33162; *World War II*, 7741 Miller Drive, SE, Suite D2, Harrisburg, PA 20175; *WWII Military Journal*, P.O. Box 28906, San Diego, CA 92198.

Collectors' Clubs: American Society of Military Insignia Collectors, 526 Lafayette Ave, Palmerton, PA 18701; Association of American Military Uniform Collectors, P.O. Box 1876, Elyria, OH 44036; Company of Military Historians, North Main St, Westbrook, CT 06498; Imperial German Military Collectors Association, 82 Atlantic St., Keyport, NJ 07735; Orders and Medals Society of America, P.O. Box 484, Glassboro, NJ 08028.

Dexterity puzzle, Atom Bomb, silhouette of Japan, A. C. Gilbert Co., 1946..........................150.00
Dogtag, scarce early version with next of kin name/address, ...10.00
Drinking glass, Remember Pearl Harbor, artwork of Pearl Harbor and Hawaiian Islands, warships, and aircraft, 4-3/4" h..........65.00
Helmet, painted, US Navy Seabees, M1, mint 450.00

War ration book, $5.

Medal, campaign and service medal, orig box...............................25.00
Poster, Under the Shadow of Their Wings Our Land Shall Dwell Secure, 2 naval aviators in life vests with air battle scene in background, 37" x 27" 180.00
Postcard, Three Dirty Dogs Remember Pearl Harbor, Axis leaders portraits, unused...............30.00
Punch-out kit, Model Battleship, 7" x 10", full color envelope with scene of battleship on open sea, colorful thin cardboard sheet, Reed & Associates, early 1940s, unused..............................45.00
Salt and pepper shakers, pr, figural, Gen MacArthur, glazed ceramic, 2" x 2-1/2", tan hat, long yellow pipe....................................85.00
Sheet Music, *What Do You Do In The Infantry* 15.00
Songbook, *Army Song Book,* 1941, 64 pgs................................30.00
View-Master reel, Naval Aviation Military Training Division, hand-lettered, #51, Fiat G-50 Italian fighter................................29.00

❖ Wrestling Memorabilia

The last sport of this edition is one that involves fewer players than team sports, but is physically demanding. It has also created a unique kind of memorabilia for its collectors and devotees.

Reference: Kristian Pope and Ray Whebbe Jr., *Professional Wrestling Collectibles,* Krause Publications, 2000.

Periodicals: *Sports Cards Magazine & Price Guide*, 700 E State St, Iola, WI 54990; *Sports Collectors Digest*, 700 E State St, Iola, WI 54990.

Autographed photo, 8" x 10"
    Bill Goldberg 22.00
    Hulk Hogan 28.00
    Kevin Nash........................20.00
    Lex Lugar 18.00
    The Warlord 18.00
Beanbag toy, Diamond Dallas Page, World Championship Wrestling 7.00

Figure, L. L. Rittgers, 1941, 3 pc set, referee looking mad at standing wrestler looking down at opponent tied up in ball..........295.00
Medal, "4th 120 lb 1948," 1" h... 5.00
Pin, 1984 Olympics, Coca-Cola 2.25
Plaque, autographed
    Goldberg 45.00
    Hollywood Hogan 45.00
    Sting...................................45.00
Sports Card, WMF Superstars, foil 30.00

❖ Wright, L.G.

L.G. Wright is a curious company. It started manufacturing glass using old molds of other companies. Some of the ware were done in colors or textures not originally manufactured in a particular pattern. Some pattern glass collectors embraced this as a way to add color or another form to their collections. However, L.G. Wright also made reproductions in original colors, causing great confusion for unsuspecting collectors. Today, as their reproductions broaden in scope and color, some folks are collecting L.G. Wright wares as examples of that glass company and are not encumbered by the reproduction aspect.

Cocktail, Paneled Grape, #55, blue opalescent 25.00
Creamer and sugar, Beaded Curtain, cranberry.................160.00
Cruet, Moss Rose, white satin, hp 135.00
Epergne, aqua blue crest......775.00
Goblet
    Paneled Grape, #55, blue opalescent..........................30.00
    Wildflower, amber..............18.50
Pump and trough, carnival glass reproduction, cobalt blue .. 20.00
Sherbet
    Bull's Eye, amber 19.00
    Wedding Ring, amber 17.50
Toothpick holder, Moon and Star, amber..................................25.00
Vase, Cherries, milk glass, cranberry int., hp, 6-1/2" h 195.00
Wine, Paneled Grape, #55, blue opalescent 30.00

**Russel Wright bowl, 6"
diameter, $10.**

❖ Wright, Russel

Russel Wright was an American industrial designer who took the streamlined look to new heights. He influenced several companies and their designs, such as Chase Brass and Chrome, and General Electric.

One area where his influence was greatly felt was in dinnerware design. The Steubenville Pottery responded with a pattern called American Modern, made from 1939 to 1959. The original issue colors were Bean Brown, Chartreuse Curry, Coral, Granite Grey, Seafoam Blue, and White. Later color additions included Black Chutney, Cedar Green, Cantalope, Glacier Blue, and Steubenville Blue. Wright also created other dinnerware patterns, but American Modern remains the one most sought after by collectors.

American Modern pattern
Bread and butter plate, 6" d
    Bean Brown 10.00
    Granite Grey 5.00
Butter, cov, White 625.00
Casserole, cov
    Granite Grey 65.00
    Seafoam Blue 45.00
Celery dish
    Bean Brown 28.00
    Granite Grey 25.00
Chop plate
    Chartreuse Curry 35.00
    Granite Grey 30.00
Cup and saucer
    Coral 12.00
    Granite Grey 14.00
Dinner plate
    Cedar Green 10.00
    Granite Grey 13.00
Fruit bowl, lug
    Coral 17.50
    Granite Grey 15.00
Platter
    Coral 35.00

    Granite Grey 28.00
Salad bowl
    Granite Grey 85.00
    Seafoam Blue 90.00
Salad plate
    Coral 17.50
    Granite Grey 15.00
Salt shaker
    Chartreuse Curry 14.00
    Granite Grey 10.00
Soup, lug
    Bean Brown 27.50
    Granite Grey 15.00
    Teapot, Coral 95.00
Tumbler, Granite Grey 85.00
Vegetable bowl, open
    Coral 35.00
    Granite Grey 25.00
Water pitcher
    Granite Grey 100.00
    Seafoam Blue 185.00

❖ Wrist Watches

Got the time? The first real wrist watch dates back to about 1850, but it wasn't until around 1880 that wrist watches were the stylish element we consider them to be. By the 1930s, the idea caught on well enough that sales of wrist watches finally surpassed sales of pocket watches.

References: Kahlert Muhe Brunner, *Wristwatches*, 4th ed, Schiffer Publishing, 1999; Cooksey Shugart, Tom Engle and Richard E. Gilbert, *Complete Price Guide to Watches,* 21st ed., Collector Books, 2001.

Periodical: *International Wrist Watch,* 242 West Ave, Darien, CT 06820.

Collectors' Clubs: International Wrist Watch Collectors Chapter 146, 5901C Westheimer, Houston, TX 77057; National Association of Watch & Clock Collectors, 514 Poplar St, Columbia, PA 17512; The Swatch Collectors Club, P.O. Box 7400, Melville, NY 11747.
Gruen
    Man's, 10k wg, precision autowind, Tonneau case, black lizard band 65.00
    Man's, 14k yg, orig strap .. 300.00
Hamilton, lady's, Art Deco, bezel and shoulders set with round baguette diamonds, platinum mount, black cord strap, white gold filled clasp, minor discoloration to dial 460.00

Lorus, Mickey Mouse, c1980, band simulates animation film of Mickey walking, MIB 25.00
Movado, man's, 14K yg, tank, stepped lugs, slightly bowed sides, gold-tone dial, Roman numerals and abstract indicators, subsidiary seconds dial, worn leather strap, crystal loose 230.00
Omega, 18K yg, Seamaster, man's 250.00
Rolex, man's, perpetual, stainless steel, Air King, silver-tone dial, applied abstract indicators, sweep second hand, oyster bracelet with clasp, discoloration to dial, scratches to crystal 575.00
Tiffany & Co.
    Lady's, 18k yg, back wind, texture gold dial with black Roman numerals and abstract indicators, diamond frame, textured gold bracelet, orig box 920.00
    Man's, 18k yg, lapis lazuli color dial, stepped bezel, black crocodile strap 635.00
Uti, Paris, lady's, 18k yg, silver-tone dial, applied gold-tone indicators, leather strap with keyhole form closure, hallmarks, wear to strap 575.00

❖ Wyandotte

Playthings a kid could be rough with, Wyandotte's heavy-gauge steel toys were a favorite with children. The company began in 1921, taking its name from the town of Wyandotte, Michigan, where it was located. At first the firm just made toy pistols and rifles, but soon moved to a line of cars and trucks with wooden wheels. Wyandotte went out of business in 1956.
Airliner, 4-engine, 12-3/4" wingspan 110.00
Army truck, 22" l 115.00
Circus truck, No. 503, 11" l ... 650.00
Coupe, 1930s, 7-1/2" l 160.00
Dump truck, #122 .... 65.00
Ice truck, #348 .... 375.00
Railway Express truck, 12" l ... 85.00
Rocket Racer, #319 .... 100.00
Ship, USS Enterprise 120.00
Station wagon, Cadillac, #1007, 21" l 275.00
Submarine 165.00
Toytown Delivery, 21" l 300.00
Wrecker, 10" l 110.00

Y

For exciting collecting trends and newly expanded areas look for the following symbols:

✿ Hot Topic
☆ New Warman's Listing

(May have been in another Warman's title.)

❖ Yard Long Photos and Prints

To most collectors, a long narrow print is considered a "yard long" print. The format can be horizontal or vertical. Yard long prints first appeared about 1900, and some were used as premiums as well as advertising. Many calendars were created in this format.

Many photographs were also made in this format. These were especially popular with school groups, so that the entire student body could be included in a photo. Military units also favored this size.

Calendar
    1911, Pabst Extra, American Girl, C.W. Henning, full length, cardboard roll at bottom 350.00
    1927, Pompeian, The Bride, sgd "Rolf Armstrong" 350.00
Photograph
    1919, *U.S.S. Siboney* Arriving at US Naval Base, Aug. 8, 1919 .... 175.00
    1936, Quakertown High School, Class of '36, in front of Capital 75.00
Print
    Battle of the Chicks, Ben Austrian, ©1920 by The Art Interchange Co. of New York 250.00
    A Carnation Symphony, 1908, Grey Litho Co. 495.00
    Easter Greetings, Paul DeLongpre, ©1894 by Knapp Co. Litho 400.00
    The Greatest Moments of a Girl's Life 325.00

Hula Girl, sgd "Gene Pressler" 350.00
La France Roses, Paul DeLongpre, ©1903, advertising Spiehler's Perfume 300.00
Tug of War, 7 dogs and cats 450.00

✿ Yellow Ware

This type of utilitarian pottery has been produced in the United States and England since the early 19th century. Because yellow ware was quite durable, it became the kitchen pottery of choice, replacing the more fragile redware. Color may range from pumpkin orange to deep yellow to pale cream, and most of the pieces are unmarked. Horizontal bands in white, brown, blue, or a combination thereof were the most common type of decoration.

References: William C. Ketchum Jr., *American Country Pottery: Yellow Ware and Spongeware*, Alfred A. Knopf, 1987; Joan Leibowitz, *Yellow Ware*, Schiffer Publishing, 1985 (1993 value update); Lisa S. McAllister, *Collector's Guide to Yellow Ware*, Collector Books, 1997; Lisa S. McAllister and John L. Michael, *Collecting Yellow Ware*, Collector Books, 1993.

Yellow ware batter bowl, embossed design, $125.

Museums: Bennington Museum, VT; Henry Ford Museum, Dearborn, MI; Museum of Ceramics, East Liverpool, OH.
For additional listings, see *Warman's Country Price Guide.*
Beater jar, 3 white stripes, base chip, 5-3/4" h 170.00
Bowl, mixing
    4 bands of brown slip, 2-3/8" h, 4-1/4" dia 110.00
    Nesting set of 5, thick white stripe between thin white stripes 275.00
Dish, rectangular, canted sides, 2-1/4" h, 11" l, 8" w 270.00
Match holder, lion motif, 2 chips to the holder, 5-7/8" h, oval base 7-7/8" x 4-7/8" 280.00

Miniature, chamber pot, white band, 2-1/4" h 100.00
Nappie, 4 embossed lines, minor in-the-making imperfection, 3-1/2" h, 14" dia 110.00
Pie plate, stains, 12" dia 198.00
Pudding mold
    Ear of corn, scalloped designs on interior sides, simple gallery-like foot, oval, 4-3/8" h, 7-3/8" x 9-1/4" 170.00
    Sheath of wheat, minor rim chips, 3-1/4" h, 7-5/8" l 110.00
Rolling pin, turned maple handles, 15" l (excluding handles), 3" dia 525.00

❖ Yo-Yos

Q: What keeps coming back when you toss it away? A: A yo-yo. Few people can truly throw away a yo-yo, which means there are many examples available on today's market. In addition to vintage items, look for contemporary yo-yos featuring popular cultural figures, advertising yo-yos and commemorative examples. Yo-yo collections can be seen free of charge at The Yozeum in Tucson, Arizona, and the National Yo-Yo Museum in Chico, California.

Collectors' Clubs: American Yo-Yo Association, 627 163rd St., South Spanaway, WA 98387.
Bowling ball, Duncan Sports Line Model, #1070, MOC.......... 55.00

Duncan Imperial yo-yo, red plastic, 2-1/4" diameter, $5.

Butterfly, Duncan, green plastic 5.00
Campbell's Kids, Duncan........ 26.00
Coca-Cola, 1992 Summer Olympics 25.00
Dr. Pepper, 10-2-4 logo, wooden, red and blue 35.00
Glow Imperial, Duncan 6.00
Hot Wheels, Mattel, tire motif, red chrome hubcaps, 1990, MOC 13.00
The Iron Giant, Warner Bros., 1990 .... 12.00
Jurassic Park, 1992, MIP 21.50
Oreo Cookie 10.00
Planter's Mr. Peanut 20.00
Spider-Man, Duncan, 1978..... 25.00
Steam Genie, metal 10.00

Z

❖ Zanesville Pottery

The area around Zanesville, Ohio, was home to several potteries. The Zanesville Art Pottery started production about 1900. Their first wares were utilitarian and they soon ventured into art pottery production. The firm was bought by S.A. Weller in 1920 and became part of Weller Pottery at that time. Another popular company was Peters and Reed.

Bowl, fluted edge, mottled blue glaze, 6-1/2" d 45.00

Bowl and figural turtle flower frog, Landsun, blue tones, Peter and Reed, bowl 8" dia 154.00

Figurine, frog, marbleized, Peters and Reed, 4-7/8" h 220.00

Jar, cov, marbleized green, Peters and Reed, 4" h 330.00

Jardiniere, ruffed rim, cream to light amber peony blossoms, shaded brown ground.....................75.00

Vase

Arts & Crafts design, teal glaze, shallow base chip, 12" h 225.00

Chromal, dark blue, brown and tan, Peters and Reed, 7-3/4" h.........................220.00

Landsun, multi-color drip glaze, Peters and Reed, 11-1/4" h 385.00

Moss Aztec, embossed blackberries, Peters and Reed, 2 glaze nicks, 7-7/8" h 88.00

★ Zeppelins

Oh, those fanciful flying machines. Some folks call them dirigibles, while others refer to them as blimps. To collectors they are something to float about, especially when finding that rare piece to add to their coveted possessions.

Book

Aircraft Carrier: Graf Zeppelin, Breyer, 48 pgs 10.00

The Zeppelin in Combat, A History of the German Naval Airship Division, Douglas H. Robinson, 400 pgs, black and white photos, charges, drawings................................50.00

First-day cover, "San Francisco Greets U.S.A.S. Macon Upon Arrival at Home Base," 8 cent airmail stamp, postmarked "Moffett Field, Oct 15, 1933".....30.00

Flight Schedule, from Germany to America, c1936................. 60.00

Magazine print, German *Graf Zeppelin* flying over NY skyscrapers, New Yorker *Magazine,* Haupt, 1930, 8" x 11" image, acid-free mat................................. 125.00

Postcard, Zeppelin flying over Montevideo, Uruguay, black and white 28.00

Pull toy, *Graf Zeppelin,* Steelcraft, C-8 .... 490.00

Pamphlet, "Facts About The World's Largest Airships," $15.

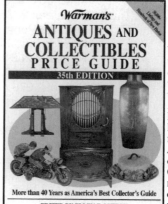